AN INTERNATIONAL RELATIONS DEBACLE

This book is a case study in international relations and contemporary history, as seen from the standpoint of a constitutional, international and human rights lawyer involved in 25 years of negotiations to agree on a federation reuniting the divided Island of Cyprus. Based for the most part on personal knowledge, the writer describes recent international attempts to settle the long-standing disputes over Cyprus and provides a warning to those who invoke UN "good offices" machinery of risks they run.

In explaining the UN Secretariat's activities, the roles played by major Powers are emphasised, together with consequential local perceptions which ultimately led to failure of the international effort. Analysis of what went wrong in that effort's later phases indicates procedural and substantive approaches needed for any renewed negotiations to achieve success. Subsequent developments until the end of 2004, including the EU's agreement to open accession negotiations with Turkey and potential positive measures, are also outlined, as are the issues which all parties should now properly consider.

Accompanying the text, which concentrates on the 2002–2004 period, is an extensive photographic record since 1954 of "the Cyprus problem" and of previous and recent attempts at negotiation. The illustrations, sometimes lightheartedly captioned, put events in context and illuminate the attitudes of significant actors in a manner no written text (other than one by a novelist) can do. The writer, in both text and photographs, frankly avows the prejudices and selectivity inevitable in any account of controversial and divisive events. But the resulting alternative narrative should facilitate a deeper understanding of the Cyprus situation than that currently afforded by the received picture, which has been presented by the UN Secretariat and certain major Powers. Such deeper understanding could assist in achieving a positive resolution of the conflict-ridden relationships in, around and about Cyprus.

An International Relations Debacle

The UN Secretary-General's Mission of Good Offices in Cyprus 1999–2004

CLAIRE PALLEY
OBE, BA, LLB (CAPE),
PhD (LOND), MA (OXON), LLD (Hon Belfast)

Former UK member of the UN Sub-Commission on Prevention of Discrimination and Protection of Minorities (1988–1998) and
Former Constitutional Consultant to the President of Cyprus (1980–2004)

OXFORD AND PORTLAND, OREGON
2005

Hart Publishing
Oxford and Portland, Oregon

Published in North America (US and Canada) by
Hart Publishing c/o
International Specialized Book Services
5804 NE Hassalo Street
Portland, Oregon
97213-3644
USA

Hart Publishing is a specialist legal publisher based in Oxford, England.
To order further copies of this book or to request a list of other
publications please write to:

Hart Publishing, Salter's Boatyard, Folly Bridge,
Abingdon Road, Oxford OX1 4LB
Telephone: +44 (0)1865 245533 or Fax: +44 (0)1865 794882
e-mail: mail@hartpub.co.uk
WEBSITE: http//www.hartpub.co.uk

British Library Cataloguing in Publication Data
Data Available
ISBN 1–84113–578–X

Typeset by Hope Services (Abingdon) Ltd.
Printed and bound in Great Britain by
MPG Books, Bodmin, Cornwall

To a great Cypriot,
Stella Soulioti

Acknowledgements

I am honoured to have worked for successive Presidents of the Republic of Cyprus and with many of its able public servants from 1979 until mid-2004. But the greatest personal pleasure has been working with the person who set me on the path of Cyprus studies, Mrs Stella Soulioti. She advised all Presidents on the Cyprus problem as Legal Adviser in the intermittent talks from 1964–1997 and as Attorney-General of the Republic from 1984–1988. Her guidance enabled me to understand the almost—but not quite—intractable character of the issues involved. It is to her that this book is dedicated.

I should like to thank five former colleagues. Ambassadors Andreas Mavroyiannis, Marios Lysiotis, and Andreas Jacovides read my typescript critically. So too did Andrea Petranyi. Moreover, after many helpful discussions, she would navigate the web to find necessary references. The photographic record could not have been compiled without her. Andreas Hadjiraftis prepared maps of the Cyprus situation, now and under the Plan. He also provided statistics on land ownership and photographs at Bürgenstock. The Office for Studies on the Cyprus Problem allowed me full use of their research facilities. Discussions with Cedric Thornberry on UN Missions and how they can go right (as in Namibia) or wrong was particularly illuminating.

The United Nations Force in Cyprus (UNFICYP) made their photographic archives available and permitted reproductions from *The Blue Beret*. *The Cyprus Weekly*, the Cyprus News Agency, and the Press and Information Office allowed extensive use of their photographs, while the CyBC provided facilities to take pictures from their news archive. I am grateful to George Lanitis for two photographs, to Panick and Pin for their cartoons and to the Council of Europe for photographs. The Cyprus Ministry of Foreign Affairs authorised reproduction of relevant UN Resolutions on Cyprus (as edited by Rolandos Katsiaounis).

The usual disclaimer about errors and opinions being solely mine is scarcely necessary. However, some of the footnotes and the photocaptioning were "inspired" by Figaro's reflection in Beaumarchais' *Barber of Seville*: "I hasten to laugh at everything for fear of being obliged to weep." In this context, it should be noted that when words are attributed to a personage captured on film, the form of the caption makes it clear whenever an actual quotation from an accompanying transcript has been used, or whether the caption merely draws ineluctable inferences from such person's conduct either at the time, previously or subsequently. In the latter event, the captioning is cast in the interrogative or subjunctive mode, or the verbs "seems" or "appears" are used. It should go without saying that all captioning is "fair comment in the public interest".

Maria Aloupa and Georgia Georgiou struggled to piece together a jigsaw puzzle of squiggles and metamorphosed them into something legible. I particularly thank the Staff of Hart Publishing for their speed in producing a volume covering events until 31 December 2004.

Finally, to Richard Hart go very special thanks indeed. He appreciated that historico-legal arguments and alternative narratives with explanation of political contexts, can, without being mere propaganda, affect attitudes both internationally and internally. He was, while not in any way sharing the writer's attitudes, willing to publish a book outside the academic mainstream. On top of that, his generosity with complimentary copies and assistance with distribution made it possible to bring this book to the attention of opinion-shapers in many States.

Contents

Table of Cases

I

Introduction and Some Historiography

THIS IS AN account of attempts by the UN Secretariat to settle the Cyprus problem between 1999 and April 2004. It is based on personal knowledge acquired through involvement as an adviser to the Government of Cyprus during those and earlier negotiations under the auspices of the UN Secretary-General. The story is not written in the UN bureaucratic or diplomatic style, which is nonetheless counter-balanced by Machiavellian private briefings by the Secretariat.[1] Nor is it a comprehensive academic account, with the addition of precise references to all documents and citation of all relevant press reports, something which only the luxury of lengthy research permits. Instead, it portrays events as they were perceived by one close to Greek Cypriot participants in the processes set up by the Secretary-General, and uses the parties' position papers in those negotiations and correspondence with members of the Secretariat to evidence the disclosures and assertions made. Unlike the Secretary-General's most recent *Report,* dealing with developments since early 2004 and renouncing any intent to give a full negotiating history of changes and clarifications[2], this writer's account will deliberately "tax the patience of even the keenest reader" in the interests of presenting the actions of the parties concerned more accurately and of correcting errors and misrepresentations in the Secretariat's *Report,* which, if not set right, will harm future prospects for achieving a settlement.

[1] Many lay-persons are ignorant of the role of press briefings, where "spin" is applied to distort the picture. For example, on 3 June 2004 President Papadopoulos first re-met the Secretary-General after the rejection by the Greek Cypriot electorate of the Annan Plan. The meeting was cordial. At the end of the meeting, while pleasantries were still being exchanged, the Special Adviser instructed the UN Secretary-General's Spokesman, who conveyed somehow to the press that the meeting had been frigid and that the only matter on which the two had agreed had been that there should be time for reflection. As regards "spin" and the recent Secretary-General's *Reports*, there was, even before these, enormous negative spin from the UN about the attitude of the Greek Cypriot side at Bürgenstock prior to "finalisation" of the Plan. Such spin continued in the period of the referendum campaign. The *Reports* themselves (*S/2204/302*, 16 April 2004, and *S/2004/437*, 28 April 2004) appeared to hypnotise the international press, a situation facilitated by briefings by some diplomats and press spokesmen for the angered Foreign Ministries of States which had believed that this Plan could be imposed on the Greek Cypriot side's elected leader and would nonetheless be accepted by its public. Despite the general expertise of the international press, it appears to the writer that the Press became myopic, focusing only on the Plan, and not on its international relations context and the motivations of those pushing for the Plan, including the Secretariat.

[2] *S/2004/437*, 28 May 2004, para 43.

No report or history is of course "objective". Participants (including UN Secretariat participants) have their own perspectives, interpretations and misinterpretations and gaps in knowledge—especially of private dealings and secret conversations—and are writing for particular audiences, always bearing in mind target audiences' predispositions and, especially in the case of a *Report* designed as a preliminary to action, known desires.[3] Nonetheless, story-tellers can and should try to keep to the facts as they know them and avoid coloration[4] and unnecessary selectivity (some emphasis and selectivity being inevitable, particularly where the story is partly autobiographical, with accounts of their own conduct and its consequences).[5] The reader of contemporary history must always bear in mind that not only is history, even when written by professional historians, non-scientific, but that all tale-tellers are also to some extent advocates. Why otherwise would they be telling the tale?[6] Tales (even Secretariat *Reports*) have political objectives.

Tale-tellers while telling their stories are also interpreters, placing their own constructions on conduct, perceiving sequences and causes and assembling their accounts with reference to frameworks and concepts they consider relevant. When seeking to provide explanations, they become inter-disciplinarians and contextualists. Thus, in the case of this tale, the assembled text is partly narrative and partly analytical, using concepts from politics, international relations, international and human rights law and even pop psychology. But,

[3] Documents (what negotiators and post-modernists call "texts") are "written by fallible human beings who made false claims, and had their own ideological agenda which guided their compilation; they should therefore be scrutinized with care, taking into account authorial intent, the nature of the document, and the context in which it was written": Lawrence Stone, "History and post-modernism" (1991) 131 *Past and Present,* 217–18. The author also referred to E H Carr, *What is History* (Macmillan, 1961), 38: "Before you study history, study the historian . . . Before you study the historian, study his historical and social background". In this context, as Peter Burke put it in *History of Events and the Revival of Narrative. New Perspectives on Historical Writing* (Polity Press, Oxford, 1991), 239: "Historical narrators need to find a way of making themselves visible in the narrative, not out of self-indulgence, but as a warning to the reader that they are not omniscient or impartial and that other interpretations besides their own are possible".

[4] If story-tellers decide to "touch up" the picture, they should do so in a manner making this activity clear, eg by indicating that a personal interpretation is being added.

[5] As President Papadopoulos wrote to the Secretary-General on 7 June 2004 about his recent *Report*: "When reading this Report, one should, nevertheless, bear in mind that it has been primarily drafted by those entrusted by you with the role of honest broker and [who] were active participants throughout the process. Through this Report they assess effectively the outcome of their own efforts, whilst at the same time attempting to portray and evaluate the attitude of the parties involved. In other words, the authors of the report play essentially the role of the judge and jury of the overall outcome of the negotiation process they presided over." It is appropriate to add that they also acted as prosecutors in the way they compiled the *Report.*

[6] The writer freely admits to advocating cautious but critical reflection on the most recent *Reports of the UN Secretary-General on his mission of good offices in Cyprus*, and, using the UN's own injunction to Cypriots, engaging in a profound and sober assessment of the potential consequences for the Secretary-General's function of good offices due to the Secretariat's conduct from September 2002 onwards in seeking to achieve a Cyprus settlement. The mythical tale, told by the Secretariat in the 28 May 2004 *Report*, is of cooperative Turks and unfairly isolated Turkish Cypriots, anxious for reunification, as opposed to obstructive Greek Cypriots.

in assembling it, the writer has striven to provide an accurate account from the available information and has sought to refrain from mere propaganda. She has not edited out value judgements, as academics usually do, concealing them by subtle weasel words or in diplomatic cotton wool (tricks those who wish subliminally to influence readers employ). If some value judgements appear harsh, or even abrasive, they are at least not hypocritical, and the reader is warned of the writer's prejudices.[7]

In the hope that international opinion-formers will reflect on the UN Secretariat's recent conduct in seeking to put a Cyprus settlement in place and in presenting its rationalisation of events—which has become received opinion—this tale-teller has, apart from introductory matter and some general comments on Secretariat *Report*-writing, told the story by way of a parallel account and critique of the Secretary-General's 28 May 2004 *Report*. This approach facilitates comparison, deals with the same pattern of issues and sets out events in the same sequence as they were described in the Secretary-General's concluding *Reports* after Annan III (26 February 2003) and Annan V (31 March 2004). The present account ends with an explanation of the reasons which moved a large majority of Greek Cypriot voters to reject the Annan Plan in its Version V, the inferences which should be drawn, developments which had occurred half a year later, and, briefly, important issues which will need canvassing in negotiations which will, indubitably, be resumed.

[7] One prejudice she does not entertain is that "the UN" should be the ultimate scapegoat when international affairs are not appropriately dealt with: the responsibility is of those who exercise decisive power ie primarily the involved Permanent Members of the Security Council and their allies on that body which they enlist. She is an admirer of certain parts of the UN bureaucracy, notably the Office of the UN High Commissioner for Human Rights and the Department of Peacekeeping, where, by-and-large, the Secretariat members concerned strive against heavy odds to pursue the Purposes of the Charter, unlike many of the inhabitants of the 38th and 33rd floors whose ideals appear to have been displaced by cynicism and political aspirations. Everything in the end comes down to particular people and their behaviour under the pressures they face.

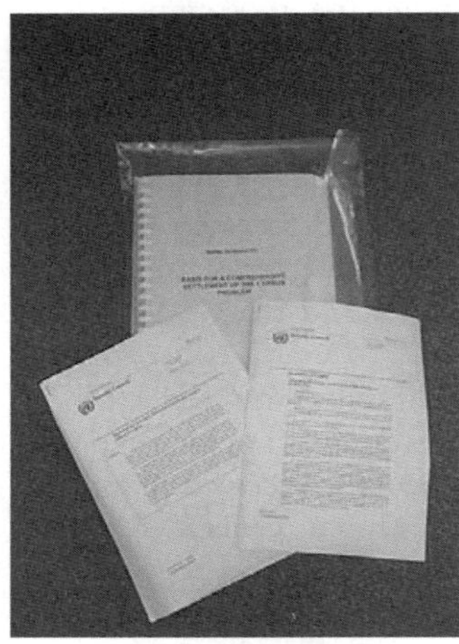

Not really sterilised, rather political products: Annan III with the Secretary-General's *Report* (S/2003/298) and Security Council Resolution 1475 (2003).

The Secretary-General and his main adviser, Sir Kieran Prendergast, Under Secretary-General and Head of the Department of Political Affairs, on 29 March 2004 immediately prior to presentation of Annan IV.

EARLIER UN SECRETARIES-GENERAL AND THEIR NEGOTIATING LEGACIES

Top left: U Thant (1961–1971), who in 1964 was crucial in upholding the independence of the Republic of Cyprus, organised the peacekeeping force, appointed the first two and only mediators and in late 1967 initiated good offices.

Top right: Dr Waldheim (1972–1981), at the UN helm during Turkey's invasion, who authorised expansion of UNFICYP's humanitarian role and encouraged inter-Community negotiations in the good offices framework of SCR 367 (1975), which resulted in the 1977 and 1979 High Level Agreements.

Bottom left: Mr JP de Cuéllar (1982–1991), who facilitated negotiations, but, by ultimately tilting to the Turkish Cypriot view, ensured their non-success under his auspices.

Bottom right: Mr Boutros Boutros-Ghali (1982–1996), whose Set of Ideas, although not pursued due to attitudes of both Cypriot sides, laid down the pattern most likely to be the basis for ultimate success in reaching a settlement.

II

The "Good Offices" Framework for Secretariat Action

THE FRAMEWORK WITHIN which the Secretariat was empowered to act as regards Cyprus was "good offices of the Secretary-General," offered by him, accepted by the leaders of the Greek and Turkish Cypriot Communities and endorsed by the Security Council. "Good offices" are an old diplomatic institution, carrying overtones of benevolence by the offeror of such services, who facilitates discussions and, if possible, negotiations between disputing parties. Successive UN Secretaries-General (and their Special Representatives) have found the institution useful to defuse threatening situations.[1] In Cyprus "good offices" were on offer from the time in early 1964 when the first Special Representative was appointed. The Secretary-General offered his own services in late 1967 and this institution facilitated inter-communal talks from June 1968. After Turkey's 1974 invasion of the Republic of Cyprus (or, as Turkey prefers to word it, her "intervention") there was a new and more extensive mission of good offices. But at no time would either Cyprus party countenance more than facilitation of discussion and production of constructive ideas, because they did not consider that any outsider, however benevolent, was the best final judge of the parties' vital interests.[2] Accordingly, until the recent negotiations, no extension of the good offices function had been acceptable in Cyprus. Elsewhere, in a more activist world of UN involvement in situations in Africa, Latin America and Asia, the Secretary-General's good offices became more extensive in character, often going well beyond mere facilitation of negotiation, with the Secretary-General (in fact Secretariat) ending up as arbiter. However, in such situations the enlarged functions had either been agreed by the parties concerned or been conferred by the Security Council under Chapter VI

[1] Under Mr J P de Cuéllar, the distinction between "good offices" and "mediation" became "tenuous". He believed the distinction to be one of nuance—depending, he claims in relation to Cyprus, "largely on whether one side or the other disliked a suggestion I put forward": *Pilgrimage for Peace, A Secretary-General's Memoir* (St Martin's Press, New York, 1997), 219–20. This fusion of the concepts was useful in affording the Secretary-General greater scope to insert his own ideas of what was appropriate, but was unacceptable to parties who did not want an arbitrator and had not agreed to appointment of one.

[2] Production of constructive ideas is a small scale activity involving making suggestions intermittently. It is very different from coming forward with a major, let alone a comprehensive, plan.

or VII of the Charter: they had not been self-appropriated or even usurped, with agreed limits on their scope being ignored. As will emerge from the account below, the Secretary-General was to usurp a jurisdiction, not conferred upon him, in order to impose arrangements, which he required should be put to referenda of the people of Cyprus voting as two separate Communities.[3]

The UN Secretariat's conduct of the Cyprus negotiations from late 2002, in early 2003 and especially in March 2004, and its subsequent conduct in reporting on what had transpired, exceeded proper limits. The Secretariat sought to mislead the international community through the Secretary-General's *Reports* and briefings it prepared—so as to pressurise a small State effectively to accept the consequences of aggression by a large neighbouring State allied to two Permanent Members of the Security Council.

The responsibility for such Secretariat conduct belongs to the Secretary-General as head of this UN organ. Obviously, although the UN Secretary-General is formally answerable for what is done or published in his name, he cannot have knowledge of all details, being himself reliant on what is filtered through to him by his aides whether in New York or elsewhere. Even where he adds his imprimatur to policies (formulated at lower levels of the Secretariat and then served up to him with appropriate embellishments to achieve the aims sought by the relevant policy initiator) the Secretary-General, by virtue of the massive demands of his office, can at best have only a limited degree of personal involvement and hence personal responsibility. In large institutions, although the roots of policies can be located in initial proposals from a particular source, the actual responsibility is always that of a number of persons at different levels, in this case of all involved members of the Secretariat, and not merely that of the originating individual, or that of the Organisation's titular, even if executive, head alone. However, since the latter has alone to carry political responsibility, it is for him to enquire at appropriate times whether he should act as a brake on, or a rubber stamp, or a positive endorser of the particular policies involved.[4] It is the Secretary-General's duty when proposals for action of any kind come to him for decision to ask:

[3] The imposition was *not* as respects the holding of referenda, which both sides had many years earlier agreed were pre-requisite for a settlement. In the "Set of Ideas" (*S/24472*, 21 August 1992), paras 63, 75, 92 and 101 there are references to such referenda on a proposed overall framework agreement on Cyprus. The imposition in 2004 was *as to the matter to put to the referenda* ie the massive Annan Plan with its many disputed provisions, inserted without proper negotiation let alone discussion, and at the briefest of notice.

[4] It is unfortunate that a misguided policy initiative has been personalised by having attributed to it the Secretary-General's name. He has been the foremost international public servant who, had he been more closely involved in the details, would not have wished his name to be historically associated with such departures from international law and human rights standards. Nor would he personally, if acquainted with all the facts, have wished to issue a formal *Report* containing so much inaccurate information and such obvious slanting. Some internal reprimands are overdue: propaganda should be well-done if it is to be effective in the long term. Moreover, although UN bureaucrats consider it part of their function to protect the Secretary-General, in this case the circumstances smack more of self-protection. Even so, it is appropriate in the "Greek" context and in the light of the moral reputation of the UN, to quote Thucydides, *History of the Peloponnesian War*, Book

> Is the Secretariat really being well-served by this proposed or current action by its personnel?

He needs to ask himself this even if, just like any other head of an institution, he has to be loyal to his subordinates, praise them publicly, thank them for their dedication—irrespective of whether this proves to have led to unhappy outcomes—and manifest public agreement with their views.[5]

In normal circumstances, revelations about recent negotiations, the contents of conversations and correspondence, and reflections on the conduct of persons involved are not made available until many years after the events concerned. But the current circumstances are far from normal: in two recent *Reports* on Cyprus,[6] and in public statements and private briefings by members of the Secretariat on the unsuccessful outcome to four years of their often intensive efforts to put a Cyprus settlement in place, which *Reports* and statements purport to rely on members' knowledge of the negotiations, animadversions have implicitly and explicitly been cast upon the conduct of the Greek Cypriot side during the Secretary-General's exercise of good offices in relation to Cyprus. Members of the Secretariat and other international public servants have even overtly criticised the Head of State of the Republic of Cyprus, doing so in a professional PR exercise. Their criticisms have adversely impacted on the reputation of the Republic's Government and have damaged the prospects for progress towards a federal settlement negotiated by and agreed to by both Greek and Turkish Cypriots. It needs adding that, in the preceding *Report* on negotiations from late 1999 until March 2003 (*S/2003/398*, 1 April 2003) a similar, although less extreme, pedagogical approach featured, with adverse comments on the conduct of the leader of the Turkish Cypriot side, Mr Rauf Denktash. This style of *Report*-writing was a departure from the UN's general practice in Cyprus. With very limited exceptions, as where there has been need for analysis of inconsistencies on particular issues,[7] the stance of the Secretariat had, ever since its involvement in 1964, been not to write critically of either side (however much the involved Secretariat members may have thought the merits justified criticism), but to concentrate on making factual statements and to

1, para 69: "And it is you who are responsible for all this. . . . When one is deprived of one's liberty one is right in blaming not so much the man who puts the fetters on as the one who had the power to prevent him, but did not use it—especially when such a one rejoices in the glorious reputation of having been the liberator of Hellas".

[5] Thus, when President Papadopoulos and the Government of Cyprus commented on the Secretary-General's *Report*, *S/2004/437* of 28 May 2004, pointing to its misleading character and serious inaccuracies (these Comments were circulated as *S/2004/493—A/58/843*, Annex) the Secretary-General naturally stood fully by his *Report*, including the narrative and analysis therein and its recommendations, disagreeing with President Papadopoulos' characterisation of the conduct of the United Nations (Letter, Secretary-General to President Papadopoulos, 15 June 2004).

[6] *S/2004/302, Report of the Secretary-General on Cyprus*, 16 April 2004, and *S/2004/437*, *Report of the UN Secretary-General on his mission of good offices in Cyprus*, 28 May 2004.

[7] For example, Mr Boutros Boutros-Ghali's *Report of the Secretary-General on his mission of good offices in Cyprus*, *S/24830*, 18 November 1992, paras 49–55, explaining the effect of Mr Denktash's positions on the right to return and the right to property.

appear even-handed in the Secretary-General's *Reports*, even though some of the persons involved did not refrain from giving negative oral briefings. Frustrating though this even-handedness in compiling official *Reports* may from time to time have been to Cypriot participants, it was a far wiser approach than employment of the currently hectoring tone of the recent Cyprus *Reports*, which *Reports* provide those parties praised (even applauded) with justifications for self-satisfaction, inflexibility and refusal to negotiate from positions perceived as being internationally approved. It must be asked: "Why did such a change in approach come about?" Regrettably, the answer can only be that members of the Secretariat had, instead of merely exercising a quasi-refereeing or reportorial function, become participating actors in the Cyprus drama, thus fusing both reportorial and participant roles. Since Secretariat *Reports* are normally regarded as authoritative, such *Reports* can only effectively be refuted where they are wrong, not by mere assertions, but by citation of documentary evidence.[8]

Students of international relations are always told that they should not reify the UN or the Security Council or idealise it: these institutions consist of States, with their own interests, and Member States when shaping UN decisions are motivated by such factors. The same kind of advice must now be given about the Secretariat as a whole: it is an international bureaucracy of public servants, alert to the wishes of its masters, the Security Council (especially some of its Permanent Members) and to those of their own nominating Governments.

[8] Of course documentary evidence has its own distortions, particular when it has been prepared for a specific purpose or for later public consumption. Nonetheless, it reflects what was actually written at the time. Relevant documentary evidence of that kind is available to the writer because, from early August 1980, she has been involved in, or closely associated with, the preparation of position papers to be submitted by the Greek Cypriot side in the talks between the Communities (whether direct talks, through Interlocutors appointed by each side or by the respective sides' "leaders," or whether indirect proximity talks under the auspices of the UN Secretary-General in the course of his good offices mission for Cyprus, with either a Special Representative, Special Adviser, or the Secretary-General in office at the time presiding). For the purposes of drafting position papers or responding to Turkish Cypriot papers, she was given access to all note-takers' records and received oral reports from Greek Cypriot participants. In the 1980–83 intercommunal talks minutes were kept by the UN and agreed by both sides. The atmosphere which developed in those talks was cordial and the minutes were promptly agreed, giving each side confidence. Pressed by both leaders in February 2004 to agree to minutes being kept, Mr de Soto declined to make UN minutes available on the basis that this would affect the sides' conduct and hamper negotiations. But he could not refuse to agree to each side having a note-taker present, as this had been the case since the start of the negotiations in December 1999, thereby undermining the rationale of his refusal. For the purposes of preparing a history of the talks and a book on Cyprus's reliance on law in its international relations, the writer was empowered to make full use of papers associated with her work in the talks. In consequence of that work, she is fully acquainted with the basis on which the talks were conducted and substantive proposals made by all parties involved. Concerned by the slanted portrayal of the talks by an institution, which the world presumes to be authoritative and impartial, she therefore decided, as a former participant, albeit at a lowly level, to rebut the UN's recent presentations and to provide a more accurate picture, even if it has its own subjectivities, especially those of a human rights lawyer. Her account cannot be "Martian," because she has so long been professionally engaged with the Greek Cypriot side, but she has striven not to provide a pale reflection of the views of her former clients.

Unless there is a Hammarskjöld or a U Thant at the helm, determined to adhere to his own line, there is also likely to be considerable external influence upon the highest executive.[9] Behind the abstract language and all institutional structures, including those of the UN, the reality is that the persons concerned are pursuing policies, which they constructed, subject to varying degrees of influence, and with which they identify themselves. If on top of this, pride of authorship is activated following disagreement with chosen prescriptions made in an attempt to do good, resentment, perhaps even fuelled by frustrated ambition for honour, often replaces attempts at objectivity. The writer believes that the assessment in her account of the Plan and of Secretariat conduct during the negotiations and in presenting the outcome shows that such factors became involved. In years to come historians will, unlike her, have access to archival material from the UN and other Powers concerned. Although they will doubtless find that some nuances of attitude and certain aspects of these institutions' internal policy-making processes have not here been precisely reflected, she is convinced that they will confirm the overall thrust of her account depicting an unhappy episode in international relations and UN institutional involvement.[10] The episode has been even more unhappy for Greek Cypriots, who, naïvely, have for four decades placed so much faith in the United Nations, forgetting that it is just another political institution.

Perhaps the most unfortunate long-term general consequence of this episode in UN history is the harm inflicted on international relations machinery. The conduct of the Secretariat in the recent Cyprus negotiations and during their aftermath casts discredit on the hitherto useful concept of "good offices of the Secretary-General" and the placing of trust in such "good offices" and in the conduct of the Secretariat.[11] This important UN function had been shaped by the first holders of the Secretary-Generalship. Distance is said to lend

[9] Such influence is, as in all cases of elected office, stronger when an incumbent is in his first term and clearly eligible for a second term. There is, however, no UN rule precluding a third term—as with the Presidency of the USA. Thus Mr Pérez de Cuéllar was apparently girding himself up for a third term until his options were precluded by African States' determination to apply geographical principles and turns to election of the Secretary-General. If Asian States were to coordinate matters properly, even the USA is unlikely to be able to ensure a third term for the current incumbent should he wish for one.

[10] The writer pondered whether to sub-title this account: "How Not to Win the Nobel Prize".

[11] UN insiders are alert to the internal bureaucratic intrigues and the politicisation within the Secretariat, but small States, outside the magic circle of the Permanent Members of the Council, do not fully appreciate the extent or consequences of this for Secretariat conduct. Certainly, Cyprus has in the past had naïve expectations. For example, when the Centre for Human Rights in Geneva had, at the request of the Human Rights Commission, prepared a *Report* on Cyprus in February 2002, it believed this would be published instead of being replaced by a version by Mr de Soto and his team designed not to offend the Republic of Turkey. This information was obtained from the Centre. Similarly, when President Clerides sought the Secretary-General's permission for former members of UNFICYP to testify on the situation in the Karpas, following this information having come into the public domain, and for release of their report on the Maronite villages to the European Court on Human Rights (sitting in 2000–2001 in *Cyprus v Turkey*) these requests were refused on Mr Zacklin's advice.

enchantment, but the actions of earlier Secretaries-General and their senior aides, looked at in historical perspective, reveal that their caution in doing nothing likely to lead to their being perceived as protagonists firmly established an invaluable international relations mechanism. At worst, that caution could lead to stabilisation without settlement, but it could sometimes lead over time to a settlement, and it did nothing to hamper reaching one.

The developments in the course of the Cyprus mission of good offices, as exercised since September 2002, show the adverse effect of alterations in the character of the institution of good offices. Once the member of the Secretariat exercising good offices becomes "a party," rather than a simple facilitator,[12] one or other side will inevitably become aggrieved, so that the conduct of the Secretariat, now itself a party, will become an issue. In so far as is possible, the Secretariat, if it is ultimately to be effective, needs to remain above the fray, without acting in such manner as to become identified with particular view-points and interests, or so as to position itself that it will inescapably be perceived as deliberately promoting those interests. Mediation and arbitration, or "bridging proposals," "completing the gaps," or "addressing the key outstanding concerns of the sides" by "improvements" by way of exercise of discretion—as the Secretariat has referred to its recent Cyprus efforts—are activities in which, despite its will to assist the parties in every way it can, and even if invited by them so to involve itself, the Secretariat is unwise to engage. Had the Secretariat refrained from embarking on activities of this kind in relation to Cyprus, it would not have ended up repeatedly regretting the loss of "unique," "historic" and "extraordinary" opportunities for reaching a settlement (in April 2003 and in May 2004). Nor would it have characterised rejection of its Plan by Greek Cypriot voters as "a major setback," or as a "watershed vote" requiring "fundamental reassessment of the full range of United Nations peace activities in Cyprus". Regret for missing "a unique and historic chance"[13] is in any event misguided, because, in international relations and in all political affairs, opportunities and the desire to seize them both go and come intermittently. Just a year earlier, the Secretary-General had also described Annan III as "a unique opportunity."[14]

Moreover, the Secretariat should not have gone so far as to debase itself by implicitly, even directly, threatening the electorate of the Republic of Cyprus with dire consequences should voters in the free and unfettered exercise of their right of internal self-determination decide, in two separate but simultaneous referenda, not to approve the Secretariat-devised Annan Plan. Regrettably, this

[12] As camouflage they may be described as a "facilitator": see eg Mr Richard Boucher on 29 January 2004, describing the role of the UN Secretary-General in his mission of good offices as respects Cyprus in State Department Press Briefing, 30 January and on 3 February 2004.

[13] Statement issued by the Spokesman of the Secretary-General on the outcome of the referenda in Cyprus, 24 April 2004, in *S/2004/437*, Annex III, p 26.

[14] *S/2003/398*, 1 April 2003, heading before para 4. "Unique" obviously does not carry its normal meaning in "UN-speak".

The Special Adviser had a UN microphone and was transmitted verbatim at length from Bürgenstock, but later the CyBC (RIK) did not invite him to educate Cypriots about distortion of details in his Plan.

Someone who never lacked microphones (including the CyBC – RIK) was Mr Denktash.

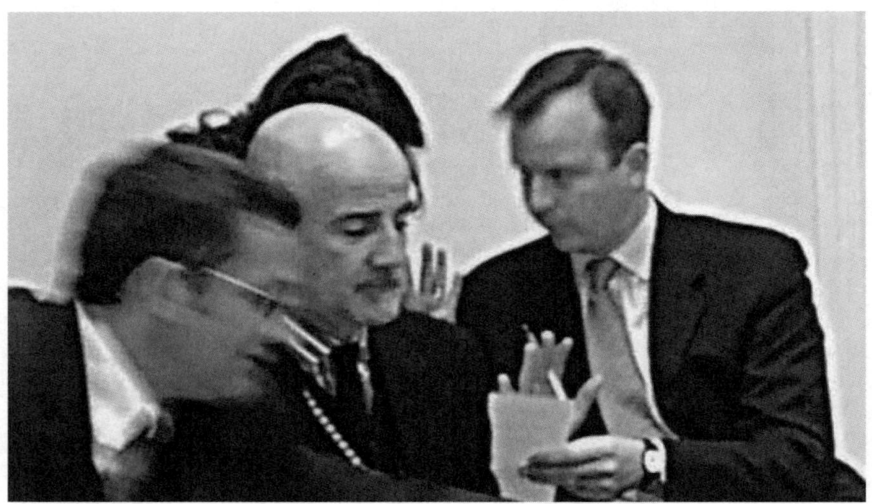

The Special Adviser, Alvaro de Soto, listening to his Special Assistant from the UN Department of Political Affairs, Robert Dann giving instructions to Melanie Redondo.

Alvaro de Soto getting further guidance from Robert Dann at a subsequent meeting.

More advice to Mr de Soto, this time from Lisa Jones in the renewed talks on 19 February 2004. Is she saying, "Do you think we should . . .?"

Below: A standard view of the UN building, emphasising its main tower, headquarters of the UN bureaucracy and a place for endless diplomatic and political meetings and networking.

Above: The UN's Dag Hammarskjöld Library where the various Annan Plans and alternative narratives by Turkish Cypriots, especially by Mr Rauf Denktash, along with copies of this book, should be accessible to all in the UN system and those who invoke "good offices". Only half the main UN building (left) is shown, while the photograph above idealises the structure, so readers can only imagine the 27th, 33rd, 37th and 38th "flaws" where those concerned with status and power are located.

The Security Council approving a resolution on 22 April 2004.

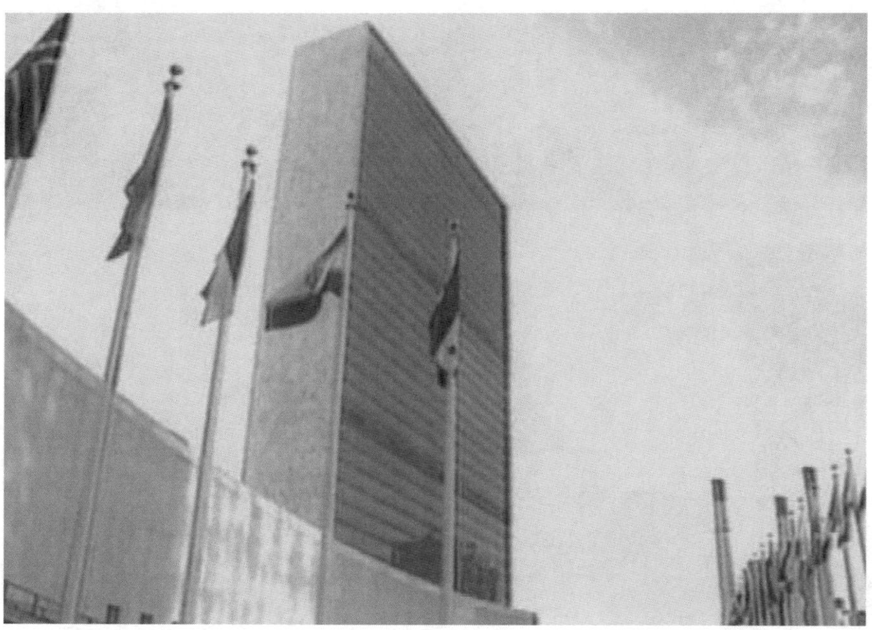

But the UN represents far more then an organisation for world security and political debate. For most people, the UN is a symbol of peace, a centre for settling international disputes in conformity with justice and international law, an institution for developing friendly relations among nations and the key body responsible for promoting respect for human rights and fundamental freedoms for all without distinction as to race or language (Article 1 of the UN Charter). That is certainly how Greek Cypriots have always perceived the UN.

implicitly "threatening" attitude continued to be manifested after the rejection of the Secretariat's Plan, with the Secretary-General's call in the *Report* of 28 May 2004 for a review of UNFICYP's mandate and concept of operations, but put in the specific context of "the watershed vote of 24 April".[15] Similarly, the people of a State should not, when they vote in a way disapproved of by the Secretariat, be told to engage in "a profound and sober assessment of their decision and its potential consequences".[16] Nor should a principal organ of the World's peace-keeping Organisation have wound up its peace-making involvement inside a Member State by demeaning itself in a petty spat with that State about whether a member of the Secretariat had been denied access to an independent, although State-funded, TV Station to air information about his Plan, which he considered had been distortedly represented in internal political debate.[17] The 28 May *Report*, at para 71, misleadingly depicted this incident by writing of "State television" and by implying that, by virtue of the media climate and Government action, the campaign for a referendum had so hampered UN informational activity that the results were not fair and free. Such a peevish descent of the Secretariat into the cockpit, its lack of scruples in making insinuations that the referendum process was being interfered with by the Government and its lapse into a fit of the sulks, because Mr de Soto lost "the game," have nothing to do with the Secretariat's real task, namely, to continue impartially to assist the parties concerned with the Cyprus problem to reach an agreed settlement in the interests of all such parties and also of world peace. The Secretariat should not have been warning, because its Plan was rejected, that there are "serious questions" and "implications for the United Nations". Nor should it have called for "a fundamental re-evaluation on the Greek Cypriot side," while simultaneously stating that "The Secretary-General applauds the Turkish Cypriots".[18] Applause is not a function of the Secretary-General. Moreover, it was inappropriate to have singled out one side for criticism because of its leader's political opposition to and presentation of the Secretariat's Plan, and to have loaded appreciation onto a political figure from

[15] *S/2004/437*, para 92. In *S/2004/756*, 24 September 2004, a Review Team proposed that the size of the UN force be reduced by approximately one-third by moving to more mobile methods of observation. No change was suggested to the mandate.

[16] Sir Kieran Prendergast's briefing to the Security Council on 28 April 2004: s/pv 4954, p 3 col 2.

[17] The Special Adviser wrote to President Papadopoulos on 20 April 2004 that a journalist who had wished to interview him "had been instructed not to interview foreigners". The President in his reply of 21 April pointed to the fact that Cyprus had a lively and well-functioning democracy in which the media are virtually unfettered and that newspapers and the media were replete with analysis and commentaries on the UN Plan. Indeed, Mr de Soto was given much space in leading newspapers and his statements were reported on the news programmes carried by the electronic media. Mr de Soto's letter of 23 April 2004, responding to the President's prompt answer to his 20 April letter of complaint, unsuccessfully attempted to claw back some ground and insisted that the good offices mission would be derelict in its duty if it failed to make available information regarding the Plan to civil society organisations. The President's points were that the media provided for freedom of expression and information and that the UN, its personnel and its agencies should not be intervening in the domestic jurisdiction of Cyprus. See also *infra*, Chapter XVI.

[18] Prendergast, above n 16, at p 3 col 3.

the other side, who, having achieved the insertion of most of his demands in the Plan, not unnaturally supported it. Indeed, it is astonishing to find comments on the behaviour of various Cypriot politicians (clearly matters within the domestic jurisdiction) scattered through the *Report*. It is not too harsh to comment that for a Secretary-General's *Report* to have taken on aspects of a fan-club circular was a grave departure from normal UN standards of reporting.

Far more serious than these lapses, however, is the reason for them. The fulsome praise in the *Report* was designed to secure an unlawful objective, namely, to recommend, on the basis that Turkish Cypriots had "undone any rationale for pressuring and isolating them," that Turkey's subordinate local administration in occupied Cyprus should be given the economic attributes of an independent state without formally recognising it. That entity would then, despite protestations in the *Report* about not assisting secession (Introduction, and paras 90 and 93), be able to function so that there was no incentive to move to reunification of Cyprus. This tactic was an attempt to by-pass a *jus cogens* rule of international law, which forbids recognition of the fruits of aggression. That rule was the reason why SCR541 (1983) and SCR550 (1984) were passed following the "declaration" of the Turkish-occupied area as the "Turkish Republic of Northern Cyprus" on 15 November 1983. Yet, although the Plan purported to be a "peace plan" in conformity with "international law" and in conformity with the Security Council's long-held vision of a settlement, not a single word in the *Report* indicated that the Republic of Turkey was and still is in unlawful military occupation of 36.4% of Cyprus, controlling that large proportion of Cyprus through 35,000 Turkish troops and her subordinate local administration. Instead, as mentioned above, the *Report* implicitly suggested that such Turkish local administration be given all benefits of international cooperation and participation in international bodies. Thus, the 28 May *Report's* para 93, and also its Summary, recommended that members of the Council

> can give a strong lead to all States to cooperate both bilaterally and in international bodies to eliminate unnecessary restrictions and barriers that have the effect of isolating the Turkish Cypriots, deeming such a move as consistent with Security Council resolutions 541(1983) and 550(1984).

This proposal is beyond the scope of the Secretary-General's good offices mission and is also in direct contravention of Security Council Resolutions and international law.[19] It continues to have serious adverse consequences by reason of encouraging States to embark on such measures, which will in turn encourage the beneficiaries not to pursue an overall Cyprus settlement, but will instead facilitate the "TRNC" remaining separate and effectively independent, both economically and politically.

[19] See Opinion of Professor Ian Brownlie CBE, "The Aftermath of the Annan Plan and the Legal Framework of the Efforts of the Secretary-General," dated 6 June 2004, and circulated to the Security Council.

III

Brief Historical Background[1]

THE SITUATION ON the Island of Cyprus has been a focus of international attention for over 50 years. Unsuccessful attempts by Greece in the early 1950s to negotiate with the United Kingdom over union of the crown colony of Cyprus with Greece led to the Cyprus situation being raised at

[1] Cyprus has probably provoked more political, international relations and historical writing per square centimetre of territory than any other problem. Reference here is made only to writing in the English language. There has been little serious study published in English by Turkish scholars on the Cyprus situation. Authors from both ethnic traditions have dwelt on and often exaggerated the wrongs inflicted on their sides by each other and by foreign powers and for this reason I have not referred the reader to their books. Nor have I referred to emotive accounts by certain foreign authors, such as Messrs Reddaway and Oberlin. Lest silence be misinterpreted, I record my view that there was wrongdoing by members of both Communities between December 1963 and November 1967, but that, after 6½ years of peace and relative normalisation, disproportionably terrible vengeance was taken by Turkey in mid-1974, which was in turn followed by two very grave mass crimes committed by members of an unlawful Greek Cypriot paramilitary group. There were similar crimes by Turkish Cypriot paramilitaries and major war crimes by the Turkish Army. The most authoritative accounts in English of the period 1954 to 1978 are: SG Xydis, *Cyprus: Conflict and Conciliation 1954–1958* (Ohio State University Press, Columbus, 1976) (based on the papers of Mr Averoff, then Foreign Minister of Greece); M A Birand, *30 Hot Days* (K Rustem and Son, London, 1985) (a distinguished Turkish journalist's account of the 1974 invasion, based on his close contacts with the Turkish Foreign Ministry); Robert Holland, *Britain and the Revolt in Cyprus 1954–1959* (Clarendon Press, Oxford, 1998) (an academic but witty study based on UK documents); R Stephens, *Cyprus: A Place of Arms* (London, 1966) (a succinct and balanced account of the history of Cyprus until 1965 by a distinguished journalist); S Kyriakides, *Cyprus: Constitutionalism and Crisis Government* (University of Pennsylvania Press, Philadelphia, 1968) (an account of the breakdown of the 1959 settlement); D W Markides, *Cyprus 1957–1963. From Colonial Conflict to Constitutional Crisis* (University of Minnesota, Minneapolis, 2001) (the breakdown, with emphasis on the role of the municipal issue and with a useful bibliography); Alan James, *Keeping the Peace in Cyprus 1963–1964* (Palgrave, Basingstoke, 2002) (an account of the start of UN peacekeeping based on US and UK documents); D S Bitsios, *Cyprus. The Vulnerable Republic* (Institute of Balkan Studies, Thessalonica, 1975) (an account until 1974 by a distinguished Greek diplomat involved in most of the events); M A Attalides, *Cyprus* (Q Press, Edinburgh, 1979) (a study of the international relations context); P G Polyviou, *Cyprus. Conflict and Negotiation 1960–1980* (Duckworth, 1980) (a study emphasising the constitutional and political aspects); and Rosalyn Higgins, *United Nations Peacekeeping. Documents and Commentary 4. Europe 1946–1979*, (RIIA, OUP, 1981). *Cyprus, 1878–1964* by Stella Soulioti (University of Minnesota Press, 2005), gives an overview of Cyprus history and deals in detail with of the period 1960–1964 during which the author was Minister of Justice. Ambassador A J Jacovides, "Cyprus: International Law and the Prospects for Settlement," *Procs of the Am Soc of Int Law*, April 12–14, 1984, and Kypros Chrysostomides, *The Republic of Cyprus. A Study in International Law* (Martinus Nijhoff, The Hague, 2000) give useful accounts of the international law aspects. These are canvassed from a Turkish Cypriot standpoint by the former "Attorney-General of the TRNC," Mr Z M Necatigil, in *The Cyprus Question and the Turkish Position in International Law* (Oxford, 1989). Because his arguments are based on selective citations from UN documents and some tainted secondary sources, some of the contentions in this otherwise authoritative study cannot be supported.

the United Nations General Assembly in 1954. In the Assembly as then composed, the Greek viewpoint that Cyprus was entitled to self-determination received little support. Soon thereafter a violent independence struggle by Greek Cypriot guerrillas commenced. In September 1955 the United Kingdom, determined to retain control of Cyprus for her own strategic purposes, held a tripartite conference with Turkey and Greece, thereby giving Turkey a platform to voice competing claims in respect of Cyprus, claims which became ever more vocal. In response to Turkish claims for partition, the UK envisaged an interim arrangement which would divide the Island into British, Greek and Turkish parts, even preparing maps for this purpose. The Cyprus situation was a major irritant in the eastern Mediterranean defensive alliance and in this deteriorating situation the USA and NATO put pressure on Turkey and Greece to settle matters amicably. Ultimately at Zurich in early February 1959 Greco–Turkish agreement was reached on creation of a Republic of Cyprus under a Constitution providing for community power-sharing. The arrangements were underpinned by a basket of interlinked Treaties (largely concerned with security issues and guarantees) between the two former imperial Powers, the United Kingdom and Turkey,[2] and Greece and Cyprus. However, the complexities of the Constitution established by the settlement, shaped by external Powers, when taken in conjunction with divisions between Greek and Turkish Cypriots, which had been deepened during the anti-Colonial struggle against the United Kingdom, and the unwillingness of Turkey to countenance any changes to that settlement, soon resulted in internal crisis. This crisis developed into intercommunal fighting from 21 December 1963, whereupon the Republic of Turkey repeatedly threatened to invade Cyprus.[3] Under Security Council Resolution

[2] Turkey conquered Cyprus in 1571 and administered it until 1878 when she assigned its administration to the UK by the Cyprus Convention in exchange for a tribute and promises of UK defence in the Caucasus region against Russia. Upon Turkey's entry into World War I, the UK annexed Cyprus. The position was internationally regularised by the Treaty of Lausanne 1923, whereby, in Article 20, Turkey recognised the UK's annexation of Cyprus on 5 November 1914. By Article 16, Turkey renounced all rights and title whatsoever to territories situated outside the frontiers laid down in the Treaty, and agreed that the future of such territories was to be settled by the parties concerned. Turkey contends that a balance between Turkey and Greece in the Eastern Mediterranean was established by the Treaty of Lausanne and was confirmed by the Treaties of 1960 eg in Letter by the Embassy of Turkey to the Member States of the European Union, 23 May 2001. The Government of Cyprus then obtained advice from three Members of the International Law Commission, Professors Crawford, Hafner and Pellet. They concluded that the Treaty

> neither provides any rights in favour of Turkey relating to the maintenance of a "balance" in the region of the eastern Mediterranean nor does it purport to establish such a balance. No rights in this regard can be derived from the Treaty and it is accordingly unnecessary to ask whether, if such rights had existed, they would have been opposable to Cyprus after its independence in 1960:

see Opinion "Does the Treaty of Lausanne 1923 Confer on Turkey Specific Rights with Respect to Cyprus?" 18 November 2001.

[3] From early 1964 a small scale civil war, instigated by Turkey to justify her intended intervention, was fought by paramilitaries of both Communities with both groups employing considerable violence. The Turkish Cypriot force was Turkish Army-officered and some of the Greek Cypriot paramilitaries had been trained by officers in the Greek Contingent. To protect Greek Cypriots

Above: Archbishop Makarios and Colonel Grivas. As Ethnarch, traditional leader of the Greek Cypriot Community from Ottoman times, the Archbishop headed the struggle for independence from British gubernatorial rule and for union with Greece (*enosis*). In complicity with Colonel George Grivas, a Cypriot Greek Army officer, the EOKA guerrilla campaign was organised, beginning operations on 1 April 1955 after it became obvious that UK policy was "never" to end British rule and Greece's first recourse to the United Nations in 1954 had been ineffective. Grivas ordered that Turkish Cypriots should not as such be attacked, despite repeated Turkish Cypriot violence to Greek Cypriots and their property in a series of riots, often after Turkish Cypriot police constables had been killed. Upon a massacre of Greek Cypriots on 12 June 1958, Grivas ordered reprisals against Turkish Cypriots. On 4 August 1958, he called for a ceasefire, and inter-communal violence under British rule ended.

Above: a symbol of widespread anti-Greek riots in Turkey on 6 September 1955. These were organised by Prime Minister Menderes and Foreign Minister Zorlu following a bomb "planted" in Turkey's Salonica Consulate-General during the 1955 Tripartite Conference between the UK, Turkey and Greece. The UK, despite Turkey's renunciation of Cyprus in the Treaty of Lausanne 1923, had invited Turkey to the Conference where Zorlu claimed retrocession of Cyprus or *taksim* (partition). The Treaty-protected Greek minority in Turkey soon fell from 100,000 to 6,000. At much the same time, Volkan, a secret para-military organisation connected with Dr Fazil Kutchuk's "Cyprus is Turkish" Association, was established in Cyprus.

Below left: Rauf Denktash, while Crown Counsel in the Attorney-General's Office (a very fair prosecutor, Greek Cypriot lawyers say) was secret civilian head of the TMT, successor to Volkan. The TMT was Turkish-officered and directed by Turkey's Special War Department. From January 1956, Turkish Cypriots attacked Greek Cypriots and their property. From June 1958, the TMT encouraged Turkish Cypriots to congregate in the north and, in places, drove Greek Cypriots out of mixed villages as a preliminary to partition. TMT continued after independence, playing a vital role in the 1963–67 civil war and gathering Turkish Cypriots into fortified enclaves to form a core of Turkish territory. Below right: Mr Denktash with Dr Fazil Kutchuk, first and only Vice-President of the Republic of Cyprus.

Above: British soldiers searching civilians, after a shooting by an EOKA gunman in Ledra Street (known to the UK press as "murder mile"). 508 persons were killed in the whole period of the EOKA campaign and its attempted suppression from 1955 to 1958, and 1,260 persons were injured. Of those killed, 142 were British, 278 were Greek Cypriots, 84 were Turkish Cypriots and there were 4 others. Of the injured, 295 were Greek Cypriots (43 being policemen) and 258 were Turkish Cypriots (108 being policemen). Included in those figures are 56 Greek Cypriots and 53 Turkish Cypriots killed in the Greco-Turkish intercommunal clashes from mid-June to 4 August 1958: cf. C.1. The Mobile Reserve of the Police Force of 542 was all Turkish Cypriot; of the 1,770 Auxiliary Police and Special Constables 1,700 were Turkish Cypriots; and of the Regular Police Force 891 were Turkish Cypriots while 932 were Greek Cypriots. Turkish Cypriots at that time were 18.13% of the population and Greek Cypriots 78.21%. (The 1960 census, taken under British rule, showed 447,901 Greek Cypriots, 103,822 Turkish Cypriots and 29,984 Maronites, Armenians, Latins and British together making 3.66%.) The Colonial authorities were not so incompetent as to be unaware of the likely divisive consequences of their recruitment policy and who was likely to be killed in a campaign attacking police and military targets.

Overpage: the pictures which follow are not of Stalag Luft IV. They are of one of the British detention camps in Cyprus in 1958 holding Greek Cypriot prisoners preventively detained under the Emergency Regulations 1955. These Regulations were the subject of the first Inter-State Case under the European Convention on Human Rights and Fundamental Freedoms in *Greece v United Kingdom*, Application No 176/56. The Regulations empowered detention, deportation (Archbishop Makarios and 3 colleagues being deported to the Seychelles), whipping, collective punishment, curfews (including closure of shops and imposition for removal of slogans), closure of schools (secondary schools for turbulence and elementary schools for flying the Greek flag), destruction of buildings and restrictions on civil and political rights. A second Inter-State Case, *Greece v United Kingdom*, Application No 299/57, alleged torture by Colonial police and

servicemen, with 29 incidents being held admissible. The Commission of Human Rights introduced the "margin of appreciation" doctrine, permitting Governments some discretion in assessing the extent of derogation strictly required by the exigencies of an emergency situation, and developed the law on exhaustion of domestic remedies. The Committee of Ministers was seized with the Commission's *Report* on the first *Case* in February 1959 and took time to decide its powers, ultimately drawing up Rules of Procedure. Just as investigations on the second *Case* were due, the Zurich and London Agreements were reached in February 1959. The Committee of Ministers then terminated consideration of the Commission's *Report*, avoiding any need to find violations (a technique re-used in 1979 regarding Cyprus's first two applications against Turkey). Thereafter, upon concerted requests by Greece and the UK, the Commission terminated the second *Case*. The Commission was satisfied that the measures were no longer being applied; that termination was a measure calculated to contribute to the restoration of the full and unfettered enjoyment of human rights and fundamental freedoms in Cyprus; that full enjoyment was "closely connected with the solution of the political problems relating to the constitutional status of the island"; and that termination was "calculated to serve, and not to defeat, the purposes of the Convention" (*Report* 8 July 1959, pp 23, 22, 21). It took 40 years before the UK would agree to the Court's Secretariat releasing the Commission's *Reports* on the law and facts. In 2002, the UN Secretariat was "inspired" by these precedents to insert in the Annan Plan a request to the European Court of Human Rights to strike out proceedings regarding property of dispossessed persons in Cyprus, thereby seeking to protect Turkey. But the Annan Plan did not provide for "full and unfettered enjoyment" of Convention rights. Nor were violations to be terminated, as they were at the end of the UK Colonial period.

C.6 and 7

Elementary school children in Limassol, their school having been closed by the Colonial authorities.

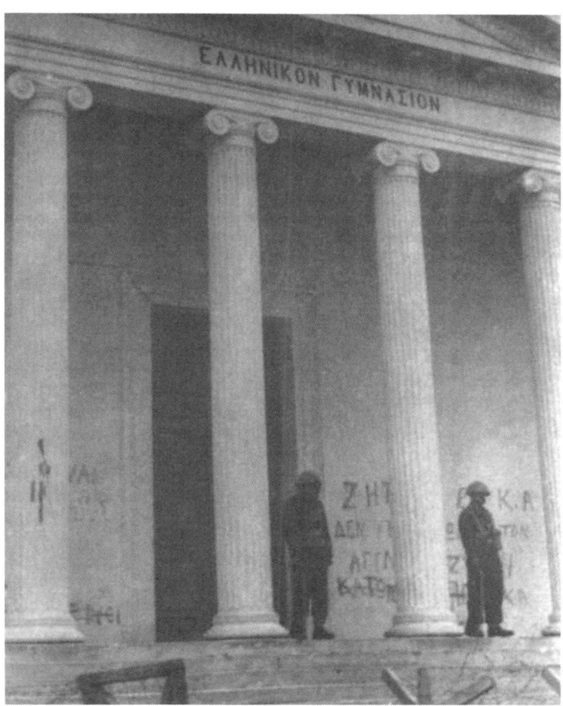

The Gymnasium in Famagusta, closed and guarded by British soldiers. Only children of the middle class rich could complete schooling by being sent to Athens.

Prime Minister Constantine Karamanlis of Greece and Prime Minister Adnan Menderes of Turkey toast each other in the Dolder Hotel after reaching the Zurich Agreement on 11 February 1959. The former described this day as "one of the happiest" in his life. A week later, on 19 February at Lancaster House, where the London Agreement on independence of a Cyprus Republic brought in the UK and provided for what were to be the 1960 Security treaties, Mr Karamanlis described Greece, Turkey and the UK as "the godfathers" of the independent Republic of Cyprus. (The phrase had not then the connotations it later acquired due to a famous film.) A "godfather" is designated a "*Koumparos*" in Greek. A second meaning of "*Koumparos*" is "best man," the term in this sense becoming applicable to another member of the Karamanlis political dynasty, his nephew Prime Minister Costas Karamanlis, in relation to another modern Prime Minister of Turkey, Mr Tayyip Erdoğan.

Prime Minister Karamanlis and Foreign Minister Averoff talking to Archbishop Makarios in London. Karamanlis and Averoff had great difficult in persuading Makarios to accept the Zurich Agreement when the Archbishop learned that Turkey was given a unilateral right of military intervention by Treaty.

THE LANCASTER HOUSE CONFERENCE

Above left: section of the main meeting showing Foreign Minister Averoff of Greece (above) with Greece's Ambassador Seferiades (the famous poet Seferis) and Turkish Foreign Minister Zorlu (below). Top right: Archbishop Makarios and George Chryssafinis; middle, Turkish Cypriot delegation, Dr Kutchuk and Osman Orek; bottom, left to right Colonial Secretary Alan Lennox-Boyd, Foreign Secretary Selwyn Lloyd and Sir Hugh Foot.

Makarios said that he could not sign, but was then subjected to duress by Greece with a threat to hold a Greek general election on denying support to the Cyprus independence movement. Knowing the UK's intention to impose the Macmillan plan leading to partition in seven years, Makarios ultimately adhered to an initial statement he had made in Greece on the basis of Karamanlis' and Averoff's verbal briefing wherein he accepted the Zurich Agreement. That Agreement, marginally expanded to give the UK security guarantee for its bases, was then reflected in a new London Agreement package. In more dignified language than is current, UK Prime Minister Macmillan described this as "a victory for all sides."

An end to imperialism? The 1960 Constitution and Treaties being signed immediately after independence of the Republic of Cyprus on the night of 15/16 October by the Republic's first President, Archbishop Makarios (left), Sir Hugh Foot, the UK's last Colonial Governor of Cyprus (centre) and the first and only Vice-President, Dr Fazil Kutchuk (right).

The complex bi-communal 1960 Constitution was difficult to operate and co-operation between the Communities was minimal. Their members had divergent aims, some still dreaming of *enosis* or *taksim*, with President Makarios wanting Cypriot independence under democratic majority rule, rather than what he perceived as "the tyranny of the minority" under the 1960 Constitution. Turkey, as a Guarantor Power, refused to consider constitutional amendments. She invoked 13 amendments proposed by Makarios at the end of November 1963 and designed to break a two-year deadlock (in which both sides had behaved obstinately, irrespective of their relative culpability) as an opportunity to intervene. Intercommunal fighting, spearheaded by the Turkish-directed TMT, broke out on 21 December 1963. This was quickly followed by Turkish Cypriot claims that the 1960 Constitution was dead, by boycott and by establishment of separate institutions by early January 1964. The TMT and ex-EOKA groups (many being in The Organisation, the largest group organised to defend the Greek Cypriot Community against the TMT and any threats to Cyprus, there being no Cyprus Army as Dr Kutchuk had vetoed a mixed Army) and the Police of Cyprus (which during the fighting divided on ethnic lines) attacked each other and each other's Communities in this period. A leading expert on conflict in Cyprus, Dr Patrick, estimated that between 21 December 1963 and 10 August 1964 (the main period of fighting) approximately 350 Turkish Cypriots and 200 Greek Cypriots and mainland Greeks were killed. To assist in restoring order, which could not be effected by either a mainly British Joint Truce Force of the Guarantor Powers or by the UN Peace-keeping Force, which became operative from the end of March 1964, General Grivas was brought back to Cyprus, with US support, to organise a disciplined National Guard in lieu of paramilitary groups. He and excess Greek troops were re-called to Greece in November 1967 when clashes between the National Guard and Turkish fighters led to Turkish threats of war against Greece and Cyprus. Subsequently, Grivas organised EOKA 'B' to bring down Makarios, who was determined to preserve Cyprus's independence as a State, instead of seeking *enosis* with Greece. Below: standing in the President's office, with its splendid traditional Cypriot ceiling later to be destroyed in the 15 July 1974 coup, and photographed on the night of General Grivas' June 1964 return to command the new National Guard, are, left to right, Polycarpos Georghadjis, Minister of the Interior (and, until it was replaced by the National Guard, leader of The Organisation), Minister of Labour Tassos Papadopoulos, Minister of Commerce and Industry Andreas Araouzos, General Grivas, President Makarios, Minister of Finance Renos Solomonides, Minister of Communications Andreas Papadopoulos, and Patroclos Stavrou, Under Secretary to the President.

Above left: Tassos Papadopoulos and Glafcos Clerides photographed in 1965. They, and also Rauf Denktash, had attended the January 1964 London Conference following the outbreak of intercommunal fighting. Earlier, all had been involved at various negotiations to settle the disputed municipalities issue. From early 1964 until the mid-1970s, Clerides and Papadopoulos, together with Stella Soulioti, constituted the core of any Greek Cypriot team of advisers in negotiations with the Turkish Cypriot side.

Above right: attending intercommunal talks between "prominent personalities of the two Communities" at the Ledra Palace Hotel from 24 June 1968 on revising the 1960 Constitution, especially the issue of municipal government. Most meetings were held tête-à-tête: left, Rauf Denktash, earlier President of the Turkish Communal Chamber, and right Glafcos Clerides, President of the House of Representatives. The talks, utilising the Secretary-General's good offices, followed the breakdown of the 1960 Constitution, civil war from the end of 1963—with Turkish and Greek interventions—and a risk of Greco-Turkish war in November 1967, after which time intercommunal fighting ceased until Turkey's 20 July 1974 invasion. Various series of talks, without results, continued until 9 July 1974, with the next meeting being scheduled for 16 July, but not taking place because of a *coup d'état* organised by the Greek military Junta on the previous day.

Below: younger Knights of the Round Table in February 1969. The first committee of experts met on matters where agreement appeared feasible. Back row: Osman Orek (former Minister of Defence) Rauf Denktash, Glafcos Clerides, Tassos Papadopoulos; middle left: Ümit Süleiman (Turkish Cypriot Interlocutor from 1977).

Above: Secretary of State Henry Kissinger and USSR Foreign Minister Andrei Gromyko used Cyprus as a venue to meet. Here they flank President Makarios at the Presidential Palace on 23 May 1974. Kissinger's and Gromyko's separate later accounts of what the former had said about his attitude to President Makarios being eliminated differ radically.

Below: President Makarios had become closely associated with Presidents Nasser and Tito in the Non-Aligned Movement. President Nasser supplied Cyprus with arms. (Western States in effect applied an arms embargo against Cyprus but not against Turkey.) Later Makarios acquired Eastern bloc arms and intelligence. Accordingly, the USA perceived Makarios as "the Castro of the Mediterranean". Greek administrations talked about eliminating him by a coup—beginning with Prime Minister George Papandreou on 18 August 1964—with the idea being pursued by Greek military Governments from 1967 onwards.

Above: the Presidential Palace 8 weeks after the Kissinger conversation with Gromyko. It was attacked on 15 July 1974 in a *coup d'état* claimed by Mr Kissinger to be "unexpected". The *coup* had been organised by the Greek military Junta, using the Greek-officered National Guard, supported by EOKA 'B' men and some figures politically opposed to Makarios.

President Makarios, having survived the *coup*, is greeted on 20 August 1974 by President Tito.

At this meeting in Ankara, US Assistant Secretary of State Joseph Sisco, Special US Envoy, asked Prime Minister Bulent Ecevit and Turkish Foreign Minister Turan Güneş at 01.45 a.m. on 20 July 1974 to "'give me 48 hours and I will bring you an American plan' . . . Ecevit's response was decisive; ' No! Mr Sisco, it is now too late. A similar meeting to this was held in this very room ten years ago. On that occasion both Turkey and the U.S. made mistakes. You erred by standing in our way, we erred in listening to you. History may repeat itself, but we are not obliged to repeat the blunders of the past. No! we will not listen to you this time' . . . Sisco burst out; 'Do you mean that I am talking here to no purpose?' Ecevit: 'Yes'. At 04.09 Mr Ecevit was told at General Staff HQ that 'our planes are on the way to their first targets'." Turkish landing craft from 31 ships moved in troops at 8.30 a.m. (MA Birand, *30 Hot Days*, pp 19–21.) Below: Turkish landing craft coming into Five Mile Beach.

Above and below: Turkish photographs of landing forces near Kyrenia at 8.30 a.m. on 20 July 1974.

C.27–29

More parachutists descending to link up with Turkish Cypriot enclaves.

Flying in equipment in US-supplied helicopters.

Turkish parachutists being dropped, and others fighting on the ground.

Above: close-up of Turkish soldiers firing.

Below: Turkish tracked vehicles bringing up infantry.

After Turkey's first invasion phase, the Guarantor Powers met in Geneva from 25–30 July 1974. Cypriots were not invited. Left to right: George Mavros, new civilian Greek Foreign Minister, UK Foreign Minister James Callaghan and Turan Güneş, Turkish Foreign Minister. They agreed to make the Geneva Declaration of 30 July 1974. This noted "the existence in practice in the Republic of Cyprus of two autonomous administrations". (See Appendix 9.) At a second Geneva meeting from 8–13 August, with Cypriots now invited, the Greek Cypriot side, given an ultimatum to accept a bi-regional (bi-zonal) or a cantonal federation (with Turkish Cypriot cantons forming 34% of the Island and with 17% of the Island to be handed over in 24 hours), asked for 36 hours to decide. This request was refused, and Turkey's pre-arranged second invasion phase commenced at 2.30 a.m. on 14 August, with Turkey occupying 35.2% of the Island. (See Appendix 5.)

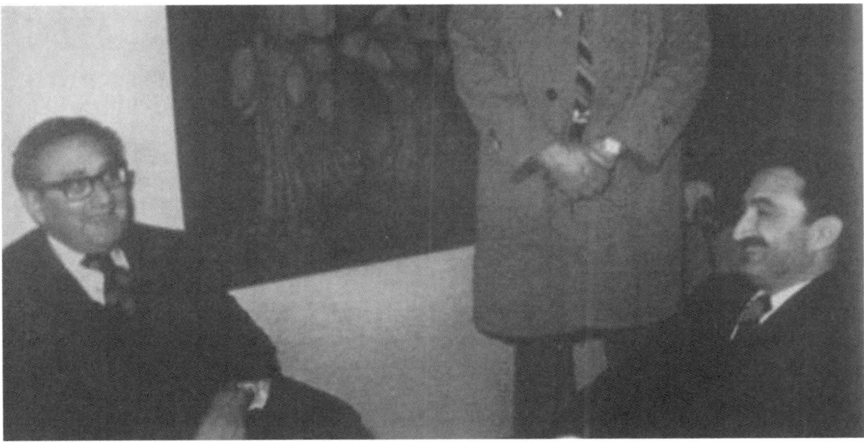

Two good friends who are *ad idem* on Cyprus: Secretary of State Kissinger and Prime Minister Ecevit. The latter regularly states his belief that he solved the Cyprus problem in mid-1974. The former, usually loquacious about his achievements, is less than forthcoming about his Cyprus role.

Advancing Turkish tanks. The latest American monsters currently stationed in the occupied area are far more powerful.

How the Turkish public perceived Turkish action: an example of Turkish postcards, with Prime Minister Ecevit top right. A similar poster was widely circulated in Cyprus.

Tanks (American supplied) advancing to capture the Mia Milia industrial suburb of Nicosia.

Bombing in Nicosia.

Above: it is only too easy to be misinterpreted in Cyprus. This cartoon, like Goya, gives messages about the evil of *all* killings, the suffering of *all* victims' families and the legacy of bitterness left. It is not implying equal extents of responsibility or proportionally equal numbers of murders. This was not the case. The missing persons' issue has not been settled, because exhumations would establish large-scale killings and war crimes by the Turkish Army, as well as atrocities by para-military groups (TMT and EOKA 'B') from the two Communities. There are also missing persons from the 1963–1967 period of intercommunal fighting. All remains should be located by the two sides, exhumed and handed to family members, so that burial with appropriate religious rites can occur. To this end, the Government of Cyprus has embarked on a programme of exhumation and identification, even though rendered difficult by non-cooperation of the Turkish Cypriot side in providing samples for DNA testing. The Turkish Cypriot side and Turkey have failed to conduct an effective investigation aimed at clarifying the fate of Turkish and Greek Cypriot missing persons, thereby continuously violating Article 2 of the European Convention: *Cyprus v Turkey*, Judgment 10 May 2001, para 136.

Secretary-General Waldheim and Under Secretary-General Brian Urquhart decided to visit Cyprus soon after Turkey's second invasion phase more or less halted on 17 August 1974. The photograph was taken on 26 August and shows (front row left to right): Acting-President Clerides, the Secretary-General, Mr Denktash and the UN High Commissioner for Refugees, Prince Sadruddin Aga Khan. Between Clerides and Waldheim is General Prem Chand of UNFICYP, and behind Denktash is Urquhart. The latter wrote: "Cyprus was divided in two. There were atrocities on both sides, many missing persons and prisoners, and a large Greek Cypriot refugee problem. UNFICYP did its best to limit the disaster, to help the helpless, to protect the civilian population, and to evacuate foreign nationals. It eventually established a buffer zone across the island and maintained complete peace between the opposing armies. In all this Prem Chand was outstanding. In an impossible situation he was fair, compassionate, and firm . . . We talked, at first separately, with Clerides and Denktash. Like the military top dog in any situation, the Turks and Turkish Cypriots resented the scrutiny of the UN peacekeeping force and its humanitarian efforts, and Denktash was both defensive and arrogant. Later in the day we brought Clerides and Denktash together for the first time since the war to discuss the island's humanitarian problems as a starting point for wider discussions on a political settlement. This meeting launched the intercommunal talks which still continue fifteen years later." (*A Life in Peace and War*, pp. 257–8.)

In the first meetings, lists of prisoners and some information about missing persons were exchanged. Left to right: Mr Remy Gorgé (a Swiss citizen, later to be Acting Special Representative), Mr Clerides, Special Representative Weckmann-Munoz of Mexico and Mr Denktash.

Left: Mr Denktash met at the Ledra Palace by Special Representative Weckmann-Munoz. Right: Mr Papadopoulos and Mr Clerides arriving for the humanitarian talks and constitutional negotiations. The constitutional talks were to end as a result of action directed by the Turkish Foreign Ministry. In January 1975 the Greek Cypriot side agreed to a federal solution and a meeting was arranged for the presentation of proposals. On 10 February, Mr Denktash was shown these written proposals and immediately postponed the meeting. On 13 February 1975 he declared the "Turkish Federated State of Kibris". Such preemptive action to abort positive developments became a feature of the process, most strikingly on 15 November 1983 with declaration of the "Turkish Republic of Northern Cyprus".

Above: Makarios was welcomed in Greece on 29 November 1974. Both Governments held talks to draw up a common policy on the Cyprus problem. President Makarios is pictured with his team: left to right, Tassos Papadopoulos, Glafcos Clerides, the President, and John Christophides, a distinguished Foreign Minister of Cyprus who did much to restore its international reputation.

Below: Upon Makarios' return to Cyprus the Archbishop addressed the largest rally ever held in Cyprus, over 200,000 people, who flocked to welcome him at his home, the Archbishopric, which had been severely damaged in the coup.

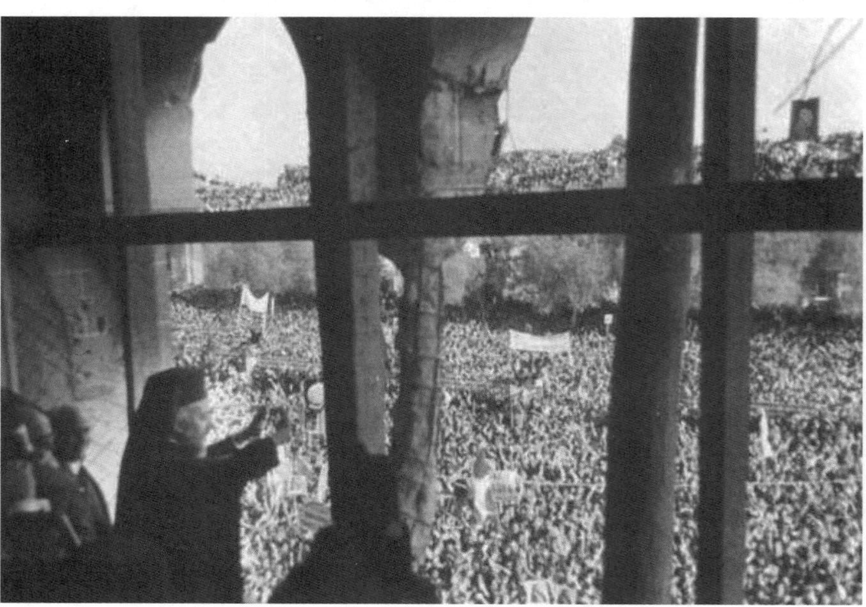

186 of 4 March 1964, UN peacekeeping forces have been (and still are) stationed in the Island.[4] Unfortunately, UNFICYP had no mandate to prevent military interventions in Cyprus by Turkey and Greece in mid-1964, 1967 and in mid-1974. American and UN good offices in the late 1967 crisis led to a withdrawal of Greek troops stationed in Cyprus in excess of the numbers fixed by the Treaty of Alliance and an end to Turkey's current threats of invasion. Subsequent Greek intervention, beginning on 15 July 1974 in a coup to eliminate President Makarios, ended following Turkey's first full-scale invasion phase, which commenced on 20 July, allegedly in response to Greek sponsorship of this coup. Although for nearly 7 years preceding these Greek and Turkish interventions there had been no inter-communal conflict, the international community acquiesced in Turkey's initial invasion on 20 July 1974, but, apart from the USA, became less complacent when Turkey in mid-August extended her operations to seize and occupy a large swathe of Cyprus territory. Despite Security Council Resolutions calling for withdrawal of foreign troops present in Cyprus otherwise than under international Treaties, Turkey's troops, even today numbering about 35,000 (sometimes as many as 40,000) have remained in occupation of 36.4% of the Republic of Cyprus.

Over the years there have been many attempts to reach an agreed Cyprus settlement between Greek and Turkish Cypriots and their "motherlands," with other Powers keeping a watchful and often interfering eye on the process to secure their own perceived interests. At first this was sought to be achieved through a UN Mediator, but, after the Plaza *Report* (*S/6253*, 26 March 1965), Turkey considered that the Mediator's functions had come to an end, claiming

against Turkey's threats, some 12,000 Greek troops in excess of the agreed Treaty numbers were from April 1964 infiltrated into Cyprus, while Turkey also infiltrated paramilitaries. In August 1964, following an attack on Turkish Cypriot coastal villages where Turkish Cypriot paramilitaries and armaments were being landed, Turkey bombed Greek Cypriot villages and threatened invasion with a large fleet, only being restrained by the risk of Soviet intervention and Security Council Resolution 193, 9 August 1964. Contemporaneous American attempts to settle the Cyprus problem by either *enosis* (union of Cyprus with Greece) or double *enosis* (the Acheson Plan for a leonine partition between Greek and Turkey) failed—as did later attempts to partition Cyprus between Greece and Turkey pursued by successive Greek Governments. At the end of November 1967, in reaction to an incident in which the Greek-commanded National Guard displaced Turkish-commanded paramilitary personnel from an area they had sought to control, Turkey threatened again to invade Cyprus and also Western Thrace. With US and UN good offices, the crisis was defused and the excess numbers of Greek troops were withdrawn, leaving Cyprus militarily undefended and still the object of international intrigues, while internally there was effectively a truce and a large degree of normalisation in the daily life of the Communities.

The complex history of the disputes and manoeuvres by the Powers and Cypriot parties are impartially and comprehensively discussed in Alan James, *Keeping the Peace in Cyprus 1963–1964*. Professor Thomas Ehrlich, one-time Special Assistant to the US Under Secretary of State, Mr G W Ball, the USA's then trouble-shooter for Cyprus, provides a good legal account, although based on the State Department's less than candid account of the facts: see *Cyprus 1958–1967* (Oxford, OUP, 1974).

[4] UNFICYP had replaced a British-commanded Joint Truce Force of troops of the Guarantor Powers which was to operate from 26 December 1963. The UN force had been agreed when the Cyprus Government rejected an Anglo–American demand for a NATO or Commonwealth force.

that his *Report* went beyond his terms of reference. Resumption of the mediator function proved impossible due to the Turkish view that direct negotiations were more appropriate. Later, direct inter-communal negotiations were initiated in June 1968 by making use of UN good offices first proffered on 3 December 1967 after the November 1967 crisis. But the parties' entrenched and divergent positions and the Cold War context prevailing until 1990 meant that success was an unlikely prospect. In the early 1990s, abortive attempts were made to achieve an overall settlement, or, alternatively, to introduce interim confidence-building measures, but all these attempts were equally unsuccessful. The Greek Cypriot side ascribed such failures to the Republic of Turkey's satisfaction with the "solution" she had militarily imposed in 1974. When negotiations were re-started, there were often moves further to consolidate the supposedly "independent" Turkish Cypriot regime (as when the "Turkish Federated State of Kibris" ("TFSK") was established by Turkey's Foreign Ministry on 13 February 1975 in occupied Cyprus)[5] so as to disrupt any negotiations, and again when the regime on 15 November 1983 (again with Turkish Foreign Ministry assistance) had been declared the "Turkish Republic of Northern Cyprus" immediately before a fresh initiative of good offices from the Secretary-General was due to be conveyed to the Turkish Cypriot side.[6]

THE DECISION TO OPEN EU ACCESSION NEGOTIATIONS WITH CYPRUS

However, on 6 March 1995, there was a crucial development. The Council of Ministers of the European Union decided that negotiations for the accession of Cyprus to the Union would begin six months after the conclusion of the EU's Inter-Governmental Conference, with such negotiations being expected to begin in late 1997.[7] This event, which would ultimately lead to Cyprus's accession to the EU, became the trigger for a series of Security Council Resolutions and Secretary-General's *Reports* and actions, and for renewed international interest in settling the Cyprus question by means of resuming direct talks between the leaders of the Island's two Communities, Greek and Turkish

[5] The then head of the Cyprus Desk at the Turkish Foreign Ministry, Mr Ecmel Baroudjou, in a series of 15 articles published in *Cumhuriyet* from 20 July 1992, described in detail the Turkish Foreign Ministry's determining role in establishing the "Turkish Federated State of Kibris" on 13 February 1975 and in drafting its "Constitution".

[6] These two moves to "independence" had been prefigured by the establishment on 28 December 1967, with the assistance of the Secretary-General of the Turkish Foreign Ministry and its Chief Legal Adviser of a "provisional Cyprus Turkish administration" to direct Turkish Cypriot affairs. This was done just when it had been agreed that the Secretary-General's good offices would be accepted to open negotiations on a constitutional settlement. In tactful but strong language, the Secretary-General reported on these developments: *S/ 8323,* 3 January 1968.

[7] This was the price of a bargain extracted by Greece from her EC partners in exchange for agreement to the 1995 EU–Turkey Customs Union Agreement with Turkey, which implied that Turkey would become an EU candidate.

NEGOTIATIONS FROM 1975–1997 IN PICTORIAL FORM
EARLIER LEADERS IN CYPRUS AND THEIR NEGOTIATING LEGACIES

Top left: President Makarios (1960–1977), who involved the UN in December 1963, secured a UN force in 1964, and made the 1977 High Level Agreement with Mr Denktash, thereby accepting a future bi-zonal and bi-communal federation and practical compromises on human rights.

Top right: President Kyprianou (1977–1988), who found settlement was not attainable when Turkey wanted the occupied area to become either an independent Turkish Cypriot "State," a loose confederation, or even better, to stay as her militarily occupied fief.

Lower: President Vassiliou (1988–1993), who brought Cyprus in from the UN-inspired cold, but was not re-elected to pursue the Set of Ideas. Later he was Cyprus's EU Negotiator.

After declaration of the "Turkish Federated State of Kibris" under Turkish Foreign Ministry direction on 13 February 1975, the Greek Cypriot side, anxious to achieve a settlement, agreed to inter-communal talks in Vienna from 28 April–3 May 1975 (Vienna I). Matters there discussed in general principle will be familiar to all concerned with the Cyprus issue. They have been debated for thirty years: powers and functions of a federal government; opening of an airport serving Turkish Cypriots (at that time the Nicosia International Airport); displaced persons; geographical (territorial) aspects; and expert committees. These meetings were followed by the Vienna II round (5–7 June 1975). Federal functions were again discussed and establishment of a joint transitional government was raised. Below left: Secretary-General Waldheim is seen, with Rauf Denktash and, right, with Glafcos Clerides, "negotiators on behalf of their respective communities" at meetings under the Secretary-General's good offices, convened in terms of SC Resolution 367 (1975) of 12 March 1975. (SC Resolution 367 remains the foundation for continuing missions of good offices in Cyprus.)

On 18 July 1975 the three Turkish Cypriot members of an agreed expert committee (Messrs Münir, Süleyman and Necati—later Necatigil) proposed joint transitional government with equal community membership, avowedly to enable cooperation pending a final settlement, but actually in order to displace the exclusive international status of the Republic of Cyprus and President Makarios' Government. That proposal was repeated at the Vienna III round (31 July–2 August 1975). (Mr Denktash remains consistent: he was murmuring such a proposal again in 2004 after the Greek Cypriot electorate's rejection of Annan V.) The Turkish Cypriot side also undertook to produce at the next meeting detailed constitutional and territorial proposals, but this did not happen then or later. However, the most important discussion at Vienna III centred on humanitarian arrangements and some limited population movement of Turkish and Greek Cypriots. These issues are so significant that they are fully dealt with in Appendix 8.

Above: it was not until Mr Pérez de Cuéllar, Special Representative 1975–77, succeeded in encouraging the Community leaders to meet on 27 January 1977 to negotiate to reunite the Island after Turkey's invasion that progress was made. President Makarios, Mr de Cuéllar and Mr Denktash are here seen together.

On 12 February 1977, in Secretary-General Waldheim's presence, a High Level Agreement, containing "Guidelines" was reached. This Agreement and the subsequent Agreement of 19 May 1979 are the only substantive Agreements the sides have reached. (See Appendix 9 for the two High Level Agreements.) Pictured are President Makarios, Secretary-General Waldheim and Mr Denktash prior to signing the 12 February 1977 High Level Agreement (the "Guidelines").

At the 12 February 1977 High Level meeting, it was agreed to resume inter-communal talks in Vienna. Assurances were given in the interval, with US intervention, that there would be meaningful negotiations on territory with presentation of serious Turkish Cypriot proposals. The Greek Cypriot side produced comprehensive federal proposals aided by their Canadian expert, Professor R St J Macdonald, and a map with specific territorial proposals. The Turkish Cypriot side produced Basic Principles to govern the constitutional structure and a 6 page list of powers of the federal government and the regional administrations. Their proposal entailed two equal political entities in a federal administration on a basis of equality with very limited federal functions, which could grow in a process they described as "federation by evolution". Their position was that there must be agreement that sovereignty of the future federation derived from the sovereign peoples of the two communities previously organised in States of their own. (That view was effectively to prevail in Annan V.)

Below left: Michalis Triantafyllides, Tassos Papadopoulos, Greek Cypriot Interlocutor, and Stella Soulioti; right, Ümit Süleiman, Turkish Cypriot Interlocutor, Rustem Tatar and Necati Ertekün. Bottom, left to right, Tassos Papadopoulos, Stella Soulioti, Pérez de Cuéllar and Secretary-General Waldheim.

D.8–10

Secretary-General Waldheim with President Kyprianou (left) and Mr Denktash (right). The "Ten Point High Level Agreement" of 19 May 1979 for resumption of intercommunal talks reiterated the 12 February 1977 "Guidelines" and various UN Resolutions. It provided for "respect for human rights . . . of all citizens of the Republic," the giving of priority to reaching agreement on resettlement of Varosha under UN auspices without awaiting the outcome of discussion on other aspects of the Cyprus problem, and it envisaged demilitarisation of the Republic of Cyprus. After a two-year break, due to Mr Denktash's insistence through his Interlocutor on agreement to various Soysal-devised conceptions about federation, unitary states, bi-zonality and security, there were amicable but fruitless talks until 1983, when the Turkish Cypriot side pulled out, because the Greek Cypriot side had encouraged the passage of GA Resolution 37/253 of 13 May 1983 on Cyprus. The "TRNC" was unilaterally declared on 15 November 1983. This was in the knowledge that Dr Gobbi, the Special Representative, was on 16 November due to present a message from the Secretary-General about immediately convening talks whose format had been under negotiation.

Mr Denktash on 15 November 1983 purports to declare the "Turkish Republic of Northern Cyprus".

The "members" of the "Legislative Assembly of the Turkish Federated State of Kibris" vote for the "Declaration".

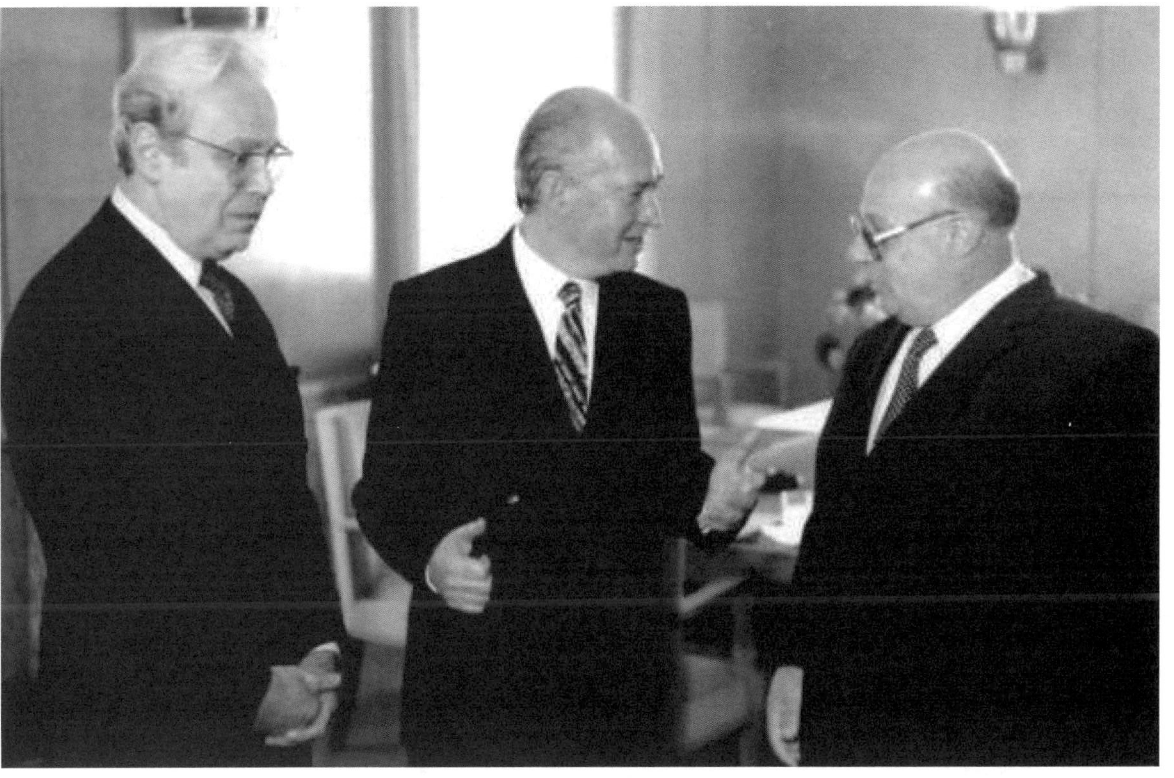

Above: a disenchanted-looking Secretary-General de Cuéllar, with President George Vassiliou and Mr Denktash. They met in Geneva on 24 August 1988, where they re-committed themselves to the High Level Agreements and agreed to meet without pre-conditions to reach an agreed settlement by 1 June 1989. (Photograph courtesy of George Lanitis.)

Above: in this cartoon, Mr Denktash says in Cypriot dialect: "If you've read it before 1st June, call me to bring more." In the many talks in 1988–9, Mr Denktash applied the allegedly agreed principle of "bi-zonality" to all his envisaged constitutional, economic and security arrangements, while the Greek Cypriot side rebutted his contentions. A wise Special Representative, Mr Oscar Camilion, did not criticise the parties for explaining their positions and answering each other, even lengthily. If international public servants take on arduous and ultimately boring tasks, it remains their duty to respect the parties' rights to hold opinions that differ and to read the papers carefully, as Mr Camilion did.

WHEN THE USA PROVED A GENUINE FRIEND TO BOTH TURKEY AND CYPRUS

Above: President George Bush Senior and President Turgut Ozal of Turkey at the White House on 24 March 1991. President Bush announced they had discussed the Cyprus question and that he supported Mr de Cuéllar's mandate of good offices. He mentioned his then able Ambassador working full time on the question and that both Greece (Prime Minister Mitsotakis) and Turkey wanted it settled. President Ozal pointed to the question's 27 year-long history, saying that he was working to see it solved sensibly on the basis of equal rights for the Turkish and Greek Communities in Cyprus.

Below: President Bush being received by President Ozal in Ankara on 20 July 1991.

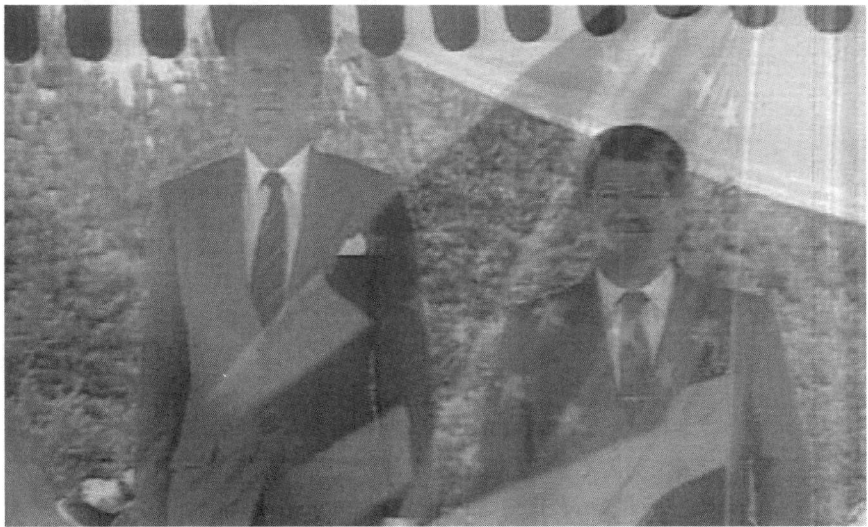

Below: President George Bush and President Ozal at their Ankara press conference, following the 20 July 1991 meeting. This was held in a strategic context broadly similar to that of 2004, although Turkey had then made a "pivotal contribution" to bringing Saddam Hussein's invasion of Kuwait to an end. President Bush mentioned the need not to break up Iraq in response to Kurdish claims. He also talked of "building a path to peace in Cyprus" and making reconciliation between Greece and Turkey possible. This was not a situation, President Bush continued, "where the US can dictate. Nor would it attempt to dictate terms". He added that Turkey was fully committed to negotiating "a settlement which is acceptable to the Turkish Cypriot and Greek Cypriot peoples." For this to be achieved, "political equality, bi-communality, bi-zonality and the maintenance of Turkey's right of guarantee are vital to a just and viable peace-settlement". His view was that SC Resolution 649 (1990) was the "necessary framework for such a settlement". For his part, President Ozal referred to the need for "political equality" of the two Cypriot Communities.

Left: President Vassiliou and Secretary-General Ghali at the UN venue for official hand-shaking on 15 July 1992 shortly before presentation of the Ghali Set of Ideas on the same day.
Right: Mr Denktash with Mr Süleyman on 17 July. When asked by the press whether the Secretary-General would produce a map, Mr Denktash, to show his seriousness about the issue of territory, pulled out a tourist map of the "TRNC". (This picture was taken immediately thereafter.)

Above: on 12 November 1992 emerging from the last meeting of the talks (supposed to be resumed in March 1993), Mr Denktash declared that he accepted 90% of the Set of Ideas but that 10% was unacceptable. (The rub was that all the crucial parts were in the 10%.) He had on 7 November already told the press that his views were so distant from the Set of Ideas and the other side's position that he did not think the UN could "bridge" them. The previous day he had explained that his concept was two independent States cooperating between themselves.

After months of negotiation, Special Representative Joe (CJ) Clark, former Prime Minister of Canada, assisted by Gustave Feissel, the Secretariat's Cyprus expert, and other technical experts, on 21 March 1994 finalised a package of confidence-building measures, particularly the re-opening of Varosha under UN administration and the re-opening of Nicosia International Airport for unhindered flow of persons and goods. The picture is of Joe Clark (third from left) with Gustave Feissel (second from left) meeting Rauf Denktash again on 23 March 1994. Denktash told him that re-opening Varosha and Nicosia International Airport were not commensurate. (This has contemporary parallels to attitudes as regards "direct trade" and Varosha.) Mr Clark, in consequence, announced his inability to get Turkish Cypriot agreement to the Draft and reported negatively to the Security Council. Upon this, Mr Denktash's position "evolved," although he demanded his clarifications be inserted in the 21 March 1994 Draft Ideas. In response, acting on National Council advice, President Clerides declined to engage in further negotiations.

Above: Prime Minister Çiller (heading the Erbakan / Çiller coalition), President Demirel and Abdullah Gül, Minister of State Responsible for Cyprus (ie the detailed Turkish direction of Cyprus) on the occasion of the 20 January 1997 Turkey–"TRNC" Declaration of Solidarity. This "Protocol" was in response to the EU's willingness to consider Cyprus's EU membership application. It was designed to provide a framework for "TRNC" integration into Turkey.

Below: signature of the 20 January 1997 "Protocol," with President Demirel and "President" Denktash engaging in exchanges of the Protocol and coming closer.

Above: a mover and a shaker, Richard Holbrooke, with President Clerides in New York on 8 July 1997 immediately before UN-organised direct talks at Troutbeck. Mr Holbrooke is still around, hoping to shake things up.

Above: the Secretary-General, with President Clerides and Mr Denktash, moving towards another fiasco at Troutbeck. Special Representative Cordovez brings up the rear. Due to take place between 9–13 July 1997, the talks broke up a day early. An EU leakage had indicated that accession negotiations with the Republic of Cyprus would proceed irrespective of whether there was a Cyprus settlement. Moreover, Turkey would not be in the group of EU applicants with whom discussions were to be held, a point confirmed in the Commission's *Agenda 2000*, published on 16 July. An angered Turkey encouraged Mr Denktash to pursue his views about two separate States in Cyprus.

Below: direct talks meeting at Glion-sur-Montreux on 11 August 1997, which Mr Denktash attended despite a further Turkey-"TRNC" Joint Statement on a visit by Prime Minister Ecevit on 20 July 1997. The Joint Statement announced determination to deepen integration measures and the uselessness of resumed negotiations. Sitting on the left, Mr Denktash is waiting to throw a spanner in the works in response to the EU's "bombshell" (*Agenda 2000*). To the right, Mr Markides, President Clerides and Mr Gustave Feissel, then Acting Special Representative, whose drafting skills have since the late 1980s, and especially in the 1990s, led to Ideas, Sets of Ideas, Draft Joint Statements at Troutbeck, and a Draft Joint Statement at Glion. These found their fruition in Mr de Soto's Preliminary Observations in July 2000 in Geneva and ultimately in Annan I. "The DNA" is Messrs Feissel's and Pérez de Cuéllar's, scarcely Greek Cypriot, although Mr de Soto introduced a large Turkish Cypriot element.

Professor Soysal, then Mr Denktash's chief adviser (but Mr Necati Ertekün and Mr Olgun were also there hovering in the background) at Glion on 11 August 1997. He explained that, depending on the EU's decision at the year-end on the Republic of Cyprus's membership application, the "TRNC" would decide on measures of integration with Turkey—like those of Cyprus with the EU—and on whether there was any point in pursuing the present process. The UN was to blame for attaching its hopes to the European process.

Below: Mr Denktash was to take Professor Soysal's clairvoyant views seriously. Here he is being interviewed on 19 November 1997 in Nicosia by Messrs Cordovez and Feissel. He indicated that negotiations could not proceed.

D.30–31

"President" Denktash on 15 August 1997 effectively announcing failure of the Glion talks. The transcript records: "EU threw a bombshell while we were negotiating in Troutbeck by reporting that the process for making Cyprus a member of the EU—in spite of the fact that the conflict for 34 years has been whether Greek Cypriots can represent Cyprus as a whole—and decided to proceed to negotiations at the end of this year." He added that, at Mr Cordovez' request, he would not destroy the UN talks process and would watch what the EU decided at the end of the year. "Division will be finalised if they accept Cyprus." He would think about whether to participate in talks in March 1998. Mr Denktash objected strongly to attempts to destroy "our vested right as a co-founder partner and to destroy the political equality between the two Motherlands". A subsidiary complaint was that there were too many [Cyprus] co-ordinators involving themselves: he was spending all his time "explaining the Cyprus problem to people who knew nothing or very little about it". This explains why he thought it necessary to subject the then Sir David Hannay (and many others) to history lessons.

Below left: here are two of Mr Denktash's able Turkish Cypriot advisers also at the meeting, Mr Necati Ertekün, formerly "President of the Supreme Court of the TFSC" and later "Foreign Minister of the TRNC" (who, before he withdrew from Republic of Cyprus office, was Mr Justice Münir, Judge of the Supreme Constitutional Court) together with Mr Ergün Olgun. As a distinguished lawyer, Mr Münir always carried a big briefcase full of dense and lengthy papers, like members of the Greek Cypriot side.

Above right: Turkish Cypriot leader Rauf Denktash, right, during a joint press conference with Turkish Foreign Minister Ismail Cem in Nicosia on 24 July 1998. Mr Denktash proposed setting up a confederation of equal states as a way to end the 24-year-old division of Cyprus. Mr Cem declared this offer had Turkey's full backing. In March, Mr Denktash had told Special Representative Cordovez that it was necessary to approach matters based on "acknowledgment of the existence of two fully functioning democratic States on the Island". This Turco-Turkish Cypriot stance meant that for 2 years and 4 months there were no talks meetings.

Above: Yiannos Kranidiotis, Deputy Foreign Minister of Greece, responsible for Cyprus becoming an EU Member State, at a crucial EU summit with UK Foreign Secretary Douglas Hurd, Hans Van Den Broek, EU Enlargement Commissioner and UK Prime Minister John Major.

Below left: Yiannos Kranidiotis with Foreign Secretary Robin Cook when the United Kingdom claimed to operate an ethical foreign policy. (It was certainly a great deal more ethical then than it is now.)

Below right: Yiannos Kranidiotis with Van den Broek.

Above: Greece's new foreign policy: all Foreign Ministers are frequent flyers abroad for their countries. Here Greece's Foreign Minister was flying at home (Samos) for the edification of Turkey's Foreign Minister, Ismael Cem, who watched his host, George Papandreou, doing the *Zeimbekiko*, a folk dance of Turkish origin, on 24 June 2001.

Below: an amused audience, with Mr Cem standing centre in a grey suit.

Cypriot. It was widely perceived that EU accession negotiations would facilitate a Cyprus settlement.[8] Nonetheless, just as earlier attempts to resurrect serious comprehensive negotiations had been attended by failure, the Secretariat's attempts, although backed by major Powers on the Security Council and, towards the end of this phase, even by the Heads of State of the "G8," did not succeed in getting Mr Denktash to return to the negotiating table.[9]

[8] SCR1062(1996), 28 June 1996, §13; SCR1092 (1996), 23 December 1996, §17; SCR1117 (1997), 27 June 1997, §§7–9 and 14; SCR1217, 22 December 1998, §§ 6–9; and SCR1250 (1999), 29 June 1999, §§ 2–7. Particularly important *Reports* on the framework of direct negotiations were *S/1996/1055,* 17 December 1996, §§12 *et seq,* and *S/1999/707*, 22 June 1999, the latter of which showed that, after abortive direct talks in 1997 and a shuttle mission, the Secretariat believed that the time had come to focus on the core issues. Simply put these were, in the Secretary-General's view:

> (a) Security (b) distribution of powers (c) property and (d) territory. A compromise on these issues would remove the remaining obstacles to a peaceful settlement (§8).

These issues were in fact the agenda (with "Constitution" being substituted for "distribution of powers") for the comprehensive negotiations under the auspices of the Secretary-General called for in SCR1250 (1999), as to which negotiating principles (still binding) were set out in §7 of the Resolution. Later still the pretentious vogue word "governance" was used as the rubric to cover all constitutional matters and a ragbag of associated topics.

[9] Direct talks between Mr Clerides and Mr Denktash as the two Community leaders had commenced at Troutbeck from 9–12 July and continued at Glion-sur-Montreux from 11–15 August 1997, where, however, the Turkish Cypriot leader declared, in view of the EU's publication of *Agenda 2000*, envisaging negotiations on the Republic of Cyprus's EU entry, that he could not enter into any formal understandings or agreements (*S/1997/973*, 12 December 1997, paras 4–6). Thereafter, despite the efforts of Mr Diego Cordovez, then Special Adviser, the process of negotiation could not be resumed (*S/1998/518*, 16 June 1998). From 16 October 1998, the Deputy Special Representative in Cyprus began a sequence of confidential meetings with both leaders, described as "shuttle talks" and in which neither side was made aware of the views expressed by the other side. Whilst this enabled the UN to understand each side's views, it could not lead to any agreement and the Secretary-General, as indicated in the preceding footnote, decided, with backing from the G8 for a comprehensive negotiation, to invite the leaders to negotiations in the fall of 1999. It took time and developments to persuade Mr Denktash and the then Government of Turkey to agree to this. These events are described in an animated and illuminating fashion in Lord Hannay's *Cyprus. The Search for a Solution* (London and New York, I B Tauris, 2005), received as this text was being dispatched to the publishers. Had there been time, the writer would have enlivened this with revelations from his highly readable account of his role, the ups and downs of negotiations from 1996 to 2003 and his frank comments on persons involved. His book emphasises the international and regional contexts, and his frame of reference is clearly the creation of better international relationships between the Powers concerned by the ongoing Cyprus situation. Of particular interest are his accounts of the positive action by UK and US diplomats in that period to ensure that comprehensive negotiations for a Cyprus settlement got onto and were kept on the road, and of the diplomatic moves to assuage the Republic of Turkey's injured feelings when it saw itself as having been let down by the European Union in December 1997. Lord Hannay's was a major contribution to bringing a Cyprus settlement into the realms of attainability, and should be acknowledged even by those (like the writer) who disagree with certain of his interpretations and historical assertions. For the latter, he cannot be reproached for choosing between the conflicting accounts in the absence of an authoritative study covering the last 50 years. Nonetheless, he tends to see things "top-down," too logically, and with a degree of dismissiveness towards Cypriots' (of both sides) own characterisation of certain issues as important to them. All experts need to learn that logic and politics are not necessarily congruent.

CYPRUS'S PROGRESS TOWARDS EU MEMBERSHIP TRIGGERS TALKS

Towards the end of 1999 it became apparent that, at the forthcoming Helsinki European Council to be held on 10 and 11 December 1999, the Republic of Cyprus's application to become an EU Member State could be attended by success independently of whether the Cyprus problem was solved or not.[10] This led the Secretary-General, despite his consciousness "that there had been many false dawns," to re-assess the prospects for re-starting Cyprus settlement talks. He explained

> [T]he new circumstances included the adoption by the Security Council of resolution 1250 (1999), the four guidelines of which provided a clear and realistic framework for negotiation, the evolving Greek–Turkish rapprochement, the European Council decision in December 1999 at Helsinki that opened the door to Turkey's candidature for accession, as well as the prospect for the enlargement of the European Union by up to 10 new members, including Cyprus. The European Union factor in particular offered a framework of incentives to reach a settlement as well as deadlines within which to reach it.
>
> (*S/2003/398*, 1 April 2003, para 6)

Having formed this opinion, with cooperation from Turkey now facilitating the holding of resumed talks, the Secretary-General, on 1 November 1999, appointed as his Special Adviser on Cyprus Mr Alvaro de Soto.[11] Mr de Soto put

[10] The Helsinki Presidency Conclusions of 10 and 11 December 1999 read:

> 9.(a)The European Council welcomes the launch of the talks aiming at a comprehensive settlement of the Cyprus problem on 3 December in New York and expresses its strong support for the UN Secretary-General's efforts to bring the process to a successful conclusion.
> (b)The European Council underlines that a political settlement will facilitate the accession of Cyprus to the European Union. If no settlement has been reached by the completion of accession negotiations, the Council's decision on accession will be made without the above being a precondition. In this the Council will take account of all relevant factors.

[11] Mr de Soto is an able and lively Peruvian national and member of the Secretariat, who joined it as a protégé of Mr Pérez de Cuéllar, on whose approaches he often appears to have modelled his own—especially as regards not always making full disclosure; the view that "good offices" involve not merely exploration of suggestions but full mediation and even imposition of his own views by way of finalisation; the tactic that "it will be all right on the night"; willingness to accept settler participation in referenda (cp Western Sahara); and sketchy approaches to economic and social issues and land transfer schemes—as in El Salvador, where Mr de Soto was architect of the peace settlement. Mr de Soto's Central American experience, where the agreed methodology was mediation and the outcome a peaceful revolution, was inappropriate for application to the Cyprus situation, where "mediation" has since 1965 been anathema (for both sides); where "good offices" are seen as being confined to their original and limited diplomatic scope; and where the consistent aim of one side (the Greek Cypriot side) had since 1963 been to prevent a revolution/rebellion and the aim of the Turkish Cypriot side has been to achieve this. Apparently, Mr de Soto did not have much sympathy for incumbent governments, a characteristic rendering a successful outcome to a process which he shaped unlikely once "all the chips were down". Testimony about Mr de Soto's and Mr de Cuéllar's approaches appears in Marrack Goulding, *Peacemonger* (London, John Murray, 2002) at pp 20 *et seq* and 211 (Western Sahara) at 237–46 (El Salvador). Mr Goulding was Under Secretary-General in charge of Peacekeeping Operations from 1986–1993 and head of the Department of

together a team of young and able assistants, mainly lawyers.[12] He also invited Mr Clerides and Mr Denktash, the respective leaders of the Greek and Turkish

Political Affairs from 1993–1997. Mr de Cuéllar's autobiography, *Pilgrimage of Peace*, pp 426–30, confirms Mr Goulding's view of Mr de Soto, whom both authors praise highly, although Mr de Cuéllar reveals that Mr de Soto was criticised by the US Government, himself admitting that Mr de Soto's sympathies were with the reformist FMLN. Mr de Cuéllar's attitude to mediating when he wanted to and the giving of conflicting accounts were experienced by the Government of Cyprus. In late 1984 it was given a different version of what was presented by Mr de Cuéllar's staff to Mr Denktash. In March 1986 it was given assurances, falsified within a few days, when a document which the Greek Cypriot side agreed he could produce on the basis of it being "the twin brother" of what their Interlocutor had been shown, was radically different, having been altered to meet all Mr Denktash's objections. The document was rejected after careful study in May 1986, when the Secretariat briefed all States against Cyprus and Cyprus was politically isolated, just as she was in May 2004 following Secretariat briefings.

In evaluating officials' conduct it is necessary to bear in mind that such persons are not merely office-holders with a special administrative history, but that they have particular characteristics, opinions and ambitions—for example, to be perceived as having settled one of the world's longest outstanding political problems. Mr de Soto is now turning his attention to the Western Sahara, but the issue of settlers may also defeat him there. According to a report in *Phileleftheros*, 5 September 2004, Mr de Soto was visiting Morocco to convince the authorities not to introduce settlers to vote in the referendum, now taking a position the opposite of that he had taken as regards Turkish settlers in Cyprus. Another impediment to settlement arising from Mr de Soto's experiences is that while these have equipped him to be a skilful advocate of political schemes to assist in reaching solutions to international problems, his desire to achieve settlements seems to lead to his relegating what he probably considers to be too inflexible rules of international law. Certainly, he did not find the approaches of Cyprus political leaders who are lawyers congenial or appropriate in trying to "broker a deal". It is regrettable that, before agreeing to Mr de Soto's appointment, the Cypriot sides did not fully appreciate Mr de Soto's politicised approaches and the negotiating model he would employ in which, although commencing softly-softly, he would, as in El Salvador, ultimately put on pressure to finalise a single text, which in earlier phases, via his team of young lawyers, whom he controlled, was shown in parts to each side with "shuttles" between the sides, during which meetings each side would separately be manipulated and pressed into making a particular compromise. Nor did the sides fully appreciate that the Secretary-General and Mr de Soto would develop special roles for "the motherlands" (Greece and Turkey) and the USA and the UK (and very occasionally other Security Council members), with the States concerned being separately used to pressure the parties as requested by Mr de Soto, but without taking maverick initiatives. The EU also acquired such a role, especially in the later stages. Mr de Soto was extraordinarily influential in that he was the prime figure in briefing Member States' diplomats as to the progress of the negotiations and the conduct of the parties, with the USA's and the UK's local representatives regularly being closeted with him.

[12] Mr de Soto's team included Mr Robert Dann of the UN Department of Political Affairs, a young Australian and a skilful drafter of Talking Points and plausible reasons for controversial, even unjustifiable, actions, who will doubtless rise high in UN circles. The main legal adviser was Mr Didier Pfirter, a Swiss diplomat, who was proud of his handiwork on the Constitution. He looked puzzled when the writer remarked to him in John Cleese-like fashion after publication of Annan I, with its property proposals, restrictions on the right of return and grant of citizenship to Turkish settlers, "Well, that's 50 years of development of international humanitarian law down the drain then!" Yet Mr Pfirter, on behalf of the Swiss Foreign Ministry, had been one of the co-sponsors of a resolution amending what became para 8 b (viii) of the Statute of Rome, so as to strengthen the provision making the transfer of settlers a war crime. He managed, somehow, in his subsequent activities as regards the provisions of the Annan Plan, to reconcile his thorough knowledge of the International Criminal Court with jurisdiction over war crimes, including the deportation of parts of the population of an occupied territory and the transfer by an occupying Power of parts of its own civilian population into the occupied territory, with provisions he and his colleagues working on the Plan proposed in order to legitimate nearly all Turkish settlement in Cyprus. As an undergraduate, Mr Pfirter took a degree in Philosophy and Islamic Studies.

Two more young Australian lawyers, Mesdames Madeleine Garlick and Lisa Jones, both with experience in the former Yugoslavia and interested in property issues and the situation of

Cypriot Communities, to participate in proximity talks in New York and Geneva, commencing on 3 December 1999.[13]

Special envoys were designated by several Governments to monitor the negotiations and to keep in contact with the Secretary-General's Special Adviser, Mr de Soto. Of these, an important role was played at the inception by the then Sir David Hannay, the British Special Representative for Cyprus, active from early 1996 until May 2003.[14] For a time Mr Richard Holbrooke was Presidential emissary, ceasing to act in 2001.[15] Ambassador Alfred Moses was appointed in his place, while Ambassador Thomas Weston was appointed as Cyprus Special

displaced persons (refugees), were at various times involved. They too must have had some difficulty in reconciling the provisions they had drafted for the Plan and their personal views expressed in their chapters in Scott Leckie (ed) *Returning Home: Housing and Property Restitution Rights of Refugees and Displaced Persons* (Ardsley, NY, Transnational Publishers, 2003). Miss Garlick believes that return is driven by individual rights, supported by an institutional mechanism for return and that there should be restoration of property rights to create freedom of choice (*ibid*, p 80). Miss Jones, while doubtful about restitution of property after long periods of absence, and while having an inclination to public ownership, believes that the fundamental rights of affected persons to freedom of movement and to the right of choice of residence, even where there are security considerations against their return, should not hastily or wrongfully be taken away: *ibid*, p 223.

The team as a whole, under Mr de Soto's direction, assembled the Annan Plan out of earlier proposals in abortive negotiations (especially the "Set of Ideas" of 1992 and Mr de Cuéllar's preceding proposals in June 1989, which were more restrictive of human rights). They ingeniously added provisions, particularly on property rights, return to their homes of displaced persons and political rights, all designed to withstand scrutiny by the European Court of Human Rights and to facilitate the making of bland statements that there was a proper balance between competing concerns with respect for human rights. His team was assisted by the Legal Department of the UK Foreign Office, and Mr de Soto could also always fall back on advice from Mr Ralph Zacklin, an old stalwart of the UN legal department, to circumvent the need to make embarrassing choices or to take any stand. One need not be so cynical as to agree with the view that you can always find a lawyer to argue anything, but there is no doubt that "in house" lawyers are subject to greater psychological pressures to put forward arguments and proposals convenient for their [political] masters and "flexibility" tends to become second nature. This is why the Lord Chancellor's Advisory Committee on Legal Education and Conduct of the Legal Profession for so long resisted claims by "in house" lawyers that they had the requisite independence to have the right to appear in higher courts in England and Wales.

[13] There is a detailed account of the talks and subsequent negotiations until 11 March 2003 in *Report of the Secretary-General on his mission of good offices in Cyprus, S/2003/398*, 1 April 2003.

[14] As the United Kingdom's Ambassador to the UN in New York from 1990 to 1995, Sir David, later His Lordship, would, claiming to speak for the P-5, even give instructions to Secretaries-General (see Goulding, *op cit* n 11, pp 179–80 and 317). He did not bear any contrary views, let alone those of "fools," gladly, and his manner was didactic and imperious, which did not assist in making his diagnoses and injunctions palatable, even when they were intellectually impeccable. Of course, Sir David was not a draftsman: drafting was for the UN legal team, given assistance from time to time by Foreign Office legal advisers or former legal advisers, the first draft of the Constitution being by Mr Henry Steel. Sir David's role was political, giving diplomatic guidance. He also tutored Mr Blair in 1997, shaping his perceptions of the Cyprus problem.

[15] The views of such personages are always revealing. Mr Holbrooke, later the USA's Ambassador to the United Nations, but named as Presidential emissary in June 1997, declared on 3 November 2003:

> The long-standing plan, which I have been closely associated with, was a three-pronged approach: first, to get the EU to invite Cyprus to join the EU; second, to use this to push the

Co-ordinator for the United States of America. Mr Weston was the main channel from early 2001 (the end of the Clinton Administration) through which the United States expressed its views and sought to influence the process. High level direct involvement began in February 2004, when the highest officers of state of the USA applied pressure—even telephoning and seeking to flatter local Cypriot political figures. Secretary of State Colin Powell contacted President Papadopoulos on 1 February, later telephoning personalities at lower levels. He was also in regular touch with the Prime and Foreign Ministers of Greece and of Turkey and with the UN Secretary-General.

One of the questions the Security Council and Secretariat should now reflect on is whether it is wise for a small group of Permanent Members and possibly other States to become too closely associated with a particular mission or mandate, in which event they can distort procedure and outcomes in their interests.

An important but unfortunate guideline for the UN negotiating team was reputedly laid down at the outset by Sir David. He apparently outlined appropriate tactics to achieve a settlement: matters should not be forced until the very last minute; at that stage, both sides should have a plan put in front of them and have their heads knocked together; and then they should be told to accept or else . . . Whether the story is or is not apocryphal, this tactical procedure was to be followed in all phases of the negotiations.[16]

two Cypriot communities into a productive negotiation that would produce the long-sought bizonal, bicommunal federation; and third, to open accession talks for Turkey to join the EU: "The United States and Turkey: Mending Fences?", www.washingtoninstitute.org/media/turgut/holbrooke.htm.

This declaration is inaccurate in so far as it does not disclose that, until the European Council's Helsinki Conclusions of 10 and 11 December 1999, the USA pressed EU States to impose prior solution of the Cyprus problem as a pre-condition for Cyprus's accession. The Council rejected this approach, spelling out that settlement was not a pre-condition, but that the Council would "take account of all relevant factors". Mr Holbrooke was apparently inspired to think along these lines by what he saw as settlement of the Northern Ireland problem by reason of common UK and Irish membership of the EU bringing about a solution. The "Irish Problem" may have been ameliorated by cessation of violence, but it has not been solved, continuing in a different form, as do all political problems. Only chemists can properly speak of "solutions".

[16] Paradoxically, the now Lord Hannay would not have approved of putting on the pressure in a referendum without adequate time for consideration by the Cypriot public, saying in the Twenty-seventh Thomas Corbishley lecture, "Cyprus: Missed Opportunities and the Way Ahead," delivered in September 2003, that things need not be decided by 1 May 2004. He repeated his view to the Cyprus Broadcasting Corporation on 4 February 2004, stating that President Papadopoulos's arguments that the people needed to know the Plan's contents before referenda were reasonable. Such an approach, differentiating between initially "squeezing" the leaders and subsequently pressurising the public, might have avoided the debacle of the rejection of the Plan on 24 April 2004. The need, so as not to besiege the Cypriot people and to avoid artificial deadlines, had repeatedly been emphasised by President Papadopoulos, who again pointed out after the referendum how inadequate and counterproductive the tactics had been (Letter to the Secretary-General, 7 June 2004). However, Mr de Soto, temperamentally and experientially committed to tactics of this kind, stuck to the decision to press ahead with a referendum soon after "his" finalisation of the Plan was provided for in New York on 13 February 2004. See Chapter X below.

The enormous Secretariat effort embarked upon did not achieve its objective, as the Secretariat was regretfully to observe when the process which had begun in December 1999 ended in April 2004 with rejection by Greek Cypriot voters of a package prepared by a team of Secretariat staff and seconded experts. That objective had been "to reunite Cyprus in time for accession to the EU on 1 May 2004."[17]

[17] Briefing by Prendergast, n 16 above, p 3 col 1. Although the "context of balanced incentives" for accession of Cyprus to the EU and the opening of Turkey's path towards that goal (*S/2004/437*, para 79) may no longer be present, the UN objective in terms of the relevant UN Security Council Resolutions, as yet unaltered, should have been (and should still be) comprehensive negotiations until a just and lasting settlement is agreed, rather than a target date, which is replaceable, even if less easily achievable because of changed incentives.

The package in its final form, Annan V, with its many Appendices and Annexes can be found at www.annanplan.org. The Secretary-General's 1 April 2003 *Report S/2003/398* can be found at http://daccessdds.un.org/doc/UNDOC/GEN/N03/305/59/PDF/N0330559.pdf?OpenElement and his 28 May 2004 *Report S/2004/437* at http://daccessdds.un.org/doc/UNDOC/GEN/N04/361/53/PDF/N0436153.pdf?OpenElement

Main Events: June 1999-April 2003

1999

22 Jun:	Report of the Secretary-General to the Security Council on his mission of good offices in Cyprus (S/1999/707)
26 Jun:	Security Council resolution 1250 (1999)
1 Nov:	Appointment of Alvaro de Soto as Special Adviser to the Secretary-General on Cyprus
3-13 Dec:	First session of proximity talks, New York, with Glafcos Clerides, the Greek Cypriot leader, and Rauf Denktash, the Turkish Cypriot leader
10 Dec:	Helsinki European Council

2000

31 Jan-8 Feb:	Second session of proximity talks, Geneva
5-12 Jul:	Third session of proximity talks, Geneva
24 Jul-4 Aug:	Continuation of third session of proximity talks, Geneva
9-26 Sep:	Fourth session of proximity talks, New York
12 Sep:	Statement by the Secretary-General to the parties
1-8 Nov:	Fifth session of proximity talks, Geneva
8 Nov:	Secretary-General's oral remarks to the parties; Mr. Denktash declines invitation to participate in further proximity talks

2001

14 May:	Secretary-General addresses a gathering of European Union Ministers for Foreign Affairs, Brussels
28 Aug:	Secretary-General meets Mr. Denktash in Salzburg
5 Sep:	Secretary-General invites leaders to new and reinvigorated phase of talks; Mr. Clerides accepts; Mr. Denktash declines
Nov:	Exchange of letters between Mr. Clerides and Mr. Denktash leads to agreement to meet face-to-face in the presence of a United Nations representative
4 Dec:	Meeting between Mr. Clerides and Mr. Denktash, United Nations Protected Area, Nicosia, in the presence of the Special Adviser results in agreement to begin direct talks
5 Dec:	Mr. Clerides dines at the residence of Mr. Denktash, north Nicosia
29 Dec:	Mr. Denktash dines at the residence of Mr. Clerides, south Nicosia

2002

14 Jan:	Office of the Special Adviser opens in Cyprus
16 Jan:	Direct talks begin, United Nations Protected Area, Nicosia
14-16 May:	Secretary-General visits Cyprus
6 Sep:	Secretary-General meets the leaders in Paris
3-4 Oct:	Secretary-General meets the leaders in New York; leaders agree to create technical committees
7 Oct:	Mr. Denktash undergoes surgery in New York; direct talks do not resume until January 2003
11 Nov:	Secretary-General tables his proposed Basis for Agreement on a Comprehensive Settlement of the Cyprus Problem
18 Nov:	Mr. Clerides agrees to negotiate on the Secretary-General's plan
27 Nov:	Mr. Denktash agrees to negotiate on the Secretary-General's plan
7 Dec:	Mr. Denktash returns from New York to Cyprus
10 Dec:	Secretary-General tables a revised Basis for Agreement on a Comprehensive Settlement of the Cyprus Problem
12-13 Dec:	Copenhagen European Council

2003

7 Jan:	Technical committees begin meeting
15 Jan:	Direct talks resume
16 Feb:	Tassos Papadopoulos is elected to succeed Mr. Clerides
23-25 Feb:	Secretary-General visits Turkey and Greece
26 Feb:	Secretary-General arrives in Cyprus and formally tables his further revised Basis for a Comprehensive Settlement of the Cyprus Problem
28 Feb:	Mr. Papadopoulos and Mr. Denktash accept the Secretary-General's invitation to meet in The Hague
10 Mar:	Secretary-General meets with Mr. Papadopoulos and Mr. Denktash in The Hague.

Proximity negotiations in New York commenced on 3 December 1999, with the Secretary-General hoping there would be "serious discussion and meaningful dialogue". The pictures are of the separate sets of posed handshakes by "President" Denktash and President Clerides with the Secretary-General. Each was shown where to stand to shake hands and there was even a degree of practising for photographic purposes with a false start (shake not good enough for the photographer). So . . . shaking hands is often a fabricated propagandistic act, at least in UN circles. This New York meeting was where the intensive UN effort of the last 4½ years started.

Before the virtual end of half-time. The UN "good offices" team for the negotiations (photographed on 26 February 2003 at the UN Protected Area with the team then in play, including the New York elements). Left to right: Alvaro de Soto, Melanie Redondo, Lisa Jones, Madeleine Garlick, Robert Dann, Kofi Annan, Kieran Prendergast, Didier Pfirter, Sven Koopmans, Laura Vaccari, John Furnari and Peter Schmitz.

TIME-WASTING IN GENEVA

Entry into the Palais des Nations for the third session of proximity talks in Geneva by "President" Denktash, Professor Soysal and "Prime Minister" Ertuğruloğlu, on 25 July 2000. Obviously the talks are going nowhere.

Chewing the cud with Greek Cypriots in Chambesy on 26 July 2000 is one of Mr Denktash's despised "co-ordinators," Sir David Hannay, with President Clerides and Foreign Minister Cassoulides.

Above: Mr Denktash on 28 July 2000 tells the press: "I don't think it's Mr de Soto's duty to give us documents." Asked about the American and British involvement in the talks. He responded: "I think they're all acting in concert, together. They're helping each other."

Above: President Clerides, accompanied by Foreign Minister Cassoulides and Ambassador Zackheos, was encouraged to persist by Prime Minister Simitis on 7 September 2000 at the UN's Millennium Summit before President Clerides attended the 4th session of proximity talks in NY from 9–26 September 2000. "The millennium for Cyprus will come too—some day," is what the Greek Prime Minister obviously believed. (By "Millenium" he would have meant a period of happiness and benign government, and not a thousand years more.) But the New York proximity talks also got nowhere.

Above: the undertakers of the talks, Mr de Soto and Sir Kieran Prendergast after the last meeting of the sides on 8 November 2000 in Geneva, where the Secretary-General asked the sides to "reflect" on future steps, pointing out that "at the end of the day it is for the parties to agree". Nearly all of 2001 was also wasted because Mr Denktash, supported by Turkey's Prime Minister Ecevit, declined to meet.

Below: Ambassador Alfred Moses, replacement (as if anyone could be) for Richard Holbrooke, and US Ambassador Bandler calling on President Clerides on 9 January 2001 to encourage him to pursue the talks process, despite nil results so far. Ambassador Bandler was important in shaping the Bi-Communal Development Programme (see pp 52–55).

Left to right: Enlargement Commissioner Günter Verheugen, UN Acting Special Representative Zbigniew Wlosowicz and President Prodi of the EU Commission in the UN Protected Area during a Cyprus visit from 25–26 October 2001. As the likelihood of EU membership for Cyprus increased, so did pressures on Turkey to encourage revived intercommunal talks. This was *A Tale of Two Memberships*.

Turkey's Prime Minister Ecevit with "President" Denktash in 2001, not long before approaching EU events would require a Turkish policy change and Ecevit's instructions to Mr Denktash to take the initiative in suggesting face to face talks with Mr Clerides. Turkey contended that only a reunited Cyprus could enter the EU (as did the USA). From Turkey's standpoint, if talks could be used to insist that a Cyprus settlement must come first, so much the better. Mr Ecevit exploited Turkey's position by asserting in November 2001 that, if Cyprus entered the EU without a solution, Turkey would annex Cyprus.

He was supposed to be "a fly on the wall", as Mr Denktash kept reminding him. In November 2001 Turkey agreed with Mr Denktash that he should suggest direct talks to Mr Clerides. President Clerides accepted the Denktash suggestion, provided the UN was present. It was then agreed at the Special Representative's home on 4 December 2001 that the Special Adviser, who had described himself as having "the fly" role only, could use his notebook. Two square meals at each others' houses on 5 and 29 December 2001 fuelled the talkers. (See the 5th colour picture centre.)

Above: but already Mr de Soto had his first slip-up on 4 December 2001, when on a rainy day he went forward to read an announcement from the Special Representative's steps. It was an augury of how the talks would end.

A benevolent fairy godfather Alvaro de Soto, looks on at two old friends genuinely shaking hands as they meet on 16 January 2002 for the first direct talks since August 1997 at Glion. Probably de Soto is hoping that some old fashioned magic will work wonders.

Above: the Greek Cypriot team at the beginning of the talks on 16 January 2002 at the UN Protected Area Nicosia (premises courtesy of UNOPS). Right table: Alecos Markides, Glafcos Clerides, Pantelis Kouros and Michalis Papapetrou.

Below: left to right, in the Turkish Cypriot team are Ergün Olgun, Rauf Denktash and Osman Ertüg; in the UN team are Didier Pfirter, Alvaro de Soto and Robert Dann, with Pfirter whispering a comment to de Soto.

When the talks started, Mr Denktash demanded "equality" and sovereignty for both sides. (Perhaps now he can have half the blanket and half the EU benefits.)

With Mr Denktash demanding two equal States, loosely linked, under a federal roof, there were suspicions about the US, which had pressed for these talks. Effectively, 2 years later at Bürgenstock, Mr Denktash was to get much of what he wanted. Greek Cypriots still perceive the USA as supporting partition *de facto*.

Stocktaking at the UN in New York on 10 March 2002 on the lack of progress. From left: Professor Soysal, Mr Denktash, Mr Clerides, Mr Markides, Mr Kouros (obscured), Mr Papapetrou, Mr Mavroyiannis, Mr Pfirter, Mr de Soto, Mr Annan and Sir Kieran Prendergast.

US Special Envoy Weston again encouraging the talkers on 21 March 2002. (Maybe it's easier to joke with President Clerides, whereas Mr Denktash's grip is fearsome.) Left: with President Clerides. Right: with "President" Denktash and Ambassador Bandler.

More stocktaking in New York on 10 April 2002, with Mr Denktash apparently getting a wigging from the Secretary-General over 2 days of talks.

It's like water off a duck's back: Mr Denktash smiles as he leaves with Professor Soysal.

Educating Cypriots No. 1: Lord Hannay at the University of Cyprus.

Educating Cypriots No. 2: Ambassador Weston at an American Hellenic Institute forum on 16 April 2002 lecturing to the Greek *diaspora*.

Educating Englishmen: High Commissioner Lyn Parker and Lord Hannay on 13 February 2002, about to receive a history lesson from "President" Denktash.

E.25–27

Below: although this looks like another history lesson by Mr Denktash to the Secretary-General, Mr Denktash apparently received a headmasterly chat in Nicosia on 15 May 2002 on the first visit to Nicosia by a Secretary-General since the 1979 High Level Agreement.

Below: a night at the round table lubricating relationships. On leaving Cyprus the next day, 16 May, the Secretary-General was to state that he had encouraged a "give-and-take basis," with focusing on the core issues, determination to make peace by the end of June, things to be put in writing and Special Adviser de Soto to assist. The "giving" turned out to be all by the Greek Cypriot side and the "taking" by the Turkish Cypriot side, without any response on territory. The UN, perhaps anticipating the same old story, declared to the press that in conducting this process: "We are here to help steer the leaders to an agreement . . . not to impose any ideas or conclusions on them".

A pleased Secretary-General getting sealing symbolic handshakes on 15 May, agreeing to his proposal for intensified negotiations and prompt dealing with core issues. But the effects of his headmasterly chat only lasted three weeks, when the Turkish Army objected to Mr Denktash being "a good boy" on Security issues and he invoked the "nothing is agreed unless everything is agreed" rule. Talks meant to settle core issues by the end of June had settled nothing.

IV

The Purported Negotiations From December 1999 to March 2003

THE UN'S OFFICIAL *Report* on the negotiations from 3 December 1999 to 11 March 2003 was provided in *S/2003/398*. The writer's "counter-report" now explicitly adds political aspects, which official *Reports* for the most part overtly shun, and continues the story up to date (18 December 2004). Since the UN's earlier *Report* of 1 April 2003 was relatively fair (even if its approach in criticising Cypriot participants can be faulted) only a summary, filling in a few gaps, is necessary.[1] In brief, in the first year, 2000 AD, five short sessions of proximity talks were held, whereupon Mr Denktash, leader of the Turkish Cypriot Community, declined further to participate. However, a year later, as Cyprus's EU accession approached, Turkey required Mr Denktash to propose face-to-face meetings. These occurred in Nicosia from 16 January 2002 until the end of September 2002. On 4 October 2002, the leaders agreed in New York with the Secretary-General that a comprehensive settlement had to be

> a complex, integrated, legally-binding and self-executory agreement, where the rights and obligations of all concerned are clear, unambiguous and not subject to further negotiation.[2]

In order to achieve that objective, it was agreed to appoint two bilateral Technical Committees to finalise Laws and Treaties applicable under the new state of affairs. The finalisation of Laws was necessary because a large number of important Laws, without which the State could not function, required approval by fixed proportions of members of the future federal legislature hailing from each constituent state, and therefore might under the proposed Constitution be impossible to enact. This provision for extensive "special majority" approval was the brainchild of the UN team. It was accompanied by an ineffective deadlock-resolving mechanism (in the shape of empowering the Federal Supreme Court, using restraint, to enact Laws). However, Mr Denktash

[1] Since writing the above Lord Hannay's detailed account of the 1996–2003 negotiating period has been published. It is enlightening and fun to read, with many "home truths" about the various participants.

[2] Statement of the Secretary-General, 4 October 2002.

did not appoint members of the Committees until the end of December 2002. As the Secretary-General's *Report* states, the process had not moved forward largely due to Mr Denktash's approach. It was only in January and February 2003 that progress was made at the Committees, but this was still subject to control at the higher political level as the Turkish Cypriot side explained to Mr de Soto, and, towards the end of February, Mr Denktash instructed the Committee's Turkish Cypriot experts not to continue work.

THE SPECIAL ADVISER'S NEW ROLE

In moving the political negotiating process forward in 2002, third party assistance was considered to be indispensable and was now provided by the Special Adviser, who sought to help the parties in a way which did not hamper their ability to negotiate freely. With encouragement from the Special Adviser, the Greek Cypriot side had by the end of May 2002 made major concessions to Turkish Cypriot views. Account was taken of Turkish Cypriots' concerns as to the origins of a future republic by accepting that the co-founders of the new state of affairs would be Greek Cypriots and Turkish Cypriots through referenda as constituent acts. The Greek Cypriot side accepted the Turkish Cypriot views on power relationships between Greek and Turkish Cypriots, governmental structures and competences in the new federation, including the reservation of residuary power to the units, and the 1960 Treaties' continuance, so as to ensure security for Turkish Cypriots.[3] The Greek Cypriot side found the compromises on power relationships easier to make than in earlier years, because many matters within federal competence would be decided in Brussels if Cyprus became an EU Member State, so that the occasions on which Greek and Turkish Cypriot politicians might clash would be greatly reduced.[4] Greek Cypriots also indicated the possibility of a package deal in which, if a substantial majority of displaced Greek Cypriots could return to territory coming under Greek Cypriot administration, fewer Greek Cypriots would be reinstated to their properties in the future Turkish Cypriot state. Yet no joint progress was

[3] See particularly *Minutes of Greek Cypriot Note-taker*, 14 May 2002. Later, on 2 July 2002, the Special Adviser was given an "Evaluation by the Greek Cypriot side of the Current Round of Talks for the Solution of the Cyprus Problem," which set out the security concessions which even included retention of the Turkish and Greek Contingents specified in the Treaty of Alliance 1960, but without a Cypriot military element; the acceptance of two equal Communities each administering <component states>; limited federal competence; a requirement that executive decisions needed support by a minimum number of Ministers from both Communities; abrogation of the 1960 Constitution; and a new Constitution, embodying a new political partnership between the two Communities in the context of a <common state>, which would be bi-zonal as regards the territorial aspect and bi-communal as regards the constitutional aspect, which Constitution would come into force upon approval in two separate Community referenda.

[4] It was estimated that over 60% of decisions within federal competence would be taken in Brussels.

made in the first half of 2002, because Mr Denktash used the talks in order to present his "visions" ie theoretical analyses of the proposed governmental system, with agreement on his overall concept being a pre-condition to negotiation on any concrete issue. Territory and its return was not discussed, while the Greek Cypriot side would not discuss property unless territory was discussed.[5] Accordingly, the Special Adviser from June 2002 began suggesting compromise formulations, and, through a work programme, encouraged the leaders to explore issues hitherto largely ignored, in particular the linkage between the size of the territory of each constituent state and the number of displaced persons able to return to the other constituent state. This linkage had been emphasised as early as 22 October 1981, when the then Special Representative, Dr Hugo Gobbi, reported on the overall state of the negotiations. Linkages and "trade-offs" became from June 2002 a prominent feature of the Special Adviser's "approach" in discussions.

GREEK CYPRIOT CONCESSIONS INDICATED TO THE UN

The making of concessions throughout this period by the Greek Cypriot side, accompanied by continued "flexibility on areas of concern to Turkish Cypriots," was acknowledged by the Secretary-General at a meeting with Mr Clerides on 6 September 2002 in Paris, although the former warned that even more flexibility (ie concessions) would be needed if serious negotiations were to begin with Mr Denktash. It may with hindsight be asked whether it was wise to rely on UN advice and whether too many concessions were made too early by one side only, but Turkey was stone-walling, and it was the Greek Cypriot side which wanted a settlement. At this time, the concept of a "virgin birth" (or the "optical" appearance of a new State, providing a fresh start for both sides) was finally agreed by the Secretary-General and Mr Clerides. Picking up on what the Greek Cypriot side had already conceded in the talks, the Secretary-General suggested that

> the two sides should, by constitutive act, first through negotiation, and then by its approval at separate referenda, bring into being an entirely new state structure and a solid foundation for a new Cyprus, via the comprehensive settlement and the new constitution. Now, I pointed out to Mr Denktash that, since Cyprus will not only have a new constitution and a new name, but also a new flag and a new national anthem, it will, for all practical purposes, look like a new state. Optically speaking, it would be a fresh start for both sides. The continuity of the State, however, would not be an

[5] This was because the two issues were seen as inter-linked and the subject of counter-concessions. If the Greek Cypriot side were first to agree to major aspects of Mr Denktash's "global exchange of property" scheme, without at the same time having secured return of territory to Greek Cypriot administration, Greek Cypriot public indignation would have been uncontainable.

> issue, since Cyprus would continue to be a member of the UN, its application to the EU would be followed through, and its treaty obligations would continue.[6]

To what extent this "new state of affairs" and its legal effect had earlier been made clear to Turkey or to Mr Denktash on the Secretary-General's visit to Cyprus on 15 May 2002, when the concept was floated with Mr Denktash, has not been revealed, but certainly it was put to him at the Paris meeting (together with an explanation of all the other openings made by the Greek Cypriot side on security, equality, bi-zonality etc). In effect, the Secretary-General was suggesting to the two leaders that the settlement should provide for the foundation of the new state of affairs in a manner which was such as to accommodate both sides' approach to this question. The Secretary-General's *Report*, *S/2003/398*, 1 April 2003, paras 18, 19, 62 and 63, succinctly explains the two sides' approaches and the way in which the UN team proceeded to avoid an endless debate on concepts and visions:

> 18. The starting positions or visions of the parties during the proximity talks and the direct talks were far apart on all main issues. Mr Clerides, invoking Security Council resolutions, favoured a solution based on a State of Cyprus with a single sovereignty and international personality and a single citizenship, comprising two politically equal communities as described in the relevant Security Council resolutions, in a bi-communal and bi-zonal federation. Mr Denktash favoured a solution in accordance with what he regarded were the realities, proposing a Confederation of Cyprus founded by two pre-existing sovereign states. The Confederation would have a single international legal personality but would be sovereign only to the extent that sovereignty was given to it by the founding states. By the time of the direct talks, Mr Denktash had put the term "confederation" to one side, preferring to speak of a new Partnership State of Cyprus, the overall concept remaining the same. The dispute was clear—would a solution be one pre-existing state which would continue in existence and federalize itself under a new Constitution, or two pre-existing states which would found a new confederal or partnership structure? The dispute took the form of a Gordian knot of conceptual and terminological issues to which I will return.
>
> 19.The difference in overall vision was matched by major differences on all core issues. On governance, the Greek Cypriots, emphasizing the need for workability and unity, proposed a free-standing federal government with representation based primarily on population ratios but with effective participation of both communities in decision-making. The basis would be a federal constitution. The Turkish Cypriots, emphasizing the need to prevent domination and maintain their separate status and identity, opposed any free-standing central institutions, proposing instead channels of cooperation and coordination between the institutions of two separate

[6] See Précis from the meeting of the Secretary-General with Mr Glafcos Clerides, Greek Cypriot Leader, Paris, 6 September 2002. A clear explanation of the methodology proposed and the reasons for it at that time is given in the Secretary-General's 1 April 2003 *Report*, paras 62–67 and 72–77. (In the "new Europe," where Cyprus is an EU Member State and will for some time have been such when a settlement is reached, the "virgin birth" concept should be irrelevant, but Turkish Cypriot sensitivities about Turkish Cypriot "independence" and rights to self-determination may keep it on the agenda.)

> but juxtaposed states, with numerical equality and consensus decision-making. The basis would be an international treaty with international arbitration in the case of disputes . . .
>
> 62. I referred earlier to the Gordian knot of conceptual issues, as much psychological as practical in nature, which divide the parties. It relates to the legal and political interpretation of the past and present as well as visions of the future, is born of bitter historical experiences and recurring nightmares, and is reflected in disputes over labels. It was therefore necessary to cut this Gordian knot by addressing issues relating to terminology, the coming into being of the new state of affairs, and sovereignty.
>
> Terminology
>
> 63. As far back as the proximity talks, I asked each leader to put labels to one side and focus on them at the end. The Greek Cypriot preference was for terminology based on a federal government with federated states, provinces or cantons. The Turkish Cypriot side spoke of a confederation during the proximity talks, a position which was refined by the time of the direct talks into a partnership state composed of partner or constituent states. It was also vital for the Turkish Cypriot side that the name of the state not be "Republic of Cyprus"—something the Greek Cypriot side was prepared to concede.

It should be added that, in internal discussions, the Greek Cypriot side had from the outset of the negotiations decided that, if a fair settlement were reached, it would be easy to put forward (or accept) proposals avoiding difficulties about "sovereignty" (a topic on which Turkey has held emphatic views since the Treaty of Lausanne); about avoiding labels of "federal" and "confederal"; and generally about conceding any "theology" which Mr Denktash desired. Doubtless the UN team appreciated this reasonable attitude in 2002, but later exploited it when imposing an unfair settlement in 2004.

Because the Secretary-General had asked the parties to put labels aside, although each side set out proposals in long papers, there was relatively little discussion about whether each side's proposals should be characterised as constituting a federation, a confederation or a unitary state, debates which had marked all talks from 1979 onwards and had prevented the development of concrete proposals to meet each side's concerns. In the talks from 1998 onwards—as indicated by the Secretary General—the Turkish Cypriot side had overtly sought a "confederation". In March 1998 he told the then Special Adviser, Mr Diego Cordovez, that there were 2 separate states and that "the realities" must be the basis.[7] This claim was pursued in Mr Denktash's 31 August 1998 proposals, and he thereafter persisted with his demand for a confederation, not in name, but in effect. Obviously, different State and governmental forms when analysed by political scientists shade by degrees into one another in their degrees of centralisation of functions and power and there are similarities between different forms of States. From this political and functional standpoint, federal and

[7] *S/1998/410*, 19 May 1998, Letter from the Secretary-General to the President of the Security Council.

confederal labels are, in general, irrelevant. Thus, political scientists saw the unitary State of the Republic of Cyprus as established in 1960 as *functionally* federal, because of the special political roles accorded the two Communities, although in legal terms the Republic was not a federation.[8] The Greek Cypriot side had begun the 1977 inter-communal talks with proposals for a highly centralised federation, moving over the years, particularly in 2000–2002, to a very de-centralised one. The various Annan Plans (I, II, III and V—IV not being characterisable as a Plan, but as a mere dress-rehearsal for producing Annan V) were all for such a loose federation, which could work only if there were in practice to be comprehensive co-operation and co-ordination activities between the units and the federal centre. These were provided for in Co-operation Agreements (virtually treaties between the Federal Government and the constituent states, or with each other) the three most significant, namely, on External Relations, European Union Relations and Police Matters, being part of the Foundation Agreement, with Constitutional provision being made for conclusion of further Co-operation Agreements by way of a procedure akin to agreeing and ratifying a treaty.[9] The most distinctive feature of any confederation also marked the Plan from its first presentation: namely, the requirement of consensus for there to be decision-making in the federal sphere. The form of the consensus was not to be separate majorities from each constituent state—a requirement long argued for by the Turkish Cypriot side as late as March 2004. Instead, there had to be approval of any executive measure by at least 50% of the voting members from each constituent State ie 1 of 2 from the TCCS and 2 of 4 from the GCCS in the Presidential Council. On the legislative level, there had, for relatively unimportant measures, to be support from at least one mother-tongue Turkish speaking Senator and a mother-tongue Greek-speaking Senator, while, for all important measures, there had to be positive votes by both 10 of 24 mother-tongue Turkish-speaking Senators and 10 of 24 mother-tongue Greek-speaking Senators, as well as a simple majority of Deputies in the lower federal chamber of Deputies. It is not an unfair assessment to claim that the UN team's handiwork resulted in a State which was federal—and thus in accordance with the 1977 and 1979 High Level Agreements on Cyprus, the Security Council's Resolutions and the EU's requirements that Cyprus be a

[8] This was because there was a single State, without autonomous *territorial* sub-units enjoying certain governmental powers and functions independently of the central government. Because the Communal Chambers enjoyed some governmental power which was not removable by constitutional amendment, there were nonetheless some similarities with a federation. Lawyers and political scientists analyse "federations" in different fashions. Lawyers look not at functions and how political forces operate with federal characteristics (ie "federalism" according to political scientists), but look for criteria such as the *locus* of sovereignty; whether the central and provincial/cantonal units have distinct and different governmental powers which are not easily alterable; whether there is a single State, even if units possess degrees of international capacity etc. They are particularly concerned where questions of competence and legality arise, requiring decision as to which of two laws, enacted at different levels and conflicting, is to prevail. Over the years, each side had ample material to argue the law and politics of various State forms—and did so.

[9] See Annan V, Annex I, Article 16, an Article which had been in all versions of the Plan.

single State—but which would operate in crucial respects like a confederation, requiring representatives from the units to agree to new decisions, Laws and *inter-se* treaty arrangements—and this even in the EU sphere and in external relations in terms of the Co-operation Agreements. But nobody wanted to listen to or to make such arguments.[10] Understandably, they wanted a deal on Cyprus, which would have been obstructed by labelling of that kind, or by theoretical analysis of the extent to which the long-standing criteria for a settlement had genuinely been met.

The Secretary-General, when proposing a by-passing of the various conceptual difficulties on federation, confederation, sovereignty and bringing the new state of affairs into being, asked Mr Denktash to negotiate on the core issue of territory—which he had refused do—and to meet his own property concerns by negotiating territory and property together, as suggested by Mr Clerides. Indeed, the Secretary-General reiterated what Mr de Soto had earlier told Mr Denktash about the UN's willingness to advocate a very strict property regime, including a low number of reinstatements. He also put forward the UN view that for every governmental decision to be taken there would have to be a requirement of "a particular fraction of each side" for the decision to be taken.[11] On this last point, he had merely told Mr Clerides in Paris that there were reasonable governance formulations to bridge the gap between the parties on whether there should be inability of the Greek Cypriot numerical majority to impose its will on the Turkish Cypriot numerical minority.

A new development in Paris was that the two sides agreed with the Secretary-General that he should make "bridging proposals" between the positions advanced by the two sides and (via the Special Adviser) formulate a written proposal to provide the basis for a comprehensive settlement. The leaders were to commit themselves to finalising negotiations on this with UN assistance by the end of February 2003, and thereafter to submit the finalised Plan to simultaneous referenda for approval, so that a new state of affairs could come into being, with a reunited Cyprus able to sign the Treaty of Accession to the European Union.

The role of the Special Adviser was not that of a mediator or arbitrator. (Nor indeed was such a role within the scope of the Secretary-General's good offices mission.) He was merely to make "bridging proposals". There had been no UN Mediator for Cyprus since 1965, when Mr Galo Plaza, the then Mediator (who had succeeded Mr S Tuomija as the Mediator appointed under SCR 186 (1964)), had reported on Cyprus (*S/6253*, 26 March 1965). The Plaza *Report* had been rejected by the Republic of Turkey, which at the same time objected to his continuation in office. As indicated earlier, instead of appointment of a further UN Mediator, Turkey and the Turkish Cypriots wished to move to talks

[10] Except Mr Denktash, who did not want a settlement detracting from the "TRNC's" independence from all things Greek Cypriot. Of course, independence from Turkey was quite another matter. He would have been happy to see the "TRNC" become Turkey's 82nd Province, as various joint "TRNC"–Turkey Declarations from 1997 made clear.

[11] This was a reversion to Mr de Cuéllar's 1989 Ideas and a confederal element.

without a mediator (*S/7191*, 10 March 1966, p 33), so no further Mediator was appointed. Mediation in the course of good offices was an alternative repeatedly excluded by the leader of the Turkish Cypriot Community, Mr Denktash. From time to time during the many years of inter-communal negotiations from 1968 onwards he had complained that there had been no agreement to mediation whenever he considered that the Secretary-General had gone beyond the scope of his role of good offices by making proposals of his own. Indeed, this limitation on the scope of good offices was recognised by the present Secretary-General after Mr Erdoğan had at Davos on 24 January 2004 raised the question of appointing a mediator or the acceptance of arbitration by the Secretary-General. He reportedly indicated to Mr Erdoğan that no such function was envisaged in his mandate[12].

It is appropriate here, lest it be forgotten because of later attitudes, to record the goodwill towards the people of Cyprus, comprising both Communities, shown at the inception of the negotiations by the United Nations personnel involved. They began with a determination to allay the fears and meet the concerns of both Communities as much as possible. However, because the two sides were so far apart on issues of principle, especially on human rights questions, it became necessary, if agreement of the Republic of Turkey and the Turkish Cypriot leadership was to be secured, especially when the latter parties did not at that time desire a Cyprus settlement, to move away from principle and to attempt to devise practical arrangements. Doubtless those concerned were alert to the fact that principle may fail to achieve results—as regrettably has been the case in Bosnia Herzegovina, where the right of refugees to return to their homes in safety has largely been a paper right more honoured in its breach than in its observance. The UN's Cyprus team wanted to get people back home, but not at the cost of inflicting suffering on current occupiers. In addition, as they got entangled in the Cyprus problem and its personalities, their sympathies became engaged with the grievances of both sides. Although "minority problem" is a concept rejected by the Turkish Cypriot leadership (for the reason that minorities do not have the right of self-determination) the Turkish Cypriots are a numerical minority on the Island, perceiving themselves as excluded and oppressed. Conversely, the Greek Cypriots are a minority in the region in relation to Turkey. That there is a double-minority problem is not however appreciated by most outsiders, who have tended to empathise with Turkish Cypriots as the local "underdogs" and ones that bark less at strangers, as well as having fewer juicy economic bones to chew. Their disadvantages are more visible, while the sufferings of Greek Cypriot displaced persons are receding, as all historically inflicted wrongs do over time. It was perhaps too easy in applying ingenuity to find ways around the two sides' competing claims to occupancy and ownership of property to move by one degree after another so far from the principles governing the right to property and the right of refugees to return to

[12] *CNN Turk*, 26 January 2004.

On 6 September 2002 in Paris, President Clerides accepted a formula for sovereignty for each side in a solo tête-à-tête with the Secretary-General, thereby according Mr Denktash's demand for this. President Clerides had earlier agreed to the Secretary-General's formula for "equality". Yet, Mr Denktash remained silent on any territorial give-back—as the Turkish side had done ever since April 1977 at the Vienna meetings, despite promises then by US Envoy Clark Clifford to the Greek Cypriot side, in exchange for which it had accepted federation and territorial division. That major unreciprocated concession had been engineered to secure US lifting of its arms embargo on Turkey. This time, US activity was designed to give effect to US policy on Turkey as a Middle East ally and to further her EU membership.

Above: "There will be 'Egalité, liberté, fraternité'," the Secretary-General on 6 September 2002, would seem to be assuring President Chirac as he explains how his Special Adviser intends to proceed.
Below: a different kind of diplomatic hand-shaking as another Permanent Member thanks the Secretary-General for his briefing and takes pre-emptive defensive measures paralysing the forearm of any handshaker.

THE DAY THE POLITICAL WORLD CHANGED

Immediately before.

The first plane hit the first tower a couple of minutes earlier.

The second plane about to hit the second tower.

The events of 11 September 2001 left nothing political unaffected. The Cyprus settlement process was soon to be blown off course, or, at minimum, the path to peace was deviated from when changed US policy in 2002 towards Afghanistan, Iraq and the Middle East generally, made accomodation of Turkish interests a higher priority.

their homes in safety that these principles were no longer applicable in reality, lip-service merely being paid to them.[13] The same phenomenon applied in relation to other principles laid down in UN Resolutions and intended to form the basis of any Cyprus settlement, eg a single sovereign state, territorial integrity of Cyprus, a single citizenship, and a special concept of equality between the Communities—with equality of status, but, because of their numerical differences, not equality of power in all governmental institutions. The imperceptible changes in attitude and moves in position of the UN team as they became more and more "practical," then led team members to final positions which went well beyond the parameters of even the most flexibly applied principles and rules of international human rights law.[14] It should be added that these departures from principle by the UN appear initially all to have been made in good faith in an attempt to bring Turkey on board, because, until Mr Ecevit was replaced by Mr Erdoğan, the Government of Turkey fully supported Mr Denktash in his opposition to the Plan as it had by then been developed.

At this point it is necessary to answer a fashionable criticism, especially among diplomats and international relations professors that lawyers are inflexible and bad negotiators.[15] What these complaints really mean is that lawyers object to purely political choices which override fundamental principles, thereby making it more difficult for decision-makers to do just what they see fit. It is a myth that lawyers insist on every technical particle of the law being observed: they too are flexible, just as UN and EU lawyers ultimately proved to be in proposing compromises or ways around problems.[16] Nonetheless, so far

[13] This is the writer's personal opinion. Distinguished Cypriots in President Clerides' team thought differently, concentrating on the fact that a majority of refugees (54%) would be able to return to their homes in the future Greek Cypriot <component state>, and that although certain current users and improvers of property were given rights against dispossessed owners, this was both politically necessary to achieve a settlement and a proper humanitarian approach. Taking that attitude, the then Attorney-General, Mr Markides, played an important role in drafting the UN's property proposals to meet Turkish Cypriot concerns that such persons be protected.

[14] A danger afflicting UN bureaucrats is that they appear to lose the ability to distinguish between creative ambiguity and dishonesty.

[15] This attitude is manifested for example in the Hannayism: "The lawyers should be on tap: not on top". The same notion can be found in one of Mr de Soto's favourite Shakespearean quotations: "First, let us kill all the lawyers". This stance applied not only to the Greek Cypriot team, but also to certain of the Turkish Cypriot team, his own team of lawyers if they stood on principle and the lawyers of the EU who at first stood in his way. The Legal Service of the Council of the European Union four months after the referenda again stood in the way of Mr de Soto's prescription for measures to permit direct international trade by Turkish Cypriots. See Opinion of the Legal Service No 11874/04, 25 August 2004 on a Proposal for a Council Regulation to circumvent the unanimity voting required by Article 1(2) of Protocol No 10 to the Act of Accession. The Opinion considered that proposed use of Article 133 EC would amount to misuse of powers (*détournement de pouvoir*).

[16] This was certainly the attitude of Mr Markides, as adviser to President Clerides, and indeed the President's own attitude. He too was a lawyer, as was Mr Papapetrou, the then Government Spokesman, who as a Presidential adviser and team member consistently supported the Plan as the best solution likely to be on offer. It is convenient to make the point here that lawyers, seconded to the Special Adviser's team by Governments, gave a great deal of help from February to April 2004 in revising all essential federal Laws and regulations and in scrutinising all treaties which would bind the UCR upon its coming into being.

as concerns Greek Cypriot lawyers engaged in the negotiations, it is remarkable that the international community criticises the "legalistic" approach taken in negotiations.[17] Law has been the Republic of Cyprus's only weapon throughout the last 30 years against the Turkish Army of occupation. It surely cannot be suggested that, rather than emphasis on legalities, other approaches should have been employed: political approaches were constantly made, but were from the weak position of a small State partly occupied by a large neighbouring military Power, while UN Resolutions did not even use the word "occupied," lest Turkey be offended. Terrorism was, as a matter of principle, discouraged from the outset—as was perpetuating the refugees' suffering in "camps" at individuals' cost in order to publicise Cyprus's claims. Instead, they were re-housed as soon as possible. In any event, terrorism, although it would have kept Cyprus's cause on TV screens throughout that lengthy period, would have earned just international condemnation and have provoked terrible retaliation by Turkey. The only weapon Cyprus chose to employ was reliance on the legal principles which bind the international community—principles whose name that community too often hesitates to speak. But there was not obstinately blind adherence by the Greek Cypriot side to principle: many compromises were offered by the Greek Cypriot side (and only by it) to meet Turkish Cypriot and Turkey's aspirations.[18]

A notable example of the Greek Cypriot side's willingness to compromise was the negotiation in September by a group, consisting of Mr Markides, Professor Soysal and Mr Pfirter, of a framework for agreeing what treaties would bind Cyprus in the new state of affairs; what legislation would be in force; how existing "Laws" in the "Turkish Republic of Northern Cyprus" and the Republic could be given legal effect; and how past debts would be dealt with. Thus difficult legal issues, involved in a potential State succession, were dealt with in a way that would satisfy both side's positions.[19]

[17] For the most recent criticism, alleging "a legal siege mentality" see the Netherlands Ambassador to Cyprus, Mr Gevers, as reported in *The Cyprus Weekly*, 16–22 July 2004.

[18] Indicatively, such compromises included changing the Constitution of Cyprus so that it would no longer be a unitary but instead a federal state. This federation would be bi-communal (based on the two Communities) and bi-zonal (confined only to two units, without there being several cantons, or provinces to have a number of balancing power centres). Such federal state would be so decentralised that it would effectively be a confederation, with each unit (called a "constituent state" to meet Mr Denktash's wishes) enjoying foreign affairs competence and participating in the exercise of federal foreign affairs and EU competences by way of Co-operation Agreements on the Belgian model. Unlike that model, residuary power would belong to the units. A rotating and collective presidency was accepted in principle, partly using the Swiss model. It was also accepted that many displaced persons would not return to their homes or retain their properties. It was agreed that the unlawfully exploited 1960 Treaties should continue in force etc. These compromises had been indicated to the UN by the time of The Hague meeting on 9 March 2003, by which stage neither Mr Denktash nor Turkey had accepted the Plan.

[19] These issues were politically highly charged because of both sides' differing views on sovereignty, continuity of the Republic of Cyprus etc, but it was necessary to decide them. As early as June 1992, President Vassiliou had put forward a mechanism to avoid difficulties on the same issues, but this became irrelevant along with the Set of Ideas early in 1993.

V

Annan I and Annan II

Turning back to the task now falling upon the Special Adviser and which required him to start moving away from pure principles, it will be recollected that in October 2002 the two sides agreed to an enhanced role for the Special Adviser in relation to making "bridging proposals". His team of lawyers then devised a draft Plan, on which they had long been working. The document was a patch-work of compromises, and was later to be known as "the Annan Plan". By letter, dated 6 November 2002, the President of the European Union, the then Prime Minister of Denmark, Mr Rasmussen, requested that the Plan be presented, and the Special Adviser on 11 November 2002 presented the first public version of the Plan (Annan I). This was a UN construction following bi-lateral talks, and it had not been negotiated between the parties concerned.[1]

ANNAN I

The UN Plan proposals were summarily set out in a proposed Foundation Agreement, with a propagandistic preamble and 14 Articles simplistically describing the main aspects of the Plan. This Agreement was written as the Plan's international marketing tool. Only when the details in the Annexes (Constitution, Constitutional Laws, Legislation, Co-operation Agreements, Treaty List, Territorial Arrangements, Treatment of Property, Treaty related to the New State of Affairs, Matters to be Submitted to the Security Council and Requests to the EU with respect to the Accession of Cyprus) were studied—and who, apart from the interested parties would undertake so arduous a task?—did the devils and the innumerable imps in the details emerge. Were the Foundation Agreement to be signed, as the UN envisaged, this would have been the first stage of a rocket speeding the proposed Constitution to the Cypriot

[1] Mr de Soto appears to have been of the view that bi-lateral talks with him or with members of his team, followed by amendments made by his team after such bi-laterals, constituted "negotiations". What happened was "brokering," without the principals dealing directly with each other, and with "glosses" or "omissions" in relation to their views being communicated by the broker to the other side. It was believed that sides will "whisper in the ear of an intermediary what they will not say to each other". Upon discovering the Plan's likely contents, President Clerides vehemently objected in letters of 24 October and 5 November, threatening not to sign. Even prior to Annan I dissent was thus made clear.

Communities. If they approved, the first stage would fall away, and a new state of affairs would then be established, in which the Constitution and associated arrangements would govern Cyprus for the future.[2]

The new state of affairs kept in being the 1960 Treaties made upon Cyprus's independence, but modified them to tie Cyprus more closely to Turkey. No unilateral change to the new state of affairs was permissible.[3] Internally there would be a federal state of Cyprus consisting of two 'component states'[4] and this was claimed to be "modelled on the status and relationship of Switzerland, its federal government and its Cantons".[5] The two-unit federation, with very limited powers conferred on the federal centre and with the two units "sovereignly" exercising all powers not vested in the federal government, was largely confined to EU and foreign affairs, central banking, federal finance, and internationally related matters, such as aviation, navigation and communications. Even in these spheres the units had considerable competence.[6] Federal

[2] Later, this Foundation Agreement disappeared and instead the same title, "A. Foundation Agreement," was used to cover Main Articles (the "marketing tool") to which there were Annexes containing the UCR's Constitution, Constitutional Laws, Federal Laws, Co-operation Agreements, Treaties binding the UCR, Territorial Arrangements, Treatment of Property, Reconciliation Commission and Coming into being of the New State of Affairs. Separate from these were: B. Constituent State Constitutions; C. Treaty on matters related to the New State of Affairs in Cyprus; D. Draft Act of Adaptation of Accession of the UCR to the EU; and E. Matters to be Submitted to the UN Security Council for Decision. The material was substantially similar, but the changes were because no "agreement" was reached, and it was also desired to drop out of the picture "the stages" of the rocket, which were covered with UN "fingerprints," these being burned up on take-off. The rocket metaphor is the UN's or Lord Hannay's.

[3] Some constitutional changes were permissible upon separate constituent state referenda since provision for this was made in the Constitution, but fundamental change was proscribed by Basic Articles of which there were two. These identified the UCR and the constituent states, and set out the principles of their organisation and certain other principles insisted upon by the Turkish side (bizonality, political equality and equal status of the States etc), together with some bland references to "the rule of law, democracy and representative republican government".

[4] On 26 February 2002 the term "constituent states" was substituted. In the following text, where abbreviation can conveniently be used, reference to the "Greek Cypriot component state or constituent state" will be made by "GCCS" and to the "Turkish Cypriot component state or constituent state" by "TCCS". In Annan III the nomenclature "Turkish Cypriot State" and "Geek Cypriot State" was adopted following direct talks early in 2003 when this concession was thought necessary by the Greek Cypriot side to move quickly to an agreement before Cyprus was due to sign the Accession Treaty. That nomenclature is ambiguous and I have not employed it because it creates the impression of there being two independent States, something the "TRNC" has been exploiting. "TCCS" more accurately reflects the status of the two federal units as "constituent states".

[5] This was a major distortion. The fact of many Cantons, several different linguistic and ethnic groups, different political and social structures, the non-coincidence of cleavages along religious lines, differences in the method of election and operation of the executive, constitutional conventions, relative competences of the units, and other aspects of the Swiss Constitution make this camouflaging statement impossible to sustain. A Swiss constitutional lawyer would have to have slipped off the north face of the Eiger and emerged semi-conscious before he could *bona fide* make such a generalisation having regard to the realities of Switzerland. The Secretary-General's 1 April 2003 *Report, S/2003/398*, at paras 83–84, was in contrast, honest, pointing out differences from the Swiss system.

[6] The constituent states could appoint representatives and conclude agreements on commercial and cultural matters. In Annan V this power was interpreted as including power to agree on economic investment and financial assistance by Turkey (Article 18 of the Constitution). The Co-operation Agreement on External Relations also indicated that economic agreements by the TCCS with Turkey were permissible.

competences in EU and foreign affairs and in police matters were to be exercised under Co-operation Agreements and Constitutional (framework) Laws on the Belgian model, to be agreed by the legislatures of all 3 governmental structures. Allegedly Cyprus was to be de-militarised, but this referred only to internal Cypriot forces, and the 1960 Treaties were modified to permit long-term stationing of large numbers of Turkish and Greek troops in Cyprus (a "4-digit figure", unspecified, was the Plan provision at that stage), while the Turkish Army of Occupation would, in phases, withdraw, with some currently occupied territory being transferred to the Greek Cypriot "component state".[7]

So far as concerns government in Cyprus there was to be a bi-cameral legislature, with its Senate consisting of equal numbers of representatives from each "component state" and with its lower house of 48 requiring to have at least one-quarter of its membership from each of the two units. (In fact, Turkish Cypriots, discounting Turkish Cypriot emigration and ignoring Turkish mainland settlement, would have amounted to about 18.2% of Cyprus's indigenous population.) Weighted voting was required for many important matters beyond those matters standardly requiring upper house approval by a simple majority in federations. Thus two-fifths of sitting Senators from each unit (ie effectively 10 Turkish Cypriot and 10 Greek Cypriots) had to be in the Senate majority approving treaties touching on unit competences, laws and regulations on aviation and maritime matters, approval of the budget and taxation (including transfers to the "component states"), election of the executive (the Presidential Council) and filling of vacancies, Cyprus citizenship, immigration and other matters specified in the Constitution or its empowering provisions.[8] In case of potential deadlocks, the Supreme Court could, apart from its normal judicial functions, resolve the deadlocks on an interim basis.[9] Such Court was to be composed of 3 Greek and 3 Turkish Cypriots and 3 non-Cypriots.

The executive was to evolve over transitional periods running over 5 years, in the first year of which the leaders of each side would be Co-Presidents, acting by consensus and appointing 6 heads of department. Complex provisions

[7] Two alternative maps were appended to Annan I. In terms of percentages of territory they did not radically differ from each other, or from Dr Gobbi's 1981 map, or Mr Boutros Boutros-Ghali's map of 1992. Where they differed considerably from each other was in the allocation of economically attractive coastline areas and ones of symbolic significance to Greek Cypriots, notably the Karpas Peninsula, which inspires religious feelings and is a place of pilgrimage. Percentages of territory can be misleading: much of the area offered for return consisted of semi-desert plain not susceptible of economic irrigation. What was important is that both maps contained the former population centres of Varosha and Morphou as well as some large villages. The map with the Karpas was far more attractive to the Greek Cypriot side.

[8] Other matters where the Constitution empowered change or action, but required special majority voting, were the composition of the Federal Parliament; impeachments; and the composition of the public service (at least one-third of the public servants at every level had to hail from each constituent state). In later versions, the composition of the judiciary and extension of the terms of members of office of the Supreme Court as appointed by the Secretary-General were also governed by special majority decisions or Laws (Annan V, Articles 36.1 and 45.2).

[9] This conferment of executive and legislative power to resolve hotly-disputed political issues was a suggestion emanating from the Greek Government.

governed an initial joint executive Headship of State, which, after 18 months, would lead to rotation between the Co-Presidents every 7 months. Thereafter a six-member Presidential Council, elected from a single list by weighted voting in the legislature, would collectively govern for 5 year terms. The President and Vice-President of the Council would be from different 'component states' and these offices would rotate among the Council members, holding ten-monthly terms of office. The Council membership would have to be proportional to the number of citizens of each 'component state', subject to at least two members hailing from each such 'state'. Decisions were to be by consensus, failing which at least one member from each 'component state' must have supported the decision (ie one of the 2 members from the TCCS must have voted positively, as must one of the 4 members from the GCCS).

Although there was to be one citizenship of Cyprus, there were also to be separate 'component state' citizenships and each 'component state' could impose limitations on the establishment of residence of persons not holding such citizenship. The Constitution purported to enshrine respect for human rights, but its provisions and the annexed federal Laws set out restrictions on residence, the right of establishment, the right to property and the principle of non-discrimination to such an extent as to nullify these as regards the past and to emasculate them for the future. There was to be a Reconciliation Commission to promote understanding, tolerance and mutual respect between Greek and Turkish Cypriots[10].

Prefaced by a long preamble, setting out in the main references to Turkish and Turkish Cypriot philosophical approaches to a settlement and what was needed, proposals were made in a Protocol (for inclusion in the Treaty of Accession to the EU of Cyprus) which the Secretary-General summed up. It

> would have provided for extensive derogations and long transitional periods relating to the application of the *acquis communautaire*, mostly in favour of the Turkish Cypriots. These far-reaching provisions arose from careful consultation between the European Commission and the United Nations, building on the policy of accommodation adopted by the European Union in view of the unique situation in Cyprus.[11]

[10] Such a Commission was regarded by the Secretary-General as very important. It was, and the unjust provisions of the Foundation Agreement made it even more essential were there to be any hope of removing bitterness and resentment arising out of past events and the settlement itself, a fresh cause for conflict.

[11] *Report*, *S/2003/398*, 1 April 2003, para 95. Lord Hannay, in *Cyprus, The Search for a Solution*, pp 106–7 and 134, makes it clear that the Enlargement Commissioner, Mr Verheugen, agreed with him "to keep in check attempts by Greek Cypriot hardliners to use the *acquis communautaire* to rule out certain types of solution in the settlement talks." In formulating derogations, Mr Verheugen gave support to measures to ensure that Greek Cypriots would not, through application of the *acquis*, gain outcomes they could not get the Turkish Cypriots to accept at the UN negotiating table. Since "he was precluded from clearing his lines in advance with Member States . . . he and his officials therefore had to make a judgement cold on what they though the EU market would bear": *ibid*, p 172. The agreement and Mr Verheugen's subsequent conduct is further discussed at pp 56 *et seq* below.

The overall effect of the Foundation Agreement was loosely to link two largely ethnically homogeneous constituent states in a federation, where any decision-making could occur only with positive support from representatives of both units in the federal organs and where the executive was elected on a single list by weighted voting, having been elected by representatives hailing from both constituent states. The UN did not go further and insist on cross-voting for election of representatives in the legislature, considering that the "single list" election for the executive was sufficient guarantee for support from both Communities for the UCR's Government. The arrangements were a triumph for theorists of conflict resolution, but a disaster for prospects of a functioning government. While they sought to encourage elite bargaining for executive office between members of the ethnic groups, the same devices precluded from representation in government large sections of public opinion in both Communities, a factor encouraging revolutionary attitudes.[12] Moreover, the arrangements as a whole were so complex that, absent an iron determination to make them work—a feature not in evidence hitherto in Cypriot history—the likelihood of the new "indissoluble partnership" (as per Article 2 of the Foundation Agreement) and of the state of affairs persisting appeared remote.

ANNAN II

Following publication of Annan I on 18 November 2002, President Clerides had, in a long letter, indicated willingness to negotiate and at the same time sought many "clarifications". On 27 November, Mr Denktash indicated his willingness to negotiate. Accordingly, further separate consultations were conducted with both sides. There were also intensive discussions with the Foreign Ministry of Turkey, with the Greek Foreign Ministry being kept in the picture and, as usual, there was close consultation with the USA and the UK. The outcome was a revised Plan (Annan II), published on 10 December 2002, immediately before the European Council was due to take decisions at Copenhagen on 12 December 2002 concerning EU enlargement. The international pressures on both sides to agree were enormous, the Greek Cypriot side being implicitly threatened that it would not be permitted to accede to the EU (non-settlement being a "relevant factor"), while Turkey was threatened that the Republic of Cyprus would be permitted to accede. But the revisions were not even-handed: seen overall, the changes to Annan I, made before the Copenhagen summit, began to tilt the

[12] Mr Glafcos Clerides, later President Clerides, made possibly his greatest contribution to stability and peace in Cyprus by his founding of the Democratic Rally Party and bringing most Greek Cypriots with right wing nationalist beliefs into politics and subsequently into the House of Representatives. To make this possible the Republic's electoral system was wisely altered by the House of Representatives to adopt proportional representation, resulting in fair representation for a large sector of public opinion at that time unrepresented. A system designed to exclude large sectors of opinion from holding public office is indefensible in a democracy, however much their political views may be disapprobated.

balance further than the existing "compromises" in the "bridging proposals" even though, for the sake of "face," some relatively minor changes were made in response to Greek Cypriot representations.[13]

A major change to Annan I was made in respect of the system of voting in Cyprus, so that, unlike in other European States, voters would not vote in their place of residence for federal institutions, but would vote according to the status they had as citizens of one of the "component states" ie Greek Cypriots living in the Turkish Cypriot "component state" would vote in the Greek Cypriot "component state" for federal representatives, but not where they lived.[14] The concept and consequences of internal "component states" citizenship were also fleshed out in a Constitutional Law providing for restrictions on residency, while dual component state citizenship was prohibited. These changes were designed to ensure that Turkish Cypriots controlled the elections of Senators and Deputies from the TCCS in the Federal Parliament.

There was to be a total moratorium on Greek Cypriot residency in the Turkish Cypriot component state for 4 years,[15] with an ultimate limit on Greek Cypriots constituting more than 28% of the population.[16] "Ceilings" on reinstatement of property were specified (9% overall in each constituent state and 14% in any municipality or village).

Provisions regarding Turkish settlers in the Law on Cypriot Citizenship were altered to allow a larger number of persons to remain.[17] Annan I had not specified the size of the list of persons who could remain. President Clerides had earlier, in direct talks in 2002, offered to accept 30,000 persons in total. Turkish settlers are such a major issue with Greek Cypriots—and also with many Turkish Cypriots who do not culturally identify with mainland Turks—that a separate explanatory Chapter is necessary. The changes made in Annan II as regards settlers are set out in Chapter VIII.[18]

[13] The sides now began to hear arguments skilfully prepared by Mr de Soto's team, telling each side what they had supposedly gained. Sometimes the same claims were listed as gains for each side. (The last of these exercises was to be in *S/2004/437*, 28 May 2004, paras 44–57, setting out improvements allegedly "inspired" by the two side's concerns.)

[14] Compare Articles 11 (Annan I) and 12 (Annan II). In Annan IV and V the voting system was further to be changed as regards the Senate in order to meet Turkish demands for ensuring retention of ethnic Turkish control. See *infra*.

[15] Previously there had been a slow process of return: 1% per annum in the first year and with returnees thereafter rising 3% every 3 years. The effect of the change was that no Greek Cypriots could return for 4 years. In year 5, if 8% of the population was Greek Cypriot, limitations could be imposed. But this was the same outcome as with the earlier rises of 3% *per annum*. So Greek Cypriots lost the right of return for 4 years but with no compensating gain. Restrictions on returning Greek Cypriots could also be imposed for 15 years as a transitional measure.

[16] This had been 33 ⅓% under Annan I.

[17] Annan I had, over and above the list, provided that 18 year old persons born in Cyprus and who had permanently resided there for at least 7 years, as well as persons married to a Cypriot citizen and permanently resident for at least 2 years, could be UCR citizens. Annan II disposed of the birth in Cyprus requirement, also increasing the list to 33,000.

[18] See Chapter VIII below. Some readers may wish to read this Chapter at this stage because the settler issue became prominent from the time of Annan II. See also Appendix 6, Table F.

According to the Secretary-General's 1 April 2003 *Report*, the Turkish Cypriot side did not comment on the maps in Annan I. In Annan II the Secretary-General therefore dropped the alternative map showing the territory of the United Cyprus Republic and its "component states", which had been provided in Annan I, putting forward only one map. This envisaged that the tip of the Karpas peninsula would be part of the Greek Cypriot "component state", such map better respecting the criteria of allowing a majority of displaced Greek Cypriots to return to their homes under Greek Cypriot administration, while affecting the lowest possible number of current inhabitants. Another change in Annan II permitted imposition for 3 years, rather than for 1 year, of extensive "safeguard measures" to protect the Turkish Cypriot "component state's" economy in the event of Cyprus's EU accession. Natural resources, including water resources were made Federal in order to give the TCCS control (though weighted majorities) over Cyprus's water resources, which were mainly in the GCCS. As indicated above, some less significant Greek Cypriot requests indicated in the "clarifications" were also met in order to show that there was balance.

POLITICAL CHANGES IN TURKEY

Those involved in the talks on the Greek Cypriot side believed that the aim of the UN modifications made at that time was primarily to assist the incoming Turkish Government. A new and moderate Islamic party had come to power in the Turkish elections of 3 November 2002, but its leader, Mr Erdoğan, had been unable to stand for the Turkish Grand National Assembly because he was disqualified due to an earlier conviction for an offence involving the reading out of a poem proselytising Islamist sentiments, and so dramatically worded that it violated Turkey's rigorously secular criminal law. In the interval until Mr Erdoğan could be held eligible to stand, despite his conviction, and be elected to the Assembly, Mr Gül was appointed Prime Minister, while the Turkish Army regarded the election result with evident distaste.[19] As an adroit negotiator, Mr

[19] Mr Erdoğan was elected on 14 March 2003, thereafter taking office as Prime Minister, with Mr Gül then becoming Foreign Minister. The Turkish Army and President Sezer gradually accommodated themselves to the governing role of the Justice and Development Party. It is simplistic to think that there is an old and a new Turkey because of the change of Government. Turkey's Foreign Ministry has maintained its long-standing Cyprus policy and the Turkish Army, always consulted, has acquiesced, even if some differences in emphasis and detail remain. Basically, Turkey has the same attitude to the Island of Cyprus, regarding it as being within her sphere of influence, even a protectorate, and as a pawn in Turkey's chess game with the European Union, of which Turkey aspires to become a member. The difference is that the Erdoğan Government is anxious to join the European Union, not least as a buttress against the Turkish Army, whereas many other Turkish politicians believe EU membership negotiations to be a premature move for which the Turkish people and the Turkish economy are not ready. All would, however, acknowledge that a Cyprus settlement will, when Turkey's EU entry occurs, have to be agreed and accompanied by the return to Greek Cypriot administration of some of the excess territory occupied by Turkey, a point made by former President Evren in 2002.

de Soto would have been unwilling to press this not yet stable Government for measures which would have weakened its standing vis-à-vis the Turkish Army. Indeed, the UN Secretariat and major Powers in the Security Council saw it as important to stabilise and buttress that Government and to ensure that Army hostility to it did not intensify. In any event, the UN team had always considered that Turkey had to be cajoled into a settlement and given every possible concession, because she invariably adopted maximalist positions and inflexible attitudes—as the international community learned in all negotiations with Turkey from the late 1930s onwards.[20] Accordingly, a shift in the impartial stance the UN had taken from 1999 now occurred. The shift was made yet more manifest with the changes as between Annan II (10 December 2002) and Annan III (26 February 2003), which tilted even further towards Turkish requirements. That development was caused by the fact that the Iraq war was impending, with Turkey's assistance being desired by the two Permanent Members of the Security Council who were virtually directing the Secretariat in conducting the Cyprus negotiations.[21] This international background to the negotiations must be appreciated because that situation led the UN Secretariat, which had hitherto been playing a more traditional refereeing and good offices role, to change stance and to take any action it deemed fit to meet Turkey's demands.

[20] For example, in relation to Syria, dealings with France, the United Kingdom and Germany. Mr Harold Macmillan in his autobiography, *Riding the Storm*, (London, Macmillan, 1971) at pp 672–74, wittily describes Turkish negotiating tactics (still current) and his own ability, necessary in the circumstances, to wield " a long knife," a capacity today's UN, US and UK negotiators have not acquired—against Turkey at least.

[21] Ambassador Daniel Fried, a senior State Department official now at the National Security Council, at a public meeting in Washington on 26 June, 2003, declared:

> When we were trying to persuade Turkey to allow the passage of our troops through its territory into Northern Iraq, we offered Turkey two incentives, several billion dollars in grants and loans, and Cyprus, in the form of the Annan Plan.

When Turkey refused passage, the billions were dropped; however, the Annan plan survived, until it was dropped by the Cypriots on 24 April. See: http://www.state.gov/r/pa/prs/dpb/2004/32860.htm.

VI

Factors Encouraging a Secretariat Belief That it Could Shape a Settlement

IT IS CONVENIENT here to indicate the factors encouraging the Secretariat in its belief that a Cyprus settlement devised by it could in effect be imposed at the Copenhagen EU summit meeting, which took place on 12 and 13 December 2002.

GREEK CYPRIOT ATTITUDES

So far as concerns the Greek Cypriot side, the Secretariat knew that its collective leadership, headed by President Clerides until 16 February 2003, was determined to secure reunification of the Island. (Such determination was to be adhered to just as firmly by the Greek Cypriot leadership headed thereafter by President Papadopoulos, even though the detailed arrangements which President Clerides and President Papadopoulos might be prepared to accept differed.) The Secretariat well knew of Greek Cypriot fears that, were the Greek Cypriot side to act in a manner which could be perceived by third parties as obstructing a Cyprus settlement, this could then be seized upon by certain EU States and EU Commissioners, who had reservations about Cyprus's accession, as a justification for denying Cyprus EU membership.

THE GREEK CYPRIOT LEADERSHIP'S ATTITUDE AT THE TIME OF THE COPENHAGEN SUMMIT

It is appropriate here to explain the general attitude of the Greek Cypriot side's leadership immediately prior to and at the meeting in Copenhagen even after Annan II had been published on 10 December 2002—accepting, as always, that views were not monolithic. Despite the adverse changes in Annan II, the proposed settlement was finely balanced as between the two sides' interests. It was still subject to negotiation until the end of February 2003, and much improvement was expected in the interval when, for the first time, serious negotiations would commence. Writing as one present at Copenhagen, Annan II would, in my view, despite the Greek Cypriot side's considerable reservations, even reluctance, and rejection by some members of the National Council, in the last resort have been accepted in order to ensure that Cyprus would be permitted to accede to the EU. But the desire for EU membership alone would not have been the only conclusive factor. As the Plan then stood—and bearing in mind that improvements were hoped for—there were the following positive aspects: there would be a permanent lock on future Turkish (and Greek) immigration, with only small quotas permitted, thus ensuring long-term maintenance of the demographic balance on Cyprus; demilitarisation was to occur, with the numbers of Turkish and Greek troops to be stationed in Cyprus in the interval still subject to forthcoming negotiations between Greece and Turkey;[1] both sides maintained their views on the scope of the Guarantor Powers' rights of intervention, but there had been no assertion in recent years by Turkey that she was entitled unilaterally to exercise this right by military means; the federal structure seemed good enough for EU purposes and a large proportion of issues likely to occasion internal disputes would be decided in Brussels, while there was, at this time, no indication of the extent of the future restricting impact on Foreign Affairs and on the EU competence of the Federal executive due to adopting the Belgian model of Co-operation Agreements (which impact came as a considerable shock in January 2003 when the model was pushed to its limits and was accompanied by support of the UN team for Turkish demands, which were opposed by the Greek Cypriot technical team); there had been no study of the financial implications of the Plan by the UN or by either side, and, apart from the general notion that federations are an expensive form of government and that there would be large expenditures on property compensation for those who did not have their property returned to them, the future burdens were not appreciated by the politicians involved;[2] the Greek Cypriot side also knew that the Plan permitted long leases of property (on the 1992 Set of Ideas model) and considered, being encouraged in this belief by the UN legal team, that large numbers of displaced persons would retain their property; moreover, they were of the opinion (having obtained expert legal advice from two members of the International Law Commission, Professors Crawford and Hafner) that there were reasonable chances that individuals, whose property rights and rights to return to their homes were interfered with by provisions of the Plan, might

[1] A figure of between 2,500 and 7,000 troops for each of Turkey and Greece was to be inserted in the Additional Protocol to the Treaty of Alliance.

[2] Regrettably, advice to the Greek Cypriot side ever since 2000 that it was essential to secure expert economic and fiscal reports was not acted upon. Economics is a boring discipline to most politicians and lawyers. Only the late President Kyprianou had the foresight to seek advice from international experts on fiscal federalism. As regards the recent series of talks, it was not until late in 2003 that the Greek Cypriot side requested experts to report. Mr Marcus Kyprianou, then Minister of Finance and son of the late President, asked them not to embark on an exercise pointing out the Plan's deficiencies, but to make constructive proposals to render the Plan workable—an indication that the Government of President Papadopoulos was serious in its desire to negotiate improvements in the Plan.

succeed in claims to the European Court of Human Rights or to the European Court of Justice (the Greek Cypriot side had not concealed its views on that issue, emphasising to the UN, especially in July 2000, that no Cyprus Government could agree to violating individual rights as part of a settlement and that, even if did so, this would be unlawful); the EU *acquis* would prevail over those provisions of the settlement which were contrary to the fundamental principles of EU law since the settlement was not to constitute "primary law" of the EU; although there remained unhappiness about the 30 month transitional period of executive Co-Presidency, it was believed that this would be further modified in negotiations (as indeed it later was at Bürgenstock, because it was in no-one's interest that the settlement soon collapse); the federal Laws and associated regulations would be modelled on Laws of Cyprus as they were in 1963 (which the Turkish Cypriot side then accepted) or as harmonised by agreement with the EU (and not as they were later to be ie much modified by the UN at Turkish Cypriot insistence); treaties binding Cyprus would be Cyprus's existing international obligations, since there was not thought to be a State succession[3] and there was no conception that any of Turkey's treaties with the "TRNC" would be adopted; nor was there any conception that the UN would insert provisions—as it did later—interfering with Cyprus's sovereignty over its waters, continental shelf and air-space; there was no provision reaffirming the UK's claim to the Sovereign Base Areas by way of an Additional Protocol to the Treaty of Establishment;[4] and there was hope that the territorial map in Annan II, making the Karpas and certain areas near Morphou part of the Greek Cypriot "component state," would not be altered in any major respect. Taking all these aspects together, the Greek Cypriot side, doubtless with much hesitation, but nonetheless appreciating that the Plan conferred considerable benefits which Turkey would not earlier have remotely contemplated, would, if put in a position where agreement was necessary to achieve EU membership, have accepted the Plan. Mr Denktash's rejection however avoided the need to make that choice.[5] The proof of the likelihood of ultimate acceptance, if necessary, was President Clerides' dispatch of Mr Markides to be present near the summit

[3] An Opinion to this effect was given by two members of the International Law Commission, Professors Crawford and Hafner: see "Legal Position of Cyprus under the 'Basis for Agreement on a Comprehensive Settlement of the Cyprus Problem'," 21 November 2002. They concluded that the Plan provision that the "UCR" *is* a Member of the United Nations made it clear that the State of Cyprus as it would emerge from the settlement would not be a new State nor would there be a succession of States. Had there been a new State, the UCR would have had to acquire UN membership as did Serbia and Montenegro.

[4] Indeed, the Republic of Turkey at this time was much opposed to reaffirmation of the Treaty of Establishment which provided for the establishment (in UK law) of the Republic of Cyprus and involved the UK in the common defence of the Island. Whenever the Treaty of Establishment was mentioned, as in Article 1.3 of the Foundation Agreement in Annan II, there was much gnashing of Turkish Army teeth.

[5] Many Greek Cypriots opposed to the Plan as unlikely to be functional described Mr Denktash as "the best Greek Cypriot we have". Mr Denktash had sent Mr Tahsin Ertuğruloğlu, "Foreign Minister of the TRNC", to Copenhagen. On 13 December 2003 the latter declared that the Plan was so unacceptable that there was nothing to negotiate about.

meeting, with authority to negotiate. The writer does not doubt that, if necessary, Mr Markides was authorised to accept Annan II—although he would not do so in advance, rejecting advice to that effect by Lord Hannay. Nor does the writer doubt that Lord Hannay said to Mr Markides—like other diplomats who advised Greek Cypriot acceptance of earlier UN proposals—that the Plan should be accepted at Copenhagen so as to guarantee its proposals were not worsened and would be finalised as the Greek Cypriot side desired. Certainly Annan II was "the least bad" of the Annan Plans, but it is submitted that any prediction of no worsening if Annan II were accepted would have been falsified, just as were predictions of diplomats giving similar advice in earlier negotiating phases. President Kyprianou had on 12 April 1985 accepted Mr de Cuéllar's Draft Agreement on Cyprus and Draft Statement by the Secretary-General on the Agreement on Cyprus. However, in March 1986, the Draft Agreement was adapted to meet all Mr Denktash's and Turkey's demands. In April 2003, Cyprus agreed to the EU Accession Treaty; in March 2004, the Enlargement Commissioner and the UN insisted that Cyprus's terms of accession be adapted and that she accept a far worse Plan, Annan V, even threatening a Member State of the EU with dire consequences if she failed to agree to the changed Plan as modified to meet Turkey's demands. Whether or not such remarks were made by Lord Hannay in Copenhagen, the bait was not taken and that hook of acceptance was avoided. "Worsening" of the Plan was inevitable, so long as Turkey had to be induced to accept it. Thus Greek Cypriot unilateral acceptance of the Plan would not have precluded changes being later demanded by Turkey and the Plan's overall balance being altered. Indeed, acceptance at Copenhagen would have made subsequent rejection, even with the changes demanded by Turkey incorporated, seem unreasonable. Since the Greek Cypriot side has never accepted the Plan in any version, it remained free to reject it.[6] Subsequent indication of the Greek Cypriot side's willingness to accept Annan II did not protect the Greek Cypriot side from adverse changes. In his 1 April 2003 *Report*, para 49, the Secretary-General stated that President Clerides had in late January 2003 indicated to Mr Denktash (in front of the Special Adviser) that, should they not be able to agree on changes by the end of February, "he would be prepared to sign the Plan [Annan II] as it stood". That did not stop the "worsening" imposed in Annan III on 26 February and 8 March 2003 and the final denouement of Annan V.

[6] Annan V could thus, conscientiously, be rejected. Even then, foreign commentators supporting the Plan have criticised the Greek Cypriot side, contending that *they would have accepted it at Copenhagen* and could not, properly, change their minds. The facts are that the Greek Cypriot side did not unilaterally accept the Plan there, while nearly all members of the National Council, which regularly met in Copenhagen, were against acceptance, whether unilateral or bilateral. Such commentators also ignore the fact of the massive changes from Annan II to Annan V, mostly to the disadvantage of the Greek Cypriot side, making Annan V, in effect, a very different Plan.

THE REPUBLIC OF TURKEY'S ATTITUDE

So far as concerns the Republic of Turkey, although settling the Cyprus problem was not a condition of the EU's agreement to opening membership negotiations with her, settlement was at the stage of Copenhagen thought in practice to be a political requirement.[7] Turkey then wished to synchronise a Cyprus settlement with the EU firmly giving her a date for commencing negotiations on Turkey's membership. Indeed, in this connection her political leaders spoke—as they still do—of Cyprus as Turkey's "trump card". At the same time, Turkey feared that: if a Cyprus settlement and a date for opening EU negotiations could not be synchronised, Cyprus might be permitted to enter the EU; Turkey might not be given a negotiating date; and the Republic of Cyprus would be in a position to block Turkey's EU application, if negotiations subsequently began.[8] Turkey was clear that she did not want the Republic of Cyprus in the EU, unless it was on Turkish terms and in accordance with her desired timing.[9] Yet there were other considerations influencing Turkey in the direction of reaching a prompt settlement: on 10 May 2001 the new European Court of Human Rights (following a landmark *Report* in the last case before the former Commission) had in *Cyprus v Turkey* reaffirmed the law as earlier established in *Loizidou v Turkey*. In 1996 and 1998 the former Court's judgments in

[7] As things have moved on, by 2005 the view of many EU Member States was that settlement of the Cyprus problem was a matter to be settled *during* Turkey's accession negotiations and possibly only at the end of that process ie a position Turkey sometimes takes.

[8] In his 7 April 2004 Declaration urging a "resounding no" to the Plan, President Papadopoulos stated that he supported Turkey's aspirations to be given an early date for the start of accession negotiations. The Foreign Minister, Mr Iacovou, later gave the UK Government assurances that it would not place any obstacle in the way of Turkey being given a start date for negotiations on EU membership: HC Debates, 6 July 2004, Mr MacShane, Minister for Europe. Whether this attitude would persist if Turkey manifested hostility to Cyprus was an open question. President Papadopoulos was reported as hoping that by 17 December 2004 it would be possible to back Turkey's EU bid, but also as stating that the Government of Cyprus had a right to veto and expected Turkey to abide by its obligations: Cyprus News Agency, 10 October 2004. In November 2004, it was agreed, after consultations with Greece, to leave the position undecided until December, and to evaluate Turkey's response to requests that she honour her obligations to Cyprus. Greece was much opposed to any use of the veto by Cyprus, suggesting a phased process of improvement in Turkey's relations with Cyprus was a better alternative. Cyprus did not veto. The EU Council agreed to open negotiations on 3 October 2005. Prior to this, Turkey was to finalise adaptations necessary to the Ankara Agreement to take account of the EU's current membership, including Cyprus: see Brussels Presidential Conclusions, 16–17 December 2004, para 19, and Turkey's Declaration.

[9] Turkey circulated legal Opinions indicating that Article I of the Treaty of Guarantee and other provisions precluded Cyprus's accession to the EU until such time as both Turkey and Greece were members. A battle of legal Opinions and pamphlets was waged for several years from mid-1997. The Opinions obtained by the Government of Cyprus are reproduced in *Cyprus and European Union Membership. Important Legal Documents* edited by the Attorney-General of Cyprus, Alecos Markides (Nicosia, 2002). Turkey herself has, in pamphlets and in Security Council and General Assembly documents, disseminated Opinions by Professor M H Mendelson QC of 6 June 1977, 21 July 1997 and 12 September 2001: see A/56/451, S/2001/953.

Loizidou had laid down general legal principles concerning property right violations and interferences with homes in occupied Cyprus. Turkey now risked facing large numbers of human rights claims in respect of homes and properties of dispossessed Greek Cypriots and the possible ordering by the Court of payment of a massive total amount in damages.[10] Due to her not satisfying the Court's judgment in the test case of *Loizidou v Turkey*, Turkey's situation in the Council of Europe was becoming increasingly embarrassing.[11] She appreciated that pending and unsettled claims for large-scale human rights violations would render the opening of EU membership negotiations impossible. For these reasons, Turkey insisted with the UN Secretariat upon insertion of provisions in the Plan prescribing the dropping of all cases before the European Court of Human Rights, the substitution of Cyprus as defendant for all future cases, and the payment of compensation for Turkish violations of Greek Cypriot rights to be by the Greek Cypriot constituent state. Indeed, on 9 March 2004, before Annan V was "finalised", Turkey, through the Turkish Cypriots, proposed that the Plan should provide that she must be indemnified should the European Court of Human Rights hold Turkey responsible for property violations in Cyprus. Despite these factors militating throughout the period from May 2001 onwards in favour of a Turkish policy of settling the Cyprus question, Turkey's political structure at that time meant that decisions were slow and difficult to take. The higher governmental levels in Turkey, especially the military leadership and other elements of what is known as "the deep state" behind the formal political office-holders,[12] were undecided whether EU membership was such a priority that Turkey should sacrifice any of the territorial gains she had made in Cyprus following her mid-1974 aggression. There was the further consideration that Turkish Army governmental power could no longer be "formal" (as it then was and, to a lesser extent since 2004, still is) in Turkey as an EU Member State. Those who thought along those lines believed, not without reason,[13] that the Committee of Ministers of the Council of Europe would tolerate Turkish non-compliance without insisting on remedial action, or that they would gladly be

[10] *Loizidou v Turkey, Reports of Judgments and Decisions* 1996–VI, pp 2227–38 (Merits Judgment, 18 December 1996), reiterated in *Loizidou v Turkey (Article 50)*, Judgment 28 July 1998, and *Cyprus v Turkey* , Application No 25781/94, Judgment 10 May 2001.

[11] Turkey only complied with the Judgment of 28 July 1998 nearly 5 ½ years later, after engaging in numerous Committee of Ministers and Parliamentary Assembly debates—on 2 December 2003.

[12] "Deep state" is the translation of the Turkish term "*derin devlet*". It refers to the military-bureaucratic complex which controls the State of Turkey irrespective of which party (and consequently government) wins the Turkish elections: Ahmet Djavit An, "The Turkish Cypriot Political Regime and the Role of Turkey," *European Movement—Cyprus Council* (Nicosia, March 2004) p 14.

[13] Although the European Commission of Human Rights had reported on 10 July 1976 on massive violations of human rights in 1974 and on 4 October 1983 as to continuing violations of human rights in Cyprus, the Committee of Ministers considered it sufficient action merely to authorise publication of the Commission's *Reports*. The first *Report* was made public (declassified) on 20 January 1979 only because it had become available to the press. The second *Report* was made public by Resolution DH (92)12 on 2 April 1992, 8 ½ years after its adoption by the Commission.

diverted from taking action by Turkey's introducing some ingenious device.[14] In contrast, the Erdoğan/Gül Government favoured a more active approach to Turkey joining the EU, not least because EU human rights standards of religious toleration and democracy would protect it against the power of the rigidly secular Turkish Army and would require changes in Turkish law and practice infringing religious freedom and democratic rights.

TURKISH CYPRIOT ATTITUDES AND THEIR DEVELOPMENT

The Turkish Cypriot Community in late 2002, when Annan I and Annan II were presented, was by and large opposed to a settlement and ignorant of the benefits which the EU could bring it. Mr Denktash and his "government" were aligned with the Turkish Army and older nationalist political figures in Turkey, while more than 50% of the population were settlers from Turkey. Settlers were then strongly opposed, especially as they feared that they would be required to return to Turkey. Nonetheless, had a settlement been agreed by the Government of Turkey in December 2002, the Turkish Cypriot subordinate local administration, being wholly dependent on Turkey, would have had to accept it.

Later, in the second half of 2003, after an extensive EU information and assistance programme, and EU-funded pro-Annan Plan propaganda campaigns orchestrated by NGOs, who were also UN-assisted, with Turkish Cypriot opposition political parties being aided by funds from abroad, the Turkish Cypriots were alerted to the benefits of Cyprus's forthcoming accession to the EU. Elections in the occupied area on 14 December 2003 led to a political upset, with pro-EU, pro-settlement left wing parties obtaining marginally over 50% of the votes. In the event, in accordance with guidelines from Ankara, a coalition of left and centre-right parties was then established. By January 2004, the major figures in this coalition, Mr Talat and Mr Serdar Denktash, were being promoted by certain Western States and the UN as constituting the new leadership of Turkish Cypriots. The reality (a phrase much used in other contexts by Mr Rauf Denktash) was and is that such political figures still remain under the authority of Mr Rauf Denktash as "President of the Turkish Republic of Northern

[14] This device was to be manifested soon after the failure of the March 2003 Hague meeting to achieve adoption of Annan III. On 30 June 2003, Turkey's subordinate local administration purported to enact "Law 49/2003," having on 23 April 2003 re-organised the crossing arrangements, thereby enabling Greek Cypriots to visit the occupied area and Turkish Cypriots to visit the Government-controlled area. "Law 49/2003" provided for an Immovable Property Determination Evaluation and Compensation Commission to which persons could apply for compensation for their property on the assumption that an expropriation had taken place . On this basis, it became possible to argue that a domestic remedy in that area was now available and had to be exhausted. Turkey raised this line of argument before the European Court of Human Rights and a test case, *Xenides—Arestis v Turkey*, Application No 46347/99, was heard on 2 September 2004. Lower sums will be payable if this device is upheld, and applicants will have to use not only the "TRNC Commission," but will have thereafter to proceed to "TRNC Courts" on appeal before applying to the European Court of Human Rights.

Cyprus". The status of Messrs Talat and Serdar Denktash had first been elevated in February 2004 by the UN, which described itself in the Secretary-General's 28 May *Report* as dealing with the two newcomers and with Mr Rauf Denktash "as a triumvirate who together spoke for the Turkish Cypriot side".[15] Messrs Talat and Serdar Denktash then represented the Turkish Cypriot Community at what the UN now chose to call the Bürgenstock "negotiations" from 23–31 April 2004, at the end of which period the Secretary-General "finalised" his Plan. It has suited the Secretariat to describe these gentlemen as "political leaders" and as part of "a triumvirate," in particular asserting that Mr Talat and Mr Serdar Denktash have "led the Turkish Cypriot team in Bürgenstock and since".[16] The reality is nonetheless that the actual "leader" of the Turkish Cypriots remains "President" Denktash, who, inconveniently for the UN, is opposed to the Annan Plan. Had Turkey at any time wished to object to the Plan and on any ground, it would soon have transpired that Mr Denktash was and is "leader," and that neither of the persons currently cultivated by certain permanent members of the Security Council and by the Secretariat is "leader" of the Turkish Cypriots, even if they have been nominated by Mr Denktash to hold high "offices of the TRNC". The paradox is that, after the international standing accorded these leaders, soon after their return from Bürgenstock, in consequence of some party resignations they no longer commanded a majority in the Turkish Cypriot "Assembly".[17] Despite his loss of a legislative majority, the Government of the USA announced on 27 May 2004 that it was recognising Mr Talat as "leader" of the Turkish Cypriot Community and that it no longer recognised Mr Rauf Denktash as leader.[18] But all these events were in the future and were not foreseen at the time of formulating Annan I, II and III, however encouraging they may have been for the UN when preparing to finalise Annan V.[19]

ATTITUDES OF THE USA AND HER ALLIES

The policies towards Turkey and Cyprus of the United States of America, which have been fully supported by the United Kingdom and also in recent years by

[15] *S/2004/437*, para 15.

[16] Prendergast, Briefing to the Security Council on 28 April 2004, pp 2–3.

[17] On 17 July 2004 a motion of no confidence vote in the "TRNC Assembly" was not passed on the basis of 25 votes to 25 votes.

[18] On 26 May 2004, the Spokesman, Mr Richard Boucher, questioned about Mr Denktash's role, replied: "All I'm saying is we regard Mr Talat as the leader of the Turkish Cypriot community" (see http://www.state.gov.r.pa.prs.dpb.2004.32860.htm).

[19] The redoubtable Mr Rauf Denktash was from 1994 onwards seen as the major obstacle to a settlement, especially during periods when he had full backing from Turkish Governments and the Army, many of whose senior personnel had served in Cyprus and had developed special sympathies with Turkish Cypriots, also acquiring personal interests there. In October and November 2004, as "President of the TRNC," Mr Denktash was offering mandates to Turkish Cypriot politicians to form a Government and in a position to determine when an election would take place—despite his "deposition" as leader by the remaining superpower.

Germany and her Foreign Minister, Mr Joschka Fischer, were crucial factors affecting the negotiating climate and UN actions.[20] The USA has always perceived Turkey as a stabilising factor in the Eastern Mediterranean and in the Middle East. She wanted Turkey to become an EU Member, tying her firmly into Europe. US support of Turkey has invariably increased whenever there has been instability in the Middle East and Western Asia. Thus Turkey's significance was magnified after 11 September 2002, and re-emphasised after the invasion of Afghanistan, where Turkish forces played an important replacement role. Turkey's co-operation was to become even more pivotal with the invasion of Iraq and American plans for a general Middle East "reconstruction".[21] Accordingly, the Secretariat was heavily pressurised by the USA to secure a Cyprus settlement which would meet Turkey's demands while simultaneously enabling her to circumvent any remaining political hurdles in the path of her getting a date to commence EU membership negotiations.[22] Unless

[20] There are over one million German citizens who are Turks and a further two million are eligible for citizenship. Turks in Germany have, by a large majority, supported Chancellor Schroeder's party, rather than the Christian Democrats. Turkish electoral support is decisive, because the electoral margin between winning and losing office is narrow.

[21] The USA's two reliable Middle East friends, Turkey and Israel, have "partnerships". Turkey and Israel cooperate in matters military, especially in respect of Israeli supply of modern equipment for the Turkish Air Force and Army. Israel reciprocates even to the extent of spying activities for Turkey in Cyprus: two members of the Israeli Secret Service were arrested in Cyprus in 1999 for espionage, but were deported to Israel following inter-Governmental discussions. Israeli–Turkish civilian trading links are also important. Turkey's second "partnership" is more significant in shaping US policy towards Cyprus. In the USA, through effective activities by her consultants, Turkey has come to enjoy in Congress and in the State Department the support of the American Jewish lobby. Backed by the Pentagon, because of her strategic position, and backed in Congress by the Jewish lobby and by all concerned about Islamic fundamentalism and potential Iranian threats, Turkey has virtually unlimited American backing in the new age of unadulterated *realpolitik* (neo-conservatism), especially where there are likely to be beneficial side-effects for American allies, such as Israel and Morocco (in relation to the legitimisation of settlers and their ability to be involved in self-determination exercises). There is an even more crucial sphere as regards Israel, for which the Annan Plan would have been a powerful precedent. This is "the right of return" of the 1948 Palestinian refugees and their rights to reclaim their property. Israel and the US believe that these are matters for which compensation is the only appropriate remedy. Restitution, they believe, cannot be given, and departure from the general restitution rule, they contend, is justified by the public interest in achieving peace. Israel would not agree to a settlement which, by requiring full scale return and restitution of Palestinians, led to the destruction of the Jewish character of the State of Israel, especially in an atmosphere where large sectors of Palestinian opinion retain the beliefs set out in the original Palestinian National Pact. If there is to be "peace," compromises on the extent of return, as under the Annan Plan, will be necessary. It is unlikely that most Islamic States, sympathetic to Turkey and the "TRNC," critical of Greek Cypriots for rejecting Annan V, and not themselves renowned for their upholding of human rights, appreciated these aspects of the Plan: most were taking a diametrically opposed position on similar issues before the International Court of Justice in the proceedings regarding the construction by Israel of the Wall on the West Bank. Their anger, were the Annan precedent to be applied to Palestine and Israeli settlers, would be unbounded.

[22] Thus the Secretary-General was urgently summoned to the White House for talks with President Bush on UN-related issues, particularly Cyprus and Iraq. He also met the US Secretary of State, Mr Colin Powell, and the National Security Adviser, Dr Condoleeza Rice. The Secretary-General was on 3 February 2004 given his "marching orders" in the Oval Office and told to organise immediate resumption of talks which must end with his acting like a mediator and finalising his Plan. The Secretary-General had been sounding out Turkey, Greece, Germany, the EU Commission President and College of Commissioners and President Papadopoulos before his meeting with

Turkey was perceived to have "clean hands," her continuing occupation of Cyprus and violations of human rights on the Island would have precluded EU membership. The policy of achieving "clean hands" status for Turkey was to come to dominate the negotiations and UN actions, ultimately leading to the fiasco of Annan V and its voting down by Greek Cypriots in the April 24 referendum, although the policy appears, as things currently stand, to have been successful in absolving Turkey of blame for anything (including her continuing occupation of 36.4% of the Republic of Cyprus), earning her only plaudits.[23]

The anxiety of the USA and her allies that Turkey should become an EU member was not confined to their concerns about Turkey's strategic importance in the Middle East. The USA, and the Foreign Office in particular, saw Turkey as crucial in the future directions that EU development was likely to take. Turkey's membership would give the EU more of the character of a free trade area, hamper further moves to integration and terminate Common Agricultural Policy of the kind now current. Turkey would be a supporter of transatlantic relationships and of the continuing predominance of NATO: her Governments would be inclined to discourage development of autonomy in the field of European Security and Defence Policy, with displacement of NATO and an end to dependence upon it. Thus Turkey's accession would be important in tipping the balance between the Federalists and the Atlanticists. For all these reasons, the UK and America were determined that Turkey's desires should be accommodated in a settlement of the Cyprus problem in order to facilitate Turkey's EU entry.[24]

When the US Government adopts a policy—in this case settlement of the Cyprus problem in the context of furthering peace between Turkey and Greece and ensuring Turkey's future EU membership—it also wills the means to ensure success. It should be recollected that, apart from the long-term policy aims

President Bush, but it was the latter's insistence which decided a hitherto cautious Secretary-General to send his 4 February 2004 invitations to resumed talks.

Future historians of US foreign policy and the disappearance of its exceptionalist characteristics, with total reversion to *realpolitik*, will doubtless document the activities and influence of a small core of associates, Messrs Wolfowitz, Grossman, Perle, Abrams and Haas, upon the Cyprus problem and similar situations and be able to assess whether the forfeiture in foreign policy areas of the USA's moral stature was in the long run productive, even for the USA itself.

[23] Compare: The Atlantic Council of the United States, "Turkey on the Threshold: Europe's Decision and US Interest, Policy Paper," August 2004, p 14, which comments on Turkey's "positive role in promoting a settlement" and implies that EU Member States should *not* "balk at starting accession talks as long as Turkish troops remain in the north, thus technically 'occupying' the territory of an EU member". The word "occupation" was also in inverted commas. One may ask the riddle: "When is an occupation not an occupation?" The answer is "When it's a Turkish occupation." Former Ambassador Bandler payed a role in drafting the Paper.

[24] One of my colleagues in the Greek Cypriot side's negotiating team wrote an interesting "think-piece" fully explaining how Turkey would acquire great power over the EU: see Andreas D Mavroyiannis, "Cyprus and Europe: Hostages to Turkey," in *Kathimerini*, Athens, 18 April 2004. The Foreign Office (or rather its previous Colonial Office "wing") should recollect that when it sought from 1955 onwards to "use" Turkey, that State ended up in control of the situation, with UK policy hostage to Turkey—as explained by Professor Holland in *Britain and the Revolt in Cyprus 1954–1959* (Oxford, 1998).

already indicated, certain events in 1996–1997 made the US Government alert to the need for prompt application of a policy of achieving peaceful Greco–Turkish relations and of settling the Cyprus problem. These events were: a potential naval clash in late January 1996 between Greece and Turkey over the Imia islets in the Dodecanese island chain, followed by competing territorial claims between Turkey and Greece, and a Turkish Army landing on an Imia rocklet, which only US mediation defused by achieving agreement that both Greece and Turkey should withdraw their forces from the area; Cyprus's entry into a contract on 4 January 1997 with the Russian State Company Rozvorouzenie for the purchase of and future stationing in 18 months of an anti-aircraft anti-missile defence system with surveillance capacity over Turkey (which was to be placed on Mount Olympus, Troodos, next to UK installations, and which would have given Cyprus, with Russian technicians, important information-gathering capacity); the intended rendering operational of a military airbase at Paphos, with stationing there of Greek fighter aircraft; and Turkey's decision, announced on 20 January 1997 by President Demirel and Mr Rauf Denktash, to re-establish Turkish military supremacy over Cyprus.[25] These events had be evaluated in the disturbing context of continued Balkan instability in Bosnia-Herzegovina, Serbia including Kosovo, Albania and the Former Yugoslav Republic of Macedonia; of Greek sympathies and aid for Serbia and of Turkish sympathies and aid for Albanian ethnic groups. All this would have been seen in relation to volatilities in areas to the east and south of Turkey. The necessity for engineering a Greco–Turkish peace must have been obvious to State Department analysts. Such a peace would provide a central buffer of stability between the volatile northern Balkans and the areas east and south of Turkey. But achieving such a Greco–Turkish peace entailed as a pre-condition settlement of the Cyprus problem, rather than leaving the Cyprus pot "on the back-burner," as was the tendency when initiatives for settlement or confidence-building measures had been unsuccessful—as had transpired after mid-1994.[26] Accordingly, initiatives to settle the Cyprus problem, already required for other policy reasons, were accelerated in mid-1997. (They were of course paralleled by diplomatic efforts to engineer better Greco–Turkish relations, which in that period continued to deteriorate in an atmosphere of Turkish military threats and political threats to promote union between Turkey and the "TRNC".)

[25] The 1997–1998 follow-up to these events is set out in "Timeline of Political Developments," in Annex VII, 8.6, of *Final Report. Cyprus Bi-communal Development Program Evaluation*, 25 May 2004, submitted by Development Associates Inc to the United States Agency for International Development (USAID). The *Final Report* set out this material in explaining the background to the Bi-communal Development Program (BDP) agreed between USAID and UNDP in March 1998.

[26] Only subsequent historians will be able accurately to establish whether the "forward" Greco–Cypriot joint defence policy was designed to alert major Powers to the need not to be complacent about relative lack of tension and acceptance of Turkey's continuing military domination in the Aegean and Eastern Mediterranean areas. It is certainly possible to interpret the 1997 missiles and air base crises and the Republic of Cyprus's announcement in October 1998 of plans to create a naval base as a message: "Do not forget about the Cyprus problem".

For a Cyprus settlement to be reached and to receive the necessary internal approval of both Communities in popular referenda, it was, quite apart from encouraging negotiations between the concerned parties, essential that general public attitudes of inter-communal rapprochement and of favouring a settlement be created. The US Government, with its experience around the world in manipulating public opinion in developing countries, then decided that an adjunct to its Cyprus settlement policy was required in the form of a flexible programme to create pro-peace, pro-settlement attitudes and, as a necessary incidental, to assist in creating the social and political structures that would facilitate growth of these attitudes, and empowerment of those who adopted them. If such action has the blessing of the Government of the country in which aid is given for these purposes, and the action is transparent—at least to the Government concerned—it cannot be said that the action constitutes improper interference in the domestic jurisdiction of the affected State. The USA had to its hand an instrumentality for encouraging pro-settlement attitudes. Since 1975, encouraged by the Greek lobby in the USA, funds of approximately $15 million *per annum* had been expended on rehabilitating displaced Cypriots and other forms of humanitarian aid.[27] When such needs were met, funds continued to be made available for infrastructural and cultural programmes benefiting both Communities, eg medical and veterinary facilities, the Nicosia sewerage project, rebuilding the walls of the old city, preserving the cultural heritage etc. The US Government in March 1998, through the United States Agency for International Development (USAID) then agreed with the UN Development Program (UNDP), which had hitherto administered US aid funds in Cyprus, upon a Bi-Communal Development Programme which would spend some of the annual Economic Support Funds to support the peace-making process in Cyprus.[28] As the original BDP grant agreement stated, it was anticipated that the grant would facilitate the two Communities working together on projects and that the bi-communal nature of the activities "will create an environment more conducive to a peace settlement". For this purpose, the UN Office for Project Support (UNOPS) set up a Project Management Unit (PMU) in Cyprus to implement the BDP. This was necessary because UNDP, which had decided no longer to operate in Cyprus, delegated responsibility for implementation of the BDP to UNOPS, and only participated to a limited extent

[27] Such sums in the Cyprus context of a population of about 800,000 are not small. As the *Final Report*, p 12, notes, such an annual sum (totalling $60.5 m in the period 1998–2004) was significant, especially as a budgetary supplement to projects that might be difficult to fund though tax revenues. If only $8 million over the period was used for influencing attitudes, this represents $10 *per capita*. According to the State Department Spokesman, Mr R A Boucher, on 4 November 2004, the sum spent by the State Department for bi-communal programmes since 1998 was $6.4 million [ie about $8 per capita]. See http://www.state.gov/r/pa/prs/dpb/2004/37819.htm. This figure is also given in the Preface to the *Final Report*, at p x, para 2 h, which refers to "investment" in "bi-communal accomplishment" through NGOs. See also p 33.

[28] These funds are currently earmarked by Congress in annual appropriations for three programs: the BDP; the Cyprus America Scholarship Program, implemented by the Cyprus Fulbright Commission (in conjunction with its own Scholarship program) and managed by the Department of State; and the Bi-Communal Support Programme, also managed by the Department of State.

The radome (protecting surveillance antennae) in the clear atmosphere on top of Mount Olympus. If the S-300 missiles had been put in place nearby, their far more powerful radar system would have interfered with reception on the UK site. Moreover, Russian technicians would have been next door neighbours and also near to a second UK site on Troodos, important for interception of signals from the Arab world.

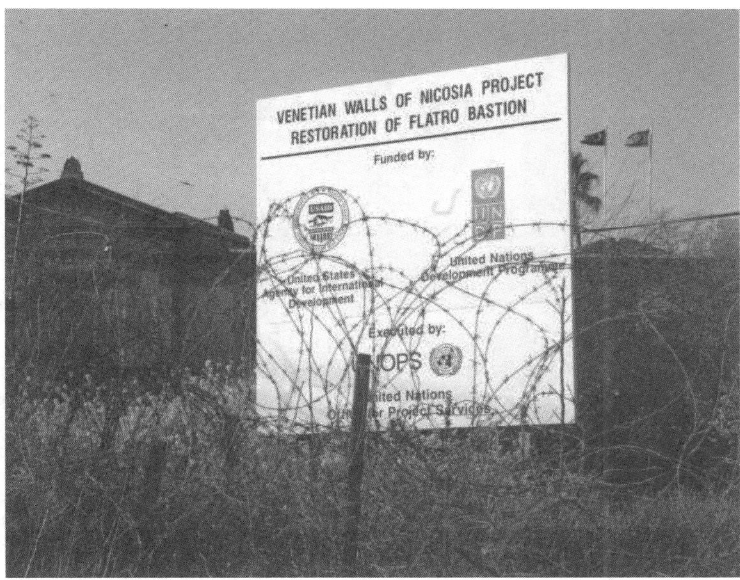

This was an important and legitimate cultural project, *inter alia* providing cover for more doubtful ones.

An important American comes visiting. Here Under-Secretary of State Marc Grossman calls on President Clerides on 4 December 2002 shortly before Annan II and the impending Copenhagen summit. Mr Grossman was accompanied by Ambassador Klosson and Councillor Renz, the latter two being responsible for overseeing the Bi-Communal Development Programme under which there were attempts at attitude manipulation and voter-education.

Subordinate local administrator "President" Denktash returns to Cyprus on 7 December 2002 after major heart surgery in New York. Fortunately, he has fully recovered and is his old self.

in approving and advising on larger projects under the programme.[29] The continuation of funding for projects, especially the infra-structural ones, which still required completion, was welcomed by the Cyprus Government under the then President, Mr Clerides. It is doubtful whether the Government appreciated the full intention underlying the BDP of engaging in social engineering. It was thought that a Programme having the aim of inter-communal rapprochement (which is how the BDP was presented) was desirable. It was not thought that creation and stimulation of growth of non-governmental organizations (NGOs), which had not been a feature of Cyprus life, could do any harm: indeed those in office may have thought that the growth of such organisations might encourage Turkish Cypriots to take attitudes more critical of the policies then followed by the occupation regime. Certainly, the long-term intentions of those who established the programme of creating changes in attitudes to "governance" and "civil society," and of promoting political change were not appreciated.[30] Nor did the Cyprus Government (or Turkey's subordinate local administration) envisage that ultimately the NGO members, who had been politically awakened, would have such an impact as they did in the occupied area,[31] or that the spending under the BDP would be envisaged as shifting from mid-2002 away from infrastructure projects to supporting "good governance," strengthening "civil society organisations," undertaking activities developing tolerance and reconciliation and "supporting the media to promote peace and reconciliation".[32] Ultimately,

[29] According to the *Final Report*: "The circumstances led to the PMU becoming something akin to a 'proto-governmental agency' backed by the political will of both the UN and the US Embassy" (pp 42–43).

[30] "Development was not the objective of the program," which was "bi-communalism": *Final Report*, p vii. The hope was that persons could be convinced to "vote for peace" through promoting bi-communal collaboration and reconciliation and developing active constituencies for peace in both Communities. Thus when ultimately a final UN Plan emerged, they would vote for it. The Secretariat, closely associated with UNOPS and with the Special Adviser later operating from UNOPS' Nicosia premises, was parti-pris to this policy. Mr de Soto's final comment after the referendum (we will know "in the fullness of time") was, significantly, picked up by the *Final Report* team in closing its prefatory remarks on the success or otherwise of the BDP in convincing Greek Cypriots to "vote for peace".

[31] There is no doubt that the NGOs in the occupied area played an important part in the growth of opposition to Mr Denktash and in the pro-settlement party winning "local elections" in June 2002. By 14 December 2003, in the "elections for the TRNC parliamentary Assembly," the outcome was that the "electorate" in even numbers returned "representatives" favouring and "representatives" opposing the Annan Plan—a point noted in the *Final Report*, Annex 7, 7–8. In the Preface, at p iv, it is stated that the BDP was able to develop an active constituency for peace among the Turkish Cypriots: "Turkish Cypriot NGOs, many of them supported by BDP, were active proponents of the settlement, and helped to convince others that this was their best hope to enter into the modern world."

[32] See *Final Report*, p 19. At p viii, e. the *Final Report* stated:

> The desire to avoid negative publicity or the appearance of political interference may also explain the predominance of grants to health (30%) and environment (19%) NGOs, particularly in the first three years of the project. As BDP became more established and the political constraints relaxed, funding shifted to peace/Mediation NGOs (11%), the latter made mostly in 2002/3 . . . As the possibilities of a settlement improved in 2002, the Special Initiative grant was established permitting the beginnings of a more directive program that remained within control of the Embassy-PMU decision makers.

working closely with the Special Adviser, some funds were used to provide information about the Annan Plan and to encourage support for it.[33] Policy under the BDP was controlled by the US Embassy. This gave "political guidance on all BDP projects".[34] As matters developed, it became clear that supporting "the peace-making process in Cyprus" was not only an expression of the US commitment to a peaceful settlement, but also to a working relationship with the US as a principal player in UN affairs.[35] The *Final Report* emphasised the prime role played by the US Embassy in grant-making, observing that, unsurprisingly, in a political programme largely financed by the United States,[36] primary consideration would be given to "foreign policy interests of the US Government" in perceptions of the programme and its expected benefits. But, in any event, "the interests of the US Government and the UN in this instance are substantially convergent".[37] Thus, before Copenhagen, the BDP, in conjunction with the US Embassy in Nicosia, was geared up to approve Special Initiative Grants, ie "target of opportunity projects or for *ad hoc* projects which might not receive the approval of the authorities".[38] Such projects required relatively small amounts of capital, but had "a significant impact".[39] A Contingency Plan was prepared for BDP in mid-2002, before the EU's Copenhagen summit when Cyprus's EU accession was to be decided upon, so as to be able to address critical areas in case of a settlement. (These areas remained valid in mid-2004.)[40] This active preparation for evolution of a settlement Plan and its implementation, and its funding by the USA in close consultation with the Special Adviser, go some way to explaining the US Government's confidence in late 2002 that support had been engineered from opinion leaders and NGOs in Cyprus for any settlement

[33] See Chapter XVI below.

[34] *Final Report*, p 5; and also p viii, showing that US Government representatives in the Embassy were "substantially involved in decisions throughout the project approval and implementation process". Elsewhere the BDP is described as "a political program" (p 18, twice).

[35] *Ibid*, p 5.

[36] \$60 million though USAID and \$500,000 contribution from UNDP.

[37] *Ibid*, p 14.

[38] *Ibid*, p 18. The reference is to the Government of Cyprus and the Turkish Cypriot Humanitarian Relief Mission, the humanitarian aid body of the "TRNC". Both, separately, were to act as project approving bodies. They were kept uninformed on a "Need to know basis" of Special Initiative Grants (*ibid*, p 10). Quite apart from the Special Initiative Grants, it appears that neither side was told about specific projects or given any details about grants afforded to the other side. This information had been repeatedly requested by the President of the Cyprus Red Cross Society because the Society cannot be associated with political activities.

[39] *Ibid*, p 22.

[40] *Ibid*, p 19. There were 4 "strategic priorities for BDP assistance": facilitating physical communications and developing "joint regulatory . . . systems" for use of common resources; spurring economic growth; supporting "good governance through assisting in the establishment of the common state organisation (the federal state), and promoting improved local government that interacts with civil society through participatory mechanisms"; and strengthening "social cohesion and mutual respect by strengthening civil society organizations, by undertaking activities that develop common values, non-discrimination, tolerance and reconciliation (eg through education, human rights activities, dispute resolution), and by supporting the media to promote peace and reconciliation."

which the UN achieved. It likewise explains the UN team's confidence that they would be able to achieve public approval for any settlement they finalised.[41]

ATTITUDES OF THE HELLENIC REPUBLIC

Greece, as a Guarantor Power and the emotional "Motherland" of Greek Cypriots, was far less active a party than she could have been. She had made belated amends to Cyprus by threatening to use her EU veto in respect of the enlargement process if this did not result in Cyprus's accession.[42] Greece, by her then Junta's organisation of a coup on 15 July 1974 against President Makarios and installation of Mr Sampson as replacement President, had provided Turkey with the pretext she had long awaited for invading Cyprus. After abortive consultations with the UK's Wilson Government, in which Turkey had suggested that the UK's SBAs and Forces be used in cooperation with Turkish Forces to take over control of the Republic of Cyprus, Turkey unilaterally purported to intervene under Article IV of the Treaty of Guarantee.[43] By making Cyprus's EU membership likely, Mr Simitis' Government thought it had done sufficient by way of atonement and that other Greek interests now came first. Greece needed a rapprochement with Turkey, as in 1930 and in 1959. This would enable her to reduce her massive defence expenditures, avoid incidents threatening war by a bellicose Turkey, which stated that were Greece to extend her territorial waters this would be a "*casus belli*," and which had reacted in the same fashion over a Greek rocklet, Imia, in 1996 which the then Prime Minister of Turkey, Mrs Ciller, claimed was Turkish. She had made similar threats in 1998 about the stationing of missiles in Cyprus, a policy formulated as part of Cyprus's and Greece's joint military policy. The Simitis Government was determined to settle the Turko–Greek disputes in the Aegean about delimitation of the territorial waters and continental shelves (or exclusive economic zones) of Greece and Turkey and possibly even to achieve agreement on joint exploration; it was equally determined to settle disputes about control of airspace; and it was anxious to encourage trade and joint tourism ventures with Turkey.

During the period of the Copenhagen summit, Mr Simitis addressed the National Council and in effect told the Cypriot leadership that they must "get it

[41] There is no innuendo that the recipients to whom this aid was targeted were other than *bona fide*, seeing the projects which they initiated and which were supported with BDP funding as being in the public interest in furthering rapprochement and peace. They did not suspect that they were being used.

[42] The decision to threaten use of the veto was the work of the late Mr Y Kranidiotis, Deputy Minister of Foreign Affairs of Greece, who died in an air accident on 14 September 1999. Mr Kranidiotis, son of a distinguished Cypriot public servant, was thought likely to end his career as President of the Republic of Cyprus.

[43] The lawfulness or otherwise of such intervention has comprehensively been examined by Professor R St J Macdonald: see "International Law and the Conflict in Cyprus" (1981) *Can YB Int Law* 3.

done with" and agree to Annan II. An indication of Greece's determination that issues with Turkey be settled finally is that, for at least the last year (2003–2004), secret talks between Greece and Turkey have been proceeding. There is no evidence that Mr Karamanlis' Government will have a policy different from that of his predecessor, Mr Simitis.[44] It appears that all that Greece will now do is give Cyprus Governments neutral advice of the character: "Don't make waves. Don't unnecessarily raise issues. This is the best deal you can get. Rely on your forthcoming (now current) EU membership and make that functional". Without positive Greek Government support (always an important internal aspect) Cyprus Governments face difficulties in making contentious political choices. For example, although this incident occurred later, during the 10–13 February 2004 discussions in New York, since Greece (still under Mr Simitis' Government) took the view that the Secretary-General should be accorded a large discretion, believing that the Cyprus issue must now be settled, President Papadopoulos could not reject the "finalisation role" accorded the UN Secretary-General on 13 February 2004, even though there were some members of his team who by then advised against trusting the UN not to usurp competence. The UN Secretariat was well-apprised that Greece was anxious that the Cyprus question be settled without further delay.

ATTITUDES OF THE EU COMMISSION

The European Union's executive organs also desired a settlement, being reluctant to accept a "divided" Cyprus (in which there could not be full application of EU law, but in which there would instead be complex suspensory arrangements and border control problems, as well as foreign relations difficulties with Turkey, an important candidate State and partner in regional military alliances). Because of Greek extraction in 1995 of a bargain from EU Member States that, in exchange for concluding a Customs Union Agreement with Turkey, the EU would open membership negotiations with Cyprus after conclusion of the Inter-Governmental Conference on institutional changes necessitated by enlargement, Cyprus had become a candidate. Moreover, there loomed in the background the threat of a Greek veto to the whole enlargement process if Cyprus were not accepted as a candidate State. There were continuing regrets at this outcome among certain Member States (expressed even today, with some of their politicians going so far as to say Greek EU membership was also a mistake). Certain Commissioners were less than sympathetic to the Greek Cypriot side. The EU Commissioner for Enlargement, backed by other Commissioners, kept sending the message that the EU would accommodate the terms of a Cyprus settlement. Lord Hannay's book, earlier cited on this point, reveals that Mr Verheugen had decided to allow UN negotiations to settle all issues and not

[44] Mr Karamanlis won the Greek elections on 7 March 2004.

to permit the requirements of the *acquis* to cut across the provisions of a settlement under UN auspices. At all events, the Seville European Council in June 2002 decided to "accommodate" a UN settlement in the terms of accession for a reunited Cyprus. However, this accommodation was to be "in line with the principles on which the European Union is "founded".[45] Clearly it is a sensible, economic and just rule (which should be applied in practice) that parties engaged in parallel or overlapping negotiating processes with different international organisations should not be able to reach a bargain in the first process to be completed and then nullify it in the other set of negotiations. The parties have agreed and should not renege. Conversely, if there has been some imposed and involuntary arrangement to which the parties have not agreed, they should be free and not considered as seeking an unfair advantage, or as estopped, if they seek to pursue their interests in the other negotiations. Failure to draw this distinction by Mr Verheugen and Lord Hannay at the time they agreed that a UN settlement should prevail in the future EU accession arrangements was natural because in early 2002 it was envisaged that a UN settlement would first be agreed. To continue to insist that a subsequent UN-imposed settlement should be binding and should entail alteration by an extensive Protocol of Cyprus's existing EU accession terms, agreed with the EU, after Turkey and the Turkish Cypriots had twice rejected opportunities to agree on a settlement on Cyprus (at Copenhagen and at The Hague), however, goes far beyond the need to see that international negotiations do not cut across one another. Moreover, although a degree of "accommodation" was permissible, this was to be in line with the fundamental principles on which the EU had been founded. The Seville Conclusions did not permit discarding or major inroads into certain of those principles, as was ultimately to occur at Mr Verheugen's instance. This final step, which occurred on 31 March 2004, was an extraordinary abandonment of fundamental principles by the Commissioner most responsible for upholding them during the lengthy enlargement process. Only extraneous political considerations (perhaps from Germany, his nominating State) can explain such conduct. At all events, from mid-2002 onwards EU Commissioners made it clear that the EU was willing to make *every possible accommodation* in Cyprus's terms of accession, and hinted that this included not only long transitional

[45] Presidency Conclusions—Seville, 21 and 22 June 2002, para 24:

> The European Union's preference is still for the accession of a reunited island. The European Council fully supports the efforts of the Secretary-General of the United Nations and calls upon the leaders of the Greek Cypriot and Turkish Cypriot communities to intensify and expedite their talks in order to seize this unique window of opportunity for a comprehensive settlement, consistent with the relevant UN Security Council resolutions, it is to be hoped before the conclusion of the negotiations. The European Union would accommodate the terms of such a comprehensive settlement in the Treaty of Accession in line with the principles on which the European Union is founded: as a Member State, Cyprus will have to speak with a single voice and ensure proper application of European Union law. The European Union would make a substantial financial contribution in support of the development of the northern part of a reunited island.

arrangements, but also permanent derogations from the fundamental principles on which the EU is based (read here EU human and economic rights standards) to facilitate Turkey's acceptance of a Cyprus settlement. This willingness was determinedly reinforced by Mr de Soto, who, in conjunction with Turkey, the US and the UK, pressed the EU Commissioner for Enlargement to accord the fullest accommodation, even to the extent of permitting the settlement to override fundamental EU principles by virtue of being made "primary law". Such "accommodations" were opposed by Cyprus as being a diminution of the rights which the Republic had sought to acquire when she applied for EU membership. But, as indicated, the policy of making virtually unlimited "accommodations" ultimately prevailed and resulted in further major changes by 31 March 2004 in Annan V. As has already been explained, Annan I and II had contained provisions for extensive derogations and long transitional periods relating to the application of the *acquis communautaire*, mostly in favour of Turkish Cypriots and arising from careful consultation between the European Commission and the United Nations, and these had, with minor alterations, been reproduced in Annan III. However, in Annan V a momentous alteration occurred. This was despite the Secretary-General having written to President Papadopoulos at Bürgenstock a few days earlier that "legal certainty" was provided as regards future immigration to the Island (ie in respect of future Turkish settlement of Cyprus) by a Federal Law providing for limitation of future immigration of Greek and Turkish nationals. His letter also stated that the UN had worked closely with the European Union to accommodate Greek Cypriot concerns. Nonetheless, the Secretary-General did an about-turn, endorsed by the EU Enlargement Commissioner.[46] A safeguard, designed to stop Cyprus being flooded with work-seekers from Turkey when she joined the EU, was abandoned. This was to be a major reason for many Greek Cypriots not approving the Plan in the 24 April 2004 referendum.

Reverting to the situation as it was towards the end of 2002, and the factors then operating, the EU Council meeting at Copenhagen in December 2002 was thought to be a favourable conjuncture for the UN-devised Plan to be accepted

[46] Shortly before the referenda and afterwards, there were acrimonious public remarks by his spokesman, alleging that the Enlargement Commissioner, Mr Verheugen, had been "cheated" into believing that the Government of Cyprus would support the final Plan. So far as concerns the President, such remarks can have had no application, because he had always reserved his position, requiring certain changes before agreeing to lend his support to the Plan. (His fundamental and consistent position had been set out in his letter of 28 February 2003 just before assuming office.) It is feasible that other Cypriot political personages may have provided the Commissioner with assurances to such effect when they held office or even after they no longer held State office. They may also have been misinterpreted. Nuances are easy to get wrong when neither speaker shares the same mother-tongue language.

If Lord Hannay's account of Mr Verheugen's decision to permit a UN settlement to prevail over fundamental EU principles is accurate, the "person" who should feel "cheated" is the Republic of Cyprus (and its citizens) whose "birthright" as a EU state was to be cut down, so that, unlike other Member States, its citizens would not enjoy the full benefits of membership and fundamental rights protection. Indeed, according to Lord Hannay, what the Turkish Cypriots would agree to at the UN table was to determine the scope of application of the *acquis*.

by all parties, who risked losing much if the then incomplete Plan was not in principle adopted. (That incomplete version—Annan II—was, it will be recollected, only to be finalised in January and February 2003.) However, the shaky new Turkish Government and Turkey's Foreign Ministry had not yet persuaded the Turkish Armed Forces to accept the envisaged Cyprus Plan, so that no solution was reached at Copenhagen in mid-December 2002. Significantly, the European Council re-confirmed its firm preference for the accession of a re-united Cyprus at the same time as it took the decision to accept EU enlargement with a Cyprus in which there would be a temporary suspension of the *acquis* as regards the areas not currently under the control of the Government of the Republic.[47]

[47] This temporary suspension was ultimately effected by Protocol No 10 attached to the Accession Treaty of 16 April 2003. The Treaty was ratified on 14 July 2003 and Cyprus entered the EU on 1 May 2004. The provisions of Protocol No 10 and the extent to which unanimous voting (ie with Cyprus's assent) is required for EU measures in Cyprus affecting such areas has become highly controversial, with the UK Foreign Office pressing for qualified majority voting in certain cases and the taking of measures under other provisions of the EU Treaty (eg Article 133) to avoid the unanimity clearly required by Article 1.2 of the Protocol.

Education for Erdoğan. Less than a fortnight after his election victory on 3 November 2002, Mr Erdoğan and an entourage of 150 senior military and civilian personnel land on the long runways of Geçitkale (Lefkoniko) Military Airport on 16 November. The Airport was funded by US military aid to create facilities for a rapid deployment force. Mr Erdoğan upon election had spoken "out of turn," so needed to be educated about the views of the Turkish Army and its protégé, Mr Denktash. Mr Erdoğan came away saying that two sovereign independent States were the basis of any common State and that, based on the London-Zurich Agreements, there must be simultaneous accession to the EU of Turkey and Cyprus.

Below left: Turkish-EU relations had meanwhile been strengthening. Here is the short-term Foreign Minister of Turkey in the Ecevit Government and also in the Gül Government, Sina Sükru Gürel, with Enlargement Commissioner Verheugen in Brussels. Below right: Mr Gürel having a last look at his speech for the 15 November 2002 "independence" celebrations in the "TRNC," which were accompanied by the usual display of military might and American weaponry. In summary, he will say *inter alia*: "a nation had been subjected to an attempt to erase it from history; in reality there are two sovereign states; and new plans for economic integration are ready." Two months earlier he had told the UN General Assembly on 14 September that there had been "a war between two distinct peoples" and that EU membership for Cyprus would lead to "tension in the Eastern Mediterranean".

Danish Prime Minister Rasmussen welcomes President Clerides to Copenhagen for the EU Council Meeting of 12–13 December 2002. Former President Vassiliou, as Cyprus' EU Negotiator, is happily looking on.

Mr Solana appears to be telling Turkey's Foreign Minister Gül (who is putting on a brave face, having unsuccessfully objected to Cyprus' EU entry before an internal settlement and before EU agreement to Turkish membership): "Keep smiling. Don't worry. 2004 is just around the corner." Top row, left to right: Chancellor Schroeder, the then Prime Minister of Portugal, Manuel Barroso, and the then Prime Minister of Poland, Leszek Miller. Bottom centre: Pat Cox of Ireland, then President of the European Parliament.

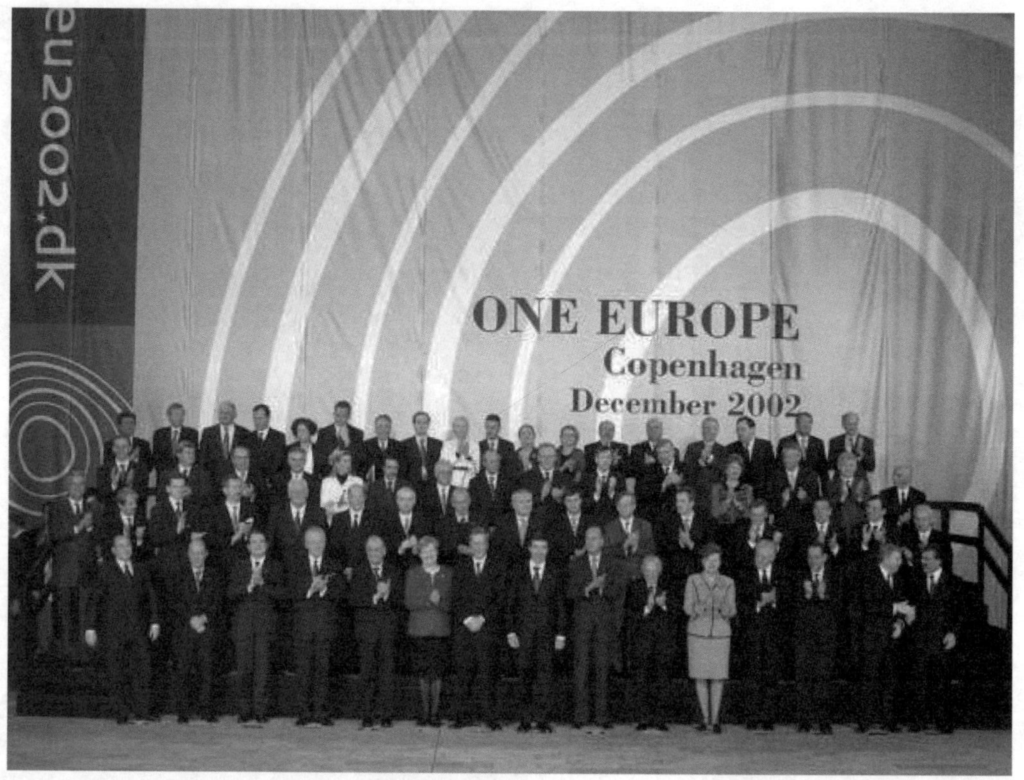

The historic Copenhagen group photograph. Bottom right, Pat Cox also offers his friendship to Abdullah Gül while Presidents, Prime and Foreign Ministers are concentrating on clapping "One Europe". (Formerly regarded in Cyprus as a friend of all Cypriots, Cox was later, to the surprise of many, to be among the most vehement in condemning a majority of Greek Cypriots for voting "No".)

President Clerides' finest hour: announcing on return from Copenhagen that Cyprus will be an EU Member. Moreover, he had not agreed to Annan II, already of concern to the Greek Cypriot public. Surrounded by, left to right: former President Vassiliou, Foreign Minister Cassoulides, Attorney-General Markides, Government Spokesman Papapetrou and Deputy Minister to the President, Pantelis Kouros. Former President Vassiliou had done great service to Cyprus in negotiating its EU entry.

Above: "We're all very glad to see you are better" is what President Clerides appears to be saying (and definitely did) to "President" Denktash, when they arrive on 15 January 2003 for the first leaders' meeting since early October 2002. By now, Mr Denktash had authorised his members of the technical committees to commence work.

VII

The Next "Deadline" for Imposing a Settlement and Annan III

DESPITE TURKEY'S FAILURE to accept the Plan and the "acceptance" of Cyprus at Copenhagen as a Member of a to-be-enlarged EU, a second UN helter-skelter rush then began to put the Plan in place before 28 February 2003. This was "Plan B," since agreement between the sides had not been reached before the accession decision at Copenhagen. Accordingly, in its conclusions, the Council expressed strong preference for accession of a reunited Cyprus to the European Union. Moreover, the Council welcomed the commitment of Greek and Turkish Cypriots to continue to negotiate with the objective of concluding a Comprehensive Settlement of the Cyprus problem by 28 February 2003 on the basis of the UN Secretary-General's proposals. In pursuance of this, the UN, after consultation with Turkey, again made changes meeting Turkish concerns. Again too the UN team, on 26 February 2003, "plonked" on the tables of each Cypriot party its revised Plan. At this point it should be explained that, from the outset, the UN team had described the forthcoming Plan as "the Plonk" and themselves as "the Plonkers". This language was not mere facetiousness, but a reflection of the arrogant tactics and conduct of the Special Adviser's team and its belief that it could at the last minute impose arrangements it had devised.[1] But, in the main, the changes related to matters which Turkey and the Turkish Cypriots wanted.[2] Indeed, the Secretary-General's 1 April 2003 *Report*, para 54, stated that

[1] If they were honest with themselves, they should have recognised that what they were producing was bad wine, newly bottled.

[2] The Turkish Cypriot constituent state was increased from 28.5% to 29.2% of the territory of the UCR, with a coastline of 52% (up from 41%). That would include the entire Karpas peninsula and virtually all land north of the Nicosia-Famagusta road. The percentage and coastline increases were effected by dropping the earlier alternative territorial map and doing a deal with the UK Government to surrender some unwanted parts of the Sovereign Base Areas, while having the simultaneous advantage of reinforcing and removing any doubts about validity of the Treaty of Establishment by virtue of an Additional Protocol. Bi-zonality was strengthened, with internal constituent citizenship status now being controlled by the constituent state, so that Greek Cypriots who wished to return to the TCCS could be excluded from residence, or, if permitted to return, from political participation. Moratoria on their re-assuming residence would be extended. At the same time the Plan was changed so that more Turkish settlers could stay in Cyprus.

Perhaps the most revealing example of UN duplicity is the way in which the changes made by Annan III on 26 February 2003 as regards the settler issue were explained by the UN in the separate

Annan III's further refinements were "particularly addressing the basic requirements of the Turkish side". On a symbolic level there were changes in nomenclature, which both sides agreed in the political meetings in Nicosia, notably the name of the federal state, "the United Cyprus Republic," and the name of the federal units, no longer described as "component states" but as "constituent states." In yet another change, to which the Greek Cypriot side agreed in order to conciliate Mr Denktash in relation to his "visions," the constituent states were denominated as "Greek Cypriot State" and "Turkish Cypriot State" (with capitals), these being the names proposed by Mr Denktash. This terminology was ambiguous, permitting the interpretation that the constituent states were international persons who could sovereignly act. Nonetheless, as indicated above, in this text the constituent states are referred to as the Greek Cypriot constituent state (GCCS) and the Turkish Cypriot constituent state (TCCS).

The most serious change was substitution of a new map according to which the whole Karpas peninsula would be part of the TCCS. This was done because the Map in Annan II had "most strongly" been objected to by Turkey and Mr

arguments it presented to each side. Unfortunately for the UN's credibility, papers setting out those arguments were leaked by the sides. See Chapter VIII below on the Question of Turkish Settlers.

A further example of UN double-dealing is given in relation to an alleged improved right of return of the 7,000 Greek Cypriots from Karpas villages, with those above the age of 65 years being able to establish residence in years 3–6 of the moratorium on return. However, not only would these returnees fill up the quota of return (7%, 14%, 21% limits on residence by the 7th, 11th and 16th years respectively after the settlement) but such returnees would be caught by the Plan's separate property provisions. They would therefore be unlikely to obtain their homes and properties. Thus in practice the right of return would be nugatory. Having told the Turkish Cypriot side how the quota would be filled by 65 year old persons returning and that the moratorium would now be extended, the UN explained to that side as follows:

> *Note also*: As provided in the property regime, the earliest that a currently occupied house would be reinstated to its original owner would be five years after entry into force of the agreement (three in the rarer cases of uninhabited properties). (Treatment of Property Affected by Events since 1963, Article 17). Therefore, while they are not caught by the moratorium on establishment of residence after two years, the over-65-year-olds would still have to wait a further three years minimum in most cases before any property was reinstated—if indeed the properties will be reinstated, which in most cases they probably will not be due to the operation of the general provisions of the property scheme ("Annan III": Additional points).

The UN allowed the Greek Cypriot side to think that the right of return of Karpasians had been improved.

Other important changes were: the special majority requirement for passing laws through the federal Senate (approval by 2/5 of Senators for each constituent state) was now to cover adoption of laws and regulations for Cyprus' exclusive economic zone and the contiguous zone (of particular interest to Turkey); a new procedure, inspired by Turkish Cypriot suggestions, regarding treaties concluded prior to the Foundation Agreement was introduced, while two Turkey-"TRNC" treaties were listed, thus clearly establishing the principle of continuity from the "TRNC" to the Turkish Cypriot state. More such treaties could be listed. Provision was made for larger fiscal transfers to the constituent states; requirements for notification of troop movements were reduced; special rules were proposed to ensure entry of Turkish nationals to the EU, etc.

The number of Turkish and Greek troops under the new "demilitarised" order was to be 6,000 for each of Turkey and for Greece. (Annan II had envisaged a range from 2,500 to 7,500 and the Greek Cypriot side in the January 2003 talks had indicated it would accept 3,000 each.) The UN agreed to double this figure and inserted it because Turkey was insisting on large troop numbers.

Denktash.[3] The new map permitted slightly more returns of displaced people, but gave less coastline and territory to the GCCS.[4] A gesture by the UK, offering to give up slightly less than half of the area of the SBAs (largely in favour of the GCCS), resulted in leaving the balance in relation to percentages of territory held by each constituent state virtually unaffected.[5]

ANNAN III ¼

After Annan III of 26 February, "Corrigenda and clarifications" (so extensive that the result could even have been described as Annan III ¼) emerged on 7 March 2003. By a new Article 49 to the Constitution, the Secretary-General now envisaged that many major Laws would not be finalised, instead providing that, until such time as Laws were passed, there should be *ad interim* exercise of a majority of federal functions by the constituent states.[6] The net effect was that, in many respects, there would for up to 8 months be a joint government conducted by the constituent states, rather than federal government. There were also symbolic changes desired by the Turkish side and some further substantive changes.[7] These "corrigenda" too were "plonked" at the last minute before President Papadopoulos. He had been elected on the first ballot as President of the Republic of Cyprus on 16 February 2003 and took over as "leader of the Greek Cypriots" from Mr Clerides. His campaign had been marked by extensive criticism of Annan II and he had a mandate to negotiate, at the very least, major changes in the Plan. (When the Corrigenda were delivered, the President was actually on his way to The Hague to meet the Secretary-General again.) He had earlier met the Secretary-General in Cyprus on 27 February when the

[3] *S/2003/398*, 1 April 2003, para 115.

[4] The TCCS would have slightly more than 58% of the coastline of the Republic, as it had in 1960. After SBA adjustment, the TCCS would have 54.3% of the whole Island's coastline.

[5] This gesture in effect gave the Greek Cypriot side little it did not already in practice enjoy: the inhabitants of the SBAs are Cyprus citizens and, under Appendix O to the Treaty of Establishment, effectively the same law and privileges afforded to citizens living in the Republic are accorded persons in the Bases by SBA Laws. Without "the gesture," the Plan would have needed further adjustment in favour of the Greek Cypriot side to restore the balance. Thus the gesture was in a sense sleight of hand, really upsetting the true balance. It is also the case that in December 2002 the Greek Cypriot side, dealing simultaneously with many issues in rapid succession, did not appreciate the full significance to the UK of legitimating the 1960 Treaties by the gesture. It became a referendum issue only in 2004. See Chapter XVII below.

[6] The areas concerned were Aliens, Immigration and Asylum; Excise; Aviation and Airspace Management; International Navigation, Territorial Waters and Continental Shelf; Water Resources; National Resources; Communications (electronic); Meteorology; Intellectual Property; Antiquities; Federal Elections (!); Pensions; Official Languages; Federal Offences (Terrorism and Drug Trafficking); and Federal Impeachment (!). Laws should all be passed either by the Federal Parliament or by judicial edict 8 months after the settlement came into force.

[7] Among these were clarifications about: each constituent state's ability to limit establishment of residence by persons from the other constituent state; enhancing the validity of actions taken in the occupied area; some economic protections for Turkish Cypriot businesses; and the extent of fiscal transfers to the constituent states.

President had made critical analytical comments on the previous day's "Plonk" ie Annan III of 26 February 2003, and had reserved the Greek Cypriot side's position on it, as well as earlier objections by the Clerides administration to Annan I (confirmatory letter, 28 February 2003 to Secretary-General). President Papadopoulos was emphatic about the paramount necessity for workable constitutional arrangements and properly studied financial arrangements.[8] This crucial letter set out the main concerns of the Greek Cypriot side and made it clear that the President's readiness to support the Plan depended on these issues being satisfactorily dealt with.[9] He also remained concerned by other substantive issues, but undertook that, if the Turkish Cypriot side did likewise, he would not reopen the substantive provisions of the Plan (for example, the decision-making arrangements). Meanwhile, it was quite clear that Mr Denktash would not accept the Plan. To avoid rejection occurring immediately, the Secretary-General tried to create more time by inviting both sides to meet him at The Hague on 10 March. He proposed that they sign a "commitment to submit the Foundation Agreement to separate simultaneous referenda in order to achieve a Comprehensive Settlement of the Cyprus Problem". He also indicated that acceptance of the invitation and signature would imply that they would support the Plan. President Papadopoulos accepted the invitation, but made clear that he did not believe the Plan was ready to go to referenda. Reluctantly, Mr Denktash also travelled to The Hague, where he informed the Secretary-General that he was not prepared to put the Plan to referendum.

It is also appropriate to note that, even by this stage, the Turkish Government had not been willing, despite agreement with the Secretary-General that it should do so, to discuss in detail with Greece revised security arrangements under the Cyprus security Treaties of 1960, and had rebuffed Greece's first two attempts to discuss these issues (*S/2003/398*, para 50).

[8] See Letter, President Papadopoulos to Secretary-General, 28 February 2003. The UN had devised a Plan which was economically illiterate and which would have made the United Cyprus Republic and the Greek Cypriot constituent state bankrupt. As one present at the Technical Committees of January and February 2003, the writer well recollects the initial resistance of the UN to involving officials of the European Central Bank—of course at Greek Cypriot request—and the gradual awakening of the UN legal team to the fact that there were serious issues involved. In responding to President Papadopoulos' letter, the UN had the impertinence to say that the deficiencies in their Plan were due to lack of input from the Cypriots. It is testimony to the young team's inexperience that they could have thought it appropriate to put forward a constitutional plan without proper economic study preceding its provisions and underpinning its proposals. Only in the two months prior to the March 2004 meeting at Bürgenstock, did the UN acquire economic experts to study the major problems. It then adopted some (but far from all) of the experts' recommendations. The UN property expropriation scheme had to be completely re-jigged. The writer puzzled the UN team by describing the arguments of the advocate of the bonds scheme as being of the calibre of a double-glazing salesman encouraging a purchaser. Perhaps in Switzerland, where this is essential, double-glazing salesmen are less like time-share touts.

[9] The letter is reproduced as Appendix 3. It is so important as a touchstone of what the Greek Cypriot side required and is of such public interest that I have, despite a general decision not to reproduce texts of letters to and from the UN, included it. It is far better for readers to have the actual text, rather than a précis by the writer of the main material incorporated into it from a paper written by her for Mr Markides, still Attorney-General and assisting President Papadopoulos.

The outcome was that no agreement on a settlement was reached at The Hague, where the Secretary-General met President Papadopoulos and Mr Denktash. The final blow to prospects of agreement arose when the Republic of Turkey, "citing previously unmentioned constitutional reasons," on 10 March at The Hague stated its inability to make a commitment to the security provisions in the Plan. This commitment had been required of Turkey by the Secretary-General. She was to confirm that, upon approval of the Plan in the referenda, she would sign the Treaty on Matters Related to the New State of Affairs, thereby amending the 1960 security Treaties (*S/2003/398*, para 58). Turkey's failure to confirm was because Article 90 of the Turkish Constitution, required that any treaty be ratified by a Law of the Turkish Grand National Assembly. Furthermore (not then mentioned but later to prove significant), any Law could be referred back to the Assembly by the President of Turkey under Article 89. It would then require re-passage in identical form or it would again be referred back.[10] In early April 2004, these Turkish Constitutional requirements were again sought to be kept in play for exploitation by Turkey in Annan V, which was only "clarified" or "corrected" after firm protest by President Papadopoulos once he had been armed with legal advice which would have justified refusal to proceed with the referendum on the Greek Cypriot side—or would, had the facts been disclosed and the referendum nonetheless proceeded, have resulted in a 100% "No" vote.

[10] Lord Hannay speculates that Turkey suddenly found these difficulties on 10 March 2003 because of the failed vote over the proposal authorising US troops to move through Turkey into northern Iraq in the event of hostilities there. This is unduly generous: the reference back and ratification provisions of the Turkish Constitution were often invoked and the Turkish Government knew that in any event it had to get around them.

Above: a new broom with a somewhat different team meets the UN on 19 February 2003. Left to right: Alecos Markides, President Elect Papadopoulos, Kypros Chrysostomides, Toumazis Tselepis; and the UN team, Lisa Jones, Didier Pfirter, Alvaro de Soto and Robert Dann. Mr Papadopoulos had, together with outgoing President Clerides, met Mr de Soto at the Presidential Palace on the previous day.

Below: on 24 February 2003, before presenting Annan III, the Secretary-General, de Soto and Prendergast had visited Athens to see Prime Minister Simitis and Foreign Minister Papandreou (right). Professor Papadimitriou is at the end of the table (left). The visit was to ensure that despite President Papadopoulos' election on 16 February 2003, giving him a mandate to improve Annan II, the "children" in Cyprus would come out to play.

The High Commissioner and the Plenipotentiary: a few weeks earlier on 27 January 2003 Lord Hannay came to push the UK's message of keeping the show on the road. Here, with High Commissioner Parker and the Deputy Minister to the President, Mr Kouros, who seems resigned to the forthcoming election result, Lord Hannay leaves the Presidential Palace.

The Secretary-General visits Cyprus on 26 February 2003 to present Annan III. Here he meets the outgoing and incoming Presidents. Mr de Soto is relishing the occasion.

President Elect Papadopoulos in Mr Denktash's iron grip on 26 February 2003 as the teams are brought out for "a photo opportunity". To Mr Papadopoulos' right are the Secretary-General's shadow, Sir Kieran Prendergast, and outgoing President Clerides. It is appropriate to quote Brian Urquhart's comment on the negotiations for the 1977 High Level Agreement (*A Life in Peace and War*, p 275):

> "On Denktash's arrival the group assembled for photographs in the jovial joshing atmosphere that often characterises the beginning, but very seldom the end, of negotiations in Cyprus".

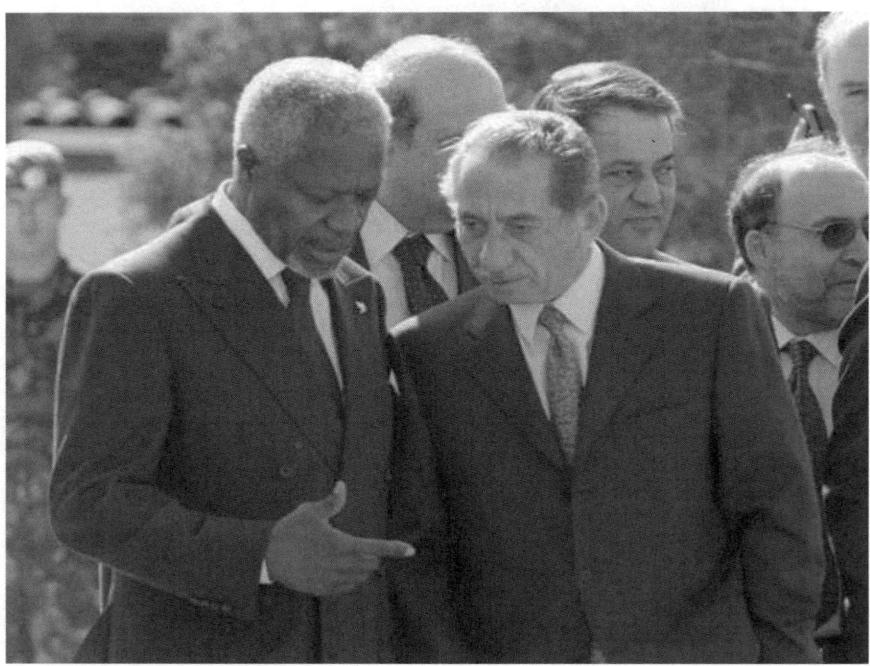

The Secretary-General has a quiet word on 26 February 2003 with President Elect Papadopoulos.

Photographed by UNFICYP inside the centre at the UN Protected Area on 26 February 2003, are three Cypriots who have sometimes been friends and sometimes political sparring partners for 40 years. They are with a slightly edgy Secretary-General, who is soon to present Annan III.

Unwonted hesitation for Mr Denktash. The Secretary-General appears to be telling him, while handing him Annan III: "It isn't infectious you know."

President Papadopoulos also appears reluctant to be bitten.

An old hand gets a courtesy call from the Secretary-General and Mr de Soto and handles the souvenir of his cooperative and forthcoming attitude far less gingerly.

Above: exterior of the Peace Palace at The Hague (location of the International Court of Justice) where all the parties met on 10 March 2003.

Ambassador Ziyal was there to say Turkey could not commit herself to the Plan for previously unmentioned constitutional reasons.

Above: President Papadopoulos told the Secretary-General of his conditions for putting Annan III to referendum: the people must know what they were being asked to vote for, so the gaps in the Plan and legislation must be filled; there needed to be agreed security provisions; and time was required for a proper public campaign on any referendum. If the other side did not re-open substantive provisions of the Plan, he would do likewise. But Mr Denktash said 'No'. (See colour picture 10, central section.)

Microphones (including RIK ie CyBC) for the Secretary-General, announcing "We've come to the end of the road" on 10 March 2003.

A down-hearted Secretary-General leaving the Peace Palace after Turkey and Mr Denktash refused to commit themselves to Annan III.

VIII

The Question of Turkish Settlers

THE ISSUE OF Turkish settlers remaining in Cyprus and of further Turkish immigration flows were to be crucial factors in most Greek Cypriots' decision to reject the Plan. There were three aspects: the large number of settlers who would be permitted to remain in Cyprus under the Plan; the large number of Turks who would in future be permitted to settle in Cyprus; and the participation by current settlers in the referendum in the Turkish-occupied area.

SETTLERS WHO COULD REMAIN IN CYPRUS UNDER THE PLAN

As regards the number of Turkish settlers already in Cyprus, the Government of the Republic had long been monitoring the problem. The idea of a census of both Communities suggested by Mr Boutros Boutros-Ghali[1] had been rejected by the Turkish Cypriot side, as had been a recommendation by the Parliamentary Assembly of the Council of Europe following a report by Mr A Cuco proposing that a census be conducted by the European Population Committee, so as to replace population estimates with reliable data. The Government of Cyprus in August 2002 estimated Turkish settler numbers to amount to over 115,000 persons. Since that time their numbers have been augmented, especially by reason of "unlawful" construction workers and others who have overstayed tourist visits without any action being taken against them by the "TRNC authorities". In approaching the problem, the Greek Cypriot side believed that, although the transfer of sections of the civilian population of an occupying Power to occupied territory is a violation of the Fourth Geneva Convention, Article 49.6, and a war crime (now also governed by Article 8 of the Statute of the International Criminal Court), the consequences for individual settlers of long standing should nonetheless be examined in a humane fashion. The USA's, the UK's and the UN's starting position was that all Turkish settlers must remain in Cyprus, and that their repatriation to Turkey could not

[1] *S24472*, 21 August 1992, Appendix to the Set of Ideas, p 45, para 13.

be required or enforced. Lord Hannay on television so told Greek Cypriots, drawing upon himself considerable odium.[2]

The Greek Cypriot side, despite its willingness to take humanitarian considerations into account, urged that the great majority of settlers should leave Cyprus. Mr Denktash, on 31 August 2002, declared that there were only about 30,000 Turkish settlers: persons who had gained citizenship of the "TRNC" should be accommodated. Mr Clerides then made a major concession. He agreed that, subject to these being the correct numbers, he would not go into the past, but would accept the principle that whoever was "a citizen" of either side would become a citizen of the new federation.[3]

Annan I thereafter provided for "a list agreed by the parties" of citizens, with their spouses and children; *plus* persons born in Cyprus and permanently resident there for seven years who had reached the age of 18 years; *plus* persons married to Turkish Cypriots; *plus* both categories' minor children permanently resident in Cyprus and, *in addition*, permitted the grant of permanent residency to further persons, such permissible number being up to 10% of the number of resident Cypriot citizens who had the internal "component state" citizenship status of the Turkish Cypriot State. Thus there would, at the very least, be 69,000 settlers at the time of the Plan coming into force entitled to remain in Cyprus.[4] This was a far greater number than the Greek Cypriot side had been willing to agree to. They had envisaged the list as incorporating the entitled categories which were now separately referred to in Annan I.

Despite going far beyond the original Greek concession by virtue of the Annan I provisions, Annan II further increased the potential number of settler stayers by changing the formula to *33,000* persons; *plus* the Turks married to Turkish Cypriots (16,000); *plus* young persons who had permanently resided in Cyprus for 7 years before turning 18 (no longer needing to have been born there)

[2] Doubtless he believed this was necessary education of the public in Cyprus. But timing of unhappy revelations dictates that they be made when they are off-settable by gains and by persons who have the capacity to persuade the local public of the overall merits of a package. That no-one could enforce the return of, say, 100,000 persons was a matter for the negotiators. It was not one for logical pronouncements by a person perceived as a representative of the former Colonial Power. In any event, Lord Hannay did not view the issue as one of "settlers," a term he considered disobliging and "pejorative". They were Turkish nationals who were "immigrants" to north Cyprus given "Turkish Cypriot nationality" (by a non-existing State): *ibid*, p 43. Diplomats choke over such words as "settlers" and "occupation".

[3] This figure of 30,000 Turkish settlers to be accorded UCR citizenship was honoured by President Papadopoulos in his March 2004 proposals on citizenship, despite his concerns about the effects of Turkish settlement and hostility among the Greek Cypriot public to any settlers being permitted to remain. In order to give humanitarian protection to persons who needed it, he was prepared to go "Thus far. But no further". However, the UN draftsman, obviously believing that all settlers should remain, had in the interim in Annan III added new provisions permitting more mainland Turks to remain in Cyprus. See *infra* on the Annan III changes.

[4] This figure would presumably be composed of 30,000 listed persons; say 16,000 Turks married to Turkish Cypriots by 2002; 8,000 persons born in Cyprus, now 18 years old and permanently resident for 7 years; and 15,000 to be granted permanent residence as 10% of the TCCS citizen population.

an estimated 16,000; *plus* the latter two categories' children (estimated to add another 2,000). Also entitled to remain in Cyprus, but by way of permanent residency, was a number equivalent to 10% of persons with Turkish Cypriot "component state" citizenship status (15,000). Under Annan II the number of future citizens and permanent residents therefore totalled about 82,000 settlers.

Further major changes were made by the UN in Annan III on 26 February 2003. The Turkish Cypriot side was told by the UN:

> *Annan III: Turkish Cypriot Perspective* (pp 1–2) . . .
> During consultations between the United Nations and Turkey, it was made clear that it was important that 60,000 "settlers" be assured Cypriot citizenship. This has more than been achieved. First, 45,000 will be entitled to citizenship based on their inclusion in a list. Second, in addition to this, persons married to Turkish Cypriots will be entitled to citizenship (this is an addition to the ideas circulated prior to the presentation of the revised plan, and will no doubt number many thousands). Third, approximately 15,000 additional persons will be able to get permanent residency and thus citizenship over time. Fourth, the 18,000 students and academic staff will be unaffected.

The figure conveyed of persons who would stay was thus 96,000.[5]

The Greek Cypriot side was told by the UN:

> *Greek Cypriot concerns raised re proposed settlement Annan III*, Annex III Attachment 4,
> Article 3.6 . . .
> 5.
> - Instead of the open-ended formula on *settlers* (which, according to GC calculations would have given citizenship to 60,000 or more Turks) there is now a lump sum of only 45,000 settlers getting citizenship, ie clearly less than expected under Annan II and little more than one third of the 115,000 settlers estimated by the GCs to be in Cyprus;
> - The lowering of the number of Turks who can get citizenship by implication also lowers the number of those getting permanent residency (and citizenship at a later stage) since the percentage is based on the number of citizens;
> - The number of future Turkish immigrants is cut in half, ie 5% of TC citizens rather than 10% provided the GC accept same cap for Greeks (which is unlikely to ever become operational);
> - The number of years of permanent residence required to be eligible for citizenship is raised from seven to nine years, providing a further brake on the number of settlers who can become citizens (this is probably the outer limit of what would be compatible with a European Human Rights concept);[6]

[5] This figure would be made up by 45,000 on the list; 18,000 Turks married to Turkish Cypriots by 2003; 15,000 permanent residents (assuming only a population of 150,000 TCCS citizens); and 18,000 students and staff.

[6] [This would not seriously affect the situation, entailing only that Turks who immigrated *after 1998* would have to wait a further 2 years for UCR citizenship. If written by Mr Pfirter, formerly of the Legal Department of the Swiss Foreign Ministry, the remarks on what European human rights concepts require are strange. Switzerland, party to the European Convention on Human Rights, does not grant citizenship even to second generation workers, and has not faced legal difficulties.]

- Finally, it is clearly stipulated that years spent as student or temporary academic staff do not qualify for the citizenship requirement.

The impression given was that not many more than 45,000 settlers could stay as citizens. However, as has been indicated above, the net effect of Annan III as regards citizenship and residence of settlers and stayers was when carefully analysed: 45,000 settlers with citizenship; *plus* 18,000 by now married to Cypriots and their children; *plus* 15,000 permanent residents acquiring citizenship in 4 years; *plus* 18,000 resident academic staff and students. Thus there would be a total of *96,000* citizens and residents who had come from Turkey. A further change as regards spouses of Turkish Cypriots and their children was that the residence requirements were dropped, so that Turkish persons married to Cypriots and who had then moved to Turkey kept Cyprus citizenship, as did their children.

Another important aspect was the quota provision for future immigration. Annan III made it clear that the quota was a rolling one, not a one-off operation of a 10% residence grant. When re-drafting to make the quota permanent, a 5% limit was imposed. The rolling quota operated at any time to permit Turkish nationals to immigrate until Turkish nationals reached 5% of TCCS citizens. Thus, once the earlier settlers became Cyprus citizens four years after the Agreement came into force, they would not be regarded as Turkish nationals (by a footnote instructing that any dual nationality, ie of Turkey, be ignored in calculating the population base for the quota). Thus, in 4 years' time, about another 10,000 Turkish nationals could immigrate to Cyprus assuming the number of TCCS citizens had reached 200,000. This rolling quota of 5% had been strongly opposed by Mr Markides in a meeting on 20 February 2003 with Mr Pfirter. Mr Markides emphasised that the Greek Cypriot side's position was that granting of residence to Greek and Turkish nationals to reside in Cyprus "should be restricted to 10% once and for all and should not be revolving".

In light of these provisions, it was unsurprising that the Special Adviser's own legal adviser, Mr Pfirter, stated at a conference on "The Annan Plan: Myths and Realities," at Bögaziçi University in Istanbul on 17 July 2003, that:

> the Plan does not foresee that anybody will be forced to leave

and that those who left would be persons choosing to do so and getting compensation. (The payment of compensation to persons who did not receive permanent residence had been a Greek Cypriot suggestion inserted in Annan II.) Mr Pfirter's statement was made after Annan III (26 February 2003) had altered the formulae for the stay of settlers and other Turks as citizens or as lawful residents. By the time of Annan V (31 March 2004), which did not further change the provisions governing the numbers of settlers and residents authorised to remain in Cyprus, a conservative estimate of Turkish nationals permitted to stay, either as citizens, permanent residents or lawful residents, or to immigrate within four years,[7] was about 106,000.[8]

As the Greek Cypriot side pointed out, the majority of such persons were male and were well-trained Turkish Army reservists, so that, despite demilitarisation, Turkey would have an army in waiting in Cyprus, merely requiring air drops of equipment and some target practice.[9] Turkish settlers would also be (as they are now) a majority on the electoral rolls of the Turkish Cypriot constituent state, and would therefore control its government.

Yet another aspect giving rise to concern was that the more settlers could stay, the fewer Greek Cypriots would be reinstated to their homes and properties within a reasonable time. This was because even non-Cypriots, as well as Cypriots (with many settlers becoming Cypriots under the Plan) were given rights as current users of property and improvers of property. Depending upon their financial means to acquire homes and the availability of alternative Government-provided accommodation, Turkish settlers could stay for up to 8 years after the settlement came into force in Greek Cypriot-owned property and this was possible even in areas to come under Greek Cypriot administration. They could, if they had substantially improved property in the TCCS, acquire

[7] At Greek Cypriot request, the UN provided that, for purposes of calculating the quota, dual nationals (ie persons retaining Turkish or Greek citizenship) could *not* be counted as Cyprus citizens holding TCCS or CCCS internal constituent citizenship status (as in Annan III). This made the quota slightly smaller unless dual nationals renounced their other nationality.

[8] The increase in numbers was due to population growth and to counting in the 5% quota. At para 60 of the Report the drafters of the Plan used student debating society style logic to assert that about half of the Turkish settlers, which the Greek Cypriot side claimed were approximately 115,000 in number, would not receive citizenship or residency and would have to leave Cyprus. This was UN disingenuousness of a high order, effectively claiming that only between 55–60,000 settlers could stay and implying that the Greek Cypriot statistics on Turkish settlement were false. As regards the number of Turkish settlers, the 115,000 figure was accepted by the Rapporteur of the Council of Europe Parliamentary Assembly's Committee on Migration, Refugees and Demography, Mr Laakso, in his 2 May 2003 Report, para 2. In Recommendation 1608(2003), adopted on 24 June 2003, para 2, the Assembly also accepted this figure.

[9] They were a major security concern: see Greek Cypriot side's position paper, 8 March 2004. The figures given above refer to "lawful" settlers under the Plan and not to "unlawful" overstayers under "law of the TRNC," who were estimated to be 40–50,000 people by the Turkish Settlers Association: *Kibris*, 9 May 2004. On 7–8 September 2004 in Ankara a "Protocol" was signed, setting out rules governing employment and registration of Turkish citizens in the "TRNC". "Unlawful over-stayers" could register at the Turkish "Embassy" and acquire social security rights and work permits: *Bayrak Television*, 12 October 2004. According to the "Minister of Interior of the TRNC," there were 35,000 illegal workers and 20,000 would be registered, with 15,000 leaving the Island. Registration was to occur within 75 days: *Kibrisli*, 17 October 2004. On 9 and 11 December *Afrika* asserted: ferryloads of entrants were arriving at Kyrenia to meet the "Protocol" deadline. By a December "Law," overstayers were "legalised". Adding 40,000 overstaying workers (excluding their families)—figures confirmed by the Cyprus Government—would, when added to the 2003 settler population (120,000), the Army (37,000) and Turkish Cypriots (87,600), make 197,000 Turks and Turkish Cypriots ie 29% of Cyprus's population, with a 2.27:1 Turkish: Turkish Cypriot ratio. *A fait accompli* on this scale, consolidating Turkish settlement and encouraging further settlement until 2005, is a crime under the law of international armed conflict. Those who facilitate such a crime have individual criminal responsibility. Although the International Criminal Court does not have jurisdiction, as Turkey has not ratified the Statute of Rome, courts of the Republic of Cyprus do have jurisdiction.

title and, in the areas to be adjusted, could also do so unless the dispossessed owner paid out for the improvement, while, if the property was one used for income generation, the improver would virtually automatically acquire a 20-year lease.[10]

Greek Cypriot concern about the scale of Turkish settlement in Cyprus was heightened by the Turkish Cypriot proposals of 15 March 2004, made under the guidance of Ambassador Ziyal, Permanent Under-Secretary of the Foreign Ministry of Turkey. In these proposals, the Turkish Cypriot side had demanded that a list of 50,000 persons, *plus* their wives and children, be given Cyprus citizenship without a 7 year residence requirement. This list was to be *in addition* to the 18,000 Turkish settlers who had married Turkish Cypriots, and who would therefore acquire Cyprus citizenship. From these proposals it was apparent that there were 68,000 Turkish settler families, quite apart from other categories of Turks who would get residence permission. The Greek Cypriot side was also conscious of the situation of "overstaying" Turkish mainland workers present in the occupied area, of whom it was then (before recent further immigration) estimated that between 40,000 and 50,000 were "illegally" present in the "TRNC". Despite Turkish requests for all settlers effectively to remain, one of the Federal Laws attached to Annan V provided that Turkish nationals residing in Cyprus were bound to leave Cyprus within one year at the latest from the entry into force of the Agreement if they did not receive permanent residence.[11]

FUTURE FLOWS OF SETTLERS FROM TURKEY AND GREECE

A major Greek Cypriot concern was future flows of Turkish settlement. In Annan III, provision for a small permanent fixed quota system, governing immigration of Greeks and Turks to Cyprus, was inserted, although the Greek Cypriot side had on 20 February 2003 told Mr Pfirter it would not accept this because granting of residence should be once and for all as regards the 10%, and there should be no revolving provision. Ignoring this strongly expressed objection, Annan III provided that once the number of Turkish nationals who were Cyprus permanent residents had reached 5% of the number of resident TCCS citizens, no further immigration could at that stage then be authorised by the Aliens Board. (The same rule *mutatis mutandis* applied to

[10] Similar provisions were made in Annan I–V, but were more invasive of dispossessed owners' property rights in Annan V. See Chapter XV for a full explanation.

[11] Their stay would after such period become illegal and they would have to be expelled: Federal Law on Aliens and Immigration (2004) section 3 (Foundation Agreement, Annex III, Attachment 5, Law). The Secretary-General's *Report*, para 50, explaining improvements inspired by the Greek Cypriot side, in contrast said persons who did not acquire permanent residency under the Law had to leave in 5 years. Since the *Report* was later, it may be that Turkey obtained a delay of stay in some provision somewhere enabling such persons to remain under the immigration quota which would have come into operation (see below). The rush to "finalise" meant that some untidy ends were left. Such a provision could be relevant to the Turkish workers whose "legalisation" was announced on 17 October 2004 and the many others who were still to arrive.

TURKISH MIGRATION

A widely-circulated post-card on sale in Turkey, featuring those responsible for the conquest of Cyprus in 1974: above right, Prime Minister Ecevit, and left, the senior Turkish General involved.

Turkish settlers arriving in Kyrenia after the invasion.

In the Karpas, formerly Greek Cypriot-inhabited villages, whose populations had been driven out or been pressurised into leaving because of oppressive conditions, were re-populated with Turkish settlers. Both sides in the talks have agreed to take a humanitarian approach to protect long-stayers and young people who know no other home than Cyprus. But the sides differ about whether *all* settlers can stay—which is Turkey's demand.

Turkish women workers whose families settled near Morphou. A new town nearby will be built to house persons who settled in Morphou. It will be surrounded by most of the orchards and agricultural land, with a run-down old Morphou being returned to Greek Cypriot villagers. (See U.16 for a satellite photograph of the boundary.)

Greek nationals.[12]) However, when the number of Turkish nationals did not amount to 5%, the quota again became available until the 5% level was reached—and so on.

The purpose of the system with its proportionally equal treatment of Turks and Greeks was designed permanently to maintain demographic balance on the whole Island and had, after lengthy discussion with Mr Markides, been introduced for this very purpose, especially since the UN and EU were applying this principle to the TCCS upon Turkish insistence.[13] On 26 March 2004, Ambassador Ziyal demanded that the quota system fall away upon Turkey's EU entry. The UN accepted this demand, changing the Plan in Annan IV and V. However, to reassure the Greek Cypriot side, it claimed that a new mechanism, applicable after Turkey's EU entry or 19 years, whichever was the earlier, would safeguard the demographic ratio. The mechanism was that

> the United Cyprus Republic, in consultation with the Commission, may take safeguard measures to ensure that the demographic ratio between Greek Cypriot permanent residents speaking either Greek or Turkish as mother tongue is not substantially altered.[14]

The Aliens Board would, by that time, be equally composed of members from each constituent state (3:3), no longer having two non-Cypriots to hold a balance. Once the UCR decided to consult the European Commission, consultation

[12] See Annan III, Annex III, Attachment 5. Federal Law on Aliens and Immigration, section 2.3. To divert attention from Turkish settlement of Cyprus, Mr Denktash, from time to time, claimed that the Government of the Republic had unlawfully engaged in large-scale settlement of Greeks and Lebanese (30,000 of whom temporarily sheltered in Cyprus during the Lebanese civil war). These assertions did not correspond with the facts. In the 40 year period 1964–2004 only 2,295 persons were naturalised, including 373 Greeks, nearly all spouses of Greek Cypriots, 360 Lebanese, 58 Russians and a few Georgians (3 in 2001–3, earlier numbers being so negligible as to fall in the residual category "all other nationalities"). Yet propaganda influences even experts—Dr Brewin on 19 October 2004 implying to the UK Foreign Affairs Committee that people from the Black Sea (Pontiacs) affected the Greek Cypriot referendum. Under the Plan, submission by each side of a comprehensive list of persons to become UCR citizens was made optional. All grants of citizenship by the Government of Cyprus, were made under the 1967 Citizenship Act or Annex D. Nonetheless, the Greek Cypriot side decided, in order to avoid any arguments about validity of citizenship, problems of succession to nationality if they were raised, and issues of statelessness, to submit a conclusive list of all persons registered or granted Cyprus citizenship from late 1963 to March 2004. Submitted in March 2004 the list contained 18,699 names and data regarding persons' original status, birth places and dates of arrival in Cyprus. Most were Cypriots (Greek and Turkish alike) who had lived abroad or their descendants. As regards foreign residents, 63,348 temporary or permanent permits were in force for work, retirement or holiday home stays. There are also an estimated 20,000 illegal workers—because Cyprus is a first magnetic landing point in Europe from the Middle East and Asia. Many illegal immigrants have made first landings in the occupied area and have then been permitted to proceed to the SBAs or the Government-controlled area.

[13] The demographic balance arrangements proposed for Cyprus could properly be described as "a double Åland Islands solution," protecting the TCCS against swamping by Greek Cypriots and the UCR against swamping by mainland Turks. Annan V altered this balance. The Turkish Cypriot Community continued to control entry to the TCCS, but stopping immigration from Turkey required their consent too.

[14] Draft Act of Adaptation of the Terms of Accession of the United Cyprus Republic to the European Union, Article 3.2.

would need to be conducted through the Federal Ministry of European Union Affairs, thus requiring Presidential Council approval, including the positive vote of a Minister hailing from the TCCS. Should measures be agreed with the Commission, giving effect to them would require UCR regulations. These in turn would require approval by 10 Cypriot Senators whose mother-tongue language was Turkish.[15] Thus Turkish Cypriot politicians, with an electorate consisting of a majority of Turkish settlers and their descendants, would have to vote in support of restricting Turkish immigration once Turkey joined the EU.[16] Unlike the UN papers telling the Turkish and Turkish Cypriot side what they had gained as regards settlers by Annan III, the papers as regards Annan IV and V were not leaked. However, an educated guess at what they would have said is:

> After 19 years or when Turkey joins the EU the limitation on immigration of Turkish citizens will end.

SETTLERS AND THE REFERENDA

As soon as he became the Greek Cypriot side's leader in February 2003, President Papadopoulos had raised the general questions surrounding settlers, making particular reference to their participating in any referendum on a new settlement and Constitution for Cyprus.[17] The matter was again raised by the President with the Secretary-General on 22 March 2004 shortly before the end of the talks in Nicosia, having earlier been raised in a meeting attended by Mr Denktash, to which reference to the *Western Sahara* Case was made. Yet the Secretary-General (obviously guided by Mr de Soto) was unwilling to open the matter. This was despite the *Western Sahara* Case [1975 ICJ Rep 12], and the precedent of East Timor having been drawn to his attention (in relation to it being inappropriate for a UN Secretary-General to approve a referendum result in a self-determination exercise where settlers constituted the majority of voters). The Secretary-General's response indicated that he considered that his role was merely formally to declare the result. He explained that he had no functions as regards the voting process in the referendums and that this was a matter purely for the parties. He explicitly rejected any supervisory role in relation to

[15] All immigration regulations under Article 25 2 (c) of the UCR Constitution have to be approved in this way.

[16] It was symptomatic of the guile with which the *Report* was written to have implied, as its para 50 did, that this change was made to meet the Greek Cypriot concern that the quota permitted a regular filling: the numbers allowed in under the quota as filled over the years would be infinitesimal in comparison with those who would, under the Plan as finalised, be entitled to settle in Cyprus. Indeed, para 50 was so carefully written by the Secretariat that it did not even use the phrase "Turkish settlers," whereas what was at issue was future Turkish immigration.

[17] This he did on 27 February 2003, confirming his position to the Secretary-General by letter on 28 February. (See Appendix 3.)

the referendum process or scrutiny of electors' rolls.[18] He did not consult the Security Council to extend his mandate, which he doubted extended to taking up the issue of settlers' voting and which Cyprus had therefore suggested he should do. Nor, having asserted that there was no practical way to ascertain matters before the referenda, did he take up the issue at Bürgenstock with the Greek Cypriot side, as he had been requested to do.[19] The Greek Cypriot side had prepared simple proposals, based on indications in the "electoral rolls" and also on the "lists" of future UCR citizens, which each side was due to supply, and which lists were required to set out birthplaces, date of arrival in Cyprus etc. Those proposals would, in a practical manner, have enabled speedy resolution of doubts as to entitlement to vote, but the Greek Cypriot side was not given the opportunity of putting its specific proposals to the Secretary-General. They had been prepared to show further flexibility by permitting settlers who were married to Turkish Cypriots to vote, because, under normal circumstances, such persons could have obtained Cyprus citizenship. But the issues were not resolved, because the Secretary-General raised one objection after another to discussing the issues, finally contending that objections to voting by settlers undermined a fundamental parameter of his Plan—and this despite the fact that he was, at Turkey's demand, prepared to alter another fundamental parameter. (That parameter was the voting and representation rights of constituent state citizens, in respect of which there would now be ethnic voting—registration for voters to be based on mother-tongue language—and ethnic representation in the Senate, in which there would, in consequence, be weighted voting on an ethno-linguistic basis.) Indeed, in para 62 of his *Report*, the Secretary-General, in justifying his refusal to act, repeated that he could not undermine a fundamental parameter of the Plan, citing in addition "apparent impracticability".

The Secretariat was adamant in maintaining the attitude that it must thwart the application of international law governing self-determination, repeatedly declining to respond to the Greek Cypriot side's requests to apply international law. When President Papadopoulos had raised settlers' participation just before going to Bürgenstock—having had no response to earlier requests to discuss the issue—and had asked the Secretary-General to circulate his letter, together with an Opinion on the issue by 18 of the world's leading international and public lawyers on the unlawfulness of settlers voting,[20] the Secretariat briefed Security Council members that there was a last minute attempt to torpedo to the talks. When President Papadopoulos responded, evidencing repeated Greek Cypriot objections from the outset of the series of talks, the Secretary-General was

[18] Letter to President Papadopoulos, 23 March 2003.

[19] Letter, President Papadopoulos to Secretary-General, 25 March 2004.

[20] The Signatories to the Opinion, dated December 2000, were: Professors Georges Abi-Saab, Dieter Blumenwitz, Jean-Pierre Cot, James Crawford, John Dugard, Pierre-Marie Dupuy, Lori Fisler-Damrosch, Cees Flintermans, Thomas M Franck, Christopher Greenwood, Gerhard Hafner, Vaughan Lowe, Donald M McRae, Alain Pellet, Joel Rideau, Henry G Schermers, Bruno Simma and Christian Tomuschat.

forced to acknowledge that the Greek Cypriot side had consistently objected on this ground.[21] Yet again, on 30 March at Bürgenstock, objection was made by the Greek Cypriot side to the Secretary-General in person as regards Turkish settlers voting in the referendum, but the Secretary-General was unwilling to take action.[22]

This treatment of Turkish settlers in Cyprus by the Secretariat and under the Plan is a regrettable precedent. The prime mover in this UN policy, Mr de Soto, obviously the inspirer of the Secretary-General's letters on this topic, has been appointed as Special Representative for the Western Sahara, where he may, as he did in Cyprus, push for arrangements obscuring the role of Moroccan settlers à la Mr Pérez de Cuéllar and Mr James Baker III in order to achieve a "political solution". Certainly the decision in the Annan Plan not to interfere with settlers participating in the referendum of Turkish Cypriots would have been welcomed by Morocco as regards the Western Sahara.

The "settler question" in Cyprus, as dealt with by the UN in the Annan Plan, would also have provided a convenient precedent for Israel and the West Bank, and these and other associated elements of the Annan Plan are, as already indicated, likely to be relied on by Israel and lawyers close to the US State Department in order to deny the right of return of Palestinian refugees and their claims to return of their land. The intervening Advisory Opinion on 9 July 2004 of the International Court of Justice on *Legal Consequences of the Construction of the Wall in the Occupied Palestinian Territory* may however afford Palestinians some protection against such arguments.

Although these questions regarding settlers raised major issues of humanitarian law, the diplomatic envoys working with the UN Secretariat, notably Lord Hannay, as previously indicated, right from the start of the negotiations relegated these and other human rights legal issues as being relatively insignificant. The UN team only changed its tune, and then to a limited extent, after the then European Commission and the European Court of Human Rights had found that denial of homes and properties to dispossessed persons, even if used by other persons (settlers and Turkish Cypriots), constituted violations of human rights. Both in this connection and in relation to all the settler issues (in particular that of settlers voting) reference to President Clerides' statement to Mr De

[21] See Letters of President Papadopoulos to Secretary-General, 22 March and 25 March 2004 and Secretary-General to President Papadopoulos, 23 March and 26 March 2004. President Papadopoulos' 22 March letter had appended the Opinion of 14 December 2000 from the jurists on the unlawfulness of settlers voting.

[22] The *Report* attempted in its para 62 to conceal UN pusillanimity. The explanation was now given that the

> Greek Cypriot proposal for strictly limiting the vote in the referendum in the north, to persons who were members of the two communities in 1963, as defined in the 1960 Constitution, and their descendants—a proposal which, aside from its apparent impracticability, would require the Turkish Cypriot side to accept the Greek Cypriot side's interpretation of the legal situation prior to the coming into being of the new state of affairs would have been contrary to the concept of the plan that neither side be required to do so.

Soto on 24 July 2000 at Geneva remains relevant. The President advanced a reasoned argument about the illegality of settlers, referring to relevant international instruments (the Fourth Geneva Convention, Article 49.6, etc.). The President concluded by saying:

> . . . The Greek Cypriot side expects UN representatives who are assisting in the settlement of disputes to do so in the spirit of the Purposes in the UN Charter, that is, to see that the dispute is settled in conformity with principles of justice and principles of international law. I do not believe there should be silence about remedying these grave breaches of international law.[23]

Although the UN and its officials are supposed to operate under international law, they relegated such law in the interests of pushing though the Plan. In this context of pushing through the Plan, it should be added that many of the Turkish Cypriot voters (who, in so far as they voted "Yes", were applauded by the Secretary-General) were to Mr de Soto's knowledge settlers, and that such settlers knew that *under the particular Plan* they could stay in Cyprus—some 42,000 settlers having been listed as Cyprus citizens.[24] The Turkish settler vote was therefore cultivated by Mr Talat.[25]

After the referenda, Cyprus public servants prepared tables listing villages in the occupied area together with their populations—as evidenced in the "TRNC

[23] This paragraph was contained in a paper by the President responding to Mr de Soto's Preliminary Thoughts of 12 July 2000, setting out a large number of suggestions, themselves vague and requiring clarification, for a settlement. A triggering factor for the writer's suggestion for such a paragraph was a lunch arranged to discuss property issues, with Mr de Soto's two legal advisers and a member of the Greek Cypriot team in July during the talks. Mr Pfirter disputed the rights to property and to return of refugees and the opinion of ten leading jurists on these issues, to which he was referred by the writer. When challenged, he claimed that he had discussed the matter in Strasbourg with members of the European Court of Human Rights, who had indicated that *Loizidou v Turkey* was not binding on the new Court and might well not be followed. The writer queried the propriety of talking to judges who would have to hear the case of *Cyprus v Turkey*, which had just been reported on by the Commission and was clearly destined for the Grand Chamber. Mr Pfirter thereupon quickly changed tack, claiming that this had just come up when he called on his former academic and diplomatic seniors. Strasbourg seems a long way to go for a social chat, in which discussing *sub judice* matters with judges likely to be involved was, as any lawyer knows, not proper conduct.

[24] Such Turkish settlers, who would become UCR citizens, could then freely move to EU States, eg the United Kingdom, as workers. So also could those accorded permanent residence if they had been present in Cyprus as workers for 7 years. The immediately eligible number would have been at least 80,000 persons under the Plan.

[25] He had worked with a Famagusta settler leader, Mr N Cevikel, and did so until the referendum was concluded, whereupon Mr Cevikel, having achieved a positive outcome for Turkey and for his supporters (who were on the relevant "list"), withdrew his support for Mr Talat's "government". This withdrawal led to that "government" not having a majority in the "TRNC Assembly" and to a decision to hold fresh "elections," which Mr Erdoğan then discouraged, as reported in *Halkin Sesi*, 9 July 2004. If and when new elections will be held, was in late November 2004 still open, and a theatre of "President" Denktash commissioning persons by turns to form a "Government" was still being engaged in.

The estimates of the Cyprus Statistical Service (given to the UN on several occasions at UN request) were that only 87,600 Turkish Cypriots had remained in Cyprus, whereas there were 115,000 Turkish settlers at the end of 2001. See references in Chapter XV below.

census" of 1996 ie indicating Turkish Cypriots and Turkish nationals (settlers). The tables also indicated "Yes" and "No" voters in the 2004 referendum and their percentages. All villages where Turkish nationals formed more than 80% of the population in 1996 (30) were then listed by the writer in Table E (see Appendix 4). This Table shows that large numbers of voters in predominantly settler-occupied villages voted "Yes," with 12 of these villages returning majority "Yes" votes, some by large margins, and this being the case even assuming that *all* Turkish Cypriots supported the Plan. (That assumption is evidently false in view of Mr Rauf Denktash's and Mr Serdar Denktash's opposition to the Plan.) Why such "Yes" votes were cast and the precise proportions of "Yes" and "No" voters who were Turkish and Turkish Cypriot is undeterminable, absent a proper survey. However, the positive reasons for settlers supporting the Plan could have included the following:

(i) Approval of the Plan's overall provisions;
(ii) Support for Mr Talat's RTP party and other small parties supporting the Plan;
(ii) Support for Mr Erdoğan's view and the majority view of the Turkish Armed Forces that the Plan should be approved;
(iv) Rights given by the Plan to large number of settlers to remain in Cyprus as UCR citizens or as permanent residents;
(v) Rights given UCR citizens (many being settlers) to enter the EU labour market;
(vi) Rights to acquire title to property if they owned significant improvements;
(vii) Rights to acquire alternative accommodation and social housing if permitted to remain resident;
(viii) Effective ability, due to the Plan's property provisions (see Chapter XV), to sell properties settlers had been allocated or had bought and, if they were touristic areas, to sell on to developers at considerable profit.[26]

There was support from settlers for the Plan, even when they lived in areas subject to territorial adjustment: Acheritou (28.5% being in favour), Prastio (31.3%) and Gaidouras (39.6%). There was even a 61.8% "Yes" vote in Avlona in the Morphou area. In those Karpas villages where Greek Cypriots were accorded a right of return after only 2 years from entry into force of the settlement and in unlimited numbers (provided they returned within 6 years of the Plan coming into force) there were still large numbers of settlers in support of the Plan.[27]

[26] Such areas included most of the Karpas villages; many sea-facing villages in the Trikomo District (Dhavlos, Flamoudi, Kalograia); sea-facing hill villages in the Kyrenia district; and villages near Cape Kormakiti.

[27] Vasili (72.9%), Melanarga (25.5%), Ayia Triada (25.4%) Leonarisso (51.9%) and Rizokarpaso (42.3%). These percentages of "Yes" voters include those Turkish Cypriots who also voted "Yes", but in most villages Turkish Cypriots were a relatively small proportion of the population. See Table E in Appendix 4.

All who wish to turn a blind eye to Turkish settlers, to the illegality of their presence, to the unlawfulness of their voting in violation of the principle of self-determination, and to the interferences with Greek Cypriot rights of property by way of expropriation (and/or requisition) in order to provide housing and other amenities for them or other persons, now need to consider the *Advisory Opinion* pronounced on 9 July 2004 by the International Court of Justice. Although not binding, it is of high persuasive authority for all UN Member States. That *Opinion* (approved by 14–1 of the Judges' votes),[28] will be a significant factor when Annan V is reconsidered and becomes a complete new Mark VI model, perhaps in consequence doing much less dishonour to the Secretary-General's name, should this be retained as nomenclature.

[28] The distinguished American Judge, Professor Buergenthal, dissented as to the propriety of giving an Opinion, although he indicated that he would not have dissented as to many significant substantive views of the Court, notably the violations of humanitarian law by reason of organising implantation of settlers and interfering with property rights unless the latter could be justified for purposes of self-defence which needed more thorough investigation in his view.

SOME THINGS CHANGE BUT OTHERS REMAIN THE SAME

Ledra Palace Hotel, photographed shortly before the crossings between the Turkish-occupied and the Government-controlled areas were opened by the Turkish Army and the Turkish Cypriot side to allow relatively free passage after nearly three decades of Turkish closing off of the occupied area to Greek Cypriots and of prohibiting most Turkish Cypriots from visiting the Government-controlled side. The barbed wire marks the crossing area and "the green line" between the sides. This was once Nicosia's only luxury hotel. After 1974 it was occupied by UNFICYP, used for accommodation of Force members as an intercommunal talks venue until 1983 and also for humanitarian meetings. The building is an UNFICYP-controlled "neutral area," long a meeting place for family reunions of those living on different sides of the cease-fire lines when the Turkish Cypriot side would permit them. It remains a venue for meetings of politicians from the two sides and for intercommunal social occasions organised by UNFICYP.

Turkish Cypriots waiting on 24 April 2003, the day the Turkish Cypriot side announced opening of the barrier at the Ledra Palace crossing controlled by the Turkish Army, with "TRNC police" *in situ*.

Young Turkish Cypriots at the Rocca Bastion hopeful for a better future. (Only a couple of years earlier, this had been a location from which stones were thrown from the part of Nicosia walled city held by Turkey at passing Greek Cypriots.)

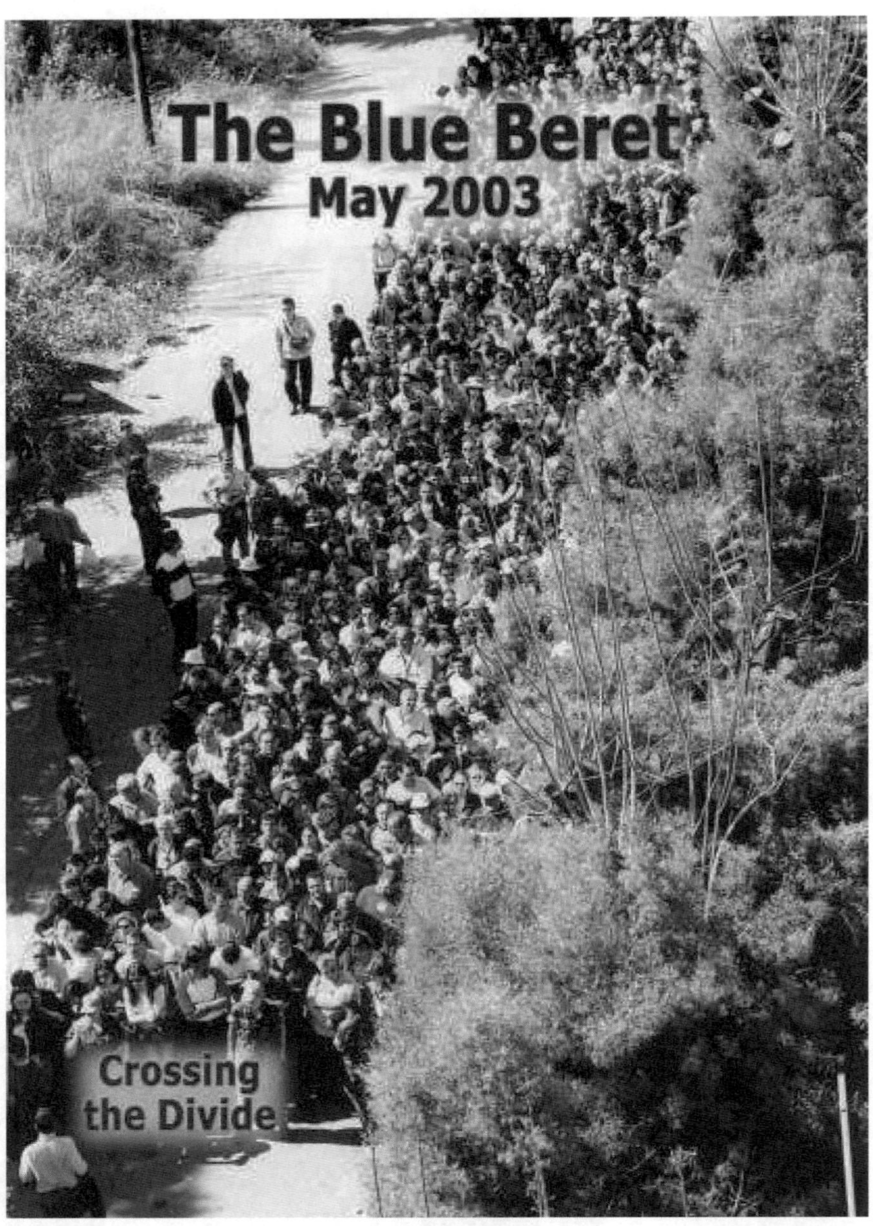

Acknowledgements to the UN Peacekeepers. This is the cover of their magazine, *The Blue Beret*. UNFICYP did a wonderful job in devising the best strategy to get people through the crossings as quickly and safely as possible. On the Greek Orthodox Easter holiday weekend of 2003 some 18,000 people passed through the Ledra Palace crossing point in one day.

Greek Cypriots and their families queuing on 25 April 2003 to visit the occupied area to see their homes nearly 29 years after they had fled or been expelled.

Things settle down to a steady flow.

Prime Minister Erdoğan's head is camouflaging the fact that the "Northern Cyprus Republic" is "Turkish". He is accompanied by Mr Eroglu, then "Prime Minister of the TRNC".

Was this visit a diplomatic one? Yanks have arrived in Kyrenia on 9 May 2003, while Mr Erdoğan was on his way there. More American tourists will be flying into unrecognised airports if current American studies bear fruit. Centre is Ambassador Klosson.

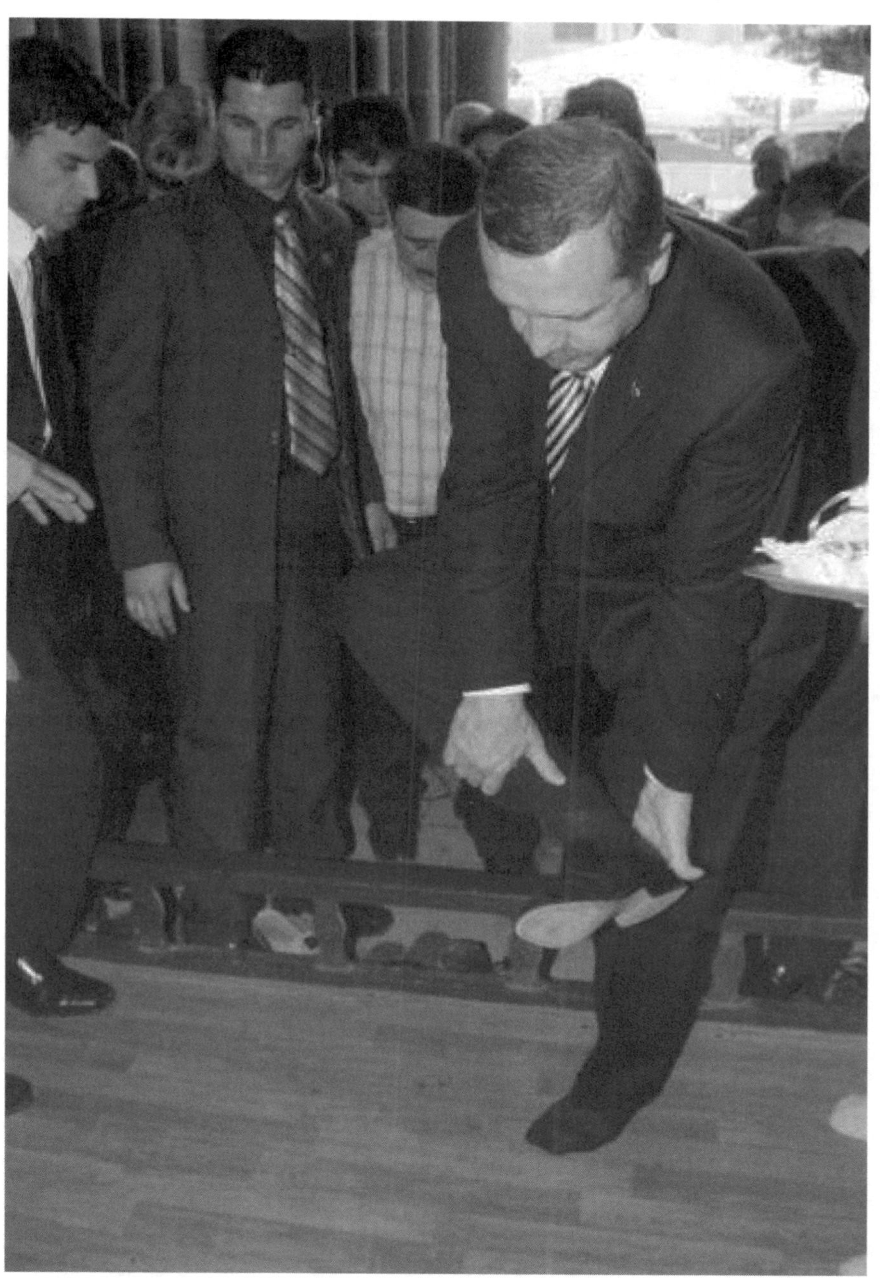

The Prime Minister of Turkey entering the Nicosia mosque on 9 May 2003.

Ambassador Weston visiting "President" Denktash on 13 June 2003 to encourage him to pursue an Cyprus settlement. ". . . He will not be moved . . ."

The US knows he knows how to say "No". "Are you really telling US what's good for Cyprus?" Ambassadors Weston and Klosson seem to be thinking as they look at President Papadopoulos on 13 June 2003.

What are these two civilian politicians, the Prime Minister of Turkey and the "President of the TRNC," doing with Turkish generals in a massive military parade by the Turkish Armed Forces in "technically occupied" Nicosia on 15 November 2003, designated the "TRNC's Independence Day"? Answer: it's the 20th anniversary of "Independence" under Turkey's effective overall control.

IX

The Secretariat's Handiwork and Presentational Tactics

ABSENCE OF DIRECT NEGOTIATIONS BETWEEN THE SIDES AND THE UN CONCOCTION OF THE PLAN

IT MUST BE emphasised that there had been no serious direct negotiations between the sides other than the face-to-face meetings in Nicosia from January to the end of September 2002 and some not very serious meetings in Nicosia in January and early February 2003, although at these there was genuine discussion about the name of the federation and the constituent states. In general, in consequence of Mr Denktash's positions, discussions had been largely non-concrete and about his "visions" (theoretical views of the nature of the State, the governmental system and issues of legitimacy). The Turkish Cypriot leader's views could not be left unanswered, so the Greek Cypriot side responded by showing that the concepts were outside the agreed framework of the talks, combining this analysis with pleas that discussions begin on specific issues. In this way, the meetings from January to April 2002 were wasted. Largely due to Mr de Soto's pressure, there was then a limited degree of negotiation on some security issues, during which the Greek Cypriot side accepted a proposal actually dictated by Mr Denktash. However, after consulting Turkey, Mr Denktash then withdrew the accepted proposal, taking the view that all matters had to be looked at together at the end of the process. The result of this effective failure to negotiate meant that the Plan was the product of the UN team, which, in the period until November 2002, *bona fide* sought to meet the fears and suspicions of both sides, talking to them about what it was considering proposing, and concocting a Plan by using bits of old Secretary-General's advisers' proposals from the 1977, 1981–1982, 1984–1986 and 1989–1992 negotiations, by balancing the two sides' concerns as expressed in their proposals of 2001–2002, by fleshing out those elements, and by inventing devices which the UN team thought could allow both sides to save face.

UN ASSERTIONS ABOUT THE CHARACTER OF THE PLAN

Because the Plan in part reflects earlier negotiations on Cyprus, Mr de Soto has described it as having "the stamp of the Cypriot DNA". This was a marketing exaggeration, put forward at a time when the balance and relationships in the Plan had moved far away from the earlier proposals (themselves put forward by UN officials, particularly in the de Cuéllar Ideas of 1989 and the Ghali "Set of Ideas" of July 1992) and from certain specifics set out in UN Resolutions on Cyprus.[1] Bland words were used by the UN to assert that the Plan conformed to

[1] In general, each successive set of proposals by UN officials with the passage of time became less accepting of Greek Cypriot claims and leaned closer to Turkish Cypriot positions. There was one exception, the "Set of Ideas" of Mr Boutros Boutros-Ghali, which had been greatly improved by the new Secretary-General, who had respect for international law and accepted that functionality and workability were necessary elements in any Constitution. The 1992 Ghali Set of Ideas was greatly modified in the proposed constitutional arrangements. The outcome was a barely federal state with minimal federal competences, and with federal decision-making, both executive and legislative, requiring positive participation by representatives from both constituent states, a reversion to the de Cuéllar Ideas. The representatives would in practice be ethnic (this being formalised permanently as regards the Senate in Annan V, although Mr Pfirter had suggested this expedient already on 20 February 2003 to Mr Markides, who had emphatically rejected it, insisting that if the UN did this in Annan III, there must be complete freedom of residence and that all time frames needed reconsideration). The Annan Plan, by insisting on effective participation of members hailing from both constituent states in every decision, abandoned the principle of functionality, which the UN had accepted in 1992. (Under the Set of Ideas, there was to be a 7:3 executive, with majority decision-making, but with vetoes available in important spheres to protect Turkish Cypriot interests.) Moreover, under the 1992 Ghali Set of Ideas, the *effective* mass expropriation of much Greek Cypriot-owned property and denial of the right of return to most displaced persons was not contemplated. In contrast, in the Annan Plan, human rights (earlier referred to mainly in the context of "the three freedoms of residence, establishment and property") were subjected to restrictions greatly reducing the scope of the rights as regards freedom of residence and of establishment and the right to property, while permitting discrimination. Again, only in the Annan Plan were Turkish settlers accorded rights to social housing and to stay as citizens or permanent residents of Cyprus in large numbers. Likewise, it was only the Annan Plan which provided for effective disappearance of the Republic of Cyprus, with its replacement by the "United Cyprus Republic". Furthermore, this latter entity started life bound by Treaties and Laws giving Turkey far greater competence in relation to Cyprus than anything hitherto suggested.

The February 1993 Presidential election lost the best settlement possibly on offer to Cyprus, and the 2004 Plan, if genuinely "the best on offer," showed how far Turkey had been able to persuade her allies to support a policy of continued violation of human rights. As indicated above, the de Soto solution had reverted to provision of his mentor's Ideas in 1989: Mr de Cuéllar had envisaged ceilings on the rights of return and on property so as to guarantee each Community a clear majority of the population and land ownership in its area as well as positive participation by representatives of both Communities in every governmental decision: see *Pilgrimage for Peace*, *op cit*, p 229. The years of careful negotiation by former President Vassiliou and Mr Oscar Camilion (the then Special Representative and a distinguished Argentinean political personality), resulting in protecting human rights while safeguarding Turkish Cypriot concerns, were thus thrown away. Mr Clerides' incoming Government encouraged the UN to pursue confidence-building measures and much UN energy was expended in trying to devise arrangements acceptable to both sides. Mr Denktash in his inimitable style drew out this process in cliff-hanging "Yes" and "No" fashion and it ended when President Clerides refused to continue with it in mid-1994: *S/1994/629*, 30 May 1994 and *S/1994/785*, 28 June 1994, Letter, Secretary-General to President of the Security Council.

This was, the writer submits, a wise decision: had the CBMs process been finalised there would have been "Famagustaisation" of the Cyprus problem ie the problem would effectively have been these, that it was "carefully balanced," "fair," "viable," "meets all concerns of the parties," "conforms to the parameters of a solution and the Security Council's vision for a settlement," and that "all changes are within the Plan's parameters and well balanced".[2] In support of such assertions, when briefing the Security Council on Annan V, Sir Kieran Prendergast put forward as evidence

regarded as no longer requiring international attention on the basis that return of Famagusta's Greek Cypriot-owned Varosha suburb to UN administration in exchange for opening of Nicosia international airport to enable direct flights carrying tourists to the "TRNC", would, in most States' view, have disposed of the main issues by providing for the return of about one-quarter of the displaced Greek Cypriots and by facilitating Turkish Cypriot economic development. In late 2004 parallels developed between what was envisaged by the UN in 1994, with the airport now desired to be opened not being the Nicosia Airport, but Ercan in the "TRNC". (The re-opening of Nicosia Airport was always a foolish suggestion: internationally known as a dangerous airport for landings and take-offs, it required enormous expenditures; and it had in the 20 years since 1974 been partly enveloped by residential areas.) Pressures in this direction, not labelled "confidence-building measures" were continuing at the end of 2004. History does not, as one is always told, repeat itself, but in the somewhat different circumstances of 2004 the same Turkish Cypriot objections were raised to the Republic of Cyprus making arrangements to facilitate economic development of the Turkish-occupied area. What Secretary-General Ghali wrote on 30 May 1994 is, *mutatis mutandis*, equally valid in describing the attitude of the collective Turkish Cypriot leadership towards measures proposed by the Greek Cypriot side or ones it has indicated willingness to implement by appropriate means. Mr Ghali reported:

> 53. For the present, the Security Council finds itself faced with an already familiar scenario: the absence of agreement due essentially to a lack of political will on the Turkish Cypriot side. While it can be understood that the Turkish Cypriot community has sometimes felt that its unhappy experience in the years before 1974 justified its unforthcoming approach on key aspects of the proposed bizonal and bicommunal federation, I find it difficult to understand why similar reluctance should have affected the Turkish Cypriot leadership's approach to a set of eminently reasonable and fair proposals that would bring substantial and tangible benefits to its community without in any way compromising its security or its basic political positions.
>
> 54. As it is, the attitude adopted by the Turkish Cypriot leadership will certainly bring with it grave consequences for the well-being of the Turkish Cypriot community, which will have to forgo the benefits that the package would have brought to it: the direct air shipments of cargo to and from countries other than Turkey; the similar direct flights for passengers and tourists; the jobs and contracts that would have flowed from construction in Varosha and the restoration of Nicosia International Airport; the businesses that would have been established in Varosha and Nicosia International Airport; the international assistance that could have amounted to tens of millions of dollars; the arrangements on entry documents for Turkish Cypriots travelling overseas, which would have had an important practical and psychological impact; direct access to the tourist markets of Europe and the world. The Turkish Cypriot community will now forgo the 20 per cent increase in its gross domestic product that it had been authoritatively estimated would have flowed from implementation of the package. Gone will be the economic momentum, the additional jobs and opportunities that would have enabled many young Turkish Cypriots to work and raise families at home in Cyprus instead of emigrating overseas.

As at the date of writing (end November 2004) it is not the case that aviation and airports policy has been discussed, but this is obviously a matter both sides will soon have to address. It is an issue bigger than opening another international airport and needs to be seen in its EU financial and competition policy context.

[2] As regards these UN standards, since they are in the main loose-textured, it is relatively easy to make such assertions without fear of contradiction. However, certain specific requirements had to be circumvented by devices in the Plan, eg the requirement for a *single* Cyprus citizenship, the return of all displaced persons to their homes in safety, the removal of foreign personnel, a single sovereignty of Cyprus etc.

for this the wide acceptance by "pro-solution forces" that the Plan's "overall balance" was preserved in its final version. Two comments sum up the value of such assertions: "They would say that, wouldn't they?" (using the words of a notorious young Englishwoman); and to single out "pro-solution forces" was to forget that *all* Greek Cypriots, whether voting "Yes" or "No" to the Plan, are "pro-solution".

The Plan's authors were well-acquainted with rhetorical devices, most notably the giving of a positive impression by a half-statement or a half-description. For example, it was said that the Plan required there to be participation by persons hailing from each constituent state in all decision-making; it was not said that no executive decision could be taken without 50% of the members hailing from each constituent state separately approving such decision. Again, gaps in protection (for example in relation to rights of property) were not mentioned, whereas emphasis was placed on the positive aspects of the same matter in the Plan, although these were minimalistic.

THE UN'S CONCEALMENT OF TURKEY'S INITIAL FAILURE TO COMMIT HERSELF TO SIGNING THE NEW SECURITY TREATY INTO FORCE

It is not going too far to say that the device of *suppressio veri, suggestio falsi* was sometimes employed to describe various situations. For example, Sir Kieran reported on 28 April 2004 to the Security Council that

> the Secretary-General received from the guarantors the commitments required of them authorizing the submission of the plan to referenda and subject to its approval and completion of the internal ratification procedures, to sign into force the Treaty contained in the Plan.[3]

The reality is that by 7 April 2004 Turkey had not given the required commitment to sign into force the Treaty, and the Secretariat, having raised this with Turkey, which chose to do nothing to correct the situation, then decided to "understand" Turkey's non-compliant letter (which failed to give the commitment that she would "sign into force" the Treaty) as the equivalent of honouring the commitment. Thus the Secretary-General sent Turkey a formal letter of understanding to this effect on 7 April 2004. In the meantime, anticipating that the Turkish Government might "play games" with a reference back under Article 89 of the Constitution of Turkey by President Sezer of a Law passed by the Turkish Grand National Assembly[4] (which would in consequence have indefinitely postponed a settlement and have given Turkey new negotiating cards at a time when, on the 31 March re-draft of the Plan, the Foundation

[3] s/pv 4954, 28 April 2004, The Situation in Cyprus, p 2 col 2. The technique of suppressing important facts is again used in relation to the same subject in para 63 of the 28 May 2004 *Report*.

[4] See p 65 above.

Agreement would have come into force), the Republic of Cyprus obtained an Opinion from two leading jurists, one a member and the other a former member of the International Law Commission, that there was no compliance by Turkey with the commitment required of her, and that the continuing existence of the Republic of Cyprus could be at risk, while Turkey could well not sign into force the new Treaty providing for reductions in Turkish troop numbers. Moreover, by the Plan as modified on 31 March, the Republic of Cyprus's terms of accession to the EU would have been altered, with major derogations taking permanent effect, even though a settlement might not come into operation. In a letter to the Secretary-General of 8 April, President Papadopoulos indicated that the stipulated conditions for holding a referendum were thus far not met.[5] At that stage, the Secretariat thought again. On 12 April it obtained a written assurance from Turkey's Permanent Representative to the UN and on 18 April the UN re-amended the Plan by Clarifications and Corrigenda.[6] There was silence, both in Sir Kieran's briefing and in the later final *Report*, about Turkey's action to give herself room for manoeuvre, so as not to sign the Treaty into force, and silence about the Secretariat's unwillingness to do anything to secure compliance, unless compelled to take action. It is noteworthy that these legal issues were associated with the UN's last minute changes on 31 March to the "null and void clause" of Annex IX should the referenda be negative.[7] Earlier, the UN had tinkered with the same clause, actually removing it without any forewarning from the Plan in the Annan III version of 26 February 2003. Only President Papadopoulos' strong objection by letter of 28 February 2003 had resulted in the clause being reinstated by the Corrigenda of 8 March 2003. (See p 269 below, Appendix 3, L and O.)

[5] See Letter, President Papadopoulos to Secretary-General, 8 April 2004, appending Opinion by Professor James Crawford SC, FBA, LLD, and Professor Ian Brownlie CBE, QC, FBA, LLD, "Transition to the Unified State of Cyprus under the 'Comprehensive Settlement of the Cyprus Problem'," 6 and 7 April 2004. The Secretary-General in his 31 March letter sending the two sides the Plan as finalised had written that the referendum was dependent upon the Guarantor Powers' commitments being duly given.

[6] Main Article 13 and Annex IX, Article 1 paragraphs 1 and 2 were amended by inserting wording requiring that the Treaty on matters related to the new states of affairs be signed "into force". A new clarification No 42a explained that not only must there be an instrument of acceptance or ratification but "all necessary internal requirements; including any promulgation of any relevant act of Parliament [must] have been completed prior to signature". Likewise, the Draft Act of Adaptation of the Terms of Accession of the United Cyprus Republic to the European Union, Article 9, was amended to make it clear that the adaptation would only occur upon entry into force of the Foundation Agreement.

[7] Turkey was concerned that the Turkish Grand National Assembly should have the Plan brought before it for approval "only after the Turkish Cypriots had given their verdict on the Plan" (*S/2004/437*, para 54). That was contrary to the procedure agreed that the guarantor Powers' commitments be given *before* the referenda. It may be that the UN draftsmen were trying to square this circle. But, in doing so, they left large gaps giving rise to new Greek Cypriot concerns. Through such gaps the TGNA and President Sezer could escape the new Treaty, while Cyprus would be left in total uncertainty.

UN MISCHARACTERISATION OF THE PLAN

Equally misleading is the reference by the Secretariat on 28 April 2004 to the Security Council's support in Resolution 1475 of the Secretary-General's "carefully balanced plan" as a "unique basis for future negotiations". In the 2004 context, this is doubly misleading. First, even if the Plan could arguably have been described as carefully balanced in March 2003 when Resolution 1475 was passed, by March 2004 the Plan had been so altered in favour of Turkey's strategic demands and her doctrine of bi-zonality (*apartheid à la Turquie* in Cyprus) that it was by now entirely unbalanced. Second, the Plan as corrected in March 2003 was to be a "basis for further negotiations," but further negotiations, other than on two relatively insignificant aspects,[8] did not occur. Instead, there was imposition of a Plan devised by Mr de Soto and his team, although they sought to disguise both this imposition and their preceding and constant close consultation with the Republic of Turkey.

UN OBFUSCATIONS

In Secretariat comments, even if purporting to describe the Plan's provisions, there was obfuscation. The miles of small print and complex concepts in the Plan (novel devices of Mr de Soto's ingenious team) often hid what was important. For example, the "constituent state citizenship status" concept, which the Greek Cypriot side long resisted, was portrayed as innocuous,[9] but, in the way it was employed in the Plan, it was designed to allow restrictions on political rights, on rights of residence and on economic and property-acquisition rights of "non-citizens". Again, the complex provisions about property ownership, deliberately now split from the right to reside, were designed to withstand potential European Court of Justice and European Court of Human Rights examination of violations of property rights in possible legal challenges. The political citizenship rights were similarly so designed. Nonetheless, remaining

[8] First, the provision in the Plan for actual establishment of a primary instance federal court, rather than stipulation for its later establishment by a federal Law; and, second, enlargement of the federal executive by three non-voting members and consolidation into twenty month periods of rotation of the offices of the President and Vice-President of the Presidential Council (rather than rotation among all six of its members, each for a 10 month term). This change was so effected as not adversely to impact on the relative overall proportion of time for which each constituent state member (in practice Community) would hold office. Article 29.4 of the Constitution was tidied up to provide that at meetings of the European Council the President should be accompanied by the Vice-President, although the UN's re-rubber-stamping of the Cooperation Agreement on European Union Affairs which it claimed to have "finalised" in February 2003, overriding Greek Cypriot objections, left the issue of Cyprus's representation in EU bodies in a most unsatisfactory, even laughable, state.

[9] "Citizenship" of units of federal states in Western Europe has a long historical background, as in Switzerland and Germany, where there were separate States before federations were established.

anxious that the European Court of Justice might still overturn the Plan's arrangements in these respects, the Republic of Turkey sought to secure yet further changes in Annan V on 31 March 2004 at Bürgenstock.[10] The UN gave way and amended the Plan,[11] with the EU Commissioner for Enlargement agreeing that the Commission would recommend to the EU Council of Ministers (upon a request by the Co-Presidents of the new Cyprus federation—which they were mandated by the Plan to make) that the Council accommodate the terms of the settlement. The outcome would be significant derogation from the fundamental principles on which the EU was founded, including its human rights law, by adapting Cyprus's terms of accession before Cyprus entered the EU on 1 May 2004. The major derogations and transitional arrangements departing from EU fundamental principles would be set out in a Draft Act of Adaptation of the Terms of Accession of the United Cyprus Republic to the European Union, placing them beyond legal challenge in courts applying EU law.

Such derogations and transitional arrangements were certainly not negotiated, other than between the UN, the relevant EU Commissioner or Commissioners, the Republic of Turkey and Powers sympathetic to the latter. Cyprus was adamantly opposed to making these derogations and extensive transitional arrangements "primary law" of the EU, thereby in effect permitting long-term discrimination against Greek Cypriots. The Greek Cypriot side had, as already indicated, on 26 March 2004, only five days earlier, received a written assurance from the UN Secretary-General that the UN had had Cyprus's concerns on these aspects in mind. It should be recollected that a major motivation for Cyprus seeking to become an EU member was that EU principles and standards would govern the situation in Cyprus in all spheres in which EU law was relevant. Nonetheless, Turkey's wish to derogate from such standards, and her ability, with diplomatic backing from the UK and the USA, to persuade the UN team and EU Commissioners involved to fall in with her wishes, resulted in a decision of the relevant EU decision-makers to meet such wishes.[12] To do this

[10] This had been Mr Ziyal's Point 6 (see Appendix 1).

[11] See Annex IX: Coming into Being of the New State of Affairs, Article 6, The European Union; and Attachment 2: Letter to the President of the Council of the European Union.

[12] The "de Soto Plan" (a more appropriate title than "Annan Plan," which attaches the name of the highest international public servant to a tainted Plan) was sold by its progenitor to Commissioners embarrassed by the prospect of Cyprus acceding to the EU as a divided State in which there could be difficulties in honouring promises which President Prodi (accompanied by Commissioner Verheugen) had made on 15–16 January 2004 to the Turkish Government about economic benefits not being denied to Turkish Cypriots even if the Plan were not to be accepted. On 28 January 2004 the Secretary-General discussed Cyprus with President Prodi and the EU College of Commissioners. To persons acquainted with the absence of restrictions on trade between the FDR and the GDR (and the important actors were many of them German), Greek Cypriot reluctance to facilitate trade must have seemed unreasonable. The difference is that one part of Germany was not seen as responsible for displacing persons and then exploiting their properties. (Indeed, most German politicians have put pragmatism first, overlooking property claims by East Prussians and Sudetenlanders.) Nor was international trading capacity assessed as a factor facilitating independence. In addition, for many years before reunification there had been internal trading. Since the Copenhagen Summit in December 2002, and probably even before then, the EU Enlargement Commissioner had proceeded on the assumption that there would be a Cyprus

it appears that they had to persuade their own lawyers, who (as widely reported in the Turkish press) had contended that to make these derogations "primary law" was legally impossible.[13]

"WHAT I TELL YOU THREE TIMES IS TRUE"

The positive accounts given by the Secretariat of the Plan's substantive content are misleadingly convincing to all but initiated experts who are capable of appreciating the qualifications that need to be made in relation to the Secretariat's statements. The author of *Alice in Wonderland* made the pertinent remark:

> What I tell you three times is true.

Lewis Carroll also made Humpty Dumpty scornfully say:

> When I use a word it means just what I choose it to mean, neither more nor less.

These observations apply to the making of assertions by the Secretariat in and in respect of the Plan. For example: that the Republic of Turkey, *inter alia*, is committed to international law and the Principles of the UN Charter (*Report*, Appendix E); that the Plan envisages *one* independent and sovereign state, when it speaks also of two constituent states of equal status who "sovereignly" exercise powers, including large external relations competences; that the division of Cyprus is ended when it is perpetuated by provisions which provide for permanent ethnic separation of the people of Cyprus into two constituent states in each of which there is forever to be predominance of different linguistic groups ethnically identified; when, instead of safeguarding the identity of Cyprus, the possibility is cleared for flooding small Cyprus by massive immigration of work-seekers from a neighbouring underdeveloped country with a population of about 80 million people by the time Turkey accedes to the EU and becomes its largest Member State; when it is claimed that there are not one-man "vetoes," but, in reality, unless one of two Turkish Cypriot Ministers votes for

settlement, an assumption which it appears was encouraged by certain Cypriot political figures with whom he or his staff negotiated. The Commission as a whole would not have wanted non-settlement in so far as this would be a complicating factor for Turkey's being given a negotiating date. If the latter were to be refused, this should be on grounds other than non-settlement of the Cyprus problem. There was therefore every incentive to accommodate the de Soto Plan, especially as its proponents were then sanguine of its acceptance. It should be added that most leading Greek Cypriot political figures and the public generally had not turned *against* the Annan Plan even after The Hague meeting on 9 March 2003, although by electing President Papadopoulos a majority indicated they wanted changes in the Plan. The turning point for public opinion came in late February and early March 2004, when it became apparent that the USA, the UK and the UN were pressurising the Greek Cypriot side, and that Turkey and the Turkish Cypriot side were likely to secure major alterations to the Plan which they were demanding. Only then did the general public enter into serious informed debate about the contents of the Plan and begin in-depth analysis of its provisions.

[13] See eg *Kibris*, 16 March 2004, regarding a meeting of EU and Turkish legal experts in Ankara.

a decision, no federal government decision can be taken; when it is claimed that there is machinery to resolve deadlocks, when this means telling politically unqualified judges to take political decisions to solve the matter, but to do so with restraint; when it is said that the Plan fully respects human rights, whereas it uses technical language and exceptions, giving with one hand and taking with the other, to ride roughshod over the human rights of return to homes, to properties, to settle and to establish businesses in the TCCS; when it talks of paying compensation, whereas what is happening is self-payment through long-term sale of part of dispossessed persons' property; when it is said that the Plan is economically and financially sound, whereas, although considerably improved at Greek Cypriot insistence after UN initial reluctance in January 2003 to look at financial problems, there still remain doubts about the inherent financial risks, due to excessive burdens imposed by the Plan on the federal government and on the GCCS;[14] when it is suggested that the Plan is to be fully and faithfully implemented, but the UN refuses to give its own guarantee for this, being unwilling to apply Chapter VII of the Charter for *this* purpose, ie it will not mandate "upholding action"—a mandate which would have the political effect of preventing unilateral intervention by Turkey—and which did not need to specify any enforcement action, such a matter only, if at all, potentially arising in the event of continued Turkish violation of the Plan. Instead, the Plan went in the opposite direction to UN enforcement, with a statement contending that UN action would not prejudice the Treaties under which Turkey claims power to intervene. The Plan was thus so framed as to confine any mandatory prohibition to arms sales.[15] Far from the UN being "robust" and holding parties to their commitments, it has in the past and now again declined to undertake this responsibility. The UN has asked Cypriots to show "hope" and "vision," claiming to await a call from Cyprus to reunite and reconcile Cyprus in safety and security. That request would have been more meaningful if the UN had made proposals genuinely ensuring safety and security for Cyprus, rather than merely offering exhortations, by-stander-type involvement and a history, even very

[14] The final *Report* on the Plan (*S/2004/307*) gives the impression of improving functionality (para 44) and of indicating that the Plan represented a solid and workable economic basis for reunification of Cyprus (Annex II, para 9). The *Report* failed to explain that important recommendations by the Technical Committee on Economic and Financial Aspects of Implementation (which had only been appointed at Greek Cypriot request) had either been changed or not included in the final, fifth Annan Plan and the accompanying fiscal or financial Laws. All these Committee recommendations had been *agreed by the Technical Committee's members, including the Turkish Cypriot experts* (on financial issues concerning property there had been some disagreement). But Annex II, while it indicated that *implementation of the Committee's recommendations* would ensure a workable economic basis for a reunified Cyprus, was silent as to the Plan's departures from these important recommendations. The details of the departures are set out below when discussing Greek Cypriot concerns following presentation of Annan IV on 29 March 2004 at Bürgenstock.

[15] The mandatory prohibition on arms sales was one of the few Greek Cypriot requests accepted by the UN. The writer drafted a request for this, bearing in mind Turkish Cypriot requests over the years for a comprehensive ban on weapons. It was reported that in the informal Security Council discussions preceding presentation of a draft Resolution on 21 April 2004 Members were made aware that the Permanent Representative of Turkey opposed there being such a mandatory prohibition.

recently—as in relation to the Strovilia area—of refusing to stand firm when commitments have been breached by Turkey.

WHICH SIDE REALLY MADE COMPROMISES?

The truism that in any negotiations there must be compromises has been used to reproach the Greek Cypriot side for having had serious objections to the Plan. Had there been genuine negotiations, as opposed to imposed arrangements dressed up as negotiations, such as occurred with the current Plan, more compromises would have been made by all concerned.[16] As things stand, the Greek Cypriot side to this very day sees no compromises by Turkey—unless it can be said that an offer in future to return a part of the territory of a State unlawfully occupied by her, and removal of part of her unlawfully present army of occupation are compromises. Equally, the Turkish Cypriot political leadership has not compromised, unless it is said that acquiescing in the use of neutral formulae to describe the coming into being of the new state of affairs (which permits it still to maintain that its view was adopted with relevant institutional structures), rather than insisting on recognition of the "Turkish Republic of Northern Cyprus's" unlawfully declared independence (condemned by Security Council Resolutions and contrary to the *jus cogens* rule as to non-recognition of the fruits of aggression), is a compromise.[17] Virtually all the specific requests or

[16] In his *Report*, paras 75–79 the Secretary General condemned the Greek Cypriot political leadership for its failure to prepare the people for compromise and for adopting a less flexible policy, while at the same time praising the Turkish Cypriot and the Turkish Government for its recent change of heart after Mr Erdoğan on 24 January 2004 had made commitments to the Secretary-General. The Greek Cypriot leadership, irrespective of who has been the President of Cyprus, has consistently been willing to compromise. It has accepted that there will have to be a degree of departure from law and full observance of human rights standards on a temporary basis, but it has not accepted the wholesale abandonment of such standards—as in the Plan. It has agreed over the years to some departures from functionality, with slower, more cumbersome and more expensive machinery, enabling brakes to be applied, but it has always insisted that government machinery must ultimately be workable. Compromises it will make, but it will not make sacrifices of such an extent that the Greek Cypriot electorate effectively surrenders and abdicates from all potential exercises of power. In short, the Greek Cypriot leadership will not commit suicide, either at Turkish or at UN insistence. It is easy to be free with words and accuse the Greek Cypriot leadership of failure to compromise and of failure to educate its people to make concessions. What must be concentrated upon is the concessions which were asked of them in the Plan—concessions which no State Member of the Security Council would accept in relation to the governance of its own country and the rights of its people. Chiding of this kind is mere cant. Had the Secretariat genuinely assisted the parties to engage in negotiations, it could have successfully encouraged both sets of leaderships to adjust their views and demands and to reach a settlement which they could in good conscience have promoted and for which they would have sought popular support. This is the task to which the Secretariat should revert.

[17] The public impression was created before the Islamic Conference Organization was asked to upgrade the "TRNC's" status and call it the "Turkish Cypriot State," as in the Plan, that such entity would implement parts of the Plan. Mr Talat, however, has refused to do so, declining even to adopt the proposed TCCS Constitution, which remedied some of the major human rights deficiencies of the "TRNC Constitution": *Cyprus Mail*, 9 June 2004.

demands of the Turkish Cypriot political leadership (invariably made in full agreement following consultation with, and even subject to the direction of, the Republic of Turkey) as to the situation in Cyprus were effectively met in the Plan without need for compromises by them or by Turkey. The compromises (or, more properly in most cases, sacrifices) were imposed by the Plan on the Greek Cypriot side, in particular as regards: a doubtfully functional form of government, in which Greek Cypriots would be under-represented; security arrangements which did not begin to allay Greek Cypriots' fears; territorial arrangements combined with restrictions on residence—precluding large numbers of Greek Cypriot displaced persons from returning to their homes for many years if ever; and very considerable loss of property rights, supposedly satisfied by so-called "compensation," but which in reality would amount to delayed self-payment from the proceeds of future sales of the owners' assets.

THE SECRETARY-GENERAL'S PARTIAL SIGHTEDNESS

Subsequently to the approval of the Plan by 64.91% of *those who voted* in the referendum held in the Turkish occupied area (77,646 persons),[18] the Secretary-General applauded Turkish Cypriots for approving his Plan "notwithstanding the significant sacrifices that it entailed for many of them". Certainly, nobody wishes to move his abode. However, those Turkish Cypriots who would under the Plan eventually have had to leave Greek Cypriot-owned properties earlier allocated to them by the Turkish subordinate local administration were, in terms of the Plan—unless they had significantly improved such properties, when they could acquire the relevant property with loan assistance—to be provided with adequate accommodation of a high standard. They would also be assisted with new forms of livelihood by a Relocation Board. Indeed, the UN was bruiting it about in Nicosia that the Turkish Cypriot population of Morphou (about half the total of the number of Turkish Cypriots to be moved) preferred to acquire their own homes in a new location—understandably, as would any self-respecting person aware that they were living in the house of refugee. Even then, they would keep agricultural land nearby. Although since 1974,[19] Turkish

[18] A further 41,973 persons (35.08% of those voting) voted "No". In addition, 15.64% of the "electorate" did not vote and 1.27% spoiled their ballots. In fact, *only 54.05% of the Turkish Cypriot "electorate" voted "Yes"*.

[19] And also in the period 1964–1967, during the unrecognised civil war in Cyprus, accompanied by continuing Turkish threats of invasion and the Government of Cyprus's responses thereto. Rather than militarily attacking Turkish enclaves, the Cyprus Government policy was strictly to regulate materials capable of military use or for building fortifications. Movement controls were applied by both sides, with the Government controls all being lifted by the end of 1967. The tale of "eleven years of Turkish Cypriot suffering" (1963–1974) has nonetheless convinced the international community, largely due to the default of the Greek Cypriot side in openly explaining what did and did not occur between 1963–1967, because, until Mr Clerides openly admitted to errors and misjudgements, it was not policy of earlier Governments to make any admissions. Mr Clerides actually made an admission about wrongdoing by both sides as early as the London Conference in January 1964, but his was an exceptional attitude.

Cypriots have certainly suffered economically, this relative deprivation has several causes. In part it was because the Government of Turkey and their own political leadership, in pursuit of a policy of Turkish ethnic concentration in the occupied area, compelled Turkish Cypriot families to migrate from the Government-controlled part of Cyprus in 1975 by blocking reunion of released prisoners of war with their families and requiring their release only in the occupied area (which the Turkish Army closed off) and by then pressurising their families and all other Turkish Cypriots to leave the Government-controlled area.[20] Since that time, the vast majority of Turkish Cypriots have been in locations militarily occupied by Turkey, where they have been subjected to the disadvantages of Turkey's economy, which has exported inflation to the occupied area. Turkey has controlled the economy of both the initial "TFSK" (13 February 1975 – 15 November 1983) and the "TRNC" (15 November 1983 onwards) by direct policy instructions, by conditional or tied expenditure grants, by introduction of the Turkish lira and by controls by the Ziraat Bank, a subsidiary of the Central Bank of Turkey. Despite the occupied area containing over 70% of the productive resources of Cyprus at the time of the Turkish "intervention," and the Turkish Cypriot population living or who moved there consisting of well under 20% of Cypriots, the northern economy was, in consequence of Turkey's management, run down—as well as being adversely affected by initial looting and transfer to Turkey of most valuable movable equipment.[21] The international community learned from South Africa that the only really effective commercial sanction had been denial of access to short-term financial markets, causing unmanageable cash-flow problems.[22] But this difficulty has never troubled the "TRNC," because Turkey has provided a large proportion of its budget and its development programmes. Availability of finance from other sources will primarily relieve Turkey of this burden.

Inability of the secessionist entity to enjoy the economic benefits of an independent State was the result of Turkey's aggression and continuing occupation. A "State" which is the result of aggression cannot be recognised. Economic "suffering" and "isolation" (the terms now fashionable) are not

[20] Over 41,000 Turkish Cypriots moved from what was later to be known as the Government-controlled area to the area occupied by Turkey between 20 July 1974 and 1976. This movement was encouraged or directed by the Turkish Cypriot political leadership and Turkey. In and after the course of Turkey's various invasion phases about 21,000 persons moved to or remained as released prisoners of war in the occupied area. About 11,000 Turkish Cypriots were flown from the British Sovereign Bases Areas to Turkey and then directly onwards to the occupied area. This was agreed following the implicit threat of Turkey commencing further hostilities if the UK did not agree to this move. About 9,000 family members (largely from the Paphos area) were moved upon an explicit threat in August 1975 by Mr Denktash of a new invasion phase if this move was not agreed. The International Red Cross declined to involve itself in such a move, so this was assisted by UNFICYP.

[21] The *Report* of the European Commission of Human Rights, 10 July 1976, para 480, found looting on an extensive scale by the Turkish Army and others and loading of movables onto ships bound for Turkey.

[22] Goulding, *op cit*, pp 19–20.

Greek Cypriot-imposed, or a result of the Greek Cypriot side's unwillingness to accept the Secretary-General's Plan.[23] It is more than time that "the Turkey factor" was brought into focus. All Cypriots have been victims of the Republic of Turkey, and the responsibility for nearly all economic, emotional and physical "suffering" in Cyprus—other than the hardships of everyday life—lies with Turkey,[24] as does "the plight" of Turkish Cypriots, to which the Secretary-General refers. It needs to be recollected that much of their relative economic deprivation is due to the fact that they have been economically squeezed out of their own labour market by low-paid Turkish migrants.[25] To the extent that trade has been hampered, this has not been by "sanctions," which do not exist, but by undue commissions by Turkish middlemen; by the fact that Turkish Cypriot businesses produce too small a volume of goods and agricultural products to organise efficient exports other than to or through Turkey, where similar Turkish products are in competition with Turkish Cypriot goods and produce; and to the expenses of transportation of goods from ports without the volume of trade to make shipping from them

[23] The inappropriateness of the propagandist language of "suffering" needs to be evaluated against *per capita* incomes in much of the world, including Turkey. "Isolation" has more of a "political" and international "sports participation" connotation. But it is deliberately emotive language designed to inspire sympathy. Since 1997, well-advised by PR consultants, Turkey and the Turkish Cypriots have been using this language, most prominently in a "Joint Declaration between the Republic of Turkey and the Turkish Republic of Northern Cyprus," signed in Ankara on 20 January 1997 by President Demirel and Mr Denktash. The Declaration announced that to end the continued "isolation" of the "Turkish Republic of Northern Cyprus" Turkey was taking "the necessary steps to ensure the integration of the Turkish Republic of Northern Cyprus with the international community." For the future, Turkish Missions would incorporate "TRNC" diplomats and they would "attend any international meeting concerning Cyprus where the Turkish Cypriot people do not have a voice". The desire for participation in their own right in international bodies can only be met if persons from the entity desiring this have appropriate national status required by the constitutions of such bodies, eg ICAO, the World Telecommunications Union, the International Maritime Organization etc. "Unrepresented peoples" and "secessionist movements" throughout the world could otherwise invoke the same language. Individuals are always penalised by political struggles. But "independent" sports participation by the "TRNC" has been a demand, accompanied by rejection of suggestions that Turkish Cypriots be part of Republic of Cyprus sports teams.

[24] And of course with local paramilitaries from each Community who, in the course of fighting between late 1963 and 1967 and in mid-1974, sometimes behaved in an unlawful and brutal manner. Generally neither side prosecuted wrongdoers on the basis that an amnesty would ultimately be agreed, while evidence was not made available, and members of paramilitary groups had political links with persons of influence. Their "impunity" will continue as the Plan, although permitting the Reconciliation Commission to enquire into facts and events and to hold public or private hearings, provides that the Commission shall have no prosecutorial and other criminal legal function or power: Annex VIII, Article 3.2.

[25] *Kibris*, 9 May 2004, reveals that the Association of Settlers from Turkey believed that there were 40,000–50,000 unauthorised Turkish workers in the occupied area. This situation was brought about by introducing unrestricted freedom of movement between the occupied area and Turkey as part of the policy of integration of the "TRNC". Earlier officially authorised waves of Turkish settlement had the same effect of making Turkish Cypriot labour uncompetitive. In 2003 the Laakso *Report* estimated that only 87,600 Turkish Cypriots remained in the Turkish occupied area. See p 173 below.

economic.[26] The situation was made worse after declaration of the "TRNC" when this entity decided to use its own "certificates of origin" for exports of agricultural produce rather than those of the Turkish Cypriot Chamber of Commerce, which the European Community had agreed with the Cyprus Government should be accepted so that Turkish Cypriots could benefit under the EU–Cyprus Association Agreement by sharing in quotas of Cyprus goods given preference. Ability to benefit from a quota share was thus lost[27].

[26] It is unfashionable to make such comments, but sanctions generally have the effect of building up internal industry. That this did not occur was due to Turkey's economic policies and the cultural predisposition of the Turkish Cypriot elite to engage in professional and administrative rather than entrepreneurial activities. The one sphere in which Turkish Cypriot economic development was hampered was tourism, due to the virtual absence of direct flights to a relatively more distant holiday destination, and, in the first years after the invasion, due to individual Greek Cypriot hotel owners' threats of litigation if Greek Cypriot-owned installations were exploited. These threats became ineffective in 1978, when the English courts ruled that they had no jurisdiction to entertain litigation for trespass on immovable property abroad. Of course, given Cyprus's entry into the European Union on 1 May 2004 and the subsequent coming into force of Regulation 44/2001 on jurisdiction and the recognition and enforcement of judgments in civil and commercial matters, foreign trespassers could find themselves being sued in Cypriot courts, with the resulting judgments being enforced against them in their (EU Member) State of origin. (A suit likely to have this effect was the subject of a first judgment in the Nicosia District Court on 9 November 2004. In *Apostolides v Orams*, an English couple who had built a house on land owned by a displaced Greek Cypriot were ordered to demolish it.) In any case, neither the absence of flights nor property owners' exercise of their rights to litigate is a matter of "sanctions". The first is caused by the fact that the "TRNC" cannot become a member of ICAO, and the second is an individual right, with which Governments may not interfere, exposing themselves, should they seek to do so, to charges of violating Article 13 of the European Convention on Human Rights.

[27] See below pp 247–8, which explain that since the beginning of May 2004 facilities for Turkish Cypriot trading through the Republic's machinery have been made available. Further measures are under consideration, so long as problems of "recognition" of the "TRNC" can be avoided. Similar offers were made in the 1981 confidence-building suggestions, but were rejected by the Turkish Cypriot side on the basis that this involved "recognition" of the Republic.

X

Renewed "Negotiations" From February–April 2004

TOWARDS THE END of 2003, as the time for Cyprus's accession to the EU rapidly approached, the European Council, meeting on 12–13 December 2003, urged immediate resumption of the negotiation process. President Papadopoulos, emphasising the shortness of time available, also requested the Secretary-General to call for an immediate resumption of talks, with the aim of reaching a more functional and viable solution to the Cyprus problem within the parameters of the Secretary-General's existing Plan, and with this as the basis for meaningful and substantial negotiation.[1] USA policy-makers were also stirring themselves on the Cyprus issue. Ambassador Weston visited Ankara on 19 December, where he stated that

> there is a very great degree of coincidence of interest between Turkey and the United States on the need for a settlement and on how to get to a settlement.[2]

Then, on 26 December, President Bush wrote to Prime Minister Simitis of Greece, underlining that a Cyprus solution would benefit not only both sides of the Island but also the security interests of Greece and Turkey. The President believed that

> At this moment, there is a window of opportunity to achieve a solution, so that a united Cyprus can join the European Union. We must not allow this window to close.[3]

President Bush also wrote with similar purport to President Papadopoulos on 9 January 2004, on the same day that his Press Secretary announced that he would welcome Prime Minister Erdoğan to the White House on 28 January 2004, giving

> an opportunity to deepen our strategic partnership with our NATO ally, Turkey on ... Iraq, Afghanistan, Cyprus, Eurasia, the Greater Middle East . . .

[1] Letter, President Papadopoulos to Secretary-General, 17 December 2003.
[2] Skyturk interview, 19 December 2003, http://ankara.usembassy.gov/westskyt.htm.
[3] Athens News Agency, 3 January 2004.

Meanwhile, the Secretary-General temporised, still requiring

> to feel confident that a resumed negotiation would actually result in a finalized plan being submitted for approval at separate, simultaneous referenda and why I would expect from all concerned the commitment which I spelled out in paragraph 148 of my April report, which was fully supported by the Security Council in Resolution 1475 (2003).[4]

It should be explained that the shortness of time available for negotiations before Cyprus's accession was not the fault of the Greek Cypriot side. Throughout 2003, the Greek Cypriot side had reiterated its willingness to resume negotiations so that these would, at the latest, be completed by 1 March 2004, leaving two months for a proper campaign prior to referenda preceding Cyprus's EU entry on 1 May 2004. In contrast, in that period Turkey did not want resumption of negotiations. Nor was there great pressure by others concerned. As the Secretary-General observed: "most of 2003 was a fallow period" in relation to the Secretary-General's good offices (*S/2004/307*, para 6). This inactivity was because certain Powers and the Secretariat (in particular Mr de Soto) believed it necessary, in order to achieve results, to put the parties into a Camp David-like situation under intense pressure there and then to reach a settlement, ie they planned for last minute knocking of heads together à la Hannay. It is an inescapable inference that the deadline was artificially created. They were not, as a preliminary, willing to pressurise Turkey as an important, but not altogether stable, Power in the Middle and Near East. In the event, after intense internal Turkish discussions between her Foreign Ministry and her Army, a decision was ultimately taken to resume negotiations and, subject to Turkey's desires being met, to agree a settlement, failing which, Turkey would in any event appear co-operative in EU eyes. This decision was taken on 23 January 2004 when her National Security Council (the formal State body containing senior Turkish military personnel among its members and thus expressing Turkish Army views) accepted the policy proposed by the Turkish Foreign Ministry that Cyprus negotiations should be reopened and that the Plan should be taken as "a reference" on the basis of "the realities existing in Cyprus".[5] Thus

[4] Letter, Secretary-General to President Papadopoulos, 8 January, para 148, reads: "In my view, a solution on the basis of the plan could be achieved only if there is an unequivocally stated preparedness on the part of the leaders of both sides, fully and determinedly backed at the highest political level in both motherlands, to commit themselves (a) to finalize the plan (without reopening its basic principles or essential trade-offs) by a specific date with United Nations assistance, and (b) to put it to separate simultaneous referenda as provided for in the plan on a date certain soon thereafter."

[5] The *Report,* para 7, stating that the Government of Turkey was putting together the elements of a new policy on Cyprus, combined with the approving references to new Turkish Cypriot leadership (paras 6, 15, 76 and 87), is designed to obscure the fact that the Plan had incorporated Turkey's policy of two separate "sovereign" ethnically-composed States in Cyprus, only loosely linked together, and that Turkish demands for this were, by technical legal drafting, satisfied in the final version of the Plan, even though their adoption is inconsistent with the framework laid down by 30 years of UN Resolutions on Cyprus and the 1977 and 1979 High Level Agreements between the two Cypriot sides. As "finalised," the Plan in practice, though not explicitly, reflected what the

on 24 January at Davos, Prime Minister Erdoğan was able to confirm to the UN Secretary-General Turkey's desire that he should take an initiative. In consequence, the only heads now seen as requiring to be knocked were Greek Cypriot ones—an event which transpired at Bürgenstock.

THE INVOLVEMENT OF THE EU

Preceding this crucial Turkish decision, there had been a flurry of meetings between concerned Powers and institutions. Turkey required certain assurances before making her decision, and the Secretary-General needed to feel sufficiently confident to invite the beginning of negotiations. The Secretary-General's 28 May 2004 *Report* briefly mentions discussions with the Government of Turkey, the Greek Cypriot leader, President Papadopoulos, the Government and Leader of the Opposition of Greece and the European Union. The meeting which seemed to tip the subsequent Government-Army discussions in Ankara towards negotiations took place on 15–16 January 2004. The Republic of Turkey sought assurances from the President of the European Commission, President Prodi, on several issues, in particular, whether

(i) The European Commission statement that the EU would accept and include the terms of an agreed Cyprus settlement in the *acquis*, still held, even if recent Council of Europe (CoE) conclusions had indicated the EU's desire for the terms of agreement to be in line with EU principles;
(ii) Once negotiations got underway using the Annan Plan, the Commission would be prepared to end the exclusion-embargo against the "north";
(iii) If the Turkish Cypriots approved a settlement agreement in a referendum, but this agreement was rejected by the Greek Cypriots what would happen; and

Turkish National Security Council and Mr Denktash have always called "the realities in Cyprus". Whereas some of Mr Denktash's demands flagrantly contradicting the Security Council's Resolutions were put aside by 18 March, his authorised agents, Messrs Talat and Serdar Denktash, were kept under his orders and those of Turkey's Foreign Ministry via Ambassador Ziyal, present in New York and in Nicosia and at the Bürgenstock negotiations and giving continuous policy directions. Ambassador Ziyal saw that the Turkish Cypriot side concentrated on key provisions, demanding that the Plan be changed: to meet Turkey's security interests; to enhance the Turkish Cypriot constituent state's power to restrict Greek Cypriots from living, conducting business or acquiring property there; and to empower its government to act independently in spheres which should have been exclusively federal. What had been abandoned was mere "theology" and "rhetoric" about "sovereignty" and "separate status" in pursuit of achieving concrete provisions, which in effect achieved what the theology implied, other than recognition of the "TRNC". The latter policy could be "put on ice", to be resurrected at a juncture deemed appropriate, such as the eventuality of the Plan being rejected, or, if accepted, when it later proved unworkable in practice. Nonetheless, Turkey began making new moves to obtain "recognition" for the "TRNC" well before the referenda, preparing the grounds for upgrading the status of the Turkish Cypriot Community in the Islamic Conference Organization to a "Turkish Cypriot State". Although she succeeded in obtaining this significant name change, the "Turkish Cypriot State" was still only accorded observer status.

(iv) If agreement was reached could anything prevent the Greek side from claiming that certain elements of that pact went against European law.[6]

Mr Erdoğan reportedly told Turkish journalists that President Prodi led him to believe that

> whether a settlement is reached or not, the next step would be the lifting of the embargos against the TRNC.[7]

This meeting also explains the conduct of the European Commission after 29 April 2004 in attempting to forge ahead with unilateral actions in Cyprus, despite legal objections that Protocol No 10 to the Act of Accession requires unanimity for such decisions. Looking with hindsight at the 15–16 January 2004 EU–Turkey meeting and the assurances then given, it can be seen that Turkey would gain EU credibility for appearing forthcoming on Cyprus by opening negotiations, and that Turkey would also gain the occupied area economic benefits to which it had not been entitled due to the self-inflicted wound of the declaration of the "TRNC" in 1983.

Turkey, as a result of the understanding reached, had by now gained so much that she no longer needed to be generous in a Cyprus settlement, with the meeting with the EU resulting in a disincentive to Turkish generosity and to reaching a compromise settlement. In consequence, Turkey made maximalist demands (with which the US and UN could see nothing wrong) and these ultimately led to rejection of the Plan by Greek Cypriots. In all probability, Turkey may have been aiming at that outcome, knowing how strong her position was after 15 January 2004, and that it would be advantageous to retain some cards up her sleeve in case the EU did not accede to her request to commence membership negotiations. Only when EU membership was certain to become "a reality," would Turkey be willing to settle the Cyprus problem in exchange for her new EU status.[8]

[6] *Phileleftheros*, 1 February 2004.

[7] *Milliyet*, 3 February 2004.

[8] Two more factors may be speculated to have been behind Turkey's intransigence. First, the Turkish Army, concerned by the impact of the Iraq war on Turkish security, believed that its continued large-scale presence in Cyprus was essential and that therefore the Plan must be so modified by insertion of Turkish demands that it would be rejected by Greek Cypriots. This view was taken by Gregory Copley in a presentation to a seminar conducted by the American Hellenic Institute, "Cyprus—The Road Ahead and US Interests," on 19 May 2004. Second, Turkey is always well-informed about and astute in assessing Greek Cypriot public opinion. Thus the Turkish Foreign Ministry appreciated soon after the New York meetings that Greek Cypriots would reject the Plan. In such circumstances, Turkey must have believed that she should not waste negotiating cards by making pointless concessions which would at a later stage be "pocketed," with more being demanded. She certainly appreciated the state of Greek Cypriot public opinion by the time of the Bürgenstock meetings.

INTERNATIONAL PRESSURES TO RE-OPEN NEGOTIATIONS

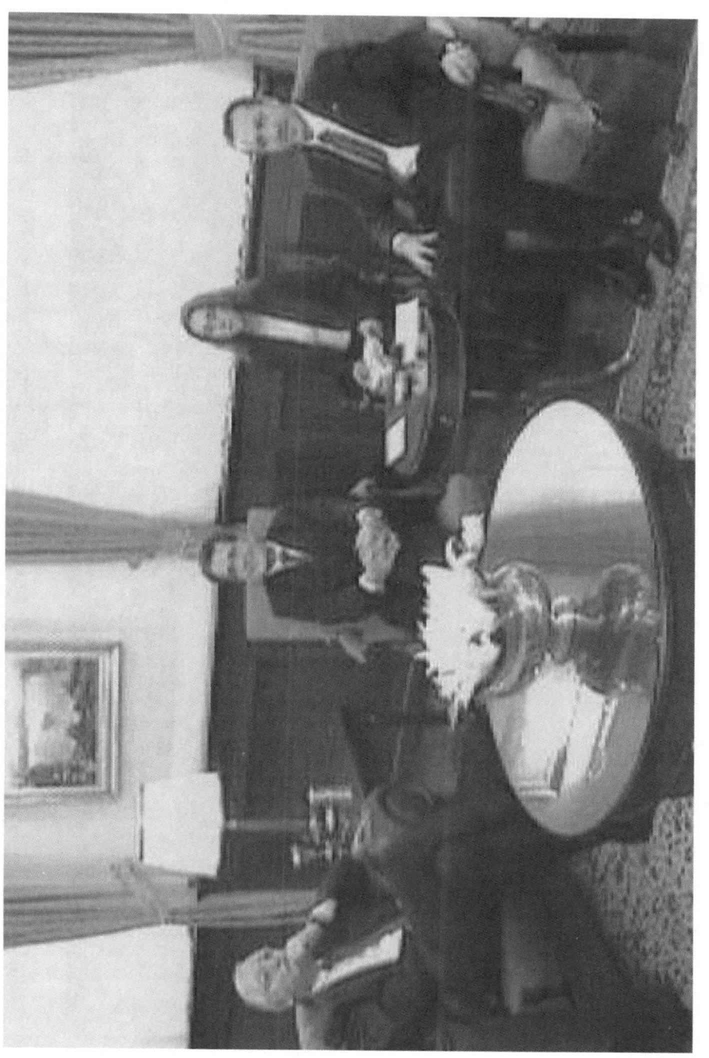

President Prodi visits Ankara on 15 January 2004. Much kissing and hugging precedes and ends his meeting with Prime Minister Erdoğan, together with Commissioner Verheugen. President Prodi, apparently happy with their mutual undertakings, states: "We have discussed Cyprus". He adds: "Settling the Cyprus problem is not a pre-condition" for Turkey's EU accession negotiations. Perhaps a thoughtful Mr Verheugen (left) is considering what further concessions, especially on "primary law," will have to be made to Turkey. This visit was followed up on 23 January by an Ankara trip by Germany's Foreign Minister Joschka Fischer to encourage Turkey.

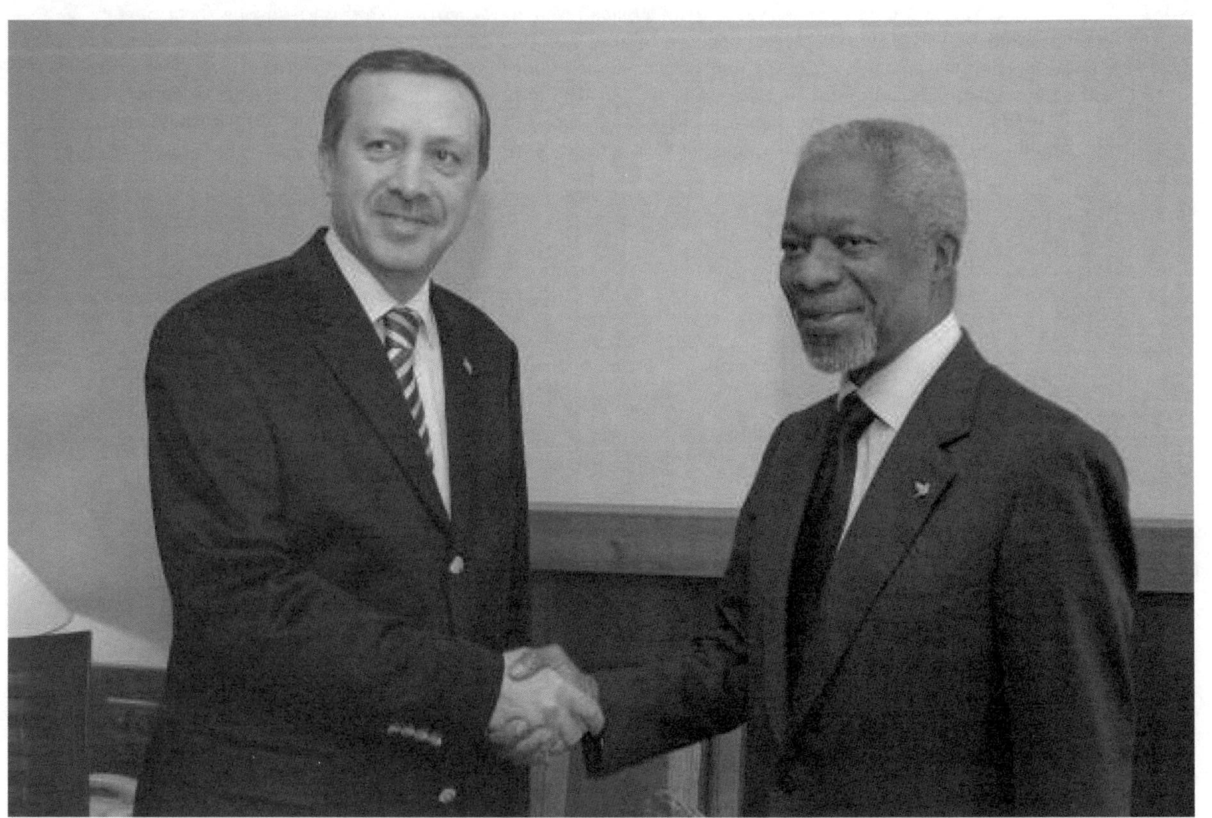

Above: Secretary-General Kofi Annan (right) meets Recep Tayyip Erdoğan, Prime Minister of Turkey in Davos on 24 January 2004, learning of Turkey's new cooperative stance.

Pomp and circumstance in Ankara to welcome Chancellor Schroeder on 23 February 2004, with a Turkish "goose-stepper" accompanying them past parading troops.

Business accomplished, Chancellor Schroeder and a happy President Erdoğan, doing a thumbs up, button their jackets for another diplomatic handshake under a looming Atatürk portrait, but kissing, unlike with Mr Prodi, is off-limits. Germany, under Chancellor Schroeder, is a strong supporter of Turkey, both as regards her attitudes to Cyprus and to Turkey's EU accession.

On 3 February 2004 the UN Secretary-General with Secretary of State Powell at the White House, being offered a friendly hand.

THE INVOLVEMENT OF THE USA

The other significant meetings involved Prime Minister Erdoğan, first at Davos with the Secretary-General and with US Secretary of State Colin Powell on 24 January 2004. Mr Erdoğan then visited the USA to meet President Bush at the White House on 28 January. He also met Secretary Powell again and Dr Condoleeza Rice. Mr Gül, Turkey's Foreign Minister, joined the meetings. The White House Spokesman commented that the President was pleased with Turkey's decisions regarding a Cyprus solution and called on the Greek Cypriot side to show similar political will. Praising the Annan Plan as fair and balanced, he repeated the USA's readiness to help, an attitude manifested by the special involvement of the busy Mr Powell, and the activity of the USA's Special Envoy, Mr Weston. Mr Powell telephoned President Papadopoulos urging resumption of the talks in the first or second weeks of February. Already Mr Powell had "apprised the Secretary-General of the US's support," as the Secretary-General revealed while still in Brussels where he talked to the EU College of Commissioners.

Ultimately, the Secretary-General was summonsed by telephone on 2 February to the White House for a meeting on 3 February to discuss UN-related issues, notably Cyprus, Iraq and Libya, and, not to put too fine a point on it, received his "marching orders". On 4 February, there followed his invitation to the Cypriot sides and to the Guarantor Powers to talks in New York on the resumption of negotiations. State Department officials were much in attendance there, although not mentioned in the *Report,* just as American diplomats were also present, again unmentioned, at Bürgenstock. The Secretary-General, having stood out against the USA over the Iraq intervention, needed now to pay attention to the USA's desires. This was an occasion on which the saying "Who pays the piper, calls the tune" applied.[9] Be all this as it may, the combination of the USA's pro-Turkey (in the context of Iraq and Middle East reconstruction) policy prevailed. US wishes were reinforced by the EU's desire to see an undivided Cyprus enter the EU, which wanted to rule out any potential Turkish grievance that absence of a Cyprus settlement would impede Turkey's own request for the opening of EU membership negotiations—and, at minimum, to preclude such a grievance, irrespective of whether Turkey's request was or was not on other grounds acceptable. The conjunction of USA pressure and EU support (two Permanent Members from the EU plus Germany and Spain were in the Security Council) made it impossible for the Secretary-General to refuse to re-open the negotiations, even if he may at that stage not have felt great sympathy

[9] Only future historians will know if and what other pressures played a part. Certainly there appears to be less interest in investigating the knowledge and the participation of high-level UN officials in skimming billions of dollars from revenue from Iraqi oil sales by various devices. It should also be remembered that a further term of office of the Secretary-General is, as Mr Boutros Boutros-Ghali discovered, subject to US veto.

for either party, just like Sir Brian Urquhart who briefed a UN staff member going to Cyprus on a mission:

> Each side is worse than the other.

THE FEBRUARY 2004 NEW YORK MEETINGS

On 4 February 2004, the Secretary-General, having discussed matters with President Bush and heard the latter's desire that he should settle the Cyprus problem by himself adopting the role of a mediator, now, and with a sense of urgency, called for resumed negotiations, observing that a solution was the only means by which Cyprus could enter the European Union united on 1 May 2004, and that it would, as well as solidifying rapprochement between Greece and Turkey,

> advance the prospects for the opening of accession negotiations between Turkey and the European Union.

At the same time, the Secretary-General stated that he had been assured both by the Turkish Prime Minister and by President Papadopoulos that any changes sought to the Plan

> would remain within the parameters of the Plan.

The Secretary-General further declared that he would maintain the Plan's overall balance. He therefore invited the leaders of both Cypriot Communities to New York on 10 February to begin negotiations. His letter also set out a proposed procedure or scheme of work

> to finalize the plan (without re-opening its basic principles or core trade-offs),

with acceptance of the invitation being treated by him as a commitment to finalise the Plan (ie in the way indicated, which precluded re-opening of basic principles and core trade-offs).[10] The most significant provision in the proposed procedure was that if, in negotiations between the parties by dates specified in the letter, the text of the Plan did not emerge completed, the Secretary-General would make "indispensable suggestions to complete the text".

In the corridors of the New York meeting, the USA and the Guarantor Powers were actively present and influenced the proceedings. They pressed for the

[10] At Davos Mr Erdoğan had suggested that, given the Plan's complexities and the time scale, it might be best to agree on a "reduced text," taking from the Plan major issues, which he described as basic principles, maps and constitution, and to go to a referendum on such framework. There had also been talk of a potential high-level agreement. The Secretary-General's proposal that the basis for negotiations be the 26 February 2003 document as clarified on 8 March put paid to these alternatives. They were, however, significant in indicating that Turkey was not at this stage sure that she wanted an overall solution: her preferred timing was December 2004 when it would be known one way or the other if she had been authorised by the EU to open membership negotiations. If not, her incentives to settle the Cyprus problem would be greatly diminished.

NEW YORK 10–13 FEBRUARY 2004

It's "Follow my Leader" as "President" Denktash enters UN Headquarters in New York on 10 February 2004, with his team in tow (behind him, left to right, Mr Olgun, Mr Talat and Mr S Denktash).

The teams which assembled in New York for the 10–13 February 2004 procedural discussions. Left to right: the Turkish Cypriot team, Ergün Olgun, Serdar Denktash, Mehmet-Ali Talat, Rauf Denktash; and, beyond the Secretary-General, Tassos Papadopoulos, Glafcos Clerides, Tasos Tzionis and Andreas Mavroyiannis.

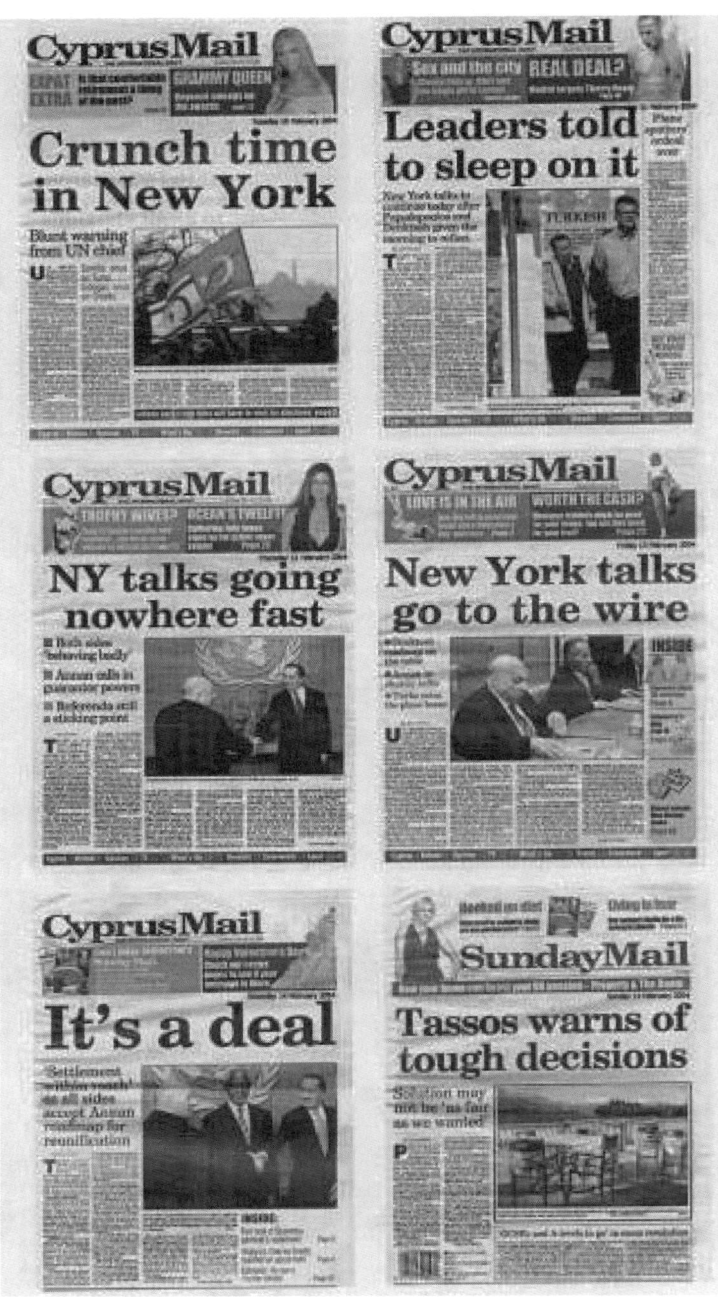

Cyprus Mail

Crunch time in New York

Blunt warning from UN chief

Cyprus Mail

Sex and the city

REAL DEAL?

Leaders told to sleep on it

TURKISH

Cyprus Mail

TROPHY WIVES?

OCEAN'S TWELVE

NY talks going nowhere fast

Both sides 'behaving badly'

Annan calls in guarantor powers

Referenda still a sticking point

Cyprus Mail

LOVE IS IN THE AIR

WORTH THE CASH?

New York talks go to the wire

INSIDE

Cyprus Mail

It's a deal

'Settlement within reach' as all sides accept Annan roadmap for reunification

INSIDE:

Hooked on diet

Sunday Mail

Tassos warns of tough decisions

Solution may not be 'as fair as we wanted'

The pro-Annan Plan *Cyprus Mail* and *Sunday Mail* reflect the intensity of the 10–13 February 2004 New York talks. (Courtesy of *The Blue Beret.*)

Above: American "brokers," Ambassadors Weston and Klosson, visited President Papadopoulos and Foreign Minister Iacovou on 11 February 2004 at the Waldorf Towers, pressuring the Greek Cypriot side to agree to the Secretary-General's being given a discretion to finalise his Plan.

Above left: afterwards, Ambassador Weston tells the press whether negotiations will go ahead is all dependent on the Secretary-General's estimate of the degree of cooperation he gets from both sides. Above right: Alvaro de Soto, accompanied by Messrs Dann and Pfirter and Ms Jones, on the same day tells CyBK (RIK) and Antenna TV stations' reporters anxious to interview him that they are "familiar faces". He too had come to persuade President Papadopoulos to accept the Secretary-General's proposed procedure.

Friday, 13 February 2004, an inauspicious day, when the Secretary-General, symbolically holding hands yet again, announces that talks between the leaders will resume in Nicosia. If they do not agree, he will, following persistent disagreement, make indispensable suggestions so as to finalise his Plan, which the leaders are then to put to two separate simultaneous referenda.

Ambassador Ziyal, Permanent Under-Secretary to Turkey's Foreign Ministry, explains on 13 February 2004 in New York that the Turkish Cypriots had immediately accepted the Secretary-General's text and also two amendments suggested by the Greek (or possibly the Greek Cypriot) side, but not a third which Turkey did not agree, so the Secretary-General had used his discretion not to accept it. He added: "We will have to achieve a win-win situation, which will help not only our integration with the EU, but at the same time the very good relationship, I will say the friendship, we have with Greece now."

Secretary-General to be accorded the powers of an arbitrator or mediator, but this was not acceptable to the Greek Cypriot side.[11] In intense discussions, the procedure suggested in the 4 February 2004 letter was slightly revised, with it being separated out into clear Phases. The Cypriot parties were to meet in Nicosia in a first Phase from 19 February to agree on changes in order to complete the Plan in all respects so as to produce a finalised text by 22 March 2004. All concerned were to seek only changes that fell within the parameters of the Plan. In the absence of agreement, the Secretary-General would, in a second Phase, convene a meeting of the two sides (later arranged to be at Bürgenstock for 24 March) with the participation of Greece and Turkey, in order to lend their collaboration in a concentrated effort to agree on a finalised text by 29 March. These were not to be quadrilateral meetings. Although Turkey pressed for this, she met firm Greek Cypriot refusal, an attitude in this case supported by Greece.

The Secretary-General described a third Phase as follows:

> As a final resort, in the event of a continuing and persistent deadlock, the parties have invited me to use my discretion to finalize the text to be submitted to referenda.[12]

Later, he reported to the Security Council that

> The procedure enlarged the role foreseen for me, from completing any unfinished parts of the Plan ("filling in the blanks") to resolving any continuing and persistent deadlocks in the negotiations.[13]

The Guarantor Powers also committed themselves to this process, while the European Union assured the Secretary-General that it would accommodate a settlement and would offer technical assistance.[14] Once the text of the Foundation Agreement was finalised, the three Guarantor Powers would confirm by 9 April 2003 that, upon approval of the Foundation Agreement at two separate simultaneous referenda, they were committed *to signing into force*

[11] Mr Erdoğan had specifically asked for this when he had met the Secretary-General in Davos on 24 January. On 26 January 2004 Mr Gül, Turkey's Foreign Minister, was reported as saying that speeding up the process required "a very strong and neutral mediator—one who Turkey will attach importance to". The Press speculated that former Secretary of State James A Baker III might replace Mr de Soto. Apparently, when Messrs Erdoğan and Gül had met Mr Bush at the White House on 28 January, they had suggested that US Secretary of State Colin Powell should act. He, however, had his hands full elsewhere. It is possible that Turkey, as a fall-back position, wished at the same time to encourage Mr de Soto to pay due regard to her desires, well-knowing that the Secretary-General wanted to continue with a good facilitator (Mr de Soto) while accepting support from States such as the USA and the UK. At all events, Mr Erdoğan had to accept that mediation did not fall within the purview of the Secretary-General's good offices. Had a new mandate been sought from the Security Council there was always the potentiality of a veto. Thus the sides had in New York to agree (subject in the case of the Greek Cypriot side to duress occasioned by the international pressures) to confer the needed authority.

[12] Statement by Spokesman of the UN Secretary-General, 13 February 2004.

[13] *S/2004/437*, 28 May 2004, para 12.

[14] The UN was less than happy about this involvement, not anticipating that the EU—via Commissioner Verheugen—would turn out to be as pliable as it did at Bürgenstock. In any case they regarded arranging a settlement as their "turf".

the Treaty on Matters Relating to the New State of Affairs (the security Treaty on troop reductions and guarantees of the settlement) and would complete their own internal procedures necessary to provide the commitment.[15] Thereafter, the sides would submit the text of the Foundation Agreement, which was to be a package of the finished Plan, various federal Laws and the constituent state Constitutions, to separate simultaneous referenda conducted among Greek Cypriots and Turkish Cypriots. (These referenda took place on 24 April 2004.) This was not described as a fourth Phase, although it clearly was, and generated controversy in Cyprus both as to the conduct during the relevant period of the UN and foreign Powers who favoured the Plan, and as to the opposition to the Plan by President Papadopoulos and others.

THE UNITED KINGDOM'S ATTITUDE

The UK Foreign Office kept a low public profile in this, although there was, as always, close contact with American allies, and a keeping in touch through missions abroad with Turkey (where there was a special team), Greece, the Government of Cyprus and the Turkish Cypriot political leadership. There were also publicised meetings between Mr Straw, the UK's Foreign Secretary, and Prime Minister Blair with Mr George Papandreou, the Greek Foreign Minister, on 22 January 2004. With the current quantum of summitry or just-below summitry in international organisations, there were also other opportunities for the Foreign Office to express its viewpoint on the desirability of manifesting political will to finalise the Plan. Although superficially less involved than the USA, the UK Foreign Office, as the driving force behind the Plan (originally via Lord Hannay), did all it could to ensure that arrangements were made to get the Plan put into place. The closeness of the UK and US was to be manifested at Bürgenstock: the Government of Russia had asked to be present, but was told that only parties involved could attend. When the United States envoys arrived they came as part of the UK delegation.[16]

A further aspect requires mention. Once upon a time, the UK operated an independent foreign policy. Today, apart from heavy US influence, UK Missions in Brussels, Strasbourg, New York, Ankara and Nicosia should have fluttering on their flagpoles not only the Union Jack, but also the Turkish crescent and star. Turkey feeds in policy requests, setting the foreign policy agreed, which is then, using the UK's status and standing, pursued by UK diplomats, who are adept at influencing Secretariats of regional and international organisations. It

[15] It is in this last respect that Turkey reneged on 6 April 2004, causing Cyprus to have to pressurise the UN into enforcing the commitment and embodying safeguards for Cyprus's continued existence in the text of the Plan should Turkey not ratify the new Treaty. See pp 84–5 above.

[16] After strong protests by Russia, the Secretariat invited her to be present, subject to considerable restrictions on the extent of her participation.

is all very well to cook up schemes in the Anglo–Turkish kitchen. The risk is that one day there may be a falling out . . .

THE SCOPE OF THE SECRETARY-GENERAL'S DISCRETION TO "FINALISE"

The $64,000 question is "Why did the Greek Cypriot side agree to the Secretary-General finalising the text and to then putting it to referendum irrespective of whether the sides agreed with the Secretary-General's finalisation and without their leaders' consent having been obtained to the Plan?" The short answer is that the Greek Cypriot side genuinely wanted a settlement with reunification of the Island; the New York negotiations had indicated that the scope of the Secretary-General's role was limited; and they knew that the final word on the Secretary-General's conduct would be by the people of Cyprus through citizens' direct and personal votes at the referenda.[17] Some members of the team, however, trusted the Secretary-General to use discretion in good faith and within the agreed limits. They accepted that this discretion should extend beyond filling in gaps (which his 4 February letter had indicated was all he would do). They took this view because Annan III was not acceptable as it stood and they (as indicated on 27 and 28 February 2003) considered it as just a basis for negotiation. If intense negotiations brought about sufficient convergence between the sides' views as to necessary changes, filling the gaps was a sensible and harmless exercise. If there was no convergence, the Secretary-General would still be empowered to alter the text, but they believed he would be persuaded by reasonable arguments to make the changes the Greek Cypriot side urged in order to have a functional settlement. They also pointed out that the widening of the Secretary-General's role had the corollary that the referenda were even more important and that both sides were reserving their rights prior to the referenda to say whether the Secretary-General's exercise of discretion was in their view properly exercised. This corollary was a clear understanding, appreciated by both sides in New York.[18] Other members of the team believed they had no option but to trust the Secretary-General, even if they were walking into a trap.[19] The Greek Cypriot side at the outset considered formally recording its understanding of what the scope of the Secretary-General's assumed role would be, but did not do so, because it would by implication have been insulting to the Secretary-General,

[17] See Declaration by the President of the Republic, PIO Press Release No 6, 7 April 2004.

[18] Thus President Papadopoulos' critical analysis of the finalised Plan on 7 April 2004 would have been paralleled by a similar Turkish or Turkish Cypriot analysis had the Secretary-General exercised his discretion to change Annan III in the ways sought by the Greek Cypriot side. The understanding on this point was forgotten by the UN when, to their chagrin, the President's powerful TV address brought out the finalised Plan's negative aspects for Greek Cypriots. See *infra*.

[19] The international furore had his good offices been rejected would have been so damaging that the Republic of Cyprus's position as the State of Cyprus could have been thrown open to reconsideration by angered States.

either by giving him a lecture on his duties, or by indicating possible mistrust of him, or, more accurately, of his team. Nonetheless, when indications emerged from Mr de Soto's attitudes in Nicosia that he assumed that the procedure agreed in New York gave the Secretary-General unfettered discretion, it was decided to table a paper "Talking Points (UN categorisation of 15 March 2004)," dated 17 March. In this paper, the Greek Cypriot side pointed out the limitations under which the Secretary-General's discretion to finalise the text was to be exercised, notably that suggestions must be "indispensable," made following persistent deadlock, without re-opening any agreed trade-offs or core issues, within the existing parameters of the Plan, within the framework of the UN Charter and in conformity with international law. It is necessary here to outline the Greek Cypriot side's understanding as to what was permissible by way of "finalisation" in order to appreciate Greek Cypriots' reaction to the text as ultimately "finalised" (*de facto* by the team under Mr de Soto).

The Greek Cypriot side's understanding of what had been agreed in New York on 13 February 2004 in relation to changes and completion of the Plan, was based on the intensive discussions which had been carried on over 4 days. A UN communiqué, Statement by the Secretary-General's Spokesman, recorded the modifications to the initial procedures suggested in the Secretary-General's letter of 4 February 2004, which remained applicable in so far as they had not been expressly altered. It is misleading to imply that the communiqué of 13 February reflected the terms of the agreement, since this brushes aside the important limitations still binding and set out in the 4 February letter, which must be read together with the communiqué.[20] The Greek Cypriot side believed that the commitment undertaken by the parties was as follows:

(i) They would be "negotiating in good faith on the basis of . . . [your] Plan" (Spokesman's Statement, 13 February §2). In relation to this undertaking the correlative is that they were not committed to negotiating on any basis other than the Secretary-General's existing Plan or on matters not grounded in the Plan.

(ii) In the negotiations, the parties would seek to "agree on changes and to complete the Plan in all respects within the framework of the Secretary-General's mission of good offices, so as to produce a finalized text" (*ibid*, §3), while, as regards the changes to be agreed, "All concerned would only seek changes that fall within the parameters of the Plan" (Letter, 4 February 2004, p3 §(ii)).

(iii) Should the text not emerge completed from the meetings, including any where Greece and Turkey collaborated, and there be continuing and persistent deadlock, discretion would become exercisable, whereupon

[20] See *S/2004/437*, paras 12–14, implying that the terms of "the 13 February agreement" were set out in the Spokesman's statement. Of course, to the extent that the communiqué stated "In addition the parties have agreed on the other suggestions contained in the Secretary-General's invitation of 4 February 2004," this analysis can in a Procrustean fashion be said to be technically true.

> the Secretary-General would "make any indispensable suggestions to complete the text. Naturally . . . with the greatest of reluctance" (Letter, 4 February 2004, p 4 (vi)). Obviously, the correlative of this statement is that the Secretary-General would only be making suggestions that were "indispensable" to complete the text, so that he would not have *carte blanche* to insert what might merely appear to be reasonable, or to add an improvement asked for by one or other side or thought up by his team. For a suggestion to be "indispensable," it would have to be imperative and of such importance that the relevant part of the Constitution or any attachment, eg a Law, would otherwise be inoperative or unworkable. Accordingly, only in very limited circumstances would the Secretary-General insert a suggestion in the text. A prior condition to any insertion was that there should have been "a persistent and continuing deadlock": thus issues on which there was such deadlock would necessarily have been subject to the parties' consideration for a period of time in which deadlock had persistently continued. In the event some of the purported "finalisations" had not been put to the Greek Cypriot side, eg the removal of the permanent limits on immigration from Turkey and Greece, until they appeared in Annan IV on 29 March and were petrified in the text of 31 March 2004. There was in fact to be the briefest of ultimatums, followed by *fiat* of the Secretary-General, a perversion of what had been agreed in New York.

It is important to recollect the background against which the Greek Cypriot side after considerable hesitation and internal debate reluctantly accepted the New York procedure. Governments of the Republic of Cyprus had previously always welcomed the assistance of successive Secretaries-General in their good offices missions, relying on their integrity and the constraints of the Charter framework within which the Secretariat operates. Heavily pressed in New York at UN Headquarters by interested Parties and their envoys, as well as by the Secretariat, to agree to the procedure proposed, the Greek Cypriot side believed that the Secretary-General must keep in mind the UN's Purposes and Principles, consequently ensuring that his proposals or suggestions to complete the text were in conformity with the principles of justice and international law, and would promote and encourage respect for human rights without distinction as to race. The Greek Cypriot side still at that stage viewed the Secretariat as an organ charged under the Charter to achieve its Purposes. Only subsequently did it appear that the Secretariat considered its functions were constrained by the parameters of the Plan, which its members had prepared,[21] so that breaches of international law should therefore be ignored: as with tolerating voting by Turkish settlers in the internal self-determination exercise of the referenda and

[21] Although in other contexts, when it suited them, these parameters of the Plan were ignored—as when the Secretary-General "finalised" Turkey's demands, for example, on Community (linguistic) representation in the Senate, permanent presence of Turkish troops in Cyprus etc.

confirming the Turkish Cypriot referendum result despite settlers' illegal participation (see *S/2004/437*, para 62); and as with the Secretariat's view that it should not modify the Plan to reflect international law prohibiting unilateral intervention, unless Turkey and the Turkish Cypriots agreed (see *ibid*, para 61).

Moreover, the Greek Cypriot side found it difficult to credit that the UN Secretariat would not always have in mind Article 2.7 of the Charter. It did not believe that the Secretary-General would require a Member State and its people to submit to a settlement which was in conflict with that State's own domestic human rights system. It was particularly mistaken in considering that the Secretariat would promote universal respect for and observance of human rights without distinction as to race in terms of Article 55 of the Charter. Above all it found it inconceivable that a Member State would be required to submit to a settlement which was not in accordance with Charter Purposes and Principles and rules of international law prohibiting discrimination, with such settlement instead entrenching ethnic and cultural discrimination.

In the last resort, it was in the context of their beliefs about the UN as a guardian of international law and human rights that the Greek Cypriot side had accepted and understood the framework established by the Secretary-General in his 4 February letter, as modified by his Spokesman's Statement of 13 February 2004. They therefore trusted that, when the Secretary-General completed the text of a comprehensive settlement Plan to be put to separate and simultaneous referenda (so as to ascertain the free choice of the people of Cyprus as to their constitutional, political, social and economic future), only indispensable suggestions in conformity with international law and international human rights law would be made. The Greek Cypriot side never for one instant contemplated that the Secretary-General would arrogate to himself an unfettered discretion to insert any provisions he deemed fit, as he ultimately did, amending the text and inserting new provisions outside the existing parameters of the Plan, some devised by members of his team working on the Plan in order to meet Turkey's demands and others being "improvements" actually devised by Turkey or the USA and the UK. In fact, the Greek Cypriot side, when they agreed to the procedure settled in New York on 13 February, had hoped that negotiations would proceed at such a pace, and with such serious intent to achieve a workable settlement, that use of the Secretary-General's discretion by way of making "indispensable suggestions" would prove to be unnecessary, and all that he would be left to do was fill in minor gaps, thereby relieving him of the burden he had professed reluctance to assume. Alternatively, if agreement between the sides did not emerge, they hoped to persuade the Secretary-General of the reasonableness of Greek Cypriot proposals for changes to Annan III, and, failing that, to fall back on the decision of the electorate in the referenda. Even so, the Greek Cypriot side repeatedly made it clear to Mr de Soto in the course of discussions in Nicosia that it only expected the Secretary-General to make "indispensable" provisions and to fill in gaps to complete the Plan, this Greek Cypriot position being formally recorded on 17 March 2004.

The UN "good offices" team, anxious to get things up and running, called on both leaders on 18 February 2004. Above: President Papadopoulos, flanked by Tasos Tzionis and Marios Lysiotis. Below: The UN team with Mr Denktash and two future triumvirs (Messrs Serdar Denktash and Mehmet-Ali Talat, left and right respectively).

Below: the EU comes marching in. Putting their best feet forward for the EU are Enlargement Commissioner Verheugen and local representative Adriaan van der Meer as they arrive (uninvited?) at the UN Conference Centre on 19 February 2004 for the opening of the resumed talks.

An EU–UN get-together. But the EU can only show their flag by their not altogether welcome presence at the reopened talks on 19 February 2004. Left to right: Adriaan van der Meer (local representative), Günter Verheugen, Alvaro de Soto and Robert Dann.

Above: "But this is my territory," Alvaro de Soto appears to be saying to his EU colleague.

Enlargement Commissioner Verheugen getting together with and sympathetically listening to "TRNC Prime Minister" Talat's concerns on Verheugen's brief Nicosia visit on 19 February 2004. The Enlargement Commissioner told the press that the solution could not violate democracy, the rule of law and human rights, adding "We are willing to accommodate a settlement provided it does not violate the basic principles of the European Union". Asked what if proposed derogations did exactly that, he replied: "But this is a hypothetical consideration, because the whole exercise here is about democracy and the rule of law and human rights."

Kibrisli view of Alvaro the Champ.

Bridging Proposals.

Making it happen as in Harry Potter – the *Selides* view.

Pictures courtesy of *The Blue Beret*, February 2004.

Paying homage to the stars and stripes. The two leaders arrive on 19 February 2004 for the renewed negotiations organised by the USA.

Mr Talat again plays "Follow My Leader" on 19 February 2004 as the talks resume in Nicosia.

Another great photograph(er) at the UN Conference Centre on 19 February 2004.

The first political meeting on 19 February 2004, but has Ambassador Tzionis lost yet another unread paper prepared at his request?

From left to right: the future triumvirate, Denktash Mark II, Denktash Mark I, and the real son, Serdar Denktash, on the first day of the resumed talks in Nicosia on 19 February 2004.

One step ahead. The Turkish Cypriot side usually arrived first. This is the meeting on 24 February 2004 where the Greek Cypriot side can be seen taking from their briefcases "dense and lengthy papers, one after another, explaining the changes sought and annexing proposed textual amendments," so that by mid-March a "vast bulk of the material was on the table"—according to the de Soto-Dann report circulated in the Secretary-General's name.

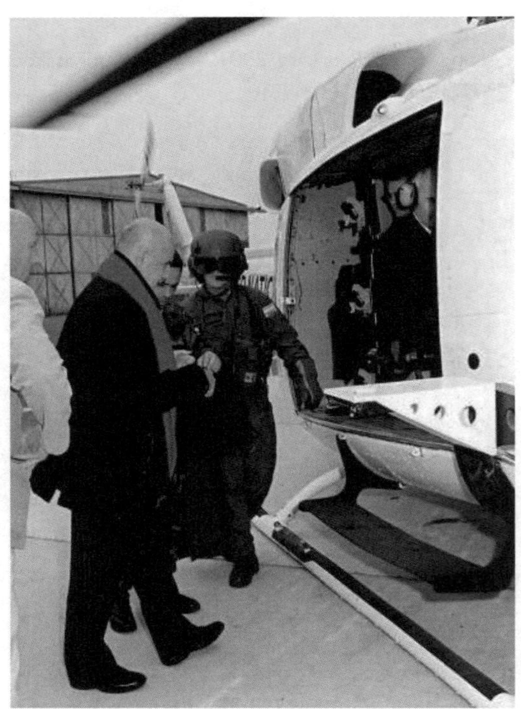

Alvaro de Soto about to enter for the start of yet another cold but heart-warming get-together in Ankara. Didier Pfirter and Robert Dann are already inside.

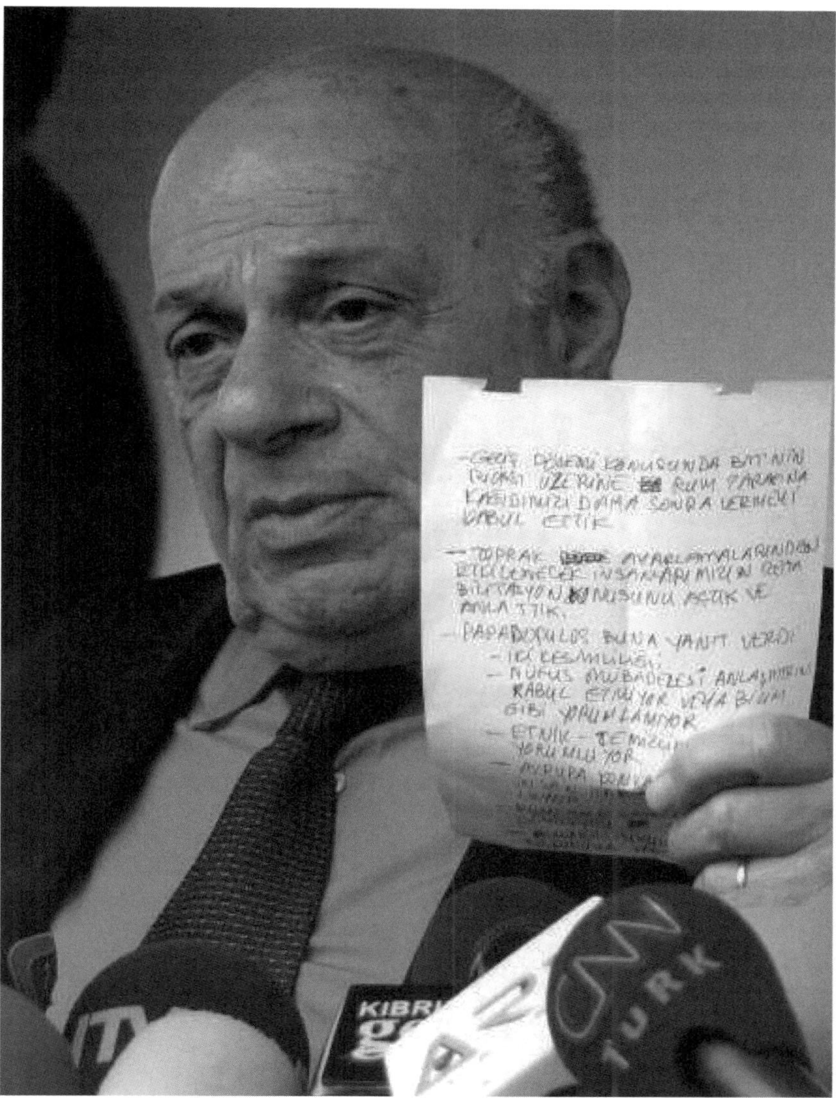

Mr Denktash, in his usual mode, briefing the press about what happened on 5 March 2004 with notes on the meeting. At UN request, he had delayed presenting transitional proposals; he had explained needs for relocation and rehabilitation of "our people" affected by the territorial adjustments; and, as regards "bi-zonality" and the "Exchange of Populations Agreement," claimed either Papadopoulos does not accept it or interprets it differently. The UN had demanded a "black out" on what happened in the talks. They were blind to Mr Denktash's daily extensive briefings on television, flouting their demand, but, when the Greek Cypriot side provided some material to reassure its public on controverted issues, the UN cast the main blame on it for leaking information.

On 8 March 2004 the EU Troika, with Messrs Verheugen and Solana, met Messrs Erdoğan and Gül in Ankara. The next day the Turkish Cypriots, under Ambassador Ziyal's supervision, revised their Cyprus proposals, making them less extreme. Below left: Messrs Solana and Verheugen; right, Foreign Minister Bot of the Netherlands; bottom left, Foreign Minister Gül; bottom right, Foreign Minister Cowen of Ireland sitting on the left.

N.19–22

Permanently parked limousines of Permanent Members at the UN Protected Area, with their passengers planning with or being briefed by Mr de Soto.

The end of the Nicosia talks on 22 March 2004. Mr Talat, about to proffer his hand, which will, genuinely and without posing, be accepted by President Papadopoulos. Who was briefing Lord Hannay about attitudes after he had resigned? Could it have been the gentleman in the middle?

The end of the Nicosia talks on 22 March 2004 before departing to Bürgenstock. What has happened to the teams? Its understandable when Mehmet-Ali Talat of the Republican Turkish Party stands shoulder to shoulder with Toumazos Tselepis of Akel, but how has Tasos Tzionis, Director of the Republic's Central Intelligence Service, gotten inside the Turkish Cyprus team? Left to right, Seniha Birand, Osman Ertüg, Ergün Olgun, Lisa Jones, Tasos Tzionis, Robert Dann, Rauf Denktash, Zbigniew Wlosowicz, Alvaro de Soto, Tassos Papadoupoulos, Didier Pfirter, Andreas Mavroyiannis, Mehmet-Ali Talat, Menelaos Menelaou, Nicos Emiliou, and Toumazos Tselepis.

XI

The Nicosia Phase (19 February–22 March 2004) and Mr De Soto's Tactics

A. NEGOTIATIONS IN THE TECHNICAL COMMITTEES

Financial aspects of the Plan

EXPECTING SUBSTANTIAL NEGOTIATIONS to occur in Phase 1 in Nicosia and hoping that changes could be agreed with the Turkish Cypriot side, so that completion of the Plan would occur by 22 March 2004, the Greek Cypriot side proposed a Technical Committee on Economic and Financial Aspects of Implementation. Having appreciated the economic and fiscal deficiencies in Annan III, the Government of the Republic had itself engaged four independent leading experts on fiscal federalism and the economics of federations to make suggestions for improvements necessary to ensure that the Plan would be workable. Their Report[1] was to lead to complete reworking of the economic and financial aspects of the Plan. Cooperation between Greek Cypriots and Turkish Cypriot experts and with the UN team, assisted by international experts, thereafter led to a significant Technical Committee Report, agreed by both sides except as to the property financial provisions.

Other major tasks at the technical level, at which Committees and various Sub-committees operated, were to finalise the body of incomplete Federal Laws, to agree on treaties binding the United Cyprus Republic and to make proper financial arrangements for relocation and rehabilitation of Turkish Cypriots vacating Greek Cypriot-owned property, for property compensation, and for loans to facilitate acquisition by individuals of properties they could buy under the Plan. The latter aspects were remitted to the Economic and Financial Aspects Committee, whose agreed report was reflected in the final Plan, although, as indicated above, the Greek Cypriot side remained concerned that

[1] "Economic aspects of the Annan Plan for the Solution of the Cyprus Problem," Draft Report, by Barry Eichengreen, Riccardo Faini, Jorgen von Hagen and Charles Wyplosz, 17 January 2004, and, in final form, Report to the Government of the Republic of Cyprus, 24 February 2004.

the Plan in some important respects did not adopt important recommendations agreed by the Committee,[2] and that the guarantees then required of the Federal Government for compensation and for loans were unduly burdensome and likely to damage the international creditworthiness of the future UCR.

Federal Laws

The Greek Cypriot side had been gravely concerned by a number of important Federal Laws as finalised by the UN team in February 2003. At that time the UN finalised provisions governing all decision-making procedures in Laws and Co-operation Agreements in accordance with Turkish Cypriot demands. Most draft Laws had been submitted by the Greek Cypriot side (because the Turkish Cypriot side had not engaged in drafting Laws until January 2003 due to political instructions and it had been instructed to let matters alone after March 2003). When both sides' legal teams re-started active work in February 2004 there were again differences of position. In the majority of significant cases, the UN team adopted Turkish Cypriot (effectively Turkish) amendments as being "indispensable" in order to complete particular Laws.[3] A notable adoption by the UN of Turkish positions related to the Law regarding the Continental Shelf of Cyprus, section 3.2 of which effectively provided that Cyprus could not even explore, let alone exploit, her continental shelf right along her northern and much of her eastern coasts until such time as Turkey agreed to a demarcation, or indicated that she did not contest any adjacent areas of territorial waters. A

[2] During the referendum campaign public concern in Cyprus about financial arrangements arose because for so long these issues had not been properly tackled in the Plan and this concern took time to die down, not completely disappearing because many thought the Plan still inadequate in such respects. The UN team was nonchalant about these issues and regarded economic debate during the campaign as being mere stirring up of exaggerated objections to the Plan.

[3] The UN team had earlier—and frequently in 2003 as well as before the 2004 negotiations—told the Greek Cypriot side that they intended to finalise the Laws in accordance with the drafts they had received from the Greek Cypriot side, nearly all Laws being lodged before The Hague meeting. This UN argument was brought up regularly when the Greek Cypriot side objected to other issues. It ran thus: "Keep quiet! You are going to get the kinds and provisions of Laws you want." It needs emphasising, as one of the team concerned in 2003, that the Laws were technical and without political overtones. The politics were introduced when the Turkish Cypriot side sought, on political instructions, to insert blocking mechanisms in some Laws or to object to the Law on Turkey's instructions. Maritime laws were the subject of particular consideration by Turkey. The Turkish Foreign Ministry on 21 April 2004, as reported by Ankara Anatolia news agency, stated that "the Ministry and concerned institutions closely monitored issues mentioned in the annex of the Annan Plan, especially the federal laws of the United Cyprus Republic on maritime and shipping matters since the preparation phase of the Plan". The Ministry added that it had exerted efforts to reach a conclusion on those laws in line with its views. It also pointed out Turkey's views on transit of warships through territorial waters of Cyprus and its opinions on economic zones and the continental shelf, observing that it had succeded in inserting in Annan III (26 February 2003) a requirement of weighted voting (ie approval by at least 10 Senators from the TCCS) for passage by Cyprus of regulations governing the contiguous zone (24 nautical miles) and any exclusive economic zones. At some points Turkey's and Cyprus's contiguous zones virtually abut, so that the Turkish navy would not have an extensive area of neighbouring high seas in which to manoeuvre.

lay-person could describe the resulting situation as being such that Cyprus had "no continental shelf" vis-à-vis Turkey.

Federal "treaties"

There were also interferences by the UN by way of finalising the list of "treaties" to bind the UCR. This was both at Turkey's direct instance and at the Turkish Cypriot side's request when it repeated the Turkish demands as to the Republic of Cyprus's Agreement with the Arab Republic of Egypt on the Delimitation of the Exclusive Economic Zone, dated 17 February 2003. On 2 March 2004 Turkey issued a Note objecting to this Agreement.[4] Direct Turkish complaint was made to the Secretary-General. She contended that it damaged the balance between Greece and Turkey established by the Treaty of Guarantee and the Foundation Agreement. She also contended that agreement with Egypt on a median line, instead of on equitable principles, was prejudicial. Turkey was here attempting to further her own future claim against the UCR that there should not be a median line between herself and Cyprus in the Eastern Mediterranean and Cilician Seas, seeking to claim most of the sea-bed between the two States.[5] Following Turkey's objection, the UN noted a reservation by Turkey to the Treaty on Matters related to the New State of Affairs in Cyprus to the effect that her acceptance of the Treaty in no way indicated the validity or legality of the Agreement with Egypt.[6] However, the Treaty on the New State of Affairs was not supposed to be subject to any reservations.

Turkey's objection to the Agreement with Egypt was paralleled by a Turkish objection to application of the Convention regarding the Regime of the Straits, with Protocol, signed at Montreux on 20 July 1936. Turkey has always wanted to diminish the general effects of this Convention and in particular to justify restrictions placed on Cyprus-flagged ships. Now she persuaded the UN not to list the Montreux Convention as a Treaty binding the UCR on the basis that the Republic of Cyprus was not a party. The UN adopted Turkey's line, although admitting that the matter was in doubt. In fact, there should have been no doubt: under Article 8 of the Treaty of Establishment, to which Turkey was also a party, the Republic of Cyprus succeeded to the UK's international rights, benefits and obligations (ie under the Montreux Treaty)—just as Cyprus in any event did under the general international law of State succession. Turkey had been notified of Cyprus's formal declaration of continued applicability on 18 March 1969 and had made no objection. The UN lawyers nonetheless

[4] 54 Law of the Sea Bulletin 1095. Turkey did not recognise this Agreement or any changes in legal rights effected by it. Moreover, she contended (as she had often done in other contexts) that there was no single authority competent to represent Cyprus as a whole, thus objecting to Cyprus's exercise of treaty-making power.

[5] See Ref: 2004/TURKUNO DT/4739.

[6] Annex V to Annan V, 31 March 2004, p 117, n 2.

adopted Turkey's view that notifications sent under the Convention to Cyprus, even by Turkey herself, and that a meeting in Paris of High Contracting Parties attended by Cyprus and called by the Depositary Authority, but not attended by Turkey, were "informal". The UN lawyer involved, Mr Hoffmeister, therefore insisted on knocking the Montreux Treaty off the list of Cyprus's treaties.[7]

This UN conduct was part of a policy adopted from February 2003 in respect of treaties to:

(i) Knock out at least some Republic of Cyprus treaties over and above any that might be inconsistent with the Foundation Agreement (the latter in any event would not, by agreement, be included on the treaty list as UCR treaties);[8]

(ii) Insert on the treaty list "treaties" by the "TRNC," so as to give the Turkish Cypriots at least this consolation prize for the future should the Foundation Agreement not be approved, thereby enabling them to contend that the "TRNC" had and has treaty-making competence, a point the US State Department has since looked upon favourably. That the UN was determined to give the "TRNC" treaty-making power appeared from the UN paper given to the Turkish Cypriot side prior to Annan III explaining to them how their concerns were being met; and

(iii) Insert on the list, as being binding on the whole of the UCR including the GCCS, "treaties" which had been designed to integrate the "TRNC" into Turkey.

It was of great concern to Greek Cypriots that Turkey could be involved inside the UCR (Cyprus) by the latter "treaties". For example, the "Co-operation Agreement on Civil Aviation, Coastal Security and Search and Rescue" interfered with the exclusive jurisdiction of the federal Government on such matters, thus infringing Cyprus's sovereignty. The Agreement provided for a common aviation and airspace management policy, while section 12.6, under certain circumstances, permitted Turkish military action in Cyprus. The UN also accepted as binding on the UCR the "Co-operation Agreement with Turkey on Coastal Security" of 19 September 2002. This gave Turkey rights with regard to "management of man-made installations at sea," to "the controlling of drilling activities and cable/pipe application activities of third countries in the maritime authority zone" and to "the use of marine life". Again the UN listed the "Agreement with Turkey on Search and Rescue at Sea," which involved

[7] He was doubtless acting on New York's and Mr de Soto's instructions. Such "hatchet jobs" were often his task. See also footnote 9 below and p 140 below on his activities as regards the Constitution of the GCCS at Bürgenstock. He was ubiquitous and obviously enjoying his role.

[8] This policy was inconsistent with the UN undertakings prior to and in November 2002 that the Republic's treaties would remain in force, in particular as evidencing that there was no State succession, something which persuaded the then Greek Cypriot team to accept the Plan's provisions regarding treaties and the lack of risk to continued existence of the Republic under another name.

participation by Turkish military units or assets in search and rescue operations in Cyprus's jurisdiction.[9]

The extensive "insertions" in the Law regarding the Continental Shelf and also the acceptance by the UN of the "TRNC's Co-operation Agreement with Turkey on Coastal Security" were remarkable in the context of an international organisation charged with upholding international law. Such provisions are not only contrary to international customary law rights of Cyprus but are in conflict with the UN Declaration on Sovereignty over Natural Resources. Other provisions (such as those in the "TRNC"–Turkey "Co-operation Agreement on Civil Aviation," affecting airspace management) interfered with the sovereignty of Cyprus and the competences of the federal government.

The SBAs and guarding UK "rights"

The UN, upon UK objection, rejected two Greek Cypriot proposals for clarifications in the new Protocol to the Treaty of Establishment. The Protocol was to be an integral part of the Plan, and, *inter alia,* provided for the UK, through a UK-designated expert (eg an Admiralty Surveyor), to re-delimit the SBAs' territorial waters. Participation by a Cypriot expert was rejected, despite the fact that Cyprus's waters were in effect simultaneously being re-delimited.[10] A further Cyprus proposal that the Protocol should clarify that the UK's SBAs did not make it a "coastal state" for purposes of the Law of the Sea Convention Articles 55 and 76 (exclusive economic zone and continental shelf respectively) was also rejected by the UN on UK representations. The Plan therefore left the

[9] The Greek Cypriot side strongly protested to Mr Hoffmeister about the listing and delisting of Treaties in accordance with Turkey's desires, but was met by superficial technical justifications. The minutes of the meeting (kept by a Greek Cypriot participant) indicate an unsympathetic attitude by Mr Hoffmeister. The writer has discovered an interesting phenomenon where there is a small legal academic elite which gets involved in a single question. The phenomenon is designated "Forsthoff's and Heinze's Revenge" and relates to the impact which these two academics have had on German legal circles as a result of their accounts of their experiences in Cyprus from 1960 to 1963 when Professor Forsthoff presided over the Constitutional Court and Dr Heinze was his Assistant. The writer has not yet met a distinguished German lawyer who has not heard of their views, which are hostile to Greek Cypriots and need to be balanced by corrective accounts.

[10] The current delimitation is provided for in the Treaty of Establishment, Article 1, read with Annex A Section 3. As newly re-delimited, the UK might well, without further ado, extend its territorial waters to 12 nautical miles in breadth, whereas currently the SBA's waters are three nautical miles. A significant pointer of the UK's intentions to act unilaterally and without possibility of challenge is that the Additional Protocol, Article 9, provided that any disputes about its interpretation or application should be resolved by consultation and "shall not be referred to any international tribunal or third party for settlement". This contrasted with Article 10(b) of the Treaty of Establishment, which required reference for final decision, failing a non-negotiated arrangement, to a tribunal composed of a Chairman nominated by the President of the ICJ and four other representatives nominated by the Guarantor Powers and Cyprus. Because of Turkey's failure to recognise the Republic of Cyprus, such tribunal might not contain a Turkish representative and this problem would have needed addressing. However, the UK wished altogether to reject the notion of judicial resolution of disputes.

UK in a position to contend—although this view is disputed by Cyprus—that she is a "coastal state" entitled to those rights, and thus entitled to control exploration and exploitation of large parts of the Eastern Mediterranean to the south of the Sovereign Base Areas of Akrotiri and Dhekelia, where preliminary surveys have indicated the likelihood of gas and oil discoveries. Although the UK could not herself exploit such areas, by reason of a Declaration forming part of the 1960 settlement, she could, as things stand, preclude the Republic from granting licences.[11] If the UK were to claim 12 mile-wide waters, she would then, under the Law of the Sea Convention, be subject to correlative international responsibilities for maritime policing and supervision.

Last minute major changes to Laws

Major alterations to the Plan were made in the small print of Laws, many of which were subject to "finalisation" by the UN legal team even in the last days immediately preceding the referenda. For example, although it was indicated that it would be introduced, the provision for increased Turkish immigration to Cyprus was buried in the Law on Aliens and Immigration. This contained further ambiguities indicating that Turkish settlers could be brought in and given TCCS citizenship.[12] Restrictions on Greek Cypriots' right to reside in the Turkish Cypriot constituent state had to be searched for in the Constitutional Law on Internal Constituent State Citizenship Status and Constituent State Residency Rights. Major changes, not clarified until the afternoon preceding the referenda, were made in the Law on the Election of Members of Parliament in order to bring the "Community" concept into elections for and voting in the Federal Senate. Members of the Public Service of the Republic were not accorded protection of their service benefits until two days before the referendum.[13]

[11] It was agreed, when drafting the Treaty of Establishment, that the UK retained sovereignty over the SBAs and that the purpose of their retention was for military bases only. As part of the independence package, the UK then was to make a unilateral Declaration. This was transmitted to the President and Vice-President of Cyprus, who noted its contents. (See Appendix O to *Cmnd 1093*, July 1960, pp 201 *et seq*.) The UK Government declared their intention not to develop the SBAs "for other than military purposes"; not to set up or permit the establishment of civilian commercial enterprises; and to invite the Republic to issue licenses for mining and prospecting and to collect and keep any revenue and fees derived, all such action of the Republic being subject to consent and control of the SBA authorities.

[12] Upon enquiry of the UN being made by the Greek Cypriot side, the Greek Cypriot side was informed two days before finalisation that this had been a drafting error, and, because of time constraints and pressures, it had not earlier been notified, but that the error was now being corrected. Such had become the suspicions as to what the UN was doing that it was wondered whether this correction would have been made had the Greek Cypriot side not noticed the problem. The UN by now certainly appreciated that including such a provision would have very negatively affected Greek Cypriot public opinion in the impending referendum.

[13] Mr de Soto accused the Government of stirring up civil servants to oppose the Plan. The reality was that their trade unions were the source of opposition on the basis that their members' service benefits were as yet unprotected and they would be denied career prospects due to the high proportion of posts at all levels allocated to Turkish Cypriots under the Plan. As soon as the

Akrotiri SBA coastline at Curium. The SBA-s form 2.6% of the Island, but their coastline is 9.6%.

Above: signs near the controversial and heavily guarded new antenna in the Akrotiri SBA. It is a High-Frequency Over the Horizon Radar with a 3,000 nautical miles radius. The antenna forms part of an anti-missile umbrella covering most of the former Soviet Union and the Arab States and was installed following "9/11th" to upgrade the facilities which had existed since about 1970 with the latest technology. Integrated with other radars, it supplies data to a command centre for information and control used for NATO purposes, and provides a complete "Air Situation" picture, not only for the Nicosia FIR, but for the greater Middle East and the Caucasus region. At Ayios Nicolaos (attached to the Dhekelia SBA) there are facilities operating in conjunction with installations on the UK sites on Mount Olympos and at Troodos (occupied in terms of the Treaty of Establishment 1960). The Ayios Nicolaos and Troodos facilities acquire information

from geo- and meo-satellites which cover 70% of the earth's surface. Relevant satellites have "footprints" on Cyprus (including those operated by Russia). Cypriots consider the new antenna to be a health hazard and object to its location in a wetland environment which is of special scientific interest next to Akrotiri's salt lake and bird sanctuary. Below: the older still operative antennae at Akrotiri SBA. All these "facilities" are why Cyprus's geo-strategical position is so significant to the USA, the UK and NATO.

B. NEGOTIATIONS IN NICOSIA ON THE POLITICAL LEVEL

On the political level (as opposed to the technical level), there was, as already indicated, genuine negotiation on only two issues. The first was the size of the Federal executive and the method of its representation in the EU so as to ensure the ability of Cyprus to speak with one voice. As regards the *size* of the Federal executive there was agreement, but as to its ability to speak with one voice in the EU no agreement was reached.[14] The second was the creation of a first instance federal Court to ensure that litigation on constitutional and federal administrative law issues could be dealt with by an appropriate judicial body. On other vital aspects there was no negotiation, even though the Greek Cypriot side in making proposals had meticulously kept within the parameters of the Plan, with many of its suggested amendments being of a purely technical character.

Proposals by the Turkish Cypriot side

In contrast with the Greek Cypriot side's restraint in formulating proposals, the Turkish Cypriot side, backed by Turkey, frittered away time by producing proposals well beyond the Plan's parameters. Such proposals should have been ruled out by the procedure agreed in New York—had the procedural limitations been properly applied by the UN. Nonetheless the Turkish Cypriot proposals required answer, especially the extensive suggestions made by the Turkish Cypriot side on 24 February 2004 for "Strengthening of Bi-zonality and Bi-nationality, Safeguard Measures, Derogations and Citizenship, Security and Matters Related to the Coming into Being of the New State of Affairs". The making of these proposals had been coordinated with the Turkish Foreign

UN settled the matter, the President announced that civil servants were protected, even though it was unclear whether the UCR or the constituent states had to foot the relevant financial burdens. The UN admitted that there were constitutional issues about which government was financially responsible but declared that there was no time to clear a Constitutional amendment with "the motherlands"—clearance being required because they were guaranteeing the Constitution.

[14] There was negotiation on the Co-operation Agreement on European Union Affairs, but certainly no agreement. The respective positions remained far apart and a bridging proposal by Mr Pfirter was merely to insert in the text a slight and inadequate change to resolve deadlocks (using the same general mechanism except that a swifter procedure was envisaged). Certainly Cyprus would not be able to speak with one voice. Indeed, most of the time she would have no voice at all and would have to abstain from voting. The Co-operation Agreement, as the Greek Cypriot side had pointed out in February 2003, confused competence and representation, which are different issues. A meeting presided over by Mr Pfirter to discuss the Co-operation Agreement was held between the two Greek Cypriot experts, Ambassadors Mavroyiannis and Emiliou, and Mr Olgun, who opposed changes. The UN criticised the Greek Cypriot side, contending that the Agreement had already been "finalised" because it had been appended to Annan III (at which stage the UN had knocked out strong Greek Cypriot objections and had accepted Turkish Cypriot positions). The Greek Cypriot experts believed that the Agreement insisted on by the UN would render Cyprus impotent in the EU, and to no avail pointed out that "finalisation" was only due to occur at Bürgenstock.

Ministry and cleared with the National Security Council (the formal body on which the Turkish Armed Forces are represented). Public corroboration of this fact was provided by a leaked Turkish Foreign Ministry paper, publicised on 29 December 2003 and thereafter partly published on 7 January 2004 in the Turkish newspaper, *Cumhurriyet*. When these materials, showing total correspondence with Turkish Foreign Ministry and Army policy decisions, were drawn to his attention by President Papadopoulos, Mr de Soto professed ignorance—although the UN monitors press reports closely, summarising all significant matters for use both locally and in New York.

As to the substance of these proposals, the Turkish Cypriot side sought recognition of the "TRNC" in devious ways, demanded massive EU derogations and transitional arrangements, insisted on a right for all Turkish settlers to remain and sought to diminish the scope of any UN peace-keeping force's mandate. Apart from their suggestions in a couple of paragraphs, the changes to the Plan demanded by the Turkish Cypriot side were then demonstrated by the Greek Cypriot side to be well beyond the Plan's parameters, subverting its basis, upsetting its delicate balances between respect for the human rights of refugees and the needs of persons who currently use their houses, seeking to legitimise ethnic cleansing and land confiscation, and virtually completely abandoning refugees' rights.[15] Mr de Soto, when appealed to by the Greek Cypriot side, and even after a formal letter of objection on 26 February 2004, requesting him to rule the Turkish Cypriot proposals out of order as contrary to the agreed procedure, disclaimed any responsibility "to judge" the parties' proposals.[16] Nonetheless, the Greek Cypriot side, trusting that the Secretary-General himself would honour the agreed procedure at the "finalisation" stage, did not withdraw from the talks—which they could quite legitimately have done—but stated that they would not delay the referendum, even though the agreement made in New York had been breached.[17]

The Turkish Cypriot proposals took some time to be "consolidated" ie revised. Consolidation occurred on 9 March in Ankara, although the decision was not at this stage conveyed to the Greek Cypriot side. Some minor points

[15] Comprehensive written reasoning was presented on 25 February 2004 by the Greek Cypriot side.

[16] Mr de Soto was not interested in the fact that the Turkish Cypriot proposals were outside the parameters of the agreed negotiating process or that they contravened its core provisions, or that they were contrary to fundamental principles or to important "trade-offs" previously agreed by President Clerides and his team. He wanted the sides to bargain on whatever was served up to them, irrespective of what had been agreed was the scope of any negotiations. He considered the paper "a demolition job," believing that the Greek Cypriot side should be attempting to convince the Turkish Cypriots of the wisdom and benefits of adhering to the Plan, which he must have known was an impossible task, rather than showing that Turkish Cypriot proposals were outside the agreed scope of negotiations. In Mr de Soto's "finalisation" for the Secretary-General, he himself did not adhere to the Plan's parameters.

[17] The Secretary-General wrote thanking them for not withdrawing. This letter was from the very same Secretary-General who "finalised" some of these proposals a few weeks later, inserting them in the Plan on 31 March 2004.

were omitted one day after an EU Troika delegation visited Turkey for consultations on Turkey's EU candidature.[18] Ultimately, the Greek Cypriot side was to find most of the Turkish Cypriot "consolidated" proposals incorporated in the Plan by the Secretary-General on 31 March 2004. Indicatively, those incorporated were: lowered ceilings for the number of Greek Cypriot refugees entitled to return to reside in the Turkish Cypriot constituent state; limitations on re-instatement of their properties as regards owners of non-residential property (such limitations now to be put into effect in another manner); ethnic differentiation between Communities on linguistic criteria as the basis for Senate elections and composition, as a consequence of which there would be weighted *ethnic* (Community) voting on certain categories of Laws and regulations;[19] extensions of the timetable for reduction of Turkish military forces in Cyprus; and effective removal of limitations on Turkish immigration to Cyprus once nearby Turkey, with its by then 80 million population, joined the EU. Mr de Soto, only partly accurately, pointed out that what he chose to describe as "the improvements" in the final Plan "while not agreed, reflect the material put forward in intensive negotiations that restarted on 19 February this year".[20] The questionable aspects of his statement are that whether a change is to be characterised as an "improvement" is highly subjective; there had been no intensive negotiations; and much of "the material" (the proposals made) was outside the parameters of the Plan and submitted contrary to the agreed procedure. Despite all this, the material had been permitted by him to go forward, and was ultimately characterised by Mr de Soto and his team as "key concepts and trade-offs of the past few years," which they then adopted. The fact is that such material negated key concepts and trade-offs, and that no return bargains (trade-offs) to meet Greek Cypriot concerns were exchanged for such UN gifts to Turkey.

MR DE SOTO'S NICOSIA TACTICS

In commenting on this first Phase in Nicosia, Mr de Soto told the Security Council on 2 April 2004 that each side blamed the other for lack of progress in the direct negotiations there and in his "shuttle" between the leaders from 15 March 2004. What had in fact happened was as follows: at the start of the Nicosia Phase, Mr de Soto had selectively assembled substantive points made by the two sides in their respective "Talking Points" presented in New

[18] Led by Mr Brian Cowen T D, Irish Minister for Foreign Affairs, with Mr Bernard Bot, Netherlands Foreign Minister, the EU High Representative for Common Foreign and Security Policy, Mr Javier Solana, and the Enlargement Commissioner, Mr Günter Verheugen. They met Messrs Erdoğan and Gül and the Turkish Chief of Defence on 8 March.

[19] The consequential change in the Law regarding voter registration with separate voters' rolls was not pointed out by the UN. The Greek Cypriot side, only upon specific enquiry by the writer, discovered a few days before the referendum that such provisions were to be inserted in a Law.

[20] Briefing to the Security Council, 2 April 2004, p 2.

York on 10 February 2004. On that day, the Secretary-General, knowing that the Turkish Cypriot side intended to produce an outline list of substantive demands which had been agreed with the Turkish Foreign Ministry, at 10 minutes' notice asked the Greek Cypriot side to produce a list of substantive demands (a tactic on which Mr de Soto and the *Report* were silent). Since it had been invited to New York to discuss only procedure and not substance, the Greek Cypriot side then had to dash off a provisional outline document, unless it was to refuse to produce a document. Exploiting the production of this provisional document, Mr de Soto grouped the sides' New York "Talking Points" as four "clusters" of issues, suggesting that the sides "concentrate" on his "clusters," which he had so grouped as to indicate that there should be bargaining inside each cluster. However, this tactic of trying to confine the sides to the clustered issues was rejected by both Mr Denktash and President Papadopoulos, the latter wishing systematically to look at the core themes of the Plan which had never been discussed as a whole. Moreover, the Greek Cypriot side was not willing to discuss matters which fell outside the scope of the procedure just agreed in New York, and, since Mr Denktash's 10 February Talking Points for the most part went beyond the substantive parameters of the Plan, discussion of these was not acceptable.[21] After heated conversations, Mr de Soto's clusters then became only an outline agenda to facilitate the parties.

The Special Adviser next adopted a different tactic. Having been frustrated over his attempt to begin trade-offs through "clusters," Mr de Soto waited until the sides had laid out their proposals, and then on 15 March submitted Talking Points on which he would "shuttle". These Talking Points he listed in two categories. The first category attempted to get the two sides to discuss

> changes on the substance where one party or the other, or sometimes both, are seeking *changes that affect the balance of one of the parameters of the Plan or to respond to a demand from the other side for such changes* (emphasis added).

He made it clear that he looked for trade-offs here "within or between issues" and that the sides should prioritise changes. In his second category, he sought to discuss practical matters, so as to enable the Plan actually to work and for both sides to get what the Plan promised them. The Greek Cypriot side, relying on the Secretary-General's undertakings in his 4 February 2004 letter that the parameters of the Plan should not be altered, refused to make proposals which would have that effect, and declined to be lured into opening up the first category by prioritising any matters within it. The Greek Cypriot side was nonetheless anxious to discuss the practical matters to make the Plan work and therefore made proposals covering the second category, cooperating with the

[21] Mr Denktash's Talking Points of 10 February set out demands for strengthening bi-zonality, permanent derogations from EU law, continued military presence of Turkey, return of fewer Greek Cypriots, and Community representation and separate majorities in governmental organs of the Federal State. Coordinated with the Turkish Foreign Ministry, most demands were well outside the parameters of Annan III.

Special Adviser.[22] The Special Adviser's new tactic of presenting the Turkish Cypriot demands in his "Talking Points" (although they were mostly outside the Plan's parameters) and of suggesting that the two sides start bargaining on these was therefore frustrated, so again trade-offs on such issues could not be proposed by him.

THE REPORT'S MISDESCRIPTION OF EVENTS IN NICOSIA

In describing those events in Nicosia, the *Report* at para 20 claimed that the Greek Cypriot side

> declined to prioritise its demands, despite my Special Adviser's request of 15 March to both sides to do so.

The *Report* at para 19 also claimed that in mid-March

> The Turkish Cypriot side replaced their initial papers with a less far-reaching set of proposed textual amendments, described as a priority list.

The "replacement" papers from the Turkish Cypriot side were sent by the UN to the Greek Cypriot side only on 19 March (Letter de Soto to President Papadopoulos), but there was no indication whatsoever in this letter or in the papers that there was any "priority". Mr de Soto's letter merely listed the attached documents by their titles eg "Consolidated list of Turkish Cypriot Proposals (revised text)," dated 18 March 2004. As already indicated, most of these proposals remained outside the Plan's parameters, but the Special Adviser ignored this fact. When reporting on the Special Adviser's conduct of the negotiations, the Secretary-General's *Report* (at para 19) however asserted that

> In suggesting agendas for meetings, and in pursuing discussions of the items clustered for consideration, my Special Adviser left aside Turkish Cypriot demands which were clearly outside the parameters of the plan.

Thus, the *Report* gave a misleadingly favourable impression of the Special Adviser's tactics.

Mr de Soto's evident frustration at the failure of his various tactics in Nicosia was reflected in the *Report* on the Nicosia Phase in the form of propaganda designed to create the impression that the Greek Cypriot side had attempted to sabotage the talks by presenting a "vast bulk" of materials. The facts are very different from the assertions made in the *Report*. The Greek Cypriot side had always worked for a stable and enduring solution and a fully considered

[22] Such issues were not "*secondary issues*," as the Report indicates at para 26, but were major issues (implementation of the Plan and the question of whether there would be a long transitional period of joint government by the constituent states, rather than by the federal government). Inconsistently, in the context of "the main improvements to the Plan," the *Report*, paras 44–46 describes these aspects as being "significantly improved".

constitutional settlement. As indicated, there had not been any proper consideration by the UN's team of young lawyers of economic and financial matters, or of changes necessary in light of Cyprus's impending EU membership. The property scheme, much of the Constitution, and the Plan as an integrated whole had never been directly discussed by the two sides. The Greek Cypriot side therefore took at face value and as being genuinely necessary Mr de Soto's proposal to both sides in his paper, "Clusters of Issues," 20 February 2004. He had written:

> The UN suggests that each side explain in concrete terms, including with non-papers as necessary, the actual changes they want to the Plan, taking the Clusters in turn during the coming meetings.

Accordingly, the Greek Cypriot side presented specific changes and reasoned explanations why these were necessary. They dealt with the major aspects of the Plan which they had, ever since President Papadopoulos' letter of 28 February 2003, stated needed to be changed; they raised other issues consequential upon the Turkish Cypriot proposals (as the Greek Cypriot side explained to Mr de Soto); they raised crucial issues arising from the Technical Committees' work (eg refusal to accept, at Turkey's instance, that Cyprus had a continental shelf); they objected to the "treaties" between Turkey and her subordinate local administration, which were aimed at integrating the occupied area and Turkey, now being applied to all of Cyprus; and they pointed out some significant drafting defects in the Plan and its Annexes. The future Constitution, the economy and the long-term rights of hundreds of thousands of Cypriots were at stake.

Nonetheless, the *Report* snidely criticised the Greek Cypriot side for its serious approach to the negotiations. Paragraph 8 ironically claimed that the Secretary-General had been reassured by President Papadopoulos that he did not want "forty or fifty" changes to the Plan. Paragraph 19 referred to "the virtue of concision" of the Turkish Cypriot proposals (substantially altering key parameters of the Plan). Paragraph 20 favourably contrasted Turkish Cypriot behaviour with the conduct of the Greek Cypriot side, which took each issue in turn (as invited to do) and produced "dense and lengthy papers one after another". Paragraph 20 also stated sarcastically that, "As they continued to present papers, it became apparent that the 10 February 2004 paper summary of Greek Cypriot demands was far from exhaustive".[23] This last comment was inserted in the *Report,* despite the fact that in a meeting of 22 February immediately after Mr de Soto had presented his paper "Clustering of Issues," President Papadopoulos had emphasised that the 10 February "Talking Points" had not comprehensively stated the issues. It was fortunate that the word "etc" had appeared in the hurriedly prepared 10 February paper. Reliance had to be placed on this in a heated conversation with Mr de Soto, who sought to exclude

[23] This was a reference to the "Talking Points" summary extracted in New York at 10 minutes' notice upon request of the Secretary-General.

from discussion in the talks all topics not expressly mentioned in the "Talking Points". In answering him, reliance had also to be placed on SC Resolution 1250 in giving overriding guidance as to the scope of the talks.[24]

The *Report* made repeated criticisms of the Greek Cypriot side's handling of the negotiations in Nicosia. Its reference (at paragraph 22) to "the vast bulk of the material" has already been mentioned. To this was added an innuendo (effected by quoting the Turkish Cypriot side) that the Greek Cypriot side was "filibustering". Again (at para 37), the *Report* exaggerated the scale of Greek Cypriot proposals and complained that a consolidated list of demands ("which ran to 44 pages") had not been presented until 25 March 2004. Had the Special Adviser conscientiously read the papers presented in Nicosia, he would have known what was proposed. What happened on 25 March was that a three page list of proposals was provided by the Greek Cypriot side at the UN's request. The 44 pages referred to in the *Report* were appended to this list. They consisted of legal texts, including all wording to be deleted (ie crossed out texts) and each amendment was placed in its relevant context of legal provisions, so that the UN draftsmen could easily understand each amendment without unnecessary cross-checking. The actual text of the proposed amendments would, without the contextual materials, have been approximately 6 pages of changes to the 9,000 pages of the Plan and its Annexes. These comments in the *Report* prove that Mr de Soto did not take the need for negotiations in Nicosia seriously, knowing that he could in a couple of weeks' time exploit the discretion afforded to the Secretary-General to impose his own text.

[24] The reports of this conversation are reminiscent of the story of what was discovered in a deceased Cambridge lecturer's notes. In the margins, there were intermittent notations: "Raise voice. Argument weak."

XII

The Bürgenstock Meetings—Phases 2 and 3

IT HAD BEEN agreed that there were to be two distinct Phases of procedure at Bürgenstock. The initial Bürgenstock Phase (Phase 2 as agreed in New York) was designed to be an intense effort to finalise a text with the Turkish and Greek Foreign Ministers present to lend their collaboration. However, it had been decided in New York that these Powers were not to be parties in the next Phase (Phase 3), when the Secretary-General was to finalise the text of the Plan.[1] The UN deliberately blurred the Phases, aided by Mr Erdoğan's late arrival on the day Phase 3 started. The Secretary-General invited Greece and Turkey to remain there, allegedly in consultation, although Turkey used the opportunity to press its demands, to which the UN acceded on 31 March 2004, quite contrary to the agreed procedure. This blurring of the Phases was a tactic planned all along by Mr de Soto, enabling Turkey (aided by the USA and the UK) to dictate the terms of the settlement.

THE UN AND THE USA DISPLACE MR DENKTASH AS "LEADER OF THE TURKISH CYPRIOT COMMUNITY"

Prior to the meetings at Bürgenstock, the leader of the Turkish Cypriot side, Mr Rauf Denktash, refused to come to Bürgenstock, something the Secretary-General's *Report* (para 26) played down as merely a "mini-crisis". After consultation with the Turkish Government, which was in constant contact with the USA and the UN, Mr Denktash ultimately conferred full negotiating authority on Mr Talat, "Prime Minister of the TRNC," and on his son, Mr Serdar Denktash, the "Foreign Minister," to attend at Bürgenstock in his place. Negotiations, throughout the many years of intercommunal talks when they occurred at high level, were always by "the leaders"—as stipulated in numerous Security Council Resolutions, notably SCR 1117(1997) and SCR 1250(1999), which applied specifically to the current talks process. "Leader" was

[1] This point is deliberately omitted from the *Report,* which in para 13 asserts that a main issue dividing the parties at the end was "the way in which the role of Greece and Turkey in the culminating phases of the process would be presented".

not defined in the Resolutions, but, from the outset and in practice over the years, the President of the Republic of Cyprus (and in his absence or illness the Acting-President) was treated as "leader of the Greek Cypriot side". As concerns the Turkish Cypriot side, Mr Denktash, who had in 1973 been "elected" as "Vice-President" in purported elections, was always treated as "leader". Both "leaders" were repeatedly chosen by their Communities in the elections/ "elections", which took place at intervals over the next 30 years as "Presidents" of the Republic of Cyprus / "TFSK later TRNC," thus having the legitimacy of popular support and of being recognised as "leaders" by their respective Communities. However, the UN and various Powers now tried to persuade the Greek Cypriot side to treat Messrs Talat and Serdar Denktash as "leaders." Yet, in reality, Mr Rauf Denktash remained leader of the Turkish Cypriot Community, able at any time to withdraw his negotiating authority or to veto decisions. Accordingly, the Greek Cypriot side would not agree to an opening session of "leaders". Mr de Soto nonetheless wished to arrange a "photo opportunity" with all present. Not only would this have given an incorrect impression as to the status of Messrs Talat and Serdar Denktash, but it would also have been misleading as to the status of Turkey and Greece at the meeting.[2] Thus Greece also disagreed with the proposed arrangement. As already indicated, Turkey's demand for quadrilateral meetings had been a matter raised and rejected in New York, but she again insisted on such meetings at Bürgenstock (*Report*, para 33). In light of the difficulty about arranging meetings, the Greek Cypriot side then agreed to a proposal by Mr de Soto to attend a meeting at 6 pm on Wednesday, 24 March. This meeting was announced as due to take place by both the Greek Cypriot side and the UN. Two hours before the time it was planned to take place, it was cancelled by the UN. When the Greek Cypriot side told Mr de Soto that the cancellation was unwise because the meeting had been announced to the press, he replied: "Please from now on let the UN make the announcements". Although Mr de Soto was told that the Greek Cypriot side was willing to meet with Messrs Talat and Serdar Denktash for discussions, and he had indicated that he would come back to this issue, he never did so—presumably because the Turkish Cypriot side wanted recognition as "leaders," rather than to have to engage in negotiations with the Greek Cypriot side. For her part, Turkey wanted to emphasise and enhance her role by insisting on quadrilateral meetings. These events were glossed over by Mr de Soto, who merely told the Security Council, when briefing it on 2 April, that there was a difference of views of the parties as to appropriate "format," so that it was

[2] The Greek Cypriot side's refusal to have an opening ceremony/"photo opportunity" was, typically, misrepresented by the UN. Lord Hannay, who not being there, had this on hearsay, wrote of President Papadopoulos "refusing to shake Talat's hand and declining any direct contact with the Turkish Government". The lie to this statement is provided by the photographs at Bürgenstock: see C.P. 21–22, Q.12–16.

difficult to arrange direct meetings.[3] There were a couple of private discussions at Bürgenstock between President Papadopoulos and Mr Serdar Denktash, commenced at the former's initiative, and not organised by or through the UN.[4]

What is clear is that the UN took a decision in effect to displace Mr Rauf Denktash as "leader". The *Report* on the talks (at para 6) stated that the December 2003 vote in the Turkish Cypriot Community "brought to the fore a new Turkish Cypriot leadership". However, this new Turkish Cypriot "leadership" did not in fact replace Mr Rauf Denktash, who had been present in New York at the 10–13 February meeting. It was he who had on 24 February in Nicosia presented his positions (which were well outside the parameters of the Plan). During all talks until 22 March 2004, he had appeared as "leader," and Messrs Talat and S Denktash has thus far merely been members of Mr Rauf Denktash's negotiating team. The Greek Cypriot side was not told by the UN team, either in New York or thereafter, that there was a leadership "triumvirate," only learning of this new institution in para 15 of the 28 May 2004 *Report*.[5]

Mr Denktash was also "displaced" as Turkish Cypriot "leader" by the United States State Department which, after the referenda, issued a written statement saying that it considered Mr Talat to be the Turkish Cypriot "leader" and that it no longer recognised Mr R Denktash as "leader": *New York Times*, 27 May 2004. Mr Talat had already been accorded this leadership status when he met Mr Colin Powell on 4 May 2004, with the State Department Spokesman, Mr Richard Boucher, subsequently describing him as having the role of a leader.

[3] See also *Report*, para 33. Apart from a couple of purely social gatherings under UN auspices, the Cypriot sides twice briefly met directly when they were gathered together to be greeted by and said farewell to by the Secretary-General. No meeting was arranged between Mr Talat and President Papadopoulos. The UN simply fell down on its job—probably because it intended to exploit the procedure of finalising the text by imposing whatever it deemed fit. Its large team in Bürgenstock was working until all hours on "finalising" the Plan, although obviously a great deal of UN work on modifying Annan III must have been done in Nicosia while the negotiations there were proceeding. There is an attempt in the *Report*, especially its para 37, to blame the Greek Cypriot side for not consolidating its demands, not indicating priorities and not using opportunities for open and frank dialogue at Bürgenstock. The thrust of this is that non-negotiation was the fault of the Greek Cypriot side. The reality is that, because the Special Adviser had been angered by the failure of his tactics in Nicosia and knew that he would be given a free hand, doubtless having been given instructions by his seniors in the Secretariat to use the Secretary-General's discretion to achieve his desired outcome, he decided to let matters float and to do nothing about organising a negotiating process in Bürgenstock. That anger (and the anger of his protégées) comes through in the *Report* with its hostility, leading to constant criticism of the Greek Cypriot side and unwillingness to accept that there were good reasons for its conduct. The reasons for non-prioritisation will be explained below.

[4] Prior to Bürgenstock, the President and Mr Serdar Denktash had also met privately and were to do so again after the 24 April referenda. See *Cyprus Mail*, 14 September 2004, reporting an announcement by the Republic's Government Spokesman, who did not give details as to the place and time of these meetings. There were also some meetings between Mr Denktash and Greek Cypriot advisers.

[5] Some members of the UN team had a fondness for drawing parallels with Roman institutions in relation to their Cyprus proposals in explaining the federal Constitution, eg "a collective Presidential Council with rotating chair," inspired by the Swiss model, itself transposed by Napoleon, following the model of the Roman triumvirates: *S/2003/398*, p 18, n 7. The UN did not however record the parallel between the final Roman office held by Julius Caesar and the role of the Secretary-General when finalising the Plan.

This was extraordinary interference by the USA within the domestic jurisdiction. It is for the Turkish Cypriot Community to appoint its own leader, and not for foreign States to appoint and anoint one. Mr Denktash still has a mandate as leader from the Turkish Cypriot Community, which he has continuously enjoyed since 1973. If such foreign king-making conduct is accepted, the next step could be an announcement that the USA is treating Mr X, leader of the largest political party in the House of Representatives, as having the role of leader of the Greek Cypriot side.[6]

PRESSURES BY THE SPECIAL ADVISER ON THE GREEK CYPRIOT SIDE TO PRIORITISE

Mr de Soto, both when briefing the Security Council on 2 April and in ghosting the *Report,* had cast blame on the Greek Cypriot side for its failure to prioritise in Nicosia and for its failure to do so at Bürgenstock. He did so in far-ranging criticism: refusing to engage in dialogue, filibustering in Nicosia and refusing to prioritise, which he harped upon. In describing this alleged Greek Cypriot default in relation to his own conduct, Mr de Soto claimed to the Security Council that, when the meeting between President Papadopoulos and the new Turkish Cypriot leadership did not occur, negotiations took on a more informal character and the UN tried "to broker areas of understanding".[7] In his "brokering" activities the Special Adviser used States with envoys at Bürgenstock and

[6] Irrespective of whether one agrees with Mr Denktash's views, it is extraordinary that the UN and the USA should treat him as a roadblock to be removed on the path to a settlement. Such removal, apart from its wrongfulness, would not in any event result in settlement, because new roadblocks tend to emerge—in this case the foolish impatience of the UN, the US and the EU to rush matters so they would be settled before 1 May 2004, leading to the "crash" on 24 April 2004.

[7] Briefing to the Security Council, 2 April 2004. The Secretary-General's 16 April 2004 *Report* at para 5 described the UN activity as trying "to build bridges through consultation with all parties, in which it explored compromise suggestions and sought to ascertain the priorities of the parties and where they might be prepared to show flexibility to achieve them". In his 28 May 2004 *Report*, para 34, there is a statement that, because direct meetings were impossible to arrange, "the UN shuttled between the parties to the extent possible" in an effort to broker areas of agreement. Para 35 declares that these efforts were complicated by the fact that Mr de Soto had difficulty in meeting the Greek Cypriot leader at Bürgenstock, due to Mr Papadopoulos' other commitments in Bürgenstock and Brussels. This statement has no foundation. Mr de Soto showed signs of pique when, upon his arrival at Bürgenstock on 23 March, he asked to see the President at 7 pm, but the National Council had been convened to meet at that time in order to examine the "authorisation" granted by the "leader" of the Turkish Cypriot Community, Mr Denktash, to Mr Talat and Mr S Denktash. The President's office replied that he was available to meet Mr de Soto at 8 pm. At 7.45 pm, Mr de Soto stated that he could not meet the President at 8 pm. Nevertheless, the meeting took place at 10.45 pm. As to the absence of the President in Brussels, Mr de Soto knew long before the Bürgenstock meetings that the President would be attending the EU Summit Council on 25–26 March and that in his absence, Mr D Christofias was fully authorised to act in the President's stead. It is untrue that the Special Adviser had difficulties in meeting the Greek Cypriot side at any time, and such statements can only be designed to mislead. It is apparent that the UN activity described in the *Report* was not what is known as "honest brokering". Instead, the *Report* is an attempt to mystify and to conceal the UN's failure to perform its function of good offices.

some members of his team to press the Greek Cypriot side and some of that side's delegates into bargaining with a view to accepting the Turkish Cypriot proposals, which were outside the parameters of the Plan. The Turkish Cypriot demands were, *inter alia*, for permanent stationing of Turkish troops in Cyprus; for a switch from the core bargain that political rights be based on place of residence and not on ethnic identity; for bi-zonality and bi-nationality restrictions to continue after Turkey's EU accession; and for return of fewer Greek Cypriot displaced persons. The Greek Cypriot side, having no expectation, in view of what been agreed in New York (letter of 4 February 2004 as modified by the Spokesman's Statement of 13 February) that the Secretary-General would use the limited discretion conferred upon him to insert in the Plan new matter going beyond its existing parameters, therefore continued to decline to provide priorities to facilitate bargaining on these demands.

In contrast with this approach the Secretary-General (in the person of Mr de Soto) appears to have seen himself as having *carte blanche* to push for bargains on all proposals of any kind. This is apparent from para 32 of the *Report*, where it is explained that, since it might fall to the Secretary-General to finalise the Plan, there was a duty on the parties (the Cypriots) to impress upon the UN their key priorities and to indicate what changes they might be prepared to live with to accommodate the other side.[8] But the negotiations had a framework, which should have been observed by all parties, not least by the UN.

Superficially, it is arguable that the Greek Cypriot side's refusal to prioritise was unreasonable. Indeed, the UN, the US and the UK made every effort to create a perception by the international community of Greek Cypriot unreasonableness in this respect. However, the Greek Cypriot side was not being negative, formalistic, or rigid in declining to prioritise. Prioritisation was a difficult exercise involving complex decisions, because there were major interrelated points in connection with each strand of the Plan (functionality of the Constitution, security, implementation of the territorial settlement and other aspects, property and residential rights, the situation under EU law etc). It was impossible to assess the consequences of particular "concessions" or "priorities"—all aspects of the Plan being interconnected—until such time as the whole picture could be seen: specific points could not sensibly be singled out without appreciation of the overall balance.

Moreover, to have given priorities would have opened Pandora's box. It would necessarily have implied that, if some Greek Cypriot priorities, or even parts thereof, were inserted in the final text by the Secretary-General, there would then have been agreement by the Greek Cypriot side to his "balancing" such insertions with other insertions satisfying Turkish demands—whereas these demands were nearly all beyond the Plan's parameters.

[8] That he expected unlimited bargaining is clear from further criticism of the Greek Cypriot side in paras 37 and 66 for not prioritising or engaging in give and take with Turkey and the Turkish Cypriots.

Mr de Soto's purpose in seeking prioritisation was to manoeuvre the Greek Cypriot side into appearing to have agreed to what he chose to insert in the Plan so as to avoid the real conclusion, namely that he would be imposing its provisions by picking and choosing. In rationalising this activity, the Special Adviser claimed to balance what he gave each side, but the issues were unrelated, and he had failed to concentrate on substance, or to have regard to principles of the UN Charter and international, human rights and humanitarian law. Whilst the Special Adviser's effort to "simplify" things and to meet time constraints by obtaining priority lists, making his choices easier, was to this extent understandable, the Cyprus problem was not a matter to be dealt with in such a simplistic way, with the UN exercising discretion to choose between parties' "key priorities".[9]

It needs to be added that the claim in paras 21 and 66 of the *Report* that the Greek Cypriot side had not engaged in "trade-offs" and in give and take was in any event a false generalisation: the Greek Cypriot side had suggested making particular trade-offs—as for example in relation to its request for UN administration of the territories to be adjusted, offering in exchange full rehabilitation of affected Turkish Cypriots and intense work to achieve this end. This suggestion was rejected by the Turkish Cypriot side. Subsequently, a Greek Cypriot suggestion to trade-off Community representation in the Senate for removal of restrictions on resumption of residence in the TCCS by Greek Cypriots was not accepted. Moreover, a general proposal for trade-offs made on 20 March by President Papadopoulos in Nicosia was not taken up.

The implication that in contrast, the Turkish Cypriot side was generally willing to engage and compromise is equally inaccurate. The only issues on which they were willing to do so were the composition of the Presidential Council and its functioning and a federal first instance court. All the important Greek Cypriot proposals about security, implementation, the period of transitional government, EU representation, treaties, Laws, property and Turkish settlers were flatly rejected.

THE SPECIAL ADVISER'S ATTEMPTS TO COMMIT THE GREEK CYPRIOT SIDE TO HIS PLAN

At Bürgenstock the Special Adviser adopted another disingenuous tactic to create a perception of Greek Cypriot assent to the Plan. Mr de Soto sent, together with papers on the draft Plan,[10] a Commitment document on 25 March 2004.

[9] Paras 32 and 37 of the *Report* make it clear that this was what the UN was seeking to do.

[10] These included a framework to update the Plan's text on questions of "legal security and transition" raised in the talks (giving the Greek Cypriot side some hope), new draft provisions on the European Union and an Annex on Coming into being of the New State of Affairs with draft letters (raising concerns on the Greek Cypriot side). The "Talking Points" assured the sides that those were merely draft works in progress "for comment, consideration and negotiation".

His purpose was (although he subsequently disavowed this) to get both sides to sign this Commitment and thus effectively to commit themselves to the forthcoming Plan, at least to the extent that they could not publicly oppose it.[11] The Greek Cypriot side declined to be inveigled in this way into implicitly endorsing a Plan which had not been scrutinised, was not available in final version and consisted of multiple complex annexes and disputed provisions. Mr de Soto well knew that devices to achieve signature were out of order. Ultimately, at Bürgenstock, Mr de Soto was reluctantly forced to accept that signature was not required.[12] This was glossed over in the *Report* (at para 36), where the Commitment was described as "a framework for signing an agreement should one emerge by 29 March". At the same time the claim was made that the framework had not been reacted to and the *Report* writer took the opportunity, by remarking that the Greek Cypriot side had instead publicly indicated concern about it, to make a further innuendo about press leaks by the Greek Cypriot side.[13] The *Report* does not accurately reflect the facts. Mr Christofias on 26 March confirmed to the National Council that Mr Vassiliou, a former President of Cyprus and a member of the Greek Cypriot team, had, on behalf of the Greek Cypriot side, notified Mr de Soto that there could be no signature, because this had not been agreed as part of the procedure in New York: all that had been arranged as regards agreement was that the "finalised" text would be put to referenda. After Mr Christofias' confirmation that the UN had been so notified, a public announcement was made. Not content with the distortions already referred to, the writer of the *Report* inaccurately asserted that only on 30 March did the Greek Cypriot side for the first time communicate views on a framework for signature, although, as explained above, this had been done by 26 March.[14]

[11] This partly explains Mr de Soto's and the Secretariat's rage when President Papadopoulos advised rejection of the Plan on 7 April 2004. They seem to have assumed that, if the President had not expressed his views, the Plan would have been approved, especially in view of the general international pressures which they had orchestrated. Such an assumption overlooked the many reasons why Greek Cypriots rejected the Plan and which they were more than capable of independently assessing.

[12] He was questioned by the Press long after he had been notified of the Greek Cypriot side's refusal to sign the Commitment and refused to indicate whether or not there would be a signature, keeping the Press guessing virtually until the end of the Bürgenstock meetings.

[13] Similar smears appeared in paras 23–24. In Nicosia there was daily public disclosure as to events at the talks in Mr Denktash's press briefings. It was impossible in the prevailing political mood for the Greek Cypriot side to have left the Greek Cypriot public doubting whether issues of the utmost importance had been addressed when Mr Denktash was being reported at length on these subjects.

[14] Because of the UN tactics of seeking to procure a signature, the Greek Cypriot side thereafter insisted on it being recorded when it received from the UN the authenticated texts of the federal Laws on 23 April (which texts were to be signed by the coordinators of each side's team, the UN Chairman of the Technical Committee on Laws and Treaties and the relevant EU Expert in relation to each Law and constituent state Constitution) that such signing only "verified the authenticity of the respective text . . . as finalized by the UN Secretary-General with the subsequent adaptations made by the United Nations. Authenticity bears no weight as to the substance of the respective text" (*Record*, 23.4.2004).

More attempts were made after presentation of the Commitment at Bürgenstock to persuade the Greek Cypriot side to produce a list of priorities to enable "trade-offs" on matters outside the existing parameters of the Plan. Repeated messages to this effect were given by foreign Powers' diplomats, especially those of the USA and the UK. Efforts to this end intensified after Ambassador Ziyal of Turkey's Foreign Ministry, on 26 March 2004 conveyed a list of "Final Points" to Mr de Soto, demanding that the changes requested by Turkey "be made by the UN Secretariat".[15] It is appropriate here to note that the request to the Secretary-General to finalise came only from the Republic of Turkey and the Turkish Cypriot side. The Secretary-General did not "act at the request of the parties," as claimed in his *Report* invoking the New York arrangements. No request to him to finalise was made by the Greek Cypriot side—or, for that matter, by Greece. Be that as it may, Turkey's requests were all ultimately to be met, with the Secretary-General telling Mr Erdoğan, now Prime Minister of Turkey, upon his arrival at Bürgenstock on 29 March that 9 of his 11 requirements had been completely agreed by the UN team and that the other two were virtually met.[16] All Turkey's requirements, which actually numbered well over 20, because some of the Ziyal Points were in effect "headings" reflecting changes earlier privately demanded from and discussed with the UN (eg property, security, bi-communal / bi-national configurations and bi-zonality) were accorded by 31 March 2004, this being effected by virtue of the UN's departure in Annan V (31 March) from what it had given the parties to understand in New York, namely, the limited role of the Secretary-General in exercising discretion to finalise the Plan.

[15] Ambassador Ziyal' s "Final Points" are appended to this book as Appendix 1.

[16] In order to obscure the UN bias in the adoption of nearly all Turkey's points, para 40 of the *Report* states that there had been a misreading by the media on the Greek Cypriot side, based on information dribbling out of the talks, of what the Turkish side had apparently sought and obtained. There was no misreading by the Greek Cypriot side of what Turkey had sought or gained. The Turkish requirements were listed in Mr Ziyal's 26 March paper. Moreover, the extent to which they were accorded is confirmed by information from the Turkish side about what the Secretary-General told Mr Erdoğan on his arrival at Bürgenstock about having been already given 9 of the Ziyal Points, with the other 2 virtually already being met. This winning the game was reflected in Turkish newspapers in conjunction with boasts by Mr Erdoğan about his scoring, like the footballer he once was. So extensive were these boasts that he had to be warned that this was counter-productive. Mr Erdoğan is a dynamic personality, radiating charisma even when surrounded by a phalanx of praetorian guards. Turkey is fortunate in having a Prime Minister who automatically attracts a sympathetic hearing, unlike those whom the UN team nicknamed "The Shrek" and "Papadoc". However, Mr Erdoğan was misguided in thinking the final whistle had been blown at Bürgenstock. That was merely half-time. There will be more play in the second half, plus "injury time," in the EU–Turkey Accession negotiations.

Comparison of the Ziyal "Final Points" with the Plan confirms that what was sought by Turkey was given by the UN. The last Points were fully given on 31 March, namely, accommodation of the settlement by adapting "primary law" of the EU, so that the settlement prevailed (ie its discriminatory provisions could not be challenged in the European Court of Justice); and it was agreed that troops under the Treaty of Alliance could stay indefinitely unless otherwise agreed.

THE PRESENTATION OF ANNAN IV ON 29 MARCH 2004

On 29 March 2004 the Secretary-General had presented Annan IV. He described this Mark IV Version as incorporating "improvements"[17] sought by the parties while maintaining the overall balance of the Plan and addressing "key concerns of the parties that had been expressed in the negotiations". In presenting this greatly revised Version IV, he described it as "an overall bridging proposal," using such language to make the draft Plan appear a constructive aid to both parties. At the same time, the Secretary-General invoked 131 Federal Laws (largely consisting of uncontroversial translations by the Greek Cypriot side into English of existing Laws currently in Greek, many of which were as they had been in 1963 before the Cyprus crisis and even as they were in Colonial days, apart from Laws necessary for EU purposes of harmonisation, most of which latter Laws had been though a clearing process with the EU). The Greek Cypriot lawyers' drafts formed the basis for discussion in Technical Committees where the Turkish Cypriot side was determined to build in procedures it wanted to enable blocking of regulations and decisions and to secure participation provisions at every governmental level. In the event, the UN tended, without good legal cause, but in pursuit of political reasons, to adopt Turkish Cypriot proposals of this kind, even though the Constitution, as set out in the Plan, did not give such rights. Astonishingly, the Secretary-General claimed that the production of the Laws by the Technical Committees showed that the settlement was not "imposed". The reality is that whatever was significant in the Laws was imposed by the UN at Turkish Cypriot and Turkish insistence. It is relevant to recollect that the very necessity for preparing these Laws in advance of the United Cyprus Republic coming into existence was due to the UN-devised legislative procedure. This required weighted majorities for enacting most federal Laws (ie support by two fifths of the sitting Senators from each constituent state) and was accompanied by an ineffective deadlock-resolving mechanism giving the Supreme Court discretion to make an interim decision. Such machinery did not ensure that Laws to enable the United Cyprus Republic to operate would be in place—something essential in view of experiences from 1961–1963, when the Turkish Cypriot members of the House of Representatives used the legislative procedure under the 1960 Constitution to prevent the passage of Laws, in particular tax Laws.[18] It is a fair comment that the UN, in "finalising"

[17] This choice of language was skilfully made in order to pick up on comments by Greek Cypriot political figures, including President Papadopoulos, as to their aim in any negotiations ie to "improve" the Plan for both sides.

[18] The Turkish Cypriot justification put forward was that the Greek Cypriot side had not under Article 173 of the 1960 Constitution passed a Law providing for separate municipalities. The Greek Cypriot side's position was that separation was practically impossible and that the requirement was subject to review 4 years after enactment, justifying refusal to proceed. Both sides negotiated and reached an agreement before Christmas 1962, but this was repudiated by the Turkish Cypriot leadership on Turkey's orders. For Turkey, the significance of municipalities was as a method of

the Laws, inserted provisions which the Turkish Cypriot side, usually at Turkey's insistence, would have demanded as conditions for passage had the measures been federal Laws actually requiring passage. For example, the changes to the 49 Laws in Attachment 11 to Annex III, namely, "Federal Laws on International Navigation, Territorial Waters and Continental Shelf," had been carefully monitored "since the preparation phase of the Plan" by the relevant Turkish Ministry, and the UN accepted the proposed Turkish changes, although Turkey was not a Party to the Law of the Sea Convention or to some of the other Conventions involved and insisted that her views on Law of the Sea matters be adopted.[19] The net effect of the manner in which the UN chose to finalise the future Federal Laws was that this subverted the purpose of yet another core bargain of the Plan. The Greek Cypriot side had agreed to accept the complex legislative procedure for passage of Laws on the basis that necessary Laws would be in place from the time of coming into operation of the UCR. They had certainly not agreed that such Laws would be dictated by Turkey, or would contain provisions of a kind which the Turkish Cypriots could dictate under the future legislative procedure, thereby making the bargain as to enactment of future Laws in considerable measure pointless—in that the bargain on the method of passage of Laws and the offsetting of this by advance enactment of Laws had been intended to prevent the Greek Cypriot side from being held to ransom, whereas the UN had now, in advance, given effect to Turkey's extortionate demands, voiced directly and also through the Turkish Cypriots.

maintaining the Turkish Cypriot Community as an entity and exercising control through it—as explained by D Markides in *Cyprus 1957–1963. From Colonial Conflict to Constitutional Crisis* (University of Minnesota, Minneapolis, 2001).

[19] Turkish Foreign Ministry statement on 21 April 2004, as reported by Ankara Anatolia news agency. The Law of the Sea was a matter on which Mr de Soto was expert, having been engaged in the negotiations for the Convention on behalf of Peru.

SELECTED SHOTS OF A BUSY COUPLE OF DAYS OF INTERNATIONAL WHEELER-DEALERING—ANNAN IV

Pro-Rauf Denktash anti-Plan anti-imperialist demonstration outside the Bürgenstock compound on 29 March 2004. Did they know that he was being "deposed" by the UN and the USA? Inside, the Greek Government Spokesman was announcing: "Half an hour ago President Bush spoke to Mr Karamanlis." He added that the Prime Minister has spoken to Mr Verheugen and that Mr Karamanlis would be meeting with Mr Erdoğan. Did the Greek Cypriot side know what was going on?

Cypriots from all sides of the political spectrum talking at Bürgenstock. The Greek Cypriot Right and Centre-right talk to two of the Turkish Cypriot "triumvirate": from left to right Mr Talat, Mr Koutsou (back to camera), Mr Cleanthous and Mr Serdar Denktash before presentation of Annan IV.

Alvaro de Soto patting Serdar Denktash's hand on 29 March immediately before presentation of Annan IV, assuring him that all will be well.

Above: the Greek Cypriot side look somewhat apprehensive. Front row from left, former President Clerides, President Papadopoulos and Mr Christofias; and second row, former President Vassiliou, Mr Cleanthous, Mr Anastasiades (obscured), and Mr Omirou, all Members of the National Council.

"Do you think we should start?" the Secretary-General seems to be asking the Head of Political Affairs just before presentation of Annan IV on 29 March 2004. Left, Greek Cypriot side; right, Turkish Cypriot side; and far right, Turkey. The Greek team is seated with their backs to the camera.

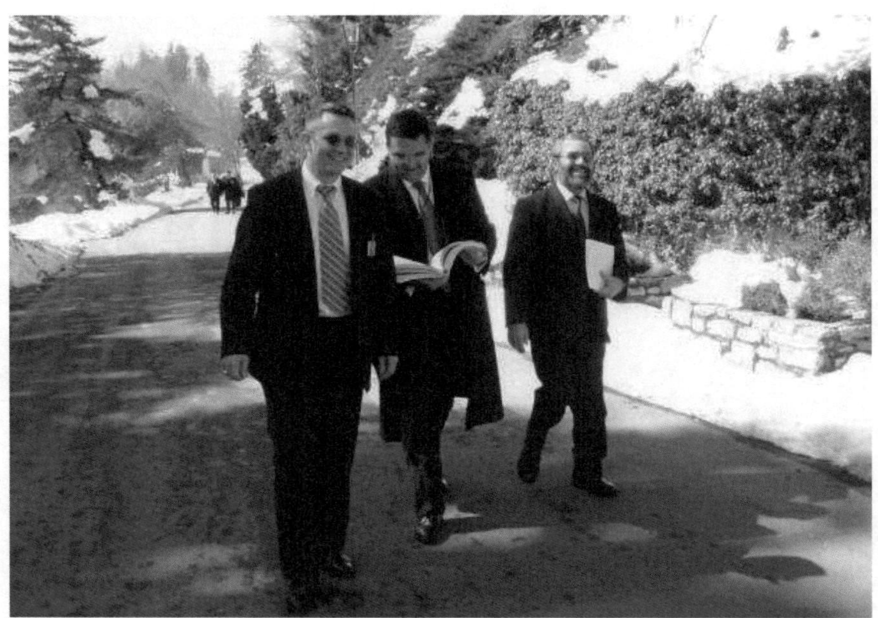

Mr Pfirter after delivering his handiwork at Bürgenstock on 29 March 2004, with Mr Demetris Stefanou, Special Adviser in the Greek team, and Ambassador Tzionis, who had just told Mr Pfirter what the referendum result would be if this was how the Plan was "finalised."

Is Alvaro de Soto explaining to the Secretary-General and Kieran Prendergast how to set off an avalanche and create a "lose-lose" situation?

Educating the press: Alvaro de Soto at Bürgenstock on 29 March 2004 at a press conference on Annan IV. He declares: "This is not a proposal. This is not a take it or leave it firm text that will go to referendum. The Secretary-General has given the participants time to examine the proposal." He then described the consultation as "a form of negotiation" with a view to making a decision on 31 March.

Later that day, US State Department Spokesman, Mr Richard Boucher, who had served as Ambassador to Cyprus between 1993 and 1996, suggests it is a "win-win" for all sides and adds: "We started to do our own work with the parties to try to gain acceptance for his [the Secretary-General's] proposals. We join the Secretary-General in urging the parties to seize this opportunity to secure better opportunities for all Cypriots." (He was later to defend State Department and USAID attempts through UNOPS to engage in "voter-education".)

Below: Alvaro de Soto apparently telling Günter Verheugen outside the lift near the Secretary-General's suite on 30 March about the importance of informing the Secretary-General that he will concede that the Agreement can become "primary law," thus over-riding fundamental principles on which the EU was founded. Leopold Maurer is behind Verheugen's back and Kristin Schreiber is in the left-hand picture.

Below: the immediately following meeting between Mr Verheugen and the Secretary-General. It will shortly be agreed that Mr Erdoğan will get his desires on derogating from the EU's fundamental principles.

Above: Messrs Talat and Serdar Denktash were also consulted by the Secretary-General on 30 March after Annan IV. Here Mr Talat is seen with the Secretary-General. According to the transcript, Mr Talat says: "Reading all those pages . . . Finding out the entanglements . . ."

XIII

"Finalisation" of Annan V by the Secretary-General and the Preceding Phoney Consultation

PHASE 3 BEGINS

THE PRESENTATION OF Annan IV on 29 March 2004 marked the start of Phase 3 of the process in which Phase the Secretary-General was to finalise the text of the Plan. He declared that he wished to do so in consultation with the parties, accordingly inviting the Greek Cypriot side and the Turkish Cypriot side to comment. It is doubtful how meaningful any consideration could be, with such brief notice being given for commenting on a massive document interspersed with new proposals. Nonetheless, on 30 March, the Greek Cypriot side provided comments on the Plan.[1] At this point it is necessary to note that undue status has been given to "Annan IV". It was just a "mock-up" or "dummy run" with a few provisional suggestions, made 2 days before the real Plan (Annan V) was to be introduced. The document enabled the UN to claim that it had sounded out the parties on possible changes to Annan III.[2]

CHANGES REGARDED AS IN PART POSITIVE BY THE GREEK CYPRIOT SIDE

In the Greek Cypriot side's view, the UN team had made limited concessions as to three significant practical points. The first of these had been in relation to the Greek Cypriot proposal to ensure proper administration, by means of UN involvement and control, of the areas to be de-occupied by Turkey. In order to facilitate the UN in this task, a partial delegation to the TCCS had even been suggested by the Greek Cypriot side. Overall UN administration and overall control had been proposed, so as to afford UN interim protection of such areas, to ensure they were not desertified and to provide some physical guarantee by way of UN presence that transfer of the territory would actually be effected on the due date

[1] These are appended as Appendix 2.

[2] In Table F there is no analysis of Annan IV, because the real comparison that must be made is between Annan III and V, ignoring the "dummy run" of Annan IV.

to the Greek Cypriot constituent state. Initially, the UN team had been inclined to reject the proposal outright, but, because of the Secretary-General's long peace-keeping experience, provision was then made in the Plan for the UN to take over such areas shortly before handover became due. However, this gave little protection against interim destruction of property or neglect of the infrastructure, and left open the contingencies that the later phases of transfer would not occur, or would be delayed by Turkish and Turkish Cypriot demands for re-negotiation of the transfers—eg due to delay in providing alternative accommodation—and for continued stationing of Turkish troops. Indeed, the Greek Cypriot side saw harbingers of such demands in Annan IV, Annex VI, Territorial Adjustments. When the UN had amended Annan III in Annan IV to provide for "enhanced UN supervision" in the last few months before the areas to be adjusted were handed over to the GCCS, the Plan was, at Turkey's insistence, revised to extend by six months the phasing of the territorial adjustments, so that Phases 4–6 would only be completed 3 ½ years after the Foundation Agreement came into force. The Greek Cypriot side also saw the simultaneous strengthening of the functions of the Relocation Board (Article 7), with targeted financial assistance, requirement for provision of public and low cost social housing and programmes for restoration of livelihoods of relocated households—especially when taken in conjunction with remarks by Mr Denktash that relocation could not be effected within the Plan's time-limits—as indicating that delays and pressures for changes to the timetable would be supported by the UN, just as it had already extended the date for territorial adjustments.

The second of the significant practical points on which the Greek Cypriot side had requested change was to ensure a reduced period of transitional government for the United Cyprus Republic, with effective federal organs to be in place from the outset. The transitional period was reduced from 30 months to what the Secretary-General considered would be a two-month period on the assumption that a Presidential Council could promptly be elected by the federal Parliament. In any event, the changes made far from satisfied the Greek Cypriot side's request, especially since some variations, particularly that giving the Turkish Cypriot side "numerical equality" in holding the office of President for the first five years after expiry of the transitional period, were now inserted. The changes provided for a Co-Presidency for a transitional two-month period in which the Co-Presidents would rotate each month as Head of State.[3] In this transitional

[3] The Secretary-General substituted a new provision in place of the long-agreed provision that the Greek Cypriot and the Turkish Cypriot "leaders" were to be the initial Co-Presidents. They were to be confirmed in office by each constituent state's legislature as soon as constituted, or the legislature was to elect another person to the office. The substituted provision provided that

> The Co-Presidents shall be persons whose *names are communicated* to the Secretary-General of the United Nations no later than two days after successful referenda or, in the absence of such communication, the *head of government* of the relevant state (emphasis added).

As indicated, prior to this provision, President Papadopoulos and Mr Rauf Denktash would have been Co-Presidents. Now there was silence as to *who* would decide and effect the communication period there was also to be an equally composed Council of Ministers and an equally composed Parliament. According to para 52 of the *Report*, this equality was

> to offset the alterations made to the transitional government to accommodate the Greek Cypriot side's concerns.

To emphasise the "equality" aspect, the Turkish Cypriot side was accorded the theological language it had long been seeking to have inserted in the Plan, namely, that

> neither side may claim authority or jurisdiction over the other.

The numerically equal composition of the federal transitional institutions departed from the long-established Security Council position on a Cyprus settlement. "Equality," according to the UN Resolutions, does not mean "numerical" equality but refers to two politically equal communities as defined by the Secretary-General in his *Report* of 8 March 1990.[4] This rejection of "numerical equality" in office-holding had been insisted upon by the Greek Cypriot side, which, representing over 80% of the Cypriot population, did not accept that "equality" meant dividing all State offices and control down the middle between the two sides. No consultation occurred with the Greek Cypriot side on these UN alterations. Nor was there any consultation about the most important Ministries in the Transitional Council of Ministers being allocated to Turkish Cypriots eg Foreign Affairs and Defence and Trade and Economy—and all this at a time when the 37,000-strong Turkish Army of occupation remained and the fledgling United Cyprus Republic had not risen to its feet.

Although the transitional period of "numerical" equality of office holding by persons hailing from each Constituent State (in effect Community) was, on the face if it, only for two months, the small print of the Plan revealed that a major

(perhaps Secretary of State Colin Powell or Mr Erdogan?). There was also deliberate exclusion of Mr Rauf Denktash in the fall-back provision, because he would not be "head of government" of the TCCS, but "head of state," while Mr Talat, under the mixed parliamentary-presidential system of the TCCS, would be "head of government". This substitution by the Secretary-General demonstrates the UN team's determination to shape Cyprus's governmental arrangements, ignoring agreements between the Cypriot sides and irrespective of the wishes of Turkish Cypriot people who had "elected" Mr Denktash by substantial majorities over the years and who would not have understood that, in this buried-away provision, he was being "deposed".

[4] A series of Resolutions from SCR 716 (1991) to SCR 1251 (1999) adopted the Secretary-General's definition in *S/21183*, Annex I, para 11. This read:

> The political equality of the two communities in and the bi-communal nature of the federation need to be acknowledged. While political equality does not mean equal numerical participation in all federal government branches and administration, it should be reflected *inter alia* in various ways: in the requirement that the federal constitution of the State of Cyprus be approved or amended with the concurrence of both communities; in the effective participation of both communities in all organs and decisions of the federal Government; in safeguards to ensure that the federal Government will not be empowered to adopt any measures against the interests of one community; and in the equality and identical powers and functions of the two federated States.

"balancing change" covering 5 years, ie the term of the first elected Presidential Council, had been inserted. Annan V, Article 41.5 of the Constitution provided that the symbolic office of President and that of Vice-President of the Presidential Council would, for the first 5 years, rotate every 10 months between two Council members, not hailing from the same constituent state and elected by the Council. Thus, each would enjoy three 10-monthly terms.[5] The President, accompanied by the Vice-President, would represent "the Presidential Council as Head of State," eg at the European Council, or the UN etc. Rotation of the Presidency had been a major concession by the Greek Cypriot side on the basis of a carefully worked out Article 27.1 of Annan III. That Article would have resulted (absent a change in Community politics) either in a 3:2 Greek Cypriot to Turkish Cypriot ratio of office-holding, or in a 4:1 ratio (on the basis of treating the Annan III Article—which is ambiguous in this respect—as applying to each 5-year Presidential Council separately). Under Annan V there was to be a 1:1 ratio, yet a further concession to Mr Denktash's and Turkey's views on numerical equality of office-holding.

A third significant aspect of the changes requested by the Greek Cypriot side had been to enlarge the size of the federal executive to facilitate its performing the many functions of a Member State inside the EU and to have continuity of representative contact with EU bodies. This was effected in the Plan by adding 3 non-voting members to the Presidential Council and by changing technical details as to how rotation of the office of President between members from the constituent states would occur. The proportional share based on rotation was retained (the Greek Cypriot side had not asked for any change here). This rotation would, according to Annan V, be between the Council President and Vice-President only. Annan V was also to provide that the President must be accompanied by the Vice-President at meetings of the European Council, a replacement for a provision that the two members of the Presidential Council responsible for European Union Affairs and External Relations, who were not to be from the same constituent state, were to attend.

Obviously, other points were also requested by the Greek Cypriot side and were accepted in Annan V, but most suggestions had not been made in Greek Cypriot interests alone: they had been advanced in the interests of all Cypriots in order to iron out potential deficiencies in the UN Plan, eg to have a federal court of primary jurisdiction in place, rather than overloading the constituent state court system with cases and appeals and only in future legislating for federal first instance jurisdiction; to provide workable fiscal and economic arrangements; and to establish a tolerable and workable property acquisition and compensation scheme. (The latter two aspects had been disgracefully deficient in the Plan proposed by the UN in Annan I, II and III.)[6]

[5] See UCR Constitution, Article 41.5 read with Articles 26.1, 27.1, and 29.1.

[6] In *S/2004/437*, paras 44 and 48 and Annex II, para 9, these "improvements largely inspired by Greek Cypriot concerns" were briefly outlined.

A SHATTERING OF GREEK CYPRIOT ILLUSIONS

Overall, the draft Plan presented on 29 March had been far worse than the Greek Cypriot side had imagined possible. The Plan (Annan IV) now provided for "bi-zonality" in the sense of creating permanent separation on an ethnic basis, and it effectively brought the whole of Cyprus into Turkey's sphere of influence.

When, responding to the Secretary-General's last minute request for comments on Annan IV, the Greek Cypriot side, without prioritising its concerns in its 30 March 2004 paper,[7] expressed its fundamental disagreement with particular draft provisions. In particular, it pointed out that, if the UN were to *change* the basis of representation in the Senate to a communal basis—something the Turkish Cypriot side had hitherto *bitterly* opposed, but which it now demanded together with Turkey[8]—and if, furthermore, there were to be further reduced caps (ceilings) on the number of Greek Cypriot refugees permitted to return, then, in lieu, more territory, with its population able to return under Greek Cypriot administration, should be allocated to the Greek Cypriot constituent state (the Karpas, Kythrea, Saint Barnabas and Salamis). It was, it should be added, still being said in the corridors that Turkey was contemplating such an adjustment, while on his US visit in late January, Mr Erdoğan had make public speeches that he would be flexible on territory "give-backs," both at a Harvard seminar and at the National Committee on American Foreign Policy. The UN had even shown certain Greek Cypriot delegates supporting the Plan a map straightening the "borders" (as desired by the Turkish military, a point repeatedly made by the Turkish Cypriot side) and providing for a large federal zone, comprising much of the areas to be adjusted, plus the Karpas, Kythrea and some other areas which the map in Annan III had envisaged would form part of the Turkish Cypriot constituent state. The impression prevailed as a result of these factors and Turkish tactics that Turkey would, in exchange for her requests, make territorial concessions when Mr Erdoğan arrived. If he had a map making territorial concessions in his briefcase, Mr Erdoğan was not compelled to open this, while the mysterious UN federal zone map evaporated.[9] Instead, Mr

[7] "Initial Reaction and Proposals for Trade-offs of the Greek Cypriot side on the United Nations Revised Plan of 29 March 2004". See Appendix 3.

[8] This "fix" as regards Senate elections, composition and voting procedures was put forward and accepted by the UN to ensure permanent ethnic control by Turkish Cypriots, even if the demographic pattern in the Turkish Cypriot constituent state were to alter. Turkish Cypriot control was to be achieved by excluding Greek Cypriots who were citizens of the Turkish Cypriot constituent state from being federal public representatives in the Senate and from electing them. The technical method of achieving this was by specifying voters' lists and representation based on whether Greek or Turkish was the voter's mother-tongue language.

[9] In para 59 of the *Report* an attempt was made to shift responsibility to the Greek Cypriot side for failure to change the territorial arrangements shown on the map attached to Annan III. Thus para 59 stated that the Greek Cypriot side did not discuss their own ideas even informally with the UN. Yet, in para 22, the *Report* admitted that the Greek Cypriot side had constantly pointed to the fact that the Turkish Cypriot side had failed to produce any territorial proposals, leaving the Greek

Erdoğan expressed concern that too many Greek Cypriots would return to the Karpas peninsula, making it effectively a Greek canton, and demanded a further restriction on returns of Karpas refugees. He achieved this restriction in Annan V on the next day. Mr Erdoğan had committed himself to the Secretary-General at Davos on 24 January "to be one step ahead in the efforts for a solution" (and also said the same thing to President Bush on 28 January). The Secretary-General's *Report* (in para 18) naïvely praised Mr Erdoğan for this. The *Report's* writers should have appreciated that this language was used in its sense of tactics to outwit his "Greek counterparts," rather than as indicating willingness to make generous offers to assist in settling the problem.

ATTITUDES AT BÜRGENSTOCK

Bringing parties together in negotiating summits is usually thought to have a positive catalytic effect. This effect did not occur at Bürgenstock. Not only are the Cypriot parties' fears and suspicions long-standing and deep-rooted, but there was a special offsetting factor. The Republic of Turkey enjoyed powerful diplomatic momentum, so that her Government was unwilling to make concessions which it did not perceive as necessary. Turkey was being and still is backed in blunderbuss fashion by the USA and in a somewhat more sophisticated and devious manner by certain European diplomats and political figures. Had there been a fly on the wall in the dining room of that luxurious resort, it would have seen and heard Western envoys and Secretariat members cultivating, flattering and trying to co-opt the Turkish and Turkish Cypriot sides and the political leadership of parties in the Republic of Cyprus thought to be pro-Plan or convertible. Particular warmth was shown by the Secretary-General to Mr Erdoğan, it being pointed out how close the UN and Turkey had become over the period of the negotiations. (Mr de Soto and some of his team had regularly shuttled to Ankara for talks with the Turkish Foreign Ministry and camaraderie, obvious to all observers, had been developed.)

The Greek Cypriot and the Hellenic Republic negotiating teams were also present, but more separate from the diplomatic intriguing and also from each other. Greece had in 1974 learned the unwisdom of dictating policies to Cyprus, although this did not preclude the giving of advice which was largely quietist,

Cypriot side in the dark. The UN was well aware that the territorial aspect, combined with the number of displaced Greek Cypriots to resettle under Greek Cypriot administration, was a constant and major concern of the Greek Cypriot side. Territory was always being brought up by the Greek Cypriot team. The UN team also knew that, in the absence of the President in Brussels, Mr D Christofias, acting as leader of the Greek Cypriot side, at three separate meetings with Mr de Soto and the representatives of two Security Council Permanent Members, had on 26 March 2004 raised the territorial issue again and the Karpas area in particular. The *Report* nonetheless stated at para 40 that "the first occasion that the Greek Cypriot side expressed interest in specified pieces of additional territory" was 30 March. This misleading paragraph was designed to excuse the UN for doing nothing to meet Greek Cypriot territorial requests.

including the advice to give priorities as desired by Mr De Soto. Earlier, she had encouraged the Greek Cypriot side to make only practical proposals within the Plan's parameters—advice which was followed.

During the Bürgenstock summit, it quickly became apparent that Turkey's insistence on her positions, and her diplomatic clout with the USA, Western Europe and the UN, would result in changes to the Plan in favour of Turkey. In contrast, only those Greek Cypriot proposals not inconsistent with Turkey's demands and her strongly held views on the "principle of bi-zonality" would be "finalised" by the Secretary-General.[10] Moreover, earlier trade-offs (most notably the permanent quota limitations on Turkish and Greek immigration to Cyprus, which had been inserted earlier to meet Greek Cypriot concerns) risked being set aside at Turkey's behest. Negotiating tactics of "talking trade-offs"—as Mr de Soto had wanted the Greek Cypriot side to do, so as allegedly to be able to give it some things it wanted—could only marginally have impacted on the prevailing political forces.[11] It is certainly true that this opportunity for a comprehensive settlement was lost. But such loss was not—as it has been characterised by the Secretariat, the USA and the UK—due to any failure of the Greek Cypriot side to negotiate at Bürgenstock, or to refusal of its leader to sign any document committing himself to a Plan imposed by the Secretary-General, or to his advice to Greek Cypriot voters to answer with "a resounding 'No'" in the referendum, or to Greek Cypriot voters' own individual decisions in large numbers to reject the Secretariat's Plan. The opportunity was lost because no negotiations were arranged by the UN at Bürgenstock and because, crucially, Turkey, with powerful Western backers, was too greedy in insisting on her strategic and territorial aims in Cyprus.[12] Meanwhile the Secretariat, tired of the frustrations of "the Cyprus game,"[13] must have been determined to end what it

[10] The Secretary-General's *Report* of 1 April 2003 had in paragraph 98 explained that Turkish and Greek Cypriot views on what "bi-zonality" meant were fundamentally different, with the Greek Cypriot side always insisting that acceptance of two units in a bi-zonal federation meant only that there would be two distinct zones administered by Turkish Cypriots and Greek Cypriots respectively. The Greek Cypriot side, during the negotiating period in Nicosia, requested that the Plan should refer to the Secretary-General's explanation where "bi-zonality" appeared in the text in order to ensure that the philosophy of *apartheid* could not be used to interpret the Plan. The UN team rejected this request—not surprisingly in light of their finalisation of the provision in the Plan reflecting the Turkish view of the scope of "bi-zonality".

[11] In para 66 of the *Report* it was suggested that the Greek Cypriot side might have been given what it wanted had it complied with the Special Adviser's negotiating wishes. This is fallacious, because the Secretariat and the two Permanent Members of the Council active in the talks process wanted Turkey to get what she desired. What the Greek Cypriot side wanted conflicted with Turkey's demands.

[12] Alternatively, she pushed for demands reflecting those aims, well-knowing that their satisfaction would certainly provoke the great majority of Greek Cypriots into voting for rejection of the Plan at the forthcoming referendum.

[13] See Brian Urquhart, *A Life in Peace and War* (London, Weidenfeld and Nicolson, 1987) 279. The frustration felt by distinguished members of the Secretariat as regards unending deadlocked talks on Cyprus is graphically expressed at pp 259–60. Sir Brian is also reported to have quoted from *Romeo and Juliet*, "a pox on both your houses," after lengthy UN attempts to assist Cypriots on the ground by means of a package of confidence-building measures had been rejected by both sides. His autobiography shows that how particular leaders and sides in a dispute are perceived becomes a

saw as interminable and fruitless procedures. As with all motives, it is difficult to prove those of the Secretariat: the persons concerned had worked so long and hard on the Plan that they may have become myopic, convinced that they were producing a "just solution"; they were certainly arrogant, believing that they could, with assistance from certain Cypriot parties, convince the people of Cyprus to approve the Plan irrespective of its "justice"; they knew that a settlement in Cyprus suited the policies of certain Permanent Members and would be a success which the UN Secretariat needed; and they had become hostile to President Papadopoulos, who stood up to Mr de Soto, who in turn became determined "to break" him. At all events, the UN Secretariat decided to exploit the discretion afforded to the Secretary-General at the 10–13 February 2004 New York meeting. The arrangements made there—even if they had to be abused to achieve this outcome—had provided the mechanism necessary to force submission of the Secretariat's package Plan to referendum without an endorsement by the leaders of the two Cyprus Communities.[14] It does not appear that human rights, international law and UN Resolutions on Cyprus were at the forefront of their concerns: a political deal with Turkey was their desire.

significant factor in the degree of sympathy they and their policies elicit from international civil servants who deal with them. Similar responses to the Cyprus situation and the two sides' leaders were manifested in Dr Waldheim's autobiography, *In the Eye of the Storm* (London, Weidenfeld and Nicolson, 1985) at 92. Dr Waldheim was often tempted to throw up his hands in frustration at failures to risk compromises and the fact that although horses can be taken to water they cannot be made to drink. Mr de Cuéllar was also frustrated and observed that surely more than perfection was needed in a negotiation to bring about agreement between the Communities.

[14] By this time the UN team did not care about meeting even the most reasonable wishes of the Greek Cypriot side. As a mechanism to resolve deadlocks, the Federal Supreme Court was to be endowed with power to take decisions if necessary. With some reluctance, the leaders of both Communities accepted, that, for a period, 3 foreign judges and a foreign registrar might be necessary to hold a balance in the Court which was otherwise equally composed of Greek Cypriot and Turkish Cypriot judges from the constituent states. The UN then consulted the sides with a list of possible candidates. The Greek Cypriot side selected from amongst these distinguished listed jurists a judge with an outstanding reputation for impartiality and great regard for human rights, but Mr Pfirter argued strongly against nominating that judge (whose name the UN had listed) and urged a different nominee. Accepting this under pressure, the Greek Cypriot side then asked—this telephone conversation occurring before the Bürgenstock meetings—that another distinguished listed jurist should fill one of the other judgeships. The UN ignored this request and then, on 30 March, put forward its own nominees, using the specious excuse that it was too late to check (by a telephone call?) whether the other persons on their own recent list were available, and explaining that the "short list," which consisted of the names they were now submitting and of which "short list" the Greek Cypriot side had not been told, had been agreed to by the other side. These crucial judicial-cum-governmental posts were meant to give both sides confidence, and not to be an occasion for imposing persons who would be suspect because of the way in which they had been appointed and concerns whether they were cronies. This arrogant imposition of the UN's nominees gave the lie to what the UN team kept professing in earlier stages of the process, namely, that it was not a "Take it or leave it exercise," but a serious process designed to reach agreement. Equally, it flatly contradicted the Secretary-General's professions on 28 February 2003 that he did not want to be seen to be imposing things on a Sovereign Member State of the UN, an assurance he gave President Papadopoulos. In *S/2004/437*, Annex II, para 11, the *Report* falsely declared that the international judges "were selected in close consultation with the parties".

The UN team had little more than cosmetic care for human rights. It had been proposed that not only religious minorities, but also the Roma minority (known as the "Gurbet" by the Turkish Cypriot Community), should enjoy similar protection to these minorities. The European Court of Human Rights in *Cyprus v Turkey*, 10 May 2001, had found evidence that individuals who were members of the Roma minority had been subjected to violations of human rights in the Turkish-occupied area.[15] When the Turkish Cypriot side objected to the proposed protection for the Roma, the UN team removed this from the Plan. The Roma would have had a Deputy in the Federal Chamber of Deputies, who would have been counted against the quota of members from the TCCS—just as the 3 Deputies from the Maronite, Latin and Armenian Communities would be counted against the GCCS: Constitution, Article 22.5. The net effect of the finalised Plan was to reduce the number of Greek Cypriot Deputies by these 3 deputies in the Chamber, while leaving the Turkish Cypriot Deputies unreduced in number.[16]

The UN team's lack of concern for human rights was also manifested in the way in which they, at the last minute at Bürgenstock, produced a Constitution for the Turkish Cypriot constituent state, modelled in large measure on "the TRNC Constitution." In many respects this TCCS Constitution was non-compliant with the European Convention on Human Rights and Fundamental Freedoms. The Turkish Cypriot side had not honoured the New York agreement to produce a Constitution consistent with the Plan by 12 March. At the last minute, the UN produced a TCCS Constitution on 27 March at Bürgenstock, giving the Greek Cypriot side a brief opportunity to comment on it. The purpose of seeing each side's Constitutions had been to reassure the two sides, who were to vote on these in the referenda, that the essential building blocks of the federation, namely, the constituent states, would be properly governed in accordance with law and human rights standards. The draft TCCS Constitution now produced had to some extent had been "cleaned up" by four UN lawyers who had received a mere re-draft of the "TRNC Constitution," which grossly

[15] The writer was involved in gathering testimony for the Commission and at the hearing. One simple and uneducated Roma woman, who, for her protection, had to give evidence anonymously, and who obtained asylum in the United Kingdom, was the most moving witness she has ever heard: in parts of the witness's sworn evidence she (like Shylock) enquired whether she too was a human being entitled to dignity and respect. The majority of the Commission and Court took the view that Roma must first have recourse to "TRNC Courts". It needs adding that in the *Case of Denizci and Others v Cyprus*, Application No 25316 of 1994, Judgment of 23 May 2001, the Court held that the Police of the Republic of Cyprus had assaulted Roma in their custody and awarded damages as just satisfaction. The UN had in Annan I and II provided for safeguarding the rights of religious "and other minorities". The "other minorities" were knocked out in Annan III, but they were put back and the Roma were explicitly given safeguards in Annan IV on 29 March 2004. The Roma and the "other minorities" together with their safeguarding disappeared again on 31 March in Annan V. However, Maronites resident in Kormakiti were given a special right by Constitution Article 11.5: they could, within Kormakiti village, freely sell and buy land like long-term Turkish Cypriot residents.

[16] The Plan had also provided for all the named minorities to be represented in constituent state legislatures: Main Article 4.3.

conflicted with human rights standards and with the Plan. Analysis by the Greek Cypriot side showed that there remained inconsistencies with the Foundation Agreement and major conflicts with the European Convention on Human Rights. Although the UN received these comments on the night of the very same day it had first exhibited the TCCS Constitution to the Greek Cypriot side, it declared the next morning at a meeting with two Greek Cypriot team members (its EU expert and the writer, which meeting was chaired by a young EU-seconded German lawyer, Mr Frank Hoffmeister) that it was now too late for any objections to be considered.[17] Mr Hoffmeister, with extraordinary effrontery, insisted "as part of the vetting process" on an unnecessary degree of editing of the Greek Cypriot side's Constitution, introducing some theoretical German federal concepts at the beginning of the Constitution, which had been prepared by the former Attorney-General of the Republic, its former Chief Justice, other judges, and several international experts in long meetings with full discussion—to some of which the writer was privy. The provisions of the GCCS Constitution were not inconsistent with the Foundation Agreement or the European Convention, which could have been the only basis for vetting. The German federal model was irrelevant. What motivated this action was the UN's desire to be able to say to the Turkish Cypriot side that the GCCS Constitution had also been re-drafted by the UN. The young Chairman also disputed the need for a comprehensive statement of Human Rights in the Constitution, especially for educational purposes, and would not accept that it should secure all the rights which were in the 1960 Constitution (suitably amended), which rights were required by the Treaty of Establishment, Article 5, to be secured so that rights were comparable to those set out in the European Convention on Human Rights and Protocol No 1. At his insistence, proven, detailed and carefully considered human right provisions were deleted from the GCCS Constitution. Subsequently Mr Pfirter had the bright idea of attaching a "Catalogue of Human Rights and Fundamental Freedoms" to the UCR Constitution as its Appendix 5, claiming (in para 49 of the Report) that this was inspired by the Greek Cypriot side's concerns. The UN probably belatedly appreciated that the European Convention on Human Rights and Fundamental Freedoms needed properly to be reflected in the Federal Constitution, rather than containing a

[17] An interesting fact about the particular young man is that it was he who had first prepared derogations from the *acquis communautaire* in a draft Protocol required to be attached to the Act of Accession and it was he who, within the UN team, sought the continued expansion of these derogations in close liaison with the EU Department of Enlargement, pushing the line that they were necessary despite their discriminatory character. As was indicated at p 110 above, he was also involved in the UN's rejection of the Treaty of Montreux as one binding the UCR on the basis of a Turkish objection that the Republic of Cyprus was not a Party—although, as a matter of international law, the Republic had succeeded to the rights and obligations under this Treaty governing the Straits, since Turkey had not within a reasonable time objected to Cyprus's succession, and as Article 8 of the Treaty of Establishment 1960 (to which Turkey was Party) provided that all international obligations, responsibilities, rights and benefits heretofore enjoyed by the UK "shall henceforth be enjoyed by the Government of the Republic of Cyprus." He had also insisted on listing Turkey–"TRNC" agreements giving Turkey jurisdiction in certain maritime and aviation matters.

mere reference to it. It may also be that they took on board the Greek Cypriot side's comments, which had explained why the Constitution of the TCCS was in many respects not in conformity with the European Convention. Such deficiencies could be overridden by inserting an equivalent in the UCR Constitution, which would then prevail. This last minute wheeze the UN team put forward as a selling point in their information for the Greek Cypriot electorate. As for the TCCS Constitution redrafted by the UN, the Turkish Cypriot side, while after Bürgenstock and the referenda demanding implementation of the economic benefits of the Plan, refused to adopt the draft TCCS Constitution, although it gave the world (including the Islamic Conference Organisation before its May 2004 meeting) the impression that this Constitution would be adopted.

It was apparent both in Nicosia and in Bürgenstock that the Secretariat believed that sufficient support from certain Greek Cypriot political leaders and an intensive information campaign would "materialise," and result in popular approval. Thus the UN team had no hesitation in "finalising" the Plan without making a serious high-level effort to organise negotiating sessions. It is not an unfair assessment to say that the UN team believed it could do just what it liked and dictate any solution it chose, irrespective of the views of the Greek Cypriot leader and his advisers.

The UN team must have been fortified by the consoling thought, had they contemplated a negative response in either of the forthcoming referenda with the settlement not being approved, that a major, if subsidiary, aim, shared by the UN, the USA and the UK, would have been achieved. That aim was to manifest to the EU that the Republic of Turkey had been cooperative and was desirous of settling the Cyprus problem, so that her continuing occupation of Cyprus should not be invoked to deny her application for a commencement date for EU membership negotiations. The final Plan was thus tailor-made for Turkey's convenience, not for settlement of the Cyprus problem. In the final analysis this drafting and "finalisation" had resulted from a political deal by certain Western Powers, the EU Commission and the Secretariat with Turkey.[18] The reference point was certainly not international law or individual justice to Cypriots.

THE "PLONKING DOWN" OF ANNAN V AND THE SECRETARY-GENERAL'S USURPATION OF AN UNFETTERED DISCRETION

On 31 March 2004, Annan V was "plonked" down. It met all Turkey's requests, especially as regards derogating from EU law by way of requesting the EU to endorse the Foundation Agreement and to accommodate its terms by adapting Cyprus's existing terms of Accession before 1 May 2004 in a way which would

[18] According to the Secretary-General's Spokesman, Mr Fred Eckhard, quoted in the Turkish newspaper *Radikal,* 11 May 2004, "the last effort of the UN . . . was meticulously worked out with the USA and the EU . . ."

result in the adaptation of "primary law" (thereby making the settlement perpetually unchallengeable, despite its discriminatory characteristics). Likewise, Annan V met Turkey's geo-strategic military and economic demands, whereas the improvements secured by the Greek Cypriot side can only accurately be described as practical changes, protecting the interests of all parties by enabling the proposed arrangements to function more effectively. Indeed, they were in the interests of the UN, because as a matter of PR as well as of common-sense, the UN Secretariat would not have wanted their vaunted settlement, assuming it to have come into force, to have collapsed within a short period, especially when a UN Mission would be in the field and calls for Security Council action would follow since the Council would remain seizable at any time.

A remarkable change in Annan V of 31 March (which has never been properly explained by the UN) was also introduced at the last minute to facilitate internal political debate in Turkey and to give her a margin of manoeuvre as regards binding herself.[19] On 29 March, in Annan IV the draft settlement had, by virtue of the prescribed conditions for bringing the Foundation Agreement into force, provided some assurance to the Greek Cypriot side that the settlement would be *signed into force* by Turkey. But, as already indicated, on 31 March even that assurance was taken away by a redraft of the "null and void" clause in Annex IX of Annan V. Only protracted complaint and a hint that a referendum could not be held without restoration of the safeguard[20] caused the UN, in the Corrigenda and Clarifications of 18 April 2004, to take action to ensure that Turkey must *sign the new Treaty into force*, or the settlement would become null and void.[21] Major incidents, particularly this one, the effective removal of the safeguard against massive long-term immigration from Turkey, and the subordination of the fundamental principles of the EU (achieved by persuading the responsible EU Commissioner into permitting a derogation on an ethno-linguistic basis and extensive discriminatory transitional arrangements to become part of EU "primary law")[22] led to mistrust of Mr de Soto's team.[23] The

[19] See *Report*, para 54, which explained that the changed mode of entry into force of the settlement had been to address Turkish concerns that the Turkish Grand National Assembly should only have had the question of approval of the settlement brought before it *after* the Turkish Cypriots had in their referendum given their verdict on the Plan.

[20] This hint was justifiable on the basis of the Secretary-General's letter to President Papadopoulos dated 31 March 2004, observing that holding of the referenda was dependent on receipt of the relevant commitments by the Guarantor Powers, and the non-provision by Turkey of the required commitment by the due date.

[21] See pp 84–5 above.

[22] In fairness it should be added that the EU Troika and also President Prodi had on their January 2004 visits to Ankara probably decided that every demand by Turkey for the adaptation of Cyprus's Act of Accession should be granted. Thus the Enlargement Commissioner, who was there with the Troika, may in reality not have needed any pushing.

[23] The *Report* asserts in para 42 D that the draft Act of Adaptation of the UCR's accession to the EU contained in the Plan and accommodating the settlement was "in line with the principles on which the EU is founded". In reality, the Draft Act, annexed to the Plan, was adapted *so as not to apply these principles, and so as to override them*, this being achieved by virtue of "adaptations" departing from these principles, which adaptations were made "primary law" of the EU.

Secretary-General, now purporting to exercise an unfettered discretion and ignoring the limitations imposed upon his competence by the New York arrangements, inserted such "improvements" as he deemed fit. "Indispensable suggestions" had been forgotten about. So had genuine "trade-offs".[24] Such conduct breached the understanding between the Cypriot parties and the Secretary-General that the "parameters" would not be altered (except by agreement). The Secretary-General had not been given a blank cheque to add, alter or omit whatever he thought fit, using a free hand and effectively usurping power to rewrite key criteria, specifications, conditions, restrictions etc to meet key concerns of either side. If anyone doubts the impropriety of the Secretary-General's action and lack of authorisation, they should ask themselves what the Turkish and Turkish Cypriot response would have been had the Secretary-General acted in this fashion to alter parameters of the plan which had been incorporated into earlier versions to meet Turkish Cypriot concerns. Turkish anger would have been uncontainable had the Secretary-General dumped the concept of constituent state citizenship; removed the restrictive quotas on Greek Cypriot displaced persons returning home; abandoned the requirements of weighted voting in the Senate and positive support by representatives hailing from the Turkish constituent state in all decision-making; insisted upon compulsory repatriation to Turkey of all settlers not married to Turkish Cypriots; removed the provisions permitting current users to acquire title to property; or required the prompt departure from Cyprus of all troops not stationed in Cyprus under the Treaty of Alliance. To have made such changes would have been outside the parameters of the Plan. That is why the Greek Cypriot-side did not make requests for them, even though it was more than dissatisfied with those provisions.

THE UN'S PRESENTATION OF THE PLAN TO THE INTERNATIONAL COMMUNITY

Mr de Soto presented a rosy picture of version V of the Annan Plan to the Security Council on 2 April 2004.[25] The Observations in the subsequent *Report*

[24] It is astonishing to read para 59 of the *Report* with its contention that, because on 29 March the Secretary-General had in Annan IV inserted a "bridging proposal" (giving the Turkish Cypriots and Turkey their demand for "community" representation in the federal Senate), this major "bridging *proposal*" should be treated as conclusive (water under the bridge!) and as not off-settable against territory. This was logic-chopping of a high order, quite contrary to the procedure envisaged, and an attempt to excuse the UN team for a failure, which, perhaps more than any factor other than the large number Turkish settlers remaining and entitled to come in after Turkey's EU entry, led to the adverse vote by Greek Cypriots in the referendum.

[25] In the vulgar language of some conflict resolution practitioners, Mr de Soto kept describing the Plan his team had produced as a "win-win" formula. Such language is more appropriate for a salesman in the marketplace, rather than being a serious analysis of the package he was ultimately able to impose through the intermediacy of the Secretary-General, cheered on by certain Western Powers.

of the Secretary-General on 28 May, drafted by the Secretariat, are of similar character. Paragraphs 43 to 57 were written to show how "balanced" the Plan was and how much it had been improved to meet Greek Cypriot and Turkish Cypriot concerns. The *Report* was also written, doubtless with the assistance of some experienced "fudgers" on the 38th, 37th and 33rd floors, to mask the Secretary-General's improper exercise of discretion, which had gone well beyond his agreed authority, since he did not have discretion to make "improvements" to address key concerns.

ANNAN V: COUNTDOWN TO A MASSIVE MISFIRING

Above: countdown at 13:53:43 on 2004:03:31. Things are not going too well for the Greek Cypriot side. President Papadopoulos with the Secretary-General and Prendergast.

Below: The UN rocket will soon be launched. It is 23:28:34 on 2004:03:31.
Here de Soto gets his long-desired "photo opportunity". Left to right: Alvaro de Soto, Special Representative of the Secretary-General on Cyprus, Serdar Denktash, Member of the Turkish Cypriot delegation, Tassos Papadopoulos, President of the Republic of Cyprus, Costas Karamanlis, Prime Minister of Greece, Secretary-General Kofi Annan, Recep Tayyip Erdogan, Prime Minister of Turkey, Günter Verheugen, Member of the European Commission, Mehmet-Ali Talat, Member of the Turkish Cypriot delegation, and Abdullah Gül, Turkey's Minister for Foreign Affairs.

OTHER IMPORTANT WORKERS AND NETWORKERS AT BÜRGENSTOCK WAITING FOR ANNAN V

Above left: Behind the scenes. Mr Verheugen's chief legal adviser, Pieter Kuijper, waiting for Annan V. Although earlier statements had been made that the Foundation Agreement could not become "primary law" overriding the fundamental principles on which the EU was founded, his boss, backed by the dignitaries contacted by Messrs Erdoğan and Gül, "sold the pass" on this issue.

Above right: Ambassador Necip Egüz of Turkey, an able Turkish diplomat and long-time head of the Human Rights section in Turkey's Foreign Ministry. The writer has a soft spot for him: he confirmed his suggestion, kindly given years ago in Geneva at the UN Sub-Commission on Human Rights, that she should inform him before visiting Turkey.

Below: Mr Satya Tripathi, Chairman of the Technical Committees, checking on 31 March 2004 the letters the Secretary-General is sending the parties upon presentation of Annan V. The need for a precautionary omission was overlooked: the letters still contained a sentence making holding of referenda dependent upon the Guarantors providing a commitment that they would sign into force the Security Treaty relating to the new state of affairs. That sentence enabled President Papadopoulos to insist on Turkey honouring her commitment, while on 15 April 2004 Turkey's President Sezer was still demanding that the Plan's key derogations must, as a test of EU sincerity, stay in effect whatever the referendum outcome.

Above: the UK delegation. Right, a low key High Commissioner, Lyn Parker, with left, Ambassador Weston talking to Dominick Chilcott, Director of the EU Department at the UK Foreign and Commonwealth Office.

Below: another snap of two leading members of the "UK delegation". Ambassador Weston is talking to the Deputy Prime Minister of Turkey, Mr Adullatif Sener, with Ambassador Klosson craning over Weston's left shoulder. (Ambassador Mavroyiannis of Cyprus anxiously waits behind Ambassador Weston's right shoulder.)

Above: A UN worker and a networker relaxed after their labours—Lisa Jones with Mr Weston, enjoying a chat.

The Greek Cypriot side's press educators: workers who communicate the things that count. From right: Dr Chrysostomides (Golden Mouth in translation) and Marios Karoyian—the Government Spokesman and the Presidential Spokesman respectively.

Those who made things functional—rather than the personages. The Greek Cypriot production line at Bürgenstock oiling themselves and waiting. From left to right: Panikos Koumnas (organiser), Andreas Hadjiraftis (territorial statistics and mapping), the writer, Maria Aloupa, Maria Papanicolaou and Anastasia Constantouris (word processing experts).

"[R]efusing [at Bürgenstock] to shake Talat's hand and declining any direct contact with the Turkish government," David Hannay, *Cyprus, the Search for a Solution*, p 243. This Orwellian "diplomatic-speak" about diplomatic manoeuvring will mislead non-diplomats. Some corrective photographs appear as pictures in the coloured central section. Here are some more:

People who had no direct contact on 31 March 2002 at Bürgenstock. Watched by the Secretary-General, President Papadopoulos is laughing at Erdoğan's translated comments in the jovial group. Mr Talat is back to camera.

As the camera moves, Serdar Denktash can be seen laughing too, but the Secretary-General appears embarrassed. Is he thinking "They should have been given time to negotiate, instead of de Soto rushing to finalise things"?

Serdar Denktash and Papadopoulos continue their conversation, while the latter wonders what's delaying things. Prime Minister Karamanlis (background) must surely be thinking about his helicopter being kept waiting, while the Secretary-General looks depressed.

The Secretary-General turns to his agent responsible for the situation.

Serdar Denktash and Tassos Papadopoulos are still engaging in friendly conversation, while de Soto is telling Annan: "The deed is done" ie the documents are ready for presentation. A nearby journalist heard this Shakespeare lover utter Macbeth's damning words.

Messrs de Soto and Annan. While the Cypriots talk, these gentlemen know what they are going to do to them. Soon, all will be seated for presentation of Annan V.

AN INTERESTING JUXTAPOSITION AND DUPLICATION

Koumparoi at Bürgenstock on 31 March 2004: left to right, Prime Minister Erdoğan and Prime Minister Karamanlis with (back to camera) Turkey's Foreign Minister Gül. This was at the Park Hotel. Remember the Dolder Hotel and two other *koumparoi*?

Seated now and a last word by the Secretary-General before presenting Annan V. A satisfied Frank Hoffmeister is sitting behind the Secretary-General and above his station.

Messrs Verheugen and Maurer snapped with Ms Kristin Schreiber as they listened, with straight faces, on 31 March 2004 at the very moment the Secretary-General was saying: "Cyprus will be a full member of the EU, based upon the rule of law, democracy and respect for human rights."

Left: the conductor of the UN orchestra and Head of the UN Department of Political Affairs, Sir Kieran Prendergast, shakes hands with Prime Minister Erdoğan on 31 March 2004 after presentation of Annan V. Mr Erdoğan has been given all 11 of Mr Ziyal's requested Final Points, including making the agreement EU "primary law," after having said on leaving Ankara for Bürgenstock that, if this issue were not solved, settlement would be "left to another spring" and, before that, having telephonically conversed with President Bush, President Prodi, Prime Minister Ahern, Chancellor Schroeder and President Chirac, while Prime Minister Blair had sent the UK Ambassador with a friendly and heart-warming message to speed Mr Erdoğan off at Essenboga Airport. Right: meanwhile, the Secretary-General has advanced to shake hands with the US- and UN-anointed new leader of the Turkish Cypriot side, a satisfied Mr Talat.

Alvaro de Soto on 31 March 2004, announcing Annan V. (This time the CyBC transmitted his full press conference.) Mr de Soto held up the map in the Plan. Then, answering a question about a possible "no" in the referenda, he observed: "The people are sovereign. *That means they don't want to come to terms* and if they don't want to come to terms on a basis which most of the world, the Security Council, the EU considers to be reasonable, then what can we do? We can't impose it." (This is evidence that he meant what he repeated in late April and May 2004, about Greek Cypriots not wanting a solution.)

Below: a happy Mr Erdoğan starts his press conference after Annan V. The clock had been stopped, so he was talking in the early hours of 1 April 2004.

The transcript reveals Turkey's Prime Minister saying: "The Turkish side always say that they are in favour of a just and fair peace in Cyprus." [At this point the microphone could take no more. It literally fell apart . . .]

When the microphone was fixed, Prime Minister Erdoğan continued: "And all our actions have been developed in accordance with these statements. . . We always say that there were two different nations and two separate democracies in Cyprus and that as constituent states they would be establishing a mutual new State. We were determined in ensuring the guarantorship right of Turkey and we ensured that . . . the two sides . . . have conducted very effortsome and detailed negotiations . . . As a result, the Secretary-General of the UN has made fourth revisions on this plan, based on the negotiations and mutual decisions to permit the peoples both to decide. . . Of course many important personalities of international policy-making of the world have contributed immensely to this stage. Therefore I would thank Heads of Government and Prime Ministers of all those countries who have contributed their assistance to this process." He particularly mentioned, *inter alia*, his long discussions at Bürgenstock with the Prime Minister of Greece, Mr Costas Karamanlis. Talking of what Turkey had achieved in the Plan as regards policies developed "after consulting all Turkey's institutions" (he had been asked if he had consulted the Army) Mr Erdoğan said:

1) the Agreement would be primary law of the EU;

2) the policy of bi-zonality was applied;

3) the Turkish Cypriots and State were adequately protected;

4) the national integrity of the Turkish Cypriot Community was to be protected;

5) the presence of the Turkish military on the Island would continue, even after Turkey became a full member of the EU;

6) there was strengthening of security and guarantees;

7) the prosperity and economic development of Turkish Cypriots was ensured;

8) those individuals based on the motherland, but living on the island – their rights would be protected. [These 8 points précis Mr Ziyal's 11 Final Points.]

The Prime Minister explained that his approach had not been based on "give and take". The approach was that "historical problems of the past, remain in the past and the people of the United Cyprus Republic live in peace together". He believed the parties had reached a mutual understanding on the basis established by the UN Secretary-General, which would help deepen the important relationship with Greece and ensure peace in the southern Mediterranean area. "A new road map for Cyprus has been drawn in Bürgenstock."

Because his "dear friend Costas" was "waiting for his helicopter" but wanted to say a few brief words before departing the scene, the Turkish Prime Minister cut short the questioning. But before stopping he had to say why he did not thank Mr Rauf Denktash. Mr Erdoğan responded: "He is owner of the family, the father of the family. We have a special place for him in our hearts. He is landlord. I don't want to keep Costas," and he rushed from the podium, arms outstretched, calling "Costas".

Apparently, even at about 1 o'clock in the morning, it was impossible to keep his helicopter waiting, so "my dear friend Costas" had a few brief words before also rushing off.

Mr de Soto (at the 4940th meeting of the Security Council on 2 April 2004, after an invitation to address the Council under Rule 39 of the Provisional Rules of Procedure), stumbling through the libretto by the Australian duo, Dann and Jones, who accompanied him to this briefing on the Plan, with composer Dann giving him an extra sheet to sing, commending the efforts of leaders and "the strong support of Greece and Turkey". At the end, Special Assistant Dann followed this up with further advice to the songster.

Q.29–31

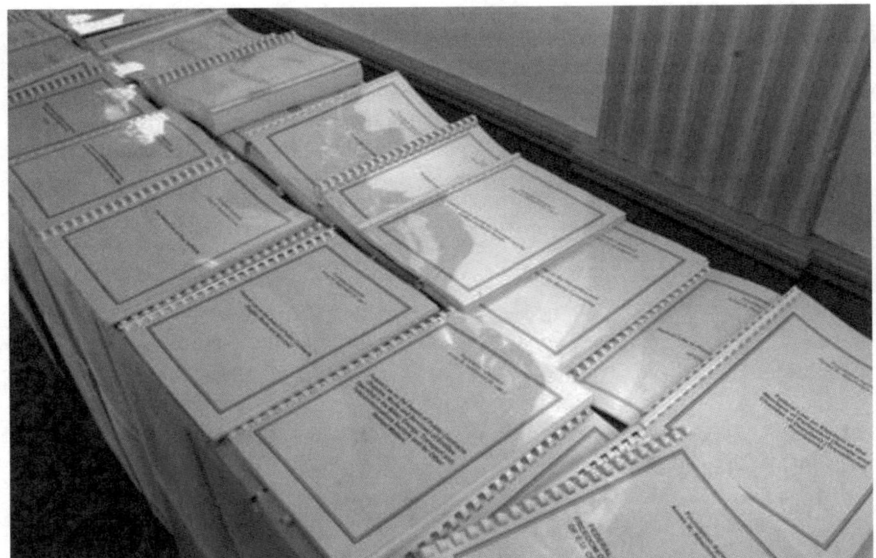

Parts of the 9,000 plus pages of the Plan, photographed at Bürgenstock (above) and in Nicosia (below). (Revisions kept coming until two days before the referenda.) Mr de Soto told the Cyprus public on 4 April 2004, arriving back after reporting to the Security Council on the 2nd: "The product is on the table." Above all, he appealed to the people to *read the Plan.*

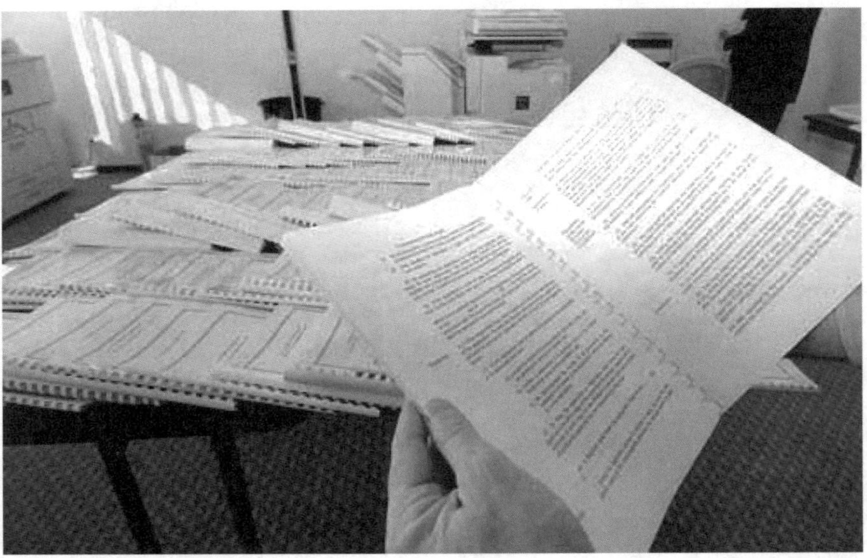

XIV

The Greek Cypriot Side's Analysis of the Real Effects of the Plan

AN EXAMINATION OF the "significantly improved" Plan as regards "functionality of the federal government" (para 44 and Annex II, describing the work of the Technical Committees) shows that the Greek Cypriot concern for functionality covered all areas of operation of the United Cyprus Republic in its proposals: *inter alia* those regarding federal legislation and its practical application; the Central Bank; fiscal and monetary policy; curtailing of the various transitional periods; the ensuring of conformity with EU obligations; the administrative structure and functions of the federal government; the decision-making process at all levels; the territorial aspect; and the issue of the missing persons.[1] The Greek Cypriot side's suggestions, viewed as an integral whole, had the objective of achieving the "functionality and workability" of the solution, thus ensuring its viability and smooth operation.[2] Those objectives (functionality and workability) could not automatically result from adopting a few elements of the Greek Cypriot proposals while simultaneously meeting the new Turkish Cypriot demands, which had nothing to do with functionality. The implication in para 44 of the *Report* that the "functionality and workability" requirement had been seriously addressed by the limited changes made is therefore incorrect. As already indicated, the changes regarding the federal executive in primarily federal jurisdictional matters were inadequate to deal with all problems, while the transitional arrangements still gave rise to much concern, as did the EU arrangements. Indeed, the Greek Cypriot side did not

[1] It must be emphasised that all the Greek Cypriot side's suggestions concerning functionality not only remained within the parameters of the Plan, but were designed not in any way adversely to affect the rights afforded by the Plan to Turkish Cypriots.

[2] "Functionality," "workability" and "viability" have over the years almost become slogans in Cyprus in relation to the character of the settlement sought. What is meant, even if the usage is etymologically incorrect, is that any arrangements should provide for offices, duties and functions which are appropriate. In other words, they should be suitable for the purpose for which the institution is required. By "workability" is meant working/operating/smoothly-running institutional arrangements for relevant governmental machinery, for example, the structure and procedures for decision-making and rules ensuring conformity with EU obligations. By "viability" is meant that institutional arrangements would continue to operate effectively even in times of political difficulty and that there would not be crises and defaults (especially financial ones).

believe that the Plan and its cooperation arrangements would have ensured that Cyprus could effectively operate within the EU as a Member State. Moreover, it retained serious doubts as to whether the Final Plan was compatible with the *acquis communautaire*. The European Commission, other than the Enlargement Commissioner and his team, had *not* thoroughly examined the final Plan—having earlier examined Annan I and II, but not the considerably altered subsequent versions of Annan III, IV and V in any degree of detail. Indeed Annan V was a last minute *fait accomplis*, taken on trust by the international community.

It should be recollected that emphasis on "functionality and workability" by the Greek Cypriot side has been a constant: they have been the major criteria of the Greek Cypriot side ever since negotiations on a federation began early in 1976 after Turkey's invasion. It needs to be appreciated that, when there has been a long background of disputes and suspicion, continued operability of the governmental system is essential. Without it, any new arrangements will collapse as they did under the 1960 Constitution, but in a much more serious fashion.

CONCERNS ABOUT GUARANTEES FOR IMPLEMENTATION OF TURKEY'S OBLIGATIONS

The Greek Cypriot side's grave concern about failure of the UN to "finalise" adequate provisions for implementation is best reflected in a letter by President Papadopoulos to the Secretary-General following publication of his 28 May *Report*. Paragraph 46 of the *Report* had described the limited additional assurances the Secretary-General had proposed to the Security Council. These had not addressed the Greek Cypriot side's request that the UN be involved *throughout the period* preceding transfer of the territory due to be readjusted, so as to secure the return of such territory *in good order*. Since all UN administration was merely to be for the future, until such time as this actually became operative, there could be delay, refusal to hand over territory due for return and refusal of withdrawal of Turkish troops. Of course, the decision as to the scope of the assurances was taken by the Secretariat in consultation with the US and the UK, who were the sponsors of Resolutions on Cyprus, but the outcome was failure by the Secretary-General to request a more effective Security Council mandate.

The President's letter of 7 June 2004, partly repeating points more fully made in the Greek Cypriot paper on security of 8 March 2004, showed how strongly the Greek Cypriot side felt about this failure:

> Acceptance and implementation of the Plan would have had profound consequences. Given that all parts of the Plan constituted an integral whole and were of equal importance, it was imperative that before embarking on its implementation all the proper iron cast guarantees should have been in place that each and every party concerned would comply with all of its obligations arising therefrom.

Regrettably, contrary to the Secretary-General's aims in formulating the Plan, the arrangements for implementing territorial adjustments under Annan V would have resulted in a "win-great risk of losing" situation and not in a "win-win" situation, as intended by the Secretary-General. The arrangements, as envisaged under Annan V, would have given the Turkish Cypriots real and considerable benefits governmentally, politically, internationally, economically, security-wise etc, from the very first day of the Foundation Agreement coming into operation. In contrast, the two benefits for Greek Cypriots, namely territorial adjustments and reductions in the size of the Turkish Army in Cyprus, would not begin immediately, and would have taken a number of years to be phased in.

In this way, the implementation of the Plan, especially those provisions of crucial interest to the GCs, would have been contingent . . . [on] Turkey's good will, which, for the last 30 years at least is far from forthcoming even in embryonic form. When for the last thirty years, due [to] lack of good will on the part of the Turkish side, no progress whatsoever has been achieved in relatively simple issues of [a] profound humanitarian nature such as the investigation of the fate of the missing persons, it would be very imprudent to rely on Turkey's good will for the full, prompt and proper implementation of a Plan purporting to provide a comprehensive solution to the Cyprus problem.

More importantly, the present Turkish Government, despite its efforts to present an image of a country ready to cooperate and respect the norms of international law, continues its unjustified hostile policy against Cyprus. Using its right of veto, Turkey continues to hinder the accession of Cyprus to a number of technical international organizations, amongst which [is] the OECD. The commercial fleet of Cyprus, a Member-State of the European Union, is still denied the right to approach any Turkish ports. The most recent and illustrative action of this deliberate Turkish policy was the extension of its customs union agreement to nine of the ten new members of the European Union, the tenth being Cyprus which was unreasonably excluded at the very moment when Turkey aspires to future membership in the EU.

Under these circumstances, one must logically wonder how much trust and confidence the Greek Cypriots can place on vague promises, in the absence of concrete and ironclad guarantees, that Turkey will fulfill all its commitments under the Plan. Experience has unfortunately been pointing . . . [in] the opposite direction, since no signs by Turkey of an ending of its hostile acts against Cyprus are witnessed.

CONCERN ABOUT TURKEY'S CLAIM TO A UNILATERAL RIGHT OF MILITARY INTERVENTION IN CYPRUS

Another matter of the greatest concern to the Greek Cypriot side was Turkey's claim to a unilateral right of military intervention in Cyprus under Article IV of the Treaty of Guarantee 1960. The Government of the Republic has consistently maintained, ever since Cyprus became independent in 1960, that Article IV did not confer a right of military intervention, whether by any of the Guarantor Powers unilaterally, or whether by way of collective military action on their part.[3] In contrast, the Government of Turkey has always maintained that the Treaty conferred rights of unilateral military intervention and actively invoked these "rights" in 1963, 1964 and 1967 and from 1974 with continuous effect, stationing up to 40,000 troops in Cyprus from the time of her 20 July 1974 "intervention" to the present day. Because the Republic of Turkey has not accepted the compulsory jurisdiction of the International Court of Justice, the Republic of Cyprus has been unable to litigate the lawfulness of Turkey's interventions in Cyprus. The Foreign Minister of the Republic has challenged Turkey to accept the Court's jurisdiction by agreeing to a submission. Indeed, in 1992, during the discussions on the UN Set of Ideas, then President Vassiliou suggested that the scope of rights of intervention by the Guarantor Powers should be determined by way of an Advisory Opinion requested by the appropriate UN organ.[4] Neither suggestion was acceptable to the Republic of Turkey. In view of repeated Security Council Resolutions calling upon both sides to take no action exacerbating the situation, the Republic of Cyprus has hitherto refrained from denouncing the Treaty of Guarantee, the Treaty of Alliance and the Treaty of Establishment, although it has reserved its rights either to terminate or denounce the Treaties, whether as null and void *ab initio*, or because of their essential breach by unlawful military interventions, or by failure to honour the obligations of guarantee and the mutual defence obligations which are inextricably interlinked in this basket of Treaties. As the Secretary-General's recent *Reports*[5] note, during the 2002 negotiations the Greek Cypriot side, had, without prejudice, agreed to discuss the continuance in force of the relevant Treaties and their modification by Additional Protocols. It was willing even to extend the scope of the Treaty of Guarantee to cover the Constitutions of the "component states" (later "constituent states") so as to provide reassurance to the Turkish Cypriot side that diplomatic intervention and other non-military lawful forms of intervention were permissible. This was an enormous extension of the scope of application of the 1960 guarantee, granting an upholding competence to the Guarantor Powers in respect of all spheres of government, including governmental arrangements under the Greek Cypriot constituent state's Constitution.[6]

Despite its willingness to discuss the Treaties continuing in force, the Greek Cypriot side remained concerned about the right of unilateral military intervention asserted to exist by the Republic of Turkey. For this reason, it had in June 2000 obtained an Opinion from leading international lawyers that there was no right of military intervention by the Guarantor Powers either individually or

[3] The Greek Cypriot delegations in the earlier talks in 1959 and 1960 finalising the Cyprus Treaties and the 1960 Constitution, which incorporates the Treaty of Guarantee, took the same view.

[4] *S/24830*, 19 November 1992, para 32. President Vassiliou also suggested that any other basic legal issues should be subject to an *Advisory Opinion*.

[5] See *S/2004/37*, para 61, and *S/2003/398*, para 120.

[6] The suggestion for this extension was made by President Clerides in the security discussions. He genuinely wished to put Turkish Cypriot concerns at rest, but such generosity was not reciprocated. Since Mr Denktash ultimately rejected the security package then under discussion, President Clerides' concessionary offer fell away. However, the UN held the Greek Cypriot side to it from Annan I onwards.

collectively.[7] Because access to the International Court of Justice was not possible unless Turkey agreed to submit to the jurisdiction, and it was desirable to obtain further confirmation of the unlawfulness of unilateral military intervention by one of the Guarantor Powers, the Government of Cyprus held a Consultation of independent jurists of international renown at The Hague in December 2000. The outcome was an Opinion, "The Treaty of Guarantee and the Legality of the Use of Force in Cyprus," dated 14 December 2000.[8] Having obtained this re-assurance as to the illegality of any unilateral intervention, the Greek Cypriot side did not, in the security discussions in Nicosia in May–June 2002, seek to clarify Article IV of the Treaty of Guarantee.

In para 61 of the Secretary-General's 28 May 2004 *Report,* the Secretary-General put forward the facts that the Greek Cypriot side had not proposed changes to the Treaty and that there were understandings reached in 2002 as justification for the Plan not being changed to reflect international law.[9]

Apart from the fact that there was no discussion of Article IV and its scope and no agreement in Nicosia in 2002 on this, another point needs making in relation to the Secretary-General's reliance on what he claimed to be an understanding in the internal Cyprus meetings in May–June 2002. The Treaties concerned four States. It had been agreed that Greece and Turkey were to discuss security, and this would certainly have led to discussion of Article IV. Turkey, for a lengthy period, did not co-operate in holding such talks and then would not engage in serious discussions either in 2002 or 2003 (*S/2003/398,* para 50).

[7] Opinion, "Article IV of the Treaty of Guarantee and the legality of the use of Force," by James Crawford SC and Christopher Greenwood QC, dated 25 June 2000. Intervention was only possible pursuant to authority under the UN Charter. The Opinion confirmed the views of Professor Hans Kelsen in an Opinion given to the UN in May 1959.

[8] The independent jurists signatory to the opinion were: George Abi-Saab, Dieter Blumenwitz, Antonio Cassese, Jean-Pierre Cot, James Crawford, John Dugard, Pierre-Marie Dupuy, Lori Fisler-Damrosch, Cees Flintermans, Thomas M Franck, Christopher Greenwood, Gerhard Hafner, Vaughan Lowe, Donald M McRae, Alain Pellet, Joel Rideau, Henry G Schermers, Bruno Simma and Christian Tomuschat. In addition, four further leading international lawyers, one a member of the International Law Commission and one a former member, were present and agreed with the Opinion, but, at Cyprus's request, were not party to it because they had been Counsel to Cyprus in proceedings against the Republic of Turkey or had regularly advised the Republic of Cyprus.

[9] The *Report* of 28 May 2004 relies on para 120 of the 1 April 2003 *Report* to claim that there was agreement to no change being made. But that paragraph made no such statement. It is unwise to make assertions allegedly supported by references which, when checked—as in this case—falsify the particular assertion. The writer has checked all minutes of the talks to confirm that the issue was not discussed in meetings between the two sides. An alternative explanation for the Secretary-General believing that there was an undertaking that military intervention under the Treaty of Guarantee would not be raised could be that Mr de Soto or one of his team in an off-the-record conversation persuaded President Clerides and his team not to do so. Assuming that to be the case, once the Turkish Cypriot side raised the right of military intervention on 8 March 2004 in Nicosia, any understanding or agreement about not raising the issue fell away. In any event, the Greek Cypriot side now had another leader, who was fully entitled to raise the issue, and, since no overall package had been agreed, all matters were re-openable. The *Report's* explanation was merely an attempt to cover up UN pusillanimity on this issue. Perhaps relevant is the further fact that the US State Department, to the knowledge of the Secretary-General, takes the view that military intervention under Treaties is lawful—this being particularly relevant to the Panama Canal—and that collective intervention is also permissible in circumstances over and above those specified in the Charter.

The result was that the alternative avenue for clarifying the scope of Article IV through Greece as Co-Guarantor Power, so that it was consistent with international law, could not at that time be used.

Subsequently, when the negotiations between the two Cypriot sides resumed in Nicosia in February 2004, the Turkish Cypriot side, in its position papers, expressed the view that the Treaty of Guarantee empowered military intervention. Accordingly, on 8 March 2004 in its "Talking Points" on "Security—Ratification of the Treaty related to the coming into effect of the Foundation Agreement," the Greek Cypriot side rejected the Turkish Cypriot side's view on military intervention and insisted in response that the Treaty did not empower any such intervention.

Soon thereafter, in the first serious security talks in which Turkey was willing to engage with Greece, the unlawfulness of military intervention was raised by Greece. In response, Turkey insisted that she was empowered to intervene militarily and unilaterally.

Aware of Turkey's insistence on a right of unilateral military intervention when she talked to Greece, the Greek Cypriot side at Bürgenstock on 30 March again asked the UN to ensure clarification that the Treaty did not empower this. It had by now become apparent, as the package was finally being put together, that the principle that "nothing was agreed until everything was agreed" needed to be invoked on this important issue. The principle is basic to all international negotiations and Mr Denktash had himself invoked it as regards security in order to abandon what he had proposed in May 2002. As explained above, the Additional Protocol to the Treaty of Guarantee would greatly have expanded the scope of the powers of intervention of the Guarantor Powers. In light of the Turkish attitude, the Greek Cypriot side therefore took this opportunity to object on 30 March to expansion of the Treaty of Guarantee. The Secretary-General in response declined to modify either aspect of his Plan, expanding the scope of the Treaty of Guarantee, and failing to clarify rights of the Guarantors thereunder. At first intending on 30 March to insert a clarification concerning unilateral military intervention, the Secretary-General, under pressure by Mr Erdoğan, dropped his proposal. He explained (in his *Report* para 61) that his refusal to clarify the situation regarding unilateral military intervention was because of absence of agreement to change the Plan. The *Report* was written so as to convey the impression that the matter had been agreed in 2002 and constituted a binding agreement that the Treaty of Guarantee would not be clarified. As pointed out, no such agreement was made in the talks. If, nonetheless, there really was an agreement, it is passing strange that the Secretary-General, while unwilling to modify this particular "understanding" was willing at the very same time to alter other crucial agreed provisions at Turkey's insistence.

Following the Bürgenstock meeting, the Government of Turkey circulated to the Turkish General National Assembly a paper asserting that the Plan gave Turkey "the right of intervention" either alone or together with the UK and Greece. Since clarifications were still being finalised by the UN Secretariat, the

Greek Cypriot side, on 15 April 2004, demanded that the matter, which involved a *jus cogens* rule of international law, must now be clarified. It submitted to the UN the Opinion by the 19 independent jurists on the unlawfulness of unilateral intervention under the Treaty of Guarantee. The Secretariat, however, evaded the issue by referring—as in did it the Report—to a political factor, Cyprus's EU membership, as creating a "different context" from earlier years, conveniently remaining blind and deaf to the fact that Turkey was still intervening in Cyprus, being in military occupation of 36.4% of the Republic of Cyprus. Even if the argument can be mounted that the Greek Cypriot side was estopped by its 2002 silence from raising this issue, such an estoppel did not apply to Greece's proposed clarifications—made at the proper time and on the first opportunity to raise the issue, as well as at a time when Turkey was publicly claiming a right of military intervention. UN pusillanimity about this issue of military intervention was sought to be masked by another of Mr Pfirter's bright ideas: when the Plan was finalised, he proudly claimed as his handiwork an addition in the preamble to the Treaty on the New State of Affairs (bringing the settlement into force and the Additional Protocols to the security Treaties). His contribution, in lieu of clarification, was to insert the preambular clause

> Committed to international law and the principles of the United Nations Charter.

But this insertion added nothing in law or in fact. All UN Member States are *ipso facto* so committed. It was merely a device to try to escape tackling the issue. That the Secretariat of the Organization committed to the Purposes and Principles of the UN Charter should have substituted evasive for real action was an abdication of its responsibilities.

However, the Government of Cyprus did not drop the matter even after the Secretariat, pressed again by Cyprus and presented with the jurists' *Opinion*, had declined to insert a clarification as to the unlawfulness of military intervention, failing to deal with the question when, on 18 April 2004, it completed its last "finalisation" of the Plan. Cyprus then took a further step, seeking, in representations to Members of the Security Council, that there should be a strong Resolution under Chapter VII of the Charter, which should incorporate a triggering-off mechanism for intervention.[10] Cyprus's representations

[10] On 20 April 2004 a letter and accompanying Memorandum was sent to the Permanent Representatives of States members of the Council. Commencing the letter with yet another objection to adopting a Resolution prior to the referenda (which could affect the outcome), Cyprus *inter alia* asked for the UN Settlement Implementation Mission in Cyprus (UNSIMIC) to be established under Chapter VII of the Charter; for the Security Council Committee due to be established to have power to monitor the implementation of the Foundation Agreement and to take measures in the event of non-compliance; for the Secretary-General to submit 3–6 -monthly reports linked to the phases of implementation; for the Council to remain seized of the situation with a view to full implementation of the Comprehensive Settlement; for an implementation mechanism for Article IV of the Treaty of Guarantee, which would refer to Article 2(4) of the Charter, combined with a provision that Guarantor Powers would take no action without prior authorisation of the Council; to strengthen UNSIMIC's mandate regarding return of territory; and to add that the adjustment of Turkish and Greek forces was with the objective of total withdrawal.

were unsuccessful because certain Permanent Members supported the Republic of Turkey's opposition to such a procedure.

A further excuse for not effecting a change was given by the Secretariat at para 61, which claimed that by 2004 the context was:

> totally different . . . from the 1960s and 1970s, namely, the full membership of the United Cyprus Republic in the European Union.

In effect, the Secretary-General claimed to have decided that his Plan should not state the law laid down by the Charter, because, on the present facts, he was of the opinion that such law was irrelevant. This was a strange conclusion: Turkey was and is still intervening in the Republic of Cyprus, currently remaining in military occupation of 36.4% of its territory and stationing there over 37,000 troops from the Turkish Mainland Army. Those numbers have been and are increased from time to time to about 40,000, as they were earlier in 2004. To this day, the Turkish Army Commander controls the occupied area through the presence of the Turkish Army and through his overall command of both the "Turkish Cypriot Police" and the "Turkish Cypriot Security Forces" (civilian control being suspended by "Transitional Article 10 of the "TRNC Constitution"), as well as through his participation, together with the Ambassador of Turkey and the Turkish-appointed Commander of the "Turkish Cypriot Security Forces", in the Committee which meets each week with the "President," Mr Rauf Denktash, and the "Prime Minister," Mr Talat, to direct executive decisions of the "Turkish Republic of Northern Cyprus". This Turkish occupation and control has continued even since the Republic of Cyprus became a full Member State of the EU. On this basis it may be enquired of the Secretary-General: "What is different from 1974?" Doubtless the USA's comment would be that the presence of Turkish troops in northern Cyprus is now merely "technically" an "occupation".[11]

It needs emphasising that the Republic of Cyprus's attitude in insisting on clarification as to the unlawfulness of unilateral military intervention was not mere legalism or an insistence on its ideological positions: there remain real threats to Cyprus from Turkey. As President Papadopoulos pointed out to the Secretary-General following the latter's 28 May 2004 *Report* and his view expressed in para 61:

> We share the view that membership in the European Union adds to the general feeling of security and we hope that Turkey's European aspirations will lead her to display more respect for international law norms and the implementation of UN resolutions. However, it remains an uncontested fact that we still have serious security concerns as a result of the presence of Turkish occupation troops and Turkish overall behavior. Recent illustrations of the latter are the Resolutions relating to Strovilia, that required the withdrawal of Turkey's occupation troops a few meters away, that had not been complied with. Even more disturbing and insulting, for the United Nations itself, is the unheeded call by the Security Council for Turkey to lift the restrictions imposed on UNFICYP.

[11] Compare Atlantic Council, Policy Paper, August 2004, pp 14–15.

When regard was had to the expanded rights of Turkey as Guarantor Power, to the permanent stationing of Turkish military forces in Cyprus, to Turkey's view as to the extent of her rights of intervention, and to her objection to creating a triggering-off mechanism under Chapter VII of the Charter to ensure Security Council supervision of the alleged right of military intervention, President Papadopoulos could only respond to the equivocations in the *Report* on the unilateral military intervention question that

> this issue has been of paramount gravity for our side
> (Letter of President Papadopoulos to the Secretary-General, 7 June 2004, p 2).

THE PERMANENT STATIONING OF TURKISH TROOPS IN CYPRUS

Paragraph 47 of the Report was equally misleading in indicating that the Greek Cypriot side's concerns about significantly reducing troop levels under the Treaty of Alliance had been met. The original Additional Protocol No 1 to the Treaty, as agreed in 1960, had provided for 650 Turkish and 950 Greek troops. The Plan now brought these up to 6,000 for each of the two Alliance Powers, Turkey and Greece. That greatly increased number of Turkish troops was to be kept in Cyprus until 1 January 2011, after which time 3,000 Turkish troops were to remain until either Turkey's accession to the EU or 1 January 2018, whichever was the sooner. Thereafter, the Turkish and Greek Contingents provided for by the Treaty of Alliance would remain, ie 650 Turkish troops and 950 Greek troops. The UN asserted in the *Report* (para 55) that the reduced number of troops to be stationed in Cyprus between 2011 and 2018 had been an "improvement," finalised *in exchange* for permanent stationing of 650 troops. This was not an "improvement" Greek Cypriots desired. In effect 650 troops constitute a permanent bridgehead, and the Turkish Contingent of that very size had been used as such in late 1963 and again in 1974. The *Report* (at para 47) claimed that this would be "a symbolic presence," and that there was merely to be stationing of "symbolic force levels" (at para 55). Such symbolism was a derogation from the UCR's sovereignty and a vital psychological factor in determining the Greek Cypriot public's perception of the Plan. The failure of the Plan's authors to appreciate the depth of Greek Cypriot feeling is illustrated by para 47 of the *Report*, which indicated that this symbolic presence, even after Turkey's EU membership, was in order to meet Turkish Cypriot concerns. As indicated above, the paragraph had added that this was in exchange for reducing the number of 6,000 troops envisaged by Annan III on which the parties were negotiating. However, the Greek Cypriot side had not agreed to contingents of 6,000 troops for each of Greece[12] and Turkey, and no Greek Cypriot (even those who

[12] Greece will be unhappy to have to incur the considerable expense of keeping 6,000 troops in Cyprus to balance the Turkish contingent. If she does not station such an "equalising" contingent, Greek Cypriots, who will have been disarmed under other Plan provisions, will be greatly concerned by the imbalance in Turkish troop numbers.

voted "YES") could see the provision for stationing of 650 Turkish troops after 2018 or Turkey's EU entry as other than according Turkey a permanent military presence in Cyprus, which she had insisted upon ever since the Greco–Turkish meetings in Zurich in February 1959. The blindingly obvious "symbol" for all Cypriots (including Turkish Cypriots) is that Turkey has military rights in and over Cyprus. Such rights should not have been accorded by the UN in light of modern international law, even accepting the Secretariat's crassness in failing to appreciate the true symbolism involved in this provision. Perceptions are all in such situations: whereas the UN saw the matter as one of "indefinite" stay of Turkish troops and a "symbolic presence," Greek Cypriots saw it as being "permanent" and a symbol of Turkey's military rights over Cyprus.[13]

CONCERNS ABOUT FUNCTIONALITY IN THE ECONOMIC AND FISCAL SPHERE

Whereas persons of a Panglossian state of mind may believe that Turkey's claims to rights of military intervention pose only fanciful risks for Cyprus, there should in contrast be no doubting that every State requires functional governmental, economic and fiscal arrangements. Nonetheless, para 44 of the *Report* gave a particularly misleading impression of improving *functionality in the economic and fiscal sphere* and of indicating that the Plan represented a solid and workable economic basis for reunification of Cyprus (Annex II, para 9). The *Report* failed to explain that important recommendations by the Technical Committee on Economic and Financial Aspects of Implementation (which had only been appointed upon Greek Cypriot insistence) had either been changed or had not been included in the final, fifth Annan Plan and the accompanying Laws. Indicatively, the "Record of Recommendations of the Technical Committee on Economic and Financial Aspects of Implementation," submitted by the UN on 25 March 2004 to the two sides, had noted that "the Cyprus Pound mentioned in the Plan is the current Cyprus pound". This note was not included in the accompanying Central Bank Law attached to the fifth Annan Plan, leaving uncertainty as to what the future currency would be. As the Plan stood, nothing on the URC's currency was agreed. Since the UCR was expected within a relatively short period to adopt the Euro, to have to introduce a new "UCR pound" in the interval would have been yet another costly complication. Alternatively, there could have been circulation of foreign currencies, without a

[13] Article 3.3 of the Draft Additional Protocol provided for 5-yearly reviews by the three Alliance Powers (Turkey, Greece and Cyprus) "with the objective of total withdrawal". But this was whitewash, because the same Article provided: "This will in no way undermine the provisions of the Treaty of Alliance and its Additional Protocols, and *the rights* and responsibilities conferred thereby". Turkey's agreement was a pre-condition to any reductions. A footnote in Annan IV, hinting that there could be revision of numbers by earlier agreement, which was attached to Main Article 8.1.b when it envisaged that ALL Turkish and Greek troops would be withdrawn unless otherwise agreed, was also deleted on 30 March. Presumably this was due to Turkish objections.

national currency, but this would have entailed no UCR control of the money supply. This omission by the UN was in response to Mr Ziyal's insistence on developing measures for effective preservation of bi-zonality (his Point 10). It was a departure from Annan III: in the 8 March 2003 Corrigenda, No 10, the UN had stated (in relation to an amendment of Article 32.1 of the Constitution as regards the Central Bank) that this was being effected

> in order to avoid the need to change the Constitution when the Euro replaces the Cyprus pound as the currency of the United Cyprus Republic.

In his 1 April 2003 *Report*, para 124, the Secretary-General had been even more explicit:

> The plan foresees that the Cyprus pound would be the currency of the United Cyprus Republic.

Another aspect of this Turkish insistence on bi-zonality (in this instance in the sense of two equal states with equal representation)[14] was shown in the Plan's structural approach to the organs of the Central Bank. Already in Annan III, it was clear that, apart from the possibility of one non-Cypriot member, Bank organs would be equally composed of members hailing from each constituent state, rather than being appointed on the basis of expertise. In Annan V, an important recommendation of the Technical Committee was ignored. All the experts (Turkish and Greek Cypriots and international members alike) had recommended that in the future Monetary Policy Committee (ensuring currency

[14] Agreement from 1977 on a federation which would be "bi-zonal" ie would consist of two zones each predominantly administered by one Community was elevated by the Turkish side under Professor Soysal's tutelage into the "principle of bi-zonality". This principle had many meanings and interpretations, varying according to the circumstances in which the Turkish side was arguing for its implementation. Such a "principle" was rejected by the Greek Cypriot side, which insisted that it had agreed only to a two-unit federation with the character above described, and that it had not agreed to ethnic homogeneity or to any form of *apartheid* since displaced persons, having regard to "practical difficulties," were to return home. Nor had the sides agreed to equal division of all offices of state on ethnic lines; to permanent economic separation; or to "security" aspects of "bi-zonality", all of which were aspects of "bi-zonality" as developed by the Turkish side. In earlier negotiations, the differences over the scope of "bi-zonality" (and also over other concepts such as federation, confederation, sovereignty, people/peoples of Cyprus and "security"—with prior agreement on their interpretation being insisted up by the Turkish side as a pre-requisite for engaging in discussion of concrete proposals) had led to unending conceptual debate. Outsiders (such as one British Minister of State, Sir Ian Gilmour) failed to appreciate that words became weapons, and naïvely expressed irritation at "The tyranny of words" when in Cyprus negotiations the Greek Cypriot side responded to Turkish development of the concepts as applicable principles for any settlement. Because the Secretary-General requested the two sides in any revived negotiations not to engage in conceptual debate and to move beyond verbal gymnastics, the Greek Cypriot side, in the direct talks in 2002 and again in the Nicosia talks in February–March 2004, apart from briefly recording its opposition to "the principle of bi-zonality" and its purported applications (but only when such issues were raised by the other side) attempted to concentrate on concrete provisions. This avoided fruitless wrangling, but it left the path open to the UN to adopt Turkey's views on "bi-zonality," which it did, even inserting the "principle of bi-zonality" in the first Article of the UCR Constitution and, in Version V of the Plan, fully applying this principle in pursuance of Turkey's demands as made by Mr Ziyal (Point 10).

stability) the Greek Cypriot side should have a majority of members. The Central Bank of Cyprus had responsibly managed the Cyprus pound since 1960, while the Turkish Cypriot side had operated under Turkey's direction and still so operates, using the Turkish lira, with its commercial banks requiring total restructuring, if not closure. Indeed, the recapitalisation and reorganisation of the banking system in the occupied area by the Bank of Turkey, which is responsible for the existing situation, is necessary, if there is to be economic development of the TCCS. Yet the final version of the Plan provided for equal representation of Greek Cypriots and Turkish Cypriots on the Monetary Policy Committee. Moreover, the Technical Committee had recommended that the branch of the Central Bank in the TCCS should be closed one year after the entry into force of the Foundation Agreement, subject to the possibility of a contrary recommendation from a working group including IMF and EU experts. In contrast, the Plan left open the possibilities of maintaining the branch in the TCCS and of widening its responsibilities. This too was in response to Mr Ziyal's Point 10 ("Measures should be developed for effective preservation of bizonality"), leading the UN team to provide for establishment of a separate branch of the Central Bank in the TCCS.[15] Such a development could seriously undermine effective application of monetary policy. Monetary policy cannot be divided up: a single centralised decision centre is essential. Only if a branch were to be confined to being a service provider and information-gathering centre would its establishment be justifiable. Of even more concern was failure to implement another recommendation: the Technical Committee had recommended that

> An advisory Council should be created to serve as the main coordinating vehicle between the federal and constituent states to define a joint fiscal policy stance and contain and manage new borrowing by an Internal Stability Pact within the MSC

and had proposed detailed provisions on the functions of this Macroeconomic Stability Council and on the borrowing limits of all levels of government.[16] But the Plan and the accompanying Laws only referred to the possibility of setting up an MSC with an advisory role by a later federal Law, whereas it is necessary that a Central Bank have authority to contain aggregate deficits, ie the sum of the deficits of the federal government and of the governments of the constituent states. Again, the Technical Committee had tackled the issues of prevention of harmful tax competition and taxation of commuting workers, vital in a small Island where changes of residence will be restricted by law and commuting will be a norm, yet the fifth Plan and Laws were silent on these points. Finally, the Committee had defined federal economic policy, whereas the Plan did not touch upon this major issue. As already indicated, these recommendations had been

[15] See Annex III, Attachment 6: Federal Law on the Central Bank of Cyprus, section 73.

[16] These issues have caused major difficulties even in federations without the legacy of ethnic resentment, which will for many years be the backdrop to decisions in the new Cyprus federation.

agreed by all the Committee's members (Turkish and Greek Cypriots and international experts) in order to ensure a workable economic basis for a reunified Cyprus. A further matter which was not dealt with in the Plan was the lack of provision precluding federal institutions from supporting or guaranteeing sub-federal authorities' external debt service. Where such guarantees have been given, there have been disastrous debt build ups, followed by defaults.[17]

CONCERNS ABOUT RESTRICTIONS ON THE RIGHT OF RETURN OF DISPLACED GREEK CYPRIOTS AND ABOUT LIMITED RESTITUTION OF GREEK CYPRIOT-OWNED PROPERTY

There remained major Greek Cypriot concerns about restrictions on the rights of return of displaced Greek Cypriots and about the very limited restitution of Greek Cypriot-owned property, which contrasted with the picture presented in the *Report* to the international community (and by certain members of that community) of there being extensive reinstatement of property to its dispossessed owners and a very large-scale return of dispossessed persons.[18] These matters are examined in Chapter XV.

CONCERNS ABOUT THE TURKISH SETTLER QUESTIONS: MOST TURKISH SETTLERS COULD REMAIN IN CYPRUS AND MANY MORE COULD COME IN FUTURE

The large number of Turkish settlers who would remain in Cyprus and future flows of Turkish settlement were discussed in Chapter VII. Of particular concern were changes made in Annan IV and V to govern future immigration from Turkey. The changed Plan now provided a complex mechanism, requiring the agreement of Turkish Cypriots, to stem the flow of Turkish settlers once Turkey had joined the EU, or after 19 years from the time the Foundation Agreement had come into force, whichever was the earlier. This mechanism was substituted for small permanent fixed quotas applicable *mutatis mutandis* to Turkish and Greek immigration. These quotas had been sought by the Greek Cypriot side. Under the substituted mechanism, "safeguard measures" were permissible to ensure that the demographic ratio between those resident Cypriots whose

[17] The writer is indebted to a paper of 4 October 2004 by Professor Charles Wyplosz, "The Economic Aspects of the Annan Plan: Suggestions for Further Improvements," in which he points out that some important questions remain either ill-treated or ignored in Annan V and that some of the changes introduced are "bound to be a serious source of difficulties".

[18] Exaggeration of this kind was a *forte* of the USA. Mr Cunningham, representing the USA, told the Security Council on 21 April 2004, when seeking its endorsement for the Plan, that the settlement "provides for the return of more than 120,000 Greek Cypriot refugees to their former homes, a comprehensive property compensation and restitution system and the withdrawal of almost all Turkish troops from the island." See *S/PV,4947*, UN Security Council, 59th year, 4947th meeting, 21 April 2004, p 3.

mother-tongue language was Greek and those whose mother-tongue language was Turkish was not substantially altered.[19] The Aliens Board, by this time equally composed of members from each constituent state,[20] would have to consult the European Commission through the Federal Ministry of European Union Affairs, thus requiring Presidential Council approval. Measures agreed with the Commission would then require UCR regulations. Those would in turn require approval by 10 Turkish Senators (since all immigration regulations under Article 25.2.c of the UCR Constitution have to be approved in this way). Thus the substituted mechanism, instead of protecting the demographic basis on a certain and permanent basis of small fixed quotas, was dependent for its operation on Turkish Cypriot politicians, themselves dependent on an electorate consisting of a majority of Turkish settlers and their descendants. Such politicians would have to vote for restricting Turkish immigration once Turkey joined the EU or 19 years had passed.[21]

BENEFITS ACCORDED TURKEY BY THE PLAN

As regards the Secretary-General's "improvements largely inspired by Turkish Cypriot concerns," these were in reality inspired by the Republic of Turkey wearing the mantle of the Turkish Cypriot side and the *Report* was silent about the benefits to Turkey accorded by the Plan. It is therefore appropriate to quote President Papadopoulos' letter to the Secretary-General of 7 June 2004. He wrote:

> Let me just outline just some of the benefits gained by that country under the finalized version of the Plan. Turkey true to her past role demanded (and obtained) divisive bi-zonality provisions, strategic economic benefits, and "security" arrangements, with sufficient troops, even if reduced in numbers, to allow her again to intervene militarily through a bridgehead in Cyprus, a right Turkey still insists she enjoys, and [these and] her continuing role make full independence impossible. Although, scarcely touched on in the Plan and then only by reference, Turkey's powers of intervention and supervision are in reality enormous, because of its continuing military presence in and near Cyprus. She has also insisted, through the Turkish Cypriots, on binding the UCR by treaties which they entered into with her and which provided for the integration of the Turkish Cypriot constituent state into Turkey, persuading the UN to accept this and a new right for the Turkish Cypriot State and Turkey to make agreements on investment and provision of financial assistance. Turkey had also insisted on

[19] It later emerged that the relevant Constitutional Law as finalised put the ratio on a different basis, protecting Turkish (and *mutatis mutandis* Greek) language-speakers against there being speakers of any other languages. This had the side-effect (in fact purpose) of reducing the number of Greek Cypriots who could return. See Chapter XV below.

[20] In earlier years, there would be foreign members "holding the balance".

[21] Greek immigration to Cyprus has never been large and it was not contemplated that even the small quota permitted would be filled: the issue of Greek immigration altering the demographic ratio would never arise. Between 1963 and 2004 only 373 Greeks were naturalised.

> putting a brake on the UCR's economic development by securing provisions in the Law on the Continental Shelf that prevent the UCR from exploring and exploiting her maritime resources in the seas of Cyprus whilst interfering with the Treaty between Egypt and the Republic of Cyprus on the Delimitation of the Exclusive Economic Zone, which is an ill-omen as to how Turkey would in future have operated. Another such example is the imposition of the "Cooperative Agreement on Civil Aviation with Turkey" on Cyprus over the strong objection of the Greek Cypriots. This "treaty" would have imposed on Cyprus a common policy with Turkey in civil aviation thus making changes in the management of Cyprus air space subject to Turkey's consent. It would have also allowed Turkey to take all necessary actions (even military action) in the event of any threat to aircraft passengers, airport or aviation facilities.
>
> In the aforementioned list, which by no means is exhaustive, the greatest benefit for Turkey, secured to the detriment of both Greek and Turkish Cypriots and consisting [of] a clear departure from the provisions of Annan III, has been the stationing of Turkish troops on the island in perpetuity.
>
> All these new provisions clearly serving Turkish interests and aims in Cyprus explain to a large extent why the Plan was overwhelmingly rejected by the Greek Cypriots, approved by the Turkish Cypriot side and so emphatically endorsed by the Turkish Government. The Greek Cypriots have every right to wonder how the United Nations, the very guardian of international law, could adopt proposals inspired by the Turkish side, which deliberately and unjustifiably limit the sovereignty exercised by one of its Member States. In other words, the main objection by the Greek Cypriot community to the Plan was the fact that foreign interests, primarily Turkish ones, were satisfied, instead of those of the Cypriot population, Greek and Turkish Cypriots alike.

Apart from the benefits to Turkey outlined by President Papadopoulos, Turkey achieved a major enhancement of her position in relation to UN peace-keeping operations in Cyprus. This was not made explicit in the Comprehensive Settlement documents, but emerges from careful scrutiny of the Treaty on matters related to the new state of affairs, Article 2, read with "E. Matters to be submitted to the UN Security Council for Decision," setting out proposals for the new mandate for UN peacekeeping. The Treaty, Article 2, provided for a Monitoring Committee of Turkey, Greece, the UK and Cyprus. This Committee was to monitor the implementation of the "*Settlement*" ie including the eventual mandate decided upon by the Security Council under E (above). The mandate itself recognised the Monitoring Committee, which would be UN-chaired and provided with administrative support. The Treaty, Article 2.4, as revised in Annan V, also included a new provision that

> The Monitoring committee shall request the United Nations to bring to its attention any significant change the United Nations may wish to make in its peacekeeping operation.

The effect of Article 2.4 was to ensure there could be no change in UN peace-keeping operations without consultation with Turkey. In practice, Turkey has, however, always been consulted. What was more significant was the implied consequence of the structure set up by the Treaty and UN force mandate read together: "*the United Nations operation*" is what would be conducted in Cyprus, subject to its implementation being monitored by the Monitoring Committee. Thus there could not be international peacekeeping other than by the UN, even by delegation by the UN, *unless Turkey consented to this*. This would preclude either an EU or a NATO peacekeeping operation without Turkey's agreement—unless Chapter VII of the UN Charter were to become applicable and to be invoked, when the decision could be exclusively that of the Security Council.

"IMPROVEMENTS LARGELY INSPIRED BY TURKISH CYPRIOT CONCERNS"

Turning now to the *Report's* account (paras 51 to 57) of the specific "improvements largely inspired by Turkish Cypriot concerns," a permanent ceiling on the potential number of Greek Cypriot residents was effected by subtle drafting, based on percentages of mother-tongue language speakers. This provision, also designated as a "safeguard clause," was presented in the *Report* in conjunction with gross over-estimates of the number of Greek Cypriots who could return to their homes in the Turkish Cypriot constituent state (para 51). At the same time there was a major departure from the earlier core agreement reached in 2002 whereby citizens could vote for all political institutions in their place of residence. Those Greek Cypriots who had been permitted to return to the TCCS would have their political rights diminished. This diminution was effected by resurrecting the Community concept (in the form of linguistic differentiation) to prevent Greek Cypriots living in the Turkish Cypriot constituent state (and who would of course not be mother-tongue Turkish speakers) from voting and for standing for the federal Senate in their place of residence. The effect was to guarantee that Turkish mother-tongue speakers would always have 50% of the seats and would thus be enabled to block decisions in the federal Senate.

Another "improvement" was that there was to be a short-term departure from the specified proportions of members from each constituent state in the transitional federal executive and legislature, with both being composed of equal numbers of representatives from the two constituent states, despite their very disparate populations. Although this equality of numbers of representatives was to apply only at the outset and for a short period, it involved a major matter of principle as to power-sharing ratios and symbolised "the principle of bi-zonality" in operation.[22] The *Report* asserted that this change was to balance the fact that transitional government was to be for a shorter period. The reality was that a joint government and numerical equality had been demanded by Mr

[22] Equality in holding the office of President and Vice-President of the Presidential Council was however to persist for a further five years, ie throughout the life of the first elected Presidential Council after the equal Co-Presidency had ceased.

Denktash since as early as 1975. He had, in Annan II and III, in the transitional period effectively been given what he had sought by way of joint government to show that the "TRNC" and the Republic of Cyprus had jointly created the new UCR. Thus, in the UN view, Mr Denktash had now to be compensated, with the *Report* asserting that a "balance" was due from the Greek Cypriot side since the transitional period had been much shortened in order to ensure governmental stability—this of course really being in the interests of all Cypriots and of the UN, which presumably did not want the settlement immediately to collapse. Where assertions are concerned, anything can be asserted to "balance" anything: there were no real scales in Mr de Soto's hands—not scales of justice anyway.

A further "improvement," effected by stratagems, related to "the legal security" of the settlement, which was described by the *Report* at para 53 as being a Turkish Cypriot concern. In reality, the concern was that of Turkey (see Mr Ziyal's Point 11), seeking to protect herself from responsibility before the European Court of Human Rights and to accord her nationals economic privileges even in the EU, which would be unchallengeable before the European Court of Justice. The Plan's human rights provisions as regards rights to property had been shaped following an earlier discreditable episode in the history of the European Court of Human Rights and of the UN when Mr Pfirter spoke to some of the Court's judges and officials about how to formulate provisions excluding the Court's jurisdiction in relation to property claims by displaced persons. His ideas envisaged enabling the Court technically to avoid hearing new and pending cases against Turkey in respect of human rights violations in Cyprus, the incentive for the Court being an easing of its concern that it might become a compensation tribunal for property cases from Cyprus. Officials of the Council of Europe Secretariat and the Directorate of Human Rights were later party to similar discussions with the UN Secretariat. This was not so offensive as discussions with Court personnel, but it is nonetheless odd that the treaty authority for a human rights Convention, charged with the duty of upholding it, should engage in discussions as to how effectively to diminish its protective scope. Such an authority should not act as a rights-avoidance consultant.

Another alleged Turkish Cypriot concern was that there be a larger number of police in the "TRNC". In fact this demand had been formulated by the Turkish Army to keep in play members of the to-be-demilitarised "Turkish Cypriot Security Force" (*Cumhurriyet* 7.1.04). According to the *Report*, the UN in its "finalisation" permitted for a period an increased number of such police, as opposed to the number proposed in earlier versions of the Plan. This was a departure from the principle of demilitarisation of Cypriots, transforming military personnel into a larger TCCS police force.[23]

[23] The Turkish Army paper requesting this increase of the TCCS police force made it clear that the reasons were military, rather than economic hardship to demobilised servicemen or a need for more policing, both of which are sensible arguments for such a temporary policy subject to there being adequate international supervision of the police force.

PROVISIONS OF THE PLAN WHICH REMAINED UNCHANGED

In his *Report*, paras 58–62, the Secretary-General provided reasons for his not changing certain provisions of the Plan, which failure had led to controversy. Since the failure to alter territorial allocations as between the constituent states (ie to change the map annexed to the Plan) has already been explained, as has been the real responsibility for this failure, and since the question of Turkish settlers entitled to remain permanently in Cyprus has been fully discussed in Chapter VIII, it would be tedious to dwell yet again on these issues. It is, however, necessary to refer again to the Secretary-General's decision to approve the referendum of Turkish Cypriots, even if Turkish settlers voted, bearing in mind that they constituted a majority on the electoral rolls. This was a serious infringement of international law, the rule as to self-determination being *jus cogens*. To cover the UN's pusillanimous attitude, para 62 of the Report attributed the Secretary-General's decision to take no action to the fact that this issue was outside the parameters of the Plan, on the basis that it would have required the Turkish Cypriot side to have accepted the Greek Cypriot side's interpretation of the legal situation prior to the coming into being of the new state of affairs.[24] The view that settlers cannot vote in an internal self-determination exercise was not merely a legal interpretation by the Greek Cypriot side, but is established international law, and, despite the *Report* sliding over this, not even using the phrase "Turkish settlers," and claiming that the Plan (or its wording) governed the situation, the issue remained a matter of international law. Had the Secretariat conformed with such international law, it would have insisted on following the principles laid down in the *Western Sahara* Case, and by the precedent of UN action as regards East Timor. The subsequent development of delivery of the International Court of Justice 9 July 2004 Advisory Opinion on the *Legal Consequences of the Construction of the Wall in the Palestinian Territory*, may in future prevent the Secretariat from hiding behind alleged ambiguities and lack of specific provision. But that *Advisory Opinion* had not been delivered when the UN Representative to the Western Sahara, Mr de Soto, persuaded his master, the Secretary-General, to ignore problems posed by the presence of settlers.

[24] This was yet another new reason advanced *post hoc* for the UN not having enforced international law. With the *Report* writer's unlimited ingenuity, more justifications would doubtless have emerged, given time.

THE "INDEPENDENT TRNC" REMAINS THE SAME

Above and below: "President" Denktash taking the salute and parading at another typical "Independence Day" celebration.

Soon after his inauguration as President of Turkey, Mr AN Sezer visited the "TRNC" to show Turkish support for it. He called on 26 June 2000 for the "TRNC's" "recognition"; and for a two-state confederation in which two States could cooperate and work together under the same roof. Sitting with two Turkish protectors, "President" Denktash photographs yet more Turkish protectors. He must have a magnificent photograph collection of American military hardware being operated in Cyprus by the Turkish Army.

15 November 2001. Taking yet another Turkish tank for granted in a period when the Turkish military were omni-present: "Independence" ceremonies then were less civilianised and more military, with high-ranking Turkish Generals and Admirals prominent, such as the Turkish Land Forces Chief, the Commander of the Turkish Naval Force, and/or the Chief of the General Staff being present and sending messages. To his credit, Mr Denktash is never seen in uniform, always being immaculately tailored in civilian suits. But large Turkish Army formations are there, even if, as a policy matter, their presence has in recent years been made less obvious by confinement to the very extensive areas in the "TRNC" from which the public are excluded.

Under Turkey's protective guns, "President" Denktash stands for Turkish tanks to parade past him.

Turkish Airforce F-16s at Lefkonico (Geçitkale) Air Base. Thanks be to "the good ol' US of A".

Above: The Foreign Minister of Turkey arrived early on 20 July 2004 to celebrate the 30th anniversary of Turkey's invasion. He appears "fed up" at having to engage in these Ruritanian ceremonies. But soon he and his wife enjoy the "ex-leader's" company, even if "President" Denktash proceeds in his "independence" speech to give a lecture on "our right of sovereignty" being preserved—of course not against Turkey, but as against the Republic of Cyprus.

Mr Gül and "Prime Minister" Talat point to Turkish protectors in the sky.

General Tevfik Özkilig, Commander of Turkey's Army in Cyprus, salutes his real master, Foreign Minister Gül on 20 July 2004.

One of the protective Turkish tanks in the 20 July 2004 parade. 300 tanks and 293 armoured personnel carriers (each carrying 12–13 soldiers) are stationed in Cyprus. They are largely American-supplied. The strength of the Turkish Army in Cyprus in 2004 was 36,000 soldiers, while there were a further 2,500 soldiers in the "Turkish Cypriot Forces Command."

R.12–13

Look who's here. To the right, another godfather, earlier displaced by the Turkish Army's "white coup" of 1997, but specially honoured in Mr Denktash's speech and warmly embraced by Mr Gül is former Turkish Prime Minister Erbakan who had appointed Mr Gül in the Çiller coalition. According to Mr Denktash, the esteemed Erbakan and Mr Ecevit (whom Mr Denktash had telephoned the previous day, 19 July 2004) together achieved "our salvation". Mr Erbakan is sitting with the then "President of the Supreme Court," Mr Taner Erginel, and Mr Serdar Denktash. The lower picture shows three generations of the Denktash dynasty: left to right, "Foreign Minister" Serdar Denktash and son, and former Turkish Prime Minister Erbakan being embraced by "President" Denktash.

It's not much different when two triumvirs, "President" Denktash and "Prime Minister" Talat, celebrate years of independence with their military protectors.

Here "President" Denktash is enjoying parading with high-ranking Turkish officers.

R.16–17

XV

The Right of Displaced Persons to Return to Their Homes in Safety and the Right to Property

THE SECRETARY-GENERAL'S GENERAL APPROACH TO PROPERTY ISSUES

The Secretary-General explained his approach to property issues as follows:

Properties affected by events since 1963

107. Almost half the population of Cyprus lost properties as a result of intercommunal strife or military action between 1963 and 1974 and the unresolved division of the island since that time. The Greek Cypriot side advocate a solution based on full respect for property rights so that all displaced persons, from either community, would have the right to have their properties reinstated. The Turkish Cypriot side argued that property claims should be settled through liquidation by means of a global exchange and compensation scheme, meaning that no displaced persons, from either side, would have the right to have their properties reinstated.

108. International developments since the Second War, both Cyprus-related and others, favour a settlement based on respect for individual property rights. In recent years the European Court of European Court of Human Rights has taken decisions recognizing the property rights of Greek Cypriots in the northern part of the island and allocating damages at the expense of Turkey. Thousands of similar cases are pending before the Court.[1] In making any suggestions I took into account these developments and the positions adopted recently by the United Nations and the international community in the former Yugoslavia, but also the fact that the events in Cyprus happened 30 to 40 years ago and that the displaced people (roughly half of the Turkish Cypriots and a third of the Greek Cypriots) have had to rebuild their lives and their economies during this time.

109. The way out of this conundrum of conflicting legitimate claims of owners and current users had to be a compromise. My scheme administered by a property board,

[1] [The number of cases was exaggerated by Turkey to persuade Council of Europe States that she should not face financial responsibility. The UN Secretariat should have checked the facts before making such an assertion. In March 2003, when the *Report* being quoted was written, there were 400 applications, some of which were made by several applicants. Of course, there is large potential liability, but most displaced property owners had not sued Turkey, partly because of the costs and partly because they knew that trying to enforce their rights would be a lengthy and frustrating process, likely to be fruitless because of Turkey's refusal to pay. By early October 2004, there were nearly 1,400 applications, with the numbers increasing, and many property-owners involved.]

> gives priority to the claims of current users who have themselves been displaced and dispossessed of properties and allows them to obtain title in exchange for their property in the other part of the island (this would apply also to their successors in title). Similarly, anyone who has significantly improved a property would be able to obtain title provided he/she pays for the value of the property in its original state. Other properties would be reinstated to their owners—although a range of incentives would encourage dispossessed owners to sell, lease or exchange their properties or seek compensation . . .
>
> 110. Owners whose properties were not reinstated would be compensated with bonds guaranteed by the federal government and redeemable . . . from a compensation fund, to be funded by the sale of properties by the property board (the concept being that no one should obtain title to a property without paying for it through exchange or in cash). The property proposals also include detailed provisions for adequate alternative accommodation and a preferential loans scheme for current users.
>
> 111. While it is possible to differ on details, this approach, particularly when married to the territorial adjustment described below, strikes a fair balance between competing legitimate interests and individual human rights and respects the principle of bi-zonality and international law (including international human rights law and the fourth Geneva Convention.) (*Report of the Secretary-General on his mission of good offices in Cyprus, S/2003/398*, 1 April 2003.)

This succinct, and on the face of it reasonable, summary by the Secretary-General of his approach to property questions in any Cyprus settlement must have been reassuring to Governments concerned to satisfy themselves that international law would be observed.

When Governments and interested persons saw the finalised Plan's Main Article 10, Property, they must also have been satisfied, having regard to the terms in which the Article set out the position, that justice would be ensured.[2] Main Article 10, as finalised in Annan V on 31 March 2004, read:

> **Article 10 Property**
>
> The claims of persons who were dispossessed of their properties by events prior to entry into force of this Agreement shall be resolved in a comprehensive manner in accordance with international law, respect for the individual rights of dispossessed owners and current users, and the principle of bi-zonality.
>
> In areas subject to territorial adjustment, properties shall be reinstated to dispossessed owners.
>
> In areas not subject to territorial adjustment, the arrangements for the exercise of property rights, by way of reinstatement or compensation, shall have the following basic features:
>
> a. Dispossessed owners who opt for compensation, as well as institutions, shall receive full and effective compensation for their property on the basis of value at the time of dispossession adjusted to reflect appreciation of property values in comparable locations. Compensation shall be paid in the form of guaranteed bonds and appreciation certificates.
>
> b. All other dispossessed owners have the right to reinstatement of one-third of the value and one-third of the area of their total property ownership, and to receive full

[2] As explained earlier, the Main Articles were a summary of the Plan prepared by the Secretariat's legal team for marketing purposes.

and effective compensation for the remaining two-thirds. However, they have the right to reinstatement of a dwelling they have built, or in which they lived for at least ten years, and up to one donum of adjacent land, even if this is more than one-third of the total value and area of their properties.

c. Dispossessed owners may choose any of their properties for reinstatement, except for properties that have been exchanged by a current user or bought by a significant improver in accordance with the scheme. A dispossessed owner whose property cannot be reinstated, or who voluntarily defers to a current user, has the right to another property of equal size and value in the same municipality or village. S/he may also sell his/her entitlement to another dispossessed owner from the same place, who may aggregate it with his/her own entitlement.
d. Current users, being persons who have possession of properties of dispossessed owners as a result of an administrative decision, may apply for and shall receive title, if they agree in exchange to renounce their title to a property, of similar value and in the other constituent state, of which they were dispossessed;
e. Persons who own significant improvements to properties may apply for and shall receive title to such properties provided they pay for the value of the property in its original state; and
f. Current users who are Cypriot citizens and are required to vacate property to be reinstated shall not be required to do so until adequate alternative accommodation has been made available.

Property claims shall be received and administered by an independent, impartial Property Board, governed by an equal number of members from each constituent state, as well as non-Cypriot members. The Property Board shall be organized into branches in accordance with sound economic practice. No direct dealings between individuals shall be necessary.

These brief presentations of the Secretary-General's approach and decisions *ex necessitate* omitted details. However, they also concealed the real impact of the Plan's provisions on displaced persons and property owners. In part this concealment was because, as the Secretary-General emphasised on 1 April 2003, his Plan

> largely unlinks residency rights and the issue of reinstatement of property—two aspects which have often been confused in public discussion.[3]

UNLINKING OF PROPERTY AND THE RIGHT TO RESUME RESIDENCE: A DOUBLE BARRIER FOR BOTH RIGHTS

The deliberate unlinking of property and the right of return was a major factor in the Plan failing to ensure that displaced persons could in practice and thus in reality return to their homes. The Plan's drafters decided upon this unlinking on a basis the Secretary-General explained as follows:

> **Residency rights**
> 98. The issue of freedom of establishment of residence was extremely contentious. *In their wish to avoid the intermingling of Greek Cypriots and Turkish Cypriots, the*

[3] *S/2003/398*, para 101.

Turkish Cypriot side wanted the constituent states to have the unfettered right to decide who could establish residency therein—this was their concept of "bi-zonality". The Greek Cypriots argued that the Turkish Cypriot position amounted to ethnic purity and that basic human rights and the principles of the *acquis communautaire* should allow any Cypriot citizen to settle anywhere on the island, any limitations being acceptable only in the first few years—for them "bi-zonality" meant only two distinct zones administered by Greek Cypriots and Turkish Cypriots respectively.[4]

99. The plan suggests a very gradual approach to the establishment of residency by former inhabitants and other Greek Cypriots in the Turkish Cypriot State (and vice versa). Initially there would be a total moratorium, though people over 65 and their spouses (or one sibling), as well as former inhabitants (and their descendants) of four villages at the tip of the Karpas peninsula where some Greek Cypriots have remained since 1974, would be exempted from limitations after two years.[5] After six years the moratorium would be lifted, but the constituent states would be authorized to impose limitations if the number of residents from the other constituent state in any given village (including any persons over 65) reached 7 per cent, and 14 per cent after 11 years. After the fifteenth year and until Turkey's accession to the European Union, limitations could be imposed if 21 per cent of the population (including any persons over 65 or in the Karpas villages) hailed from the other constituent state. The power to impose these restrictions would have been specifically authorized by the European Union in the protocol to the Treaty of Accession.

100. It is my conviction that the dispute over this issue may have been based on unrealistic assumptions on both sides. I believe that fewer Greek Cypriots than the percentages indicated above would, in the end, wish to establish residence in the Turkish Cypriot State, meaning that these limitations would have little practical effect on Greek Cypriots, and also that the Turkish Cypriots should not look at these figures as "targets" of returns but as ultimate safeguards unlikely ever to be required. However, these figures became major sources of controversy and contention on both sides, and in each version of my plan I revised them to try to improve the plan for both. The initial approach had been an even more gradual one but with a shorter moratorium and slightly accelerated the pace to end with a limitation of 28 per cent after 15 years. My third plan introduced the concept of lifting these limitations after Turkey joins the European Union in exchange for lower limits before, and the exemption for the elderly in exchange for a longer overall moratorium . . .

[4] [Emphasis added. In the 2004 finalisation negotiations, the Greek Cypriot side requested the Secretary-General to append to the Plan, when it used the term "bi-zonality," a brief clarificatory footnote referring to this fair explanation of the different meanings attached to this word, so that the Turks' asserted "principle of bi-zonality" could not be used to interpret constitutional provisions as authorising *apartheid*. However, the Secretary-General refused to insert a reference to his own 1 April 2003 *Report*, although the rest of the Plan's text was, as a drafting technique, littered with explanatory and qualifying footnotes. In fact, as "finalised," Main Article 10 of the Plan adopted "the principle of bi-zonality," a principle the Greek Cypriot side had always rejected.]

[5] [The population of these villages had been granted special rights under the humanitarian arrangements reached by Mr Clerides and Mr Denktash in August 1975 at the third round of talks in Vienna, but these rights were not given effect despite years of successive Secretary-General's *Reports* calling for implementation. Only in July 2004 did the "TRNC Council of Ministers" decide to open a secondary level school for Greek Cypriot children of the Karpas. This decision was taken because of pressures following *Cyprus v Turkey* and discussion in the Committee of Ministers of the Council of Europe on remedial measures necessitated by the European Court of Human Rights' judgment.]

The details as to how many former inhabitants could establish residency in the TCCS and in the GCCS[6] were again changed in Annan V as finalised. This was upon Turkey's insistence. She demanded strengthening of provisions in accordance with "the principle of bi-zonality," which the UN now accepted. Consequently the UN reverted to its "even more gradual" approach, with an effective upper limit of 33.3% of the resident population not being mother-tongue Turkish speakers. This limit would have applied in the 19th year after the Foundation Agreement came into force or when Turkey acceded to the EU, whichever alternative was the earlier.[7] There were also to be lower percentages of return, with only 18% (rather than 21%) of the population permitted to hail from the other Cypriot constituent state from the 15th year until the above-mentioned alternative times. The asserted counter-balance put forward by the Secretariat for seeking this change was that the moratorium ceased from the beginning of year 6, rather than year 7. But this "improvement" (so described in para 51 of the *Report*) was further offset by counting against the quota of returnees persons from the Karpas villages and any person over 65 with his or her accompanying spouse or sibling.[8] The outcome would be that the latter categories of displaced persons would fill the quota of permitted returnees until more than 10 years after the Agreement had begun to operate.[9]

The net effect of the "de-linking" between the right of return and the right to restitution of property was to establish two barriers to return of displaced persons: they were subject to the strict quotas under the residency ceilings described above; and they were also subject to limitations on restitution to them of their property. In consequence, some persons would be permitted to return, but would not necessarily be reinstated to their homes, there being no congruence between applicability of the two rights.[10] Thus many permitted to return (being under the ceiling limit) would have nowhere to live and would not return. Other

[6] The UN mirrored the provisions for each constituent state so they were not discriminatory. Had the provisions applied only to the TCCS, they would have been open to legal challenge. The Greek Cypriot side had not asked for such restrictions to apply in the GCCS.

[7] The limitation had to be sought for, but not in the Constitution. The limitation was not properly reflected in the Main Articles, the Plan's international sales brochure, where there was only a glancing reference to "non-discriminatory safeguard measures" in Main Article 3.6. The actual provision was set out in Sub-Article 2.2 of the Draft Act of Adaptation of the terms of Accession of the UCR to the EU and in the Constitutional Law on Internal Constituent State Citizenship Status and Constituent State Residency Rights (2004), Article 8 (1)—see Foundation Agreement D, and Annex II, Attachment 3.

[8] Annan III, as part of an earlier bargain, had allowed such persons to return in year 3 after the Agreement came into force.

[9] Such old persons and returning Karpas villagers were estimated as amounting to a potential 29,800 persons by 2019 ie the 15th year, assuming the settlement came into operation in 2004. Until that year, there could be limitations once persons hailing from the GCCS had reached 12% of the population of any village or municipality.

[10] Mr Pfirter told the Turkish Cypriot side prior to the Annan III changes how much this separation of the rights to property and to return was to their advantage: they need not fear return of older Karpas former residents because they would not at the stage be able to reclaim their property, and, when current users' rights were taken into account, might not be able to get their homes and property back at all.

persons would be reinstated to their properties and homes, but would be excluded by the residency quotas. Embarrassed by this double-barrier effect, the UN effected a modification in Annan III–V to permit those reinstated to their properties to use them as second residences for holidays or weekends and to lease or sell these.[11] For those not re-instated to their homes, the Secretary-General presented an auspicious picture to the world in his *Report*, declaring:

> restrictions on the establishment of secondary residence by Cypriot citizens anywhere in Cyprus were removed.[12]

All this sentence meant was that, under the Plan, persons not reinstated *were allowed to rent* a property for secondary residence, while reinstated persons, who could not return because the ceilings stopped this, could use their reinstated property

> to temporarily stay or have a holiday in their own properties or any other accommodation anywhere in Cyprus.[13]

Elsewhere in the Plan, the Turkish Cypriot constituent state authorities were given power to restrict the *purchase* of property: persons who had not already been permanent residents of the TCCS for at least three years needed their permission. Such restrictions could continue for 15 years or until the GDP *per capita* income in the TCCS reached 85% of the GDP *per capita* in the GCCS.[14]

Although phasing of return of refugees was essential, so as to protect current occupiers of their property and to discourage disorderly return, the provisions limiting return went far beyond those needs. The extent of the moratoria and the size of the quotas in the Plan could not by any reasonable standard be said to have been necessary.[15] The real purpose was in order to prevent large-scale

[11] Mr Pfirter told the Greek Cypriot side that they had got a great concession when the Turkish Cypriot side agreed that stay should not be limited to two nights per week. The UK Foreign Office in its briefing paper "Twelve Reasons for Greek Cypriots to vote 'Yes'" stated that removal of restrictions on the number of nights Greek Cypriots could stay in their second homes was a "big picture" reason for Greek Cypriots to vote "yes" in the referendum.

[12] *S/2004/437*, 28 May 2004, para 48.

[13] Section 8 (7), Constitutional Law on Internal Constituent State Citizenship Status and Constituent State Residency Rights (2004). However, the Law did not define the "temporary stay" or "holiday" terms.

[14] Draft Act of Adaptation to the terms of Accession of the United Cyprus Republic to the European Union, Article 1.1. The 85% of GDP *per capita* requirement for removal of the limitation is, as any economist will tell you, never likely to be reached.

[15] The extent of the limitations should be recollected: apart from Karpas villagers and persons over 65 and their spouse or a sibling, there would be: a total moratorium until the end of the 5th year after the Agreement came into force; limitation of residents hailing from the other constituent state if such residents had reached 6% of the population of a village or municipality from the 6th to the 9th years; limitations if such residents had reached 12% from the 10th–14th years; and limitations if they reached 18% of the population of the constituent state from the 15th–18th years or Turkey's EU accession, whichever was the earlier (Constitution, Main Article 3.7 and Constitutional Law on Internal Constituent State Citizenship Status and Constituent State Residency Rights (2004) section 8.2). The practical effect of the provision in relation to villages which were formerly entirely Greek Cypriot inhabited and which have been only partly occupied by Turkish Cypriots and Turkish settlers, would be absurd: as regards the village of Kythrea, which

re-integration of Greek and Turkish Cypriots, because Turkey wished to maintain a predominantly Turkish-populated unit in Cyprus under her control ("bi-zonality").[16] Making light of this real purpose behind "bi-zonality," in order to sell the Plan to Greek Cypriots before the referenda and to justify it afterwards to the international community, both the Secretariat and the UK Foreign Office stated that, even when restrictions were in force, they were "highly unlikely to prevent any Greek Cypriot who wishes from returning as a permanent resident to the north".[17] The Secretariat went even further. They asserted that "over time 100,000 Greek Cypriots would be able to take up permanent residence in the Turkish Cypriot State."[18] This statement grossly exaggerated the figures without giving a time frame. The actual numbers of persons *potentially* eligible were as follows: for the first five years there was to be a moratorium, other than for persons aged over 65 years and their spouse or one of their siblings and for villagers from the Karpas who were able to return in the third year after the settlement. Between 2010–2013, 12,000–13,900 persons would have been eligible to resettle; by 2019 the maximum cumulative number who could have been eligible would have been about 45,000 persons.[19]

formerly had 2,947 Greek Cypriot inhabitants, on the assumption that there was by now a Turkish population of 1,000 persons (there were 878 Turkish and Turkish Cypriot inhabitants in 1998), only 64 of the village's former inhabitants could return by 2012 and about 136 by 2017, or slightly more if the Turkish population had increased. It should be observed that the Plan effectively consolidated the "ethnic cleansing" (compulsory demographic change) effected between 1974 and 1976. The extremes of absurdity are reached in relation to currently uninhabited villages: if one displaced person returned, limitations could be imposed until 2022, because such person would constitute 100% of the population, whereas by that date displaced persons may only reach 18% of the village's then current population, in which event limitations may be imposed.

[16] Turkey and Turkish Cypriots keep emphasising "bi-zonality," believing to this day that deep-rooted identity/ethnic conflict prevents mixed living together of Greek and Turkish Cypriots. Thus, when property issues were discussed in Nicosia, the Turkish Cypriot side would agree only to limited reinstatement restricted to residences (ie excluding businesses—see Talking Points, Comments of the Turkish Cypriot side on 12 March 2004, something they were effectively to achieve in the Plan). They resented obvious parallels with the philosophy of *apartheid* being drawn, and insisted that exchange of populations, Turkey's policy in the late 19th and 20th centuries before modern humanitarian law made such policies unlawful, was the appropriate methodology. They contended that the humanitarian arrangements at Vienna on 1 August 1975 were a population exchange agreement, giving the Vienna *communiqué* at times the unilaterally invented title "1975 Vienna Population Exchange (Regrouping of Populations) Agreement". Some Governments, until events in the former Yugoslavia, shared their views. It appears to the writer that Foreign Office policy-makers yearn for "the good old days," when ethnic problems could be "sorted out" by treaties and were prepared to devise means to achieve such effects.

[17] This was a briefing paper circulated by UK diplomats: "Twelve Reasons for Greek Cypriots to vote Yes".

[18] In a paper "It's Your Choice—know the Truth. The Annan Plan in 20 Points".

[19] Both the Secretariat and the Foreign Office made similar exaggerated assertions that "120,000 Greek Cypriots can return to their former homes under Greek Cypriot administration": "Twelve Reasons for Greek Cypriots to vote Yes" and *Report*, para 83, where "some 120,000" are mentioned as returning. However, the UN knew from official statistics provided in December 2002, based on the 1973 Census of Population, that 82,170 displaced persons would be the maximum number entitled to return. They achieved the exaggerated figure by adding an asserted growth of descendants by 40% since 1974, whereas the Statistical Service had told the UN that the 2001 estimate was 106,820 including descendants. The drafters of the *Report* (and the Foreign Office went along with them) are the kind of persons who give statistics a bad name—as the clichéd joke goes.

However, these maximum numbers of eligible persons would not in practice be able to return *to the locations* in which they had lived. This was precluded by the limitations on residence in particular villages or municipalities, which the TCCS would have imposed once the ceiling was hit, so as to avoid concentration of Greek Cypriots in particular villages where they had formerly lived. Thus many who wished to return would have had to settle in *other* locations in the TCCS.

The most serious limitation of all on re-integration of Greek and Turkish Cypriots throughout Cyprus was glossed over by the Secretary-General as being

> a safeguard clause related to the establishment of residency (*Report*, para 51).

The Secretary-General asserted that this mirrored a safeguard on immigration of Greeks and Turks to Cyprus which was "transitional" and not a derogation. But the restriction on assumption of residence by Cypriots was of a permanent character and was to be a derogation from EU Law.[20]

The derogation was given effect in the Constitutional Law on Internal Constituent State Citizenship Status and Constituent State Residency Rights (2004), which read:

> 8 (1) A constituent state may, for a period of up to 19 years following the relevant date or until Turkey accedes to the European Union, whichever is the earlier, limit, on a non discriminatory basis, the establishment of residence by Cypriot citizens who do not hold the relevant internal constituent state citizenship status.
>
> **Thereafter, with a view to protecting its identity, either constituent state may take safeguard measures to ensure that no less than two-thirds of its permanent residents speak its official language as their mother tongue.** (See Foundation Agreement Annex II, Attachment 3 (emphasis added).)

The Article had effect in perpetuity, empowering the Turkish Cypriot side to take action ensuring that no less than two-thirds of its permanent residents had Turkish as their mother-tongue language. Although the *Report*, at para 51, stated that the percentages applied as between "*Cypriot* permanent residents," the Constitutional Law as finalised did not apply the ratio *as between* Greek and Turkish Cypriot language speakers, but covered all permanent residents. Indeed, this was precisely what Turkey wanted, namely, a guarantee that the Turkish Cypriot State (TCCS) would always remain at least two-thirds Turkish Cypriot (or Turkish).[21]

These changes, inserted in Annan V at Turkey's insistence, meant that Greek Cypriots faced the virtual certainty of being subjected to an *upper* quota of

[20] See Annan V, Draft Act of Adaptation of the Terms of Accession of the UCR to the EU and the Constitutional Law on Constituent State Residency rights, referred to above.

[21] The provision was therefore even more limiting than the ceiling of one-third of the population hailing from the GCCS (the other constituent state) contained in Annan I. The Annan I ceiling was subsequently reduced in Annan II to 28%, subject to review and in Annan III had been reduced to 21%, disappearing with Turkey's accession to the EU. Such changes had been the result of "bargains" in the shuttles by Mr de Soto's team, with the Greek Cypriot side making other concessions. This was now conveniently ignored.

33⅓% of the TCCS's permanent residents. To the extent that English, German, Arabic etc language-speakers would have become permanent residents of the TCCS, they would then share in this quota, so that the permissible number of Greek Cypriots would be correspondingly lower.[22] Once the provisions were in practical operation they would have entailed that, if eligible returnees exercised their rights and the "TRNC" were to succeed in its policy of becoming a retirement and holiday home destination for European citizens,[23] relatively few Greek Cypriots who had not been displaced would have had the right of establishment. The outcome would be an aging and dying Greek Cypriot population and some visitors to their holiday homes, thereby effectively achieving the broad ethnic cleansing effect Turkey had always sought.

SERIOUS PROBLEMS REQUIRING SERIOUS REMEDIES

As the Secretary-General properly pointed out in the quoted paragraph with which this Chapter began, almost half the population of Cyprus lost properties as a result of intercommunal strife or military action between 1963 and 1974. Similarly, between 1958 and 1976, and with continuing pressures in the occupied area for Karpas inhabitants to leave, nearly half of the population was displaced. The causes of displacement of Turkish Cypriots are the subject of considerable dispute. On the basis of the rule "what I tell you 3,000 times is true," all displacement of Turkish Cypriots and their genuine resultant suffering was inflicted by Greek Cypriots. This view, which has been assiduously promoted, has undoubtedly affected international attitudes to the Greek Cypriot side. That it has prevailed is the fault of the Greek Cypriot side for not scientifically answering such assertions and analysing the extent of their accuracy, together with provision of an unqualified acceptance of some wrongdoing by certain groups within the Greek Cypriot Community. Apart from the private admissions of Mr Clerides in 1964 at the London Conference, his open statements in his 1989 autobiography, *My Deposition*, and his speech during his investiture for a second term as President on 28 February 1998,[24] there have been few such admissions, and Turkish Cypriot assertions have been left largely

[22] At the end of 2001 it was estimated that there were 9,900 non-Turkish foreign residents in the occupied area: *Estimates of Turkish Cypriots and Settlers from Turkey 1974–2001*, Statistical Service of Cyprus, November 2002, p 10. These numbers are rapidly increasing, with 2,556 foreigners having bought property in 2003 and until the end of August 2004, and there are ambitious property development promotion schemes to lure more foreign home purchasers to the "TRNC".

[23] It will be seen that even property development sales to foreigners were considered as an element furthering "bi-zonality," which is a pervasive concept affecting all aspects of the structures sought (and achieved) by Turkey, just like *apartheid* was in South Africa.

[24] See Public Information Press Release No 1, 28/2/1998. President Clerides, addressing these remarks particularly to Turkish Cypriots, said that both Greek and Turkish Cypriots had suffered a lot, harmed one another and lost their trust in each other. Now was the time to think about the future and to bequeath "a heritage of peace not a heritage of confrontation and conflict". He called on Mr Denktash to work together with him for "our common homeland".

unchallenged.[25] Although details as to the responsibility of the Cypriot parties and the States concerned are relevant for purposes of legal liability, especially their duties of reparation to

> wipe out the consequences of the illegal act and re-establish the situation which would in all probability have existed if that act had not been committed,[26]

here is not the place to set out the facts.[27] What is necessary is to look at the scale of displacement and dispossession at the end of the process, which is the starting point for analysis of the size of the current problem. Subsequent demographic change also requires examination.[28]

DISPLACED PERSONS AND TURKISH MIGRANTS

Following the Turkish invasion of mid-1974 and moves in 1976 onwards to displace inhabitants of the Karpas, there were, after the return to their homes near

[25] From 1995 to 1998 the then Attorney-General, Mr Markides, courageously submitted to the European Commission and Court of Human Rights, sitting in *Cyprus v Turkey*, a full analysis of events, setting out the rights and wrongs of the Cyprus parties, Greece and Turkey. It was unique for a Government officially to make submissions and admissions of this sort. Mr Markides requested the writer to prepare this material and refrained from deleting sections which reflected adversely on Greek Cypriots and Greece. He authorised the writer to publish the documents submitted to the Court in a volume showing the use of historical materials in litigation and the uses of law as a sword and a shield in international relations, based on a case study of Cyprus. Similar material on a history of Cyprus had been prepared in late 1986 for submission to the UK Foreign Affairs Committee, but the Cyprus Foreign Ministry decided it should not be submitted, because it could have occasioned political criticism from some sections of Greek Cypriot opinion. Thus it was that the Turkish Cypriot account remained unchallenged, leading to the then Committee's acceptance of an unbalanced historical account by Turkish Cypriot memorialists and to stimulating disproportionate sympathy for Turkish Cypriots, accompanied by an underlying tone of hostility to Greek Cypriots as being solely responsible of the situation of Turkish Cypriots. Similar sympathies have been excited among visiting diplomats and UN personnel, especially when presented with some of the Turkish Cypriot material presenting their view of events and details of their Community's real suffering. Such sympathisers are unaware that much of this was self-inflicted through the Turkish leadership.

[26] *Chórzow Factory (Indemnity) case* (*Germany v Poland*) 1928 PCIJ (ser A) No 17 (Judgment of 13 September 1928), at 47.

[27] The Secretary-General's recommendation for a Reconciliation Commission to, *inter alia*, prepare a comprehensive report on the history of the Cyprus problem as interpreted by Greek and Turkish Cypriots is essential for future understanding between the members of the Communities—see Plan Annex VII, Article 2b.

[28] Many displaced persons from both Communities have emigrated over the lengthy period. Others have died, but there will have been population growth with descendants. The latter factor has been exploited in the UN presentation of the effect of the Plan to assert that large numbers of persons can return. In fact, persons have re-made their lives and many are unlikely to return. What they want is the choice of returning and the choice of keeping or disposing of their property. That relatively few Greek Cypriots "would, in the end, wish to establish residence in the Turkish Cypriot State" was used by the Secretary-General to justify his imposition of limitations on their return. See para 100 of *S/2003/398*, cited above.

GREEK CYPRIOTS WHO WERE DISPLACED

Above: some countryside Greek Cypriots fleeing because they had heard: "The Turks are coming."

Below: Greek Cypriot displaced persons in one of the many refugee camps. (Later, Mr de Soto said there were no refugees in Cyprus. Was he being pedantically dismissive, in that they were technically "displaced persons" in UNHCR terminology, or was he ignorant, having, on good authority, claimed that he would not read history because this had distorted the views of earlier Special Representatives?)

Above: Greek Cypriot refugees' immediate needs being met.

Below: Things get more organised foodwise.

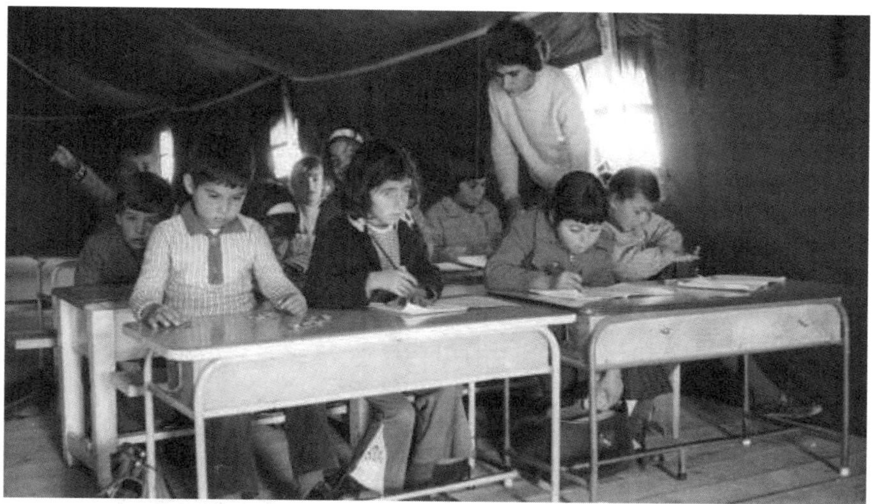

Above: schooling restarts.

Below: normal camp-life for those not at school yet.

Bottom: winter-time. There were 25,000 Greek Cypriots living in tented camps in December 1975.

TURKISH CYPRIOTS WHO WERE DISPLACED

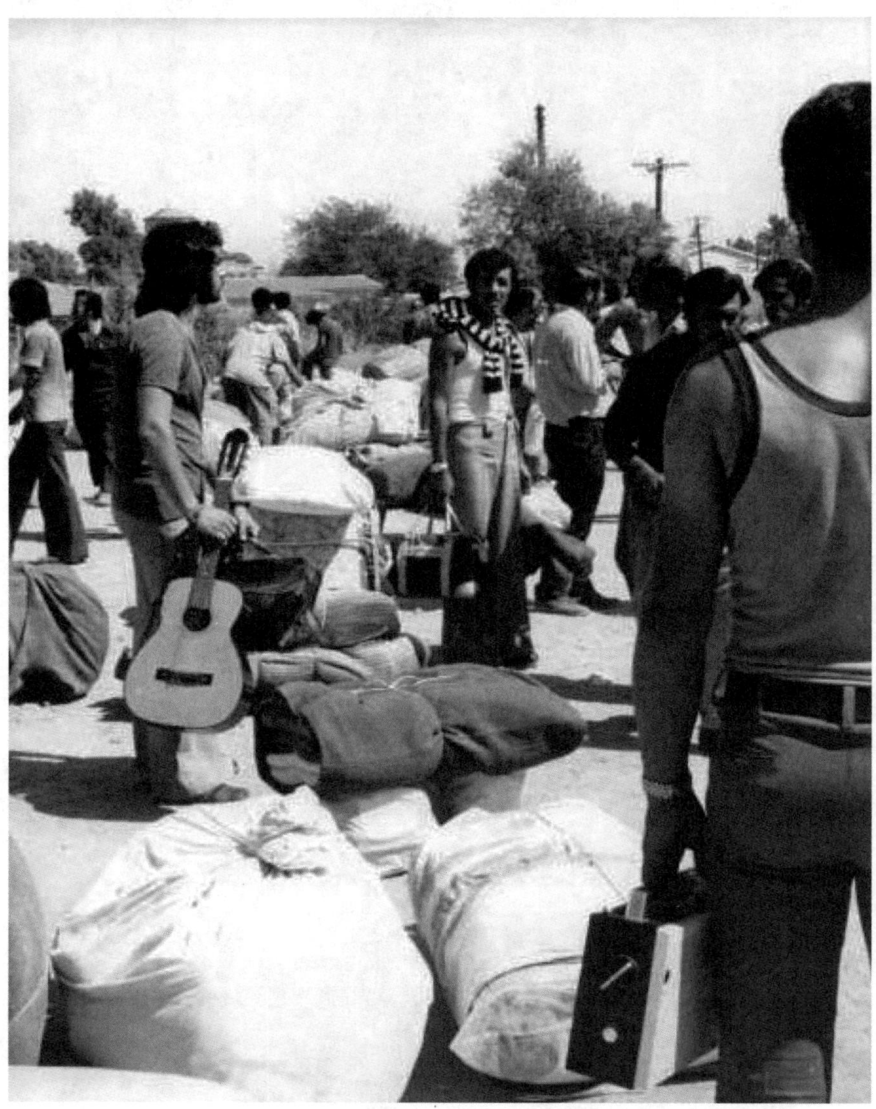

Released Turkish Cypriot detainees and Turkish prisoners of war due to be handed over to the Turkish occupation authorities. Unlike Greek Cypriots who were prisoners of war of Turkey and who came back barefooted and only with the clothes they wore, those released by the Government of Cyprus took their possessions (as did Turkish Cypriots who later moved northwards with UNFICYP). In pursuit of Turkey's policy of ethnic concentration, persons released were kept by Turkey in the occupied area and were refused permission to return to homes in the Government-controlled area.

Above: a camp of Turkish Cypriots sheltering in the Akrotiri SBA. Some Turkish Cypriots moved northwards during or after the fighting, but many remained. Subsequently in mid-January 1975, about 11,000 Turkish Cypriots in the SBAs were flown to Turkey and then transshipped to the Turkish-occupied area. This move was followed in August and September 1975 by that of a further 8,000 Turkish Cypriots, mainly women, children and old people from Paphos, whose male relatives had, upon release as Greek Cypriot detainees, been kept by Turkey in the occupied area. Both moves were effected under implicit threats of further hostilities, and, as regards the latter move, explicit mention of a "limited military operation" by Mr Denktash at the Vienna III meeting on 2 August 1975. He has since maintained that a general exchange of populations was agreed.

Below left: Turkish Cypriots being bussed from a camp to be flown by UK transport planes from the SBAs to Turkey. Right: they were moved on immediately by ship to the Turkish-occupied area.

Turkish Cypriot women and children from Tokhni village, who, on humanitarian grounds, were assisted by the Cyprus Government to move to the Turkish-occupied area. The male inhabitants, with some men from Mari and Zygi, had been rounded up by EOKA 'B' on 14 August 1974 and 50 of them were transported by bus north of Limassol, where they were shot. This atrocity and killings at the Turkish Cyprus villages of Maratha and Sandallaris, on the day after Turkey's second invasion phase commenced, still await investigation. Mutual investigations of all alleged killings and massacres were sought in late August 1974 by Acting President Clerides through UNFICYP, but were refused by Turkey. Turkey was responsible for killings on an extensive scale at many locations, including, *inter alia*, Elia (near Karavas), Palekythrou, Trimithi, Prastio, Ashia, Voni—"these being only a limited number of cases selected as representative," according to the European Commission on Human Rights' *Report*, dated 10 July 1976, on the First and Second Inter-State cases in 1977. Similarly, in *Cyprus v Turkey*, Judgment 10 May 2001, at paragraph 136, the Court found Turkey responsible for failure to effectively investigate and clarify the fate of Greek Cypriots who disappeared in life-threatening circumstances after Turkey's invasion. This finding was based, *inter alia*, on evidence about persons who had disappeared after surrendering at Lapithos (such persons having, according to Mr Denktash in a TV interview on 1 March 1996, been killed by TMT fighters), on evidence of others who were from Ashia and had disappeared from Pavlides Garage in Nicosia where they had been brought, on the evidence of persons missing from Yialousa, Strongylos, etc, etc. The long dormant Committee on Missing Persons, if it begins to operate effectively, may assist in a degree of closure in many cases. But, irrespective of the Committee's limited competence, impunity should not be permitted for anyone—Greek Cypriots, Turkish Cypriots and members of the Turkish Army alike.

the cease-fire lines of persons who had temporarily fled,[29] *163,797 displaced Greek Cypriots.*

After all movements between 1974 and mid-1977 had taken place (including movement of persons who had sheltered in the UK's SBAs and Turkish Cypriots in the Paphos area, who had remained in the Government-controlled area),[30] the Secretary-General stated that *41,700 Turkish Cypriots* had moved to the occupied area. [31]

In a series of migrations from late 1974, Turks from the mainland settled in Cyprus. In a study by the Statistical Service of Cyprus, made on the basis of demographic analysis of published data by Turkey's subordinate local administration, information in the Turkish Cypriot press and Republic of Cyprus data, it was estimated that there were *115,000 Turkish settlers by the end of 2001.*[32]

It should be added that there had, from 1974, been a high level of Turkish Cypriot emigration, resulting in a diminished number of members of the Community in the occupied area. At the end of 2001, only 87,600 Turkish Cypriots were estimated to be present in Cyprus. They amounted to 41.2% of the occupied area's 2001 population. If the number of persons in the Turkish Armed Forces stationed in Cyprus (then around 35,000) were to be added in calculating the percentage of the population who were members of the Turkish Cypriot Community, the percentage of Turkish Cypriots in the occupied area would be 35.4%, compared to 64.6% of persons who were Turkish nationals.[33] These demographic facts explain Turkey's concern in the talks that Turkish settlers should be permitted to stay. The Turkish Cypriot Community would, in Turkey's view, have been too small to retain its identity if settlers had to leave, and if Greek Cypriots were permitted to return to the TCCS in large numbers. Turkey's colonisation of Cyprus, following her "intervention" (aggression), would therefore have been ended.

[29] There were at one stage an estimated 200,000 Greek Cypriot "refugees".

[30] In Dr Waldheim's presence, Mr Denktash threatened a third invasion phase on 1 August 1975 if the Government of Cyprus did not agree that all Turkish Cypriots should be concentrated in the occupied area and were moved there. The resulting humanitarian arrangements, including provision of facilities for Karpas villagers and return of 688 expelled Greek Cypriots, are the Vienna III arrangements. They are referred to by the Turkish Cypriot side as "The Exchange of Populations Agreement" and by other more legalistic invented titles depending upon the audience. (The European Commission of Human Rights was recipient of the most imaginative title.) The Turkish Cypriots, with their possessions, were moved by UNFICYP, with the International Red Cross refusing to be party to such an act.

[31] UN General Assembly doc A 32–282, 25 October 1977, para 23. This figure correlates with the 1973 census figures of Turkish Cypriots who had been in that part of Cyprus which remained under Government control after the invasion.

[32] *Estimates of the Turkish Cypriots and Settlers from Turkey 1974–2001,* November 2002, p 11. Similar estimates were accepted in 2003 by the Council of Europe's Committee on Migration, Refugees and Demography: Parliamentary Assembly, Doc 9799, 2 May 2003, "Colonization by Turkish settlers of the occupied part of Cyprus," para 2. The Rapporteur was Mr J Laakso.

[33] *Ibid*, pp 10 and 12.

PROPERTIES AFFECTED

A crucial matter requiring the making of agreed arrangements was the future ownership or possession of properties owned by displaced and/or dispossessed persons. This was an emotive issue: Greek Cypriots felt that they would lose ancestral homes and assets; and Turkish Cypriots believed that they did not own a fair share of land, proportionate either by area or value to their population numbers.[34] They also feared that they would be economically swamped if Greek Cypriot properties were returned to their owners. The scale of the problem (as it was before the Plan and now still is) appears from TABLES A and B. These give estimated figures (rounded up) which were prepared by officials of the Republic's Department of Lands and Surveys and of the Planning Bureau.

After taking account of the UN proposal for territorial adjustments in Annan III (kept virtually the same in Annan V), according to which many villages, predominantly Greek Cypriot-inhabited in 1974, would become part of the GCCS, the disproportionately large and valuable share of Greek Cypriot-owned property in the TCCS would have been reduced. Nonetheless, there would still be "disproportionality" (see Table C, p 182), partly because in the 20th century Greek Cypriots actively acquired land.

[34] The 12.2% percentage figure of land owned by Turkish Cypriots in the Republic in 1964 has from time to time been challenged by Turkish Cypriot politicians. They have asserted it should be about 34%, a figure derived from using the 1960 census figure that 20.4% of agricultural land was Turkish Cypriot-owned, to which figure was added half the State-owned land as belonging to the equal partner Turkish Cypriot Community. Moreover, claims have been made that large amounts of property under Greek Cypriot title held in terms of the British Colonial land registration system, belong to Evkaf, the Moslem religious trust. However, any claims arising out of or purporting to arise out of British administration of Cyprus were settled in 1960 by the UK Government, which paid the Turkish Cypriot Community £1.5 million in conjunction with confirmation by a letter from future Vice-President Kutchuk and Mr Denktash that Evkaf and the Community had no financial claims against the UK or the Republic. (See *Cmnd* 1093, *Cyprus,* July 1960, Appendix U, pp 221–22.) When serious intercommunal talks were due to begin in 1979 with discussion on return of Varosha as a priority, Evkaf commenced suit in a Famagusta "court". The "court" enjoined the Turkish Cypriot Interlocutor from discussing Varosha on the basis that Evkaf was entitled to Varosha and Famagusta land owned by Lala Mustafa, the 1571 conqueror of Famagusta, which land had had been parcelled out in accordance with British reform of the Mejelle-Ottoman land tenure system. The Turkish mainland newspaper, *Aydinlik*, 18 June 1979, described this "discovery" of Lala Mustafa's ownership as a "formula to torpedo the intercommunal talks" and concluded:

> One wonders to which Pashas Athens, Salonika, Belgrade and Budapest belong. If they also belong to some Pashas, then we could reach again the gates of Vienna.

Evkaf ownership of Varosha, Famagusta and other areas was raised with the UN in 2002 during the formulation of the UN's property proposals. Tactfully, the Secretary-General's *Report*, *S/2003/398*, 1 April 398, para 112, merely stated that "the property ownership was of roughly similar proportions" to the population ie Turkish Cypriots about 18% and Greek Cypriots over 80%. This is correct as regards the Community ownership ratio of *privately-owned* land, which in 1964 was owned as to about 82.5% by Greek Cypriots and as to about 17% by Turkish Cypriots. (The 1964 figures in Table B below ie 59.2% Greek Cypriot-owned to 12.2% Turkish Cypriot-owned, related to *all* owned land in the Republic of Cyprus.)

Table A Land Ownership by Ethnic Group and Location under present situation. Land ownership in Donums for 1964 *(estimated by Department of Lands and Surveys and the Planning Bureau)*

Locations	Greek Cypriot	Turkish Cypriot	Other (Aliens)	Public	Church (1)	Vakouf (2)	Total
Occupied Area	1,405.235	391,212	6.767	551,150	58,147	2,579	2,415.090
Buffer Zone	106,860	25,199	2.494	40,384	5,466	163	180,565
Government-Controlled	2,470.289	401,496	10.011	1,165,029	72,732	11,681	4,131.238
Total	3,982.384	817,905	19.272	1,756.563	136,344	14,423	6,726.893

Table B Percentages of Land Owned by Ethnic Group

Locations	Greek Cypriot	Turkish Cypriot	Other (Aliens)	Public	Church (1)	Vakouf (2)	Total
Occupied Area	58.2%	16.2%	0.3%	22.8%	2.4%	0.1%	100%
Buffer Zone	59.2%	14.0%	1.4%	22.4%	3.0%	0.1%	100%
Government-Controlled	59.8%	9.7%	0.2%	28.2%	1.8%	0.3%	100%
Total	59.2%	12.2%	0.3%	26.1%	2.0%	0.2%	100%

(1) As stated to the Department of Lands and Surveys after 1974 as regards Kyrenia and Famagusta Districts.
(2) No records are available for Famagusta and Kyrenia Districts. The figures here given are estimates.

Furthermore, the making of territorial adjustments did not deal with other problems that would arise upon reaching a settlement—due to intervening developments between 1974 and such time. Displaced persons from the two Communities had been re-housed in homes of displaced persons of the other Community and were also using the other Community's business premises and agricultural land. Formal measures were taken by the Republic of Cyprus under the 1962 and 1966 Laws relating to Requisition of Property to control the occupation of Turkish Cypriot-owned property not personally used by Turkish Cypriots. A Committee for the Protection of Turkish Property was established by Notice No 14202 of 18 August 1975 and property of Turkish Cypriots who had left the Government-controlled area was requisitioned (see Notice No 1218, 11 September 1975). The orders made any occupation of Turkish Cypriot-owned property without Committee approval unlawful. The Committee temporarily leased land to refugees on application by them and gave incentives for land to be put to productive agricultural use. After one year of free rent, refugees were to pay rentals at 50% of the rates in force, and a fund was established, into which rental payments were made and from which repairs were effected. Subsequently, a Guardian of Turkish Cypriot Properties was established, with power to manage such property and to allocate it to Greek Cypriot displaced persons for their use. This was effected by Law 139/1991 and Government notices thereunder. This Law was based on the "abnormal situation," prevailing since Turkey's 1974 invasion with consequential population displacements, interferences with property and barriers to movement to the Government-controlled area imposed by the Turkish Army. The "abnormal situation" would be terminated upon a decision by the Council of Ministers, with interim action being justified on the basis of the doctrine of necessity—so held by the Supreme Court in various rulings. The Minister of the Interior was, during this situation, the Guardian, and the management of properties left by Turkish Cypriots was conducted by the Turkish Cypriot Properties Service under his direction. The practice, authorised by the then Attorney-General, Mr Markides, was followed until mid-2003 of permitting Turkish Cypriots, who returned to reside in the Government-controlled area and who gave 6 months notice, to obtain restitution of their property. In some cases, arrangements would be negotiated for their alternative accommodation. In other cases, properties would be acquired, especially from Turkish Cypriots who lived abroad, or they would be given permission to engage in transactions concerning their property or to sell it. Accordingly, serious disputes did not arise, or, if they did, matters were promptly settled. The situation changed after April 2003, when the "TRNC" for the first time permitted free movement of Turkish Cypriots between the occupied and Government-controlled areas. The potential impact of the new situation was serious. According to Government statistics in 2004, some 25,000 Greek Cypriots remained housed in about 5,500 Turkish Cypriot-owned homes and 30,055 hectares of Turkish Cypriot-owned land were being used for agricultural purposes.[35] The previous policy of returning properties to Turkish Cypriots or of permitting them to sell their properties was therefore changed in June 2004 on the advice of the Attorney-General, Mr Nikitas, and the 1991 Law,

[35] The press has suggested that some of the Turkish Cypriot land and premises has been used by Greek Cypriots who are not displaced persons eligible for allocation to them of Turkish Cypriot owned land: eg *Cyprus Today*, June 12–18, 2004, p 9. Such allocation and use would be contrary to the legal provisions governing use of Turkish Cypriot-owned land.

COUNCIL OF EUROPE ACTION AND INACTION

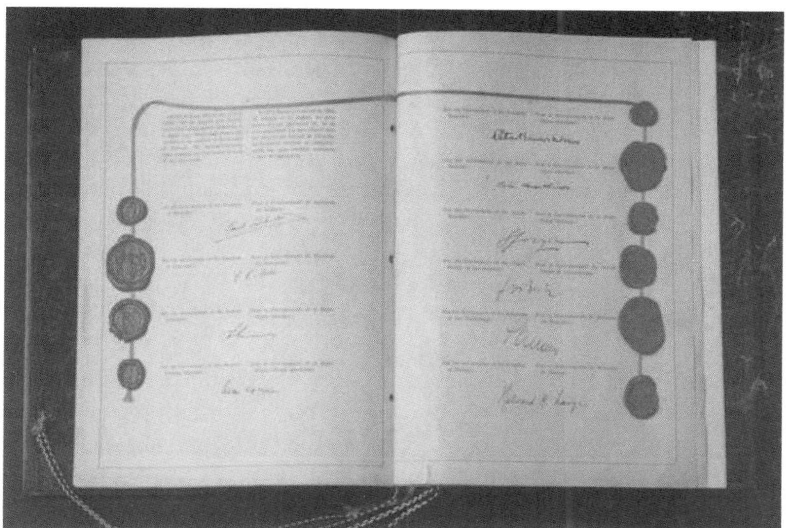

The European Convention on Human Rights and Fundamental Freedoms, signed in Rome on 4 November 1950, the basis of the world's most advanced human rights system. (This and the 6 succeeding photographs are courtesy of the Council of Europe.)

A building where human rights have been the focus of action, with development of new frontiers in freedoms. The Human Rights Building (by Richard Rogers Partnership) in Strasbourg houses the European Court of Human Rights and housed the former Court and Commission.

Towers of Babel, the Council of Europe building where bureaucrats and Member States' representatives talk and discuss, but do little effective work other than to set up expert committees for discussion and organise their meetings and specialised conferences, agree on various European Conventions, supervise execution of straightforward judgments of the Court in individual cases—even then being reluctant to push Turkey to satisfy judgments for violations committed inside Turkey, mainly against Turkish Kurds—and provide liaison and backup for the deliberative Parliamentary Assembly.

The Committee of Ministers of the Council of Europe in session. It has formulated standards, taken decisions on Commission *Reports* on violations of the Convention and supervised execution of Court judgments. But, it is essentially a political organ, even if endowed with quasi-judicial functions. Acting through Ministers' Deputies, it has ducked real challenges, especially in Inter-State Cases where the former Commission and the Court from 1977 onwards have reported or found violations of human rights by Turkey in Cyprus. This reluctance is still evident. Such passivity in the face of continuing violations of human rights will render a fifth Inter-State case by Cyprus against Turkey inevitable.

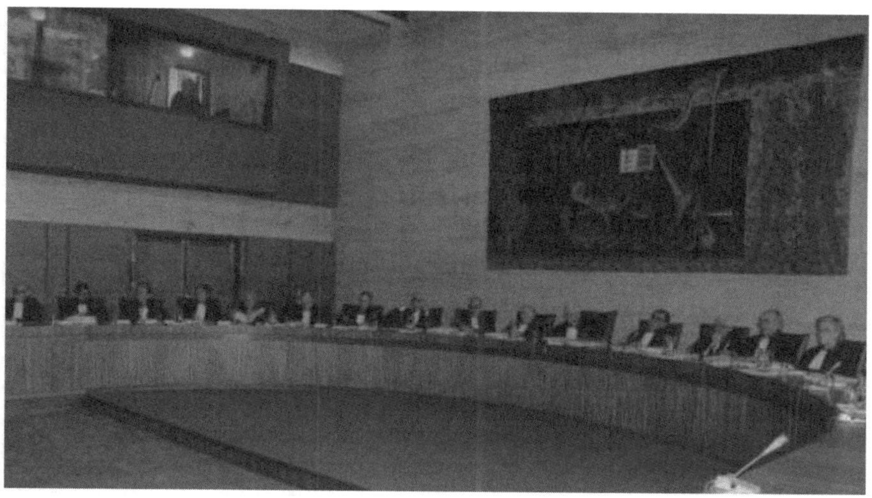

Above: the European Court of Human Rights sitting on 22 June 1994 in *Loizidou v Turkey (Preliminary Objections)* (40/1993/ 435/514, Judgment, 23 March 1995). Centre: President Rolf Ryssdal; third from left, Judge Luzius Wildhaber (later to be President of the new Court under Protocol No. 11); and right, Judge Palm. (She was to follow through with a strong partially dissenting judgment along with 5 other Judges in *Cyprus v Turkey* in the new Court on 10 May 2001, when a majority of the other Judges, although accepting most of Cyprusís complaints about Turkey's violations of human rights, declared some inadmissible on the basis that domestic remedies in the courts of Turkey's subordinate local administration had not been exhausted.)

Below: Applicant Titina Loizidou (third from left) who made legal history, claiming interference by Turkey with her property by denying her access and control since 1974. She is with her Cypriot lawyers (left, Achilleas Demetriades and Joanna Loizides) and, right, Ian Brownlie QC, who advocated applying the law of State responsibility in an extended manner to hold States legally responsible for acts and omissions in locations under their effective overall control, even if outside national territory. The photograph was taken at the hearing on Merits on 25 September 1995.

The last case heard by the European Commission of Human Rights was *Cyprus v Turkey*, Application No 25781/94, an Inter-State case. The comprehensive *Report* was adopted on 4 June 1999 and was a model "judgment", showing what a tribunal concerned to uphold human rights is capable of achieving. Over a period of nearly 40 years, the Commission created most of the jurisprudence under the European Convention on Human Rights and Fundamental Freedoms, until Protocol No 11 replaced the Commission by an expanded Court, regrettably of lesser quality. The photograph (by the Council of Europe) shows Cyprus's team at the historic hearing on 7 July 1998: front row, Polis Polyviou, Professor Malcolm Shaw, Ian Brownlie QC, and the Attorney-General of Cyprus, Alecos Markides. In the rear are Nicos Emiliou (left) and the writer (behind Ian Brownlie).

providing for vesting of the properties in the Minister during the tendency of the abnormal situation was more rigorously enforced. When some Turkish Cypriots requested return of their properties or authority to sell these and this was declined, litigation followed. In the case of *Arif Mustafa v Minister of Interior, through Limassol District*, Case 125/2004, decided on 24 September 2004, Hadjihambis J ruled that Law 139/1991 had been misinterpreted to exclude Turkish Cypriots who had returned after 1991 from reclaiming their property and then ordered that the property be restored to the plaintiff.

The case is now on appeal. Depending upon the ruling, the Law will require amendment to protect the respective interests of the persons involved.[36] The major differences between the arrangements made in the "TRNC" and those applicable in the Government-controlled area are that in the latter area, where there is guardianship, the title remains in the Turkish Cypriot owner, although such owner is temporarily (even long-term) deprived of possession. However, a right of recourse to the Republic's Courts, under Article 23 of the Constitution governing the right to property, is exercisable.[37] The *Arif Mustafa* Case shows both the practical effect of this difference and the independence of the Cyprus judiciary.

In the Turkish-occupied area, the "Constituent Assembly of the Turkish Federated State of Kibris" by "Laws 17, 32 and 33" provided for the collection, control, administration, allocation and utilisation of "aliens' property". "Aliens" included Greek Cypriots other than those who were "citizens of the TFSK". In 1977 the "Housing, Rehabilitation and Property of Equal Value Law No 33 of 1977" was passed. This facilitated rehabilitation of Turkish Cypriots who had left the south to settle in the north by allocating Greek Cypriot-owned property to them, and issuing them with "certificates of immovable property of equal value" if they agreed to assign their property in the Government-controlled area to the "TRNC Ministry of Finance". Allocated land could not be transferred for a period of 20 years. The "Law" also provided for housing and land for relatively needy Turkish Cypriots. In 1982 it was extensively amended to provide for land redistribution to Turkish Cypriots, Turkish settlers, Turkish soldiers who had served in Cyprus, and other persons. The "Settlement, Land Allocation and Equivalent Property Law No 27 of 1982" provided for "certificates of definitive possession," and also stipulated that title was not transferable for 20 years (section 18).[38] This non-transferability meant that

[36] It appears to the writer that some form of long-term requisition will need to be introduced, together with provision for fair rents supported by State subsidies to assist displaced persons who occupy properties. This will also protect owners' interests. Property not occupied by displaced persons should be returned to the owner, while a policy of negotiated purchases, combined with loans, also needs consideration.

[37] Some properties were compulsorily acquired (with resultant loss of title and compensation in lieu). Such compensation has, it appears, not been paid out by the Fund, controlled by the Minister of the Interior, into which such compensation has to be paid. These matters are currently under investigation and require regularisation.

[38] The first allocations were made on 20 December 1982: "TRNC" Housing Minister, Mr Serakinci, in *Birlik*, 21 December 1982.

Turkey could contend that there had not been a confiscation in international law, but merely control of use—an argument put to the Council of Europe's Committee of Ministers by Turkey in her Second Memorial dated 16 April 1987. That document was circulated by the Turkish Government after the Commission of Human Rights had, in Cyprus's third recourse, found Turkey responsible for continuing violation of rights to properties and homes in the occupied area. In a Memorial of 30 August 1986, Cyprus had asked the Committee of Ministers to take action of the basis of the Commission's *Report* and had drawn the Committee's attention to the "Constitution of the Turkish Republic of Northern Cyprus 1985" whose "Article 159" purported to confiscate all Greek Cypriot property "found abandoned".[39]

In 1995, by an amendment effected by "Law No 52 of 1995" the "definitive possessory certificate" was replaced by an "immovable property title deed" and the administrative practice developed of the "Land Registry" recording and issuing separate title deeds, whereas, previously, properties owned by Greek Cypriots in respect of which "certificates" had been issued were listed in a separate register and the formal Land Registry books had been kept unaltered.[40]

To persons unfamiliar with the intricacies of the "TRNC Law," available only in the Turkish language, it must have appeared that, by "administrative decisions," both the Greek Cypriot and the Turkish Cypriot sides had granted possession of "abandoned" properties to displaced persons from their Communities. That a flood of transfers of title would occur in the "TRNC" from 20 December 2002 onwards, a date after formulation of Annan I and II, appears not to have been present to the minds of the Plan's draftsmen.[41]

[39] The Committee of Ministers took no decision on the matter. On 2 April 1992 it adopted Resolution DH (92) 12 in respect of the Commission's 1983 *Report*, limiting itself to a decision to make the 1983 *Report* public and stating that its consideration of the case was thereby completed. This Resolution was requested by the Foreign Minister of Cyprus to clear the path for fresh judicial proceedings, because, so long as the matter was pending before the Committee of Ministers, Turkey could contend that this was a bar to a fresh recourse to the European Convention machinery or to another international tribunal. The pusillanimity of the Committee of Ministers, which took no action on the Commission's *Reports* of 10 July 1976 and 4 October 1983 and has merely discussed some limited aspects of the European Court of Human Rights' judgment of 10 May 2001, has been a factor encouraging Turkey in her continuing violations of human rights in Cyprus and to both Turkey and the UN taking the view that the Council of Europe would endorse provisions of the Plan ensuring that Turkey would no longer be respondent State in relation to events in Cyprus.

[40] See "Observations of the Turkish Republic of Northern Cyprus" in *Cyprus v Turkey* (Application No 25781/94), 21 November 1997, by Dr (hc) Z M Necatigil, Legal Adviser, paras 273–84.

[41] However they appreciated that some transfers to foreigners could "in theory" occur. See note 44 below. Draft Annex VII on property, Article 12 (Article 13 in Annan V), protected purchasers of Greek Cypriot-owned property allocated to Turkish Cypriot displaced persons who had themselves been dispossessed, if the property left in the south were given in exchange together with any difference in value and the purchaser and the vendor collectively had owned the property for 10 years. But this exception was understandable: displaced persons who had been dispossessed arguably needed to be able after a lengthy period to realise and dispose of assets if they made their "abandoned" property available to the Property Board, thereby enabling the Board to pay out compensation to persons adversely affected ie the Greek Cypriot owners of the sold property.

When regard is had to the general redistribution of Greek Cypriot-owned land which had occurred in the "TRNC" from 1977 onwards, to the comparative values of Greek Cypriot and Turkish Cypriot-owned land and to Turkish Cypriot perceptions as to disproportionality of land ownership as between the Communities collectively, it is unsurprising that Turkey and the Turkish Cypriot side contended that a "global exchange of property" was the only appropriate methodology. They also claimed that this was entailed by the alleged "exchange of populations agreement," subject to a potential balancing of accounts, which they claimed was in favour of the Turkish Cypriot side. This "global exchange" was opposed by the Greek Cypriot side on the ground that Governments could not override individuals' rights to claim restitution of their property.[42]

PRINCIPLES AND PROVISIONS ADOPTED BY THE UN IN THE PLAN REGARDING RETURN OF DISPLACED PERSONS AND PROPERTY RESTITUTION

The UN (along with the USA and the UK Foreign Office) took the attitude in making provision as regards return of displaced persons and restitution of property that:

(i) Turkish migrants should on the basis of humanitarian principles—many had lived for long periods in Cyprus—nearly all be permitted to remain. They should also not become homeless, and should thus be entitled to assistance by way of social housing or financial aid. (That this would effectively legitimate the consequences of a war crime, violating Article 49.6 of the Fourth Geneva Convention was not considered relevant.)

(ii) Displaced persons should be permitted to return to their former district of residence, but
  (a) in phases, with long moratoria; and
  (b) subject to constituent state quota limitations, at first based on constituent state citizenship status, and later subject to an upper limit which would be ethno-linguistically based (explained above).

(iii) Rights of individuals to their homes should be given effect by way of restitution, subject to the following exceptions where restitution was not permitted:
  (a) where the current user was a displaced person who had left property of a broadly similar value in the other constituent state which could be surrendered to the Property Board;[43]

[42] The Greek Cypriot side's opposition was based on principle, and not on the fact that an absurd exchange was being suggested, namely about £16.7 billion worth of Greek Cypriot-owned property in the TCCS (at 2002 values at comparable locations in the Government-controlled area) as against £1.6 billion worth of Turkish Cypriot-owned property in the GCCS.

[43] The property available for surrender should be worth at least two-thirds of the property sought to be acquired by the current user. In the talks, each side attempted to alter these proportions: the Turkish Cypriot side to make the value lower, so that displaced Turkish Cypriots who had

(b) where a subsequent purchaser had bought from such a user and he and the seller had collectively used the property for 10 years (thereby protecting foreigners who had acquired such properties);[44]

(c) where the land had a significant improvement ie an improvement which is worth more than the current market value of the land in its state at the time the improvement was made;

(d) where the property was owned by any company, partnership or association of persons whose shareholders or members were not close relatives;[45]

(e) where the property was used for military purposes;

(f) where the property was used for public benefit purposes; and

(g) where the displaced owner had not either built the house, or lived in it for at least 10 years, and a current user had lived in it for ten years.[46]

(iv) Rights of institutions (companies, unincorporated associations, trusts, the Church and Evkaf—the Moslem religious Trust) would be only to compensation and not to restitution, except in the case of religious sites, together with in exceptional cases other buildings or land up to 2 donums (2675.5 square metres), with special provision being made for one major Greek religious site (Apostolos Andreas monastery) and the major Moslem site (Hala Sultan Tekke). This amounted to sweeping nationalisation of corporate and religious property.[47] All property of the Church

acquired valuable properties, having left behind properties of minimal value, could acquire title; and the Greek Cypriot side to raise the necessary value of the property to be given to the Property Board in part exchange, so that fewer current users could acquire title.

[44] This encouraged sales to foreigners, which greatly increased once the Plan's property provisions were published in November 2002. Miss Garlick, in a paper entitled Annan Plan Presentation: Proposed Property Arrangements under the Annan Plan, November 2003, n 10, observed that "this provision also *in theory* entitles a foreign purchaser to retain possession of a property s/he may have bought, if the requirements are met" (emphasis added).

[45] Where an individual used a company as a mechanism to hold his property, restitution was not excluded.

[46] Annex VII, Part II, Article 16.3. This provision has overtones of the "ten-year rule" applied in Rwanda, a country which depends on subsistence agriculture but has a dreadful land shortage, unlike Cyprus. It is an inappropriate precedent to apply. In Cyprus sufficient land is available for alternative accommodation to be built in convenient locations and agriculture is not the major activity it once was. Nor, indeed, should it be encouraged as a way of life in a Cyprus which is part of the EU.

[47] Annex VII, Attachment 1, Article 1.6 and 14. There was also the exception mentioned above as regards family companies and corporations sole. In her November 2003 paper, Miss Garlick explained: "What is the rationale behind this? For the vast bulk of companies, a specific property does not have an emotional significance. What matters to the company is the financial value of its asset. Therefore, the property rights of a company can be effectively recognized and satisfied through the payment of full and effective compensation." This is a recipe for wholesale nationalisation. Miss Garlick went on to claim that "the Plan, seeks to *prioritize* individuals for reinstatement over companies." This is misleading: companies as such could not claim reinstatement. It was only where a company was a mere mechanism for individual or family ownership that restitution to one-third of the value or area was an entitlement. The UN's concern to give Turkish Cypriot individuals priority over Greek Cypriot commercial interests sits ill with the UN's concern to prioritise Turkish Cypriot commercial developments over Greek Cypriot individuals' rights to return of their land, and to give developers and improvers title. See below. Principles appear to have been abandoned when it came to Turkish Cypriot as against Greek Cypriot individuals' interests.

of Cyprus had earlier been transferred to Evkaf, the Moslem religious trust, under legislation and orders of the "Turkish Federated State of Cyprus" (predecessor of the "TRNC"). As current user, Evkaf would have been entitled to acquire such land in exchange for its Vakouf land in the GCCS, subject to payment of any difference in value. Since Evkaf owned relatively little land in comparison with the Church (which had been beneficiary from many donors and testators over centuries) most Church property would in terms of the Plan have ended up in the hands of the Property Board.[48]

(v) Effective nationalisation of property was to occur via transfer to a Property Board, which would, as a general rule, acquire all institutionally owned property, except the religious sites and private family companies, and would also acquire about two-thirds of the property of persons who had been dispossessed.[49] This insistence on what was the equivalent of extensive nationalisation of land made the property and compensation scheme so burdensome to dispossessed owners.[50] After

[48] Evkaf-owned (Vakouf) land in the area under Government control was estimated at 11,681 donums in 1964, while Church-owned land in the area to be occupied was estimated at about 58,147 donums.

[49] It will be recollected that owners could only be reinstated to one-third of the land areas they owned, or one-third of the current value of any land (whichever first applied): Annex VII, Attachment 1 Article 1.13 "Restitution entitlement". As minimum, an owner could claim his house and one donum.

[50] This extensive nationalisation through the intermediacy of the Property Board was the legacy of Turkey's desire for *global* exchange of all property between Greek Cypriots and Turkish Cypriots. Whereas it was sensible to seek to ensure that dispossessed Turkish Cypriots should be able to acquire property at least the equivalent of what they had, and also to ensure that the State had land for necessary housing schemes (although since it owned so much land, acquisition of much more was scarcely necessary) there was little need to acquire land for more than those purposes and thereafter to provide for its resale with compensation to owners being paid from these proceeds. This is "forced sale" in effect in order to reinforce "bi-zonality".

If people kept their land and were assisted, if they wished, to sell or exchange it, through accredited private sector estate agencies, the State would not have to invest about CY £100 million in a large and bureaucratic Property Board, and individuals would not have to lose 2/3 of their property in exchange for long-term "compensation bonds and property appreciation certificates," which would be diminished in value by responsibility to pay for the Property Board, with final payments being made to holders 25 years after issuance (ie from 28–30 years in practice). This is a matter which Cypriots should negotiate in their common interests. It was not helpful in resolving these issues that some of the UN team's property lawyers (eg Miss Jones) had, because of experiences in other countries, a view that divisive land questions required for their resolution "broad-based public ownership" and had doubts about the wisdom of restitution: see her chapter in *Returning Home, op cit*, p 223.

There is a remarkable gap in *Returning Home: Housing and Property Restitution Rights of Refugees and Displaced Persons* in that although Annan I, II and III with detailed property provisions had already been published, restitution for displaced Cypriots was not dealt with. On the basis of the Editor's statement, if consistently applied, that countries where problems were still being grappled with or where the political will adequately to address the issue had not been found were not covered in this virtually comprehensive series of studies, the Palestinian Case, Georgia and Turkey, should, like the Cyprus case, have been omitted from the volume. Was there a concern that if authoritative and independent NGO staff members and academics dealt professionally and impartially with the issues concerning Cyprus's displaced persons, UN agencies would be displeased, and future sponsorship would be affected? Or was the Editor "warned off" by the Secretariat, possibly the territorial adjustments proposed by the UN for transfer of administration of territory to the GCCS, the land ownership percentages in the TCCS would have been:

Table C TCCS: Figures of Land Ownership under Annan V[51]

Ownership	Area in donums	% to all UCR land	% to TCCS land	Transfers to Property Board under Annex VII AND State land
G/C Land	1,051,269	15.50	54.10	36.06
T/C Land	363,636	5.40	18.70	—
Aliens' Land	4,153	0.06	0.21	—
State Land	484,605	7.20	24.90	24.90
Church Land	37,524	0.55	1.93	1.84[52]
Vakouf Land	1,732	0.026	0.09	—
Total Land	1,942,919	28.70	100.00	62.80

The consequence of applying the Plan's property provisions to these land-ownership percentages would have been that approximately two-thirds of the land owned by Greek Cypriots in the TCCS would be transferred to the Property Board,[53] so that the Board would then acquire 36.06% of the owned

by way of the two contributors, Mesdames Garlick and Jones, who formed part of Mr de Soto's property team, with a claim that a contribution independently assessing the problems of Cyprus and commenting on the Plan's property provisions could prejudice acceptability of the de Soto Plan. Commercial sponsorship of scientific research raises doubts about the validity of findings. The same doubts should be raised about the veritable industry of social science "think-tanks," conferences and NGOs sponsored by Governments and foundations supporting their policies.

[51] Compiled by the Department of Lands and Surveys, using the Cyprus map 1:50,000, an analysis of the Annan line and the administrative boundaries of the Communities to compute percentages of the Communities falling into the TCCS. These percentages were then applied to the 1964 land ownership figures. Accuracy is to ± 3%. (Only by a very-time consuming process of examining the cadastral plans and individual properties in relation to the Annan line could precise figures be achieved.)

[52] Estimate after deduction of religious sites.

[53] One third of land owned, or at minimum a house and one donum (1,337.76 sq metres), was to be reinstatable. Houses would be reinstatable only if they had been lived in by the dispossessed owner for 10 years (the "10 year rule") or had been built by him. Thus displaced persons who in 1974 were under 10 years of age were disentitled to claim the family house, as were purchasers of houses after about September 1964. Since reinstatement claims would be determined in 2009 (assuming the Foundation Agreement came into force in 2004), only heirs who were then over 45 years old would be entitled to reinstatement. There were also restrictions on reinstatement of agricultural land—mentioned below. The effect would be that at least two-thirds of the Greek Cypriot-owned property would be acquired by the Property Board.

There is doubt whether this one-third reinstatement entitlement was to be calculated on all land owned, or was first to have deducted from it land which was compulsorily acquired by a current user from the owner or by a significant improver of the property. In any event, if the reinstatement land in the TCCS. Unless sold by the Board,[54] or the life of the Board was extended annually by the Supreme Court, such land was to be transferred in 10 years to a Compensation Trust. Church land, apart from any exchanged with or paid for by Evkaf, was also to go to the Board (ie up to 1.93% of owned land in the TCCS, say 1.84% excluding the religious sites). Together with the existing State land (24.9%),[55] the Board (and thereafter the Compensation Trust) would own approximately 62.8% of land in the TCCS, ie 36.06% formerly Greek Cypriot-owned, 1.84% formerly Church-owned, and 24.9% of State land. Such a situation was not one likely to improve the individual incomes of Turkish Cypriots, unless they were "given" discriminatory capital gains by way of ability to buy land from the Board (or later from the Compensation Trust) at a large discount,[56] which they then used to produce income. The interim situation would have been that a very high proportion of land would be in public ownership, whether as State land, or as Property Board or Compensation Trust land, and this situation would have continued unless there were to have been large-scale discriminatory action in favour of individual Turkish Cypriot purchasers.

(vi) Return of agricultural land was restricted by provisions prohibiting subdivision into plots less than 5 donums, or less than 2 donums for irrigable land. Thus, unless a plot was 15 donums (3 × 5 donums)upon sub-division, or 6 donums if irrigable (3 × 2 donums), it could not be reinstated. Cypriots have traditionally had the equivalent of smallholdings, especially as regards irrigable land. These restrictions as to plot size would have prevented return of a great deal of agricultural land to its owners.[57]

entitlement is calculated on all land owned by dispossessed owners, the fraction of land remaining in Greek Cypriot ownership would be less than one-third, because the rights of current users and improvers to acquire title would then have to be taken into account. This would correspondingly increase the Turkish Cypriot percentage of ownership. These changes in ownership percentages as between the Communities are ignored in the discussion in the text above.

[54] Sales would be on a different and lower basis of valuation than any compensation paid, ie they would be discounted when sold to Turkish Cypriots. Compensation was payable on a "current value" formula to reflect appreciation of property in Cyprus in comparable locations in the period until the entry into force of the Foundation Agreement. Sales were to be on "market value" for comparable properties at the time of sale: see Annex VII, Part II, Article 8.2; Attachment 1, Article 1, 4 and 1.8; and Attachment 2, Article 2.b and d.

[55] Land owned by the Republic of Cyprus in the future TCCS would be owned by the TCCS unless it was on the short list of properties to be owned by the Federal Government.

[56] As indicated, some discounting was involved. This was in effect a further benefit to "secondary occupants". Principles now being developed by the international community to govern restitution of refugees' and displaced persons' property prescribe that "secondary occupants" should not be able to acquire title, let alone acquire at a discount.

[57] A donum is 1337.76 square metres. Owners could aggregate their reinstatement entitlements or sell them to other dispossessed owners from the same village. See Annex VII, Part II, Article 16.6. Nonetheless, much agricultural land would not be reinstated, especially as other villagers, if hit by the ceilings for return, would not then buy agricultural land requiring constant work.

(vii) Turkey was to be protected against claims for the violations of property rights arising out of her State responsibility, which had been found by the European Court of Human Rights in *Loizidou v Turkey* and *Cyprus v Turkey*.[58]

(viii) Restrictions on the establishment of business, industry and professional activities by returnees, and also by other Cypriots, would be permissible for up to six years after the entry of the UCR into the EU if these could cause difficulties likely to persist in any section of the economy of the TCCS. Such restrictions could be imposed for 3 months by the TCCS and prolonged on EU Commission authority.[59]

It should be apparent that although the UN purported not to adopt the Turkish and Turkish Cypriot demands for a global exchange of Greek Cypriot and Turkish Cypriot-owned properties between the Communities (constituent states) in conjunction with a compensation scheme, the provisions for taking of property by the Property Board were so extensive that there was a virtual global exchange, with compensation being the norm, rather than restitution. Annan III had provided for a 10% ceiling on return of property, but the Plan was changed at Bürgenstock. The changes had a dual purpose: they dealt with complaints by the Greek Cypriot side that some persons would get all their property while most would get none back; and the model of giving nearly everyone back some of their property *created the impression* that all individuals were being given back their property, together with some compensation. Were this impression successfully to be created, the property provisions would be more likely to withstand scrutiny by the European Court of Human Rights.[60] This change in the

[58] This immunity of Turkey was to be effected by a joint letter by the Co-Presidents to the Court and a provision that the UCR should be the sole responsible State party, with there now allegedly being a domestic mechanism to remedy property violations (the property scheme), taken together with liability imposed by the Plan upon the constituent states for acts prior to the Agreement. See Annex IV, Attachments 1 and 2; Annex VII, Part II, Article 5.2; and Main Article 12.2.

[59] D. Draft Act of Adaptation to the Terms of Accession of the UCR to the EU, Article 4. Safeguard measures. Such measures were not to be disguised restrictions on trade. This more emollient wording in Annan V replaced explicit restrictions in Annan IV, but the objective was the same.

[60] The same misleading impression was sought to be conveyed to the international community in the Secretary-General's *Report*. Thus its paragraph 48 described the changes as "providing that most Greek Cypriots would have some property reinstated in the Turkish Cypriot State [. . .] and *all* for returnees to four Karpas villages and the Maronite village of Kormakiti." This superficially reassuring picture was deceptive. First, as regards homes, only persons who *owned* a dwelling at the time it was built, or had lived in it for ten years, were eligible for reinstatement. Second, current users' rights were in many cases to prevail over the entitlements of eligible dwelling-owners. Third, current users' rights would also prevail over the rights of returnees to the Karpas and Maronite villages, so "all" their property would not be returned. Fourth, Karpas villagers (and their descendants) would have had to resume residence within 6 years of the entry into force of the Foundation Agreement or would lose their right to reinstatement (Annex VII, and II, Article 16.8). The Secretariat's presentation was deliberately bland and intended to convey to any reader unaware of the hidden technicalities and "Catch 22-s" in the property provisions that the changes in Annan V favoured Greek Cypriot property owners and had been designed to meet their concerns.

Turkey's Army symbolically flaunts its domination, with flags vandalising the Pentadactylos Range, each 462 metres long. The left flag carries Atatürk's maxim: "How happy is one who says 'I am a Turk'." The right is the derivative "TRNC" flag. Turkish Cypriot goodwill has not extended to their removal, with the flags being seen from most of central Cyprus.

"Independence" celebrations with the Turkish Army on 15 November 1996, when international pressures to start the recent series of negotiations became operative. "President" Denktash is with Lt General Kuntaci, Commander of the Turkish Armed Forces in Cyprus, and "Ambassador" Aydan Karahan, who returned as "Ambassador" in November 2004, probably with various electoral missions. Lt General Kuntaci was responsible in August 1996 for ordering the shooting of a Greek Cypriot demonstrator, who had climbed a flagpole to pull down Turkey's flag. Turkey's Prime Minister, Mrs Çiller, implied that anyone who touched Turkey's flag would suffer a similar fate.

Richard Holbrooke and "Tom" Miller on a visit to President Clerides on 4 April 1998 are not looking to see if they spilled soup on their ties. Even Holbrooke was unable to persuade Turkey and Mr Denktash to enter fresh negotiations, the latter demanding as pre-conditions prior recognition of the "TRNC" and withdrawal of Cyprus's EU application. Coming with bad news, the American visitors were less than pleased that photographs were taken.

Other important Americans were to visit Cyprus Presidents. Here Under-Secretary of State Marc Grossman and Ambassador Weston are meeting President Papadopoulos at the Waldorf Towers on 26 September 2003. Mr Grossman told the President that "the US is squarely and energetically for a solution to the Cyprus problem, a solution that is fair and good for all the parties. We ought to use the time between now and early next year, May, to see what can be done." He then referred to the positive impact for Cyprus of Turkey's EU entry.

Have any two other politicians been sparring partners for so long? (Since February 1963 on the divisive municipalities issues.) "President" Denktash and President Clerides are pictured before dining at the latter's home on 29 December 2001. Two square meals at each other's homes fuelled their will to begin direct talks in Nicosia on 16 January 2002.

Prime Minister Simitis of Greece visited President Clerides and Cyprus's National Council at their hotel on the first morning of the December 2002 European Council in Copenhagen. When the photographers left, he would tell the Greek Cypriot side to accept Annan II and to "Get it over and done with".

A new Triple Alliance? Germany, France and Turkey? That would be usurping the UK's desired role as Turkey's EU friend. Chancellor Schroeder, Prime Minister Gül and President Chirac shake hands at the Copenhagen European Council.

Later at the Copenhagen meeting, Prime Minister Blair appears to be telling his new—soon to be best—friends, Messrs Gül and Erdoğan, not to over-react to admission to the EU of the Republic of Cyprus without a Cyprus solution. He can (almost) fix anything, especially for an ally like Turkey.

The long and the short of it: France has been a loyal friend to Cyprus since February 1964. The Copenhagen summit group photograph, bottom row right to left: Presidents Clerides and Chirac, Prime Minister Rasmussen and Foreign Minister Per Stig Møller of Denmark. Prime Ministers Bertie Ahern of Ireland, Jan Peter Balkenende of the Netherlands and Jean-Claude Junker of Luxembourg are behind Mr Rasmussen.

"President" Denktash meets the Secretary-General at The Hague on 10 March 2003, informing him that he had fundamental objections to Annan III; that a new starting point was necessary; and that the parties would have to agree on basic principles. Moreover, Turkey told the Secretary-General it was unable to make the commitment his Plan required. After a last attempt to salvage the process, with Mr Denktash rejecting his proposals, the Secretary-General announced the process had reached "the end of the road".

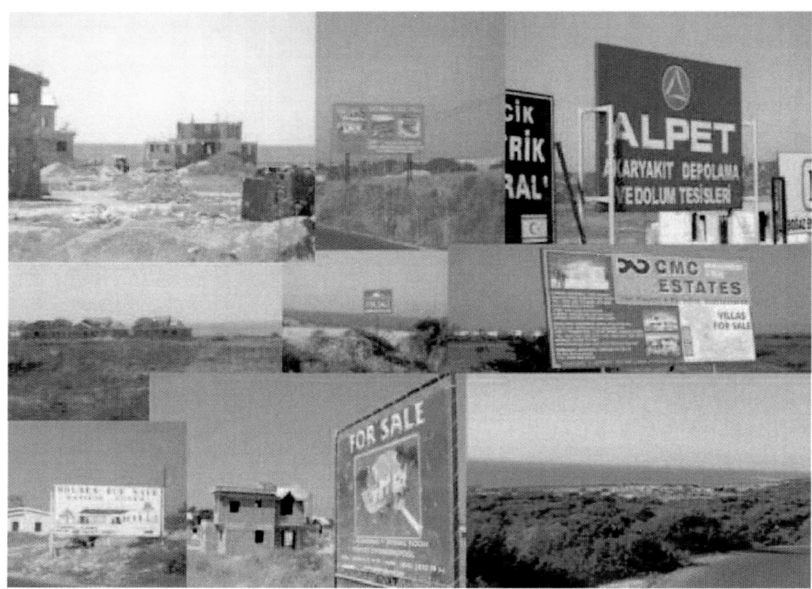

On 23 April 2003 the Turkish Army opened two crossings and permitted Greek Cypriots to enter the occupied area, where they discovered what was happening to their property. Bottom right is typical Karpas countryside. This large area, owned by the Church of Cyprus, would, as religious property, be expropriated under the Annan Plan, which protects only places of worship, the small areas forming an inseparable part of such religious sites, and cemeteries.

How long will the Karpas and its bays, where virtually extinct Mediterranean turtles lay their eggs, remain the same if there is not a federal national park?

Karpas untouched.

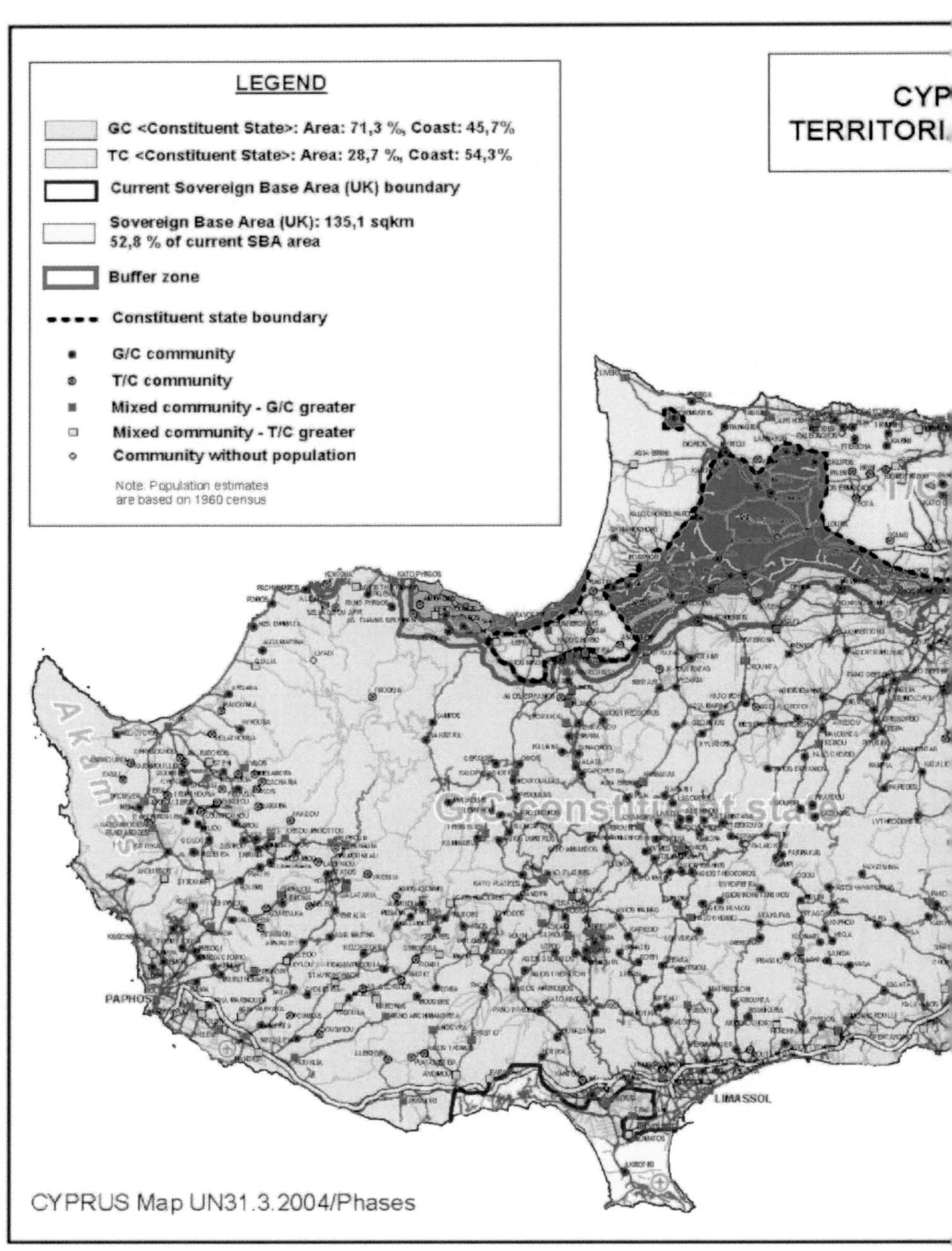

Prepared by: Andreas Hadjiraftis, December 23, 2004

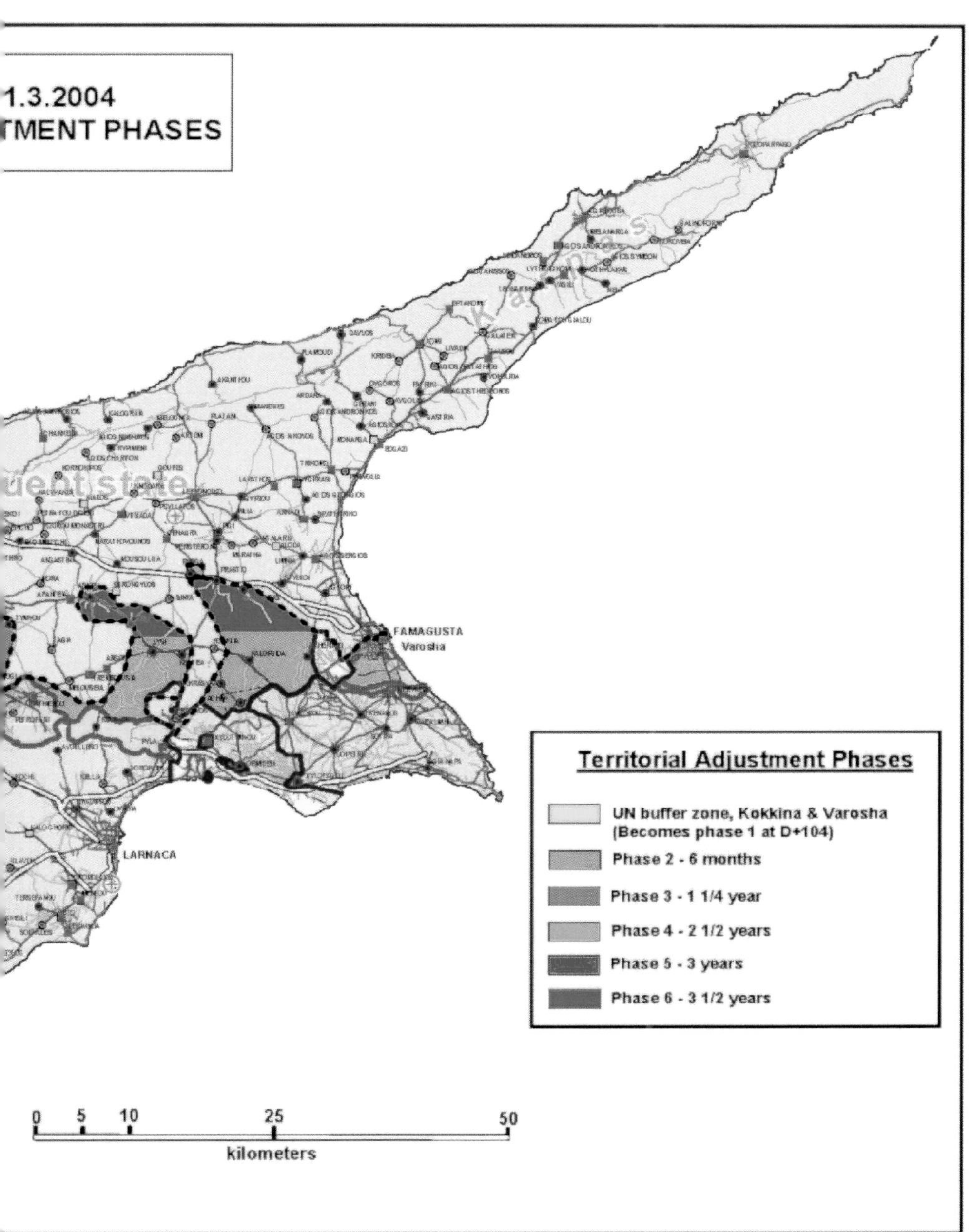
1.3.2004
TMENT PHASES
FAMAGUSTA
Varosha
LARNACA
Territorial Adjustment Phases
UN buffer zone, Kokkina & Varosha
(Becomes phase 1 at D+104)
Phase 2 - 6 months
Phase 3 - 1 1/4 year
Phase 4 - 2 1/2 years
Phase 5 - 3 years
Phase 6 - 3 1/2 years
0
5
10
25
50
kilometers

ACH: MAP-UN3.13.2004/Ph

President George W Bush at the White House on 28 January 2004 with Prime Minister Erdoğan. Transcript: "I've been looking forward to this meeting because Turkey is a friend and an ally in America. We talked about Iraq and the United States' ambition for a peaceful country, democracy and one that is territorially integral. . . . He briefed me on the Cyprus problem and I appreciated his trying to find a solution to a long-standing dispute; and the Prime Minister's determination to fight terrorism." President Bush's father, when President, supported Turkey and her Kurdish policy to keep her on side on Iraq, but did not do so at the expense of Turkish gains in Cyprus.

President George W Bush with the Secretary-General on 3 February 2004 at the White House. Transcript: "We've just had a really constructive dialogue about a lot of issues. . . . The world is changing to the better and the UN is playing a vital role in that change. We talked about Iraq, Afghanistan, Pakistan, India, the Middle East, the continent of Africa and other issues. We've got a lot of work to do, and we will have to focus on certain areas . . . We are going to work closely together." Iraq was certainly a focal area. On 4 February, the next day, Mr Annan invited the Cypriot leaders and the Guarantor Powers to New York to agree how to finalise the Secretary-General's Cyprus Plan.

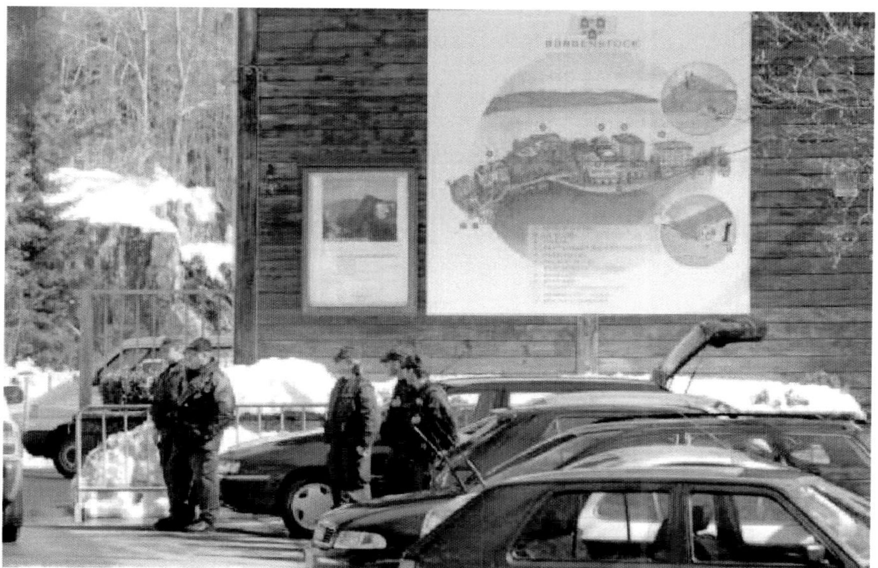

A Swiss Camp David, Bürgenstock. But the Americans arrange things better: even if they "bully," they organise negotiations, unlike the UN.

The Plan's godfather, Alvaro de Soto, sussing out the landscape during the Bürgenstock caper.

Former President Clerides tells yet another joke to National Council members on 29 March 2004. The real joker, Annan IV, was yet to come. Left to right: President Clerides (back only), Nicos Anastasiades, Dinos Michaelides, Kypros Chrysostomides and President Papadopoulos.

The Secretary-General and Sir Kieran Prendergast on 29 March 2004 after dropping the bomb of Annan IV, walking past Cyprus's shattered Government Spokesman, Dr Chrysostomides. The green leaves are not an olive branch.

Orwellian "diplomatic-speak," likely to mislead the public by Lord Hannay: as the text explains, the Greek Cypriot side declined a "photo opportunity", designed to change Mr Rauf Denktash's status as leader and to alter the basis of Phase 3 of the talks so as to make Turkey a party, rather than a collaborator. These pictures, taken on 31 March 2004, show good inter-country contact and even direct contact between Prime Minister Erdoğan and Mr Papadopoulos.

On this occasion the camera wasn't lying.

C.P.22 and 23

The two "*koumparoi*" (friends who act as best man at a wedding), Prime Ministers Erdoğan of Turkey and Karamanlis of Greece at Bürgenstock on 31 March 2004. Foreign Minister Gül has his back to the camera. Will the "Motherlands'" children fall in with maternal parental wishes?

Alvaro de Soto bids Mr Talat, "Prime Minister" of the "TRNC", a despondent farewell on 26 April 2004. Is he reflecting on happier days before he took steps precluding his winning the Nobel Prize for his Cyprus activities?

A lesser Version II of Mr Denktash, Mr Talat, appears to be giving a lecture on his favourite topics to Deputy Assistant Secretary of State Laura Kennedy on 24 July 2004, namely, Turkish Cypriot "isolation," the necessity for "direct trade" and how air-flights bringing tourists from the USA would help.

The more things change, the more they remain the same. Celebrating the 30th anniversary of Turkey's invasion and occupation of Cyprus on 20 July 2004: the Turkish Armed Forces present "President" Denktash on parade.

Was this just another diplomatic handshake on 17 December 2004, or was it an augury of impending "courageous" decisions by Prime Minister Erdoğan and "normalisation" of relationships between Turkey and Cyprus?

property provisions was made by the UN Secretariat at Turkey's insistence: on 26 March 2004 Mr Ziyal had demanded that the "Turkish Cypriot proposal regarding the property issue (1/3) should be accepted" (see Appendix 1, para 2).

The Plan in its Version V was also changed to meet Turkish demands for reinforcement of "bi-zonality". The changes further limiting the right of return (the right to reassume residence), which had been Mr Ziyal's Final Points 1 and 10, have already been set out. The provisions regarding minimum size of land for reinstatement have also been mentioned. There was, however, one further major change to a provision long objected to by the Turkish side. The Plan in Versions I–III had provided that owners might retain their ownership of property if, before its reinstatement, they had leased property to current users or to persons hailing from that constituent state.[61] They would then retain ownership and such leased property would not be counted in the ownership ceilings which had at that time been applicable.[62] Turkey demanded and got elimination of this provision, thereby considerably reducing the potential amount of Greek Cypriot-owned land in the TCCS and reinforcing bi-zonality. A replacement for the lease provision was inserted, which further reinforced "bi-zonality" by compelling persons reinstated to more than 100 donums to offer the excess amount of land on lease for a minimum period of 20 years to any person holding citizenship of the constituent state where the land was located (Annex VII, Article 19.1). This was aimed at Greek Cypriot farmers or individuals who had bought property for development, so that Turkish Cypriots could acquire and develop such land.[63]

With all these "improvements"(to use the Secretary-General's euphemistic language) being inspired by Turkey, it was thought essential to give an appear-

[61] Annex VII, previous Article 19, as in Annan I, II, and III. Mr Pfirter from December 2002 to February 2003 kept telling the Greek Cypriot side that this provision was their major safeguard and they should accept the property provisions.

[62] Annan I, Annex VII, Article 20 with similar provision in subsequent versions.

[63] The UN Secretariat, having made these and other changes in the property provisions, was anxious to convey that the extent of property reinstatement would be far greater than it had been in Annan III and that Greek Cypriot property owners would have benefited. Thus, paragraph 48 of the *Report* misled by *implying* that the total area of land returnable "would be roughly doubled," although the fine print was careful to refer to property "eligible to be reinstated." As explained, under Annan III, there had been a 10% "ceiling" on the amount of land eligible for reinstatement, but all owners could enter into long leases, thus keeping their properties, and this did not count against the ceiling, so that the percentage of properties reinstated or kept in ownership and their total area would have been much higher than the 10% "ceiling." However, at Turkish demand, to strengthen bi-zonality, the proposals regarding long leases were removed from Annan IV and V, along with "the ceilings," so that owners could get up to one-third of their property or one-third of its value, whichever was the lower. But the rate of reinstatement would have been far lower for three reasons earlier explained, namely, the rights given to current users; the double constraints of value and area, whichever first applied; and the prohibition on reinstatement to institutions (companies and the Church of Cyprus, except as regards religious sites and family companies). Eligibility in theory there was according to the Plan, but, because of other unmentioned provisions, the overall amount of land *actually* returnable would scarcely have been increased by Annan V, if at all. Had this statement appeared in a company prospectus in New York, and not in a UN Report, the account of the effect of the property provisions would have attracted the attention of an Eliot Spitzer.

ance that there was proper discussion at Bürgenstock of a property and residency ceilings package. Such a suggestion was misleading. UN team members had talked to certain individual Greek Cypriot team members about some of the potential changes. Further discussion was expected, and the Greek Cypriot side's property team sat around in Bürgenstock waiting to be called to a projected meeting. But the call never came, so no package was discussed, contrary to the *Report*'s suggestions at both paras 37 and 48.

Before leaving these aspects of the UN's approach and Turkish demands, it is necessary to appreciate that the Greek Cypriot side, although having a fundamentally different philosophy, namely, that Greek and Turkish Cypriots should not forever be ethnically separated and concentrated in two distinct governmental units, were willing to make compromises. Thus they accepted that not everyone would be able to be reinstated and that current users would require protection. They accepted that phasing of return was necessary. They had, as early as 1992, suggested provision of alternative accommodation and employment opportunities before removal, and still accept that this is necessary.[64] They suggested provision of financial assistance ie grants for persons to return to Turkey.[65] They did not propose major changes to the Annan III property provisions, remaining within the Plan's parameters, even though they were opposed in principle to the ceilings on restitution in Annan I to III, especially the 20% limit upon restoration of land and residences in particular municipalities and the 10% limit in the TCCS as a whole. They too took a "rights-based" approach, concentrating on individual rights. What they did insist on was that individuals should have a choice between restitution and compensation, and should not be compelled, except in public interest cases of land use and in relation to current users who met certain requirements, to accept compensation.[66] They pointed to the reality that many Greek Cypriots, given the choice (which must be theirs) would not demand reinstatement or return. But this was a risk Turkey would not countenance, and the UN allowed Turkey's political "bi-zonality" concerns to prevail over individual rights concerns. It is submitted

[64] Provision of alternative accommodation is particularly essential for persons in the areas subject to territorial adjustment and transfer to the administration of the Greek Cypriot constituent state. The UN figures were 42,900 persons (who were comprised of 23,300 Turkish Cypriots and 19,600 Turkish settlers). The Greek Cypriot side accepted the need for re-housing of all such persons as set out in Annex VI, Article 5.

[65] Their suggestion for cash grants to relocate such persons to their country of origin and payable there in the sum of not less than € 10,000 per household was accepted in Annan II. For both humanitarian and political reasons, they were willing to treat settlers fairly and to meet their needs.

[66] In the Draft Principles on Housing and Property Restitution for Refugees and Displaced Persons (proposed by the Special Rapporteur, Mr P S Pinheiro, and approved at the 56th session in August 2004 of the UN Sub-Commission on the Promotion and Protection of Rights for circulation to Governments for comments) Article 15.2 stipulates that *only* where restitution is factually not possible, or when the injured party knowingly or voluntarily accepts compensation in lieu of restitution, can the remedy of compensation be used. The Draft Principles are admirable. The writer hopes that the UN's property law team will reconsider how to proceed along these lines should negotiations be resurrected and they be involved.

that "bi-zonality" (residential segregation and concentration of ethnic groups in particular areas) is not a genuine public interest allowing for limitations on human rights.

THE PLAN HAD BECOME A "PROPERTY DEVELOPER'S CHARTER"

A most serous practical aspect of the property provisions did not receive proper consideration. In formulating property provisions, the UN had sought to balance "rights" of current users and improvers of property acquired over the lengthy period since Greek Cypriot and Turkish Cypriot home and property owners had been displaced, dispossessed or had left their properties. This was a humanitarian concern, shared by all sides, because, over many years, while displaced Turkish Cypriots had been given possession of Greek Cypriot-owned properties by Turkey's subordinate local administration (the "TRNC"), a similar process had, to a lesser degree, occurred in the converse direction as regards displaced Greek Cypriots being permitted by authorities of the Republic of Cyprus to occupy Turkish Cypriot-owned property.[67] In many instances, the new users had added rooms for their expanded families, or had erected new homes and business premises on land not previously built upon. They could not properly be dispossessed without further ado: both alternative accommodation and compensation for improvements were necessary. Accordingly, apart from agreeing that alternative accommodation should be provided, the Greek Cypriot team members dealing with the settlement's property provisions sympathetically considered UN suggestions that current users who were not otherwise eligible to acquire title[68] and also significant improvers of property[69] should be able to acquire title to the immovable property involved upon payment of its value in its unimproved state. Thus, it was agreed that current users who had significantly improved property should be able to acquire title if they had made the improvement before 31 December 2001, or had acted on the basis of a building permit granted before such date. (That date was fixed because, after the interval of a year wasted by Mr Denktash's unwillingness to talk and the breakdown of initial talks, serious talks on a settlement had begun.) With the focus being on competing human rights and how to balance them, the

[67] As already indicated, the process differed in that there was no elimination of title of Turkish Cypriot owners, whereas "Article 159 of the 1985 Constitution of the TRNC" purported to expropriate all Greek Cypriot and Greek-owned property and this was given practical administrative effect by "Law 52 of 1995." In the Government-controlled area, Laws and regulations provided for Turkish Cypriot-owned properties to be held in trust by the Guardian for Turkish Cypriot Property.

[68] Eg as dispossessed owners surrendering their own property and paying for any difference in value.

[69] Significant improvers were persons who owned an improvement which had a greater value than the property they had improved as it was in its original state, eg a person who had built a house in Kyrenia, with the house, together with the land, at current values being worth £40,000, while the land, without the house, would at current values have been worth £19,500.

Greek Cypriot side did not appreciate that what was in the making was a "Property Developers Charter". In contrast, the Turkish side, which had asked for such provisions to cover activities in the occupied area, fully appreciated, as a result of its property discussions with the UN and the publication of Annan I (11 November 2002), that owners of significant improvements made before 31 December *2001,* or made on the basis of a building permit for such an improvement issued prior to that date and acted upon, could acquire title of the relevant property, subject to payment for the ground taken. In addition, any improver of property, whose improvement was worth 10% of the value of the property, could get compensation, which would be paid by the Property Board (funded by the future UCR Government). Thus, improvers could safely start building works and claim compensation if the value of their improvement was at least 10% of the total value of the property. Furthermore, such an improver could, as indicated above, claim title if the property had "significantly" been improved (ie the improvement was worth more than 50% of the value of the improvement and the property together). As a result, a building development boom in the occupied area commenced.

As the Plan was altered in Annan III (26 February 2003), Annan IV (29 March 2004) and Annan V (31 March 2004), the rights to developers and improvers were greatly increased. Improvements before 31 December *2002*, developments based on a building certificate issued before then, and *others declared admissible by the Property Board* (a new loophole) would be compensated and title could be acquired.[70] This extended date was demanded by the Turkish Cypriot side on 9 March 2004. They contended:

> the original cut-off date of 31 December 2001 would severely prejudice people who *invested* after that date, not knowing whether, and if so, on what terms a Cyprus settlement would ever be made. The substantive issue is whether the improvement was made, not when it was made" (emphasis added).

What they failed to add was that, after August 2002, Greek Cypriot-owned land allocated to persons in the "TRNC" had started becoming transferable under the "Settlement, Land Allocation and Equivalent Property Law 1982", so that many properties allocated to Turkish Cypriots and settlers had come onto the market and had been snapped up by local, Turkish and other foreign property investors.

The real "substantive issue" is that any investors knew they were building or obtaining permissions to build on property eligible for reinstatement to lawful owners. On the Turkish Cypriot line of argument, there should have been no cut-off date at all, because investors expending monies must be protected and title should be acquired, even as regards properties reinstatable to their owners. The Turkish Cypriot attitude was to a considerable extent carried through into the Plan by the UN legal team. They extended the date to 31 December 2002 (so

[70] The Board was also to have discretion in deciding cases of improvements which were "in an advance stage as at that date [31 December 2002] and completed thereafter": Annex VII, Attachment 1, note 46.

that newly transferred Greek Cypriot-owned land sold for development could benefit if the relevant building certificate had been obtained). And, even in areas due to become part of the GCCS, they extended protection to "investors" by providing that, if both the owner of a significant improvement and the owner of the property wanted the property with the significant improvement, the Property Board had to decide whether to grant the improver a 20-year lease and, in so doing, whether to treat the use of the improvement for income-generation as an important consideration. Accordingly, if an improvement was part of a development project for sale or leasing, or if a rental income was being obtained from it (thus covering holiday homes), the Board was virtually certain to grant a long lease.[71]

Because the Greek Cypriot side had no access to the occupied area,[72] it was unaware of the consequences of the provisions in the Plan, whereas these were being studied by Turkish Cypriot developers and their lawyers. Greek Cypriots had not re-analysed the property provisions which by Annan II (10 December 2002) were virtually in the form they took when the Bürgenstock meetings commenced in late March 2004. They certainly did not appreciate that, in the occupied area, property transfers were commencing and that large developments were being planned and starting, with erection of holiday and future retirement houses for expatriates, individual housing schemes, tourist complexes, etc. In effect, the right of Greek Cypriot owners to reacquire properties from which they had been expelled was in practice being displaced by a right to compensation for the land, or for the original house or building, because, in these circumstances, the Plan provided only for compensation as regards property in the TCCS, and provided for the grant of long leases of 20 years in the areas to be transferred (a period sufficient for any developer to recover his capital). Even when there were discussions, the Greek Cypriot side, concentrating on human rights aspects and on the overall balance of the property provisions, did not perceive the new and the continuing violations and "the mess of pottage" which it was going to end up getting under the Plan. All the developments in the occupied area had, in the meantime, been encouraged by the legitimisation of property transfers by the Plan by virtue of giving validity to "administrative decisions" under the "TRNC Law," by the known provisions of the Plan, and by further anticipated modifications in Turkish and Turkish Cypriot developers' interests. These facts were only reported by the Turkish Cypriot press after the extent of development had become an issue subsequent to the referenda. The "TRNC Minister of Finance," Mr Ahmet Uzun, thereupon admitted that the Annan Plan

> gave the Turkish Cypriots the incentive to build in occupied Greek Cypriot properties.

[71] Annex VII, Attachment 4, Article 3.4. Although physical alterations to property were suspended once the plan entered into force, the board could authorise their continuance (Article 5).

[72] Greek Cypriots could only start visiting the occupied area after April 2003 when the Turkish Cypriot side permitted them to cross into it.

He explained that prior to the Plan

> citizens who possessed Greek Cypriot property were thinking what would happen if they invested on this property and they were concerned. These concerns have been an important factor that stopped the investments. They were removed with the universal formulas proposed by the Annan Plan for the solution of the proprietorship problem. Everyone who possesses Greek Cypriot property today and makes an investment on it equal to the value of the property has the priority on getting its proprietorship . . .[73]

On 23 August 2004, the Turkish daily, *Milliyet,* reported that the Republic of Turkey's Deputy Prime Minister and State Minister responsible for Cyprus, Mr Abdullatif Sener, had said that

> the amount of properties that foreigners had bought in the occupied areas of Cyprus had increased by ten times during the last two years.[74]

Mr Sener observed that, only within the area of occupied Kyrenia, one million square metres of land were sold during the last 3.5 years. He pointed out that immovable properties had rapidly been changing hands after the Annan Plan was submitted to the sides in 2002. Noting that the great majority of the foreigners who buy land and properties in the occupied part of Cyprus come from Britain and Turkey, Mr Sener admitted:

> Great demand is seen as compared to previous years, on purchases in various areas especially in Kyrenia. In spite of the fact that the foreigners preferred buying properties the title-deeds of which belong to Turks, the fact that the past few years they are buying also properties the title-deeds of which belong to Greek Cypriots attracts attention.

The Turkish State Minister responsible for Cyprus added that in 2001, foreigners had bought 63,000 square metres of land in occupied Cyprus, while this annual amount increased to 290,000 in 2002, and to 613,000 in 2003. During the first six months of 2004, foreigners had bought 116,000 square metres of land in the occupied part of Cyprus.

There were many adverse effects for Cyprus as a result of this mushrooming development. The supply of land was run down as and when title was acquired. A side-effect was the sucking in of more low-paid construction workers from Turkey, increasing the number of Turkish settlers. Other provisions in the Plan encouraged the re-sale of individual properties owned by Greek Cypriots (whose properties had been allocated to Turkish Cypriots or settlers) to foreigners, either already having been improved or for improvement. That the Turkish Cypriot side was fully conscious of what was at stake by way of encouraging foreign purchasers of existing houses, and especially of newly built holiday and retirement homes, both in the future TCCS and in the occupied

[73] *Kibrisli*, 20 August 2004.

[74] In those two years Greek Cypriot-owned properties allocated under the "TRNC Law" had become transferable for the first time.

area, is clear from its 9 March 2004 proposal in the Nicosia talks for a new definition in Attachment 1, Article 1, paragraph 17, as follows:

> Bona fide purchaser: A Person who acquires an interest in affected property in good faith and for value, whether or not she knew the property to have been in the ownership of a dispossessed person.
>
> Reasons: It would be unfair for a purchaser who acted in good faith, and in accordance with local laws and conveyancing practices in force at the time and in the place where the property is located, to lose his property by reason of a subsequent change in the law and by reason only of the fact that he had not carried out significant improvements.
>
> A person who had carried out significant improvements will not be prejudiced by knowledge, actually or constructive, that the property had been owned by a dispossessed person and it is unfair to apply different standards to other bona fide purchasers.
>
> It is true that this would decrease the number of properties in the North from which the current user could be evicted, but for the new state of affairs in Cyprus to have the best chance of success, and to reduce the causes of friction, it is necessary to keep the number of *evictions* and relocations the minimum . . . (emphasis added).

This was a Turkish Cypriot proposal, which the UN did not agree to insert in Annan IV and V: perhaps by now the legal team was beginning to appreciate the significance of the Plan in destroying the right to restitution of property.[75]

The net effect was that what had been proposed as a humanitarian measure was commercially exploited and resulted in a grave attack on the rights of displaced Greek Cypriots, altogether outweighing the considerations which had influenced the UN when it had originally made such proposals. Irrespective of which way the referendum result went, the Plan and its known and anticipated provisions had been an incentive to violation of rights. As long as such provisions remain in the Plan and are regarded as a model for a future settlement, the incentive to such violations will continue.[76]

[75] Although, if this was so, it was strange that their property legal advisers should have accepted the proposal to protect those acting on building certificates issued up to December 2002, rather than 2001, and to agree the loophole for Property Board agreement to permit the acquisition of title in case of later developments. Perhaps this acceptance was a compromise, giving something in response to the Turkish Cypriot proposal, because UN lawyers, like housing NGOs, tend to be mesmerised by invocation of the concept of "evictions" and to have a knee-jerk protective reaction when "evictions" are mentioned. The writer prefers to think that UN utopian property lawyers were manipulated, rather than that they would insert anything to satisfy Turkish demands on Mr de Soto's orders, and that they did not advert to the lapse of the 20-year ban on transfers of Greek Cypriot-owned land.

[76] The relevant property provisions, which not only invade the rights of displaced and dispossessed persons, but which also act in the interim as a Property Developers' Charter, are, as modified in Annex VII of Annan V (31.03.2004):

Part II, Article 7—only damage after 11 November 2002 is covered, so that demolition before that date will be legitimated.

Part II, Article 13—protects foreign purchasers of Greek Cypriot-owner property who acquire from Turkish Cypriot displaced persons. An even more extended protection was asked for by the Turkish Cypriots on 9 March 2004.

THERE WAS NO EFFECTIVE FREEZE ON DEVELOPMENT PENDING REINSTATEMENT BY THE PROPERTY BOARD OF OWNERS

Rather than putting a freeze on unlawful development, as appears to have been the UN's inclination in Annan I in November 2002,[77] the Plan became an incentive to economic short-termism and to encouraging actions leading to expropriation of refugees' property, resulting in ultimate legitimisation of the ethnic cleansing that had occurred. This outcome was the responsibility of those who drafted the Plan's property provisions and kept amending them on Turkish Cypriot suggestions that development should be encouraged.[78] The Plan illustrates the dangers of legal dilettantism in commercial matters, accompanied by disregard for human rights of property owners. Only the UN's utopian property lawyers could so unthinkingly have devised such a Property Developers' Charter. Although Mesdames Garlick and Jones, with their insights gained in Bosnia-Herzegovina and Rwanda, may have wished to resolve the property problems, they were negligent in not understanding the consequences of their proposals in the Plan for Cyprus, a society which is commercially astute and very different from the other States in which they have worked.[79] The Plan

Part II, Article 14—significantly improved property (defined in Att 1, Article 1.15) permits transfer of title to the improvement owner when read with Att 2, Article 3 o. This provision enables the Property Board to pass regulations declaring later improvements admissible. This applies to all areas, including areas to be transferred to the GCCS.

Part II, Article 18—as regards improvements on reinstated property developers may claim compensation if the improvement is worth more than 10% of the current value of the property or CY £3,000, whichever is lower. (The sum of CY £3,000 indicates that land in the occupied area was becoming more valuable and that small improvements might not hit the 10% mark unless the provision was altered.)

Attachment 4, Article 3—relates to entitlement of improvements of a certain value; to entitlement to apply for title; and virtual certainty of being granted to a 20-year lease if the property is used for revenue-generation. This was applicable in the areas to form part of the GCCS.

[77] In Annan I, carried over into Annan II and III, there was a stipulation that significant improvements, in order to render the owners eligible to claim title, had to be made or based on a building permit issued prior to 31 December 2001. As indicated, the time was extended by Annan V, by a year, to 31 December 2002 and a loophole to cover later permission was opened through possible action of the Property Board. A footnote permitted the Board to accord these rights where property was at "an advance stage" before the cut-off date.

[78] The long-term economic gain from the kinds of development occurring was immigration to Cyprus of European retirees and holiday makers who would bring their spending power to the occupied area.

[79] If they understood the consequences, their conduct was reprehensible in a human rights context. The writer does not, however, think that they adverted to the commercial exploitation which (in Cyprus) was bound to follow. To the writer it appears that Miss Jones' perspective was shaped by her Rwanda experiences and the need, because of land shortages and violence, if there were a return of refugees, to discourage restitution, and to have nationalisation on a grand scale. One other provision has Rwanda overtones: although current occupiers need protection if they have planted crops, so that they can harvest them (as in Rwanda and in most States where tenancies end), a new Article 6 in Annan IV, Annex VII, Attachment 3, to this effect *inter alia*, is so drafted that future rental of reinstated property (which cannot be handed over because not yet due) must be paid to owners of significant improvements, even if such rental related in part to a period after reinstatement.

should have given only personal protection—and this confined to Turkish Cypriots who were currently in occupation of Greek Cypriot-owned property (and *vice-versa*); it should have frozen new commercial development of such property from the time talks had begun in December 1999;[80] and it should have excluded foreign carpetbaggers from protection.[81] If settlers were to be protected on humanitarian grounds, such protection should have been limited to the provision of temporary alternative accommodation in Cyprus, and to provision of grants upon arrival in Turkey. Settlers should not, as secondary occupants, have been given rights to apply to acquire title or long leases if they improved property—as they were by the Plan.[82] Nor should they have been entitled, after reinstatement of the property had been ordered by the Property Board, to remain for such lengthy periods in property belonging to Greek Cypriots. This long period of delay is explained below.

Even when property was subject to being reclaimed by Greek Cypriot displaced persons, the Plan's provisions for action by the Property Board were such that, in practice, subject to a qualification as regards the Karpas, the earliest time for a reinstatement order was to be 6 years after the settlement, if the property was *vacant*. If the property was not vacant, there could then be delays for a total of up to 9 years if the occupier had financial means to acquire another property. Reinstatement could be delayed for up to 8 years if the occupier was a Turkish settler (non-Cypriot); and delays could occur for an overall unlimited period if the occupier was Cypriot, but had insufficient means to acquire another property and had not been offered alternative accommodation. Only in the case of Karpas villagers returning to reside could such persons be reinstated (at the earliest) in *3 years* for *vacant* property, and for non-vacant property, in either 7 or 8 years, or at an unspecified date depending upon the means and nationality of the occupier. As Mr Pfirter told the Tusaid Seminar at Bögaziçi University on 17 July 2003, these provisions meant that the Karpas villagers would not, in practice, be able to return to their homes.[83] Thus, the Plan contained paper provisions for reinstatement of property, which would be largely illusory in practice. Due to provisions of this character, the benefits of the settlement can be properly described as "pie in the sky", which is why, unlike certain foreign commentators and the UN inventors of these provisions, most Greek Cypriots declined the delayed banquet on offer.

[80] December 2001 or December 2002 after the Copenhagen meeting were dates that should have been too late to protect new developments: developers had long been on notice that there would be a property settlement in any talks.

[81] It is noteworthy that a large proportion of the foreign purchasers of Greek Cypriot-owned properties in the Turkish-occupied area are UK citizens. Belatedly, the UK Foreign Office made occasional statements warning that there could be legal problems.

[82] See the Draft Principles on Housing and Property Restitution for Refugees and Displaced Persons, Article 14.2, which provides that legal protection afforded secondary occupants, should not prejudice the rights of legitimate owners to repossess the housing and property in question.

[83] The relevant Articles are in Annan V, Annex VII, Attachment 3, Articles 1 and 2, read with Article 17 and Attachment 2, Articles 11–13.

RECENT TURKISH MOVES TO PORTRAY PROPERTY TRANSFERS IN CYPRUS NOT AS CONFISCATIONS BUT MERELY AS POSSESSORY RIGHTS

When, after the referenda, the commercial exploitation of Greek Cypriot-owned properties and their permanent transfer to developers and foreign entrepreneurs and buyers became a matter of heated public discussion, the Government of Turkey appreciated that it risked embarrassment. It had been protected since 1977 and 1982 from international criticism that Turkey was responsible for "confiscating" such properties. This protection was by virtue of the fact that the properties were subject only to *possessory use* and were not transferable.[84] However, by the end of 2002, ownership could be transferred by those allocated the properties and by mid-2004 such transfers and subsequent development had become the focus of criticism. Turkey therefore insisted that the "TRNC Law" be amended to preserve the fiction that there was merely long-term possession. Accordingly the "TRNC Government" introduced an amendment to the "Law" to provide that there should in future be 125-year leases when properties were sold to foreigners, with intermediate re-transfer of the allocated property to the "State," which would then grant a 125-year lease to the purchaser.[85] As things stood at the time of writing (November 2004) the move was merely cosmetic: a draft Bill remained under consideration by a "TRNC Assembly committee". Were there a genuine wish to secure a settlement for Cyprus which protected property rights of dispossessed persons, the Government of Turkey would have ensured that its subordinate local administration, the "TRNC," actually changed the "Settlement, Land Allocation and Equivalent Property Law No 41 of 1977 as amended" to provide that Greek Cypriot-owned property ("abandoned property") could not be the subject of transfer of title from either the person who had originally been allocated possession or his heirs or successors: such provision would adequately protect persons who need housing protection and the right to till agricultural land, while not foreclosing the possibility of ultimate restitution to displaced and dispossessed owners of the land or house in question.[86]

[84] See p 178 above.

[85] See *Kibris*, 4 October 2004 and *Yeniduzen*, 3 October 2004, explaining that Turkey's insistence was in the context of its EU application. *Yeniduzen* added that in the first nine months of 2004 there were more than 2,000 applications by foreigners who wanted to buy property in the "TRNC".

[86] The lack of intention to stop transfers has been manifested by administrative instructions to the "TRNC Law Registry" not to reveal the background to titles: *Cyprus Mail*, 30 September 2004. Previously information would be given as to whether the property was Greek Cypriot-owned and had been allocated under "Law 41 of 1977" or had always been owned by a Turkish Cypriot or a foreigner who had acquired title before the 1974 invasion. Advertisements by estate agents in the Turkish Cypriot press feature these historic differences in title, and properties of lawful provenance are offered at higher prices. The instruction not to provide information indicated that buyers should now be regarded as *bona fide* purchasers. The counter-argument to this has to be that when it comes to property, a buyer must satisfy himself, and if enquiry cannot be made, he should anticipate problems and suspect lack of title.

WOULD A FEDERAL NATIONAL PARK COVERING NORTHERN AREAS IN CYPRUS, WHICH REMAIN UNDEVELOPED, NOT BE BETTER FOR ALL CYPRIOTS AND FOR EUROPE?

Above: an Akamas peninsula view. The peninsula lies to the north-west in the Government-controlled area, and, like the upper parts of the Pendadaktylos range and the Karpas peninsula, should be part of a federal national park for Cyprus and Europe.

Below: Part of the as yet even more unspoilt wilderness in the Karpas peninsula, with some of the best undeveloped coastline in Europe.

Above: A panoramic view of the as yet unspoiled Akamas peninsula, but the Karpas is far more beautiful, with its natural wildness, extensive bays and beaches. Below: typical Karpas scenery. This is known as Turtle Beach.

Above: the Monastery of the Apostle St Andrew at the end of the remote Karpas peninsula. For Orthodox believers it is a place of pilgrimage and for all Greek Cypriots it symbolises their cultural history for 2000 years.

Below: the Monastery's icon screen.

Yialousa: development above the sea on Greek Cypriot-owned property by the Loyal and Royal Company of Asil Nadir, a fugitive from British justice, and Sidika Atalay, who, with Mr Talat's assent, have just sold their Loyal and Royal shares to an Israeli company for ten million dollars to "develop" the Port Barbaros project (a marina and hotel complex). Many fugitives operate in the "TRNC" from which they cannot be extradited.

Dhavlos, which is threatened by development on land allocated to and then sold on by Turkish settlers. It needs to be a strictly regulated centre in a national park.

The Pentadaktylos Range above Kyrenia, which requires preservation as federal national park.

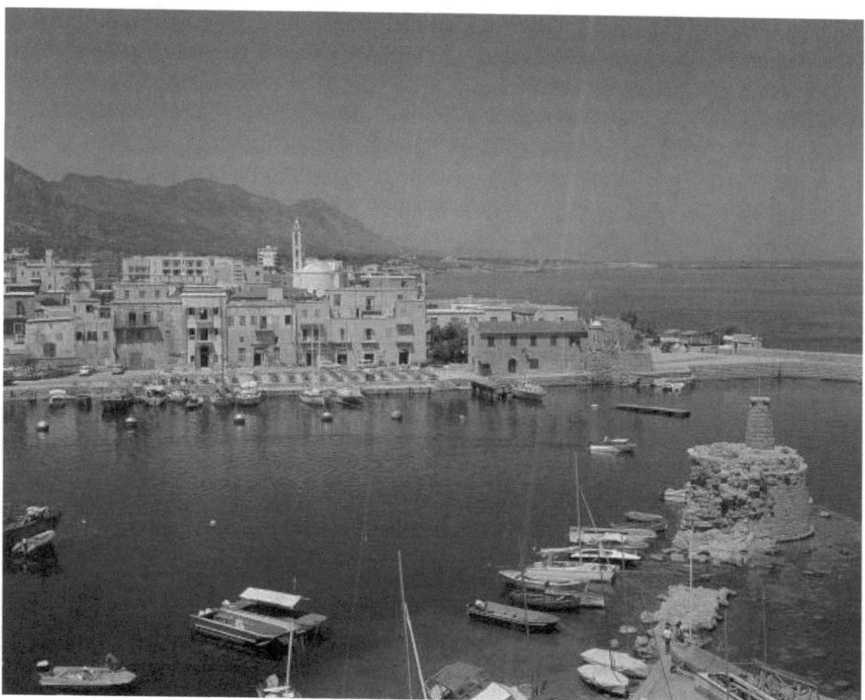

Kyrenia harbour. The town was a gem, set in an Eastern Mediterranean Riviera, and will always be dear to Greek Cypriots.

The Latin Abbey of Bellapais (13th century) above Kyrenia. This would be under the proposed federal Department of Antiquities.

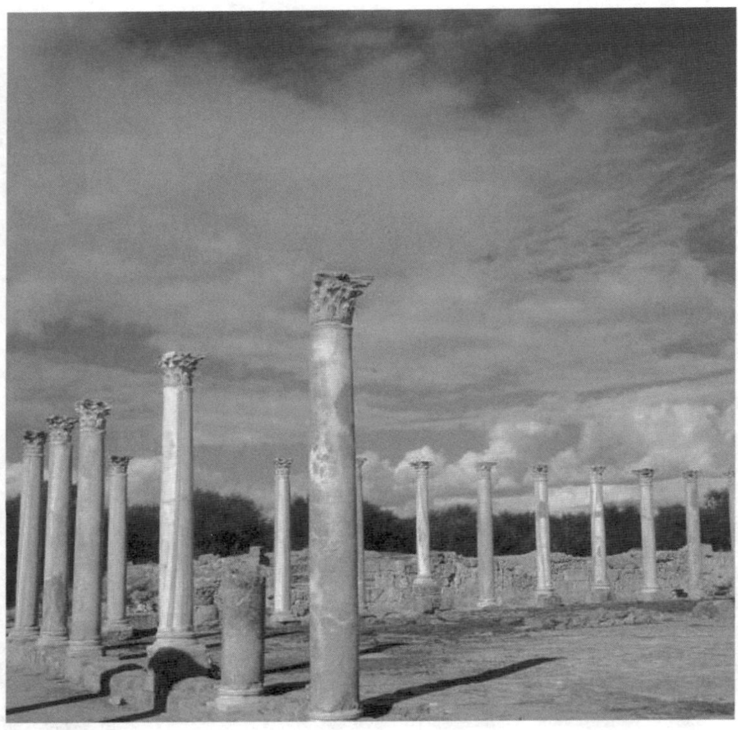

The archaeological site of Salamis near Famagusta. This too would be regulated by the proposed federal government, establishing the principle of federal protection.

Above: Lapithos (now re-named Lapta by the "TRNC"), largely Greek Cypriot-owned, where the Orams bought literally priceless land with splendid Mediterranean views, building a house and swimming pool like other retirees and holiday-makers.

Panagra, near Cyprus's north-west coast and Kormakiti, is one of Cyprus' most beautiful villages, with views of mountains and sea. It is an area mainly occupied by Turkish settlers where there was a 78% "Yes" vote in the referendum. This area, like all the Pentadaktylos chain, needs to be preserved as national park with regulated centres.

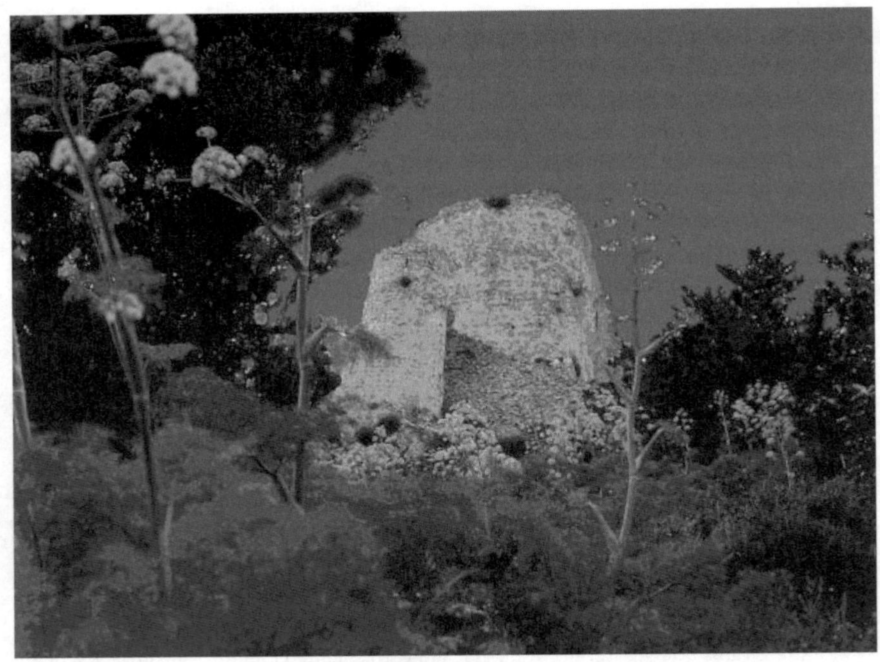

On Kantara there are also dream-like buildings. (Photo courtesy of George Lanitis.)

From space: satellite picture of Morphou town and orchards, showing the proposed constituent state boundary, which leaves the main agricultural area and western coastline in the TCCS.

The Turkish Army's handiwork on the Pentadactylos range. Photographed by satellite 450 kilometres above the earth. At the 15 November 2004 "independence celebrations" Mr Denktash, urging again the upholding of "independence," concluded: "May the shadow of the Motherland be always upon us . . . May the Turkish soldiers never leave our side. May nobody try to take away our freedom and sovereignty. 'How happy is the man who can say he is a Turk'." How long will this Reich last before a settlement?

Above: here the Prime Minister of Turkey in Cyprus on 9 May 2003 is commemorating "Martyrs of the Peace Operation" of July–August 1974 (officially entitled "Attila"). Bad taste in the 'thirties style of monstrous "heroic" sculpture is also manifested in the Government-controlled area, but, fortunately, it is for the most part obscured by buildings, unlike in the occupied area, where there are also massive slogans disfiguring the environment. Below: giant and slogan. There are others.

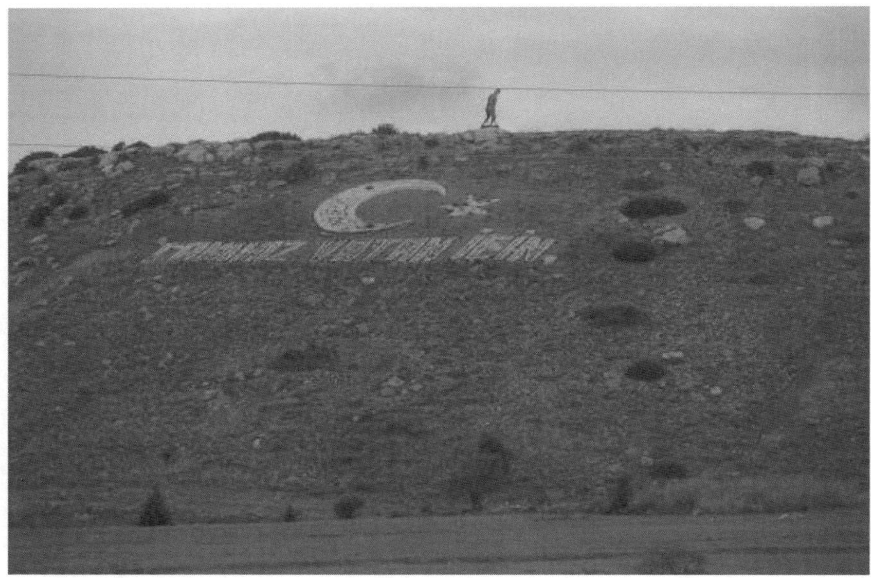

U.18–19

AN EU SIDE-WIND PROTECTION FOR DISPOSSESSED OWNERS

For many years, dispossessed Greek Cypriot owners have contemplated litigation against persons who had unlawfully taken possession of their properties in the Turkish-occupied area (pursuant to Turkey's subordinate local administration having allocated such property either to them or to earlier possessors, whose rights were subsequently assigned to them). However, foreign courts' lack of jurisdiction when the litigation concerned "land abroad" rendered action impractical.[87] The alternative of litigation in the courts of the Republic, followed by use abroad of the machinery for reciprocal enforcement of judgments, was also not invoked because of major procedural difficulties, especially difficulty in commencing proceedings by reason of inability to serve papers on potential defendants located in the occupied area, to which Greek Cypriots (including lawyers and process-servers) had no access. The problem of service was resolved by the opening in April 2003 of the crossing points, hitherto closed by the Turkish Army, while the doubts surrounding reciprocal enforcement of judgments were largely settled by the Republic of Cyprus's entry into the EU. At that stage, EU Regulation 44/2001 on jurisdiction and the recognition and enforcement of judgments in civil and commercial matters came into operation. The Regulation provided that EU Member States would, without question, enforce judgments of other Member States in the State of origin of the judgment debtor. Relying on these provisions, litigation has been commenced against foreign purchasers of illegally seized land owned by displaced Greek Cypriots. In *Apostolides v Orams*, the Nicosia District Court on 9 November 2004 issued summary judgment (the English defendants not appearing) and ordered demolition of a house and swimming pool built on a displaced Greek Cypriot owner's land. Should the defendants not succeed in setting this judgment aside or not succeed at full trial, or unsuccessfully challenge the procedure for enforcement of the Cyprus judgment in the English courts, the Cyprus judgment will be executed in England, attaching the defendant's assets in satisfaction of the claim. Such procedures may have some effect in deterring foreign purchasers from acquiring "bargains" by buying holiday or retirement homes on Greek Cypriot-owned property, which is, in European terms, relatively very cheap and discounted because of the legal risks.[88]

[87] See *Hesperides Hotels v Aegean Turkish Holidays Ltd* [1978] 3 WLR 378, in which the House of Lords held that English courts had no jurisdiction over such claims.

[88] Property owned by Turkish Cypriots or foreigners before 1974 is at a much higher price (virtually double) and this fact is advertised by Turkish Cypriot estate agents. Before there is sympathy shown to foreign purchasers who gambled that the current regime would not change, persons should recollect German exploitation of seized Jewish-owned properties. Similarly, they should ask whether the splendid undeveloped areas in States successors to Yugoslavia should be exploited by carpet-baggers buying up properties of Croat, Serb or Moslem refugees unable or too frightened to return. People who buy goods knowing that they have "fallen off the back of a lorry" do not deserve sympathy.

HUMAN RIGHTS AND HUMANITARIAN LAW ASPECTS

The Plan's treatment of the rights of displaced persons to return to their homes in safety and to restitution of their property or to compensation has been explained. Deliberately, discussion about the lawfulness or otherwise of the proposed arrangements was virtually eschewed, because the nature of the rights in question is fully set out in judgments of the European Court of Human Rights, notably *Loizidou v Turkey (Merits)* (ECHR Series A No 310 (1995) 2223), and in relevant legal literature.[89] Analysed in terms of the rights, the Plan's provisions are attempts to evade application of humanitarian and human rights law. A striking manifestation of this was an initial attempt in Annex VII, Article 5, to exclude the jurisdiction of the European Court of Human Rights. However, in Annan V, thinking better of the risks inherent in this approach, the UN team, in conjunction with Turkey, decided that Annex VII should in part be re-cast, first, so as to create the impression that all landowners would be returned part of their property, and, second, so as to convert the Property Board into a domestic remedy for all questions related to immovable property in Cyprus which owners had, between 1963 and the Foundation Agreement, left, or of which they had lost use and control in consequence of inter-communal strife, military action or the division of the Island. This alternative approach was reinforced by stipulating that the United Cyprus Republic was to be the sole responsible State Party. Moreover, the President of the European Court of Human Rights was then to be advised by the UCR's Co-Presidents of the new domestic remedy and of the UCR's sole State responsibility.[90] In a letter to the Court, they were to request it to strike out any proceedings currently before the Court concerning such immovable property—in order to allow the domestic mechanism in Cyprus to proceed.[91]

A similar move was taken to ensure, *inter alia*, that the European Court of Justice would not have jurisdiction on property questions and violation of rights in connection therewith. In this instance, the mechanism chosen was to seek to make the Foundation Agreement "primary law," prevailing over the fundamental principles of EU Law (which comprehend the European Convention on

[89] See eg Opinion on "Legal Issues arising from Certain Population Transfers and Displacements on the Territory of the Republic of Cyprus in the Period since 20 July 1974": http://www.attorney-general.gov.cy.

[90] As a further insurance that Council of Europe institutions would not in future consider that the Foundation Agreement contravened the European Convention and its Protocols, the Co-Presidents were, through the Council's Secretary-General, to request endorsement of the Foundation Agreement by the Parliamentary Assembly and the Committee of Ministers. With such endorsements, a ruling by the Court that the Foundation Agreement contravened the Convention or its Protocols was virtually unthinkable. See Annex IX, Attachment 3, letter to the Secretary-General of the Council of Europe.

[91] Annex VII, Part II, Article V; Attachment 1, Article 1.1; and Attachment V. Loss of use compensation was, according to the Plan, to be "considered" by the constituent state from which any claimant hailed: Annex VII, Part III, Article 21.

Human Rights) and any potential changes in EU law protecting property rights.[92]

Since no international judicial institution has compulsory contentious jurisdiction over humanitarian law as it applied to Cyprus in the relevant period, no action needed to be taken by the Plan in that respect.[93] Speculation about what an international Court, if it had jurisdiction, might decide is superfluous in this report. It is submitted, however, that the attempts to ensure absence of jurisdiction and/or inadmissibility in the European Court of Human Rights and the Turkish-inspired tinkering with the property provisions establish that Turkey and the UN had major doubts as to whether the Plan's property provisions and strictly regulated right of return could withstand judicial scrutiny and application of the rules of international law.

In concluding this Chapter it is appropriate to recollect the UN's cavalier attitude to property rights (and other human rights). This was conclusively established by the deliberate omission from Annan III, as presented on 26 February 2003, of Protocol 1 to the European Convention. In the talks in Nicosia, a draft Annex V, showing this omission was strongly objected to by the Greek Cypriot side. Moreover, one of the seconded EU legal experts, having been asked by the Greek Cypriot side at the Technical Committee dealing with Treaties to give advice, pointed out to the Committee and the UN team that adherence to Protocol No 1 and all the Convention's Protocols was a pre-requisite for EU membership. These objections were disregarded, with only "Protocols 2 through 11" being listed in Annex V in Annan III. Protocols 12 and 13 were also omitted. It took a public reaction from the Secretariat of the Council of Europe about Annan III to get a "clarification" on 8 March 2003 that Protocol No 1 would bind the UCR, as well as Protocols 12 and 13.

POSTSCRIPT

Lord Hannay, at the heart of UN policy decision-making on the proposed Plan, was fully aware of the evolution of property proposals from 2001–2002. He confirms that although the UN did not adopt Turkey's preference for

> a scheme based on compensation alone . . . the complexities of the UN ideas were *designed to come up with a result that was not too different from that in practice* (*Cyprus. The Search for a Solution*, p 180; emphasis added).

[92] See Plan, Annex IX, Attachment 2, Letter by Co-Presidents to the President of the Council of the European Union.

[93] The Fourth Geneva Convention, Article 49. 6, and the Hague Regulations prohibit much of the action taken, but, unless there were to be a submission by Turkey to the jurisdiction of the International Court of Justice, these matters cannot be judicially determined. For useful summaries of relevant international and humanitarian Law see K Chrysostomides, *The Republic of Cyprus. A Study in International Law* (The Hague, Martinus Nijhoff, 2000) 192–98, and L C Loucaides, "The Protection of the Right to Property in Occupied Territories," (2004) 53 *ICLQ*, 677–90. Turkey is not a Party to the Statute of the International Criminal Court, although as an EU Member State she will be expected to become a Party. Jurisdiction is not retrospectively applicable.

That outcome was because of the multiple exceptions to the right to restitution, effectively leaving displaced or dispossessed Greek Cypriots with only compensation claims. Most international personalities who condemned Greek Cypriots for voting "No" either did not understand or were misled as to the Plan's effects—effects which were admittedly "designed". Those who understood the Plan's effects and then claimed that it had fairly balanced human rights can only be adjudged hypocrites, pursuing preferred political goals while paying lip-service to international law and human rights standards. Lord Hannay provided a novel justification: he claimed that the Plan provided

> a framework for a more normal existence in the future. Decisions on residence could be taken on the same grounds as elsewhere in the world, such as job location, schools, family and not the backward-looking criterion of inherited property ownership (*ibid*, pp 184–5).

XVI

The Question Faced in the Referenda and the Run-Up

WHETHER OR NOT "justice" was done to each side's demands, and whether the settlement had been imposed by action entirely beyond the limits of the agreed procedure—even being the equivalent of an abuse of power—was not, however, the ultimate question that the two Cypriot Communities, as the people of Cyprus, had to decide. Of course, a sense of injustice entertained by either Community would remain very relevant in that its presence would potentially impede operation of the Plan by virtue of diminishing the necessary oil of goodwill. But what had been done by the UN had been done. The issue now became the future of the people of Cyprus and what most mattered for their future was whether the Plan, as a finalised product, soberly assessed, taken as a whole and irrespective of who had gained what, was likely to be workable.[1] In sum, was it fit for the purpose of organising the future political, economic and social life of Cyprus? This was the crucial question which the people of Cyprus, Greek and Turkish Cypriots, had to face in their separate simultaneous referenda.[2]

[1] Obviously, in the heated political debates which preceded the referenda, "who had gained and who had lost," provided material for arguing the Plan was unjust, especially having regard to Turkey's "gains". But the substance of the "gains" had to be evaluated in determining whether the Plan would be workable eg Turkey's rights in the military and economic spheres. To debate the "gains" was thus not manifestation of a "zero-sum" approach. Most Greek Cypriots, while emotional about injustice, are also practical when it comes to assessing the situation and taking decisions as to their political future. Nor were they "dog in the manger," unwilling to see Turkish Cypriots get benefits. It is regrettable that some analysts think stereotypically, characterising Cypriots of both sides as having a "zero-sum mentality."

[2] At Bürgenstock on 29 March, when presenting Annan IV (which was insignificantly altered in relation to the Greek Cypriot side's comments) the Secretary-General, after singling out Greek Cypriot concerns about "functionality and viability" and the Turkish Cypriot desire for "strengthened bi-zonality," had said the question for the sides, having regard to the text of the Plan, was:

> Is this revised plan better than the one on the basis of which you agreed to negotiate? Does the package of improvements meet your core concerns? Can it reassure your people and give them the courage to seize the chance of peace? Does it respect the other side's core interests?

His answer to his question was "Yes," and he hoped that the sides would act on his "vision" of a Cyprus working for all its people (Greek Cypriot notetaker's record). The Greek Cypriot side's answer to the first three questions (as is clear from its paper the next day—see Appendix 2) would have been "a resounding No," an answer publicly made by the President in his 7 April TV broadcast (see below) which was internationally criticised and internally attacked by those who wanted

REMAINING PRE-REFERENDUM TASKS IN NICOSIA AND THE REFERENDUM CAMPAIGN IN THE GOVERNMENT-CONTROLLED AREA

FINALISATION OF LAWS

Before the referenda, a huge task of adapting draft Federal Laws to accord with the final Constitution, which the Secretary-General had altered in important respects, required to be executed by a band of lawyers seconded to the UN and by the lawyers of the Greek and Turkish Cypriot sides. The UN lawyers, many of whom were generously seconded by foreign States, continued working on the Laws until the last day preceding the referenda. Corrigenda and Clarifications to the lengthy Foundation Agreement were also necessary. In these tasks, the three groups of lawyers made a massive contribution, which will assist in reaching a settlement in future negotiations so far as concerns Laws required to be in place for functionality of the United Cyprus Republic and also so far as concerns treaties which are to bind it. Nonetheless, the caveat must be entered that certain controversial provisions in particular Laws, inserted by the Secretariat[3] at Turkish Cypriot instance (dictated by Turkey's legal advisers), will require revisiting, as will the listing of certain "treaties" with Turkey.[4]

COMMITMENTS BY THE GUARANTOR POWERS TO SIGN THE NEW TREATY INTO FORCE

In this period preceding the referenda, the issue of Turkey's non-compliance with her obligation as a Guarantor Power to commit herself to signing into force the Treaty between Cyprus, Greece, Turkey and the United Kingdom related to the New State of Affairs in Cyprus, came to light. Only after considerable pressure by President Papadopoulos was the issue resolved by the Corrigenda in a fashion protecting Cyprus.[5]

the Plan (despite its negative aspects) to be approved so that a reunited Cyprus would begin to operate on 1 May 2004. At Bürgenstock, President Papadopoulos refused to sign anything, despite the UN pressing for a signed agreement to put the Plan to referendum. He would not sign, lest this be used to create the impression that he in any way supported the Plan.

[3] Since I have been so critical of certain of the lawyers seconded to Mr de Soto's team, a corrective is necessary. Messrs S Tripathi and C Harland were invariably professional and if they took a view different from the Greek Cypriot side on certain issues, no-one in the Greek Cypriot team considered that this could have been occasioned by bias. The Greek Cypriot lawyers saw these professionals as being there to help all Cypriots. They held a similar view concerning the lawyers seconded by Governments to finalise Laws.

[4] In light of the rush to finalise Laws and Treaties, Articles 48 and 49 provided for revision procedures. Regrettably, the motivating force was not just common sense, but also mistrust by the Turkish Cypriot side of drafting by Greek Cypriot lawyers. Article 49 permitted 16 members from either Federal Chamber to request review of any Law attached to the Foundation Agreement on grounds of incompatibility with the Main Articles of the Agreement or the Constitution.

[5] See pp 84–5 above.

PROBLEMS ABOUT PROTECTION OF REPUBLIC OF CYPRUS PUBLIC SERVANTS' ACCRUED RIGHTS

Another difficulty arose when public servants' trade unions became concerned to ensure protection of their members' terms of service, benefits and pensions. The conferment of the necessary protection encountered legal problems due to the UN's insistence on its "virgin birth" concept. This precluded the standard solution of referring to service with the preceding Government prior to the settlement (ie the Government of the Republic of Cyprus) because such reference was unacceptable to Turkey and to the Turkish Cypriots. The UN was dilatory in addressing the responsibility of drafting safeguarding measures in the relevant Federal Law and in the Greek Cypriot Constituent State Constitution (subsequently blaming the Government of the Republic for not itself undertaking this task and for some senior public servants having sent circulars to their juniors).[6] Meanwhile, the Republic's public servants became increasingly restive. Not only was there uncertainty, but many public servants disliked the Annan Plan itself, particularly diplomats and higher ranking officers in departments that were to be federalised under the Plan. They knew that their career prospects would be adversely affected by the disproportionate share of higher-level posts in the Federal Public Service accorded to Turkish Cypriots by the Plan (ie 33⅓% and in the case of the diplomatic service, 50% at the highest levels). The consequences were twofold: a large number of public servants indicated that they did not wish to become Federal public servants;[7] and many public servants and their families were likely, on grounds of personal financial uncertainty, to vote against the Plan. Ultimately, two days preceding the referenda, various techniques to protect public servants were devised by the UN with Greek Cypriot assistance, although these still left legally unsettled the financial responsibility as between the federation and the constituent states. The UN admitted that the latter was a constitutional issue, but considered that it could not now be settled in the Constitution because of the need to consult and obtain "the motherlands'" consent to any adaptation of the Constitution. When the

[6] Letters from Mr de Soto to President Papadopoulos, 20 and 23 April 2004. The real reason for the difficulties was the UN's inflexible determination only to use elliptical language which would permit both sides to keep their views as to the "virgin birth" of the United Cyprus Republic in accordance with the "TRNC's" doctrinaire theology that the Republic of Cyprus did not exist, having been extinguished sometime between 24 and 27 December 1963 after inter-communal fighting started and the Turkish Cypriot Vice-President and Ministers declined to meet the President and Greek Cypriot Ministers, whom they alleged had destroyed the Constitution. This last is another long (and incorrect) story which the writer will be telling in a forthcoming book. The book by Mrs Soulioti, now at press, deals with the 1963 events in detail.

[7] Ironically there was doubt whether enough Greek Cypriot public servants of calibre would wish to serve the Federal Government. The Plan, in Article 46.3 of the Constitution, had addressed Turkish Cypriot concerns, based on their view of the 1960–1963 period that Turkish Cypriots would not be appointed, by providing for a list assigning personnel to offices in the Federal Government with such list finalising structure and staffing by 16 April 2004.

issues as to terms of service were resolved by the UN, President Papadopoulos immediately issued a public announcement that all matters had been settled satisfactorily. The UN chose to describe these events and the situation prior to their resolution as "unfounded concerns generated about job security for public servants".[8] Nonetheless, had public servants not expressed concern, it is unclear whether they would have received the legal protection they eventually achieved.

UN AND OTHER ATTEMPTS TO INFLUENCE THE GREEK CYPRIOT PUBLIC'S PERCEPTIONS OF THE PLAN AND UN CRITICISM OF THE POLITICAL PROCESS IN THE GOVERNMENT-CONTROLLED AREA

The UN, once it appreciated the atmosphere prevailing in the Government-controlled area, became concerned by widespread Greek Cypriot public hostility to the Plan.[9] It is astonishing that the Secretariat should ever have thought that Cypriots, who are acutely politically conscious (many male Cypriots spending much of their lives in coffee-shop political talk), would not assess the Plan for themselves. The Island's five Greek-language television stations (one being State-funded with a State-appointed Board, but operationally independent, while the others were privately owned) analysed the Plan in endless debates by protagonists and antagonists, with the latter at first being more prominent, but with the former gradually organising themselves and speaking up in favour of the Plan. In the period immediately preceding the referenda, by which time debate on the Plan was virtually excluding all other programmes, the stations were allocating time equally as between both sets of spokesmen. There was also lively and unfettered coverage in the printed press, which gave the Plan, its pros and its cons, wallpaper coverage.[10]

The UN team, fearing that the Plan would be rejected by Greek Cypriot voters (opinion polls taken at the time of the Bürgenstock talks were already predicting a massive majority in favour of rejection), then contemplated engaging in further "voter education" and in disseminating positive approaches to the Plan. In the main, NGOs, press advertising and election "literature" were to be used to do this. Funds paid by the United States of America to support

[8] Prendergast, 28 April 2004, p 4.

[9] Many of the reasons which would move Greek Cypriots to vote "No" had been indicated by Ambassador Jacovides in an insightful paper "Cyprus—Prospects for a Solution" at the Western Policy Center conference, 26 February 2004, Washington, DC. It will be noted that these remarks were made as early as the second day of negotiations in Nicosia. In papers delivered on 18 March 2004, before Annan IV and V, Professor Van Coufoudakis and Dr K A Kyriakides set out "The Case Against the Annan Plan". It was published by Lobby for Cyprus soon after Annan V appeared. The authors considered that a vote in favour of the Plan would be "a human blunder of historic proportions" and advanced persuasive arguments that must have convinced many Greek Cypriots to vote "No".

[10] The owners of the 4 private TV stations and of the media were for the most part opposed to the Plan, but, apart from editorial policy, their views did not preclude comprehensive coverage of all views on the Plan's details and merits.

rapprochement and cooperation between the two Communities had, since 1998 and increasingly since mid-2002, been directed, under State Department control, towards attitude-shaping projects put forward by NGOs, which were encouraged by the US Embassy, and whose members, especially in the "TRNC," had often been trained by UNOPS or UNOPS-sponsored Management Studies associations.[11] By early 2004 it had become apparent that UNOPS was closely associated with the Special Adviser. (Indeed UNOPS premises were made available for the inter-communal talks and his headquarters were located there.) It was also apparent that "supporting the peace process" had metamorphosed since February 2003 into supporting the UN's specific peace Plan (Annan III, ultimately Annan V). It was this metamorphosis that overstepped the line between generous US funding of charitable activities in Cyprus with Government consent, and interference in domestic politics, by pushing for a particular political outcome, a specific policy (the UN Plan), when that very Plan was to be the subject of a referendum.[12] The 16 February 2003 election had been fought on the basis that Annan II (10 December 2002) was unacceptable and that there must be negotiation of major changes in the Plan "to improve it". The incoming President, Mr Papadopoulos, elected by an absolute majority of the Greek Cypriot electorate on first ballot, thus had an electoral mandate to negotiate "improving" changes. It was therefore all the more reprehensible for the USA and the UN (through UNOPS activity funded by the USA, keeping the USA's fingerprints off the exercise) to promote the Plan, especially as it was, from a Greek Cypriot point of view, "worsened" on 26 February 2003 by the UN within 10 days of his election and before the President had even been inaugurated (28 February 2003). The Plan was, as has been indicated,[13] to be further seriously "worsened" at UN, US and Turkey's instance by Annan V.

[11] See Chapter VI supra. The *Final Report*, p 14, refers to the NGO Support Centers and suggests that not enough was consistently done as regards NGO capacity-building. Annex 8, at 8–2, shows that from April 2003 the Management Association (Management Centre) supporting the "growth of civil society" helped or trained 353 non-profit representatives from the Turkish Cypriot side and 35 from the Greek Cypriot side. To understand the large scale of this operation, the figures of Turkish Cypriots trained as NGO representatives should be extrapolated to the USA. The equivalent would be training, with a particular political slant, of 441,250 US citizens as NGO representatives. Congress ought to be asking questions about the propriety of extensive attitude-shaping programmes in small States.

[12] Just imagine the furore in France if US funding were directed to NGOs and projects to encourage French voters not to be "anti-Islamic" and to educate them prior to a referendum on Turkey's EU membership. The same criticism would be made if a border poll were to be held in Northern Ireland and US funds were in anticipation directed to "voter education" on this issue. Similar objections would be made if, in the next Swiss referendum on EU membership, the EU were to spend funds on promoting this during the referendum campaign. Good ends do not justify improper means. It should be added that, although President Clerides, both in office and thereafter, did not oppose the Plan, had he remained in office, he too conceivably could have opposed modifications on the lines of Annan V. Had this occurred, he and his Government would have been opposed to the USA and the UN interfering in the domestic jurisdiction to promote the Plan immediately before a referendum on it or before an election fought on the issue.

[13] See Chapters IX, XIII and XIV. See also Table F (Appendix 6) for a detailed comparison of the changes introduced by each version.

The Cyprus Government was aware that UNOPS was not, despite repeated requests, informing the Planning Bureau or the Cyprus Red Cross (who were to approve projects) of what was being approved, and that UNOPS was claiming to be unable to produce accounts or to do so at any time soon. It also, in light of the enormous international and UN Secretariat pressure for a "Yes" vote, suspected that there would be a last-minute UN-directed propaganda campaign in favour of the Plan. The Government had already seen professionally prepared leaflets, such as "It's your Choice—know the Truth. The Annan Plan in 20 Points".[14] Mr de Soto was therefore asked by President Papadopoulos

> to take action to ensure that any UN involvement, whether of an agency or of personnel stationed here or visiting, in facilitating any such campaign does not in fact occur.[15]

Mr de Soto responded that this was not a matter for him as Special Adviser, implying it was for the Special Representative. (Normally, Mr de Soto did not hesitate to tread on the Special Representative's turf.) Mr de Soto then continued that, in any event, UN agencies' activities were merely informational.[16] At

[14] It did not know at that time that on 16 April UNOPS had entered into a one-week agreement with an Ad Hoc Committee to:

- — Conduct creative research and development work for the design of a public information campaign in preparation for the planned public referendum on the Annan Plan.
- — Provide short, basic, easy to understand messages on key issues in the Annan Plan.
- — Develop appropriate methods of information distribution including newspaper advertising and posters/billboards.

In the preamble to the Memorandum it was stated that:

> the UNDP Bi/communal Development Programme desires to provide funding to the Local CBO in the context of the 'Information Campaign' based on promoting the Annan Plan.

This information only came to light with publication of the project's Memorandum of Agreement and a copy of a cheque for CY£14,400 ($30,000). See *To Pontiki*, 5–7 November 2004.

[15] Letter, President Papadopoulos to Mr de Soto, 21 April 2004.

[16] As indicated in Chapter VI, the United Nations through UNOPS had organised "Governance" and "Civil Society" activities with NGOs, some of whose members (particularly Turkish Cypriots) it had assisted with training beginning in 2000, in order to encourage better inter-communal relations and a positive attitude to settlement of the Cyprus problem in terms of the Plan as first presented in November 2002, as revised on 10 December 2002 (Annan II) and then as re-revised on 26 February 2003 (Annan III). In October 2004 President Papadopoulos' request to Mr de Soto to ensure that there be no UN intervention, together with awareness that US funds were used to promote the Plan, became public. The State Department Spokesman, Mr Richard Boucher, in answer to a question about US financing, accepted that US funds were "spent to support peace on the island, spent to support rapprochement" and that the US Government had supported the agreement (the Plan): "We did go out and support it in our speeches, in our statements. And to what extent people spent money on things like *voter education*, I don't know, but I am sure everybody can account for it transparently and openly" (US Department of State, Daily Press Briefing, 20 October 2004; see http://www.state.gov/r/pa/prs/dpb/2004/37261.htm). What was remarkable is that, without the words being put into his mouth by the questioner, Mr Boucher twice referred to "voter education". After the State Department Spokesman had said there could be transparent accounting, UNOPS on 27 October 2004 belatedly put on its website very general information about programme costs and breakdowns of funding in relation to Project Partners. This was uninformative about how money was spent in shaping attitude change, revealing only that (in rounded up figures) $2.7 million were spent on Governance and Civil Society Development; $1 million on Information and

this late stage in the referendum campaign and after the President's preventive warning to Mr de Soto, there were, for whatever reason, "no surprises," and there was no last-minute large-scale UN "informational" activity or further "voter education".

It was only in October 2004 that the encounter between the President and Mr de Soto became known in the context of discussion about USA funding of pro-Plan activities.[17] During the heated public and press discussion which then followed, it came to light that USAID had commissioned this *Final Report* of 25 May 2004 on the BDP (see Chapter VI above) and that the *Final Report* was available for inspection on the internet. In the ensuing press comments and analysis of the *Final Report*, recipients of aid from UNOPS perceived themselves as under attack as disloyal, or as having been "bribed". This they, justifiably, angrily denied. Equally offensive to them is the view that they were used as "innocent pawns" when their *bona fide* desire as Cypriots to exercise freedom of expression by making information available was exploited by the USA, which, in pursuance of US policy aims, covertly provided them with funding to explain or promote the Plan. Regrettably, the course taken by the discussion directed Cypriot attention away from the only institutions deserving of criticism, namely the UN, UNDP, UNOPS and the US Government. These institutions had engaged in stealthy and deceitful manipulation of public opinion in pursuit of their political objectives, and, in 2004, the last year of the BDP, had tried to engineer the outcome of the self-determination exercise. Perhaps the most damning criticism of their conduct was in the *Final Report*, especially when regard is had to the fact that the evaluators were the subsidiary of a consulting firm (Nathan Associates Inc.) which is often commissioned by the US Government and who had therefore to phrase any criticism of that Government cautiously. The *Final Report*, in its conclusions (at pp 44/45, repeated in the Executive Summary at p.x) made a finding that

> It is important that Cypriot government representatives in any future program steering committee understand and agree with the program's objectives.

The *Final Report* explicitly added a footnote to this point (which it also repeated in the Executive Summary):

> 31. We are fully aware that there are risks to greater transparency and increased Cypriot participation. On the other hand, as has been demonstrated by USAID

Communication; $0.3 million on Special Initiative Grants; and $0.5 million on dissemination of the Annan Plan, assistance to the UN good offices mission, a Plan website, citizens' guides to the Plan and leaflets, access to information etc. In addition, there were very large sums ($12 million) in administrative costs ($6.6 in Cyprus and $5.5 million at headquarters, these not being apportioned in relation to "purposes / objectives" of UNOPS activities). As indicated, the *Final Report* at p x, evaluating the BDP, stated that $6.4 million was invested in "bi-communal accomplishment."

[17] The press had attacked Mr Christofias, President of the House of Representatives, for privately commenting that US funds had been used to attempt to secure a "Yes" vote. After these attacks on Mr Christofias, President Papadopoulos then revealed that he had made representations to Mr de Soto about the impropriety of the UN getting involved in Cyprus's domestic jurisdiction by facilitating any pro-Annan Plan campaign.

programs in other difficult environments, US programs "model" desirable values and behaviours in the way in which they are implemented.

The *Final Report* then, as its Recommendation No 2, repeated that, if there were a settlement:

> It is important that Cyprus Government representatives in any future program steering committee understand and agree with the program's objectives.

Clearly, independent professionals in the "development" sphere appreciated that development aid should not be used for surreptitious social engineering of attitudes—quite apart from their awareness that, if such conduct became known, Governments throughout the world would be reluctant to embark on internationally-funded development programmes.

A last comment needs making: even where there are attitude-shaping programmes in which people have participated or to which they have been subjected, if an issue of great significance arises for decision, many people will not decide as the agents who are shaping attitudes desire. Some persons, despite their general support, say, for peace, will assess the possibility put to them for decision either as not achieving peace, or as conflicting with other interests which they hold dear. Thus, in the case of the Annan Plan, many persons who had been participants in UNOPS' projects voted against the Plan, while continuing to believe in the desirability of peace.[18] The Plan was not assessed by them as the only way to achieve peace and rapprochement.

The UN's desire to project the Plan positively led to two incidents which have been much magnified in order to try to cast doubt on the freedom and independence of the Cyprus media, to smear the Government of Cyprus and to question the validity of the referendum result. Mr de Soto, the suggestion allegedly having been made to him by a reporter, wished to give a television address, explaining what he considered to be the correct interpretation and facts of the Plan, which he regarded as having been greatly distorted in the public discussions. His willingness to give an interview was not taken up by the Cyprus Broadcasting Corporation, and an indication was given by a CyBC Board member that in the last week of the campaign foreign bodies and personages should not be provided with airtime. Mr de Soto wrote to President Papadopoulos complaining about this incident, and was told that the Government could not direct the media, which decided such matters for themselves.[19] The de Soto incident

[18] Thus of Greek Cypriot grant recipients who answered questionnaires asking whether they would vote for the Plan (Annan III) in February 2004 (before the negative developments in Annan V), one person said they would vote against the Plan, two said they had not yet made up their minds, 4 were in favour with reservations, and 10 were in favour. Out of 20 persons who answered the questionnaires, 19 answered that bi-communality was the purpose of the BDP and 16 that their activities promoted co-operation and understanding. Likewise, of 10 Turkish Cypriot grant recipients, 8 said they would vote in favour of the Plan and 3 against. (The discrepancy in figures may be due to multiple grants to certain recipients.) See *Final Report*, Annex 5c, Q21, at 5–6 and 5–7.

[19] Letters, Mr de Soto to President Papadopoulos and President Papadopoulos to Mr de Soto, 20 and 21 April 2004.

was seized upon by international and internal actors as a stick with which the beat the Cyprus Government both before and after the referendum. The Secretary-General's *Report* (para 71) asserted that Mr de Soto had been "declined air-time on state television".[20] If the experienced and wily Mr de Soto, surrounded by PR experts, really wanted effectively to correct distortions, he would have called a couple of press conferences so that his remarks would have been highlighted, leading to debate and providing fresh opportunities for corrections. Long interviews by the saturnine Mr de Soto, overlaid on the film by subtitles translating his remarks into Greek, would not have held short attention spans or convinced sceptical listeners. He well knew this. The inference to draw is that Mr de Soto saw a heaven-sent opportunity, which had arisen because of some editorial idiocy and pig-headedness about correcting it, to cast doubt on the forthcoming result, now clearly going to be "No," and to begin building an alibi for this outcome, which had been caused in large measure by his handling of the Cyprus problem since the talks had resumed in Nicosia on 19 February 2004. He certainly exploited this single incident to the full, and international commentators have naïvely taken his interpretation of it at face value.

The second incident concerned Mr Verheugen, EU Commissioner for Enlargement, who requested a commercial television station to go to Brussels to record and then transmit a two-hour press conference by him on the Plan, explaining the compatibility of the Plan with the *acquis communautaire*, this having become a referendum issue. The station, having arranged its programmes and bearing in mind the costs, declined Mr Verheugen's suggestion. The CyBC station declined a similar suggestion.[21] There has also been much pompous huffing and puffing about this dignitary's offers not having been accepted.[22]

These events have been portrayed as tantamount to Government censorship and denial of access to the media, with failure to make information available. The Government of Cyprus had nothing to do with such incidents. Cyprus is a free and a democratic society, with free—some would even say too free—media. No Government, and not even the world's Peace-keeping Organisation, can

[20] However, the Secretary-General followed this assertion by the admission that his own message to the Cyprus people, "underlining the unique opportunity that was at hand" and assuring them of the UN's commitment to full implementation, had received extensive coverage. (It was fully transmitted.)

[21] When the Government Spokesman, Dr Chrysostomides, learnt of this through statements by Mr JC Filori, Spokesman of the Enlargement Commissioner, he emphasised that the Government had no control over the State-owned station CyBC, or over private TV stations, but publicly suggested that they make arrangements to host an interview by Mr Verheugen: Statement, 19 April 2004. Mr Verheugen subsequently made an appearance on the CyBC channel. Earlier pronouncements by Mr Verheugen had, when newsworthy, been featured in all electronic media reports and in the press.

[22] Mr Verheugen's impact, had he been provided with TV facilities, would have been insignificant. Not all politicians are favoured with telegenic personalities, and channels transmitting in German (or even in English) with Greek sub-titles would rapidly have been switched—hence the commercial decisions of the two TV stations involved.

dictate to the Cyprus media what they should or should not carry.[23] In the event, as already indicated, all TV stations transmitted a message from the Secretary-General recommending his Plan. So far as concerns availability of information, the allegations are nonsensical. The only unavailable material was that which the UN had not yet prepared, eg amendments to the Federal Laws related to the Public Service and other Laws still under finalisation. There were of course considerable amounts of misinformation circulating, such misinformation being put forward by both the pro and the con sides of the argument, something inevitable when a technical and complex subject is discussed by lay members of the public and by politicians, each with his own angle. As with all such debates, fresh manifestations of misinformation and distortion as well as provision of accurate information will occur as long as discussion continues. Nonetheless, there was widespread public understanding of the major issues, even if some technicalities were not fully appreciated.[24] But this cuts both ways: few understood that the Plan's property provisions were serving as a charter for developers and improvers of seized Greek Cypriot-owned property. They only awakened to this fact when they saw, after the referenda, how property development had mushroomed in the occupied area since 2002. They then realised that the Plan in all its versions had encouraged such development and would finally legitimate it, converting the right to property to a right to compensation in many cases, thereby denying the right to actual restitution and at the same time sabotaging the right to return.

The UN and some international commentators remarked at the time of the referendum on demonstrations by "children". Such comments show ignorance about traditional behaviour by young people in Cyprus. Secondary school students in Cyprus have always been highly politicised, as the United Kingdom found in Colonial days, ultimately closing secondary schools. That young people are civically active and committed to promoting human rights issues (and not only in respect of Cyprus itself) is something to be approved, rather than condemned. There is no evidence that the Ministry of Education encouraged demonstrations against the Plan, even if some individual teachers may have encouraged their students. The reality is that the youth of Cyprus have always advocated and acted on moral and political principles that the UN usually promotes. That they demonstrate in public and very often outside the Embassies of Powers whom they regard as pursuing immoral and unlawful foreign policies (eg on Iraq or policy

[23] Libel suits by Cypriot politicians are frequent. Scarcely a politician in Cyprus, including the President and former Presidents, has not been subject to libel and been a plaintiff. Conversely, they have been unable to insist on getting the coverage they wanted.

[24] Mr Pfirter, in an interview published in Swiss Peace Supporter, No 2, June 204, published by the Swiss Ministry of Foreign Affairs, asserted that apart from the Greek Cypriot population having "been led to expect a better negotiating position after joining the EC" the "No" vote "was caused by a strong uncertainty and confusion following a questionable campaign by the plan's opponents". The same Swiss Foreign Ministry publication asserted in a caption to a photograph accompanying Mr Pfirter's interview: "Despite *massive international pressure* the Greek Cypriots said No with a clear majority *to the reunification of the Island*" (emphasis added).

towards the Palestinians) is just a fact of Cyprus's free political life. Indeed, it often causes the Republic's Government diplomatic embarrassment and necessitates public expenditure on extra policing.

One striking aspect of the period preceding the referenda is the international criticism that was directed at President Papadopoulos, who is an elected executive President, not a judge. Even though the holder of the highest political office, he, like other persons, has the right to freedom of expression. He also had, as he pointed out in his speech to the Cyprus electorate, not only

> the heavy burden of responsibility for conducting the negotiations . . . [but] the duty to state publicly and with sincerity and frankness my own assessment of the conclusion of the negotiations and my own decision. Without any attempt on my part to impose my choice on you, but offered as a guideline to be assessed also by you. The final decision is and always has been yours. Your verdict will be expressed at the referendum of the 24th April.

These remarks were made on 7 April 2004, when the President was given air time on all television stations to express his views on the Plan. He pointed out that there were some improvements in the Plan's most recent version, but said that he would not dwell now on these aspects as they would be debated in the coming weeks. After emphasising that he was giving his personal assessment, and that responsibility for final decisions belonged to each individual citizen, he then gave a devastating analysis of the impact of the Plan as a whole, concluding with an emotional call for Cypriot voters to "say a resounding No" to it and to defend their dignity, their history and what is right.[25] The President's objection was to the particular Plan imposed, not to a plan, properly negotiated, for reunification—a goal devoutly hoped for by all Greek Cypriots. Some internal political opponents, who supported the Plan, condemned the President for his emphasis on the Plan's deficiencies and for not having given an account of its positive provisions. What was notable was that this criticism was followed by intervention by the UN Secretariat, which, in private briefings, described the President's approach as unbalanced.[26] It is extraordinary that the Secretariat

[25] Saying a resolute "No" is a cultural and historic tradition among Greeks, who believe that their dignity is important. "No" (OXI) was said by the Government of Greece to an ultimatum by Mussolini in October 1940. 28 October is a Cyprus national holiday. Those persons (such as Lord Hannay) who regard the implicit reference to this no-saying as "disgraceful" (see "Greek Cypriots must pay the price of Folly" in *E Sharp, People, Power and Process in Europe*, July 2004) have no understanding of Greek Cypriot culture or psychology.

[26] Paras 65 and 66 of the *Report* of 28 May 2004 publicly expanded on this criticism, now using first person language by the Secretary-General. He expressed surprise at President Papadopoulos' views on the unwisdom of the Plan. Yet he knew that President Papadopoulos had constantly expressed doubts since their 27 February 2003 meeting (fully recorded in the President's 28 February letter). These major doubts had been expressed when the Plan was still subject to negotiation and had not been finalised in the way it later was at Bürgenstock. The President had said nothing at his 29 January 2004 meeting with the Secretary-General in Brussels that could have led the Secretary-General to believe that he had been satisfied as to the fundamental deficiencies that had been raised a year earlier. Naturally, the Secretary-General repudiated the notion that his team had finalised the Plan at Bürgenstock with excessive regard being paid to Turkey's concerns and with too little regard

should have overlooked the fact that the Plan had not been so modified in the negotiations as to meet the conditions for the President's support of it which he had set out orally and in writing on 27 and 28 February 2003. Some of these conditions he had restated to the Secretary-General in Brussels on 29 January 2004 and he had reiterated them at Bürgenstock on 30 March, immediately before the decisions on "finalisation" of 31 March 2004.

Following the President's "vote No" television address, Mr de Soto attempted to remonstrate with the President on 8 April and threatened that he would be suggesting that the Secretary-General say certain things.[27] Mr de Soto had to be

to Greek Cypriot concerns. But, to anyone familiar with the alterations made at the end of March 2004 in Bürgenstock in Annan IV and Annan V, the Plan's balance was by now quite unacceptable. The arrangements under the finalised Plan, seen as a whole, were particularly unacceptable in view of the large numbers of Turkish settlers who would remain in Cyprus and would politically control the TCCS. That possibility had always been rejected by the Greek Cypriot side. Without settlers as the dominant voting body in the northern part of Cyprus, the Plan would have been different both in context and in practice. Moreover, the active intervention and direction of Turkey had become ever more apparent. By 2004, as in earlier years, she was explicitly claiming a right of unilateral military intervention.

[27] Mr de Soto sought to claim that the President had not negotiated in good faith. The President told him that he had no standing or basis for making such remarks. Mr de Soto's views were widely purveyed and those aware of them ask whether negotiations were conducted in good faith. The answer to this question is that President Papadopoulos, immediately upon Annan III being presented, but before his inauguration, in a letter of 28 January 2003 (reflecting joint agreement on his approach with outgoing President Clerides and with Mr Markides) agreed not to re-open Annan III. But, at the same time, his letter set out the basis on which he would be prepared to support the Plan. (See Appendix 3.) In the February–March 2004 negotiations, he made clear that he wanted improvements on Annan III so that he would be in a position to lend support. He spelled out the improvements he required in what the Secretary-General's Report described as "dense and lengthy papers". The President had earlier made it clear in New York that the Plan could be voted down, also recording in Nicosia that there were limits to the Secretary-General's discretion to "finalise" the Plan. In particular, the President proved that he would do nothing to indicate his acceptance of the Plan, most notably at Bürgenstock, where, despite heavy pressures, he refused to sign a document agreeing to submit the Plan to referenda lest signature be construed as support for it. The President did not mislead anyone, least of all Mr de Soto—unless the latter was deaf and blind or had convinced himself that he was invincible—into thinking that he supported the Plan.

The suggestion that the President was "going through the motions," or that his attitude to the negotiations was *male fide*, is unworthy. The UN well knew that he wanted "improvements" and precisely what they were, as well as what Greek Cypriot concerns were, since these were repeatedly spelled out in the Nicosia meetings and in contacts at Bürgenstock. To reiterate, he gave no undertaking that he would support the Plan in any referendum campaign should the Plan not be improved in accordance with his reasoned proposals. Had the major proposals been accepted in full, rather than only in part, and had the Plan not been "worsened"—as it was in Annan IV and V—the President would have assumed the task of persuading Greek Cypriot voters to support the Plan. In corroboration of what is here asserted, the writer can state that the President carefully scrutinised and revised every one of the proposals made by the Greek Cypriot side. He would not have devoted such care and such enormous amounts of time to this activity had he been engaging in a mere charade. Among his advisers who accompanied him to Bürgenstock were politicians and experts who believed that improvements could be negotiated there, such as to persuade the President and the majority of National Council members to support the finalised Plan.

It is more appropriate to ask whether Turkey was in good faith in the negotiations in demanding changes to the Plan which she must have known would inevitably make the Greek Cypriot side reject it. Certainly in 2002 under the Ecevit Government, Turkey, apart from meetings between Mr Ziyal and Mr de Soto, would not seriously negotiate, in contrast with President Clerides who exhibited flexibility: see *S/2003/398*, para 35. It was only after Turkey (even under the new Erdoğan/Gül informed by the President that, now the Plan had been finalised, he had virtually executed his functions as regards Cyprus. The President by no stretch of imagination could be described as having exploited his office. Apart from his one powerful initial speech, he did little to campaign in relation to the forthcoming referenda, only again taking airtime two nights before the referenda in order to answer journalists' questions. Because this was the last night on which the Electoral Law permitted campaigning (there being a one-day gap in which campaigning was impermissible) there was again criticism. The provisions of this Law of many years' standing had been enacted in order to preclude last minute opinion polls and rhetoric from unduly influencing voters, giving them a day for reflection before voting. That Law had not previously been challenged, but the President was now accused of wrongdoing, with certain political figures contemplating legal challenge. All such criticism is misconceived: Cypriots are not sheep, and the President is far from being their shepherd, driving them into pens. Cypriots listened to both sides, and made up their minds for themselves.[28] It is insulting to the Greek Cypriot electorate, that those who were disappointed by its final decision and the political consequences were not willing to accept the people's verdict in a fair and free referendum, instead attributing the result to manipulation and to governmental interference with information processes.[29] Indeed, the Secretary-General's *Report* at para 67 implied that Greek Cypriot political parties were muzzled and prevented from supporting the Plan because, being represented on the National Council (an extra-constitutional advisory body to the President), they had to decide their own positions in light of Mr Papadopoulos' speech on TV. The reality is that, because leaders were in Bürgenstock awaiting the final outcome of the negotiations on 31 March, those who wanted a "Yes" campaign did not have this fully organised until the last 10 days before the referendum on 24 April. There was no "muzzling". If Party leaders chose not to take public positions prior to the President having done so on 7 April, these were their own tactical choices in light of their perceptions of

Government) insisted on her earlier policy of linking settlement of the Cyprus issue with Turkey's European Union perspective, and Mr Denktash remained unyielding, that President Clerides took "a non-committal position" on acceptance because whether the Greek Cypriot side would sign had become "theoretical": *ibid*, para 47.

[28] The writer's former colleagues, public servants who worked on the Plan, comprised both "Yes" and "No" voters, and, whichever way they voted, were fully informed, felt free to decide as they wished, did so, and said so subsequently.

[29] It is particularly unfortunate that the Secretariat should have adopted such a stance. Its role was to facilitate a settlement by producing a Plan capable of being decided upon in the referenda. But, because of the UN team's long involvement and the enormous work they had done on the Plan, and also because they saw themselves as having negotiated a reasonable settlement and as having achieved considerable benefits for Greek Cypriots, despite Turkey's stone-walling tactics, they identified with the fruits of their labours. Such inevitable human reactions should have been kept private, and should not have been used publicly to berate Greek Cypriots for not accepting the gifts they had been brought. This point is quite apart from the political motivations of certain senior figures in the Department of Political Affairs, who were extremely close to the USA and the UK, keeping in close, even daily, contact at times, as during the 2004 Nicosia negotiations, with their diplomats, and taking policy lines favoured by these two Permanent Members.

public opinion and the views of their own political bureaux. They had no obligation to await a "go" signal from the President. In fact, most were carefully assessing the state of public opinion before deciding on the stance they would adopt. Other political personalities in favour of "yes" were immediately vociferous in support of the Plan on the electronic media and in the printed press, speaking up for seven days before the President's TV appearance. As to "balance" in media allocations of time and space, surveys by the independent Radio and Television Authority showed that more "no" proponents spoke than "yes" supporters. This was only natural, since the former reflected 75% of public opinion. Even so, in the last few days before the referendum, the television stations ensured a 50–50 division of time to supporters and opponents of the Plan.

The Secretariat's public concern about the electoral process in the Government-controlled area contrasts oddly with its repudiation of any responsibility for, or involvement in, or concern about the electoral process in the occupied area. Despite repeated requests by the Greek Cypriot side to consider preventive measures regarding illegal Turkish settler participation in voting, the Secretary-General declined to do anything, failing even to consult the Security Council.

The Secretariat apparently regarded the President as a powerful "bogeyman". In fact he is a historic personage in Cyprus with nearly half a century of political life and, like all politicians, has not only supporters, but also detractors and rivals. As a young man he was involved in giving political guidance to EOKA in the anti-Colonial struggle. When Archbishop Makarios invited a group of leading Greek Cypriots to the London Conference to assist him in standing up against the Zurich Agreements of 1959, all except the then young future President and another delegate capitulated to suasion and to threats by Prime Minister Karamanlis of Greece to hold a general election on withdrawing support from the Cyprus independence movement if acceptance of the Zurich backroom deal between Greece and Turkey was not advised by them. Greek Cypriots would be left at the United Kingdom's mercy, with the Colonial Power intending to impose the Macmillan Plan, which would inevitably lead to partition of the Island. At 25 years of age Mr Papadopoulos became Minister of the Interior in the pre-independence period, while President Makarios appointed him as Minister of Labour in Cyprus's first Council of Ministers.[30] From 1970

[30] While Minister of Labour, in the last two years before the inter-communal clashes of December 1963 and in the absence of any Cypriot Army (vetoed by Vice-President Kucuk), a time when there was Turkish provision of arms supplies, Turkish Army training of Turkish Cypriot paramilitaries and Turkey had threatened to invade Cyprus if amendments were made to the 1960 Constitution, Mr Papadopoulos, with two other colleagues, formed a Greek Cypriot paramilitary group called The Organisation. After its establishment, this group came under President Makarios's indirect surveillance through appointment for this purpose of Mr Glafcos Clerides, later President 1993–2003. The Greek Cypriot Community had from 1954 to 1958 suffered numerous violent attacks on it by Turkish Cypriots, incited by the Republic of Turkey. Under the circumstances, it was essential to have a military force to protect the Community. This is why it was acquiesced in as being the only option.

President Papadopoulos photographed during his TV address on 7 April 2004, as he advises Greek Cypriots, exercising their free choice, to say a "resounding 'No'" in the forthcoming referendum.

"The Four Musketeers" (as the team was known) at their internal farewell party on 26 April 2004. (Who was which adventurer?) *The Blue Beret* society column reported: "In addition to the UN family, Good Offices' guests included the British High Commissioner, the Dutch, German, Irish and US Ambassadors and the Swiss Charge d'Affaires—whose Governments provided funding and support to the Good Offices."

Where will Goldfinger's next operation take place? Alvaro de Soto departs UNFICYP headquarters preparatory to leaving Cyprus on 28 April 2004.

he became a member of the House of Representatives. For many years he advised Mr Clerides in the inter-communal talks. Later, as Greek Cypriot Interlocutor in the inter-communal talks from 1976–1978, he put forward in Vienna on 1 April 1977 the first Greek Cypriot proposals for a bi-communal federation, which would consist of two zones (ie the federation would be "bi-zonal"). Mr Papadopoulos has been a long-standing public representative of Cyprus in international and national bodies. In the early 1990s, as the leading partner in a Cyprus Law Office, he incurred hostility of the US Treasury and State Department, followed by attempts to establish that there had been money laundering. The US hoped to entangle him in proceedings before the Tribunal on the Former Yugoslavia on the basis that relevant UN sanctions Resolutions had been violated. This was because his firm had as clients Yugoslav Banks and the family of Mr Slobodan Milosevic, who had removed from Yugoslavia large funds still being sought for across the world as allegedly being property of its successor States or as being claimed by the Government of Serbia and Montenegro. Full cooperation was given to investigations in Cyprus by the Prosecutor of the Tribunal and by the Government of Serbia and Montenegro. All documents of the Central Bank were made available. No evidence of any wrongdoing by Mr Papadopoulos or by his firm was found, but this has done nothing to stop the State Department and others from seeking to stigmatise him. The real reason for the hostility to Mr Papadopoulos from certain Powers is that he is a man of great strength of character, who is prepared to say "No". This does not entail that he is negative or what is described as a "rejectionist" in relation to a Cyprus settlement. He will do what he thinks best for Cyprus in the circumstances. In appropriate circumstances that could well be "Yes" to a much revised Annan V or to a fresh UN or EU Plan.[31]

[31] No man is an island, and it is important to take account of those who advise the President. Apart from Mr Christofias, President of the House of Representatives and Secretary-General of the Central Committee of Akel, members of the National Council accompanied Mr Papadopoulos to New York and Bürgenstock and earlier regularly met in Nicosia—just as National Council Members accompanied President Clerides to Copenhagen, Geneva and New York and met regularly during the Nicosia talks. He also had the benefit of advice from the Foreign Minister, Mr George Iacovou, who has had unrivalled experience acting in international fora for Cyprus for most of the period since 1983. Dr Chrysostomides, the Government Spokesman, a leading lawyer trained in international law, was always on hand. On the professional level, the President had as advisers the Head of his Diplomatic Office, Ambassador Tasos Tzionis, a diplomat with an enquiring, principled yet flexible mind, who is also Director of the Central Intelligence Service; Ambassador Andreas Mavroyiannis, Cyprus's Permanent Representative to the UN in New York, an international and EU lawyer trained in France; and Ambassador Emiliou, then Cyprus's Council of Europe Representative and an expert in EU Law. The Government of Greece made available as required a number of distinguished Greek professors and public servants, among whom were Professors Papadimitiou and Tassopoulos and Mr Stefanou. Available for professional advice if required were international jurists, such as Professor Ian Brownlie QC, Professor James Crawford SC, Professor Joseph Weiler and Professor Gerhard Hafner. The writer, a comparative public lawyer, who had worked on the Cyprus problem for various Cyprus Presidents since 1979, was a member of the advisory team, as were two leading Cypriot economists, Dr Charalambous and Mr Trokkos. Many other Cypriot lawyers and experts gave unstintingly of their time to produce advice and work whenever needed. Their respective leaders were the Law Commissioner, Mrs Leda Koursoumba, and Dr Lycourgos, Head of the European Union Section of the Law Office of the

There was indeed one major attempt to manipulate public opinion in Cyprus. That attempt was by the Secretariat. Anticipating that such an attempt would be made, President Papadopoulos and his advisers had orally indicated to the UN team at Bürgenstock that, when briefing the Security Council on the outcome of the finalisation exercise and clearing with the Council that a UN peacekeeping force with an appropriate mandate would be established, the Secretary-General should not request the Council to endorse the Plan. Endorsement by the Council should occur only after the referenda. Internally, passage of an endorsing Council Resolution would have had a major impact on Cypriot opinion, especially because, over the years, Greek Cypriots have placed their faith in the Security Council and its Resolutions. Security Council decisions carry special weight among the Cyprus public, as the Secretariat was well aware. In light of this situation, the impression could well have been created, were there to have been Security Council advance endorsement of the Plan, that the Council was attempting to influence the outcome of the referenda, something that the Council could not contemplate doing in light of Article 2.7 of the Charter. When, in mid-April, it became clear that the Secretariat was pressing

Republic. The property team was Andreas Hadjiraftis, Stella Zapitis and Costas Apostolides. The basic work on Annan I, II, and III and earlier cooperation with the UN had been done by the then Attorney-General, Mr Alecos Markides, a man of exceptional intellect, willing to adopt humane attitudes and unprejudiced approaches. Mr Markides believed that, despite the adverse changes in Annan V after he had left the team, the Plan, although far from ideal, was the best that could be obtained and should be accepted to secure the practical benefits of return of numbers of refugees, property and territory under Greek Cypriot administration; a reduction in the size of the Turkish Army present in Cyprus; the economic benefits of certainty through agreeing upon a Cyprus settlement; and a start to intercommunal cooperation. Similar views were held by those who voted "Yes" in the referendum, outweighing for them their many doubts and concerns. It needs adding that former President Clerides who handled the Cyprus problem intermittently from 1962 had a unique grasp of the issues, appreciation of the rights and wrongs of both sides and was determined to settle the problem, provided that the terms were sufficiently fair.

Since the Greek Cypriot advisers have been mentioned, it should be said that the Turkish Cypriot side also had excellent advisers available. The large and effective Turkish Foreign Ministry has many skilled and experienced personnel, conversant with all aspects of the Cyprus problem and well-equipped to pursue Turkish policy aims for Cyprus. A strong Turkish team was present at Bürgenstock, while some advisers assisted the Turkish Cypriot *dramatis personae* both in Ankara and in Nicosia, including among them lawyers from the Republic of Turkey, her Foreign Ministry and other Departments. Ambassador Ugur Ziyal played a crucial role. All who dealt with him held in high respect. Mr Ergün Olgun, "Permanent Undersecretary" to Mr Denktash's "Council of Ministers," a powerful personality trained in conflict resolution, was both a political and a technical figure directing the Turkish Cypriot teams of experts, and was very close to Mr Rauf Denktash. (He was referred to as "Olgun Bey" by the younger members of his side and as "a hero" by Mr Pfirter.) Professor Mümtaz Soysal, Mr Denktash's long-standing adviser and inventor of the concept of "bi-zonality," who at one time was Foreign Minister of Turkey, played a major role in shaping Turkish Cypriot constitutional proposals, especially as to foreign affairs and bi-zonality aspects. (Certain UN personnel could scarcely conceal their view that he was poison when it came to reaching the compromises they wished to impose in February 2003.) Professor Soysal's view was that Turkish entry to the EU was being considered prematurely and that the Turkish economy would suffer seriously from adjustments needed for EU membership. An important contribution was made by Professor Rusen Ergec, a Turco-Belgian expert on Co-operation Agreements and EU matters. Finally, Mr Rauf Denktash's remarkable abilities as leader of his Community, his consistent policy over the years, his pugnacious determination and his sense of humour, should not go unremarked.

for a prior endorsement of the Plan, President Papadopoulos on 13 April 2004 formally requested the Secretary-General *not to request approval of domestic arrangements for Cyprus until these were consented to by the people of Cyprus through the referenda. He suggested that the Secretary-General should only seek contingent approval by the Council of the security aspects of the Plan.* Nevertheless, the Secretary-General's initial *Report* of 16 April, *S/2004/302*, Parts I and IV, and paragraph 12 in particular, sought to convey the impression that there had been agreement to the whole Plan being endorsed in advance of the referenda. Despite the Cyprus Government repeatedly objecting, and making it clear that it did not consent to prior "endorsement," the USA and the United Kingdom, acting in conjunction with the Secretariat, then moved a resolution in the Security Council on 21 April 2004 *to endorse the Foundation Agreement* before the referenda. In the event, the Government of Russia exercised its veto in order to ensure that the Council in no way imposed any decisions on the parties and that the referenda should take place freely without any external interference or pressure.[32] When the 28 May 2004 retrospective *Report* on the mission of good offices appeared it was astonishing to read that

> the Greek Cypriot leader did not wish the Council to take decisions—*even on security issues*—before the referenda
>
> (para 69, emphasis added)

and that only *subsequently* to the *Report* of 16 April 2004 did Mr Papadopoulos indicate his desire that the Foundation Agreement not be endorsed prior to referendum. These misstatements compelled the Greek Cypriot side to give chapter and verse showing their falsity.[33] Despite the Government of Cyprus's

[32] *S/PV 4947*, 21 April 2004, p 2, Mr Gatilov. Fourteen other Members of the Council voted in favour of the Resolution. Some States however indicated in their explanations of vote that, although they had no doubts as to the substance, they had doubts as to the timing of the initiative eg Mr Valle of Brazil. Mr Iacovou, Cyprus's Foreign Minister, made representations to the Russian Government to assist in precluding attempts to influence the electorate by a Security Council Resolution endorsing the Plan.

[33] In its comments on the *Report* at p 8, para 27, the Government wrote:

> Para 42E and para 69. These paragraphs give a false picture. President Papadopoulos did not "*subsequently*" to the Secretary-General's 16 April Report indicate his desire that the Foundation Agreement not be endorsed by the Security Council. At Bürgenstock it was made clear that the Greek Cypriot side did not believe endorsement by the Security Council should be used as a device to persuade the Cyprus public. Moreover, in para 69 the false statement is made that President Papadopoulos did not wish the Council to take decisions before the referenda "even on security issues". In fact, in his letter of 13 April (note also that this was before, not subsequent to, the 16 April report), President Papadopoulos requested the Secretary-General, *while not seeking endorsement of the domestic arrangements for Cyprus, to "put the security aspect to the Council"*. Furthermore, the Permanent Mission of the Republic of Cyprus to the United Nations, upon instructions from the Government, conveyed to all members of the Security Council, on 20 April 2004, a Memorandum with specific proposals to be reflected in the draft Resolution presented to the Council. *All proposals addressed security issues* and in particular aimed at strengthening the provisions for the implementation of the Foundation Agreement; at subjecting any right of intervention by the Guarantor Powers to prior authorization by the Security Council; "at assuring the compatibility of the Treaty of Guarantee . . . [with] the UN Charter; and . . . sought a clear statement that the objective should be the total withdrawal of foreign military forces from Cyprus." [Emphasis added.]

attempts to correct the wrong picture that has been presented about Cyprus's unwillingness to see a Security Council Resolution approved before the referenda, misapprehensions remain. It is not understood that Cyprus wanted a Resolution, affording guarantees, and which would come "into force simultaneously with the Foundation Agreement" (as the Plan required), so that any Resolution should have been contingent, coming into effect only at the envisaged time. Nor is it understood that Cyprus wanted a *mandatory* Resolution, and that, apart from the ban on weapons, the Anglo-Americans would not consider this. It is ignored that Cyprus insisted (as the Plan provided in E) that matters were to be submitted to the Security Council "*by agreement of the parties*," and that she had not agreed to *endorsement* of the Plan prior to the referenda. The fact is also ignored that negotiations in the Security Council to omit the language of endorsement and about the timing of the Anglo-American draft Resolution led nowhere, because of those Powers' insistence on their own draft.[34]

At the same time certain foreign States' Ministers and diplomats, notably those of the USA, the UK and some other EU States, together with the Secretariat, used every possible opportunity to warn the Cyprus public of the serious, even dire, consequences should voters fail to approve the Secretary-General's Plan. The warnings were not merely advice: they were implicit threats of major changes of policy and moves to quasi-recognition of the Turkish Republic of Northern Cyprus, along the lines of the Taiwan model, combined with an intention to remove any pressures on the Turkish Cypriot subordinate local administration, which might otherwise encourage Turkish Cypriots to engage in negotiations for amendments to the Plan which the Greek Cypriot side might propose.

THE RESULTS IN THE TWO REFERENDA AND THE EXAGGERATED PRESENTATION OF THE OUTCOME

The two separate simultaneous referenda held on 24 April 2004, resulted in high polls (89.25% of the electorate in the Government-controlled area ie Greek Cypriots and 84.35% in the Turkish-occupied area ie Turkish Cypriots). They produced the results shown in Table D[35].

The results of each referendum were separately presented and the totals of "Yes" and "No" votes were kept distinct by agreement of the two sides (so as not to risk any suggestion that this was a "majority" voting exercise, but only

[34] Even the usually perspicacious Lord Hannay in answering the Foreign Affairs Committee's questions as to why Russia vetoed the US–UK draft, seemed to share some of these misapprehensions, thinking that the British and Americans were doing what was in the Plan "as needed to be done" (Testimony to the Foreign Affairs Committee, 2 November 2004, p 4).

[35] Derived from statistics provided by North Cyprus Web Guide—http://www.cyprusive.com/default.asp?CID=519.

Charge d'affaires Gennady Gatilov (centre) exercises Russian's veto on a USA-UK sponsored draft resolution seeking to endorse the Annan Plan after a prior explanation of vote on 21 April 2004. In these post-Cold War days it is a long time since the Council President (in this instance German) has had, due to Russian action, to announce that "the draft resolution was not adopted owing to the negative vote of a Permanent Member of the Council". It is noticeable that most Mission personnel sent to attend the Council are of relatively low rank. Debates on the Cyprus situation seem only to involve the big players' messengers, not their Permanent Representatives.

Typical "Grey Wolf," demonstrating in the Turkish-occupied area on 21 April 2004. It was members of this ultra-nationalist group who committed acts of violence against Greek Cypriot demonstrators in and along the buffer zone in 1996 and from whose organisation the man who tried to assassinate Pope John Paul II was drawn.

Above left: Mr Denktash (like 41,972 other Turkish Cypriots) depositing his 'No' vote in Box No 125 on 24 April 2004, after much flourishing of the ballot paper to the world's press and telling them how he voted.

Above right: a serious Mr Anastasiades deposits his 'Yes' vote in a Limassol polling station.

Below: former President Clerides (like 99, 976 other Greek Cypriots) after depositing his 'Yes' vote. He stated: "Whatever the people today decide, what is really important is that we should all co-operate, because the Cyprus Republic will have to face a lot of difficulties." Asked by the press how he felt that day, his 85th birthday, he joked: "I went to see recently a 95 year-old lady, wishing her to live to 100. She responded: 'You want me to live another 5 years only'." Mrs Clerides and their daughter Kate, a Member of the Republic's House of Representatives and a strong supporter of good inter-Community relations, are with him.

Table D Voting in the Referenda of 24 April 2004

	Registered Voters	Votes Cast	Valid Votes	Spoilt	Did not vote	Yes	No
GREEK CYPRIOTS	480,165	428,587	413,680	14,907	51,578	99.976	313,704
% of electorate	100%	89.25%	86.15%	3.10%	10.74%	20.82%	65.33%
% of votes cast	—	100%	96.52%	3.47%	—	23.32%	73.19%
% of valid votes	—	—	100%	—	—	24.16%	75.83%
TURKISH CYPRIOTS	143,638	121,160	119,619	1,541	22,478	77,646	41,973
% of electorate	100%	84.35%	83.27%	1.07%	15.64%	54.05%	29.22%
% of votes cast	—	100%	98.72%	1.27%	—	64.08%	34.64%
% of valid votes	—	—	100%	—	—	64.91%	35.08%

one involving each Community in making its own separate decisions). Nonetheless, the total voting picture has here been presented to show that individuals across the population of the whole Island had diverse views as well as providing the actual sizes of each section of the Cyprus electorate. As regards the results in the Turkish-occupied area, President Papadopoulos's TV address cannot be blamed for the 41,974 Turkish Cypriots who voted "No," or the 1,541 Turkish Cypriot voters who spoilt their ballots (1.27% of the votes cast). Nor can his address be blamed for the further 15.64% of the Turkish Cypriot electorate who failed to vote.[36] In fact, rather than *64.91% of Turkish Cypriots voting "Yes,"* as the UN, the USA and the world press kept stating, *only 54.05% of the Turkish Cypriot electorate voted "Yes"*. Thus comments, which to this day are repeated by certain foreign statesmen, about an "overwhelming majority" of Turkish Cypriot voters being in favour, are mere propaganda to justify

[36] The Turkish Cypriot "electorate" is larger than it appears in the prevailing discussion of referendum results. Only 84.35% of "electors" voted. On the Greek Cypriot side 89.25% voted. This higher figure is because the Electoral Law requires persons to cast a ballot even if they "spoil" it. *As a percentage of the total electorate in Cyprus* (623,803 persons), 88.12% (549,747 persons) voted; 11.87% (74,056 persons) did not vote; 2.99% of votes cast (16,448 persons) were invalid (ie there was deliberate spoiling of ballots by a sophisticated electorate); and, of the 97.01% of *valid votes*, there was a "Yes" vote by 33.24% (177,622 persons) and a "No" vote by 66.56% (355,677 persons).

American, British, EU and UN Secretariat decisions to make economic benefits available to Turkish Cypriots.[37]

THE SECRETARY-GENERAL'S REACTION

In the event, a disappointed Secretary-General singled out for applause the 77,704 voters in the occupied area (described as "Turkish Cypriots") who had voted "Yes," for applause,[38] and called on the 313,693 Greek Cypriots who had voted "No," soberly to reassess their decision and its consequences. (No such call was made to those Turkish Cypriots, who, following the negative presentations of Mr R Denktash and Mr S Denktash, had voted "No," or had in large numbers abstained.) In this context of applause and denigration, it should be recollected that the Plan had been positively presented by politicians from *both sides,* namely by Mr Talat, Mr Anastassiades, Mr Clerides, Mr Vassiliou and Mr Markides. Messrs Clerides and Vassiliou were former Presidents of the Republic of Cyprus. Mr Markides, formerly Attorney-General, had been a recent independent Presidential candidate, while Mr Anastassiades was leader of what at the time was the largest Greek Cypriot political party. The Plan was also negatively presented by politicians from both sides, including both Mr Rauf Denktash and Mr Serdar Denktash of the Turkish Cypriot side. All the major protagonists were representative political figures in their Communities. It is also noteworthy that more Greek Cypriots voted *for* the Plan than did Turkish Cypriots: 99,976 Greek Cypriots to 77,646 Turkish Cypriots (including Turkish settlers). Having regard to the election campaign and the results, "one side" cannot properly be singled out as having unfairly presented the Plan to the public or as the one seeking reconciliation and reunification. Implications and explicit statements in the *Report* of the character described above raise serious questions about who currently writes and advises on the Secretary-General's speeches and on his Cyprus *Reports*

[37] This is a separate issue which requires proper examination irrespective of how Turkish Cypriots voted. The Government of Cyprus has agreed that benefits should be made available so far as this is compatible with not buttressing separatism in Cyprus and with not according the "TRNC" the economic status and rights of an independent State, thus encouraging consolidation of its purported secession. In an EU context (see p 247 below) the Government has cooperated in the removal of barriers to economic development and trading rights of individual Turkish Cypriots, although not in the mode which the Turkish Cypriot political leadership and Turkey desire and for which Turkish allies, notably the USA and the United Kingdom, have been pressing.

[38] He did not applaud the 99,976 Greek Cypriot "Yes" voters. It appears that the 77,646 "Turkish Cypriots" included very many Turkish settlers, because current estimates are that only about 88,000 Turkish Cypriots, including children, have remained in Cyprus. Settlers who had become "citizens" were in the list of 45,000 persons to become citizens of the United Cyprus Republic and knew that *this Plan* permitted them to remain. The speculation that settlers voted for the Plan is corroborated by Mr Talat's arrangements with Mr Cevikel to get settler support. Once the referendum was over, Mr Cevikel and Mr Talat parted company, leading to Mr Talat's "Government" no longer having a parliamentary majority. See now Table E (Appendix 4) showing extensive voting by Turkish settlers in favour of the Plan.

on his mission of good offices.[39] What has recently been written (and said) contrasts with earlier UN approaches manifesting impartiality.

On 1 April 2003, the Secretary-General had wanted the people of Cyprus to decide for themselves on their own future (*S/2003/298*, §§ 144 and 146). Yet, when, on 24 April 2004, the majority of Greek Cypriots (and a majority of all Cypriots) decided to reject his team's Plan, despite the heavy "steer" given to them prior to the referendum by the Secretary-General, he clearly disliked the inconvenient results of government by the people. Despite the *Report's* innuendoes to the contrary, Greek Cypriots in the Government-controlled area constitute a genuine democracy and their wishes, expressed in a free and untainted process, should be respected. They should not, in reflections on the process, be upbraided or accused of folly for making their own choices, and lectured about the need to reflect on the consequences of these. It was not only the Secretary-General and his Secretariat subordinates who criticised the decision of the great majority of Greek voters: a torrent of criticism came from Ministers and diplomats of foreign States in an admixture of accusations and regrets at the outcome, hedged with the qualification that "of course Greek Cypriots' views were to be respected". If even the Greek Cypriots misunderstood the Plan, as Mr de Soto asserted, most foreign diplomats were plain ignorant of the Plan's labyrinthine complexities. They had founded their views on briefings from Mr de Soto, other members of the Secretariat, or selective Foreign Office and State Department accounts. International journalists were similarly taken in.

Amazed at the initial international governmental and press reaction to the Greek Cypriot "No" vote, Mrs Stella Soulioti, a leading Greek Cypriot, who had assisted in the search for a settlement since the early 1960s, who has an irreproachable reputation for fairness among both Communities as former Minister of Justice and later as Attorney-General of Cyprus, and who is regarded by all diplomats posted to Cyprus as a great expert on the Cyprus problem,[40] wrote on 5 May 2004 a personal memo "Justice?". In particular, she observed:

> On 24 April 2004 the Greek Cypriots and the Turkish Cypriots exercised their democratic right, by Referendum, to accept or not to accept the Annan Plan for the solution of the Cyprus Problem. The Plan, as a whole, consists of about 10,000 pages: the main body, which is some 200 pages long, was finalized on 31 March 2004, whilst the remaining 9,800 pages, containing matters of crucial importance, were not finalized until the day before the Referendum. The Annan Plan is a most complex legal

[39] The head of the Department of Political Affairs, Sir Kieran Prendergast, has overall responsibility, even if drafts are sent upwards from Mr de Soto's team. Some sober reassessment about speech and report-writing tactics is required. Propaganda by professionals should neither be so blatant nor so unskilful as to be counter-productive, or be so obviously based on repeated errors of fact, as was the situation with *S/2004/437*, 28 May 2004.

[40] On his private visit to Cyprus in mid-August 2004, Ambassador Richard A Boucher, Spokesman of the State Department and Assistant-Secretary, US Bureau of Public Affairs, requested an opportunity to meet her again.

document several of the provisions of which are so involved as to need analysis and interpretation by international and constitutional lawyers of acknowledged repute and expertise.

On the Greek Cypriot side, efforts were made to give to the public as comprehensible a summary of the Plan as possible. Its provisions, its positive and negative aspects, were examined and interpreted by politicians and persons who had held high office and had participated in previous negotiations for the solution of the Cyprus Problem, and even on the Annan Plan itself, by political parties and their experts, by members of the legal community and others. Democracy was in full swing and apparent for all to see. All the television and radio stations virtually suspended their programmes to host talks, discussions and interviews with exponents of both views, the "yes" and the "no". Let it be said that, except for the Cyprus Broadcasting Station, all the television and radio stations of Cyprus are privately owned. Full coverage of all views was given by the press. In private conversations, there was only one topic.

In 24 days at best (and with no time at all in the case of some provisions) the Greek Cypriots and the Turkish Cypriots were asked to decide on the future of their country, of themselves and the generations to come. The Greek Cypriots felt that the choice was not whether or not to re-unite Cyprus: the solution of the Cyprus Problem and re-unification was their only hope of redressing some at least of the tragic consequences of the Turkish invasion and the losses they had suffered. It was not between living together with their Turkish Cypriot compatriots, which they genuinely wish, and not. They saw the choice as being between opting for a Plan which would produce a Government whose workability and viability they felt were at least dubious, in which human rights were not adequately safeguarded, which disregarded United Nations Resolutions and which gave Turkey such rights as to fetter Cyprus's independence, providing no satisfactory guarantees against a repetition of armed intervention. Above all, hung the fear that the Greek Cypriots ran the risk of losing the only security they had, that of their recognized State, the Republic of Cyprus, and of being reduced to a Community without a State. Two eventualities could lead to such a loss. One was almost immediate: within days after acceptance of the Plan in the Referendum, the Republic of Cyprus would become a "Constituent State" of the Federal Republic, thus losing its status as an independent State, while there was no guarantee that Turkey would finally ratify the Plan. The other eventuality would occur if the Plan were accepted but did not, because of its intricate nature, work in practice, leading to the dissolution of the Federal Republic.

This is not a Daumier-like view of the *Palais de Justice*, but the steps of the Supreme Court of Cyprus with Attorney-General Stella Soulioti, followed by Deputy Attorney-General Loukis Loucaides, after winning a major constitutional case on the Separation of Powers. *L'esprit des Lois* prevails in the Courts of the Republic of Cyprus, which are expert in drawing on many systems of jurisprudence.

The surroundings are not as sophisticated as those in Vienna or Paris, but these coffee drinkers too engage in political analysis all day long.

XVII

Reasons Which Swayed a Large Majority of Greek Cypriot Voters to Reject the Plan

ANALYSIS OF THE reasons for the "No" vote in the Greek Cypriot referendum will continue for a long time to come. What can safely now be written, having regard to what was said in the course of the widespread public participation in media interviews, what was indicated by exit polls[1] and the actual voting in the Government-controlled area, is the truism that some people were affected by practical or personal considerations and others by more ideological approaches. Views were far from monolithic (just as they were not monolithic in the Turkish Cypriot Community) and different persons gave varying degrees of weight to some or all of the considerations set out below. So far as concerns Greek Cypriots who voted "No," their reasoning included the following:[2]

A PLAN IN FOREIGN INTERESTS

They perceived the Annan Plan as a foreign plan, a UN construction imposed upon them, with foreign Powers pressing for adoption of its terms in their own and in their allies' interests and demanding concession after concession by the Greek Cypriot side, many of these being demanded at the last minute at Bürgenstock and thereafter being imposed by the Secretary-General. Annan V radically differed from Annan II and III and from the framework of Security Council Resolutions on Cyprus.

[1] In the Mega TV exit poll questioning those who claimed to have voted "No," 75% of persons questioned referred to "security" as their reason for voting "No"; 7% said they voted in support of the President's position; 5% referred to economic burdens; and 13% stated that they preferred to live separately from Turkish Cypriots.

[2] The reasoning is not given in any order of priority, although the reactions to international and security aspects are mentioned first.

A FOREIGN-IMPOSED PLAN

Greek Cypriots, in talk among themselves, have always commented on the arrogance of foreign Powers and "experts" who come to Cyprus with condescending prescriptions for its ills, an attitude having its roots in the international pressures prior to the 1959 Zurich Agreements and the USA's Acheson Plan of 1964 for partition of the Republic of Cyprus, with double *enosis* (union) in which the larger part would go to Greece and a smaller part to Turkey for a military Base with two Turkish prefectures in the Greek area.[3] Regrettably, as regards the recent negotiations, what was initially perceived as a good-willed UN and mainly American attempt to help Cyprus with its difficulties, was ultimately perceived as arrogant dictation to Cypriots by outsiders. In this respect, Mr Rauf Denktash's blunt objections to the conduct of the Special Adviser and of the EU Enlargement Commissioner struck a chord with many Greek Cypriots. The more foreign diplomats and international public servants exhorted and "warned" them to accept the Plan, the more Greek Cypriots resented the advice they were being given, which many considered to be improper pressures, even indirect threats.[4]

DENIAL OF CYPRUS'S INDEPENDENCE AS A STATE

Greek Cypriots were offended that under the Plan Cyprus would not in reality be a fully independent State, instead being under the scrutiny and tutelage of the Guarantor Powers, two of whom were regarded by many as still being hostile to Greek Cypriots, with, all, at different times, having intervened in Cyprus. The new Treaty on Cyprus and the Protocols to the 1960 Treaties, which were annexed to it, were to continue for an indefinite period of time and the guarantee was extended in scope beyond what had been agreed in 1960, when only the state of affairs established by the listed Basic Articles of the Constitution was guaranteed. Cyprus was in effect to be a protectorate under the Guarantor Powers. These views were held by the Cyprus man in the street—or rather the coffee shop. "Sovereignty" and its meaning have been the subject of constant

[3] Greek Cypriot mistrust in foreign Powers as regards imposing Cyprus solutions first surfaced when the public became aware of NATO pressures (via the USA) on Greece, which then negotiated in late 1958 and early 1959 to produce the Zurich Agreements, followed in turn by the London Agreement. The terms of Cyprus's independence and the unworkable 1960 Constitution were dictated by these Agreements.

[4] There were leaked suggestions that certain foreign States would recognise the "TRNC". Azerbaijan in particular was mentioned, without noting that since 1992 it has entered into agreements with the "TRNC," as also have Tajikistan and Abkhazia, without the sky falling in. Even if some Turkish or Moslem States recognise it, the great majority of States, and all concerned with the maintenance of international law, will not do so. Nor will the USA, despite current policy temptations to do so: it was historically the originator of the doctrine of non-recognition of the fruits of aggression, a fundamental rule of the modern legal order.

public debate in Cyprus since the mid-1950s: outsiders perhaps forget that political thought had its origins in Greece and that ordinary people are attached to and talk in terms of political concepts, particularly "democracy" and "sovereignty" to an extent that would be inconceivable in other societies.[5]

SECURITY RISKS

Greek Cypriots were fearful that the military arrangements for their security were inadequate:

Turkey's claims to a right of unilateral military intervention in Cyprus and the scope of its application

Greek Cypriots were apprehensive about Turkey's asserted right of unilateral intervention, especially military intervention under the Treaty of Guarantee, the possibilities of which were to be more extensive than provided in 1960, because the "security and constitutional order" of the constituent states was now also covered (preamble to Additional Protocol to the Treaty of Guarantee).[6]

Large numbers of Turkish troops to remain in Cyprus after the settlement

Greek Cypriots were anxious that after the settlement large numbers of Turkish troops (6,000) would, subject to their being reduced to 3,000 in January 2011, remain in 6 major military facilities (potential bridgeheads) either until 2018 AD, or until Turkey's entry to the EU, while the Greek Cypriot National Guard (the armed force of the Republic of Cyprus) was to be dissolved. Greek

[5] A week after noting this characteristic, the gardener caring for the writer's garden, a young man displaced from Karavas, a village near Kyrenia and whose brother is a "missing person," while having a coffee break observed that the difficulty in reaching agreement on Cyprus was that politicians when not in office behaved like Alcibiades.

[6] Reassuring a Turkish audience at Bögaziçi University on 17 July 2003 even before Turkey obtained the Bürgenstock concessions, Mr Robert Dann, Mr de Soto's aide, an architect of the Plan, and one of the main drafters of the *Report,* observed:

> This brings me to the second myth about the Annan plan, which is that it destroys Turkey's responsibilities and rights vis-à-vis Cyprus. In fact, the plan preserves and extends Turkey's rights and responsibilities as a guarantor in respect of Cyprus. Under the Treaty of Guarantee which guarantees the territorial integrity, sovereignty, I can't quite remember the phrase, of the Republic of Cyprus—that is what the Treaty of Guarantee currently guarantees—what would happen under the plan is that not only would the same features of the United Cyprus Republic be guaranteed, but so too would the territorial integrity, security and constitutional order of the constituent states. Now I don't know of any international example where there is such an extensive guarantee of a political structure not only . . . [in its] overall structure but also the structure of its constituent states.

"Independence" and "security" were the parts of the phrase which Mr Dann, not unnaturally having regard to his role, had blotted out from his memory.

Cypriots, who would be disarmed, appreciated that Cyprus was only 4 minutes' flying time from Turkey and that Turkish sea-borne troops could land easily, without the resistance they had faced from the National Guard in 1974.

An inadequate UN mandate, designed not for peace-keeping, but for mere monitoring

Greek Cypriots considered that the proposed UN peace-keeping mandate was inadequate to protect them, UNFICYP II (to be designated UNSIMIC) effectively being mainly concerned with confidence-building by way of the Mission's presence. The UN Mission would have only a minor supervisory role, without any responsibility for ensuring removal of excess Turkish troops. This restricted mandate led to Greek Cypriots feeling let down by the UN Secretariat, which had failed to recommend enforcement powers to uphold the settlement, merely recommending the monitoring of compliance with the security provisions, the monitoring of political developments regarding implementation, and the provision of advice and good offices (see Matters to be submitted to the UN Security Council for Decision). It was widely known, having been reported in the press, that the Greek Cypriot side had in the security talks and in requests to members of the Security Council asked that UNSIMIC should have mandatory powers,[7] but that these requests had not been accepted.

Withdrawals of Turkish troops and effecting of territorial transfers dependent on Turkey's benevolence and honour

Greek Cypriots asked themselves "What would happen if Turkey did not proceed with the agreed troop withdrawals?" (They asked the same question as regards the territorial transfers.) For many, the Plan was a paper legal scheme, dependent for its implementation on Turkey's goodwill.

Stationing of a number of Turkish troops in Cyprus in perpetuity

The stationing in perpetuity of Turkish troops in Cyprus, even after Turkey's EU entry or January 2018, was unacceptable, although such numbers were to be

[7] The only mandatory aspect of the proposed UN Resolution to create the peace-keeping force was an arms supply ban. This proposal came from the Greek Cypriot side, which bore in mind long-standing Turkish Cypriot demands for a weapons ban. Accordingly this request was not a concession made to Greek Cypriot views, but the meeting of a responsible request made for the benefit of all Cypriots. This mandatory provision was opposed by Turkey at the Security Council. One voter, who had decided until then to vote "Yes," explained to the writer that this was the last straw in weighing down the scales of her doubts about Turkey's *bona fides* and decisive in her switch to a "No" vote.

reduced at that stage to 650 men (in effect a bridgehead). Opposition to this was not merely based on fear, but on the principle that an independent State should not be subject to the stationing on its territory of foreign troops, especially those of a State which had invaded and occupied its territory.

Through the incessant media debates on security, members of the public became aware that security negotiations in Cyprus in May–June 2002 had not been seriously conducted so as to reach inter-community agreement, and that even the reduced numbers of Turkish and Greek troops specified in Annan III–V had never been agreed.[8] The Greek Cypriot public's overall assessment of the security provisions of the Plan was that, taken together:

(a) the provisions ran counter to the concept of ultimate *demilitarisation of Cyprus*, which had been a fundamental Greek Cypriot demand accepted in the 1979 High Level Agreement, point 7, and which had again been proposed in 1983 by President Kyprianou. Instead, the Plan proposed that Cypriots would be disarmed, while foreign military forces would remain in Cyprus;
(b) Cyprus's independence was being infringed; and
(c) Cyprus remained at Turkey's mercy.

These security factors particularly affected Akel, traditionally "a pro-settlement" party, and led it to oppose approval of Annan V.

Legitimation of the British Sovereign Base Areas in perpetuity

Greek Cypriots objected to the reinforcement of the position of the United Kingdom's Sovereign Base Areas by virtue of reaffirmation of the 1960 Treaties.[9] Many regarded the United Kingdom as having, as outgoing colonial Power, unlawfully insisted on territorial subtractions from Cyprus's sovereignty when Cyprus achieved independence, by withholding these areas as Sovereign Base Areas. A majority of Greek Cypriots in any event resented current uses to which the Bases are being put—especially their use for international military and surveillance purposes in operations in foreign States and with which operations eg Iraq, many Cypriots disapprove. A particular point of friction in recent years has been the creation of large new and upgraded antenna, perceived

[8] It did not come out that an offer by the Greek Cypriot side (which lapsed because the security talks agreement was, as the Secretary-General said, "ephemeral") had been made to allow the original Treaty of Alliance 1960 troop contingents to remain in order to reassure Turkish Cypriots.

[9] The Minister of State, Foreign and Commonwealth Office, Baroness Symons, in HL Deb, WA6, 12 May 2003, declared that the amendment to the Treaty of Guarantee reaffirmed the full pre-existing rights of the three Guarantor Powers. Article III guaranteed the rights to be secured by the Republic to the UK under the Treaty of Establishment, which sets out Cyprus's duty to cooperate with the UK to ensure effective operation of the military bases in the SBAs. The Plan also contained a new Protocol to the Treaty of Establishment (giving some territory to the two constituent states) with the result that this Protocol also reaffirmed the SBAs' existence and rights.

locally as a health hazard, and which forms part of an anti-missle umbrella covering most of the former Soviet Union and the Arab States. Other installations acquire information from satellites covering 70% of the earth's surface, passing this via Cheltenham to the Pentagon, with the UK then being able to "punch above its weight" in intelligence matters and in exchange sharing American information. Most importantly, they considered that the UK, by failing to act to protect Cyprus under the Treaty of Guarantee when Turkey invaded the Republic in 1974, and by failing to take any effective diplomatic action thereafter to reverse the situation, had forfeited her rights by not honouring her reciprocal obligations. It was also noticed that the UK had slipped in Article 9 to the Additional Protocol, so as to stipulate that disputes about its application and interpretation should be settled by consultations only, and should not be referred to any international tribunal or third party for settlement. As things now stand, the Republic of Cyprus can invoke a judicial tribunal under Article 10b of the Treaty of Establishment, or, if this is not feasible, can seize the International Court of Justice with such disputes.

LACK OF ENFORCEMENT PROVISIONS TO ENSURE IMPLEMENTATION OF TURKEY'S PROMISES TO RESTORE TERRITORY AND TO RETURN HOMES OF REFUGEES

Greek Cypriots doubted whether the Plan's benefits for the Greek Cypriot constituent state (by way of transfer of territory to it) and for dispossessed persons (by way of restoration of up to one-third of their individually owned properties or up to one-third of their current value, whichever was the lower, with restitution for companies, other than family companies, being excluded) would in practice be implemented. The Plan contained no enforcement mechanism to ensure that either the territory containing their homes would in fact be transferred to Greek Cypriot administration, or that their homes and other properties, if in the Turkish Cypriot constituent state, would actually be returned. Apart from those Greek Cypriots owning property in the area adjacent to the buffer zone, in the buffer zone itself and in Varosha and Dherynia (where transfer to Greek Cypriot administration was to occur 3 ½ months after the Plan came into force) Greek Cypriot home and property owners feared non-performance, and further feared that this would then be combined with Turkish Cypriot ploys for further negotiations and for further "adjustments" to the Plan's already restrictive provisions. In short, they felt, as President Papadopoulos put it, that honouring the obligations imposed on Turkey by the Plan was merely a matter of her "good will" and they doubted whether this existed, or, if it existed, would continue to exist once the exigencies of agreeing on the Plan and Turkey's desire to look good in EU eyes were no longer present. They believed that, if Turkey did not "get a date" for opening EU membership negotiations, the Cyprus settlement would be brushed aside on some pretext by Turkey, even if it had come into operation.

THE GREAT MAJORITY OF TURKISH SETTLERS COULD REMAIN IN CYPRUS

Greek Cypriots were angered that the great majority of Turkish settlers, whom they regarded as persons coming to conquer and seize their land,[10] should be authorised by the Plan to remain in Cyprus. They also saw Turkish settlers as culturally very different from Turkish Cypriots, changing the character of Cyprus, and turning the northern part in effect into another province of Turkey.[11] Greek Cypriots were particularly concerned that Turkish settlers would not only control the government operating in the Turkish Cypriot constituent state, but would also control Greek Cypriots through the mechanism of the Senate's extensive powers over federal Laws and regulations for the whole of Cyprus. Whereas they had come round to accepting Turkish Cypriots—updating Lord Caradon's epigram—as "Masters in the north and partners in the south," Greek Cypriots would not tolerate this situation when the persons exercising such power were to be settlers brought in by Turkey and kept in Cyprus at Turkey's insistence, with Turkey characterising the settlers as "security" for Turkey. Greek Cypriots found it particularly offensive that Turkish settlers would be permitted to vote in the referendum for "Turkish Cypriots" and that they would, being a majority of that electorate, therefore decide the future of Cyprus. They also feared that, if at any time clashes with settlers were to occur, this would provide Turkey with a pretext for intervention in the Greek Cypriot constituent state.

[10] They were alert to the fact that Turkish Army personnel were, upon demobilisation in Cyprus, granted land like Roman legionnaires.

[11] So too do many Turkish Cypriots. Until Turkish settlers became an electoral majority and taking account of their views became a necessity for politicians who sought election, Turkish Cypriot political opposition to Turkish settlers on this ground was intense. Here is an appropriate place to mention the bravery of many Turkish Cypriots who, while insisting on their politically independent and equal status vis-à-vis Greek Cypriots, have spoken out against Turkish settlement and Turkish Army control and conduct in the "TRNC". They have been persecuted. Dr Ahmet Djavit An successfully took Turkey to the European Court of Human Rights for interferences with his freedom of association. Mr Kutlu Adali, a senior official in the "TRNCs Department for Registration of the Population" and later a mordant satirist in left-wing newspapers, was murdered on 6 July 1996, two days after a widely-publicised article criticising the subjugation of the "TRNC" by Turkey. Proceedings by his widow for Turkey's failure to conduct a prompt, impartial and effective investigation into the circumstances of Mr Adali's murder, an investigation required by Article 2 of the Convention, are pending before the Court. Again, Mr Sener Levent, editor of the former *Avrupa* (Europe), its premises bombed, its ability to publish suppressed and its printing presses seized, but which has been reincarnated as *Afrika*, has been imprisoned, and, together with other critical journalists, has faced court martial proceedings on multiple indictments laid before military courts. Due to Turkey's impending application to begin EU membership negotiations, the military courts in the last week of November 2004 ruled that they did not have jurisdiction. It would be invidious to single out Turkish Cypriot politicians opposed to Turkey's direction of "government" in her subordinate local administration: all have, from time to time, been subjected to threats and to interferences with their civil rights. They have to work in the milieu in which they live, and a condescending pat on the back by a writer associated with Greek Cypriots will do them no good. Nonetheless, without naming them, I salute them all as true heroes.

FURTHER LARGE FLOWS OF TURKISH SETTLERS WHICH WOULD BE WITHOUT EFFECTIVE LIMIT AFTER TURKEY'S EU MEMBERSHIP

In the longer term, Greek Cypriots feared a continuous flow of settlers from Turkey would result from the effect of the Plan's provisions that the TCCS had the right to maintain a ratio of 66.6% of mother-tongue Turkish language-speakers vis-à-vis mother-tongue Greek language speakers, combined with the UCR's virtual inability to stop immigration from Turkey after the latter joined the EU. (This situation was occasioned by the Turko–Greek immigration provisions substituted in Annan V at Bürgenstock—see pp 157–8 above.)

LEGITIMATION OF ETHNIC CLEANSING AND ABSOLUTE DENIAL OF THE RIGHT OF RETURN OF NEARLY HALF THE REFUGEES, PLUS MAJOR IMPEDIMENTS TO RETURN OF THOSE PERMITTED TO GO HOME

Greek Cypriots live in a environment where there is a thirty-year history of demands for "justice" and "restoration of human rights," especially those of displaced persons and dispossessed persons. While Greek Cypriots appreciate—as lay persons often put it—that "a war had been waged against them and they had lost," they were unwilling to endorse what they perceived as being so grossly unjust a settlement, denying many persons the right to reside in their homes, long after these were ultimately returned to their ownership. The Greek Cypriot electorate was well aware that, even in 2023 AD, unless Turkey had earlier joined the EU, Greek Cypriots were permitted only to total 18% of the population of the Turkish Cypriot constituent state, a time 50 years after Turkey's occupation of Cyprus and her expulsion of or denial of the right of return of such persons. The overall effect of the Plan, taking account of both territory to be transferred to Greek Cypriot administration and the return of the permitted number of Greek Cypriot returnees, was that only just over half of the Greek Cypriot refugees (displaced persons) would *in principle* be able to return to their former homes. They resented the fact that in "their own country" many would be unable to live in their own homes, while very few would be permitted to set up new homes in the Turkish Cypriot constituent state. All Greek Cypriots saw this outcome as legitimation of ethnic cleansing of Greek Cypriots from northern Cyprus, while many considered that the Plan's provisions for phased return of a small proportion of displaced persons over very lengthy time periods (in which the great majority of such displaced persons would die, or be too old, or too at risk of illness to return to an inhospitable environment), was a relatively meaningless gesture to principle. Of course, they appreciated that Turkey, in terms of *realpolitik,* had most of the chips, but many Greek Cypriots thought the gestures in the Plan not worth accepting, and preferred to stand on principle. Outsiders anxious to see a settlement have looked impatiently and askance at Greek Cypriot insistence on principles. Indeed, they blame the Greek Cypriot political leadership for, over the years since 1974, not educating public opinion that the situation could not be reversed, except marginally, and for not convincing their people of the need to compromise, as the Secretary-General put it in paragraph 75 of his *Report*.[12] Leaving aside the fact that in a changing world, with changing State interests, acquisition *de facto* of a small piece of territory (occupied Cyprus) may be of less significance to Turkey than her wider interests, there is difficulty in educating the public in the middle of negotiations. Concessions need to be mutual and simultaneous, and not publicly announced before agreement has been negotiated. Internal furore can be counter-productive and needs to be avoided. The writer recollects Mr Rüstem Tatar of the Turkish Cypriot Interlocutor's team in 1982 justifying Turkish Cypriot refusal to talk about territorial adjustments. He explained that farmers in such potential areas had already refused to sow their fields. The only way, he emphasised, was for the two sides to agree an overall settlement and then to announce it, with each side telling its own people to "shut up" and to accept what had been agreed. Democratic processes, it seems, may be inconsistent with successful negotiating tactics. Certainly, it was politically impossible to tell Greek Cypriots that they must forgo many of their rights. More seriously, it would have been a mistake of the greatest magnitude. Principled claims to respect for human rights have been the only weapons the Greek Cypriot side has been able to wield in pursuing a Cyprus settlement over the last 30 years. That success on the ground has not been accompanied by vindication in principle (especially when what has been offered has formed so small a proportion of the claim made) does not indicate that the strategy of insisting on internationally recognised principles and standards is in the long run misguided. Not all will be dead by then; and even those by then deceased would have wished their heirs to return to their ancestral land and to recover their inheritances.

UNFAIRNESS AND INJUSTICE OF THE TAKINGS OF GREEK CYPRIOT PROPERTY AN AFFRONT TO GREEK CYPRIOT SELF-RESPECT

Greek Cypriots also believed that the takings of property and the compensation provisions (which would affect most dispossessed persons and many other ordinary Cypriots, who owned property but were not displaced persons, because they ordinarily resided in the Government-controlled area) were grossly

[12] Mr Pfirter in June 2004, in the Swiss Ministry of Foreign Affairs publication, "Swiss Peace Supporter", put it more strongly: the Greek Cypriot "population had been led to expect a better negotiating position after joining the EC".

unfair.[13] The cliché, "adding insult to injury" expressed their feelings: they were not prepared to forfeit their self-respect so as merely to have returned to them (if indeed it was) a fraction of the property of which they had been deprived of control nearly 30 years ago.[14] These feelings about injustice and self-respect explain why many persons, who stood ultimately to be financially better off (should the Plan be implemented) than in their present condition, voted 'No' in the referendum. There was such a negative vote even in the district of Famagusta, which contains Varosha, and to which Greek Cypriots would, had the Plan been accepted, have been permitted to return within a relatively brief period.[15]

[13] A particular grievance was that, prior to Annan V, Greek Cypriots who were willing to enter into a long-term lease of their property could retain ownership and reclaim the property after 20 years. Many had intended using this provision, which Mr Pfirter had told the Greek Cypriot negotiators at the time of Annan I–III was an important safeguard for Greek Cypriots. It had been envisaged in the 1992 Set of Ideas. Annan IV and V removed this protection and this fact was mentioned in the referendum debates.

Causing even more widespread umbrage were the provisions in the Plan imposing liability on taxpayers of the GCCS to meet claims for loss of use of properties caused by Turkey's invasion. Instead of such responsibility resting on the wrongdoing State, Turkey, the Plan transferred this to Greek Cypriots. In the negotiations on Annan I and II the then negotiating team took the view that the arrangements were probably unlawful in any event and that individuals would be able to challenge them. The manner in which Annan V was "finalised" meant that challenges by individuals would be effectively precluded by characterising the duty of the GCCS to pay in lieu of Turkey as a domestic remedy, to which, with all its concomitant appeals, recourse must first be had by claimants. Greek Cypriots have for the last eight years focused attention and even coffee-shop talk on the *Loizidou* test cases in the European Court of Human Rights (1995–1996), and on compensation for loss of use (1998), which judgments were followed in *Cyprus v Turkey* (1994–2001). Thus the Plan's shifting of responsibility was not seen as mere legal manoeuvring to exculpate Turkey (in itself infuriating to many who had been injured by her conduct) but as a gross injustice, nullifying the effects of many years of proceedings before the European Court of Human Rights. Whereas foreign diplomats in the Council of Europe may comment that Turkey should not be burdened with the large financial claims validated by the *Loizidou* case, it should not be forgotten that invasion and continuing occupation of Cyprus and refusal to return property of dispossessed persons over the last 30 years has been Turkey's own free political choice. Like other aggressors, she is now facing a "reparations" responsibility. If her allies and supporters do not wish Turkey to bear the financial burden alone, they are able themselves to contribute, rather than urging that the Court's judgments be circumvented and that the victims of violations be made to compensate themselves (40% of Greek Cypriots were displaced) with aid from other tax-paying Greek Cypriots. Emotions run high on issues such as these. Perhaps similar emotions in the interests of US corporations and Arab partners have prevented States from abolishing the compensation tribunal still making awards in respect of Iraq's continuing responsibility for compensation payments arising out of the invasion of Kuwait. Why sympathy for Turkey and not for the Iraqi people who ultimately pay?

[14] Greek Cypriots expressed the view that, if this was all they were to get, they could on such terms have settled the problem a couple of years after Turkey's invasion, without vainly striving all those long years for justice from the international community. Indeed, Annan V in its crucial elements and aspects resembles the Turkish Cypriot proposals of 9 January 1977 and 13 April 1978 formulated by Turkey's Foreign Ministry, Mr Denktash and Professor Soysal. When Mr de Soto and Lord Hannay contend that the plan was based on Cypriot DNA or ideas, they should have qualified this by explaining that the plan's roots and major features were based on Turkish ideas of a settlement.

[15] The lowest negative votes were in areas where voters in nearby villages, such as Dherynia and Mammari, immediately overlooked their fields in the buffer zone, which they would have been able to begin reclaiming 3 ½ months after the Agreement came into force. For them the personal attractions of a "Yes" vote must have been enormous.

FEARS ABOUT THE FINANCIAL BURDENS THE SETTLEMENT WOULD IMPOSE ON GREEK CYPRIOTS

Greek Cypriots were anxious that, although much had been done in the period between the New York meetings and the Bürgenstock meetings to meet their financial and economic concerns by at last incorporating properly considered financial arrangements into the Plan, large burdens (falling primarily upon them) would still have to be undertaken by the federal government. Greek Cypriots feared the costs of relocating and rehabilitating Turkish Cypriots, which would only in small part be met by international assistance;[16] they feared the costs of "equalising" the Turkish Cypriot economy with that in the Government-controlled area, with enormous development needs and fiscal redistribution being necessary; they feared the increasing costs of UN Mission operations (two-thirds being payable by the UCR after three years) with its costs being likely to be far greater than current defence spending for a conscript and therefore cheap National Guard; they considered the new UN bureaucracy for reconciliation, foreign judges and other foreign appointees and the Property Board would be expensive;[17] and they feared the massive costs of the preferential loans and mortgage guarantee and subsidy scheme, which they would, as tax-payers, ultimately be called upon to meet under the Plan's property and relocation provisions.[18] In addition to the factors already mentioned, there would be the redistribution of State revenues (the tax-base being 92% Greek Cypriot); the inflation of expenditure on government structures inevitable in a federation; and the costs of additional compensation for loss of use of property during Turkey's occupation, which each constituent state was to meet in relation to its own citizens. At first, many doubted whether these were bearable burdens for the future federation. Even after economic expertise was brought to bear on the Plan, so that the Plan in Annan V

[16] Turkish Cypriot estimates for relocation and rehabilitation cost for Turkish Cypriots were 4 billion US dollars. The European Commission organised a preparatory meeting on 15 April 2004, to discuss international financial assistance, but only 800 million US dollars of undertakings, including already pledged EU, US and UK aid, resulted. The *Report* asserts that a later pledging conference was to have been called.

[17] When outsiders wish to dismiss Cyprus, they comment on her smallness. When it comes to expenditures, they forget Cyprus's size and expect a State whose total population is the same as a mid-sized European town to fund all costs.

[18] The Plan (Annex VII, Attachment 3, Article 1) provided for preferential loans, including mortgage guarantee and mortgage subsidy systems which would be administered by the Property Board. Subject to assistance from donors, the federal government was to pay for and guarantee this scheme. It was also to fund the Property Board (a large institution) for 5 years. Loans were to be on "favourable terms" for all dispossessed owners, current users (persons authorised to use property of dispossessed owners) and owners of significant improvements. Thus approximately 50,000 persons were potential borrowers and criteria for guarantees were to be subsequently fixed by the Board's Mortgage Bureau. Experience with loans and guarantee schemes in Cyprus has previously been unhappy, with considerable burdens falling on the State due to defaults.

was much altered,[19] many Greek Cypriot tax-payers remained worried that they would have to pay a very heavy price for a settlement.[20] Nonetheless, it was apparent from journalists' interviews with voters that financial considerations, although a background worry, were not decisive in affecting voting patterns. It was principle and not materialism which was determinative in the making of choices—and this comment equally applies to those who voted "Yes": they did not do so merely for financial benefits.[21] Whichever way Greek Cypriots voted, their overriding criterion was whether they believed that the outcome would be a better state of affairs for all Cypriots in future. They thought of their children and grandchildren, and not of a piece of agricultural land, a virtually derelict house, or even a house that had been relatively well maintained.[22]

CONCERNS THAT THE COMPLEX GOVERNMENTAL ARRANGEMENTS WERE UNWORKABLE

Greek Cypriots, particularly those with knowledge of what had happened between 1960 and 1963, were concerned that the complex governmental arrangements could not work. The procedures in the 2004 Plan effectively provided for potential blocking of decisions by virtue of requiring positive support (in differing degrees) by representatives of the two States in all decision-making, whether executive, legislative or judicial. Far less complex arrangements under the 1960 Constitution had failed in the early 1960s, a time when antagonisms between the two Communities were at a much lower level.[23] The *Report*,

[19] The earlier suggestions for the Property Board to acquire property not reinstated (only 20% of residences and of the land area in constituent state could be reinstated and 10% in any given municipality) were replaced. Under that scheme the Board would have issued compensation certificates which would be subject to federal guarantee, with billions of CY£s being involved, thus making the federal Government un-creditworthy from its inception.

[20] Obviously when making generalisations about conduct and motives there are some persons whose attitudes fall outside the generalisation.

[21] Among the smears given publicity was the suggestion that Greek Cypriots from Limassol and Paphos, who were benefiting from a boom in the property market, voted against the Plan because they feared the boom would end, with development moving to Varosha and the Turkish Cypriot constituent state.

[22] It is appropriate as regards Greek Cypriot modes of thought to quote what Pericles told the Athenians who were facing the Spartans (*Thucydides* being a text in every grammar school):

> What we should lament is not the loss of houses or of land, but the loss of men's lives. Men come first; the rest is the fruit of their labour. And if I thought I could persuade you to do it, I would urge you to go out and lay waste your property with your own hands and show the Peloponnesians that it is not for the sake of this that you are likely to give in to them (Thucydides, *History of the Peloponnesian War*, Book 1, para 143).

[23] A core element of the Plan from its initial publication on 11 November 2002 (Annan I) had been the requirement of positive support by at least one of the members from each constituent state for the taking of executive decisions and weighted special majorities for passing certain important Laws and regulations, and for ratifying all treaties. This concept had not been welcomed by the Greek Cypriot side, which had urged that it was easier for Turkish Cypriot political figures, who did not

paragraph 85, mentions Greek Cypriots concerns about "risk," but only in the context of a settlement as a whole—not in the crucial context of the executive decision-making arrangements specified in the Plan as finalised.

wish to risk being publicly identified with policies favoured by Greek Cypriot politicians, to be entitled to abstain, and that only in narrowly circumscribed categories of decisions should positive support be required, even this going further than the 1960 Constitution, which did not require specified Community support in executive decision-making. They were, however, prepared to accord executive vetoes as under the 1960 Constitution and delay mechanisms. The Greek Cypriot side emphasised that the support requirement made effective deadlock-resolving machinery essential, but finally acquiesced in a mechanism whereby the Supreme Court could in extreme cases, and exercising appropriate restraint, take an *ad interim* decision until one was taken by the relevant institution of the federal Government. This foolish proposal had been a suggestion from Greece. One of the better features of Cyprus's political life has been the rigid separation of powers and the independence of the judiciary. Apart from a brief period between 1961–1963, when there were personal clashes between each side's member of the Constitutional Court, the judiciary has been unpoliticised. The writer has heard many Greek Cypriot lawyers say they would have been happy to vote for Chief Justice Zekia as President of Cyprus. Until his death, Mr Justice Zekia, a distinguished Turkish Cypriot, remained as Cyprus's member of the European Court of Human Rights.

So far as concerns Laws and treaties, the Greek Cypriot side agreed to weighted voting in a wide sphere, provided that Federal Laws to enable the federation to function *ab initio* (taxes, budget, external affairs, EU, law of the sea etc) were put in place. This is why the 131 Laws and Cooperation Agreements (running to nearly 10,000 pages) and the list of 1,134 treaties and instruments binding the UCR had to be produced.

Although the Greek Cypriot side had submitted proposals on the 1960 model based on two Cypriot Communities, on UN assurances, they accepted an overall package for governmental arrangements in which ethnicity (or Community membership) would not now be an element, with political rights being exercised on a non-ethnic basis, namely internal "component state" (later "constituent state") citizenship. This package was also accepted by Mr Denktash, who had been strongly opposed to any references to Community origins or a Community basis for the Constitution, because he wanted the "TRNC" as a "State" to be the basis.

No Government of Cyprus endorsed any full version of the Plan, such a decision not being necessary before or at Copenhagen (Annan II), or at The Hague (Annan III), although President Clerides had in January 2003 indicated his willingness to sign Annan II as it stood if Mr Denktash and he could not agree on changes. President Papadopoulos in his 28 February 2003 letter undertook not to re-open core elements of the Plan if the other side took the same stance. In fact, the core governmental package was undone at Bürgenstock, when the Secretary-General made changes providing for the federal Senate effectively to be composed of Turkish Cypriots and Greek Cypriots and for voting for the Senate to be on an ethno-linguistic basis, also requiring ethno-linguistic special majorities (two-fifths of sitting senators from each constituent state) for all important federal Laws, the budget, treaty ratification and even for *regulations* on taxation, airspace, continental shelf, contiguous zone and territorial waters (all the latter on Turkish insistence). Some of these changes only became evident after Bürgenstock, two days before the referenda, in a change to the Electoral Law. The *Report*, para 52, partly outlines this major change to the package, stating that it addressed safeguarding of Turkish Cypriots' "political equality". No balancing factor was indicated. In future negotiations, now that the core governmental package has been radically altered, so as permanently to entrench ethnicity and essentially to return to the 1960 Constitution's Community basis for voting and representation, the question of decision-making will require to be re-addressed. Certainly, many Greek Cypriot voters were conscious of decision-making problems facing the UCR if the Plan were to be approved, regarding the Plan as providing for a dysfunctional governmental system, likely to be hampered by continuing deadlocks on political issues, which would not be susceptible of resolution by judicial intervention. (Mr A Lordos in his survey—see n 28 below—found that 32% of Greek Cypriots considered it "essential" that the decision-making machinery be altered.) Many Greek Cypriots believed paralysis (cp the failure to enact tax laws from 1961 onwards) would be the outcome, followed by collapse of the federation. As Ambassador Emiliou, one of the Greek Cypriot team, commented after the referendum:

> The distance between paralysis and dissolution is a very short one (Statement, 25 April 2004).

FEARS OF TURKISH INFORMAL CONTROL AND POLITICAL INTERVENTION LEADING TO COLLAPSE OF THE UCR

Greek Cypriots perceived Turkey not as a friendly neighbour, but as a nearby threat, always ready to intervene in Cyprus's political affairs, possibly even militarily, and using Turkish settlers to dominate the political machinery of the Turkish Cypriot constituent state through informal control exercised by the Turkish Army Commander and the Turkish Ambassador in Nicosia. Had goodwill between all parties been in existence, Greek Cypriots might have considered the gamble of trying out the Plan's complex governmental system to be a risk worth taking, but, in light of their knowledge of Turkey's direction of "TRNC" governmental institutions, many Greek Cypriots found themselves unable to agree with the Secretary-General that replacement governmental institutions could work on "hope" and "vision," especially when there was bitterness by both sides over past history and when they were resentful at what they perceived as being an unjust settlement. Fear, suspicion and a sense of betrayal by the UN Secretariat, seen as acting in conjunction with the USA and the UK, both States considered by many in the Cyprus public to be hostile to Greek Cypriots, confirmed most Greek Cypriots' disbelief about the workability of the Plan and their fears of its dangers. Some even saw the Plan as being aimed at achieving the dissolution of the Republic of Cyprus, particularly those aware of events and policies in the period from early 1964, when the disappearance of an independent State of Cyprus by way of double *enosis* was the aim of the American and British Governments.[24]

SOME SCEPTICISM ABOUT ANY POSSIBILITY OF COOPERATION BETWEEN GREEKS AND TURKS IN CYPRUS

There were some Greek Cypriots, just as there were some Turkish Cypriots, who, over the more than half-century of troubled inter-communal relations, particularly from 1955 to 1976, became entrenched in their belief that the Communities cannot successfully live and work together. There were also others in both Communities, whose ideology was exclusivist, believing in long-outdated concepts such as *enosis* (union of Cyprus with Greece) or *double enosis* and *taksim* (partition of Cyprus between Greece and Turkey). But they were not large in numbers, although some of their number were vociferous,

[24] The American aim persisted until President Carter assumed office early in 1977. The British aim changed once Sir Alec Douglas-Home was displaced by Mr Harold Wilson late in 1964, although some members of the British Foreign Office remained of the view that this was the best outcome for Cyprus. These matters are confirmed by the public records of both Powers, which have been extensively cited in publications by contemporary historians writing in the late 1990s.

boisterous and even aggressive to those who disagreed with them.[25] In all societies there are always some persons with divisive ideologies and strong emotional political reactions, but the whole society must not be stereotyped by these exceptional attitudes. As one member of the Greek Cypriot team, Mr Tselepis, wrote in the Greek Cypriot side's first position paper in New York:

> Greek and Turkish Cypriots can and want to live together.

NO PROVISIONS TO DEAL WITH THE SITUATION IF THE RISKY SETTLEMENT PLAN COLLAPSED AFTER THE REPUBLIC OF CYPRUS HAD BEEN EXTINGUISHED[26]

Greek Cypriot fears about possible unworkability and collapse of the arrangements led them on to questioning, in the event of collapse, "What would happen next?". They did not want to abandon the security they now enjoyed in the Republic of Cyprus by embarking on an experimental "solution". Would there be competition for recognition between two administrations of a collapsed State? They wondered what insurance policy would be available. Whereas it is unfortunate that people look at the possibility of unhappy outcomes (or divorce), it is only human nature to want a degree of reassurance that chaos will not ensue—especially when they have already experienced grave problems, as Cypriots had from 1963 onwards. These fears about potential collapse of the Plan's governmental arrangements and what the future would then be were never addressed by the sides, partly because there were no serious negotiations, but more because discussion of partition and secession were *verboten* topics. The UN certainly did not consider it appropriate, when submitting its forward-looking Plan, to couple this with undertakings as to what would happen in the event of failure once the Plan was in place. This was entirely understandable. Turkey would not have countenanced any insurance policy acceptable to Greek Cypriots, namely, that the Republic of Cyprus would continue as the sole sovereign State of Cyprus.[27] Greek Cypriots would not have accepted that there could be recognition of the fruits of Turkey's aggression in the form of the "Turkish Republic of Northern Cyprus". A just "partition" has not been an

[25] In the Turkish occupied area, there was a considerable amount of violence by Grey Wolves opposed to the Plan. Some aggressive verbal intimidation was alleged to have occurred in the Government-controlled area.

[26] The issue of whether under the Plan the Republic continued under another name as the UCR, or would be extinguished, so that there would have been a State succession, can be argued either way. An Opinion by Professors Crawford and Hafner in late 2002 that there would not be a State succession encouraged Mr Clerides to accept the UN formulation regarding treaties binding the UCR. The Turkish Cypriot and Turkish legal advice obtained was different: there would have been a State succession.

[27] The Greek Cypriot side had, because of its concerns about possible collapse, proposed a "null and void" clause with such explicit effect, but this related only to the coming into force of the Plan.

agenda item, because any form of partition has vociferously and consistently been opposed by Greek Cypriot leaders and the public, who in the great majority believe in a re-united Cyprus,[28] while Turkey has hitherto remained determined to maintain control over the whole Island, which she perceives as essential to her security, quite irrespective of any concerns she may have about the fate of Turkish Cypriots.

DIFFICULT POLITICAL CHOICES FACED BY ALL GREEK CYPRIOTS

Many of the perceptions above set out were shared by those Greek Cypriots who voted "Yes". Obviously, the choices all voters in both Communities had to make were neither simple nor straight-forward in view of Greece's, Turkey's and Cyprus's history over hundreds of years, with attitudes much influenced by events in Cyprus from 1955, a period which had reawakened mutual fears and resentments. Those who were to vote "Yes" made the political judgment that no better Plan would be achievable, and that Annan V would be the only Plan on offer—a viewpoint expressed by the Secretariat, leading Permanent Members of the Security Council and most EU Member States, as well as by conflict resolution experts who had long been associated with the Cyprus problem and realised that Turkey was now apparently willing to return territory which she had previously been unwilling even to discuss. Moreover, the present juncture was exceptional in that Turkey needed, before December 2004, to establish to the satisfaction of the European Commission and Council that she was willing to settle the Cyprus problem[29]. Those who voted "No" made a different political assessment. They believed that the present Plan was too risky an adventure to embark upon and that its implementation could not, even in these unusual

[28] In *Can the Cyprus Problem be solved? Understanding the Greek Cypriot response to the UN Peace Plan for Cyprus. An evidence-based study in cooperation with Cymar Market Research Ltd,* by Alexandros Lordos, October 2004, pp 17–21, the author, on the basis of a survey of 1,000 Greek Cypriots in the first fortnight of September 2004, concluded that there was a gradual shift in Greek Cypriot attitudes among the youth, with a strong tendency towards the acceptance of an agreed partition. Whereas this solution was only favoured by 10% of the 65+ age group, it rose to 15% in the 35–44 age group, then 33% in the 25–34 age group and finally 40% of the 18–24 age group. The younger groups had little familiarity with Turkish Cypriots. Among those who did not want a federation were those who mistrusted Turkish Cypriots. The author concluded that, although a rising number of Greek Cypriots were beginning to favour a Two-State arrangement, this number was far from becoming a majority in the foreseeable future, with 60% among the very young being strongly opposed to such an eventuality.

[29] Diplomats aware of crucial opportunities seized—such as the Austrian State Treaty of 1955—must have seen Turkey's EU needs and change in government in late 2002 as such an opportunity. Hence, perhaps, Lord Hannay's views. Indeed, after the referenda, Mr Talat stated to a radio station:

> If Turkey gets a date from the EU, its negotiating power on the Cyprus problem will weaken because its responsibilities will increase. However, if it does not get a date, things will be very bad, because a Turkey that does not get a date by the EU will not be willing for a solution in Cyprus. . . . The Cyprus problem should be solved while Turkey is heading towards the EU. This is a condition for Turkey's final accession (reported in *Vatan*, 18 August 2004).

circumstance, be guaranteed. They considered that in the course of history Fortune's wheel offers opportunities at many different times—even if long lulls intervene—and that other Powers concerned by the Cyprus situation would not want its continuance once Cyprus had become an EU Member State. Sooner or later, they believed, there would be further moves for resumed negotiations, from which a better Plan could result.[30]

Greek Cypriots believe in principles of justice, and, although willing to reach compromises, would not agree to a settlement which they considered was blatantly unjust, uncertain of application and full of grave risks for the future. Having endured so much from July 1974, once the Plan emerged from the Secretary-General's "finalisation," the majority of Greek Cypriots could not and would not put on rose-tinted spectacles, accept the half-truths misleadingly depicting the likely outcome, or listen to bland UN and third State assurances, unaccompanied by binding promises. Had the Plan provided genuine security and certainty of implementation; if Greek Cypriots' long-term future had not been threatened in an institutional arrangement, where Turkish settlers controlled the north of the Island and would be able to block central decision-making; if Turkey did not direct decisions (as she has done for the last 30 years and manifestly did so in the so-called negotiating process); and if the Plan had been less unjust, giving a hope of authentic reunification, rather than caricaturing and simulating this, the majority of Greek Cypriots would, while maintaining their conceptions of dignity and self-respect, have considered such a Plan as the way forward for future reunification and reconciliation. But Turkey's greedy demands, US and UK pressure to accommodate Turkey, the EU Commission's decision to go along with this, and UN pusillanimity, combined to lose the opportunity in April 2004 of reaching a just and balanced settlement plan.

[30] The Greek Cypriot side has previously experienced negative UN briefings. After the breakdown of talks in New York, when Mr Denktash used as an excuse to walk out of the talks President Kyprianou's speech made in conformity with what Mr Pérez de Cuéllar had said to him about the talks being negotiations, contrary to what he had indicated to Mr Denktash, the Secretariat briefed the international press that President Kyprianou was responsible for collapse of the talks, although the real responsibility was that of Mr de Cuéllar, behaving like a mini-Dr Kissinger. After President Kyprianou in May 1986 rejected Mr de Cuéllar's capitulation on all points to Mr Denktash, the Secretariat and foreign governments unremittingly criticised the Greek Cypriot side, which survived this. New initiatives began 2 years later.

XVIII

Lessons and the Future

LESSONS AS REGARDS ATTITUDES TOWARDS THE UN SECRETARIAT

THE EVENTS OUTLINED in the writer's "report" provide several lessons. First, the UN is a political organisation, with both the Security Council and the Secretariat subject to political pressures from the most powerful members of the Security Council. Thus neither the Council nor the Secretariat (or for that matter the UN itself) must be reified or idealised.

Second, there is danger in a small group of Council Members working too closely with the UN Secretariat on particular international problems and therefore being able to inveigle the Secretariat into pursuing the policy shaped by such Powers' perceived interests, rather than by what international law and justice require.

Third, the Secretariat, pressurised into such conduct and pleasing its masters, will then hesitate to say—as it should explicitly have done, of course assuming this in fact to be the case—that

> This is genuinely the best deal we can get out of Turkey. We cannot extract better terms, since Turkey insists on her positions except to the extent of the concessions she has made. The people of Cyprus must evaluate whether settlement of the dispute in the way suggested accords with their claims and with the requirements of international law.

In the Cyprus case, the Secretariat would not speak in this direct fashion, because it had been tasked by the USA, the UK and certain other Western Powers with clearly absolving Turkey from responsibility for not reaching a settlement in Cyprus and had also been enjoined to leave Turkey with apparently "clean hands" for EU entry negotiations. Moreover, the Secretariat had so identified itself with the task given it by its masters that, when the people of Cyprus exercised their right of self-determination to reject the Secretariat's proposed settlement, the Secretariat reacted sulkily and upbraided Cyprus political representatives who had opposed its scheme.

The whole sad story revealed the Secretariat's unsuitability for achieving fair dispute settlement, and its unwillingness to uphold international law on military occupations. This failure is of consequence not only to Cyprus, but to all small States and peoples who have looked to the UN for protection from aggression and its results. It is regrettable that in future not only will it be said that protection is unlikely to be assured by the Security Council and the General Assembly, which after all only consist of self-interested States, but that it will also be properly said that protection cannot be relied upon from the Secretariat, even in matters within its competence, because the Secretariat consists of persons subject to political influence.

THE FUTURE

The people of Cyprus, Greek and Turkish Cypriot alike, have suffered many disappointments. Yet they have persisted in seeking a Cyprus settlement. They will not now cease because this opportunity—like chances in 1972, 1974, 1977, 1985, 1993 and 1994—was lost.[1] For Greek Cypriots it was a shock to read para 83 of the 28 May 2004 *Report*. Obviously, they appreciated that there would be UN and international disappointment that, after so much Secretariat effort over nearly 4 ½ years, the Secretariat's finalised Plan had been rejected by the Greek Cypriot electorate, and that the writers of the *Report* would consider this "a major set back". What Greek Cypriots found inexplicable—except as an attempt to discredit them—was the statement that

> What was rejected was the solution rather than a mere blueprint,

accompanied by the implication that Greek Cypriots had voted against the reunification of their country. This implication was reinforced by para 85 of the *Report* which raised "even more fundamental questions" about a bi-communal, bi-zonal federal solution, political equality and the sharing of power, and without using the word, accused many Greek Cypriots of hypocrisy in strongly stating their wish to reunite, although in reality seeing little gain and lots of inconvenience and risk in a settlement. President Papadopoulos wrote in response to the assertions about rejecting a solution or a settlement:

> Such a claim is unfounded and insulting. It should not be forgotten that a substantial number of those voting were refugees, 70 per cent of . . . [whom] voted "no", and who for more than thirty years have been deprived of their human rights, particularly their rights to return and to property, due to the presence of 35,000 troops and 119,000 illegally implanted Turkish settlers.
>
> Another fallacious assumption of the Report is that the Greek Cypriots are turning away from a solution based on a bi-zonal, bi-communal federation. I would be very interested to look into any credible evidence, put forth in good will, pointing out even a single reference

[1] It is open to argument whether chances were really lost, although some participants have contended that they were. There is no evidence that Turkey wanted a solution in 1972, 1974, 1977, 1993 and 1994, and there is evidence that had President Kyprianou not given Mr Denktash an opportunity to escape in 1985, he would have effected another Houdini-type act. The writer recollects a luncheon in the early 1990s with the London Ambassador of Turkey and one of his senior colleagues. Having reproached her for speaking at the UN Sub-Commission in Geneva about human rights violations in Turkey (although not voting on these because of her professional involvement in Cyprus) the Ambassador concluded by saying that such speeches harmed Cyprus, about which she obviously cared. She must, he said, understand that the Cyprus problem would only be solved when Turkey acquired EU membership. The writer accepted the Ambassador's invitation upon the UK Foreign Office's suggestion that she should hear Turkey's views. She takes this opportunity, having in this text criticised current Foreign Office attitudes, to record the absolute independence the Foreign Office accorded her between 1988 and 1998 to express human rights views which were not only critical of UK policy in Northern Ireland (to the public displeasure of the relevant Minister) but which were condemnatory of UK Western allies, as well as all the usual suspects whose activities came before the Sub-Commission. Although in consequence the Foreign Office often had to deal with third States' complaints, it twice ensured the writer's re-election. Today that elite and expert institution is being dismantled, with UK foreign policy being determined at 10 Downing Street.

> in our written proposals, submitted in Nicosia and Bürgenstock, which will support this assumption. The same can also be said for our comments submitted orally. Moreover, our firm position taken through all these years of deliberations does not justify in any way the . . . [inferring] of such a claim.
>
> In any event, I take this opportunity to emphatically reiterate, once more, on behalf of the Greek Cypriot side, the commitment of my people, as well as my strong personal one, to the solution of a bi-zonal, bi-communal federation. At the same time, I am compelled to reject the notion that the Plan submitted on 31 March 2004 constitutes the one and only, unique, blueprint of a bi-zonal, bi-communal federation. Does anybody today claim that the previous versions of the Plan, which were similarly presented as unique opportunities for the achievement of a bi-zonal, bi-communal federation, were not so?[2]

Such was the indignation among Greek Cypriots at the Secretary-General's claim that Greek Cypriots had "rejected the solution itself," that Mr de Soto subsequently speciously explained that this was not what was meant. He merely meant that the Plan offered a comprehensive plan for settlement, ready for implementation, rather than being a mere framework or set of principles for future negotiations, which was rejected.[3]

A recent evidence-based survey of Greek Cypriot attitudes has attempted to answer the question:

> What, in the end, do the Greek Cypriots want?

The author, Mr A Lordos, considered that this question could be broken down into 4 further questions, namely:

[2] Letter to the Secretary General, 1 June 2004, pp 2–3. It is astounding that para 83 of the *Report* claimed that the Greek Cypriot electorate had "rejected . . . the reunification of Cyprus, the return of a large swathe of territory, the return of most displaced persons to their homes (including a majority, some 120,000, under Greek Cypriot administration), the withdrawal of all troops not permitted by international treaties, the halting of further Turkish immigration and (if Greek Cypriot figures are accurate) the return to Turkey of a number of 'settlers'."

Benefits of the character listed in para 83 were precisely why the Plan, as it had evolved from Versions I, II and III, was kept as the basis for negotiations. It is why Version V will also be *a basis* for negotiations, although it will certainly require important modifications. However, so major are the modifications that it would be unwise to treat the Plan, which is in its own terms "void" (Annex IX: Coming into Being of the New State of Affairs, Article 1.2) as being a model. Such an approach would result in a process of chipping off protuberances here and there, accompanied by international pressures to accept the cosmeticised result, whereas everything needs consideration and in depth. If Annan V is treated as the focus, its benefits will be deliberately overstated (as they were in the *Report's* para 83) and the same distorted arguments would be pressed upon Greek Cypriots (arguments the UK Foreign Office was at the time of Bürgenstock circulating to the press). These included the assertions which later appeared in paras 83 and 51 of the *Report*. When these asserted benefits of the Plan are raised again—as they will be if Annan V is the model—there will again be deadlock. The great majority of the Greek Cypriot electorate was far from persuaded of the Plan's merits when faced with the choice of approving or rejecting it, and tinkering will not change minds.

[3] Briefing to the Security Council by the Special Adviser on Cyprus, 8 June 2004: www.un.int/cyprus/de Soto 9.6.04 htm. Since the *Report* had been written and vetted for nearly 2 months by mother tongue English-speaking professionals in the Secretariat, this explanation lacks credibility. They meant what they wrote, something made clear from paras 85 and 86 where it was-doubted whether Greek Cypriots wanted a federal solution based on power-sharing and political equality—the solution accepted since February 1977 and more fully spelled out on 12 March 1990 by Security Council Resolution 649(1990). What happened was that the *Report's* writers "went over the top" in their criticism, misjudging readers' reactions, something all writers, including this one, from time to time do, when commenting on matters in which they have been involved.

— Are the Greek Cypriots willing to accept a Federal Solution?
— Have the Greek Cypriots understood the UN Plan?
— What improvements do they wish to have made to the UN Plan?
— Are the Greek Cypriots ready for a Solution Now?

The survey was scientifically conducted and analysed. It was based on a questionnaire, the first focus being attitudes to particular improvements on the Plan. (Most of those improvements reflect reasons set out in Chapter XVI.) The survey was specifically designed to discover which changes would extract a strong "Yes" by Greek Cypriots in a future second referenda. Thus the survey investigated sets of belief about the Annan Plan and associated political issues in specific sub-groups, obtaining information about questioned subjects' ages, places of residence, education, occupation, refugee status, political party affiliation and voting in the 2004 European election. It was then possible to assess particular groups' likely attitudes to future improvements to the Annan Plan. Mr Lordos found that only a minority of Greek Cypriots (about 23%) resisted a Federal Solution, while most Greek Cypriots accepted Federation as a painful compromise, departing from their ideal of a Unitary State. He also found that about 60% of Greek Cypriots (more men, the middle-aged and the well-educated) assessed themselves as having "quite high" or "extremely high" awareness of the Plan. Only 40% of those who claimed to know the Plan extremely well voted "Yes," while 60% voted "No". Thus greater understanding would not have resulted in acceptance, even though the proportion of those who knew the Plan very well and voted "Yes" was higher than among persons not so familiar with it.

Of those who demanded improvements, 14% of Greek Cypriots wanted improvements in respect of Security and Guarantees; a further 21% wanted improvement in resettlement rights of displaced Greek Cypriots, a Federal department to oversee education of Greek Cypriots residing in the TCCS (rather than this being for the TCCS), and a permanent ceiling on the influx of Turkish nationals to Cyprus; a further 16% wanted removal of the derogation imposing permanent limits on the number of Greek Cypriots who could settle in the TCCS, a short period for limitations on property purchase, as well as demanding that the Federal Government have more control in Economic, Financial and Trade affairs. With the 19% already finding the Plan "tolerable" and the 5% who find it "satisfactory", the total who could support it, with all the above changes could be 65% (with a ± 3% error). However, he considered that three demands were so widespread that unless the Plan took these into account, it was doubtful whether it could receive approval. These were: a much earlier withdrawal of Turkish troops (demanded by 75%); more settlers should leave Cyprus (demanded by 75%); and a more equitable division of costs of the Federal state, which on the Plan were to be shouldered as to 90% by Greek Cypriots (demanded by 73%).

Obviously, survey results are considerably influenced by the form of the questions asked, especially, when complex issues are put in the form of one simple question. The results are also affected by the interpretation given to the answers. This perhaps explains the finding on the Plan's philosophy in handling the issue of functionality. The questionnaire asked whether it was "unnecessary, nice to have, or essential" "to remove qualified majorities (that is, votes in favour from both communities) from decision-making in Federal organs". The answers were that 32% found removal essential. Somewhat over that number (say 34%, the precise figure not being discernible from Mr Lordos's figure 4.10) found removal would be "nice to have"; somewhat under 20% found such a change unnecessary; and somewhat over 20% did not know. Mr Lordos concluded from these figures that the Plan's provisions in this respect are "acceptable (or at least not unacceptable) to the majority of Greek Cypriots". This depends on what "nice to have" means. It is certainly not an answer indicating acceptance of the current provisions without any changes being desirable. It should be pointed out that, although Greek Cypriots would approve equality of numbers in the judiciary (thus requiring a favourable vote from at least one judge from each constituent state), and would certainly agree to the need for support from representatives of both constituent states in the equally-composed Senate, there is, in the writer's view, doubt as to what questioned subjects would have replied had there been a specific question as regards the executive along the following lines: "Do you consider that there should be removal of the requirement that government decisions can only be taken if, in addition to approval by a majority of Ministers, at least one Minister from each constituent state has voted for the decision?" It is submitted that Mr Lordos' conclusion as to the acceptability to Greek Cypriots of the Plan's approach to functionality requires reconsideration in the light of more specific questioning in another survey.

Mr Lordos finally concluded that about 70% of Greek Cypriots strongly preferred that a new round of negotiations leading to a comprehensive settlement should begin as soon as possible and that an international initiative on the basis of the Plan would be welcomed. 67.8% of Greek Cypriots coming from all political parties believed negotiations should recommence before the watershed date of 17 December 2004, when a date for Turkey to commence accession negotiations was to be a matter for EU decision. The strong majority felt that if that watershed was missed, many years would pass in which Turkey could stall proceedings, with consolidation of partition. In his Executive Summary Mr Lordos asserted that

> This strong preference for a Solution before Turkey is given the green light from Europe, might well translate into overwhelming public support for a veto against Turkey's commencement of accession negotiations this December, if no steps are taken in the meantime to promote the comprehensive settlement of the Cyprus problem.[4]

WHAT WAS LOST BY REJECTION OF THE DE SOTO "BLUEPRINT"

What, then, has been lost by non-acceptance of the Plan? More settlers will come from Turkey, but, if they come in considerable numbers, this could (and should) be at great political cost to Turkey. In future discussions, the problems consequent upon Turkish settlement in Cyprus need to be properly addressed, reversing the UN's surrender to Turkish pressures on those issues, which went so far as to keep the phrase "Turkish settlers" out of the Plan, instead giving most settlers citizenship

[4] A poll carried out by Cyprus College's research centre found that unless there was progress on the Cyprus issue 62% of Greek Cypriots would support a veto on Turkey's accession to the EU. The figure dropped to 28% if Turkey were to recognise the Republic of Cyprus: *Cyprus Mail*, 25 November 2004.

or permanent residence, and property rights as current users or as improvers of property, and social housing in other cases.

Turkish troops (now in the vicinity of 37,000) will remain. But the number of 6,000, permitted by the Plan, and Turkey's geographical closeness to Cyprus, in any event entailed that in a day or two a number equivalent to the 37,000 troops now present could have been placed on Cyprus. The safeguard against Turkish *military* intervention in Cyprus will, as the Secretary-General in a different context pointed out, be political—Cyprus's EU membership, which she now enjoys, irrespective of the Plan.[5]

Territory will not *now* be re-adjusted, especially Varosha, but that is not a permanent loss. Turkish settlement of Varosha in the interval before further negotiations would be the death-knell to Turkey's EU membership hopes. When Turkey eventually joins the EU, she will be unable to keep the fruits of her aggression, even if that is a decade or more away. Much of Varosha already requires demolition. Most other property there, which has already been standing derelict for 30 years, requires such extensive and expensive restoration that reconstruction is likely in any event to be the best outcome. Thus, at worst, owners will suffer more delay and frustration, but not great material loss—other than hotel owners who will lose revenues which they could have earned due to earlier operation of new hotels.

Although many Greek Cypriots have, as matters now stand, lost the opportunity of relatively quick reinstatement to their Varosha properties and to properties in the buffer zone,[6] others who lost the opportunity of somewhat slower reinstatement (assuming the Plan proceeded through the implementation phases) lost far less than at first sight. This is because of the way the Plan had, at Turkish insistence, been changed in Annan III in regard to processing of land claims. Claimants of land and houses outside the buffer zone and Varosha could not obtain rapid reinstatement, because the Plan provided that returnees' claims, *even in areas to be handed to the GCCS for administration*, were to be dealt with only after the claims of dispossessed Turkish Cypriots living in such areas and also those of current users (who included settlers) had been dealt with. The Plan permitted the taking of up to 3 years for reinstatement decisions, after which there would then have followed the lengthy periods of delay permitted for current users (up to 3 years after a reinstatement order, plus an extended time limit if there was urgent humanitarian need) and provision of alternative accommodation.[7] If the Plan is re-negotiated, as it surely must be, such lengthy delays need to be reduced. Should this be agreed, apart from having been subjected to temporary disappointments, the owners will not have suffered great concrete losses, and land does not go away—unless sold in the interim to developers, who are, by any new Plan, as under the Annan Plan, given protections.[8]

[5] The political safeguards would have been greatly strengthend by a Chapter VII Security Council Resolution, providing for enforcement of the Plan. Potential Turkish intervention would have been so discouraged as not to be an issue in practice. As things stand, Turkey can indirectly use force by transferring tens of thousands of settlers to the Army-occupied area. Would the Security Council act?

[6] The villages of Achna and Petra would have been due for return six months after the agreement came into force.

[7] Annex VII, Att 4, Article 2.4 and Att 3 Articles 1 and 2.

[8] In any new Plan it is essential that exploitation of dispossessed and displaced persons' properties not be countenanced. Those responsible for encouraging this under the Annan Plan should

Perhaps the most significant loss is the delay in the start of cooperation between the two sides in federal governmental institutions and as between the constituent states. To some extent this can be mitigated by informal cooperation, both at the political and at the expert levels. Such cooperation will be encouraged in EU and Council of Europe contexts, while, internally, intercommunal meetings of all kinds are likely to become more frequent. If, despite political opposition from a few quarters, offers of cooperation are made and are not hastily rejected, reciprocal cooperation will develop, making a negotiated settlement more likely. These developments are up to Greek and Turkish Cypriots and to their leaderships, facilitated by the EU and NGOs in seizing all chances for cooperation. If this happens, the lost time for cooperation can in considerable measure be made up. An important aspect is that such cooperation will have been voluntary—not institutionally compelled.

Certain losses to individual Turkish Cypriots are in some respects greater, although not in the property sphere. Relatively few Turkish Cypriots have permanently lost their properties by reason of compulsory acquisition. Upon a settlement most will be able to recover the properties they vacated, or from which they were, over the years between 1964 and 1976, "dispossessed".[9] Current limitations, applied by Law 139 of 1991 in the Government-controlled area of the Republic on claims to re-possession of Turkish Cypriot-owned properties, are subject to legal challenge in the courts of the Republic. Until recently, Turkish Cypriots were discouraged from making such challenges by their political leadership, which favoured a scheme of global exchange of properties between Greek and Turkish Cypriots, whereas return and the reclaiming of properties by Turkish Cypriots would have undermined that scheme. However, the catalytic effect of the negotiations over the last 4 ½ years and the opening of crossings to the Government-controlled area by the Turkish Army, which had earlier restricted Turkish Cypriots' access will make individual Turkish Cypriots more willing to invoke their rights. The Greek Cypriot legal profession has indicated its willingness to act or advise in any such cases. Already one Turkish Cypriot has brought successful proceedings—although an appeal is pending. A few more cases brought by Turkish Cypriots would necessitate overdue amendments in the Law to deal with what is a complex situation of competing rights and needs and which requires regulation balancing these.[10]

compensate developers and their own foreign nationals who rushed to acquire property bargains in Cyprus—if they believe compensation is required for such persons.

[9] Many moved voluntarily, without Greek Cypriot duress. All who moved were subjected to political pressure by the Turkish Cypriot political leadership not to return, despite encouragement to re-occupy their property, including rebuilding offers, by President Makarios' Government. Numerous Secretary-Generals' reports from 1964 onwards explain that the purpose of the Turkish Cypriot political leadership was to show that Greek and Turkish Cypriots could not live together. Return home by Turkish Cypriots, who had moved in the course of intercommunal disturbances, was deterred, even to the extent of imposition of community criminal sanctions on those who cooperated with Greek Cypriots. See *S/5764*, 15 June 1964, para 13; *S/6102*, 12 December 1964, para 32; *S/6228*, 11 March 1965, para 17, and *S/6426*, 10 June 1965, para 106.

[10] The previous Attorney-General, Mr Markides, proposed fresh legislation some 3 years ago but met political reluctance to change the current Law on the basis that the return of Turkish

Turkish Cypriots still have fewer economic opportunities to trade internationally than their Greek Cypriot compatriots. This will not be because of any discriminatory measures, alleged "embargo" or "sanctions" against the subordinate local administration and its population. To the extent that any measures by the Government of Cyprus have in effect denied economic benefits to Turkish Cypriots, this has not been a denial to them *as such*, but because they are in an area occupied by a foreign Power. Moreover, because of the "TRNC's" declaration of independence on 15 November 1983, preferential quota benefits for Turkish Cypriot goods and produce, agreed between the European Community and the Republic of Cyprus to be accorded to produce and goods originating in the Turkish-occupied area by way of a procedure involving marks of origin affixed by the Turkish Cypriot Chamber of Commerce were foregone in search of independence, which it was hoped the international community would ultimately accord. Subsequently, exporters of produce in the Government-controlled area brought proceedings in the United Kingdom, challenging the lawfulness of the import into the Community of plants or plant products which did not comply with the Community's protective measures against the introduction of organisms harmful to plants and plant production and their spread within the Community. This precluded entry into the EU of certain plants and plant products from the occupied area.[11] Denial of economic benefits to them by virtue of their being in an area not under the control of the

Cypriot-owned property would not be paralleled by return of Greek Cypriot-owned property. Such an argument is based on the principle "A wrong for a wrong," and is inconsistent with the observance of human rights, a position which the Greek Cypriot side has always insisted upon. If Greek Cypriot displaced persons require to occupy the properties in question pending a political settlement or their relocation, the Republic must provide Turkish Cypriot owners who return to the Government-controlled area with alternative accommodation or premises, and change the law governing requisition so that it covers the abnormal situation, while ensuring payment of fair rents. If there are problems in raising funds for this purpose, international institutions should be approached to assist with funding or loans.

[11] The litigation concerned imported potatoes and citrus fruit originating in the occupied area. In consequence there were 3 preliminary references to the European Court of Justice: Case C–432/92, *Anastasiou and Others* [1994] ECR I–3087; Case C–219/98 *Anastasiou and Others* [2000] ECR I–5241; and Case C–140/02, *R, ex parte Anastasiou (Pissouri) Ltd and Others v Minister of Agriculture, Fisheries and Food (Interveners, Cypfruvex (UK) Ltd and Another*) Judgment 30 September 2003. The first case resulted in further issues because Turkey sought to circumvent the outcome by arranging for relevant produce originating in Cyprus to be shipped to Turkish ports and kept on board for a day for inspection and certification by Turkish phyto-sanitary inspections, and then transported onwards to the EU. The outcome was that the European Court of Justice held that in general phyto-sanitary certificates could be issued only by competent authorities at the place of origin; that, in those cases where certificates by a non-member State into which the plants or plant-products had temporarily been imported were permissible, conditions had to be met enabling proper checking of the consigned goods; that certain specific requirements for plant health and as to origin of goods could only be satisfied in the place of origin; and that the special requirement that an appropriate origin mark be affixed to plants' packaging as required by Council Directive 77/93/EEC of 21 December 1976 as amended could only be fulfilled in the country of origin of the plants concerned. Only on 15 July 2004 did the House of Lords give a judgment applying the final ruling of the European Court of Justice on the Directive. This required that plants and plant products originating from Cyprus needed to be accompanied by a phyto-sanitary certificate *issued by or under the supervision of the competent authorities of the Republic of Cyprus*. It has taken time for the EU to propose proper phyto-sanitary inspection facilities in Cyprus to deal with produce from the occupied area in order to comply with the EU's own requirements. The Republic has expressed its willingness fully to cooperate in making such arrangements.

VAROSHA (FAMAGUSTA) – STANDING EMPTY FOR MORE THAN 30 YEARS

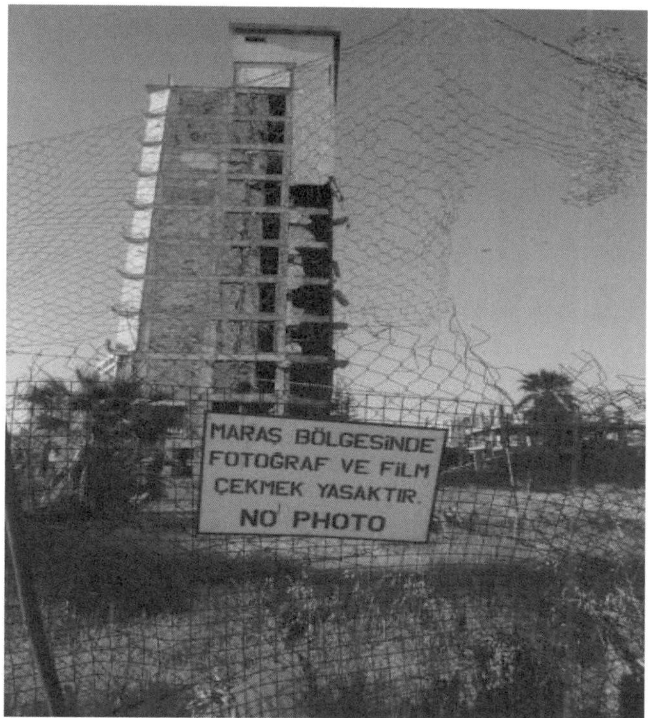

The area is fenced off by the Turkish Army, which controls the area and is regarded as responsible for it by the UN.

Even well-constructed buildings (fled from three decades ago after nearby bombing while the Turkish Army rapidly approached) will need complete renewal. (Photographs taken on 2 May 2003.)

The modern airport at Ercan, internationally unrecognised, awaiting direct flights to bring more tourists, especially Americans, contrary to the rules of the Chicago Convention (photographed on 10 May 2004).

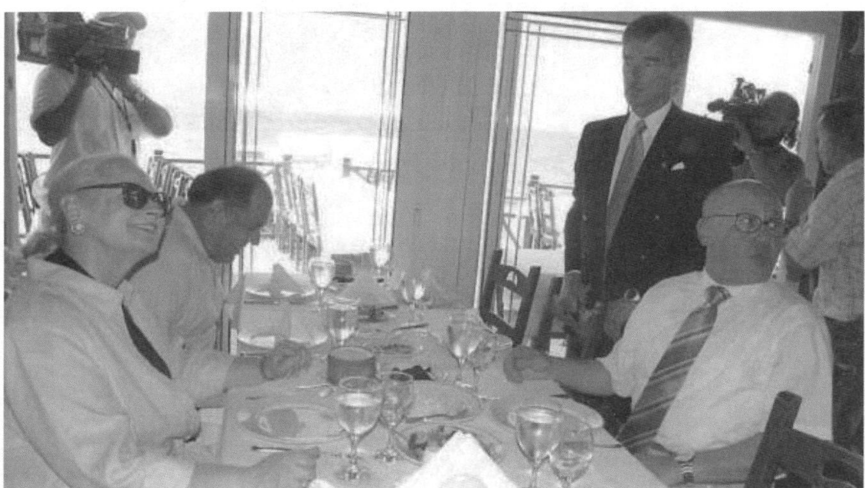

How to win friends and influence people. Foreign dignitaries and all diplomatic missions in Cyprus are well-hosted by the Turkish Cypriot side. Here, Mr Talat is entertaining Laura Kennedy, US Assistant Secretary of State, accompanied by Ambassador Klosson in Kyrenia on 24 July 2004. In late 2004 the US was considering measures to circumvent international restrictions on direct flights to unrecognised airports in Cyprus or how to persuade the Security Council to rescind or amend SC Resolutions 541 (1983) and 550 (1984).

Such entertaining often occurs in property owned by Greek Cypriot refugees who have not been compensated. Those who wish to promote good bi-communal relations and economic development should check the venue before accepting hospitality. There are plenty of other very good restaurants operating on Turkish-Cypriot owned property.

These three gentlemen (Serdar Denktash, Mehmet-Ali Talat and Mustafa Akinci photographed on 18 June 2004) were supposed to form a reconstructed triumvirate after the referenda and the collapse of some settler support for Mr Talat because of his left-wing politics. But Turkey objected to Mr Akinci coming into government (too left and too liberal). So Mr Serdar Denktash and Mr Talat have continued to govern with "elections" being delayed, while "President" Denktash sought to find a "parliamentary" leader commanding a majority. "Parliamentary elections" are due on 20 February 2005. Maybe, after "elections in the TRNC," an administration with a desire for cooperation and real partnership, rather then one seeking *de facto* independence, might come into being.

Turkish Cypriots queuing to get official documents from offices of the Cyprus Government. Soon, additional facilities were laid on for them.

Turkish Cypriots returning from a day's labour on the Government-controlled side. Largely as a result of the opening of the crossings, per capita income in the "TRNC" rose in 2004 from $5,600 p.a. to $7,350 p.a., so that, whereas earlier Turkish Cypriot *per capita* income was about one-third of that of Greek Cypriots, it had by the end of the year risen to about one-half.

The future opens up with a good use for earth moving equipment: demolishing the wall at Ayios Dhometios on 30 April 2003 to make a crossing-point so Greek and Turkish Cypriots can use their cars to visit. More crossing points are in the process of being opened to facilitate travelling workers and trade between the sides.

Republic of Cyprus has, since Cyprus entered the EU, in large part been ended by joint Republic of Cyprus and EU action so far as is compatible with EU Law. Nevertheless, the Turkish Cypriot Community leadership has discouraged[12] and still discourages Turkish Cypriots from availing themselves of facilities which have in the last few months been made accessible to them by the Government of Cyprus.[13] To the extent that Turkish Cypriots do not avail themselves of such facilities provided by the Government of Cyprus, merely grumbling that they have been or will be discriminated against, rather than insisting, by taking legal action, that any discrimination must cease, the economic wounds they suffer will be self-inflicted. It is time that Turkish Cypriots decided to make full use of all facilities provided by the

[12] The "TRNC" hindered use of facilities to such an extent that until 2002 it even sought to criminalise conduct of Turkish Cypriots who obtained Republic of Cyprus passports. As at the time of writing, hampering of commercial relationships and their general discouragement continues.

[13] This process commenced with elaboration on 30 April 2003 of a Set of Measures in the framework of the Republic's Policy vis-à-vis Turkish Cypriots. It was followed by further measures on 26 April 2004 and 16 and 30 July 2004. The package aimed at a wide range of social, economic and educational measures to ensure that Turkish Cypriots had the opportunity to make full use of their rights as Cyprus citizens and to have access to benefits which would arise from Cyprus's EU membership. They followed the 23 April 2003 decision by Turkey's subordinate local administration, which had hitherto prevented Greek Cypriots from crossing to the occupied area and Turkish Cypriots from crossing to the Government-controlled area. These restrictions were imposed by the Turkish Army, which still exercises control and from time to time interferes. The result of the Republic's measures to enable Turkish Cypriots to visit the free areas has been that more than 10,000 Turkish Cypriots arrive every day in the areas under the control of the Republic of Cyprus. This figure represents more than 12% of the population of Turkish Cypriots living in the occupied areas. Those among them who work earn, as at present, an estimated CY £150 million per year. Each day there is a significant number of daily visits of Turkish Cypriots to offices of competent authorities of the Republic, dealing with issues such as birth certificates, identity cards, passports and other administrative matters, where full service is accorded to Turkish Cypriots. Many thousands of Turkish Cypriots have visited the Republic's medical institutions (of whom a large number receive specialised treatment on a regular basis at the Cyprus Oncology Centre and the Cyprus Institute of Neurology and Genetics). Compared to April 2003, the monthly number of Turkish Cypriots treated in these institutions increased by 506%, with Turkish Cypriots visiting medical centers for care and for free drugs currently numbering about 1,350 per month.

Following accession of Cyprus to the EU, the Government, working closely with the European Union, achieved a common understanding as to how products, produced in the occupied areas, could be exported through legal ports and airports of the Republic of Cyprus. (See footnote 11 above.) Measures in essence freed intra-island trade in agricultural and manufactured goods and minerals produced in the occupied area, and made arrangements facilitating their export through legal ports and airports, although some difficulty continues at the date of writing because of EU food and plant safety requirements explained above. There have also been difficulties about transport safety requirements eg testing of trucks and lorries and certificates of drivers' competence. These have taken time to iron out and so do individual public servants' attitudes. Cypriot officials, for many years perhaps overly apprehensive about risks of "recognition," were cautious about any dealings with Turkish Cypriots and such hesitancy will take time to disappear. Greek Cypriot civil servants will be courteously assisting Turkish Cypriots long before British police stop being accused of racist attitudes.

The measures in force have not been properly exploited by Turkish Cypriots, because the subordinate local administration prefers that there be "direct trade" through illegal ports and airports. (In addition, as at the date of writing, import of Greek Cypriot goods flowing to the occupied area, required the consent of the Turkish Army.) Statements by Mr Talat, then "Prime Minister of the TRNC," made in a letter to EU Heads of Government, establish that the non-take up of Government-provided facilities is because intra-Island trade is not desired and he believed that what is required is "direct trade". Readers, in this context of Turkish Cypriots forgoing substantial economic benefits, are advised to look at Secretary-General Ghali's remarks in *S/1994/629*, 30 May 1994, para 54, at n 1, p 83 above.

Republic of Cyprus. By doing so, they will either ensure provision of proper services, or will expose as hollow Government statements that facilities are available to Turkish Cypriots. What they will not secure is "their own" facilities in their own independent state, but, if this is the grievance, it is not one about "isolation," "discrimination," or "disadvantage," but one about a political claim to independence, which even the Annan Plan did not recognise. They need to stop using the propagandistic language of "isolation," even if they have "sold" this to foreign observers; to put aside any hidden agenda of political upgrading; and to cooperate in good faith with their Greek Cypriot partners if "partnership" is what they really desire.[14]

As indicated below, inventive approaches, enabling both sides to "save face," are under consideration. As this process continues, the EU should, but not in dragooning fashion, encourage development of further facilities under its own auspices, subject to this being agreed by the Government of Cyprus. When such arrangements are being evolved, invocation of "principle" that Turkish Cypriot "authorities"[15] must be *formal* equal parties to arrangements will possibly again be a Turkish Cypriot political demand. The converse demand based on "principle" would be insistence by the Government of the Republic on itself formally running the arrangements. There have already been proposals to by-pass the latter principle by accepting that there can be action under EU authority or chairmanship once initial consent has been given in order to ensure that legalities are observed. If, rather than demands for public manifestation of claimed competence, good will is exhibited by both sides, full participation and consent to arrangements could be achieved in practice.

Although the present is technically not a "transitional period" with joint governmental arrangements, as envisaged in the Plan, there are nonetheless similarities, in that the Government of the Republic and Turkey's subordinate local administration are working separately and in parallel. They need not be constrained by formal provisions. They can and should put this time to good use by proving that they wish to and can work together towards a reunified Cyprus.

NEW OPPORTUNITIES FOR COOPERATION IN AN EU CONTEXT

Following the outcome of the referenda, the European Council stated on 26 April 2004:

> The Turkish Cypriot community have expressed their clear desire for a future within the European Union. The Council is determined to put an end to the isolation of the Turkish Cypriot community and to facilitate the reunification of Cyprus by encouraging the economic development of the Turkish Cypriot community. The Council invited the Commission to bring forward comprehensive proposals to this end, with particular emphasis on the economic integration of the island and on improving contact between the two communities and with the EU.

[14] Some persons in the Turkish-occupied area do not want partnership or economic benefits based on business cooperation between the Communities. On 29 November 2004 Polatkan Tourism in occupied Nicosia was bombed. This large tourism company works closely with Greek Cypriot companies in bringing tourists to the occupied area and in sending tourists from the Government-controlled area to Turkey.

[15] These are the subordinate local administration of the Republic of Turkey—as so held in 1996 in *Loizidou* and in 2001 in *Cyprus v Turkey*.

It was announced that the EU would recommend the use of economic assistance in the sum of 259 million Euros, earmarked for the northern part of Cyprus in the event of a settlement, to be given to the Turkish Cypriots, subject to approval in the EU budget. The Republic's Government welcomed this announcement, and indicated that it would facilitate implementation of this and other measures, provided that these were not divisive. By "divisive" they meant that the measures should not result in quasi-permanent separation, à la Taiwan,[16] as an alternative to a settlement pending the day when ultimately—say 15–20 years hence—Turkey joins the EU. On the same day, 26 April, the Government announced further measures to encourage intra-Island trade and to remove any remaining barriers (so far as compatible with EU regulations) to Turkish Cypriot products and agricultural goods coming into the Government-controlled area and being exported thereafter.

The EU attitude of encouraging economic development in the occupied area was, however, taken much further by the Secretary-General's *Report* of 28 May. In para 93 he went "a bridge too far" when he called upon the Security Council to

> give a strong lead to all States to cooperate both bilaterally and in international bodies to eliminate unnecessary restrictions and barriers that have the effect of isolating the Turkish Cypriots and impeding their development, deeming such a move as consistent with Security Council resolution 541 (1983) and 550 (1984).

This call was claimed to have been made in the context of encouraging the Turkish Cypriots and Turkey to remain committed to the goal of re-unification and

> for that purpose and not for the purpose of affording recognition or assisting secession.

A blunt and honest response was given by President Papadopoulos:

> There is no doubt that our common goal for the reunification of Cyprus will be negatively affected for ever by such proposed actions, which undoubtedly will lead to the upgrading of and creeping or overt recognition of this secessionist entity. This would be done in direct violation of Security Council resolutions 541 (1983) and 550 (1984) and the prevalent norms of established international law. The adoption by the Security Council of this particular suggestion will be paradoxical, since it will amount to an incomprehensible negation of its own categorical call to all States *'not to facilitate or in any way assist the aforesaid entity'* [emphasis added].
>
> We strongly believe that the welfare and prosperity of the people of Cyprus lie with the economic integration of the two communities and the unification of the economy of Cyprus, and not with the encouragement of separatist tendencies. In this respect, any moves or initiatives, aiming at first sight . . . [at] the economic development of Turkish Cypriots, but with evidently hidden political extensions, create nothing more than a disincentive for a solution and promote the permanent division of the island.[17]

Nonetheless, the warning that development should not be such as to encourage division was ignored in proposals made by the EU Commission—probably because of

[16] The Taiwan precedent is an unhappy one, arising from civil war, continuing competing aspirations, bitterness and foreign intervention. Intractable situations should not be exacerbated by the international community.

[17] President Papadopoulos offered cooperation with the Turkish Cypriots and assured them that the participation in benefits which they would have enjoyed had EU law applied in the occupied area would not be denied to them.

promises made by President Prodi and the Enlargement Commissioner, Mr Verheugen, to Turkey on 15 January 2004 in exchange for Turkey agreeing to re-open negotiations on Annan III. The result of the Commission's approach of riding rough shod over Cyprus Government views was complex negotiations in Brussels, with the aid package not being finalised until mid-October 2004. At the same time there were negotiations on the possibility of "direct trade" by Turkish Cypriots, which the Commission and some States sought to couple with the aid package. (This coupling was largely abandoned in mid-October.) Trade in goods between the areas not under effective control of the Cyprus Government was governed by a Council Regulation,[18] while, as indicated, the Cyprus Government had made provision for trade between the occupied area and the Government-controlled area. Further measures in most cases require approval by the Government of Cyprus and its willing cooperation in applying them. The difficulties in negotiation arose because some Commission services proposed taking direct EU action to facilitate direct trade between the "TRNC" and the EU and third States. Such action was beyond EU competence, unless effected under the procedure by way of unanimous Council decision prescribed by Protocol No 10 on Cyprus.[19]

The apparent determination of some members of the Commission to take direct action as regards trade was probably based on Turkish objections to Cyprus Government involvement in any arrangements, with this being seen against the background of promises made by President Prodi and other Commissioners early in 2004 that economic benefits would be conferred by the EU on Turkish Cypriots. There was also an attitude of querying whether Greek Cypriot intentions were genuine, accompanied by cynicism about any Greek Cypriot desire to assist or to see Turkish Cypriots assisted, and failure to understand that Greek Cypriots welcomed economic aid to Turkish Cypriots by the international community. They had (and have) no wish that Turkish Cypriots be subjected to any hardships. In contrast, they had and have every motive for encouraging foreign aid and seek to facilitate its occurrence: aid will assist in effecting economic convergence of the northern occupied area with the south, thereby making reunification more financially viable and reducing the transitional periods which will be required in which a weaker Turkish Cypriot economy will require special protective measures against competition by Greek Cypriot businesses and fiscal redistribution from Greek Cypriot taxpayers. Regrettably, a diplomatic game of blame-attribution has been played for the benefit

[18] See Council Regulation (EC) No 866 (2004), known as the "Green Line" Regulation: OLJ 161, 30.4.2004.

[19] OJL236, 23 September 2003. See Legal Opinion, Professor Vaughan Lowe and Professor Derrick Wyatt QC, 19 May 2004; and Professor Wyatt QC, "Export of Goods from the North of Cyprus to Member States and Third Countries—Status of 'Community Goods'," 21 May 2004. This legal position was disputed by the Commission, but the Legal Service of the Council (which has to pass the necessary Regulation) gave an Opinion on 25 August 2004 that such measures could not lawfully be taken except by unanimity under the appropriate provision of Protocol No 10. (See Council of European Union, 11874/04 TUR 361 ESE 10, Opinion of the Legal Service. Subject: Proposal for a Council Regulation on Special Conditions for Trade with those areas of the Republic of Cyprus in which the Government of Cyprus does not exercise effective control—Doc No 11278/04.) In mid-December the legal issues had not been resolved, with some States, notably the UK, and the Commission still urging at COREPER that Article 133 of the EU Treaty permitted the taking of a non-unanimous decision.

of EU Member States by way of Turkish and Turkish Cypriot oral representations, and by way of "non-papers," asserting that the Turkish side had taken unilateral initiatives to build confidence, whereas the Greek Cypriot side had (allegedly) blocked every positive move towards Turkish Cypriots, made proposals to create a smoke-screen of pretending to help and made improper demands on Turkey. Such a blame-game can only cause a deterioration in relations and fail to achieve a positive outcome. Graciousness and generosity have been characteristics long absent in Greco–Turkish Cypriot relationships: it is essential that both sides, despite the effort it will cost them to overcome their mutual resentments and suspicions, begin to put these aside, looking away from past responsibilities for wrongful, dilatory or inadequate responses and action towards the positive future they can share.

In the meantime, a policy of insisting that Turkish Cypriots must be provided with their own autonomous trading facilities and should not be put in a position to have to use facilities of the Republic of Cyprus continues at the date of writing. This policy raises questions as to whether the obtaining of economic benefits is really the objective of Turkish Cypriot political leaders. Ever since 1980, they have rejected confidence-building measures, including in the trading sphere, because, although causing benefits to accrue and "isolation" to end, these would not afford the Turkish Cypriot governmental entity international recognition. The time is overdue for important Turkish Cypriot political figures to cooperate in measures to begin to re-integrate the Turkish Cypriot and Greek Cypriot economies, with participation by Greek Cypriots and the Government of Cyprus. However distasteful this proposition is to Turkish Cypriot political figures, who see the "TRNC" as an independent State, until a new state of affairs is brought into being by agreement of Greek and Turkish Cypriots, the Republic of Cyprus, which has sovereignty over all Cyprus, and within whose domestic jurisdiction all lawful governmental arrangements and dealings with other Governments remain, must consent to arrangements in regional and international economic spheres. It has been regrettable that, encouraged by Turkish objections, the Commission, largely at UK Foreign Office instigation, has since June 2004 suggested that the EU act alone without Cyprus Government consent or participation.[20] Attempts from June to September 2004 by the EU Commission to exclude the Government of the Republic of Cyprus were not only improper, but were also unlawful. They illustrated that the EU's institutions, just like the UN's, are directed by States' "representatives" with particular political interests.[21]

[20] Thus, the Commission, in making proposals for the harmonisation of Laws in the future TCCS and training of its personnel to EU standards, opposed involvement and advisory participation of the Government of Cyprus, which had just completed the same process in respect of the Government-controlled area. The Government's constructive suggestion to confer authority on the EU and merely to take part in an EU, Turkish Cypriot and Greek Cypriot expert committee dealing with these issues was misconstrued and ignored.

[21] As indicated, the main proponent of qualified majority voting (to avoid Cyprus's consent) and the State most opposed to any need for unanimity was the Government of the United Kingdom. It produced arguments by the Foreign Office Legal Department in favour of invoking sections of the Treaties, which, as parts of the *acquis,* were suspended. It is paradoxical that the United Kingdom, which had for so long resisted qualified majority voting as a danger to its interests, was now strenuously arguing in all cases where it wished Cyprus to bend to its will to accommodate Turkish wishes, that, despite the provisions of Protocol No 10, majority voting applied in respect of questions requiring unanimity.

POTENTIAL DEVELOPMENTS

Although Mr Talat, then "Prime Minister of the TRNC," stated that he would take no fresh initiative to settle the Cyprus problem,[22] Prime Minister Erdoğan did not initially adopt the same stance. He hinted that, in exchange for re-opening of Famagusta Port, the fenced area of Varosha should be handed over to the UN.[23] He also declared that, as December 2004 neared, he would have other proposals to make, although these did not eventuate. The European Commission thereafter recommended on 5 October 2004 that accession negotiations be opened with Turkey,[24] with a decision to be taken by the Council on 17 December. Despite highly favourable comments on Turkey's support of the Secretary-General's good offices mission, Cyprus issues remain obstacles in Turkey's accession path. Most Member States preferred these to be decided after opening of negotiations, but the Republic of Cyprus wished to ensure the taking of prompt action—rather than facing a situation in which negotiations on Cyprus could stretch out indefinitely.[25] Following Greek advice, the Cyprus Government pressed for Turkish recognition and normalisation of relations by Turkey with Cyprus. The outcome was that the EU will over time need to examine: recognition by Turkey of the Government of Cyprus; cessation of the Turkish policy of preventing Cyprus-flagged vessels, or vessels sailing directly from legal ports in Cyprus, from calling at Turkish ports; recognition of Cyprus's FIR;[26] cessation of settler flows and attempts at legitimising settlers;[26a] an end to the continuing presence of the Turkish Mainland Army in Cyprus; an end to that Army's continued holding of

[22] *Cyprus Mail*, 9 June 2004.

[23] According to *Kibris*, 19 August 2004, the Turkish Government intended to open Varosha to returning Greek Cypriots and to administer the area itself, but it was unsure whether to proceed in light of how the Turkish generals would react. Since then Mr Talat has sounded more flexible about listening to suggestions for revisions of Annan V, but he was made to backtrack and was silenced by Mr Gül, who, as Foreign Minister of Turkey, in the run-up period to the EU decision on whether to open membership negotiations with Turkey asserted that Turkey's duties finished with finalisation of Annan V: *Hurriyet*, 23 November 2004; *Afrika*, 4 November 2004; and *Zaman*, 2 November 2004.

[24] COM (2004) 656/2, Brussels, 5 October 2004 *O/307/2004*. The Recommendation was backed up by a lengthy Regular Report on Turkey: *SEC(2003) 1201*, Brussels, 29 September 2004.

[25] Without agreement on a timetable before the opening of negotiations on Turkey's accession there could be repetition of the experiences Cyprus has faced at the Committee of Ministers of the Council of Europe—at least two decades of delay.

[26] Flight information region administered by the Republic's air traffic control system.

[26a] If reports in the Turkish press on 9 and 11 December 2004 are accurate, there has been a massive new flow of Turkish immigration to Cyprus, accompanied by measures to "legitimise" unlawful workers' presence. The purpose of this *fait accompli*, in breach of the Fourth Geneva Convention and Article 8.2(b) (viii) of the Statute of Rome, is unclear: it is a use of force because of the scale of organised crossing of Cyprus's northern international border by large numbers of men, who are Turkish Army reservists, and do so under protection of Turkey's Army; it is to keep up population levels if Turkish Cypriots leave to work in EU Member States; it is a deterrent to return of Greek Cypriots; it will ultimately mean no homes are left for returning Greek Cypriot displaced persons; it stacks the cards in Turkey's favour when demands are made of her and she has settler trumps to play; and, most seriously, because of the scale of the demographic change, it means that the electoral balance in any federation will be so gravely upset that there will not be a Cypriot federation, but a *Turko*-Greek Cypriot federation, making two States a prospect of choice for many Greek Cypriots. On 20 December 2004, Mr Erdoğan declared that any new settlement process "will either be for two separate States or a United Cyprus Republic as stated in the Annan Plan": *CNN Turk*, interviewed by MA Birand.

Varosha; an end to continuing violations in the occupied area of property rights of dispossessed Greek Cypriots etc. But the basic issue remained the need to negotiate a settlement of the Cyprus question. In order for this to happen, Turkey needs to be committed to a timetable, followed, in the event of non-compliance, with pre-agreed suspension of EU negotiations.[27] When, on 17 December 2004, the EU Council agreed to open negotiations, a timetable on Cyprus was not set as a benchmark, although it is possible that under any revised Accession Partnership the issue of a timetable may arise. One thing was, nonetheless, made clear on 17 December 2004, when Turkey was invited to open negotiations on 3 October 2005. (This will happen under the Council Presidency of the United Kingdom, presumably with Mr Blair in the chair.) Turkey will have to sign a Protocol adapting the Ankara Agreement (on a Customs Union with the EU) to take account of the EU's enlargement on 1 May 2004 by 10 new Member States of which one is the Republic of Cyprus. Turkey declared at Brussels that the Government:

> confirms that it is ready to sign the Protocol on the adaptation of the Ankara Agreement prior to the actual start of accession negotiations and after reaching agreement on and finalising the adaptations which are necessary in view of the current membership of the European Union.[27a]

When such Protocol is ratified in accordance with Turkey's Constitutional Article 90, the effect will be Turkish recognition that the *State of the Republic of Cyprus* exists.[27b] Turkey will, even if she does not recognise *the Government of the Republic*

[27] In the writer's opinion, suggestions that settlement of the Cyprus problem can be put on the agenda for urgent attention by using the process for opening of Chapters to block such opening unless Cyprus issues are dealt with are misconceived. Such conduct could well be characterised as an abuse of process by fellow Member States. Regrettably, a suggestion emanating from the Council before the Brusels summit that there be a mechanism for putting on the brakes or suspending negotiations was dropped after vehement Turkish objections.

[27a] This Turkish Declaration was the subject of intense negotiations, with the Turkish Government refusing to sign a Protocol before 17 December 2004 as initially decided upon by the Council. Indeed, Turkey threatened to walk out of the talks, because of the wording of Conclusion 19 on the Protocol to the Ankara Agreement. She demanded that there be reference to "*actual* membership of the European Union" so that she could contend that the Republic of Cyprus was only *de facto* a member, but the Council insisted on "current membership". She also wanted adaptation to the Ankara Agreement on the basis of a Cyprus solution. This too was rejected. Turkey was also generally displeased for a combination of other reasons: the demand that she commit herself in writing; the early date for signature of the Protocol; the negotiating framework; the potential restrictions on migration to European States; and the open-endedness of the process. EU States learned much about Turkish negotiating stratagems. Their response was less than favourable. All four Candidate States were individually called in to address the Council and to make Declarations. Bulgaria, Romania and Croatia completed their Declarations and were each applauded by general clapping. When Mr Erdoğan completed his Declaration, there was silence, apart from an attempt twice to clap by one State which then stopped. The explanation for such a reception was provided by a story from the corridors. The Foreign Minister of Luxembourg allegedly observed: "It's about time Turkish politicians realised that we are not carpet traders" (*Cyprus Mail*, 21 December 2004).

[27b] It is paradoxical that Turkey insists that the Treaty of Guarantee remains valid. Under Article II she guarantees the independence, territorial integrity and security of the Republic of Cyprus, yet she simultaneously claims that she does not recognise such State. All this is political theatre for internal and "TRNC" consumption. What is really meant is, first, that Turkey is unwilling to recognise the Government of the Republic of Cyprus, and, second, that she is unwilling to acknowledge the State of the Republic of Cyprus as territorially integral, because this necessarily implies that the "TRNC" is a secessionist entity, operating (at best) a *de facto* Government or a secessionist

of Cyprus, have to honour her obligations under the Protocol to the Republic. She could honour those, treating the Government of Cyprus as a *de facto* Government and dealing with it, although such a policy could not continue indefinitely, because the EU has imposed a requirement of improving good neighbourly relations.[27c] Although the paragraph setting out this requirement had in mind primarily Greece's and Turkey's Aegean disputes, it is worded without restriction, and thus applies equally to the Cyprus dispute, which could, at last, find its way to the International Court of Justice, if not settled by negotiation within a reasonable time-frame or by a possible Advisory Opinion on Turkish settlement in the occupied area.

If Turkey agrees to re-open the Cyprus question, she will have, just as Cyprus has done, to face international pressure—not from the USA and the UK, but from other EU States, who believe that a Cyprus settlement should reflect human rights standards and international law.[28] Turkey will then have to reconsider the Annan Plan and the results of succeeding in her excessive demands to such an extent as to cause Greek Cypriots to reject its final Version V. Mr Erdoğan will at that stage have to take some courageous decisions, because he will face major internal political attack from those satisfied with Turkey's gains in Cyprus and those opposed to Turkey's joining the EU because the procedure is open-ended, without guarantee of membership, and permanent restrictions on Turkish immigration to European States are likely.

Future developments towards a Cyprus settlement depend in the last analysis on the attitude EU States in the Intergovernmental Conference negotiating enlargement show to Turkey's bid and upon Turkey's response.[28a] Turkey may refuse to be put

insurgent regime in part of the Republic. Turkey appears to be seeking to revert to the situation she forced upon her co-Guarantor Powers when they made the Geneva Declaration of 30 July 1974. Upon Turkey's insistence, the three Foreign Ministers then "noted the existence in practice in the Republic of Cyprus of two autonomous administrations," although this was factually incorrect. That Declaration was thereafter relied upon as the basis of Turkish claims for a bi-zonal federal solution. In late 2004, UK and US policy was moving towards accepting that there are two *de facto* administrations or two *de facto* Governments in Cyprus. The USA wished to do this in February and March 1964, but the UK said "wait and see".

[27c] See Presidency Conclusions. Brussels 16/17 December 2004 para 20:

> 20. The European Council, while underlining the need for unequivocal commitment to good neighbourly relations, welcomed the improvement in Turkey's relations with its neighbours and its readiness to continue to work with the concerned Member States towards resolution of outstanding border disputes in conformity with the principle of peaceful settlement of disputes in accordance with the United Nations Charter. In accordance with its previous conclusions, notably those of Helsinki on this matter, the European Council reviewed the situation relating to outstanding disputes and welcomed the exploratory contacts to this end. In this connection it reaffirmed its view that unresolved disputes having repercussions on the accession process, should if necessary be brought to the International Court of Justice for settlement. The European Council will be kept informed of progress achieved which it will review as appropriate.

The Cyprus dispute is, amongst other things, also one about borders which have been violated.

[28] This was shown in COREPER, where several important States have supported Cyprus's contention that the property of dispossessed persons, who had not been compensated for the taking of their property, should not be the subject of aid to facilitate its exploitation. The UK Foreign Office opposed this provision and then tried to water it down, seeking in a series of meetings to remove a provision that would have precluded aid if there was doubt whether the property had been the subject of compensation. It was this opposition which delayed approval of the aid package until mid-October 2004, and even then it was further delayed, because some States, in deference to Turkey's desires, insisted that the package be linked with a package on direct trade.

[28a] There is to be a framework for negotiations. This was set out in para.23 of the Presidency Conclusions as follows:

to terms timeously to agree a Cyprus Settlement: "face," especially in the Middle East, can lead to ill-advised decisions. The current Cyprus *status quo* would then continue until such time that Turkey's circumstances vis-à-vis Europe and her political aspirations combined to change her present position as to the basis on which she was willing to settle the Cyprus problem. It needs adding that there needs to be less glib talk about "the Cyprus problem," which facilitates Powers being dismissive and enables them to avoid the real issue, "the Turkey problem"—a continuation of the Eastern Question.

Meanwhile, the Greek Cypriot side has been looking—and will continue to look—for openings for future negotiations in which the proposed "rights" and powers of Turkey vis-à-vis Cyprus will be revised; in which the security and independence of the people of Cyprus will be better protected, rather than, in the clichéd manner of international bargaining, too little being offered too late;[29] in which arrangements will be made to reverse the flow of Turkish settlers to Cyprus; in which homes and properties will be restored to all dispossessed Cypriots without occasioning suffering to now current occupiers; and in which there will be authentic reunification, with a functioning government, but with mechanisms to ensure that there cannot be

23. The European Council agreed that accession negotiations with individual candidate states will be based on a framework for negotiations. Each framework, which will be established by the Council on a proposal by the Commission, taking account of the experience of the fifth enlargement process and of the evolving acquis, will address the following elements, according to own merits and specific situations and characteristics of each candidate state:

- As in previous negotiations, the substance of the negotiations, which will be conducted in an Intergovernmental Conference with the participation of all Member States on the one hand and the Candidate State concerned on the other, where decisions require unanimity, will be broken down into a number of chapters, each covering a specific policy area. The Council, acting by unanimity on a proposal by the Commission, will lay down benchmarks for the provisional closure and, where appropriate, for the opening of each chapter; depending on the chapter concerned, these benchmarks will refer to legislative alignment and a satisfactory track record of implementation of the acquis as well as obligations deriving from contractual relations with the European Union.
- Long transition periods, derogations, specific arrangements or permanent safeguard clauses, ie clauses which are permanently available as a basis for safeguard measures, may be considered. The Commission will include these, as appropriate, in its proposals for each framework, for areas such as freedom of movement of persons, structural policies or agriculture. Furthermore, the decision-taking process regarding the eventual establishment of freedom of movement of persons should allow for a maximum role of individual Member States. Transitional arrangements or safeguards should be reviewed regarding their impact on competition or the functioning of the internal market. . . .
- The shared objective of the negotiations in accession.

These negotiations are an open-ended process, the outcome of which cannot be guaranteed beforehand. While taking account of all Copenhagen criteria, if the Candidate State is not in a position to assume in full all the obligations of membership it must be ensured that the Candidate State concerned is fully anchored in the European structures through the strongest possible bond.

[29] There were hints between 16 and 20 April 2004 that the Security Council might strengthen the Peace-keeping Mission's mandate. Nothing of this sort occurred, when the Anglo–American draft resolution was discussed by Council members. In June 2004 Mr Pfirter still thought that "with minor additional guarantees" prospects were good for a solution: "Swiss Peace Supporter". By 2 November 2004 Lord Hannay told the UK Parliament's Foreign Affairs Committee that he believed a mandatory Security Council Resolution was necessary: HC 1172–ii. Uncorrected transcript minutes of evidence, Question 44. He was in error in thinking that the Greek Cypriot side wanted a mandatory resolution implementing the Plan to be vetoed. They were opposed to the draft Resolution because it was *not* mandatory except as regards arms suppliers, and because it endorsed the Plan before the referendum, seeking to influence Greek Cypriot voters by virtue of Security Council approval.

suspicions or fears of domination. Here is not the place to go into the many major changes to the Annan Plan which are required to make it acceptable to a majority of Greek Cypriots, while not alienating current Turkish Cypriot supporters of the Plan.[30] In the writer's opinion, the Greek and Turkish Cypriot sides need to cover the general areas under each broad theme set out below. Some commentators assert that only 5 or 7 specific amendments should be selected for trade-offs. At the time of Bürgenstock, the very same diplomats were commenting favourably on Mr Ziyal only asking for 11 Points. However, as indicated earlier, he was in reality asking for well over 20, by elliptically referring to themes or headings. Choosing to kick only 5 or 7 "penalties" shows ignorance as to the many complex and major issues involved, simplistically taking a game strategy or even a standard negotiating model for far less complex situations as the proper way of proceeding. Otherwise, it manifests mere impatience to get things done, or, even worse, bad faith in demanding that Turkey's wishes and interest must prevail whatever the real needs may be. Each broad theme (Security, Property and the Right of Residence, Territory, Fiscal and Economic Matters and Governance) needs to be examined by the two sides. Linking all these themes, except territory,[31] is the Draft Act of Adaptation of the Terms of Accession of the United Cyprus Republic to the European Union. That especially needs reconsideration: Greek Cypriots did not wait 30 years for restoration of their human rights only to see these permanently restricted by the EU in complicity with the UN. Re-evaluation and correction of the extent of EU "accommodation" afforded in Annan V in particular is necessary to ensure that, in accordance with the Seville Conclusions, the "accommodation" is "in line with the principles on which the European Union is founded" and "consistent with the relevant UN Security Council resolutions".[32] Such consideration should take place in re-opened negotiations under UN auspices, and, in the last case, preferably with a different team, neither jaded, dispirited, disappointed, nor, regrettably, mistrusted. Since trade-offs and compromises will certainly occur at that stage, it would be unwise for either side now to declare, except in the most general terms, what it wants: there will be bargaining, and a declaration now by either side of its essential demands would harm that side's prospects in the ensuing negotiations, however reasonable it may appear to third parties to request such statements. Indeed, it is quite wrong that requests of this character are currently being made only to one side so as to establish its *bona fides*. Both sides must be assumed to be *bona fide* and to be the best judges of what they want, without having to prove to officious bystanders that they are making well-advised

[30] A good idea of the broad scope of the amendments Greek Cypriots want can be obtained by looking at Chapters VIII, IX, XIV, XV and XVII, the last briefly setting out the reasons why a majority of Greek Cypriots voted "No". Table F (Appendix 6), showing the Developments in the various Annan Versions is another indicator of what need reconsidering. Appendix 7, An Agenda for Discussion, sets out the issues which both sides need to ponder to accommodate the other's concerns.

[31] That could however be affected by decisions under the themes of Property and the Right of Residence and of Governance and by possible "trade-offs" in relation to topics under such themes.

[32] SC 361 (1974) 30 August 1974 is a Resolution which was mandatory even if there was no explicit reference to Chapter VII of the Charter. It *called* upon *all parties* to ensure the respect of fundamental human rights for every person and urged the parties concerned, who included Turkey, Greece and Cyprus "to permit persons who wish to do so to return to their homes in safety". Resolution 774 (1192) 26 August 1992 noted that both sides had accepted the right of return and the right of property.

proposals. The writer's personal view of what needs to be re-examined in unprejudiced fashion is set out in Appendix 7, An Agenda for Discussion. A necessary preliminary is prior agreement on a procedural framework to avoid another Bürgenstock debacle. Without that, it is better than no negotiations be started.

Inside Europe, Cyprus and all its citizenry, Greek Cypriots and Turkish Cypriots alike, will have greater confidence. Such confidence can only facilitate a reconciliation between all Cypriots, so essential for any new arrangements to be agreed and thereafter actually to work. If European Member States and institutions encourage cooperation rather than attempting coercion,[33] the process of reconciliation will facilitate the opening of serious negotiations.

More generally, it is not mere enunciation of a *mantra* to say that the Greek Cypriot side will continue to rely on the principles embodied in the Charter of the UN, on international law and on resolutions of the Security Council in searching for a freely agreed settlement of the Cyprus problem and for reversal of the effects of Turkey's military intervention in Cyprus.[34] It remains determined to negotiate a settlement with the Turkish Cypriot side, resulting in a mutually acceptable constitutional arrangement which will ensure that the independence and territorial integrity of the Republic are maintained in a reunited Cyprus. Greek Cypriots believe that this will best be achieved within the long-established framework of the Security Council's Resolutions establishing the Secretary-General's mission of good offices (since SCR367 (1975)) and the Security Council's position taken (ever since SCR 649 (1990)) on reunifying the Island by way of a bi-communal, bi-zonal federation in line with the Cypriot parties' 1977 and 1979 High Level Agreements. They are convinced that the recent Plan's departure from the established framework, while paying lip-service to it, was a recipe for the debacle which ensued. The UN stopped building on the progress to agreement between the Cypriot sides which had been achieved by the formulation of Annan I a month before the Copenhagen summit of December 2002—and, despite disagreement with some important details, the Greek Cypriot side, and possibly also Mr Erdoğan's Government, would agree that there had then been progress in laying down the basic structure and procedures to achieve a final settlement. Instead, the UN Secretariat allowed itself to become the engine for moving onto a different track and towards a different destination when the USA and leading EU Member States switched the points, making the objectives of negotiations stabilisation of the newly elected democratic government of Turkey, stabilisation of the uncertain Middle East situation, and bringing Turkey closer to Europe. Thus, what should have been the virtual culmination of nearly 26 years of ongoing, if intermittent, negotiations since February 1977, was, metaphorically, "derailed".

What is needed now is the giving of priority to achieving a Cyprus settlement within the long-established framework of substantive principles, instead of the

[33] The UK has learned in Ireland the lesson that coercion does not produce results. It is strange that policy attitudes have not permeated the walls between departments of state which have to deal with persons who have memories of colonial approaches. Similarly, looking at some EU foreign policy approaches in recent years, Professor Brownlie's comment comes to mind: "They had a term for it in the old days: imperialism. Now it's done collectively."

[34] As indicated earlier, the Council's Resolutions are to some extent loose-textured and open to interpretation, but they set out fundamental criteria. Upholding of principle is not iconolatry.

purported peacemakers giving priority to other extraneous objectives. Reversion to Annan I or II as a basis for negotiations may be the most practical approach. Annan III and V were mere Secretariat impositions, encouraged by major Powers on the Security Council. So far as concerns Annan II, the leader of the Greek Cypriot side, President Papadopoulos has an electoral mandate to negotiate "improvements". He cannot, if due respect is paid to the wishes of his electorate, negotiate *on the basis of Annan V* which was rejected by 65.33% of the Greek Cypriot electorate, or, put differently, by 75.83% of the valid votes Greek Cypriots cast. So far as concerns the Turkish Cypriot side, it is true that 54.05% of the electorate approved Annan V, or, put differently, 64.91% of the valid votes cast approved it. But, as recently as December 2003, the "TRNC elections" had returned representatives in even numbers favouring and opposing Annan III, so that Mr Talat, as leader of the largest party (by a small margin) then had a mandate on that Plan. To argue about precisely which Annan version should be the basis for negotiations would be foolish proceduralism: both sides have mandates to discuss and improve versions earlier than Annan V. The sensible mode of proceeding is thus to make use of all documentation, particularly the large volume of work that has been done on fleshing out details since the Copenhagen summit, when EU Members envisaged that Cyprus would agree on Annan II, subject to further negotiations;[35] and then, using Mr Erdoğan's language to President Bush and the Secretary-General in January 2004 concerning Annan III, to take as "a reference" material from all the Annan Plans, especially documentation produced subsequent to the Copenhagen submit by the UN, and also the 1977 and 1979 High Level Agreements and the 1992 Set of Ideas. Such a procedure would, admittedly, leave major issues open for decision (not *re*-decision, because the relevant provisions were not decided by the parties, but imposed by the Secretariat). But the sides are now fully acquainted with the issues and their overall context, so that each side is today in a position seriously to negotiate, and must do so if it wants a settlement. There should be no more relying on the Secretariat to do what it wants, thereby deterring genuine negotiation by the parties themselves. This is yet another reason why preliminary agreement on a procedural framework is essential.

So far as concerns Greek Cypriots, the ultimate goal to be reached in any negotiations remains unchanged, namely that of seeking a bi-zonal, bi-communal federation, so that all Cypriots may benefit from accession of their country to the EU, looking beyond the past and cooperating on the best of terms in peace and security. It is evident that many Turkish Cypriots also share that ultimate goal. The Secretary-General's 28 May 2004 *Report* should have ended with his paragraph 81. This text now takes the lost opportunity to end with his wise Observation:

> A new fluidity has developed in the interaction of the players. We have witnessed hundreds of Greek Cypriot and Turkish Cypriot public officials working cooperatively together. Political party leaders from the two sides are in regular dialogue. The people themselves are able to meet and visit each other and develop joint efforts across a once-impregnable divide. Greece and Turkey have developed trust and friendship, to the point that a major setback in Cyprus did not cause a major setback in their own relations. These precious achievements must be preserved and built upon. But they are not a substitute for a settlement.

[35] Indeed, even Annan V envisaged that there would be revisions in Laws and Treaties after any settlement.

The real Turkish Cypriot leader, "President Denktash", visited Prime Minister Erdoğan and Foreign Minister Gül in Ankara on 4 December 2004, accompanied by the rest of the triumvirate. "Presidents" and Prime Ministers sit on "thrones"; lesser officers sit on sofas. As "father of the family" and "the landlord" (Mr Erdoğan's description of Mr Denktash at Bürgenstock on 31 March 2004), Mr Denktash was kissed and hugged on arrival and again on departure. He was also about to be embraced by Prime Minister Erdoğan again (centre bottom). Any "Et tu Brute!" syndrome would only appear later.

THOSE WHO WILL BE THE EFFECTIVE DECISION-MAKERS IN THE REPUBLIC OF CYPRUS

President Tassos Papadopoulos with Demetris Christofias, President of the Republic's House of Representatives at the end of the Cyprus talks on 31 March 2004, being given a message by Dann and closely watched by Günter Verheugen. Cyprus is rife with conspiracy theory, with political cynics making the superficial claim that continuance in power is the objective of office holders. In reality, statesmen appreciate that decisions on a settlement will secure their places in history, something which, even on the personal level, will be far more significant than two further years of office holding.

Allegedly, the Greek Cypriot side declined "any direct contact with the Turkish Government" when at Bürgenstock. People who, in the not-too-distant future, will play major roles in settling the Cyprus problem, were earlier seen chatting in Brussels on 20 March 2003. Left, Turkish Foreign Minister, Abdullah Gül, and right, President of the House of Representatives and General Secretary of AKEL, Demetris Christofias.

SOME FOREIGN STATESMEN STILL ACTIVELY CONCERNED WITH CYPRUS

Above: Chairman of the EU Council of Ministers for the first half of 2005, Prime Minister Juncker of Luxembourg, listening to Prime Minister Erdoğan in translation, with Foreign Minister Gül behind.

The statesmen who hold the future of Cyprus in their hands in 2005: UK Prime Minister Tony Blair (likely to chair the EU Council of Ministers when Turkey's accession negotiations open on 3 October 2005) could be telling Chairman of the EU Commission Manuel Barroso, photographed together in Brussels on 17 December 2004, "I'll fix everything when I'm in charge".

Koumparoi getting together behind the scenes in Brussels at the 16–17 December 2004 European Council. What could "my dear Costas" be saying to Tayyip and Abdullah? In all likelihood, he said: "I told the Cypriots not to use their veto on your accession negotiations. And now I hope that you will be taking some courageous decisions about normalisation as soon as you can. You must help me too. We both know that in the EU its 'win-win' all round."

APPENDIX 1

THE FINAL POINTS CONVEYED TO MR DE SOTO BY AMBASSADOR ZIYAL ON 26 MARCH 2004

It has become obvious that the Greek Cypriot side is not prepared to engage in meaningful trade-offs exercise and therefore the changes in the Plan requested by the Turkish side will have to be made by the UN Secretariat Accordingly:

1. The percentage of the Greek Cypriots returning to the North, should be reduced from 21% to 18%. This percentage is the least we can accept.
2. The Turkish Cypriot proposal regarding the property issue (1/3) should be accepted.
3. Bi-Communal/bi-national configurations, such as 24 Turkish Cypriot and 24 Greek Cypriot Senators should be properly reflected in the Plan.
4. The restriction of 5% to be applied to the Turkish citizens to establish residence in Cyprus even after Turkey's accession to the EU should be lifted.
5. Inclusion in the Plan of the understanding of neither side claiming jurisdiction and authority over the other side.
6. The European Union should take proper action for the adoption of the settlement as the primary law of the Union.
7. The individual applications of the Greek Cypriots to the ECHR, including the ones on the loss of use should not be encouraged. Then, the United Cyprus Republic should be the sole responsible addressee for these cases.
8. Our expectations regarding the security and guarantees should be fully met.
9. Preservation of Greek and Turkish military presence on the Island even after of accession of Turkey to the European Union. (The contingents provided by the treaty of Alliance should be maintained.)
10. Measures should be developed for effective preservation of bi-zonality.
11. Turkish Cypriot citizens originating from Anatolia should not be discriminated against within the framework of a comprehensive settlement.

APPENDIX 2

30 March 2004
Initial Reaction and Proposals for Trade-offs of the Greek Cypriot Side
on the United Nations Revised Plan of 29 March 2004

Given the extremely short time provided for comments on the text of this voluminous Plan (including laws, list of treaties etc.) it has not been possible to examine properly the bridging proposals in the Plan and in all these laws and see them in the text of the Plan as a whole. From what has been seen so far, the drift of the bridging proposals is to strengthen "bizonality" in the sense of creating permanent ethnic and legal separatism and effectively bringing the whole of Cyprus under Turkey's shadow and sphere of influence.

The Greek Cypriot side reserves its right to submit further and revised comments.

The points presented below are not in any order of priority.

1. According to the procedure agreed in New York, no signing of any document is envisaged at this stage. In any event, consultations with the Greek Cypriot side were not "close" or intense but sporadic. The Greek Cypriot side reaffirms its commitment to submit the finalized text of the Foundation Agreement to a referendum.
2. Disguised permanent derogations on the rights to property and residence are not acceptable. The Greek Cypriot side demands transitional periods of determinate duration (expiring upon Turkey's accession to the European Union at the latest), including review clauses at regular intervals. A reference to a high percentage of GDP per capita (85%), would amount to a permanent derogation in disguise.
3. The draft *Treaty between Cyprus, Greece, Turkey and the United Kingdom related to the new state of affairs* and its Additional Protocols to the 1960 Treaties should be duly ratified in accordance with constitutional requirements of each party concerned prior to the signing and coming into force of the new state of affairs.

The scope of the Treaty of Guarantee should not be expanded in comparison to the 1960 agreements. It should therefore, be restricted to cover the territorial integrity, security and constitutional order of the UCR and its duration subject to review. It should also be clarified further that the Treaty of Guarantee does not empower unilateral military intervention.

The strength of the Greek and Turkish contingents that shall remain in Cyprus under the Treaty of Alliance shall not exceed 2500 men of all ranks by 29 months after the entry into force of the Foundation Agreement. All Greek and Turkish troops shall be withdrawn from Cyprus no later than 1 June 2015 or prior to that date upon Turkey's accession to the EU.

4. The Greek Cypriot side insists that the territorial transfers must actually occur as scheduled in Annan III and in accordance with the Plan's primary and core bargain.

The administration of the areas subject to territorial readjustment should be delegated to the UN (as per the G/C proposal of 1 March 2004), consecutively, upon completion of each phase. The UN's share in the administration of these areas should be strengthened.

The Co-operation Agreement should ensure effective participation and representation of Cyprus into the EU in accordance with the G/C proposals of 27 February 2004.

6. Every dispossessed owner should be entitled to reinstatement of up to one third of the land area from which they were dispossessed. The additional ceiling included in the revised version of the Annan Plan (one third of the current value) causes unnecessary complications, confuses the issue and will be the source of continuous fiction and should, therefore, be deleted.

The implied financial burden of the Mortgage Guarantee Scheme as well as the preferential loan scheme is likely to be substantial and cannot therefore be undertaken by the Property Board or the Federal Government of the UCR. International assistance and guarantee is therefore absolutely essential to ensure the implementation of these schemes.

International assistance should be administered through the establishment of a special Fund which should be established by the Central Bank and administered by the Federal Government. It should, among others, be directed towards covering the financing of the operations of the Property Board, including the proposed mortgage and preferential loan scheme as well as the relocation and resettlement costs for G/C and T/C.

7. Though the caps on permissible percentages for Greek Cypriot residents in the TCCS envisaged in Annan III were too low and very difficult to accept, the Greek Cypriot side decided not to raise the issue on the understanding that such caps, should at least, remain at the levels provided for in Annan III. Since this core issue is reopened the Greek Cypriot side asks for the caps to be defined at higher percentages than those of Annan III. (The specific percentages can be negotiated). Furthermore, the Greek Cypriot side considers that it is unthinkable to reduce the caps, as the new version of the Plan does, without at least allowing an additional number of persons, equivalent to that of the persons affected by such reduction, to return under Greek Cypriot administration and provision for the right of each Greek Cypriot to establish and own a "secondary" house without acquiring internal citizenship.

Restrictions may not be imposed by a constituent state on establishment of residence by persons not holding its internal constituent state citizenship with a view to protecting its identity so long as two thirds of its Cypriot population speak its official language as its mother tongue, and, in any event, up to 33% of residents who do not speak such official language as mother tongue shall be permitted.

8. Election and representation in the Senate should be on a constituent state basis as envisaged in Annan III.

Election and representation in the Senate on a communal basis (24/24) constitutes a major departure from: (i) the whole structure of the federal legislature as agreed in Geneva in 2000; (ii) the trade-offs done in Annan III as regards exercise of political rights by residents in their constituent states; and (iii) another core bargain of the Plan to the effect that there would be effective participation by both communities, but there was not to be effectively separate decision-making by representatives of the constituent states, who are now, in addition, ethnic in character.

The Greek Cypriot side would be, however, ready to consider this fundamental change to the Plan only in exchange of a substantial increase of the areas and the population returning under Greek Cypriot Administration (Karpas, Kythrea, Saint Barnabas and Salamis).

9. The list of Turkish and Greek nationals who are going to acquire Cypriot citizenship should number no more than 30,000 persons fulfilling the criteria provided for by the plan. In addition, settlers married to T/Cs and their descendants (estimated at 15,000) may become citizens, thus, bringing the total number to up to 45,000. Furthermore, no more than 5% should be entitled to remain through permanent residence. The 5% quota applicable must be calculated on the number of persons who are only citizens of Cyprus and not dual nationals.

Settlers should not be allowed to vote in the separate referenda to approve the settlement.

10. There should be hierarchy between federal and constituent state legal rules with the former prevailing over the latter in case of conflict as well as pre-emption in favour of the federal government in case of overlapping competences.
11. The 5 per cent ceiling concerning the residence rights of Greek and Turkish nationals should be safeguarded permanently as this has been one of the core trade offs agreed by the two sides. If the technique of transitional period followed by the possibility of safeguard measures is adopted, then it should be ensured that the federal government is under the obligation to introduce such safeguard measures upon demand of the interested constituent state.

Thus, a request by a constituent state for the adoption of safeguard measures with regard to residence of Greek and Turkish nationals, in conformity with the *acquis communautaire*, shall be binding and granted by the Presidential Council, unless opposed by a majority of its members comprising, at least, one member from each constituent state.

Similar treatment of Greek and Turkish nationals concerning entry and residency rights and the resulting special treatment of Turkish citizens with regard to entry and residence in Cyprus should not prevent Cyprus from participating fully not only in the Schengen acquis but also in the Schengen area and partaking in any future arrangements that may be agreed among the Member States.

12. Any necessary adaptations to the terms concerning the accession of Cyprus to the EU with regard to the Turkish Cypriot Community can be adequately achieved in accordance with Article 4 of Protocol 10 of the Act of Accession. The draft letter to the President of the Council reopens the highly controversial issue of "primary law" and the issue of re-ratification through national Parliaments of EU Member States which is totally unacceptable.
13. The inclusion of T/C instruments in the list of Annex V is unacceptable, given, *inter alia*, that the aim of most of these instruments was the integration of T/C into Turkey. Acceptance of these instruments will extend Turkey's influence over the whole of Cyprus in an unacceptable manner. A procedure should be devised allowing the finalization of the list of treaties at a later stage through agreement between the parties. Article 48(3) of the UCR Constitution should be deleted on grounds of legal certainty.
14. The role of UNFICYP II and of the Monitoring Committee should be reinforced in accordance with the G/C proposals of 8 March 2004.

UNFICYP II must in great measure be funded by assessed contributions under Article 17(2) of the UN Charter, just like any other similar operation. The UCR will make voluntary contributions feasible by virtue of its available revenue. The GCCS will undertake to make available the funds necessary for the temporary UN administration of the areas whose administration will ultimately be transferred to it.

15. The indirect expansion of constituent state competences in the sphere of foreign affairs (see Cooperation Agreement on External Relations, eg Articles 18, 23, 40 and 42) cannot be accepted.
16. The transitional arrangement proposed concerning the rotation of the President and Vice President for an initial five-year period cannot be accepted.
17. It should be clarified that the function of the Committee on Missing Persons under Article 54 of the draft UCR Constitution should be governed by the relevant case-law of the European Court of Human Rights.
18. Cypriot citizens cannot be denied effective legal protection before European Courts. Moreover, undue interference with judicial process before international jurisdictions is unacceptable (thus, the text of the letters in pages 147 and 156 of the revised Plan cannot be accepted). Responsibility or provision of indemnity on behalf of the UCR in respect of Turkey's liability in respect of present and future case before international jurisdictions is completely unacceptable. The Greek Cypriot side insists on the deletion of the second paragraph of Article 12 of the Main Articles.

APPENDIX 3

Nicosia, 28th February 2003.

His Excellency Mr. Kofi A. Annan,
Secretary-General of the United Nations,

Excellency,

I am writing this letter in order to confirm the main points, which I raised during our meeting yesterday and responding to your suggestion to submit them in writing. I, also, take this opportunity to make some initial comments in respect of your plan relating to the solution of the Cyprus problem, as revised on 26 February, 2003.

A. For the Greek Cypriot side "workability" of the constitutional arrangements of the "United Cyprus Republic" is of paramount importance.

In this respect, the successful outcome of the work of the Technical Committee(s) in respect of Laws, which would be put in effect as from Day 1, will greatly contribute to the "workability" of the whole Federal system.

Notwithstanding the efforts of the Greek Cypriot side, which, as until yesterday, has put on the negotiating table 60 draft laws and will continue forwarding the remaining texts in an accelerated manner during the next days, in the hope that this job will be more or less completed not later than the 12th of March, 2003, the pace of the work of the Committee(s) was not what we expected.[1]

As a result, I feel that the Greek Cypriot aspiration, ***namely that all laws and agreements in respect of all competences, of the Federal organs should be put in place and be in force as from Day 1 will not materialize, not because of its fault, but because of the other side's prevarication.***

Indeed, this is obvious, if one reads the version of your plan dated 26.2.2003 in respect of "FEDERAL LAWS" (ANNEX III), Attachments 1, 5 (see page 68), 9 (see page 72), 10, 11, 12, 13, 15, 16, 18, 19, 20, 22 (part 2, see page 91), 23, 27 and 28.

As a result, the other side has achieved one of the main political purposes of Mr. Denktash, namely that, following a solution, the Country will operate by having the two constituent states working in parallel, exercising many of the functions of the Federal Government, which will be hampered or deadlocked through the non-existence of necessary legislation.

[1] Note 1: In this respect, I would like to remind you of the following: (a) The Greek Cypriot side nominated its representatives in accordance with the timetable agreed at the meeting of New York early last October, 2002 (b) The Greek Cypriot side suggested that the Committee should work in two parallel or more sessions (in sub-committees) mornings and afternoons, but the Turkish Cypriot side insisted that in all meetings Mr. Olgun should be present, and (c) The Turkish Cypriot side has not been so far in a position even to discuss many of the drafts which the Greek Cypriot side forwarded during January, 2003.

Leaving aside the issue whether we agree or not to your undertaking to fill or complete by yourself remaining gaps, I hope that your Excellency will understand my position and accede to my request, namely that you should make clear that the work of the Committee on Laws should be completed by the 25th of March, 2002. Acceding to my request, entails suitable amendments to the notes accompanying the above Attachments. Work should not be left to be completed following a solution.

Finally, I feel that, in the interest of democratic principles, those, who will participate in voting at the referenda, are entitled to know the entire position as at the time when the Referenda will be declared.

B. *The Financial Arrangements and Economic transition.*

(i) The financial arrangements are not based on a proper study in depth. There has been no proper matching of the various Federal Government's fiscal needs so that revenues and expenditure responsibilities balance each other.

(ii) At the last minute, a vague criterion about population benefiting from a loan has been inserted. This has to be applied and there is no indication who will apply it to particular loans. There are enormous servicing requirements and, if these are to be honoured without a default by Cyprus, these issues need determining *on the facts* before revenue is allocated in a rather arbitrary manner to the constituent states.

(iii) The whole tax regime, carefully designed to meet EU needs and to keep international investment and companies in Cyprus, will be endangered and will have to be redesigned. With great difficulty the Greek Cypriots have rebuilt their economy since 1974: now the whole financial structure of the State—and resultant economic prosperity and stability—is cast into doubt.

(iv) Other uncertainties and confusing elements regarding the economy have been introduced. There is to be "economic harmonization". What does this mean? Earlier Greek Cypriot proposals set out specific institutions to make this possible, whereas they are absent in the Plan.

(v) There is a danger that the proposed obligations of the Central Bank to exchange Turkish lira with Cyprus Pounds, if they remain unqualified, may assist money-laundering.

(vi) The suggestion about "book-keeping in Euros" by the Central Bank and its implications needs working out.

(vii) Last but not least: the Plan appears to have accepted the main part of the suggestions by the Turkish side that the responsibility of servicing and paying the public debt should not be loaded onto the shoulders of the United Cyprus Republic. This entirely overlooks the questions of the vast reserves of foreign currency of the Republic of Cyprus (1.6 billion at this time, as at present advised, whilst the Reserves back in 1963 were only 21+ million pounds), which are the result of elaborate efforts of the Greek Cypriot population over the past decades. Therefore, as a result, the reserves can no longer be used for repaying the external debt, whereas, in effect, through the United Cyprus Republic, the Turkish Cypriot constituent state indirectly acquires a share in them, while at the same time, refuses to participate in sharing in a similar fashion in the debt.

C. *Settlers from Turkey*

There remains confusion about this burning political issue.

(i) As regards the number of settlers who will remain in Cyprus, it is now said that 45,000 will remain. But, because of the further provision for Turkish nationals to acquire permanent residence in Cyprus (up to a limit of 10% of the persons enjoying internal citizenship status of the northern constituent state) combined with the right of residents to eventually acquire citizenship, there will be a further large number of Turkish settlers entitled to permanent residence and, eventually, to citizenship.

(ii) There is also confusion surrounding future immigration from Turkey. A figure of 5% of the number of persons hailing from the northern constituent state is a suggested future limit. But this will be a repeated phenomenon. Each time the 5% will be calculated on the total number of persons hailing from that constituent state at that time and not only on the number of citizenships newly acquired by reason of the application of the 10% rule.

The Greek Cypriot suggestion is that the 5% should not be calculated on the total number of those hailing from the particular constituent state, but only on those who acquire citizenship after having taken advantage of the 10% or, as the case may be, of the 5% rule.

(iii) It is to be noted also that under "European Aspects" there is a provision causing further confusion: "equal entry and residency rights" for Turkish and Greek nationals. This tends to contradict the 5% rule.

(iv) There is a total absence of provisions relating to departure from Cyprus of those who have to leave Cyprus.

(v) We cannot agree with the figure of 45,000. During our preliminary discussion after Mr De Soto's letter dated 23.2.2003, we indicated that we can accept a figure of 25,000. However, in the interests of further negotiations in good faith, I inform you that the Greek Cypriot side can accept 30,000.

D. Having exchanged views with persons familiar with Schengen, the Greek Cypriot side finds it impossible to understand how the "equal entry and residency rights as Greek nationals" of Turkish nationals can be, as far as implementation is concerned, reconciled with the "Schengen Acquis". We think that the task for the negotiators is a very very difficult one. There is uncertainty as to what will happen, if it is proved to be impossible. Then, which set of rules will prevail, those of the Plan or those of the Schengen? The danger that Cyprus may be excluded from the Schengen is there. But to us such a possibility is not acceptable.

E. Karpas should be under Greek Cypriot administration. The only reason, why the other side did not accept that, is psychological. However, this is not a valid reason. The balance of the Plan has been substantially altered by reason of excluding Karpas from the Greek Cypriot constituent state. The result as concerns administration of the coast-line of Cyprus is unacceptable.

In any event, judging the Plan as it is, there is confusion and uncertainty as to the method of governance and the social, economic and cultural rights of the Greek Cypriots, who will be living in the Karpas. The Vienna III arrangements have never been honoured and, unless there are proper and clear constitutional arrangements, which for the time being are not spelled out in the Plan, the uncertainty will undermine the quality of life and the effectiveness of the rights of residence and property of the Greek Cypriots living or entitled to establish themselves in the Karpas villages referred to in the Plan.

F. There is a confused and uncertain scheme for property bonds. It is not at all certain that the scheme is viable. Few land-owners would want to exchange their property rights for dubious paper. The compensation scheme needs to be *massively* funded, externally, if it is to have any chance of success. There is no certainty about international contributions. The precedent concerning Zimbabwe is an unhappy one.

G. The issue of administration of the areas which are now in the Buffer Zone or north of it and which will come within the area of the Greek Cypriot constituent state is of paramount importance.

Our position is that the solution of the thorny problems that will emerge (such as, re-location of persons now living in this area, departure of settlers, delivery of vacant possession of properties, necessary preparatory steps so that people entitled to return to their properties will, in fact, find it possible to return as soon as the relevant transitional period expires etc) makes it imperative that the aforesaid area should immediately be handed over to the Greek Cypriot side, which, however, will delegate its administration during the various phases of the transitional period to the U.N. (and/or any other international NGO as to be agreed). If a precedent is needed for this suggestion, we refer you to Resolutions 550 and 789 of the SC in respect of "Varosha".

H. The new provisions in Article 6 of Attachment 3 (Constitutional Law on Internal Constituent State Citizenship Status and Constituent State Residency Rights) have substantially reduced the percentage of persons hailing from one Constituent State to establish residence in the other Constituent State, whilst at the same time the period of the initial moratorium as well as the periods of the relevant phases have been substantially extended. The only compensation for that is the lifting of all limitations, if and when Turkey joins European Union. This is entirely unsatisfactory because no one can predict the time when or even whether Turkey will join the European Union or not.

I. The proposed mandate of the "United Nations peacekeeping operation in Cyprus", namely "to monitor and verify compliance", "use its best efforts", "supervise activities "is not at all satisfactory.

In any event, the proposed text is far shorter than the text that was on the negotiating table, when, by reason of a retraction by Mr Denktash of what he had accepted earlier on, the negotiations did not continue, with the result that the whole chapter (as indeed all others) was never finalized between the Parties.

J. The creation of the First Instance Federal Court is necessary for the efficiency of the administration of Justice. There is still time to include its creation in the Plan. The Supreme Court should not be overburdened. The operation of a First Instance Court is especially necessary for the effective protection of Human Rights.

K. The provisions that the right of residence and the right of property will cease to be affected by any restrictions, as well as the provision that the military contingents under the Treaty of Alliance will leave Cyprus, if and when Turkey joins the EU (which is an uncertain future event) should be strengthened by a provision that the restrictions should be lifted and the contingents should depart "upon expiration of X number of years or upon Turkey joining the EU, whichever is the earlier". We suggest that "X number of years" should be fixed at 15.

L. Unfortunately, it appears that the provision of Article 1.5 at page 2 of your plan as revised on the 10th December 2002, has been omitted. We did not have any fore-warning about that. I sincerely hope that this is due to inadvertence. It is absolutely necessary that the provision should re-appear in the proper place.

M. Footnote 5 of page 15 (Article 12 of the Foundation Agreement) is substantially different from the corresponding Footnote 9 of page 15 (Article 12 of the Foundation Agreement) of your Plan as Revised on 10 December 2002. The new Footnote undermines the positions adopted by International Courts. I hope that the old Footnote will re-appear in substitution of the new, which to our side is not acceptable.

N. The omission to refer to Protocol No.1 of the European Convention of Human Rights, in respect of which we did not have any forewarning, is utterly unacceptable. The omission is, also, contrary to the positions adopted in your Plan as far as International Treaties are concerned. Protocol No.1 was ratified by Cyprus in 1962. Equally objectionable, is the omission of Protocols 12 and 13 of the same Treaty.

O. The Greek Cypriot side does not share the view that the Plan is ripe to be submitted to Referenda, prior to the Commitment by Greece and Turkey that they accept them (eg the proposed arrangement in respect of the Treaty of Alliance); otherwise, the voters are called upon to decide on a plan, which, perhaps, following the referenda, but prior to the finalisation of the settlement, may still be subject to amendments by reason of an accord between Greece and Turkey.

P. The Greek Cypriot side strongly object to the amendment effected by the plan of the 26.2.2003 of the part of plan of the 10.12.2002 relating to the Bilateral Instruments with Greece or Turkey. These instruments should be examined one by one as per your original suggestion for the purpose of agreeing a list, specifying those, which will be included in the list as binding on Cyprus.

Q. Finally, the Greek Cypriot side fully reserves its positions on all matters of substance as the same were expressed in writing at any time following the submission of your plan on the 11.11.2003. I, also, reserve my position to forward further observations, when I complete the study of your plan as revised on 26 February 2003.

Please accept, Your Excellency, the assurances of my Highest Consideration.

Tassos Papadopoulos,
President Elect of the Republic of Cyprus.

APPENDIX 4

Table E Villages predominantly occupied by Turkish settlers in 1994 (over 80%) and the referendum result in 2004

Source: Figures prepared by the Diplomatic Office of the President on the basis of the 1996 "TRNC" census and the 2004 referenda.

Key: * To be transferred to GCCS
▲ Karpas village with return of Greek Cypriots
■ Majority in favour of Plan.

VILLAGE		VOTERS	VOTED	YES	%	NO	%	TURKISH CYPRIOTS (1996)	%	TURKISH SETTLERS (1996)	%	DISTRICT/ AREA
Acheritou	*	598	513	146	28.5	360	70.2	106	12.3	758	87.7	Famagusta District
Gaidouras	*	350	303	120	39.6	181	59.7	70	13.8	438	86.2	"
Tripimeni	■	119	95	74	77.9	19	20.0	6	3.0	197	97.0	"
Marathovounos		340	303	105	34.6	193	63.7	47	8.9	480	91.1	"
Ay. Nikolaos		48	47	21	44.7	25	53.2	1	1.0	99	99.0	"
Prastio	*	717	638	200	31.3	430	67.4	106	9.9	965	90.1	"
Mosoulida		81	74	26	35.1	47	63.5	5	4.3	110	95.7	"
Kalograia		263	216	55	25.5	161	74.5	8	2.2	352	97.8	Kyrenia District
Panagra	■	76	56	43	78.0	11	19.6	13	10.8	107	89.2	"
Koutsoventis	■	13	12	11	91.7	1	8.3	1	5.0	19	95.0	"
Fptericha	■	37	34	19	55.9	15	44.1	6	11.1	48	88.9	"
Livera	■	96	83	43	51.8	38	45.8	7	4.2	158	95.8	"(Kormakiti)
Orga		109	106	45	42.4	57	53.8	7	4.2	161	95.8	" (Kormakiti)

Table E Villages predominantly occupied by Turkish settlers in 1994 (over 80%) and the referendum result in 2004

VILLAGE		VOTERS	VOTED	YES	%	NO	%	TURKISH CYPRIOTS (1996)	%	TURKISH SETTLERS (1996)	%	DISTRICT / AREA
Avlona	* ■	246	220	136	61.8	82	37.3	22	5.4	382	94.6	Morphou District
Melanarga	▲	52	47	12	25.5	35	74.5	3	3.7	78	96.3	Trikomo District
Ardhana		265	230	65	28.3	157	68.3	67	15.6	363	84.4	"
Ay. Georgios												
Trikomo	■	281	245	155	63.3	85	34.7	60	13.3	390	86.7	"
Vokolida		213	184	57	31.0	123	66.8	37	10.9	303	89.1	"
Vathilakas	■	385	296	173	58.5	122	41.2	69	11.2	545	88.8	"
Kilaminos		43	39	17	43.6	21	53.8	10	15.1	56	84.9	"
Vasili	▲	337	258	188	72.9	64	24.8	47	8.1	534	91.9	"
Dhavlos		279	234	107	45.7	120	51.3	8	1.8	440	98.2	"
Flamoudi	■	127	110	63	57.3	47	42.7	1	0.5	205	99.5	"
Ayia Triada	▲■	331	256	65	25.4	186	72.6	12	2.3	498	97.7	"
Yerani		97	81	17	21.0	62	76.5	7	4.7	141	95.3	"
Patriki		201	154	89	57.8	63	40.9	36	11.2	284	88.8	"
Ayios Ilias		232	197	93	47.2	101	51.3	20	7.9	234	92.1	Trikomo District
Leonarisso	▲■	497	395	205	51.9	180	45.6	147	18.7	638	81.3	" (Karpas)
Rizokarpaso	▲	1082	830	351	42.3	454	54.7	113	6.4	1645	93.6	" (Karpas)
Tavros	■	196	171	114	66.7	57	33.3	35	11.0	283	89.0	

APPENDIX 5

Cyprus Map with current cease-fire lines and UK Sovereign Base Area boundaries, compiled by Andreas Hadjiraftis, 8 March 2005.

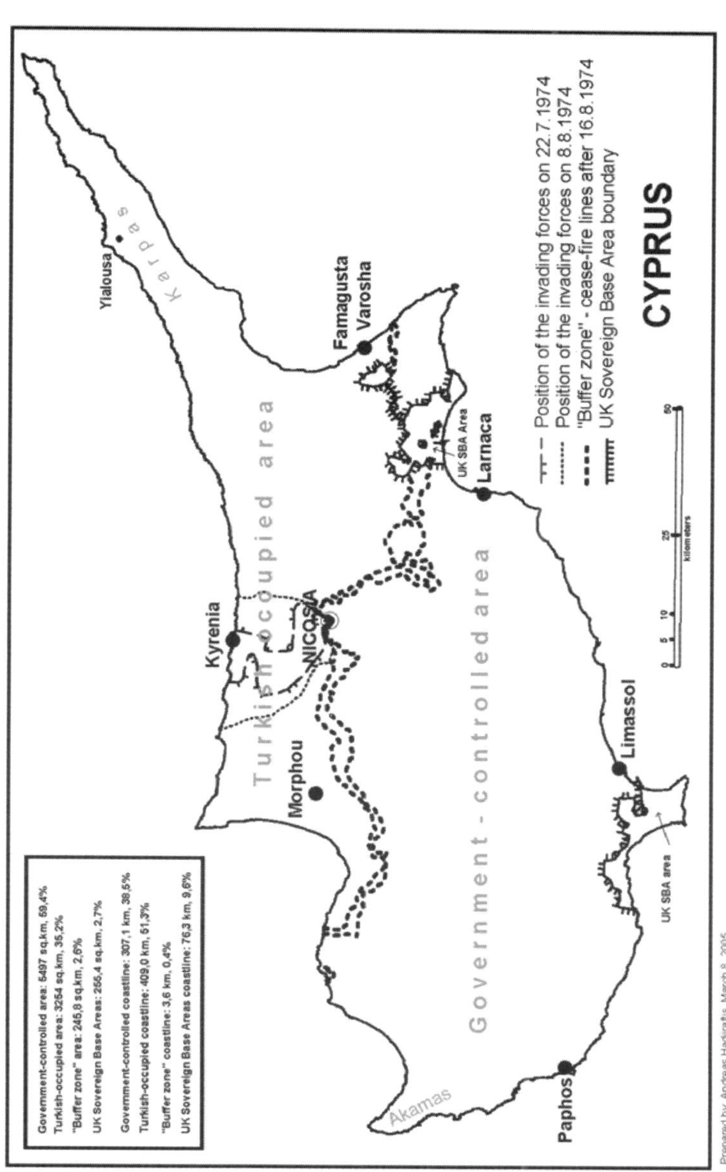

APPENDIX 6

TABLE F

DEVELOPMENTS FROM ANNAN I THROUGH ANNAN II, III AND V, ACCOMPANIED BY UN ASSURANCES THAT THE OVERALL BALANCE OF THE PLAN WAS BEING PRESERVED

NOTES:

1. Only significant changes are noted; minor "compensatory" benefits, which are of a window-dressing character, are not listed. Obviously "benefits" could be presented in an inflationary manner—as was the UN's style in explaining changes to each side.
2. Annan I was changed in Annan II "to bridge remaining gaps between the parties": *S/2003/398*, para 46. Annan II was changed in Annan III, "particularly addressing the basic requirements of the Turkish side at the same time as meeting a number of Greek Cypriot concerns in order to maintain the overall balance," and filling "all remaining gaps in the core parts of the Plan, particularly those relating to security on which Greece and Turkey had not been able to agree": *ibid*, para 54. Annan V was "the text [finalised by the Secretary-General] to be submitted to referenda on the basis of the Plan, maintaining its overall balance while addressing to the extent possible the key concerns of each side": *S/2004/437*, Summary, p 1, para 4.
3. Annan IV is not noted. This was a "trial run" two days before Annan V in order to show that there had been consultation by the UN before "finalisation".
4. The Table shows that in general the Plan was altered in each succeeding version to the detriment of the Greek Cypriot side. Such an analysis is not a manifestation of a "zero-sum mentality," treating anything "gained" by the Turkey and the Turkish Cypriot side as a correlative loss. Instead, it shows how the benefits afforded by the Plan to the Greek Cypriot side were steadily whittled down, so that the Plan ultimately became perceived as unacceptable.

DEVELOPMENTS FROM ANNAN I THROUGH ANNAN II, III AND V, ACCOMPANIED BY UN ASSURANCES THAT THE OVERALL BALANCE OF THE PLAN WAS BEING PRESERVED

	ANNAN I (11/10/2002)	ANNAN II (10/12/2002)	ANNAN III (26/2/2003 and 8/3/2003)	ANNAN V (31/3/2004)
			TERRITORY OF EACH CONSTITUENT STATE	
1.	*Two* MAPS as alternatives—human impact of the map was the overarching concern (ie number of returnees; number of TCs in historic homes affected; current users affected; property ownership; economic viability/productivity)	*One* MAP as best respecting these criteria (includes tip of Karpas)	NEW MAP ***after Turkish objections***: ***Karpas excluded.*** ***Less coastline to*** GCCS (59% **now** 49%) 2,300 more GC refugees going home. *GCCS territory* (*with* SBA addition—see below) changes from 71.5% to 71.8%. *TCCS territory* changes from 28.5% to 29.2%.	**Approximately the same—small positive adjustments.**
2.	—	—	UK offers to reduce the Sovereign Base Areas by 116 sq. km., with about 90% going to the GCCS and about 10% going to the TCCS to enable the new map to keep up the GCCS % of territory and to balance loss of the Karpas.	Same.

		[If not done there would have been major imbalance due to map change, BUT: i. SBA areas are inhabited already by Greek Cypriots who have full rights, so no real gain – only a psychological issue, with the GC side *not being really compensated in the Plan for loss of balance.* ii. *New Protocol to the Treaty of Establishment and the Treaty of Guarantee give the SBAs legitimacy*, despite their not according with Cyprus's right of self-determination and despite the UK's continuing violation of the Treaty of Guarantee and failure to consult on defence under the Treaty of Establishment.]	
		SECURITY ASPECTS	
1. *Turkish and Greek contingents, each not exceeding a* ***four digit figure*** *[1,000 – 9,999]*, shall be permitted to be stationed under the Treaty of Alliance in the TCCS and GCCS respectively. *No time limit.*	*Permanent* Figure is inserted: **2,500–7,000.**	***Transitionally only.*** Specific figure: **6,000.**	***TRANSITIONALLY:*** **6,000 *until* 1.1.2011** **3,000 *until* 1.1.2018 *or Turkey's EU accession whichever is earlier.*** ***PERMANENTLY:*** **1960 Treaty of Alliance number (950 *Greek* : 650 *Turkish*).**

ANNAN I (11/10/2002)	ANNAN II (10/12/2002)	ANNAN III (26/2/2003 and 8/3/2003)	ANNAN V (31/3/2004)
2. *Reductions of current forces*: to be phased to agreed levels (above in 1). Any excess will be withdrawn, under a *timetable commencing not later than 5 months following the signature of the Treaty on matters related to the new state of affairs in Cyprus (a security treaty, modifying the three 1960 Treaties)*. [Under Turkey's Constitution Treaty ratification is long after signature.]	Same.	Reductions of forces: commence *5 months after Foundation Agreement enters into force (ie on the day after the Secretary-General confirms approval of the Agreement in the two separate referenda).* **UPON TURKEY'S EU ENTRY ALL CONTINGENTS TO BE WITHDRAWN.**	**Same.** **TREATY OF ALLIANCE CONTINGENTS REMAIN. Review of numbers 7-yearly.**
End figure, after phasing, is 4 digit.	End figure is 2,500–7000.	**End figure is NIL FOREIGN TROOPS**	**END FIGURES ARE: *Greek troops 950;* *Turkish troops 650.***
3. *Length of time foreign (Turkish and Greek) troops may be stationed in Cyprus.* The Treaty of Alliance *is without time-limit.* *Stationing is permitted to be permanent.*	Same.	***UPON ACCESSION OF TURKEY TO THE EU ALL GREEK AND TURKISH TROOPS SHALL BE WITH-DRAWN UNLESS OTHER-WISE AGREED.*** ***No foreign troops after Turkey's EU accession.***	***Stationing of Treaty of Alliance troop numbers is permanent.***

4.	UCR territory shall *only* be at disposal of international military operations *with the consent of Turkey and Greece*. The participation of Cyprus in the European Security and Defence Policy shall respect this limitation.	*An alternative consent* is added: that of *both the constituent states of the UCR* will suffice.	**Consent of constituent states will not suffice: *until Turkey accedes to the EU, the consent of both Turkey and Greece is in addition required ie both these States and both constituent states must agree.***	Same.
5.	*Rules governing movement of foreign troops stationed in Cyprus* Notice (unspecified) to be given of troop movements of size (to be specified).	***14 days*** for ground, air, maritime movement of more than *3 military* **vehicles with a capacity of *3 passengers* per vehicle.**	***48 hours only.*** Movement of *4* or more military vehicles, 3 aircraft in a single movement, one or more military vessels ***or 100 or more troops.***	Same.
6.	*Locations and size of military facilities and training field to be part of the Agreement.*	Same.	*Not to be part of the Agreement.* To be designated by Turkey and Greece 3 months after entry into force of the Agreement. **But total area of facilities and training areas are to be specifically limited.**	Turkey and Greece must *consult* the Federal Government and relevant constituent state before designation. No fixed date. ***No limit on area* of facilities and** training areas.
7.	Each constituent state police force must not number more than 700 police personnel plus 5 *police personnel* per 1000 inhabitants.	Increased to 6 *police personnel* per 1000 inhabitants.	Same.	For a transitional period, the *TCCS* will be entitled to maintain *a larger number of police* than in the previous version of the plan.

	ANNAN I (11/10/2002)	ANNAN II (10/12/2002)	ANNAN III (26/2/2003 and 8/3/2003)	ANNAN V (31/3/2004)
8.	**Treaty of Guarantee is extended to cover the territorial integrity, security and constitutional order of the constituent states.**	Same.	Same.	**Same.**
9.	***Unilateral rights of military action.*** **Silence.**	Silence.	Silence.	**Silence – despite claim by Turkish Cypriot side that such right exists and recent Turkish official statements to such effect, followed by Greek Cypriot request for clarification.** *Secretary-General, following Turkey's objection does not clarify*. The *Report, S/2004/437*, para. 61, contends there was an understanding in 2002 that the Treaty of Guarantee would not change and that the Plan's provisions "are consistent with the Greek Cypriot side's long stated position".
10.	*Legal security* *Immediately after confirmation by the Secretary-General* of the Plan's approval at referenda the Foundation Agreement shall enter into force.	Same.	Same.	**After approval at separate referenda on 24 April 2004 *AND signature by Greece, Turkey and the UK no later than 29 April 2004* [To give the Turkish Grand National Assembly the right to**

			approve only *after* the Turkish Cypriots gave the verdict: *S/2004/437*, para. 54.]
Should the Agreement not be approved it shall be *null and void* and commitments undertaken shall have no further legal effect.	Same.	**OMITTED. Corrigenda reinserting this on 8/3/03 – after Cyprus's protest.**	If not approved at referenda, or any guarantor fails to ***sign*** by the 29 April 2004, shall be null, void and have no legal effect. [*No need to sign into force*—cp. below the duty of UCR to do this —thus ***leaving it open to Turkey to rely on her Constitution allowing return of a law ratifying the Treaty so that it would not be binding on Turkey. No guarantee Turkish troops would be reduced.*** THIS provision was amended on 18.4.2004 only at Cyprus's insistence.]
Upon entry into force of the Foundation Agreement the Treaty on the New State of Affairs (Security) shall be signed and enter into force.	Same.	Same.	*Immediately* on entry into force of the Foundation Agreement, the Treaty with Turkey, the UK and Greece shall be "signed into force" *by the Co-Presidents of the UCR*.

ANNAN I (11/10/2002)	ANNAN II (10/12/2002)	ANNAN III (26/2/2003 and 8/3/2003)	ANNAN V (31/3/2004)
		SETTLERS	
1. i. Any *18-year old* ***born in Cyprus*** who has *permanently resided* there for at least 7 *years*.	Any person who enjoyed permanent residence for *at least 7 years before reaching* **18** and 1 year in last 5 years. [BIRTH IN CYPRUS GONE]	Now in list (3 below). No longer a separate category.	Same as Annan III.
ii. Any person *married to a Cyprus citizen* who has *permanently resided* for at least 2 *years* in Cyprus.		Gone. But covered by facilitated naturalization (2 below) which does *not* require residence.	
iii. *Minor children of above* who are *permanently residing* in Cyprus.		Gone – but automatic if parent gets facilitated naturalization.	
2. i. **Facilitated naturalization by spouses of Cypriot citizens *married* for at least 2 years [NO PERMANENT RESIDENCE REQUIRED.]** ii. **Automatically minor children of above [NO PERMANENT RESIDENCE REQUIRED.]**	Same.	Same. [*Note*: this covers categories (ii) and (iii) above which on the face of it were removed.]	**Same.**

3. **PERSONS WHOSE NAMES FIGURE ON A LIST. PERSONS SHALL BE LISTED WITH THEIR SPOUSES AND CHILDREN.**	No more than *33,000 persons*, inclusive of spouses and children. Applicants included on basis of length of Cyprus residence.	***45,000** persons* inclusive of spouses and children. Priority to 18 years old persons enjoying permanent residence in Cyprus before reaching 18 and for at least 1 year in last 5 years AND their minor children.	**Same.**
4. Equal treatment to Greek and Turkish nationals as to entry and residency rights to be negotiated between *Commission, Cyprus and Turkey*.	Same.	Same, but to be compatible with the Schengen *acquis* AND the principle of equal treatment. [Note: Ambiguity whether this overrides the quota arrangements under 5 below.]	Same, but to be negotiated between **the Commission and Turkey** within 6 months. Ambiguity removed, as restrictions remain until Turkey's EU entry or 19 years.
5. If the number of permanently resident Turkish nationals has reached *10% of TCCS internal constituent state citizens*,	Same.	**MAJOR CHANGES BY RE-DRAFTING:**	Same.
NO FURTHER IMMIGRATION of Turkish nationals (*mutatis mutandis* of Greek nationals),	Same.	***Permanent limit on further immigration goes.*** **(see 6 below)**	
BUT, on entry into force of Agreement, Aliens Board to authorize grant of *permanent residence* to up this level.	Same.	**Turkish nationals to up to 10% of resident TCCS internal constituent state citizens shall upon entry into force of the FA be given permanent residence.**	Same.

ANNAN I (11/10/2002)	ANNAN II (10/12/2002)	ANNAN III (26/2/2003 and 8/3/2003)	ANNAN V (31/3/2004)
AND Acquisition of citizenship by naturalization if legally resided for *at least 7 consecutive years* (if "TRNC" admitted the person he will have been lawfully resident as past acts are legalized) *ie immediately eligible for citizenship*.	Must now *include at least 4 years after* entry into force of FA (ie presence earlier in "TRNC" can count for 3 years). *ie eligible for citizenship after 4 years*.	***9 years*** residence for naturalization still including 4 years residence after FA in force (earlier presence in "TRNC" can count for 5 years). *ie eligible for citizenship after 4 years*.	Same.
	Persons not granted permanent residence and who had lived for 5 years in Cyprus eligible for cash grants of not less than 10,000 Euros for a household of four.	**Same.**	Same.
6. **No future immigration.**	Same.	***Future immigration quota permanently accorded*** **(by redrafting):** ***rolling on-going*** **5%** ***quota of Turkish nationals (mutatis mutandis Greek)*****, subject to no further immigration under the quota if the number of persons who are Turkish nationals has reached 5% of the number of TCCS internal constituent state citizens.** **In calculating the base for the quota, dual nationals of Turkey**	**Same,** ***BUT now a transitional system ONLY to operate for 19 years or until Turkey's EU entry.*** Dual nationals shall *not* be counted in the quota base ie the size of the quota will be slightly smaller.

and Cyprus shall only be counted as Cypriot ie *as Turkish nationals become TCCS constituent state citizens (having completed 9 years residence, at least 4 being after the FA)*, a fresh quota will open up further immigration.
These quotas are permanently to operate.

***Quotas end on Turkey's EU entry or in 19 years*. IMMIGRATION IS THEN UNLIMITED** *unless the UCR in consultation with Community takes safeguard measures* to ensure that there is not substantial alteration of the demographic ratio between Greek or Turkish as mother-tongue. *This requires*:

1. Aliens Board (3 : 3) approval;
2. Approval by UCR Presidential Council (4 : 2) **with support from 1 member of each constituent state;**
3. EU Commission approval;
4. **Regulation by UCR, requiring weighted voting in Senate *ie SUPPORT BY AT LEAST 2/5 (ie 10) OF SENATORS WHOSE MOTHER-TONGUE WAS TURKISH.***

ANNAN I (11/10/2002)	ANNAN II (10/12/2002)	ANNAN III (26/2/2003 and 8/3/2003)	ANNAN V (31/3/2004)
7. NIL.	NIL.	Immigration limitations shall not apply to full-time students and temporary academic staff of universities for 7 years. [**An estimated 18,000 persons fall within this category and are given seven years residence**]	Same.
THE RIGHTS TO RETURN AND OF ESTABLISHMENT IN THE CONSTITUENT STATES AND THEIR LINKAGE WITH POLITICAL RIGHTS OF THE CITIZEN			
1. ***The constituent states may limit the establishment of residence for persons not holding constituent state internal citizenship status.*** Such limitations are of two kinds: (a) *transitional* and (b) *permanent*.	Same.	***Limitations are only transitional and cease upon Turkey's EU entry.***	***Limitations are both transitional AND PERMANENT, BEING DEROGATIONS TO THE ACQUIS COMMUNAUTAIRE.***
2. ***Transitional limitations for 20 years*** are permissible if the number of residents hailing from the other constituent state has reached:	***Transitional limitations for 16 years***	***Transitional limitations until Turkey's EU entry.***	***Transitional limitations for up to 19 years or Turkey's EU entry, whichever is the earlier.***

i. 1% of population in Year 1;	i. *Total moratorium for 4 years.*	i. *Moratorium for 6 years* (except from Year 3 for persons over 65 and their spouse or sibling and Karpas villages (Tylliria and Messaoria for T/Cs).)	i. *Moratorium for 5 years* (Same exception, *BUT such persons count in the quota of returnees and must return before Year 7 or lose right*).
ii. 4% of population in Yrs. 5–7;	ii. *8% of population in Years 5–9.*	ii. 7% *of population in Yrs. 7–10.*	ii. *6%* of population in Yrs. 6–9.
iii. 7% of population in Yrs. 8–10 Thereafter rising by 3% in each 3-year period	iii. *18% of population in Years 10–15*	iii. *14%* of population in Yrs. 11–15.	iii. *12%* of population in Yrs 10–14.
iv. *Until 20%* of population in *Yr. 20.*		iv. *21%* from Year 16 to Turkey's EU entry.	iv. *18%* of population in Years 15–18.
Permanent limitations From *Year 21* limitations after *33⅓% of population* hails from other constituent state.	*Permanent limitations.* From *Year 16* limitations after *28% of population* hails from other constituent state. Reviewable by 25 years.	*NO LIMITATION AFTER TURKEY'S EU ENTRY*	*PERMANENT LIMITATION* The constituent states may, with a view to protecting their identities, take safeguard measures to ensure that *no less than two-thirds of its permanent residents speak its official language as their mother-tongue* (a formulation which, in the TCCS, means that Greek speaking *and* non-Cypriot residents together cannot exceed 33 ½ %).

ANNAN I (11/10/2002)	ANNAN II (10/12/2002)	ANNAN III (26/2/2003 and 8/3/2003)	ANNAN V (31/3/2004)
3. *EU safeguard measures for **one year*** where free movement of persons (in the sense of establishment) threatens economic difficulties in the TCCS.	Measures for 3 ***years***.	Same.	Subsumed in another provision.
4. ***Dual constituent citizenship* permissible. However, for constitutional purposes, deemed to have citizenship at place of residence.**	***Single constituent state citizenship only*. May apply to change to state of residence after 7 consecutive years residence.**	***All change to be controlled by constituent state*. No qualification stated. (*Designed to control change to stop acquisition of political rights at federal level in* TCCS).**	**Same.**
5. *POLITICAL RIGHTS OF CYPRUS CITIZENS*			
i. *Constituent state level: **internal citizenship** of constituent state.*	i. Same.	i. *Constituent state level: **permanent residence*** (acquirable after 6 months – *residence is under TCCS control by limitation* until Turkey's EU entry. See 2 above.)	i. Same. **BUT *permanent limitations are permitted*, so 66 ⅔% *of permanent residents (ie two-thirds) speak Turkish as mother-tongue*).**
ii. *Federal level: **residency** in constituent state.*	ii. ***Federal level: internal citizenship of constituent state* [to keep TCCS control of Senate and Deputies of UCR].**	ii. *Federal level: **internal citizenship** of constituent state (controlled by TCCS* – see 4 above). Applies to (a) Senate and (b) Deputies.	ii. *Federal level.* a. ***SENATE: 50% (12 of 24) to be Turkish mother-tongue speakers* (vice-versa in GCCS).**

			b. *Chamber of Deputies*: internal constituent state citizens (citizenship controlled tightly since Annan III).

PROPERTY CLAIMS

1. *In areas not subject to territorial adjustment*, properties are reinstatable, provided that no more than i. x% of the area and residences in the constituent state AND ii. y% in any municipality or village shall be reinstated. These percentages are directly related to the agreed territorial adjustment.	"Ceilings" are attributed numbers at i. 9% overall in the constituent state AND ii. 14% in any municipality/village.	"Ceilings," because of territorial adjustment in favour of Turkish Cypriots are raised, effectively allowing more restitution of GC-owned property. Now: i. 10% overall AND ii. 20% in any municipality/village.	More even *per capita* return of land to individual owners. (But non-personal companies and institutions are still excluded; exceptions continue in favour of current users and their successors (including purchasers) of property who have been dispossessed in the other constituent state; current users who have significantly improved property can still acquire title on payment for property as unimproved. The reinstatable property is *one-third* of the area or *value*, whichever is the lower. If the claim is for a house, it goes with one donum of land. But the house must have been built by or lived in for 10 years by the dispossessed person.

	ANNAN I (11/10/2002)	ANNAN II (10/12/2002)	ANNAN III (26/2/2003 and 8/3/2003)	ANNAN V (31/3/2004)
	Same. X years after entry into force of Agreement, bonds are redeemable.		Bonds: 2/3 payable in 10 years. 1/3 payable in 15 years.	**No more property returned, but more evenly returned. The un-reinstatable property is monetarily compensated by bonds effectively payable in 27 years.**
2.	NIL.	NIL.	***In areas to be adjusted, the owner of a significant improvement may be granted a 20-year lease*** by the Property Board, the use of such improvement for income generation being a significant consideration.	**Same.**
3.	**Dispossessed owners may lease or exchange property on long-term basis (20 years). Such dealings do not count as against the "ceilings" in 1 above. *Thus many GCs can retain ownership*.**	Same.	Same.	**PROVISION DROPPED.**
4.	NIL.	NIL.	NIL.	**If the land reinstated exceeds 100 donums, a long-lease (minimum 20 year period) must be offered to any citizens of the constituent state where the land is located.**

5. NIL.	NIL.	NIL.	**Agricultural land shall not be reinstated if this requires sub-division into plots less than 5 donums (ie owner must own 15 donums before reinstatement can be given) or 2 donums if irrigable (ie 6 donums of irrigable land).**
6. Liability for serious damage or destruction of property.	Same.	**Liability only for damage *after 11 November 2002*.**	**Same.**
7. **Only significant improvements made before 31 December 2001 or based on a building permit issued prior thereto entitle the improvers to acquire title to the property improved.**	Same.	Same.	**Improvements made before *31 December 2002* allow acquisition of title. The same applies where there is proof of *engineering approval for construction* (not a permit) *or the Property Board deems the improvement admissible. Effectively the freeze on development is removed by Annan V.***
8. NIL.	*In areas to be adjusted, priority in dealing with claims* must be given by the Property Board to: i. current residents′ claim to property from which they have been dispossessed (ie resident TCs, or GCs who have already returned);	Same.	Same.

ANNAN I (11/10/2002)	ANNAN II (10/12/2002)	ANNAN III (26/2/2003 and 8/3/2003)	ANNAN V (31/3/2004)
	ii. current users of their properties (ie GCs using TC property in the GCCS; TCs in the area to be adjusted; Turkish settlers in the areas to be adjusted); iii. dispossessed owners' claims to properties in that area (ie GCs in the rest of the GCCS seeking to reclaim their property).		
		Generally The priority must be given to: i. Claims of persons currently residing in the areas to be adjusted to property from which they have been dispossessed (as in (i) above); ii. Compensation claims; iii. Current users who have been dispossessed, claiming exchange for transfer of their own title; iv. Owners of significant improvements seeking title;	Same.

		v. Dispossessed owners' claims to properties in areas subject to territorial adjustment. **vi. Other claims ie dispossessed owners in areas not being adjusted.** *N.B*: **No priority is given for return of vacant property. Claims of persons returning to the TCCS (or GCCS) are postponed until last eg Karpasians' claims to their property, although they have the right to return to the TCCS in 2 years. The order of addressing claims is to deter people seeking restitution.**	*Same.*
9. Safeguard measures where the EU's internal market (free movement of capital, persons, services etc) caused or threatened serious economic difficulties in the TCCS could be taken for ***one year*** and prolonged with consent of the Commission.	Measures to be taken for ***three years***.	Same.	For ***15 years*** the TCCS may ***restrict the rights*** of persons not resident for at least 3 years in the TCCS, and, for the same period, the rights of legal persons (companies) ***to purchase immovable property in the TCCS***.

	ANNAN I (11/10/2002)	ANNAN II (10/12/2002)	ANNAN III (26/2/2003 and 8/3/2003)	ANNAN V (31/3/2004)
10.	The federation and the constituent states shall request the European Court of Human Rights to strike out any proceedings currently before it concerning property which persons left or lost control of due to international strife or military action between December 1963 and the Foundation Agreement entering into force.	Same.	Same.	More persons will get restitution of part of their property (about 1/3 —less any exceptions) with compensation for the rest. Read with the duty of constituent states to compensate for loss of use, the likely effect was that the Court would require these domestic remedies, first to be exhausted. ***The UCR would ask the Court to strike out proceedings* against Turkey and Cyprus, adding that *the UCR was sole responsible State Party – thus avoiding all Turkey's State responsibility for violations of property rights.***
11.	—	—	—	***To preclude the European Court of Justice from challenging provisions of the Foundation Agreement as contrary to the acquis communautaire or any new European Constitutional protections for rights*** (especially property rights), ***the UCR Co-Presidents***

			were to request that the Foundation Agreement be endorsed and accommodated "in a way that results in the adaptation of primary law".

GOVERNANCE

1. *Transitional executive government* i. *Year 1. Leaders who signed the Comprehensive Settlement on behalf of the Greek Cypriots and the Turkish Cypriots to be Co-Presidents, holding office of Head of State. They exercise executive power, acting and deciding by consensus. Heads of* Departments named by them are delegated the executive power.	Same, BUT	Same. The Greek Cypriot leader and the Turkish Cypriot leader shall become Co-Presidents.	i. The Co-Presidents shall be the persons whose names are communicated to the Secretary-General by 2 days after the referenda or the "head of government" of the relevant constituent state. [**To exclude "President" Denktash "the Head of State," and to endow "Prime Minister" Talat.**]
ii. ***Year 2.*** Parliament elects Council of Ministers of 6 (effectively 4 GCCS and 2 TCCS) on a single list with special majority (2/5 of Senators from each constituent state). The Council is the Government, while	Year 2 ½. Council of Ministers becomes Presidential Council with 7-monthly rotation between President and Vice-President ie 3 terms each as President.		ii. *They act until the Federal Parliament elects a Federal Council* (Parliament would be elected on 13 June 2004, *six weeks* after FA in force). *No date* by which the Parliament, *by special majority* must elect the Presidential Council or a single list.)

ANNAN I (11/10/2002)	ANNAN II (10/12/2002)	ANNAN III (26/2/2003 and 8/3/2003)	ANNAN V (31/3/2004)
Co-Presidents are only Head of State. Decisions require support from a Minister from each constituent state. iii. *Year 4*. Council of Ministers becomes Presidential Council for 3 years, with 6-monthly rotation between President and Vice-President. Former Co-Presidents cease to hold office with office of Head of State being vested in the Presidential Council.			iii. Monthly rotation of Co-Presidents to represent Cyprus as Head of State. [The *Report*; para. 44, asserts the period of transitional Government will be "two months," but there is no guarantee of this because of need for election on a single list and special majority voting.] iv. **Interim *Council of Ministers* of *3 Greek Cypriots*, *3 Turkish Cypriots* (named 2 days after the referendum) with European Affairs, Finance and Justice and Home Affairs being headed by 3 Greek Cypriots, and 3 Turkish Cypriots heading Foreign Affairs and Defence, Trade and Economy, and Communications and Natural Resources.**

			v. *As soon as Council is elected for 60-month term*, the Presidency and Vice-Presidency shall rotate each 10 months, so each will have 3 terms.
6 years of transitional government.	Same.	Same.	**THE NET EFFECT IS THAT THERE WILL BE EQUAL ROTATION OF THE PRESIDENCY FOR 5 years and 2 months. There will also be *numerical equality* of office holding for at least 2 months between Greek and Turkish Cypriots (*ethnic*, not constituent state based) until the Council of Ministers is elected, with crucial Departments being headed by Turkish Cypriot Ministers without any agreed allocation of portfolios (which *was* to be done *by consensus* of the Co-Presidents).**
2. ***Presidential Council***: composition: i. 6 members elected by Parliament for a fixed 5-year term on a single list by special majority.		Same.	*6 voting members* Shall, unless it decides otherwise by special majority (undefined), elect 3 non-voting members.

ANNAN I (11/10/2002)	ANNAN II (10/12/2002)	ANNAN III (26/2/2003 and 8/3/2003)	ANNAN V (31/3/2004)
ii. proportional to *population* of the constituent states though at least 2 from each. Therefore 4 GCCS : 2 TCCS.	Proportional to the *number of citizens holding internal constituent state citizenship*.	Same.	One third of voting and one third of non-voting members, must hail from each constituent state ie 4 GCCS: 2 TCCS voting members AND 2 GCCS: 1 TCCS non-voting member.
iii. Consensus in Senate. If not reached, then by simple majority, but majority must comprise at least one member from each constituent state.	Same.		
3. The heads of Departments of Foreign Affairs and European Union affairs shall not hail from the same constituent state.	Same.	Same.	
NIL.	NIL.	At the European Council, the member of the Presidential Council responsible for European Union affairs shall represent the Council as Head of Government and shall be assisted by the member responsible for External Relations. [ie the division of important offices and superin-	At the European Council the President will be accompanied by the Vice-President. [ie the constituent state division is in a different form, but nonetheless there.]

		tendence of each side by the other is manifested at the European Council, and there is no real Head of State.]	
4. *Cooperation Agreements* The constituent states shall participate in the finalization and implementation of policy in *external and EU relations on matters within their sphere of competence* in accordance with Cooperation Agreements modelled on the Belgian example.	Same.	The Cooperation Agreements are extended to areas of *federal competence*. They are also extended to *police matters* in ways not earlier envisaged. **The complex Agreements make it *in practice* impossible to take timeous decisions in external relations and in EU affairs.**	**Same.**
5. Public offices at high levels in the Service are to be held in equal numbers by persons from the two constituent states and Deputies must hail from different states as well as certain senior officers eg Attorney-General and Deputy, Auditor-General and Deputy. Deputies and Heads of the 10 most senior missions (held 50 : 50) must be from different constituent states.	Same.	Same.	Same.

ANNAN I (11/10/2002)	ANNAN II (10/12/2002)	ANNAN III (26/2/2003 and 8/3/2003)	ANNAN V (31/3/2004)
6. *Legislature* *The people of each constituent state* shall elect on a proportional basis 24 members of the Senate (48 members).	Same.	Same.	**The Senate shall be composed of an equal number of *Greek and Turkish speaking senators*. They shall be elected on a proportional basis by the citizens of Cyprus, *voting separately as Greek and Turkish speaking voters*. [Ethnic voting was introduced to keep Turkish Cypriot control of the Senate should any numbers of Greek Cypriots resume residence in the TCCS.]**
7. *Special majorities /weighted voting* Most significant federal measures require passage by a special majority comprising at *least 2/5 of sitting Senators from each constituent state* in addition to a simple majority of Deputies present and voting.	Same.	Same.	***The weighted voting requirement was now made ethnic in relation to the Senate*** by the Federal Laws on Legislative Procedure. These provide for Senators, based on mother-tongue language, to vote on such basis, in effect ***requiring passage of specified measures to be approved by 10 of the 24 Turkish mother-tongue speaking Senators***

			and 10 of the 24 mother-tongue Greek speakers.
8. *Expansion of topics requiring weighted voting*: The Constitution specified areas of federal competence (which were very limited) and major topics required special majority voting.	"*Natural resources, including water resources*" was added to federal competences, with "*water resources" requiring special majority voting*. [This was to ensure Turkish Cypriots an equitable share of and control over water resources, which were mainly located in the GCCS, so that the GCCS could not regulate its own resources. Natural resources generally were not subjected to special majority voting since the Turkish side wanted the TCCS to keep control over natural resources (except water) located there.]		Same. Federal Laws governing these topics were "finalized".
	All matters regulated by the 1982 Law of the Sea Convention were added to federal competence by an interpretive note which effectively also extended ***weighted voting to these, both as***	Weighted voting was required for Laws and ***regulations*** governing the UCR's ***exclusive economic zone and the contiguous zone***. [This was at Turkey's demand.]	**Of particular concern was the finalization of the Federal Law on the Continental Shelf (Attachment 11 No. 48), section 3.2 of which provided that Cyprus could not explore or exploit her continental**

	ANNAN I (11/10/2002)	ANNAN II (10/12/2002)	ANNAN III (26/2/2003 and 8/3/2003)	ANNAN V (31/3/2004)
		to Laws and regulations. [This was a Turkish demand.]	An interpretative note clarified federal competence *as covering airspace of the UCR and the Flight Information Region (FIR), effectively extending weighted voting to this.* [This was a Turkish demand.]	**shelf unless Turkey agreed to a demarcation or indicated she did not contest any adjacent areas of territorial waters. [The UN informally told Turkey the UCR had "no continental shelf".]**
9.	*Federal Laws to be in force upon commencement of the new state of affairs in Cyprus* were to be annexed to the Agreement. [This was a Greek Cypriot demand to ensure Laws were in place and could not be blocked by the weighted majority requirement in view of past experience from 1961–1963.]	Laws on Water Resources and on Natural Resources were added to the Laws required. [To ensure the Greek Cypriot side enacted a Water Resources Law and that Federal standards were set out in a Natural Resources Law.]	Many essential Federal Laws were drafted and submitted by the Greek Cypriot side, but could not be agreed due to delays by the Turkish Cypriot side in approving a Technical Committee on Laws and to ordering to their members not to meet in the Committee later in the process. ***ADDED BY CORRIGENDA AND CLARIFICATIONS OF 8 MARCH 2003 (ANNAN III ¼)*** ***New Article 48 bis of the Constitution*** **provided for**	131 Laws were "finalized" by the Secretary-General after extensive Technical Committee meetings in Nicosia. They were "almost all on the basis of Greek Cypriot drafts" (*Report*, para. 44) BUT the Greek Cypriot side's view is that most significant "finalizations" adopted Turkish – Turkish Cypriot positions. (See below.) No longer applicable. **BUT a "light procedure" allowing revision by simple majority and reviewed by federal Supreme**

finalization and adoption of outstanding federal Laws. The Technical Committee on Laws was to become a federal committee and work "*on the basis of any drafts before the Committee on 25 March 2003*". Finalized common drafts were to be presented to the transitional Federal Parliament and be passed by it at various dates up until *15 October 2003* (ie 7 months later). If not passed, *the Transitional Supreme Court should decide the unresolved issues* and promulgate the Law by the end of *November 2003* (ie within 6 weeks).	Court was introduced by Article 49. Sixteen members of either Chamber may request parliamentary review of Laws for compatibility with Main Articles of the Foundation Agreement and the Constitution. [Turkish Cypriot demand as pre-caution.]
Functions to be regulated by such Laws would be deemed delegated *ad interim to the constituent states until the Law came into force* or the last date for Supreme Court promulgation, whichever was the earlier, subject to Laws and decisions of the Federal Parliament.	As before.

	ANNAN I (11/10/2002)	ANNAN II (10/12/2002)	ANNAN III (26/2/2003 and 8/3/2003)	ANNAN V (31/3/2004)
			[In effect there was to be *government by the constituent states in most federal spheres of competence* – 6,000 pages of draft Laws were on the table for consideration.] **Where Laws on Cooperation Agreements had been considered and the sides had taken different reserved positions, *the Secretary-General purported to "finalize" such Laws, in the majority of significant cases adopting Turkish Cypriot positions eg the Cooperation Agreements on EU Affairs and on External Relations.***	
10.		Same.		**Same.**
	Treaties binding Cyprus from entry into force of the Foundation Agreement were to be listed.			
	There was a presumption of inclusion of all multilateral	Same.	***List finalized by the UN.*** 22 multilateral treaties. ***Protocol No. 1 to the European***	1,134 Treaties and instruments binding the UCR were listed.

instruments and all bilateral instruments other than with Greece or Turkey. Either side might object on grounds of incompatibility with the Comprehensive Settlement or the Foundation Agreement.			***Convention on Human Rights is excluded (Property protection).*** **After strenuous Greek Cypriot objection the 8 March 2003 CORRIGENDA listed PROTOCOL 1. Also Protocols 12 and 13.**	**The UN refused, at Turkey's insistence, to list the Treaty of Montreux 1936 on the basis that the Republic of Cyprus was not a party. Apart from the factual and legal inaccuracy, the Treaty was not incompatible with the Foundation Agreement.**
Instruments with Greece and Turkey not related to defence should be examined and, unless incompatible with the *Settlement* or the Agreement, should be included.	Same.		**Deleted.** 2 bilateral treaties with Greece listed. 2 bilateral treaties with Turkey listed – see below.	**These Cooperation Agreements and certain other Turkey – "TRNC" Agreements listed (eg "Cooperation Agreement with Turkey on Coastal Security") infringed the sovereignty and exclusive competence of the Federal Government and were incompatible with the Agreement.**
Instruments with Greece and Turkey on defence matters should not be included unless otherwise agreed.			Deleted. Cooperation Agreement on Civil Aviation *with Turkey* and Cooperation Agreement in the Field of Air Rescue and listed. **Both these treaties related in part to defence matters, giving the Turkish Army competence to act in the territorial space of the UCR. [UN finalization despite Greek Cypriot objections.]**	

ANNAN I (11/10/2002)	ANNAN II (10/12/2002)	ANNAN III (26/2/2003 and 8/3/2003)	ANNAN V (31/3/2004)
Treaties binding on Cyprus shall be considered an integral part of the Constitution.	Same.	New provision (Article 48) for listed Treaties after entry into force of the Foundation Agreement to be objected to on grounds of incompatibility with such Agreement. If either Co-President, or Council of Ministers, or Supreme Court decide incompatible, attempts should be made with other Parties, in accordance with international law, to modify the treaty, or, failing this, to terminate as soon as possible.	**Not an integral part of Constitution but treaties to prevail over any federal or constituent state legislation.** [Greek Cypriot **request.**] ***Except treaty is not suspended* in interim (because contrary to international law) *unless the other High Contracting Party is Greece or Turkey*.**
		Constituent states may invoke a modification procedure if the scope of the treaty falls within the exclusive competence of the constituent states and *treaty is suspended in such constituent state's territory*. [All international treaties would effectively be subject to potential re-examination and termination.]	***Same*.** References to Co-Presidents consequentially deleted.

FINANCIAL ASPECTS

1. *Property compensation scheme* by "compensation bonds" from Compensation Fund with initial capital (**X**) provided by UCR, to which proceeds of disposed property and any international aid contributions are added.	Same.	**100 million Cyprus pounds initial capital by the Federal Government, which shall seek a matching contribution from international donors.** ***If Fund unable to meet its obligations, further contributions payable by Federal Government.***	**Improved scheme re compensation bonds and preferential loans scheme to provide limits on loans. To safeguard solvency and creditworthiness of Federal Government** ***further federal contributions were deleted, BUT the loan scheme is still guaranteed by Federal Government.***
Compensations bonds and interest thereon shall be guaranteed by the UCR.		**Same.**	**Interest not guaranteed,** ***although nominal value of compensation funds at maturity is guaranteed.*** **[Still a risk.]**
Preferential loans to be made to dispossessed owners, current users and owners of significant improvements who are Cypriot citizens without sufficient financial means to purchase or reconstruct property.		**Same.**	Limits on amounts at 40,000 Cyprus pounds. **[Still a serious risk.]** **Not applicable to** ***re-construction*** **of property (for purchase or** ***construction*** **only).**
The UCR shall support the scheme by funds from its budget. Donations by international and local banks and the constituent			**[Still a risk because** ***the fund is guaranteed by Federal Government*** which can seek

ANNAN I (11/10/2002)	ANNAN II (10/12/2002)	ANNAN III (26/2/2003 and 8/3/2003)	ANNAN V (31/3/2004)
states shall (if given) to the scheme also be overseen by Property Board.			backing [optional] by international financial institutions.]
2. ***Public debt*** The UCR shall not assume responsibility for debts to Greece or Turkey or for purchase of armaments.			
Special majority law *may* provide for reimbursement of the UCR by the constituent states.	Same.	For *external* debts this remains the same, *BUT*, *internally*, responsibility shall be borne for service and payment by the constituent state whose population benefited from the loan, unless the infrastructure or works which are the result of the loan benefit the whole of Cyprus, when the debt shall be paid and serviced by the Federal Government. [This ignores the issue of who is to benefit from and entitled to CY£6 billion in reserves, built up from Greek Cypriot economic activity, and	Same. **[There is no provision as to *external debt* responsibility after the UCR is in being. This requires clarification, else, under the law of State responsibility, the UCR could be bankrupted by excessive loans to the constituent states which are defaulted upon.]**

			currently held by the Republic's Central Bank.]	
3. The Central Bank of Cyprus shall *issue currency*.	Same.		The Central Bank shall *define* and implement monetary policy and regulate and supervise credit institutions. [Corrigenda, item 10, on 8 March 2003 explained that the change had been made "in order to avoid the need to change the Constitution *when the Euro replaces the Cyprus pound as the currency of the United Cyprus Republic".]*	**Despite recommendations by the Technical Committee on Economic and Financial Aspects, it is not made clear what the UCR currency shall be, leaving it open whether a new currency should be issued prior to the UCR adopting the Euro.** **[Currency instability is a serious risk.]**
The Central Bank shall exchange deposits held by Cyprus citizens and residents in Turkish lira *into Cyprus pounds*.	Same.		*Same.*	
4. *Fiscal transfers* i. The UCR shall confer on the constituent states, in proportion to their population [ie per capita] *no less than 50%* of the revenue from indirect taxation not transferred to the EU. [This is a redistribution	Same.		i. No less than *one-third* of this shall be transferred to the states in proportion to their population *BUT IN ADDITION*. ii. One-third of the VAT collected within the boundaries of each constituent state	Similar.

ANNAN I (11/10/2002)	ANNAN II (10/12/2002)	ANNAN III (26/2/2003 and 8/3/2003)	ANNAN V (31/3/2004)
from GCs and TCs as their *per capita* incomes radically differ.]		shall be conferred upon it. *Also*: this is *on the understanding* that VAT on imported goods is paid at *place of consumption*, not port of entry. [Otherwise the provision could have been unfair to Turkish Cypriots due to imports tending to be through Limassol.]	
		Moreover the UN for the first time notes. "An in depth discussion based on facts and expertise may be necessary with respect to this and other provisions in the course of deliberations on the relevant legislation."	
5. *Central Bank control and direction of monetary policy and the required extent of "ethnic" character of managing organs, rather than expertise.*			

i. Board of 3 including the Governor. ii. At least 1 from each constituent state. iii. The third member may be non-Cypriot.	Same.	Same.	Organs to be: i. Governor and Deputy Governor. ii. Board of Directors of 5—with 2 from each constituent state and *one* may be non-Cypriot. iii. **Monetary Policy Committee of 7 with 3 from each constituent state including the Government and any non-Cypriot.** **[Numerical equality of membership *and not expertise* is the basis of organizing the Central Bank.]**
iv. Law may provide for establishment of Branches in each constituent state and inclusion of Branch Directors on the Board.			Same. **[This was despite the Technical Committee's contrary recommendation that Branches could, if established, only be for information and not regulatory, and that Branch Directors should not be on the Board – for reasons of supervision, competence and independence.]**

	ANNAN I (11/10/2002)	ANNAN II (10/12/2002)	ANNAN III (26/2/2003 and 8/3/2003)	ANNAN V (31/3/2004)
			HUMAN RIGHTS ISSUES	
1.	Constitutions of each constituent state to be approved by both referenda. [The purpose was that the constitutional structure of the whole country (UCR State) and the protections for all inhabitants were to be scrutinized before being approved.]	Same.	Same.	*Verbally* the same. In fact, no opportunity was given by the UN to comment on the TCCS Constitution, which was due to be presented to the UN and exchanged for information between the sides by 14 March 2004. It was only shown to the Greek Cypriot side on *27 March*, with an invitation to comment which was accepted, with comments given the same night. But, on 28 March, Greek Cypriot comments on the TCCS Constitution's incompatibility with the Agreement and with the European Convention on Human Rights were said by the UN to be too late to be considered.
2.	NIL.	NIL.	NIL.	**The Foundation Agreement to be "primary law," thereby excluding applicability of the fundamental**

			principles of the EU and rulings thereon by the European Court of Justice in cases where the Agreement was incompatible with such principles.
3. i. Validation of past acts by any authority whatsoever.	Any authority *in Cyprus*.	Same.	Same.
ii. Request to the European Court of Human Rights by the UCR and constituent states to strike out any proceedings concerning property of displaced persons in Cyprus.	Same.	Same.	Request to strike out *to allow the domestic mechanisms* for solving these cases to proceed. **The UCR to be the sole responsible State Party as regards such issues.**
iii. Claims for compensation for acts prior to the Agreement to be dealt with by the constituent state from which the claimant hails.	Same.	Same.	Same.
4. NIL.	NIL.	*Missing Persons* **The executive heads of the constituent states shall without delay take step *to conclusively resolve the issue of missing persons*.**	Similar, with slightly different wording.

ANNAN I (11/10/2002)	ANNAN II (10/12/2002)	ANNAN III (26/2/2003 and 8/3/2003)	ANNAN V (31/3/2004)
Any claims for liability or compensation arising *from acts prior to this Agreement, shall,* insofar as they are not otherwise regulated by the provisions of the Agreement, *be dealt with by the constituent state from which the claimant hails.*	Same.	Same.	
		Claims on behalf of missing persons and their close relatives in respect of human rights violations will now no longer lie against Turkey or the Republic of Cyprus (if either is responsible) but only against the constituent states from which the victims hail. [Only if investigations are refused *after* the Agreement is in force, will Turkey incur responsibility for the violations of Article 3 of the European Court of Human Rights in relation to missing persons' relatives by reason of their continued subjection to inhuman treatment. Liability in respect of those missing persons who appear to have disappeared in circumstances indicating commission of a war crime by the Turkish Army will generally be extinguished.]	Same.

APPENDIX 7

AN AGENDA FOR DISCUSSION

1. If Cypriots are to reach agreement on a settlement, they need seriously to discuss a large number of matters categorisable under five headings: Security; Property and the Right of Residence; Territory; Fiscal and Economic Issues; and Governance. They will also need to discuss any proposed Act of Adaptation of the terms of accession of the Republic of Cyprus to the European Union. Such discussions should be intense (not in a pejorative sense) and in depth, disregarding advice by those who tell the sides to decide their future by, as it were, putting their all on six, seven, or even eleven squares. If the discussions are virtually continuous, without games being played of stopping to consult parties not present, in particular "motherlands," each side will appreciate the inter-linkages between various proposals, see alternative possibilities and envisage offsetting compromises, not only within the headings, but across them.

   The agenda below lists matters which, in the writer's view, are or should be of concern to all Cypriots. Naturally a somewhat different agenda could be proposed by a former adviser to the Turkish Cypriot side (especially by a well-known academic believing in bi-zonality or union with Turkey).
2. What are not included on the writer's suggested agenda are matters of concern to the Republic of Turkey purely in her Turkish State capacity. Although such matters relate to that State's perceived foreign policy interests, they are, it is submitted, not lawfully or properly to be taken into account in negotiations on the State of Cyprus. Turkey's sole standing in relation to Cyprus is under the 1960 Treaties, insofar as these are valid and still operative. She is estopped from relying on the Treaty of Alliance and the Treaty of Establishment to claim that her rights in relation to "common defence" are being disregarded. Other than in connection with the Treaty of Guarantee (should such Treaty be enforceable despite its continuing breach by Turkey) the Republic of Turkey has no rights. Under the Treaty of Guarantee, Turkey has not only undertaken to prohibit, so far as concerns herself, any activity aimed at promoting, directly or indirectly partition of the Island of Cyprus or its union with any other State, but she has also undertaken in terms of Article II to

   > recognize and guarantee the independence, territorial integrity and security of the Republic of Cyprus, and also the state of affairs established by the Basic Articles of its Constitution.

   That Constitution of 1960 has remained operative other than in its important inter-communal aspects. Assuming that Turkey were not in breach of the Treaty of Guarantee, she would, under its Article IV, have rights in the event of breach of the Treaty's provisions. Those rights are to consultation with the other Guarantors, the UK and Greece, and, following consultation, to take common or concerted action on representations or measures to ensure observance of the Treaty's provisions. If common or concerted action does not prove possible, Article IV reserved the rights of each guaranteeing Power to take action with the sole aim of re-establishing the state of affairs created by the Treaty.

Turkey has no other rights. In particular she has no rights to claim "balance in the Eastern Mediterranean," as explained by Professors Crawford, Hafner and Pellet (see p 14n2 *supra*), or other conjectural rights built upon the Treaty of Lausanne 1923. Likewise, the Hellenic Republic is no more entitled than is the Republic of Turkey to claim rights over and above those, *mutatis mutandis*, set out above. It is long overdue that Cypriots, who have to live with the consequences of any decisions, agreed matters without self-interested "maternal" inter-meddling.

SPHERES WHERE RECONSIDERATION IS REQUIRED AND SPECIFIC TOPICS THEREUNDER

1. ***SECURITY* (in the widest sense)**

This requires consideration of:

(i) *Treaty revision as regards the folowing treaties*:

(a) *Treaty of Guarantee to clarify*:

1. The issue of the alleged right of unilateral military intervention.
2. The scope of the guarantee and whether it covers both the federal Constitution and those of the constituent states.

(b) *Treaty of Alliance to ensure:*

1. There is speedy demilitarisation of Cyprus by withdrawal of foreign troops.
2. The final outcome is complete demilitarisation.

(c) *Treaty of Establishment to*:

1. Ensure that any bases are leased from Cyprus;
2. Provide international judicial dispute-settlement machinery (failing successful negotiation within a time-limit) as regards disputes concerning the Treaty's interpretation and application.

(ii) ***Exclusion of foreign intervention in Cyprus's internal affairs.***

This requires discussion of:

(a) A Constitutional prohibition on intervention by foreign States in the affairs of Cyprus and its constituent states.

(b) A specific Constitutional prohibition on extra-constitutional bodies operating with foreign participation and the giving of directions to the Governments of the federation or the constituent states.

(c) Police forces in the federation and constituent states being under civilian control, with Cypriots being members of such forces, subject to the requirements of EU law.

(d) Treaties which confer rights on foreign States, which rights are exercisable within Cyprus's jurisdiction.

(iii) ***The European Security and Defence Policy***

Discussion is necessary as to whether Cyprus should, as a sovereign EU Member State be entitled fully to participate in the Common ESDP, subject only to the requirements consequential upon demilitarisation of Cyprus.

(iv) ***Police***

This requires discussion of the sizes, both permanent and temporary, of:

(a) the constituent state police forces;

(b) the federal police force; and
(c) whether temporary international training and supervision is advisable.

(v) ***UN mandate for peace-keeping***
The following items require discussion:
(a) The mandate of any UN Mission or peace-keeping force and whether this should be under Chapter VII of the Charter.
(b) The scope of the mandate to uphold the peace settlement, including ability to intervene, if necessary, without a fresh mandate.
(c) The establishment of a Security Council Committee to monitor *all* aspects of implementation of the settlement, which, in conjunction with the Secretary General, shall submit 3-monthly reports to the Security Council.
(d) The enhancement of any UN peace-keeping force's administrative power and powers regarding enforcement of law and order, in particular of all areas to be territorially adjusted, subject to powers of delegation by the UN.
(e) Costs of the UN's Cyprus operation and contributions to be made by the federation and the constituent states.

(vi) ***Implementation of the Plan***
Associated with the issue of the scope of the UN mandate is that of implementation. Discussion is required as to
(a) troop reductions; relocation and rehabilitation of inhabitants from areas to be territorially adjusted; actual transfer of territory; and guarantees against failure to implement on due dates; and
(b) how to ensure persons will be allowed to return home to the unadjusted areas.

(vii) ***Transitional arrangements***
Discussion is needed as to:
(a) The initial arrangements, their duration and joint executive government.
(b) The "equality" in rotation of office between President and Vice President for *5 years*.

(viii) ***Settlers (Turkish nationals)***
This topic requires examination in light of international law earlier ignored by the UN. Specific aspects are:
(a) The stay of certain Turkish nationals on humanitarian grounds; criteria; and numbers.
(b) Limits on immigration of Greeks and Turks to maintain demographic balance and the Island's cultural character.
(c) Participation rights in any self-determination referenda.

(ix) ***Schengen***
Consideration of entry and residency rights of Greek and Turkish nationals subject to Cyprus's ability fully to participate in:
(a) the Schengen acquis;
(b) the Schengen area; and
(c) any future arrangements that may be agreed between Member States.

2. *PROPERTY AND THE RIGHT OF RESIDENCE*

A *Property*

Further consideration is needed of the property provisions to ensure that the settlement is perceived as just and as in conformity with humanitarian and human rights law. Specifically needing consideration are:

(i) Whether in general, all dispossessed owners should be entitled to reinstatement to their property, with compensation being an alternative only in exceptional cases.

(ii) What protection should be given to *current users* of homes, agricultural land and business premises, who have themselves been dispossessed of similar property of *approximately* equal value.

(iii) *Whether owners of significant improvements made* after 31 December 1999, when negotiations for settlement commenced, or of such improvements based on a permit issued prior thereto, should be protected and how.

(iv) Modes of immediately prohibiting transfer of title of or long leases of property which is owned by dispossessed persons, so as to protect dispossessed persons' rights.

(v) Whether subsequent purchasers from dispossessed owners, if they were at the time of purchase "citizens" of the area in which they bought the property, should be protected.

(vi) Whether there should be provisions in effect resulting in widespread compulsory property purchases (nationalisation) followed by compensation by bonds, and whether, where property is taken for public benefit or military purposes, the relevant Government must promptly pay the owner.

(vii) Whether *long-leasing* of agricultural, business and other property is a better option than forced sale.

(viii) What the decision-making priorities should be when determining the many property and occupation of property claims and the extent of permissible delay before restitution becomes enforceable.

(ix) Whether machinery and procedures can be created to facilitate acquisition of land in convenient locations for public and private housing, in particular mechanisms to encourage sales by reinstated owners of land.

(x) To what extent a proposed Fund for subsidised loans with federal guarantees requires revision and how best development of a property market can be encouraged.

(xi) Whether the private sector should be involved in facilitating sales, leases and property exchange, rather than this being in large part by a Property Board; and whether any Board's functions should be reduced in scope to dealing with (a) valuations and (b) compensation claims.

(xii) Whether there should be a Compensation Tribunal of nominees by the constituent states, equally composed, to decide *loss of use damages* based on international standards, with such Tribunal being funded by the Federal Government, the Government of Turkey and contributions by European States and the USA.

(xiii) What the scope should be of temporary "safeguard measures" to restrict trade, establishment of business, industry and professional activities in the TCCS and what EU procedural safeguards are required to ensure absence of abuse.

B *The right of residence*

Discussion about principles and striking a balance between competing rights is essential. This should give due weight to:

(a) Turkish Cypriot concerns to retain the Turkish Cypriot constituent state's predominantly Turkish Cypriot identity;

(b) the specific methods by which each constituent state can retain its cultural and ethnic identity;

(c) individual citizens' right of return to their homes, as required by UN Security Council Resolutions on Cyprus, and to citizens' freedom of "establishment" and residence in their own country;

(d) the methods by which each Community can ensure that a Community-based political system operates without unreasonably restricting political rights; and

(e) phased return of displaced persons and priorities in according return, with the object of avoiding instability or disorder of any kind.

3. *TERRITORY*

The sides need directly to discuss the territory of each constituent state from two different standpoints:

(a) ***Whether further territorial adjustments or special arrangements are required to*:**

(i) accommodate areas where minorities inside either constituent state are located, such as the Karpas, Tylliria and Messaoria villages. Failing such territorial accommodation, discussion (which has never occurred) is needed on the specific administrative arrangements to safeguard the rights and status of such minorities in accordance with the European Framework Convention for the Protection of National Minorities; and

(ii) avoid administrative or other difficulties due to the location of territorial lines.

(b) ***Whether federal areas would facilitate*:**

(i) co-operation in joint government of the Communities in Cyprus;

(ii) avoid the need for territorial adjustments in certain locations;

(iii) better protect Cyprus's environment, with large federal national parks in the Karpas and Akamas, and possibly covering the whole Pentadactylos Range, with ownership of the land remaining in the constituent states or existing owners;

(iv) better provide for a federal capital with joint governmental arrangements; and

(v) better provision for an international free port.

4. *FISCAL AND ECONOMIC ISSUES*

The following themes require further consideration, initially through re-constitution of a Technical Committee with international experts and with equal membership of Greek and Turkish Cypriot experts:

(i) *Central banking and currency*

Inter alia, this should address the structure of the federal Central Bank and its organs and competences; the currency; and banking supervision and stability of commercial banks.

(ii) *Economic policy*

Inter alia, this covers economic policy in general; minimum standards for Cyprus workers as to social protections and transport; labour market policy; and common development policy.

(iii) *Fiscal policy and stability*
Inter alia, this covers establishment of a Macroeconomic Stability Council; limitations on federal guarantees of external debt; and policies to avoid tax competition.

(iv) *Cost effectiveness*
Inter alia, this covers
- (a) Reduced expenditure on international personnel in Cyprus institutions (eg foreign judges and the Property Board);
- (b) UN assessed contributions for any UN Mission or Force;
- (c) The scope of federal Government guarantees for land acquisition; and
- (d) The relative burden-sharing of costs by each constituent state.

(v) *Permanent machinery for review of fiscal and economic arrangements.*

(vi) *Cyprus's use of its assets and natural resources*
Inter alia, this should cover:
- (a) competence to exploit all Cyprus's national natural resources without foreign interference, but subject to EU law; and
- (b) aviation and airports policy, particularly in relation to the number of international airports and a national carrier, again subject to EU law.

5. *GOVERNANCE*

Fully appreciating Turkish Cypriot concerns that neither side may claim authority or jurisdiction over the other, and that federal governmental organs should strive for consensus, especially by avoiding divisive policies or measures, more attention needs to be given to ensuring functionality, workability and viability *in practice*, with consequential lowering of some barriers to effective daily decision-making. *Inter alia*, the matters requiring some consideration relate to:

(i) *The legislative sphere*. If additional judicial functions are conferred on the Supreme Court, such jurisdiction should be invocable to avoid unnecessary cases of divisive voting. (The writer makes no suggestion as regards changing the scope of weighted voting.)

(ii) *Executive decision-making*. Better ways of enhancing functionality, while at the same time preventing executive decisions unacceptable to either Community require exploration, with the issue of "deadlock-resolution" also requiring re-consideration. (Proposals which could be a substitute are too complex to be explained here.)

(iii) *The judiciary*. Changes in respect of *competences and composition of the Supreme Court* require consideration, namely:
- (a) removal of the court's deadlock-resolution competence, avoiding direct judicial law-making and executive decisions;
- (b) removal of the element of foreign judges;
- (c) regular rotation of the office of President of the Court;
- (d) speedy judicial references on grounds of compatibility with the Comprehensive Settlement; and
- (e) appellate competence to ensure compatibility of legal interpretation throughout the federation.

(iv) The scope of *federal economic competence*, which requires re-evaluation.

(v) *The Co-operation Agreements on EU Affairs and External Relations* to facilitate speedier decision-making.

(vi) Some *Federal Laws, Treaties and Constitutional Laws*, which were the subject of significant disagreement between the sides.

(vii) The *Federal Public Service* arrangements, to ensure temporary flexibility and training schemes for personnel, and to reconsider decision-making procedures.

(viii) *Governance rights for "minorities"* in the constituent states (This is mentioned under territorial arrangements.)

(ix) Overall, the election and composition of representative organs in the federation and the constituent states require thorough reconsideration, so that they are such as to satisfy concerns about maintenance of an appropriate balance as to each constituent state's cultural identity, bearing in mind the 1977 High Level Agreement and the equal status of the Communities at the federal level.

6. *ACT OF ADAPTATION TO THE ACT CONCERNING THE CONDITIONS OF ACCESSION OF THE REPUBLIC OF CYPRUS AND THE ADJUSTMENTS TO THE TREATIES ON WHICH THE EUROPEAN UNION IS FOUNDED AND PROTOCOL NO. 10 ON CYPRUS*

Topics agreed under the themes Security, Property and the Right of Residence, Fiscal and Economic Issues and Governance and consequential appropriate accommodations require discussion in relation to the EU, subject to such accommodations, as prescribed by the Seville Presidency Conclusions of 21 and 22 June 2002, being:

(a) in line with the principles on which the EU is founded; and

(b) consistent with the relevant Security Council Resolutions.

CONCLUSION

The length of the Agenda should not be dismissively assessed as pedantic categorisation by "a German professor". The future life of Cypriots, indeed all the structures supporting their political, legal, economic and social forms of organisation, will be affected by any new Plan for a *comprehensive* settlement. Superficial comments by diplomats or anxious politicians, who sometimes over-simplify matters, should not deviate the two Cypriot sides from checking through the issues. They will not start from scratch: they have canvassed most aspects in the last 4 ½ years—indeed in the last 44 years. If "political will," a tired but necessary cliché, is present, the two sides could, in concentrated negotiations, forge an agreement relatively quickly. This, having been thoroughly considered and weighed, would be more durable than any "quick-fix" arrangements made to satisfy third Parties. Foreign Powers are not altruistic; their interests are other-directed; and they seek only to bury the Cyprus problem, and probably Cyprus too, as a factor which has, for too long, been an irritant in their international relations.

APPENDIX 8

VIENNA III AND THE ALLEGED "EXCHANGE OF POPULATIONS AGREEMENT 1975"

An important matter, disputed to this day, was discussed at the Vienna III meetings—in addition to the recurring issues of a loose federation, with appropriate powers and functions, and geographical aspects of a future settlement. Specific arrangements were made about certain important humanitarian issues, some of which were revealed in the Vienna III closing communiqué of 2 August 1975 (annexed to *S/11789*, 5 August 1975). This communiqué is so often relied upon by the Turkish Cypriot side (to assert an agreed general exchange of Greek Cypriot and Turkish Cypriot populations) and by the Greek Cypriot side (to secure proper living conditions for the remaining Greek Cypriots in the Karpas), that it is reproduced in Appendix 9 at pp 343–4 below.

The communiqué is referred to by the Greek Cypriot side and the UN as the "Vienna III humanitarian arrangements," and by the Turkish Cypriot side as the "Exchange of Populations Agreement 1975" (and similar more formal titles, such as the "1975 Vienna Population Exchange (Regrouping of Populations) Agreement)". The latter side's analysis is explained by Mr M Necati Münir Ertekün in his *In Search of a Negotiated Settlement*, ULUS Matbaacilik Ltd, Nicosia, 1981, at pp 38–41 and in his Appendix 31 at pp 275–81. Leaving aside the question of the illegality since 1945 of any State *en masse* overriding individual human rights of return, residence and property, it is submitted that: no such agreement was reached at Vienna (or elsewhere); even the limited arrangements agreed there as respects some persons were made under duress; and subsequent negotiations and Agreements (notably the 1977 and 1979 High Level Agreements) and later UN Resolutions contradict any assumption or interpretation that a general population exchange between Greek and Turkish Cypriot displaced persons or other parts of the respective population groups was agreed at Vienna. This submission is supported by the surrounding circumstances in which the Vienna III arrangements were made and by the UN Minutes (of which Mr Ertekün asserted in 1981 that he was unaware).

The background is that, in pursuance of Turkey's long-standing policy of concentrating all Turkish Cypriots in the northern part of Cyprus and as a result of the tragic events of mid-1974, most Turkish Cypriots had by mid-1975 left for or been moved to the Turkish-occupied area, either in small groups or as individuals, or had been assisted to move on humanitarian grounds (as in the case of those in the SBAs, certain families of released POWs kept by Turkey in the occupied area and others who had suffered). They were permitted to join the bulk of the Turkish Cypriot community. The UN figure of Turkish Cypriots who moved between mid-1974 and September 1977 correlates with the 1973 census figures of Turkish Cypriots in the part of Cyprus which remained under Government control after Turkey's 1974 invasion. UNFICYP's figure was 41,700 by the end of September 1977 (UN General Assembly doc A 32-282, 25 October 1977, para 23). The Turkish Cypriot side claims 65,000 Turkish Cypriots were displaced, but that figure is derived from adding persons who moved in the 1958 and 1963–4 periods. It would be more accurate to say that there were 65,000 *moves* of Turkish Cypriots between 1958–1976 and that, between 1974–1976, 41,700 persons who were Turkish Cypriots *moved*. (Most of those who had moved in the earlier periods had been directed to the area which Turkey would in future occupy—that area having been widely publicised from 1954 onwards—so those who had then moved there did not have to move again following the 1974 events.) Whatever the precise numbers, the lives of very many Turkish Cypriots were seriously disrupted, with some moving twice and a few three times over the whole period. Similar disruption on a greater scale occurred as regards an initial 200,000 Greek Cypriots, although, when cease-fires came into operation, some 20,000 were able to return to their homes in or near the future demilitarised buffer zone (established in December 1976, before which time the area had been referred to as "confrontation areas" or "the areas between the lines"). (Like Turkish Cypriots, some Greek Cypriots had moved in 1958, particularly from Nicosia's Omorphita suburb from whence they were driven, making it a focus for recapture in 1963.)

In the various talks from August 1974 onwards, the Greek Cypriot side's policy was that the general problem of return home of ALL displaced persons should be settled as a whole, and should not be dealt with piecemeal, except in humanitarian cases. The Greek Cypriot side believed that, if the Government agreed to transfer all Turkish Cypriots in the Government-controlled area to the occupied area, this would create a *fait accompli* leading to partition, making more difficult any return home of Greek Cypriots. When the Turkish Cypriot leadership unilaterally proclaimed the "Turkish Federated State of Cyprus" in February 1975, a major step towards partition, the Government of the Republic of Cyprus thereupon halted transfers, except those based on urgent medical reasons. However, its policy of seeking to solve the refugee problem as a whole could not be maintained when, at the Vienna III meetings, Mr Denktash demanded that all remaining Turkish Cypriots be transferred to the occupied area. UN Minutes, kept by the UN, of the meeting on 1 August 1975, record what Mr Denktash said:

> He stated emphatically that it is not his intention to throw the Greek Cypriots out of the north, but that the Turkish side was determined to have the remaining Turks, which according to their figures were 6,000 only in the south, move to the north. He said there were only two alternatives, if the Greek side refused to allow them to proceed north. The first alternative was to force them to do so by expelling the Greeks from the north, beginning with those who have already applied to the Turkish side for transfer to the south. If this measure did not prove effective, then the other alternative was a limited military operation for the rescue of the Turks in the south, which would be a regrettable development because it would cause to both sides loss of human life and heavy damages.

As a result of these threats, the Greek Cypriot Interlocutor, Mr Clerides, indicated willingness to agree that the remaining Turkish Cypriots left in the south should be moved to the occupied area, but he insisted "that he would only be able to accept this if a simultaneous movement of Greek refugees *to the north would commence*" (emphasis added).

The UN's Minutes do not show Mr Denktash as suggesting that the refugee problem had been settled by any "exchange of populations". This was a much later rationalisation. At the Vienna III talks, Mr Denktash accepted that the "refugee" (displaced persons) problem in general had to be dealt with and that this would involve territorial adjustments. Specifically asked if Greek Cypriots could now go back to Famagusta town, if the remaining Turkish Cypriots were allowed to go to the occupied area, the UN Minutes record his answer:

Denktash replied that, although the Turkish side had no intention to keep the Greek sector of the Famagusta town and though the Turkish side realised that it will have to make other territorial concessions, at this point of time, for reasons which it had explained at the previous meetings in Vienna, it could not release territory unless such release was either in the context of a general solution or as a result of the Greek side clearly accepting bi-zonal federation.

In effect, Mr Denktash was insisting on transfer of all remaining Turkish Cypriots to the occupied area, while leaving decisions on return of displaced Greek Cypriots for later discussion in the context of "a general solution". That the "question of displaced persons" was a general issue for discussion, distinct from the specifically agreed matters set out in its points 1–5, is confirmed by the text of the communiqué. An extract from it (the full text being reproduced in Appendix 9) follows.

In addition the following was agreed:

1. The Turkish Cypriots at present in the south of the island will be allowed, if they want to do so, to proceed north with their belongings under an organized programme and with the assistance of the United Nations Peace-keeping Force in Cyprus.
2. Mr Denktash reaffirmed, and it was agreed, that the Greek Cypriots at present in the north of the island are free to stay and that they will be given every help to lead a normal life, including facilities for education and for the practice of their religion, as well as medical care by their own doctors and freedom of movement in the north.
3. The Greek Cypriots at present in the north who, at their own request and without having been subjected to any kind of pressure, wish to move to the south, will be permitted to do so.
4. The United Nations will have free and normal access to Greek Cypriot villages and habitations in the north.
5. In connexion with the implementation of the above agreement, priority will be given to the reunification of families, which may also involve the transfer of a number of Greek Cypriots, at present in the south, to the north.

The question of displaced persons was also re-examined.

The specifically agreed matters had a very specific context and background, namely the general halting by the Government of Cyprus of movement of Turkish Cypriots to the occupied area after the "TFSK" had been declared on 13 February 1975 (the demand to ensure their transfer being reflected in point 1); the need to improve living conditions for Greek Cypriots in the Karpas and Maronite villages (points 2–4); the need to end pressures on remaining Greek Cypriots to leave the occupied area (point 3); and the requirement to reconsider the expulsion of certain categories of Greek Cypriots from the occupied area (point 5). This context is made clear in an unpublished UN minute on what was agreed, and which was sent as a separate note to both sides. The note reads:

CYPRUS NEGOTIATIONS IN VIENNA

Within the context of points 1 to 5 of the Press Communiqué of 2 August 1975 the following was agreed at the closed meeting of 2 August 1975:

The 788 Greek Cypriots who came to the South as a result of the Milikouri (Troodos Range) incident will be free to apply to proceed to the North. Those who will do so, will proceed to the North together with the last group of Turkish Cypriots who will move North.

Those Greek Cypriots who did not apply to go South, but were expelled from the North for security reasons will have their cases re-examined by the Turkish side.

cc: The Secretary-General
Mr. Clerides
Mr. Denktash.

The clarificatory UN note refers to a tragic incident near Milikouri village, where a group of Turkish Cypriots travelling north were intercepted by the Cyprus Police with some of the travellers being assaulted and injured. In response, Turkey expelled 788 persons, including the entire Greek Cypriot population of Dhavlos (270 persons), a beautiful location far away in the Karpas. None of the Dhavlos expellees were permitted to return. Many other Greek Cypriots had also been expelled, apart from the Milikouri "reprisals," allegedly on "security" grounds. The "re-examination" by the Turkish side of all cases, as agreed, resulted in a total of only 346 Greek Cypriots being permitted to return.

Following the Vienna III humanitarian arrangements, the Greek Cypriot side fully co-operated with UNFICYP in moving 8,033 Turkish Cypriots northwards. News reports at the time report the reluctance with which many left their homes, but an admixture of fear lest there be further conflict, community political pressures and the desire and need to rejoin male relatives kept in the Turkish-occupied area, led to nearly all Turkish Cypriots leaving the Government-controlled area under the Vienna arrangements. Only 62 remained by 8 December 1975.

In contrast, the humanitarian undertakings by the Turkish Cypriot side were not properly implemented. General conditions enabling Greek Cypriots in the occupied area to live a normal life (as provided for by point 2 of the Vienna arrangements) were not brought into being: cultivation of land by Greek Cypriots, all dealings with their produce, and freedom of movement were restricted; there was no freedom to communicate and talk with the humanitarian section of UNFICYP and with ICRC delegates; Greek Cypriot doctors or medical personnel were not permitted entry; appointments of replacement priests were not permitted; Greek Cypriot teachers were not approved to staff Greek Cypriot schools; school texts and equipment were not permitted to be brought in; and the secondary school in the Karpas was closed. Thus Greek Cypriot children were forced to leave home to attend schools in the free area. After reaching the age of 16, boys were not permitted to return home, even for holidays. A similar bar was applied to girls aged 18 years. As indicated, only 346 of the expelled Greek Cypriots were permitted to return to their homes in the occupied area. Moreover, Greek Cypriots of Yialousa in the Karpas were effectively expelled in late 1976 to settle Turkish Cypriots moved by the Turkish Army from Kokkina.[1]

The failure of the Turkish Cypriot side to end human rights violations occurring in the occupied area (or to mitigate them by the agreed humanitarian arrangements) was canvassed in *Cyprus v Turkey*, Application No 8007/77, the third Inter-state case brought in 1977 after there had been both new and continuing violations. Despite a *Report* by the

[1] See *S/11900*, 8 December 1975, paras 47–56 and *S/12253*, 9 December 1975, paras 28–40 for the Secretary-General's assessment of the failure of the Turkish Cypriot side to implement the Vienna III humanitarian arrangements.

European Commission of Human Rights on 4 October 1983, confirming the continuing violations, the Committee of Ministers took no action. The UN too virtually ceased reporting on the Karpas situation—presumably on the basis that good offices require silence about other misconduct, even grave violations of human rights, so as not "to spoil the atmosphere" for negotiations.

Only when a new UNFICYP Chief Humanitarian Officer from Austria, Lieutenant Colonel Rainer Manzl, ordered a study in 1994 of the situation did independent evidence about violations become available—although the UN tried to stop Colonel Manzl and his aide, Captain Antony O'Sullivan of the Irish defence force, from testifying to the Commission. The Secretariat also sought to prevent reliance by the European Commission of Human Rights on UN documents (such as *The Karpas Brief* prepared by the above-mentioned UNFICYP personnel) which had been leaked into the public domain. A fourth Inter-state case, initiated at the end of 1994, led to the Commission, in it last historic case, holding on 4 June 1999 that as regards Greek Cypriots living in the Karpas area there had been and still were: violations of Article 3 of the Convention by subjecting them to discrimination amounting to degrading treatment; violations of Article 9 by unjustifiable interferences with their religious life; violations of Article 10 by excessive censorship of schoolbooks; violations of Article 1 of Protocol No 1 by violating their rights to peaceful enjoyment of their possessions by preventing transmission upon death or lifetime transfer of their homes and property to their children (so the population would wither away); violations of Article 2 of Protocol No 1 by denial of appropriate secondary school facilities; violations of Article 8 by failure to respect their private and family life and home; and violations of Article 13 by reason of failure to provide effective remedies. These findings were confirmed two years later in the Court's judgment, dated 10 May 2001, as still continuing. That judgment was reached despite some limited improvements made by Turkey's subordinate local administration towards the very end of the case. As at the date of writing, although some important improvements in the Karpas Greek Cypriots' living conditions have since been made, the Committee of Ministers, charged with supervising the execution of the Court's judgment, has not yet ensured that the Court's implicit order to cease the proven human violations continuing since 1974 has been fully implemented.

So far as concerns the justification of the alleged "Exchange of Populations Agreement 1975," which was raised by Turkey (and rebutted by Cyprus), both the former European Commission of Human Rights and the European Court of Human Rights, held that, in refusing to allow the return of Greek Cypriot displaced persons to their homes in northern Cyprus, Article 8 of the Convention had been violated. The absence of justification, either by way of a global solution as regards return of properties or displaced persons, was put very clearly in the Commission's *Report*:

> 320. As regards the justifications which the respondent Government now invoke, they are not essentially different from those advanced in the *Loizidou* case. In particular, the Commission does not consider that the detailed explanations given by the respondent Government as to the necessity to satisfy the housing needs of displaced Turkish Cypriots and to consolidate the Turkish Cypriot economy justify a departure from the Court's above conclusions. Even if these were legitimate aims of public policy, the means employed to achieve them are disproportionate to those aims and no fair balance has been struck between the public interest and the individuals' fundamental rights when the latter are being denied any rights at all. By this denial

the authorities have overstepped the margin of appreciation which the Convention allows them.

321. Nor does the fact that a global solution to the Cyprus question, including the compensation of property owners on both sides and a possible return of some of them, is being sought in the framework of the inter-communal talks justify such total denial of rights in the meantime. The inter-communal talks have now gone on for decades without producing any tangible results, although they should be the instrument for putting an end to the human rights violations occurring in Cyprus. As long as this aim has not been achieved, the Commission cannot refrain from denouncing the said violations if they continue.

Apart from these judicial findings, including the finding by the Court (at para 174 of its judgment) that the intercommunal talks cannot be invoked to legitimate a violation of the Convention, the practice of both sides has been to continue to discuss in those talks (as early as the Vienna V meetings in February 1976, just six months after Vienna III) the question of return of displaced persons. In particular, at the intercommunal meetings resulting in the two High Level Agreements, the sides accepted that the displaced persons problem still required resolution. The third Guideline in the 12 February 1977 Agreement stipulated that:

Questions of principles like freedom of movement, freedom of settlement, the right of property and other specific matters are open for discussion taking into consideration the fundamental basis of a bi-communal federal system and certain practical difficulties which may arise for the Turkish Cypriot community.

In the later Ten Point Agreement of 19 May 1979, the 12 February 1977 Makarios-Denktash Guidelines and UN Resolutions were reaffirmed as the basis for talks. The latter included SCR 361 (1974) of 30 August 1974, urging the parties to search for peaceful solutions to the problems of refugees and to permit persons who wish to do so to return to their homes in safety, while SCR 367 (1975) endorsed GA Resolution 3212 (XXIXI), calling upon the parties concerned urgently and effectively to implement all parts of the GA Resolution. This had considered "all the refugees should return to their homes in safety" and had called upon the parties "to undertake urgent measures to that end". Significantly, the Ten Point Agreement also provided that

3. There shall be respect for human rights and fundamental freedoms of all citizens of the Republic.

The High Level Agreements were repeatedly endorsed by UN Resolutions. Indeed, the Resolution under which Secretary-General currently operates Cyprus good offices (SCR 1250 (1999) 26 June 1999—see Appendix 9) reaffirms all the Security Council's earlier Resolutions on Cyprus, including at least 13 earlier Resolutions endorsing the High Level Agreements, among then important framework Resolutions such as SCR 649 (1990) and SCR 774 (1992), both of which were secured by President George Bush senior's administration. Since the Agreements and the cited Resolutions provide the framework for a Cyprus settlement, they are reproduced in Appendix 9.

Reverting to the question of population movements in Cyprus, it is submitted that, apart from processes of urbanisation (with rural dwellers leaving small villages—no schooling, social life, facilities etc—which movements occurred in Cyprus just as they have in all societies which were earlier largely agricultural) population movements in

Cyprus between 1958 and 1976 were not genuinely voluntary. The Turkish Cypriot population moves to some degree involved individuals desirous of congregating as larger groups and as an entire Community. But this phenomenon, initially provoked by fears of continued inter-communal violence, was magnified by over-persuasion and intimidation by the Turkish Cypriot political leadership and the TMT, which forcibly prevented the return of most Turkish Cypriots to their homes, keeping them in enclaves, a point repeatedly made in a series of Secretary-General's *Reports*. In mid-1974 fears of renewed hostilities and possible inter-communal atrocities, as well as intense political pressure by the Turkish Cypriot political leadership and pressures for family reunion—otherwise denied—led to more Turkish Cypriot departures. Equally, so far as concerns Greek Cypriots, fears of Turkish Army atrocities, or expulsion by the Turkish Army or subjection to degrading, oppressive and discriminatory treatment, caused their flight or departure from the Turkish-occupied area. Any action agreed at Vienna was pursuant to threats of the further use of force by Turkey. None of this can be regarded as a "voluntary exchange of populations," as it has been and is today portrayed by the Turkish Cypriot side. The issue of displaced persons still requires settlement in accordance with international and human rights law.

APPENDIX 9

List of items:

1. Security Council Resolution 186 (1964) 4 March 1964.
2. Security Council Resolution 367 (1975) 12 March 1975.
3. Security Council Resolution 541 (1983) 18 November 1983.
4. Security Council Resolution 550 (1984) 11 May 1984.
5. Security Council Resolution 649 (1990) 12 March 1990.
6. Security Council Resolution 774 (1992) 26 August 1992.
7. Security Council Resolution 1250 (1999) 26 June 1999.
8. General Assembly Resolution 3212 (XXIX) 1 November 1974.
9. General Assembly Resolution 3395 (XXX) 20 November 1975.
10. Geneva Declaration of July 1974 on Cyprus, 30 July 1974.
11. Press Communiqué on the Cyprus Talks issued in Vienna on 2 August 1975.
12. High-Level Agreement of 12 February 1977.
13. Ten Point Agreement of 19 May 1979.
14. Letter, Secretary-General of the United Nations to His Excellency, Mr Tassos Papadopoulos, 4 February 2004.
15. Statement Attributable to the Spokesman of the Secretary-General 13 February 2004.

1. The Cyprus Question
Resolution 186 (1964)[1]
4 March 1964

The Security Council,

Noting that the present situation with regard to Cyprus is likely to threaten international peace and security and may further deteriorate unless additional measures are promptly taken to maintain peace and to seek out a durable solution,

Considering the positions taken by the parties in relation to the Treaties signed at Nicosia on 16 August 1960,[2]

Having in mind the relevant provisions of the Charter of the United Nations and its Article 2, paragraph 4, which reads: "All Members shall refrain in their international relations from the threat or use of force against the territorial integrity or political independence of any State, or in any other manner inconsistent with the purposes of the United Nations",

1. Calls upon all Member States, in conformity with their obligations under the Charter of the United Nations, to refrain from any action or threat of action to worsen the situation in the sovereign Republic of Cyprus, or to endanger international peace;
2. Asks the Government of Cyprus, which has the responsibility for the maintenance and restoration of law and order, to take all additional measures necessary to stop violence and bloodshed in Cyprus;

[1] Security Council, Resolutions 1946–1964, Resolutions 1–199, New York, 1966, pp 2–4.

[2] United Nations, Treaty Series, vol 382 (1960), Treaty of Guarantee, No 5475 and Treaty Concerning the Establishment of the Republic of Cyprus No 5476. *Ibid*, vol 397 (1961) Treaty of Alliance between the Kingdom of Greece, the Republic of Turkey and the Republic of Cyprus, No 5712.

3. Calls upon the communities in Cyprus and their leaders to act with the utmost restraint;
4. Recommends the creation, with the consent of the Government of Cyprus, of a United Nations Peace-keeping Force in Cyprus. The composition and size of the Force shall be established by the Secretary-General, in consultation with the Governments of Cyprus, Greece, Turkey and the United Kingdom of Great Britain and Northern Ireland. The Commander of the Force shall be appointed by the Secretary-General and report to him. The Secretary-General, who shall keep the Governments providing the Force fully informed, shall report periodically to the Security Council on its operation;
5. Recommends that the function of the Force should be in the interest of preserving international peace and security, to use its best efforts to prevent a recurrence of fighting and, as necessary, to contribute to the maintenance and restoration of law and order and a return to normal conditions;
6. Recommends that the stationing of the Force shall be for a period of three months, all costs pertaining to it being met, in a manner to be agreed upon by them, by the Governments providing the contingents and by the Government of Cyprus. The Secretary-General may also accept voluntary contributions for the purpose;
7. Recommends further that the Secretary-General designate, in agreement with the Government of Cyprus and the Governments of Greece, Turkey and United Kingdom, a mediator, who shall use his best endeavours with the representatives of the communities and also with the aforesaid four Governments, for the purpose of promoting a peaceful solution and an agreed settlement of the problem confronting Cyprus, in accordance with the Charter of the United Nations, having in mind the well-being of the people as a whole and the preservation of international peace and security. The mediator shall report periodically to the Secretary-General on his efforts;
8. Requests the Secretary-General to provide, from funds of the United Nations, as appropriate, for the remuneration and expenses of the mediator and his staff.

Adopted unanimously at the 1102nd meeting.

2. The situation in Cyprus
Resolution 367 (1975)[3]
12 March 1975

The Security Council,

Having considered the situation in Cyprus in response to the complaint submitted by the Government of the Republic of Cyprus,

Having heard the report of the Secretary-General[4] and the statements made by the parties concerned,

Deeply concerned at the continuation of the crisis in Cyprus,

[3] Resolutions and Decisions of the Security Council, 1975, Official Records, Thirtieth Year, New York, 1976, pp 1–2.

[4] Official Records of the Security Council, Thirtieth Year, Supplement for January, February and March 1975, 1814th meeting, "Report of the Secretary General on the situation in Cyprus", 20–23 February 1975.

Recalling its previous resolutions, in particular resolution 365 (1974) of 13 December 1974 by which it endorsed General Assembly resolution 3212 (XXIX) adopted unanimously on 1 November 1974,

Noting the absence of progress towards the implementation of its resolutions,

1. Calls once more on all States to respect the sovereignty, independence, territorial integrity and non-alignment of the Republic of Cyprus and urgently requests them, as well as the parties concerned, to refrain from any action which might prejudice that sovereignty, independence, territorial integrity and non-alignment, as well as from any attempt at partition of the island or its unification with any other country;
2. Regrets the unilateral decision of 13 February 1975 declaring that a part of the Republic of Cyprus would become a "Federated Turkish State", as, inter alia, tending to compromise the continuation of negotiations between the representatives of the two communities on an equal footing, the objective of which must continue to be to reach freely a solution providing for a political settlement and the establishment of a mutually acceptable constitutional arrangement, and expresses its concern over all unilateral actions by the parties which have compromised or may compromise the implementation of the relevant United Nations resolutions;
3. Affirms that the decision referred to in paragraph 2 above does not prejudge the final political settlement of the problem of Cyprus and takes note of the declaration that this was not its intention;
4. Calls for the urgent and effective implementation of all parts and provisions of General Assembly resolution 3212 (XXIX), endorsed by Security Council resolution 365 (1974);
5. Considers that new efforts should be undertaken to assist the resumption of the negotiations referred to in paragraph 4 of resolution 3212 (XXIX) between the representatives of the two communities;
6. Requests the Secretary-General accordingly to undertake a new mission of good offices and to that end to convene the parties under new agreed procedures and place himself personally at their disposal, so that the resumption, the intensification and the progress of comprehensive negotiations, carried out in a reciprocal spirit of understanding and of moderation under his personal auspices and with his direction as appropriate, might thereby be facilitated;
7. Calls upon the representatives of the two communities to co-operate closely with the Secretary-General in the discharge of this new mission of good offices and asks them to accord personally a high priority to their negotiations;
8. Calls upon all the parties concerned to refrain from any action which might jeopardise the negotiations between the representatives of the two communities and to take steps which will facilitate the creation of the climate necessary for the success of those negotiations;
9. Requests the Secretary-General to keep the Security Council informed of the progress made towards the implementation of resolution 365 (1974) and of the present resolution and to report to it whenever he considered it appropriate and, in any case, before 15 June 1975;
10. Decides to remain actively seized of the matter.

Adopted at the 1820th meeting without a vote.

3. The situation in Cyprus
Resolution 541 (1983)[5]
18 November 1983

The Security Council,

Having heard the statement of the Foreign Minister of the Government of the Republic of Cyprus,[6]

Concerned at the declaration by the Turkish Cypriot authorities issued on 15 November 1983[7] which purports to create an independent state in northern Cyprus,

Considering that this declaration is incompatible with the 1960 Treaty concerning the establishment of the Republic of Cyprus[8] and the 1960 Treaty of Guarantee,[9]

Considering, therefore, that the attempt to create a "Turkish Republic of Northern Cyprus", is invalid, and will contribute to a worsening of the situation in Cyprus,

Reaffirming its resolutions 365 (1974) and 367 (1975),

Aware of the need for a solution of the Cyprus problem, based on the mission of good offices undertaken by the Secretary-General,

Affirming its continuing support for the United Nations Peace-keeping Force in Cyprus,

Taking note of the Secretary-General's statement of 17 November 1983,[10]

1. Deplores the declaration of the Turkish Cypriot authorities of the purported secession of part of the Republic of Cyprus;
2. Considers the declaration referred to above as legally invalid and calls for its withdrawal;
3. Calls for the urgent and effective implementation of its resolutions 365 (1974) and 367 (1975);
4. Requests the Secretary-General to pursue his mission of good offices, in order to achieve the earliest possible progress towards a just and lasting settlement in Cyprus;
5. Calls upon the parties to co-operate fully with the Secretary-General in his mission of good offices;
6. Calls upon all States to respect the sovereignty, independence, territorial integrity and non-alignment of the Republic of Cyprus;
7. Calls upon all States not to recognise any Cypriot state other than the Republic of Cyprus;
8. Calls upon all States and the two communities in Cyprus to refrain from any action which might exacerbate the situation;
9. Requests the Secretary-General to keep the Security Council fully informed.

Adopted at the 2500th meeting by 13 votes to 1 against (Pakistan), with 1 abstention (Jordan).

[5] Resolutions and Decisions of the Security Council, 1983, Official Records, Thirty-eighth Year, New York, 1984, pp 15–16.

[6] Official Records of the Security Council, Thirty-eighth Year, 2497th meeting, 17 November 1983, New York, 1992, pp 3–11.

[7] Resolutions and Decisions of the Security Council, 1983, Official Records, Thirty-eighth Year, Supplement for October, November and December 1983, Letter dated 15 November 1983 from the Representative of Turkey to the Secretary-General, document S/16148, Annex, pp 91–96.

[8] United Nations, Treaty Series, vol 382 (1960), Treaty Concerning the Establishment of the Republic of Cyprus, No 5476.

[9] Ibid., Treaty of Guarantee, No 5475.

[10] Official Records of the Security Council, Thirty-eighth Year, 2497th meeting, 17 November 1983, New York, 1984, pp 2–3.

4. The situation in Cyprus
Resolution 550 (1984)[11]
11 May 1984

The Security Council,

Having considered the situation in Cyprus at the request of the Government of the Republic of Cyprus,

Having heard the statement made by the President of the Republic of Cyprus,[12]

Taking note of the report of the Secretary-General,[13]

Recalling its resolutions 365 (1974), 367 (1975), 541 (1983) and 544 (1983),

Deeply regretting the non-implementation of its resolutions, in particular resolution 541 (1983),

Gravely concerned about the further secessionist acts in the occupied part of the Republic of Cyprus which are in violation of resolution 541 (1983), namely the purported exchange of Ambassadors between Turkey and the legally invalid "Turkish Republic of Northern Cyprus" and the contemplated holding of a "constitutional referendum" and "elections", as well as by other actions or threats of actions aimed at further consolidating the purported independent state and the division of Cyprus,

Deeply concerned about recent threats for settlement of Varosha by people other than its inhabitants,

Reaffirming its continuing support for the United Nations Peace-keeping Force in Cyprus,

1. Reaffirms its resolution 541 (1983) and calls for its urgent and effective implementation;
2. Condemns all secessionist actions, including the purported exchange of Ambassadors between Turkey and the Turkish Cypriot leadership, declares them illegal and invalid and calls for their immediate withdrawal;
3. Reiterates the call upon all States not to recognise the purported state of the "Turkish Republic of Northern Cyprus" set up by secessionist acts and calls upon them not to facilitate or in any way assist the aforesaid secessionist entity;
4. Calls upon all States to respect the sovereignty, independence, territorial integrity, unity and non-alignment of the Republic of Cyprus;
5. Considers attempts to settle any part of Varosha by people other than its inhabitants as inadmissible and calls for the transfer of this area to the administration of the United Nations;
6. Considers any attempts to interfere with the status or the deployment of the United Nations Peace-keeping Force in Cyprus as contrary to the resolutions of the United Nations;
7. Requests the Secretary-General to promote the urgent implementation of Security Council resolution 541 (1983);
8. Reaffirms its mandate of good offices given to the Secretary-General and requests him to undertake new efforts to attain an overall solution to the Cyprus problem in conformity with the principles of the Charter of the United Nations and the provisions for

[11] Resolutions and Decisions of the Security Council, 1984, Official Records, Thirty-ninth Year, New York, 1985, pp 12–13.

[12] Official Records of the Security Council, Thirty-ninth Year, 2531st meeting, New York, 1993, pp 1–5.

[13] *Ibid*, Thirty-ninth Year, Supplement for April, May and June 1984, "Report by the Secretary-General in pursuance of paragraph 2 of Resolution 544 (1983)", 1 May 1984, document S/16519.

such a settlement laid down in the pertinent United Nations resolutions, including resolution 541 (1983) and the present resolution;
9. Calls upon all parties to co-operate with the Secretary-General in his mission of good offices;
10. Decides to remain seized of the situation with a view to taking urgent and appropriate measures in the event of non-implementation of resolution 541 (1983) and the present resolution;
11. Requests the Secretary-General to promote the implementation of the present resolution and to report thereon to the Security Council as developments require.

Adopted at the 2539th meeting by 13 votes to 1 (Pakistan) with 1 abstention (United States of America).

5. The situation in Cyprus
Resolution 649 (1990)[14]
12 March 1990

The Security Council,

Having considered the report of the Secretary-General of 8 March 1990[15] on the recent meeting between the leaders of the two communities in Cyprus and on his assessment of the current situation,

Recalling its relevant resolutions on Cyprus,

Recalling also the statement made by the President of the Security Council on 22 February 1990[16]calling upon the leaders of the two communities to demonstrate the necessary goodwill and flexibility and to co-operate with the Secretary-General so that the talks will result in a major step forward toward the resolution of the Cyprus problem,

Concerned that at the recent meeting in New York it has not been possible to achieve results in arriving at an agreed outline of an overall agreement,

1. Reaffirms in particular its resolution 367 (1975) of 12 March 1975 as well as its support for the 1977[17] and 1979[18] high-level agreements between the leaders of the two communities in which they pledged themselves to establish a bi-communal Federal Republic of Cyprus that will safeguard its independence, sovereignty, territorial integrity and non-alignment, and exclude union in whole or in part with any other country and any form of partition or secession;
2. Expresses its full support for the current effort of the Secretary-General in carrying out his mission of good offices concerning Cyprus;
3. Calls upon the leaders of the two communities to pursue their efforts to reach freely a mutually acceptable solution providing for the establishment of a federation that will be bi-communal as regards the constitutional aspects and bi-zonal as regards the

[14] Resolutions and Decisions of the Security Council, 1990, Official Records, Forty-fifth Year, New York, 1991, p 10.

[15] Official Records of the Security Council, Forty-fourth Year, Supplement for January, February and March 1988, "Report of the Secretary-General on his mission of good offices in Cyprus", 8 March 1988, document S/21183.

[16] *Ibid*, "Statement made by the President of the Security Council", 22 February 1990, document S/21160.

[17] *Ibid*, Thirty-second Year, Supplement for April, May and June 1977, document S/12323.

[18] *Ibid*, Thirty-fourth Year, Supplement for April, May and June 1979, document S/13369, para 51.

territorial aspects, in line with the present resolution and their 1977 and 1979 high-level agreements, and to co-operate, on an equal footing, with the Secretary-General in completing, in the first instance and on an urgent basis, an outline of an overall agreement, as agreed in June 1989;

4. Requests the Secretary-General to pursue his mission of good offices in order to achieve the earliest possible progress and, towards this end, to assist the two communities by making suggestions to facilitate the discussions;
5. Calls upon the parties concerned to refrain from any action that could aggravate the situation;
6. Decides to remain actively seized of this situation and the current effort;
7. Requests the Secretary-General to inform the Council in his report due by 31 May 1990, of the progress made in resuming the intensive talks and in developing an agreed outline of an overall agreement in line with the present resolution.

Adopted unanimously at the 2909th meeting.

6. The situation in Cyprus
Resolution 774 (1992)[19]
26 August 1992

The Security Council,

Having considered the report of the Secretary-General of 21 August 1992 on his mission of good offices in Cyprus,[20]

Reaffirming all its previous resolutions on Cyprus,

Noting that some progress has been achieved, in particular the acceptance by both sides of the right of return and the right to property, and in a narrowing of the gap by both sides on territorial adjustments,

Expressing concern nevertheless that it has not yet been possible, for reasons explained in the report, to achieve the goals set out in resolution 750 (1992),

1. Endorses the report of the Secretary-General of 21 August 1992 and commends him for his efforts;
2. Reaffirms its position that a Cyprus settlement must be based on a State of Cyprus with a single sovereignty and international personality and a single citizenship, with its independence and territorial integrity safeguarded, and comprising two politically equal communities as defined in paragraph 11 of the Secretary-General's report of 3 April 1992[21] in a bi-communal and bi-zonal federation, and that such a settlement must exclude union in whole or in part with any other country or any form of partition or secession;
3. Endorses the Set of Ideas including suggested territorial adjustments reflected in the map contained in the annex to the Secretary-General's report as the basis for reaching an overall framework agreement;

[19] Resolutions and Decisions of the Security Council, 1992, Official Records, Forty-seventh Year, New York, 1993, p 94.

[20] Ibid., Forty-seventh Year, Supplement for July, August and September 1992, "Report of the Secretary-General on his mission of good offices in Cyprus", 21 August 1992, document S/24472.

[21] *Ibid*, Supplement for April, May and June 1992, "Report of the Secretary-General on his mission of good offices in Cyprus", 3 April 1992, document S/23780.

4. *Agrees* with the Secretary-General that the Set of Ideas as an integrated whole has now been sufficiently developed to enable the two sides to reach an overall agreement;
5. *Calls on* the parties to manifest the necessary political will and to address in a positive manner the observations of the Secretary-General for resolving the issues covered in his report;
6. *Urges* the parties, when they resume their face-to-face talks with the Secretary-General on 26 October 1992, to pursue uninterrupted negotiations at United Nations Headquarters in New York until an overall framework agreement is reached on the basis of the entire Set of Ideas;
7. *Reaffirms* its position that the Secretary-General should convene, following the satisfactory conclusion of the face-to-face talks, a high-level international meeting chaired by him to conclude an overall framework agreement, in which the two communities and Greece and Turkey would participate;
8. *Requests* all concerned to co-operate fully with the Secretary-General and his representatives in preparing the ground prior to the resumption of the direct talks in October to facilitate the speedy completion of the work;
9. *Expresses* the expectation that an overall framework agreement will be concluded in 1992 and that 1993 will be the transitional period during which the measures set out in the appendix to the Set of Ideas will be implemented;
10. *Reaffirms* that, in line with previous resolutions of the Security Council, the present status quo is not acceptable, and, should an agreement not emerge from the talks that will reconvene in October, calls on the Secretary-General to identify the reasons for the failure and to recommend to the Council alternative courses of action to resolve the Cyprus problem;
11. *Requests* the Secretary-General to submit, prior to the end of 1992, a full report on the talks that will resume in October.

Adopted unanimously at the 3109th meeting.

7. The situation in Cyprus
Resolution 1250 (1999)[22]
29 June 1999

The Security Council,

Reaffirming all its earlier resolutions on Cyprus, particularly resolution 1218 (1998) of 22 December 1998,

Reiterating its grave concern at the lack of progress towards an overall political settlement on Cyprus,

Appreciating the statement of the Heads of State and Government of Canada, France, Germany, Italy, Japan, the Russian Federation, the United Kingdom of Great Britain and Northern Ireland and the United States of America on 20 June 1999 calling for comprehensive negotiations in the autumn of 1999 under the auspices of the Secretary-General,[23]

[22] Resolutions and Decisions of the Security Council, 1999, Official Records, Fifty-fourth Year, New York, 2001, p 137.

[23] *Ibid*, Fifty-fourth Year, Supplement for April, May and June 1999, "Statement of the Heads of State and Government of Canada, France, Germany, Italy, Japan, the Russian Federation, the United Kingdom of Great Britain and Northern Ireland and the United States of America", 20 June 1999, document S/1999/711, Annex.

1. Expresses its appreciation for the report of the Secretary-General of 22 June 1999 on his mission of good offices in Cyprus;[24]
2. Stresses its full support for the Secretary-General's mission of good offices as decided by the Security Council and, in this context, for the efforts of the Secretary-General and his Special Representative;
3. Reiterates its endorsement of the initiative of the Secretary- General announced on 30 September 1998, within the framework of his mission of good offices, with the goal of reducing tensions and promoting progress towards a just and lasting settlement in Cyprus;
4. Notes that the discussions between the Special Representative of the Secretary-General and the two sides are continuing, and urges both sides to participate constructively;
5. Expresses the view that both sides have legitimate concerns that should be addressed through comprehensive negotiations covering all relevant issues;
6. Requests the Secretary-General, in accordance with the relevant Security Council resolutions, to invite the leaders of the two sides to negotiations in the autumn of 1999;
7. Calls upon the two leaders, in this context, to give their full support to such a comprehensive negotiation, under the auspices of the Secretary-General, and to commit themselves to the following principles:
   - No preconditions;
   - All issues on the table;
   - Commitment in good faith to continue to negotiate until a settlement is reached;
   - Full consideration of relevant United Nations resolutions and treaties;
8. Requests the two sides in Cyprus, including military authorities on both sides, to work constructively with the Secretary-General and his Special Representative to create a positive climate on the island that will pave the way for negotiations in the autumn of 1999;
9. Requests the Secretary-General to keep the Security Council informed of progress towards the implementation of this resolution and to submit a report to the Council by 1 December 1999;
10. Decides to remain actively seized of the matter.

Adopted unanimously at the 4018th meeting.

8. The Question of Cyprus
Resolution 3212 (XXIX)[25]
1 November 1974

The General Assembly,

Having considered the question of Cyprus,

Gravely concerned about the continuation of the Cyprus crisis, which constitutes a threat tointernational peace and security,

[24] *Ibid*, "Report of the Secretary-General on his mission of good offices in Cyprus", 22 June 1999, document S/1999/707.

[25] General Assembly, Resolutions, Sessions 27–30, 1972–1975, General Assembly Official Records, Twenty-ninth Session, Supplement No 31 (A/9631), New York, 1975, p 3.

Mindful of the need to solve this crisis without delay by peaceful means, in accordance with the purposes and principles of the United Nations,

Having heard the statements in the debate and taking note of the Report of the Special Political Committee on the question of Cyprus,[26]

1. Calls upon all States to respect the sovereignty, independence, territorial integrity and non-alignment of the Republic of Cyprus and to refrain from all acts and interventions directed against it;
2. Urges the speedy withdrawal of all foreign armed forces and foreign military presence and personnel from the Republic of Cyprus and the cessation of all foreign interference in its affairs;
3. Considers that the constitutional system of the Republic of Cyprus concerns the Greek-Cypriot and Turkish-Cypriot communities;
4. Commends the contacts and negotiations taking place on an equal footing, with the good offices of the Secretary-General between the representatives of the two communities, and calls for their continuation with a view to reaching freely a mutually acceptable political settlement, based on their fundamental and legitimate rights;
5. Considers that all the refugees should return to their homes in safety and calls upon the parties concerned to undertake urgent measures to that end;
6. Expresses the hope that, if necessary, further efforts including negotiations can take place, within the framework of the United Nations, for the purpose of implementing the provisions of the present resolution, thus ensuring to the Republic of Cyprus its fundamental right to independence, sovereignty and territorial integrity;
7. Requests the Secretary-General to continue to provide United Nations humanitarian assistance to all parts of the population of Cyprus and calls upon all states to contribute to that effort;
8. Calls upon all parties to continue to co-operate fully with the United Nations Peace-keeping Force in Cyprus, which may be strengthened if necessary;
9. Requests the Secretary-General to continue to lend his good offices to the parties concerned;
10. Further requests the Secretary-General to bring the present resolution to the attention of the Security Council.

2275th plenary meeting

[Adopted by 117 votes in favour, none against and no abstentions]

9. The Question of Cyprus
Resolution 3395 (XXX)[27]
20 November 1975

The General Assembly,

Having considered the question of Cyprus,

Having heard the statements in the debate and taking note of the report of the Special Political Committee,[28]

[26] *Ibid*, Twenty-ninth Session, Annexes, agenda item 110, document A/9820.

[27] General Assembly, Resolutions, Sessions 27–30, 1972–1975, General Assembly Official Records, Thirtieth Session, Supplement No 34 (A/10034), New York, 1976, p 5.

[28] *Ibid*, Annexes, agenda item 125, document A/10352.

Noting with concern that four rounds of talks between the representatives of the two communities in pursuance of Security Council resolution 367 (1975) of 12 March 1975 have not yet led to a mutually acceptable settlement,

Deeply concerned at the continuation of the crisis in Cyprus,

Mindful of the need to solve the Cyprus crisis without further delay by peaceful means, in accordance with the purposes and principles of the United Nations,

1. Reaffirms the urgent need for continued efforts for the effective implementation in all parts of its resolution 3212 (XXIX) of 1 November 1974 endorsed by the Security Council in its resolution 365 (1974) of 13 December 1974 and to that end;
2. Calls once again upon all States to respect the sovereignty, independence, territorial integrity and non-alignment of the Republic of Cyprus and to refrain from all acts and interventions directed against it;
3. Demands the withdrawal without further delay of all foreign armed forces and foreign military presence and personnel from the Republic of Cyprus, and the cessation of all foreign interference in its affairs;
4. Calls upon the parties concerned to undertake urgent measures to facilitate the voluntary return of all refugees to their homes in safety and to settle all other aspects of the refugee problem;
5. Calls for the immediate resumption in a meaningful and constructive manner of the negotiations between the representatives of the two communities under the auspices of the Secretary-General to be conducted freely on an equal footing with a view to reaching a mutually acceptable agreement based on their fundamental and legitimate rights;
6. Urges all parties to refrain from unilateral actions in contravention of its resolution 3212 (XXIX), including changes in the demographic structure of Cyprus;
7. Requests the Secretary-General to continue his role in the negotiations between the representatives of the two communities;
8. Also requests the Secretary-General to bring this resolution to the attention of the Security Council and to report on its implementations, as soon as appropriate and not later than 31 March, 1976;
9. Calls upon all parties to continue to co-operate fully with the United Nations Peacekeeping Force in Cyprus;
10. Decides to remain seized of this question.

2413th plenary meeting

[Adopted by 117 votes in favour, one against (Turkey) and 9 abstentions]

10. Geneva Declaration of 30 July 1974
(source *S/11398*, 30 July 1974)

DECLARATION BY THE FOREIGN MINISTERS OF GREECE, TURKEY AND THE UNITED KINGDOM OF GREAT BRITAIN AND NORTHERN IRELAND

1. The Foreign Ministers of Greece, Turkey and the United Kingdom of Great Britain and Northern Ireland held discussions in Geneva from 25 to 30 July 1974. They recognized the importance of setting in train, as a matter of urgency, measures to adjust and to regularize within a reasonable period of time the situation in the Republic of Cyprus on a lasting basis, having regard to the international agreements signed at Nicosia on 16 August 1960 and to resolution 353 (1974) of the Security Council. They were, however, agreed on the need to decide first on certain immediate measures.

2. The three Foreign Ministers declared that in order to stabilize the situation, the areas in the Republic of Cyprus controlled by opposing armed forces on 30 July 1974 at 2200 hours (Geneva time) should not be extended; they called on all forces, including irregular forces, to desist from all offensive or hostile activities.
3. The three Foreign Ministers also concluded that the following measures should be put into immediate effect:
   (a) A security zone of size to be determined by representatives of Greece, Turkey and the United Kingdom in consultation with the United Nations Peace-keeping Force in Cyprus (UNFICYP) should be established at the limit of the areas occupied by the Turkish armed forces at the time specified in paragraph 2 above. This zone should be entered by no forces other than those of UNFICYP, which should supervise the prohibition of entry. Pending the determination of the size and character of the security zone, the existing area between the two forces should be entered by no forces.
   (b) All the Turkish enclaves occupied by Greek or Greek-Cypriot forces should be immediately evacuated. These enclaves will continue to be protected by UNFICYP and to have their previous security arrangements. Other Turkish enclaves outside the area controlled by the Turkish armed forces shall continue to be protected by an UNFICYP security zone and may as before, maintain their own police and security forces.
   (c) In mixed villages the functions of security and police will be carried out by UNFICYP.
   (d) Military personnel and civilians detained as a result of the recent hostilities shall be either exchanged or released under the supervision of the International Committee of the Red Cross within the shortest time possible.
4. The three Foreign Ministers, reaffirming that resolution 353 (1974) of the Security Council should be implemented in the shortest possible time, agreed that, within the framework of a just and lasting solution acceptable to all the parties concerned and as peace, security and mutual confidence are established in the island, measures should be elaborated which will lead to the timely and phased reduction of the number of armed forces and the amounts of armaments, munitions and other war material in the Republic of Cyprus.
5. Deeply conscious of their responsibilities as regards the maintenance of the independence, territorial integrity and security of the Republic of Cyprus, the three Foreign Ministers agreed that negotiations, as provided for in resolution 353 (1974) of the Security Council, should be carried on with the least possible delay to secure the restoration of peace in the area and the re-establishment of constitutional government in Cyprus. To this end they agreed that further talks should begin on 8 August 1974 at Geneva. They also agreed that representative *[sic]* of the Greek Cypriot and Turkish Cypriot communities should, at an early stage, be invited to participate in the talks relating to the constitution. Among the constitutional questions to be discussed should be that of an immediate return to constitutional legitimacy, the Vice-President assuming the functions provided for under the 1960 Constitution. The Ministers noted the existence in practice in the Republic of Cyprus of two autonomous administrations, that of the Greek Cypriot community and that of the Turkish Cypriot community. Without any prejudice to the conclusions to be drawn from this situation, the Ministers agreed to consider the problems raised by their existence at their next meeting.

6. The three Foreign Ministers agreed to convey the contents of this Declaration to the Secretary-General of the United Nations and to invite him to take appropriate action in the light of it. They also expressed their conviction of the necessity that the fullest co-operation should be extended by all concerned in the Republic of Cyprus in carrying out its terms.

STATEMENT BY THE FOREIGN MINISTERS OF GREECE, TURKEY AND THE UNITED KINGDOM OF GREAT BRITAIN AND NORTHERN IRELAND

The Foreign Ministers of Greece, Turkey and the United Kingdom of Great Britain and Northern Ireland made it clear that the adherence of their Governments to the Declaration of today's date in no way prejudiced their respective views on the interpretation or application of the 1960 Treaty of Guarantee or their rights and obligations under that Treaty.

Done in duplicate at Geneva the 30th day of July, 1974, in the English and French languages, both texts being equally authoritative.

(signed) George MAVROS
Minister of Foreign Affairs of Greece

(signed) Turan GÜNEŞ
Minister of Foreign Affairs of Turkey

(Signed) James CALLAGHAN
Secretary of State for Foreign and Commonwealth Affairs of the United Kingdom of Great Britain and Northern Ireland

11. *S/11789*, 5 August 1975, Annex. Text of the press communiqué on the Cyprus talks issued in Vienna on 2 August 1975

The third round of talks on Cyprus was held in Vienna from 31 July to 2 August 1975.

Preliminary discussions were held on the powers and functions of a federal Government on the basis of the original Greek Cypriot proposals submitted at the first round, the Turkish Cypriot paper of 21 July and the more comprehensive paper presented by Mr Clerides at this meeting. Further examination of this subject will continue in Nicosia with a view to a final discussion, together with the other aspects relating to the solution of the Cyprus problem, at the next round of talks. Mr Denktash expressed his views on the comprehensive paper submitted by Mr Clerides and also on his own proposals for a transitional joint Government submitted by him on 18 July [*see S/11770*]. Mr Clerides referred to his previous position in this regard.

A discussion of the geographical aspects of a future settlement of the Cyprus problem took place. It was agreed that Mr Clerides and Mr Denktash would have further private talks on this subject prior to the fourth round of the Cyprus talks with a view to preparing the discussion of this matter which will take place at that time.

In addition the following was agreed:

1. The Turkish Cypriots at present in the south of the island will be allowed, if they want to do so, to proceed north with their belongings under an organized programme and with the assistance of the United Nations Peace-keeping Force in Cyprus.

2. Mr Denktash reaffirmed, and it was agreed, that the Greek Cypriots at present in the north of the island are free to stay and that they will be given every help to lead a normal life, including facilities for education and for the practice of their religion, as well as medical care by their own doctors and freedom of movement in the north.
3. The Greek Cypriots at present in the north who, at their own request and without having been subjected to any kind of pressure, wish to move to the south, will be permitted to do so.
4. The United Nations will have free and normal access to Greek Cypriot villages and habitations in the north.
5. In connection with the implementation of the above agreement, priority will be given to the reunification of families, which may also involve the transfer of a number of Greek Cypriots, at present in the south to the north.

The question of displaced persons was also re-examined.

Although both sides again affirmed that they were not knowingly holding undeclared prisoners-of-war or other detainees, it was agreed mutually to extend full facilities for searches in response to information given by either side.

Both sides declare that the Nicosia international airport, which has been repaired by the United Nations under the agreement reached at the first round, can be used, as a first step, by the United Nations for its needs. Practical arrangements, including the provision of liaison personnel, will be worked out between the Force and the two sides.

The fourth round of talks will take place, due to the Secretary-General's commitments in regard to the General Assembly, at United Nations Headquarters in New York on 9 and 9 September 1975.

12. High Level Agreement of 12 February 1977

Guidelines for the Interlocutors, as agreed at the Meeting of President Makarios with Mr R Denktash at UNFICYP Headquarters, Nicosia, in the presence of UN Secretary-General Dr Kurt Waldheim on 12 February 1977: source *S/12323*, 30 April 1977, *Report of the Secretary-General in pursuance of para 6 of SC res 401 (1976).*

"5. The text of the agreed instructions (guidelines) . . . reads as follows:

'1. We are seeking an independent, non-aligned, bi-communal Federal Republic.
2. The territory under the administration of each community should be discussed in the light of economic viability or productivity and land-ownership.
3. Questions of principles like freedom of movement, freedom of settlement, the right of property and other specific matters are open for discussion taking into consideration the fundamental basis of a bi-communal federal system and certain practical difficulties which may arise for the Turkish Cypriot community.
4. The powers and functions of the central federal government will be such as to safeguard the unity of the country having regard to the bi-communal character of the State.'"

[The Guidelines were not signed, but were recorded in the UN Record of the Meeting.]

13. Ten Point Agreement of 19 May 1979

Communiqué as agreed on 19 May 1979: source *S/13369*, 31 May 1979, para 51.

Following a high-level meeting at UNFICYP headquarters in Nicosia on 18 and 19 May between the President of the Republic, Mr Kyprianou, and Mr Denktash in the presence of the UN Secretary-General, Dr Waldheim.

"1. It was agreed to resume the intercommunal talks on 15 June 1979.
2. The basis for the talks will be the Makarios / Denktash guidelines of 12 February 1977 and the UN resolutions relevant to the Cyprus question.
3. There should be respect for the human rights and fundamental freedoms of all citizens of the Republic.
4. The talks will deal with all territorial and constitutional aspects.
5. Priority will be given to reaching agreement on the resettlement of Varosha under UN auspices simultaneously with the beginning of the consideration by the interlocutors of the constitutional and territorial aspects of a comprehensive settlement. After agreement on Varosha has been reached, it will be implemented without awaiting the outcome of the discussion on other aspects of the Cyprus problem.
6. It was agreed to abstain from any action which might jeopardize the outcome of the talks, and special importance will be given to initial practical measures by both sides to promote good will, mutual confidence and the return to normal conditions.
7. The demilitarization of the Republic of Cyprus is envisaged, and matters relating thereto will be discussed.
8. The independence, sovereignty, territorial integrity and non-alignment of the Republic should be adequately guaranteed against union in whole or in part with any other country and against any form of partition or secession.
9. The intercommunal talks will be carried out in a continuing and sustained manner, avoiding any delay.
10. The intercommunal talks will take place at Nicosia."

14.

4 February 2004

Excellency,

I wish to refer to the longstanding Cyprus problem, on which there has been much discussion, public and private, in the months since the breakdown of negotiations last March at The Hague. I have given this problem much thought in the last few weeks and I have reached the conclusion that the time has come to appeal to the wisdom and statesmanship of all the leaders involved. That is why, with a sense of urgency, I am writing to you today.

You will recall that after the meeting at The Hague, I reported to the Security Council on 1 April 2003. In that report (in paragraph 147), I said that I did not propose to take a new initiative unless and until such time as I had solid reason to believe that the political will existed necessary for a successful outcome.

I further stated my view that a solution on the basis of the plan (by which I mean the document entitled "Basis for a Comprehensive Settlement of the Cyprus Problem" that I formally presented on 26 February 2003) could be achieved only if there was an unequivocally stated preparedness on the part of the leaders of both sides, fully and determinedly backed at the highest political level in both Greece and Turkey, to commit themselves to finalize the plan (without reopening its basic principles or core trade-offs) by a specific date with United Nations assistance, and to put it to separate simultaneous referenda as provided for in the plan on a date certain soon thereafter. The Security Council strongly endorsed this approach in resolution 1475 (2003).

It is in this context that I have weighed the recent expressions of political will for negotiations to resume in order to achieve a solution before 1 May 2004.

His Excellency
Mr. Tassos Papadopoulos
Nicosia

-2-

I have appreciated the strong assurances you have given me in this regard, and I was encouraged by your public statements that you would accept an invitation from me to negotiations, particularly in the light of the new determination being displayed by Turkey.

The European Union has expressed its clear preference for the accession of a reunited Cyprus and its strong support for my good offices, and has made specific commitments to encourage this. A number of governments have signaled their strong support for resumed negotiations under my auspices in order to achieve a solution by 1 May.

I am heartened by these developments, which I hope offer a real possibility that the Greek Cypriots and the Turkish Cypriots will, at last, have the opportunity to vote on their reunification and bring into being a new state of affairs in Cyprus. Clearly, a solution before 1 May 2004 is in the interests of all concerned, and in the interests of international peace and security. It is the only means by which Cyprus can enter the European Union united on 1 May 2004. It would also solidify the rapprochement between Greece and Turkey as well as advance the prospects for the opening of accession negotiations between Turkey and the European Union.

While I appreciate that the requirements laid down in paragraph 148 of my report to the Security Council may seem daunting, a number of factors have confirmed my belief that only the unequivocal commitment of all concerned to those requirements would justify a renewed effort:

- I think of the Greek Cypriots and Turkish Cypriots, who have to live with the problem every day, and whose hopes have been repeatedly raised and dashed. I do not wish to raise hopes only to see them once more dashed.

- I believe I owe it to the Member States of the United Nations to ensure that there are reasonable prospects of success before committing myself and the Organization to a new effort.

- I truly believe (as I stated in paragraph 144 of my report) that the plan I put forward, which was the culmination of a long process in which all the issues were thoroughly aired and discussed, would permit the reunification of Cyprus through an honourable, balanced and durable settlement that protected and guaranteed the basic interests and aspirations of both sides. Hence, I also believe that the parties would do well to accept the package that is before them as representing a careful balance. I recognize however that both sides wish to try to effect changes to the plan. I have been assured by the Turkish

Prime Minister and you that the changes sought by the two sides would be confined to a small number and would remain within the parameters of the plan. I welcome this, and I have indicated that, should negotiations resume, I would do my best to help the parties reach speedy agreement on changes to the plan in order to improve it for both sides, while maintaining the overall balance, since it could not be expected that either side would accept changes that altered the plan in its disfavour.

- The accession of Cyprus to the European Union is now less than three months away. There is a large amount of work that needs to be done to complete the plan before it can be put to referendum. As you know, everything indispensable must be in place to ensure that the new state of affairs in Cyprus can function from the moment a settlement enters into force. It is inconceivable that this work could be completed in the time available without the political will that I have sought.

- The referendum to be held on each side on the same date before 1 May will require extensive technical and political preparation by each side, in order that this important vote is properly conducted. Only if all parties come back to the table committed to holding such a referendum will it be possible for those preparations to be made. I note in this respect that the plan has now been before the public for some time, and they have had the opportunity to familiarize themselves with it.

I therefore wish to invite you to New York on 10 February to begin negotiations. I would take your acceptance of this invitation as a commitment to finalize the plan (without reopening its basic principles or core trade-offs) with United Nations assistance by 31 March 2004, and to put the finalized plan to separate simultaneous referenda as provided for in the plan on 21 April 2004. The procedure to be followed in order to give effect to this commitment would be the following:

i. The parties would meet in the presence of myself or my Special Adviser in order to negotiate in good faith in a spirit of give-and-take on the basis of my plan to try to agree on changes to the Foundation Agreement (including its annexes and attachments) as needed. Greece and Turkey would also meet as necessary on issues of security. All concerned would only seek changes that fall within the parameters of the plan. I and my Special Adviser would actively assist them to reach agreement up to and including 26 March 2004.

ii. The parties would appoint technical committee members right away. They would begin meeting – in parallel and in sub-committees as necessary – in the presence of the United Nations in Cyprus no later

than 16 February, in order to complete the texts of those constitutional laws, cooperation agreements and federal laws that the plan specifies must be completed prior to the referendum, and to complete the list of international treaties binding on the United Cyprus Republic.
This work would be based on the texts that were submitted to the technical committees by the end of the last process. The meetings of the technical committees for this purpose would conclude on or before 26 March 2004.

iii. The parties would agree on or before 19 March on the nominees to the transitional Supreme Court and the transitional Board of the Central Bank.

iv. The parties would immediately appoint flag and anthem committee members, who would begin meeting in the presence of the United Nations in Cyprus on 28 February, in order to select recommendations on the flag and anthem of the United Cyprus Republic to place before the leaders for their agreement and decision by 12 March 2004.

v. The parties would each provide me by 12 March with a proposed Constituent State constitution consistent with the Foundation Agreement and containing the following article:

> "(i) constituent state laws adopted pursuant to referendum together with the Foundation Agreement and this Constitution shall, as from entry into force of the Foundation Agreement, be applied in this constituent state with such modifications as may be necessary to bring them into conformity with the Foundation Agreement and the Constitution of this constituent state.
> (ii) No provision in any such law which is contrary to or inconsistent with any provision of the Foundation Agreement or this Constitution shall so continue to be in force.
> (iii) The term "modification" in the above paragraphs includes amendment, adaptation and repeal.";

and a provision specifying those laws that shall become laws of their constituent state.

vi. It is clearly desirable that the text should emerge completed from the negotiations between the parties by the dates specified above. However, should that not happen, I would, by 31 March, make any indispensable suggestions to complete the text. Naturally I would only do this with the greatest of reluctance, and indeed I very much hope that this prospect would spur the parties to approach the effort with the determination required to come to terms in a timely fashion.

vii. On the basis of the finalized text, the three guarantor powers – Greece, Turkey, and the United Kingdom – would confirm to me and each other in writing by 9 April that they agree to the Foundation Agreement being put to the separate simultaneous referenda provided for in the plan, and that, upon its approval at such referenda, they are committed to signing together with the United Cyprus Republic the Treaty on matters related to the new state of affairs in Cyprus as annexed to the Foundation Agreement, which shall be registered as an international Treaty in accordance with Article 102 of the Charter of the United Nations. The guarantor powers would complete all internal procedures necessary in order to provide this commitment by 10 April.

viii. The parties invite me, on the basis of the finalized text, to request the Security Council to take decisions as set out in the appendix to the plan entitled "Matters to be Submitted to the United Nations Security Council for Decision".

ix. The finalized text of the Foundation Agreement would be put by each side to separate simultaneous referenda on 21 April in the manner foreseen in the plan, namely by asking the following question: "Do you approve the Foundation Agreement with all its Annexes, as well as the Constitution of the Greek Cypriot/Turkish Cypriot constituent state and the provisions as to its laws to be in force, to bring into being a new state of affairs in which Cyprus joins the European Union united? Yes/No."

x. Should the Foundation Agreement be approved, it will enter into force at 00.00 hours the day after confirmation by me of such approval. Should the Foundation Agreement not be approved, it shall be null and void, and the commitments undertaken by the parties in resuming negotiations, including the submission to referenda, shall have no legal effect.

The procedural points listed above are foreseen (albeit with different dates) in the plan, and in the list of work outstanding that was provided to the parties during the previous process. I know that they may seem daunting, but I firmly believe that they must be adhered to. With the true determination of yourself and all parties, I am convinced that they can readily be met.

For my part, I will ensure that, should negotiations resume, all necessary personnel and resources from the United Nations are deployed to assist the parties in their task, and I myself will be closely engaged in the effort.

- 6 -

I hope that the parties will see the historic opportunity that is before them, and work closely with each other and with me in the time remaining to bring the healing hands of peace to Cyprus at last. Together, I know that we can transform the island from a symbol of long-standing division into a source of friendship and peace in the region. Cyprus can become a beacon of hope to people everywhere – living proof that, in the long run, the strongest stirrings of the human heart are for peace.

I look forward to seeing you in New York next week.

Please accept, Excellency, the assurances of my highest consideration.

Kofi A. Annan

STATEMENT ATTRIBUTABLE TO THE SPOKESMAN OF THE SECRETARY-GENERAL

The Secretary General wrote today to the Greek Cypriot and Turkish Cypriot leaders inviting them to come to New York on 10 February 2004 to resume negotiations on the basis of his plan. The objective of the negotiations would be to put a completed text to referenda in April 2004, in time for a reunited Cyprus to accede to the European Union on 1 May 2004.

The Secretary-General has also written to the Prime Ministers of Greece, Turkey and the United Kingdom asking them to have representatives on hand in New York on that occasion.

The Secretary-General was moved to take this initiative by his recent, encouraging contacts on the Cyprus question during his trip to Europe and afterwards. In his letters, the Secretary-General has appealed to the leaders to summon the political will needed to bring about this result in the short time available. He has also set out what needs to be done for this to happen.

15.

STATEMENT ATTRIBUTABLE TO THE SPOKESMAN OF THE SECRETARY-GENERAL

13 February 2004

Negotiations resumed on 10 February at United Nations Headquarters in New York between the two parties in Cyprus, in the presence of the Secretary-General of the United Nations.

Following three days of meetings and consultations, the Secretary-General is pleased to announce that the parties have committed to negotiating in good faith on the basis of his plan to achieve a comprehensive settlement of the Cyprus problem through separate and simultaneous referenda before 1 May 2004.

To this end, the parties will seek to agree on changes and to complete the plan in all respects by 22 March 2004, within the framework of the Secretary-General's mission of good offices, so as to produce a finalized text.

In the absence of such agreement, the Secretary-General would convene a meeting of the two sides – with the participation of Greece and Turkey in order to lend their collaboration – in a concentrated effort to agree on a finalized text by 29 March.

As a final resort, in the event of a continuing and persistent deadlock, the parties have invited the Secretary-General to use his discretion to finalize the text to be submitted to referenda on the basis of his plan.

In addition, the parties have agreed on the other suggestions contained in the Secretary-General's invitation of 4 February 2004. They have also decided to form a technical committee on economic and financial aspects of implementation, to be chaired by the United Nations.

The guarantor powers have signified their commitment to this process and to meeting their obligations under it.

The Secretary General welcomes these commitments as well as the assurances of the European Union to accommodate a settlement and the offer of technical assistance by the European Commission. He looks forward to drawing on this assistance as well as that of others in the course of the negotiations.

The talks will re-convene in Cyprus on Thursday, 19 February, with direct meetings between the two parties in the presence of the Secretary-General's Special Adviser, Alvaro de Soto. The technical committees on laws and treaties will re-convene on the same day.

The Secretary-General commends the constructive spirit and political will displayed by both parties, as well as by Greece and Turkey, to reach this agreement.

All concerned now face historic responsibilities to bring about a just and lasting peace in Cyprus. The Secretary-General wishes them well, and looks forward to working closely with them.

Index of Illustrations

Illustrations in black and white are referred to as Sets A–Z and numbered within Sets eg A.3. Coloured prints are referred to as eg C.P.9. The centre-fold map is C.P. 14–15

Index